COLLECTIONS

OF THE

ILLINOIS STATE HISTORICAL LIBRARY

EDITED BY
THEODORE CALVIN PEASE
UNIVERSITY OF ILLINOIS

VOLUME XXVI

ILLINOIS
STATE HISTORICAL LIBRARY

BOARD OF TRUSTEES

Otto Leopold Schmidt, *President*
Laurence Marcellus Larson, *Secretary*
Albert Britt

Paul M. Angle, *Librarian*
Theodore Calvin Pease, *Editor*

ADVISORY COMMISSION

Evarts Boutell Greene
William Edward Dodd
James Alton James
Andrew Cunningham McLaughlin
Theodore Calvin Pease

STATISTICAL SERIES
VOLUME III

ILLINOIS CENSUS RETURNS
1820

COLLECTIONS OF THE
ILLINOIS STATE HISTORICAL LIBRARY
VOLUME XXVI

STATISTICAL SERIES
VOLUME III

ILLINOIS
CENSUS RETURNS
1820

EDITED BY
Margaret Cross Norton
ILLINOIS STATE LIBRARY

Theodore Calvin Pease
EDITOR-IN-CHIEF OF THIS SERIES

HERITAGE BOOKS
2013

HERITAGE BOOKS
AN IMPRINT OF HERITAGE BOOKS, INC.

Books, CDs, and more—Worldwide

For our listing of thousands of titles see our website
at
www.HeritageBooks.com

A Facsimile Reprint
Published 2013 by
HERITAGE BOOKS, INC.
Publishing Division
100 Railroad Ave. #104
Westminster, Maryland 21157

Copyright © 1934 by the Illinois State Historical Library

— Publisher's Notice —
In reprints such as this, it is often not possible to remove blemishes from the original. We feel the contents of this book warrant its reissue despite these blemishes and hope you will agree and read it with pleasure.

International Standard Book Numbers
Paperbound: 978-0-7884-5106-5
Clothbound: 978-0-7884-6983-1

PREFACE

This publication of Illinois state census schedules for 1820 is a companion work to the 1810 federal and 1818 territorial censuses published in another volume of the Illinois Historical Collections. The introduction to the earlier returns presents the history of census taking in Illinois and gives tables and a map showing the population by counties in 1818 and 1820. This book contains not only the 1820 state census schedules but also notes comparing all discrepancies between the names as written in the 1818 territorial, the 1820 state, and the 1820 federal censuses. While in most instances these represent merely minor variations in spelling, there are enough marked discrepancies to indicate that all three sets of returns are necessary to compile a correct list of the pioneers of each county. Symbols have been used in both volumes to indicate names appearing in the other two censuses. In making this comparison families were not assumed to be identical unless they appeared as residing in approximately the same vicinities. Similarity of names alone was not considered sufficient unless they were quite distinctive or unless other evidence corroborated the hypothesis. Names appearing in the federal but not in the state census of 1820 are given in the notes. No attempt has been made to compare the number of members ascribed to each family, as the classifications used in the federal census are more detailed than those of the state census, and since it is to be hoped that the 1820 federal census will also be printed before many years.

The editor wishes to thank those who have given so freely of their time, criticisms and the resources of their departments. She wishes to give especial thanks to Professor Theodore C. Pease, the editor-in-chief of this series, and to his staff, Miss Ernestine Jenison, Miss Mildred Eversole and Miss Louese Ramser, without whose exceptional and painstaking accuracy many errors would have slipped into this volume. The coöperation of the assistants, past and present, in the State Archives Division have made this work possible. The successive chief clerks, Mrs. Grace B. Hanson and Miss Jean Carroll, by relieving the editor of many office details have given the opportunity for the concentration necessary; and the typists, especially Mrs. Edith D. Strain and Mrs. Helen J. Hanson, contributed much by their cheerful patience in an exacting task. Both Miss Georgia L. Osborne and her successor, Mr. Paul M. Angle, of the Illinois State Historical Library, have placed their personal knowledge and the resources of their library at her disposal in the freest possible manner.

January 29, 1934

TABLE OF CONTENTS

ALEXANDER COUNTY	1
BOND COUNTY	7
CLARK COUNTY	25
CRAWFORD COUNTY	33
EDWARDS COUNTY	55
FRANKLIN COUNTY	62
GALLATIN COUNTY	75
JACKSON COUNTY	99
JEFFERSON COUNTY	121
JOHNSON COUNTY	128
MADISON COUNTY	137
MONROE COUNTY	201
POPE COUNTY	214
RANDOLPH COUNTY	237
ST. CLAIR COUNTY	256
UNION COUNTY	293
WASHINGTON COUNTY	312
WAYNE COUNTY	324
WHITE COUNTY	331
INDEX	363

ILLINOIS CENSUS RETURNS
1820

CENSUS OF ALEXANDER COUNTY, 1820
enumeration of the inhabitants of Alexander County state of Illinois

Alexander County Nov 24 1820 Heads of Familys	Males under twenty one	of twenty one & upwards	Female under Eighteen	Female of eighteen & upwards	
[1*‡] Alexander Millikin	2	1		2	
[2 ‡] Lewis Crow		1		1	
[3*‡] Allen McKinzie	2	1	1	1	
[4 ‡] Lewis Durham		1		1	
[5*‡] Merrit Harvell	2	2	5	1	three
[6*‡] George Hacker	1	2	3	1	female
[7*‡] Absolem Hacker	3	1		1	Negroes
[8 ‡] Richard Abbey	3	2		2	under 10
[9 ‡] James M. Johnson	1	1	2	1	
[10*‡] Alexander Baggs	4	1	3	1	
[11*‡] George Oller, sen		2	2	1	
[12 ‡] John Brown		1	1	1	
[13*‡] Charles Bradley	3	1		1	
[14*‡] John Shaver	3	1	3	1	
[15*‡] Samuel M. Phillips	2	1	3	1	
[16 ‡] William Walker	1	1	2	4	
[17 ‡] Jason Fowler	1	1	1	1	
[18] William Braken	2	1	3	2	
[19*‡] Levy Graham	3	1	4	1	
[20*‡] Thomas Williams	2	1	2	1	
[21 ‡] Tapley White	2	1	1	1	
[22 ‡] Thomas Peterson	1	1		1	
[23 ‡] John Biggerstaff	3	1	2	1	
[24*‡] Levi Hughes	3	2	2	1	
[25*‡] Mark Provou	4	1	2	1	
[26*‡] Richard Brown	6	1	4	2	
[27*‡] William Smith	3	1		1	
[28] Nicholas Smith	1	1		1	
[29*‡] James Murphey	2	1	2	1	
[30*‡] William McIntosh	2	1	1	1	
[31*‡] Mathew Gaston	3	1	3	1	
[32*‡] Edmond Russel	1	1	2	2	
[33 ‡] Elizabeth Russel	2	1	2	2	
[34*‡] James McClane	3	1	2	1	

Figures and symbols preceding names have been supplied by the editor:
‡ Indicates name also in Federal Census for 1820.
*Indicates name also in State Census for Union County, 1818.

1

ALEXANDER COUNTY (Continued)

No.	Heads of families	Males under 21	Of 21 & upwards	Females under 18	Females 18 & upwards	
[35 ‡]	Robert McConel		1	1	1	
[36*‡]	Samuel Fowler	1	1	4	1	
[37*‡]	Thomas B. Peyton	1	1	2	1	
[38 ‡]	Arthur Oller	1	1		1	
[39 ‡]	John Allen		1	2	1	
[40*‡]	James Stephenson	2	1	1	1	
[41 ‡]	David McKinzie		1		1	
[42*‡]	Nathan Turpin	1	2	1	1	
[43 ‡]	Silas Durham		1		1	
[44*‡]	Stephen McKinzie	2	1	1	1	
[45*‡]	Green B. Brown		1		1	
[46 ‡]	William Parker		1	1		
[47*‡]	Maryann Smyth	1	2	1	1	
[48*‡]	John F. Smyth	2	1	3	1	
[49 ‡]	James P. Edwards	5	2	2	1	
[50 ‡]	Rheubin Stephens	1	1		1	
[51*‡]	Car Allen	2	2	3	1	
[52 ‡]	Collins M. Johnson	4	2	3	2	
[53 ‡]	William Johnson	2	1		1	
[54 ‡]	James Willis	1	1	1	1	
[55 ‡]	Martin Atherton		1		1	
[56 ‡]	James H. Rowland		1	1	1	
[57*‡]	James Tash	1	1	1	1	
[58 ‡]	Mary Tash	1		1	2	
[59 ‡]	George Oller, jun	2	1		1	
[60 ‡]	Ila Forrister		1	1		
[61 ‡]	Leonard Oller	3	1	1	1	
[62 ‡]	John Oller	1	1		1	
[63 ‡]	Simion Harvell	1	1	2		
[64]	John Oller, sen	1	1	2	1	
[65 ‡]	John Rutherford	3	1	6		
[66]	Mary Graves	5			1	
[67*‡]	Nathan Russel	3	1	2		
[68 ‡]	John Russel		1		1	
[69*‡]	James Phillips	3	1	1	1	
[70 ‡]	Stephen Butler		7			One
[71*‡]	Edmond Sutton	4	1	1	1	Slave
[72 ‡]	Henry L. Webb		1	2	2	16 year
[73*‡]	William M. Alexander		2			of age

CENSUS OF 1820

ALEXANDER COUNTY (Continued)

No.	Heads of families	Males under 21	Of 21 & upwards	Females under 18	Females 18 & upwards
[74 ‡]	John Barnet		1	1	
[75 ‡]	George Cloud	1	1	4	2
[76*‡]	William F. Holly	2	1		1
[77 ‡]	Amos Fox		3	2	1
[78 ‡]	Joel Spencer	3	1	3	1
[79 ‡]	Hardy Smith	3	1	7	3
[80 ‡]	Joshua Levingston	1	1		1
[81 ‡]	Barbary Wilcox	2	1	1	1
[82*‡]	Leroy Smith	3	3	1	1
[83 ‡]	John Rumal		1		1
[84 ‡]	Almeran Sacket	4	1	2	1
[85 ‡]	Thomas Jones	3	1	1	1
[86 ‡]	David Parks	1	2	2	2
[87 ‡]	Levin Charles	2	2	4	1
[88*‡]	William Daniel	7	3	2	1
[89*‡]	Nesbit Allen	3	1	6	1
[90 ‡]	Absolem Heddy	2	1	1	1
[91 ‡]	William Price	7	1	2	1
[92 ‡]	Peter Fury	2	1	2	1
[93 ‡]	James Berry	2	2	1	1
[94 ‡]	John Nelson		2		
[95 ‡]	John C. Jones		5		1
[96 ‡]	James Cook	4	3	2	2
[97 ‡]	Nathaniel Clark	5	1	3	2
[98 ‡]	William Wilson		1		1
[99 ‡]	Joseph E. Wilson	4	2	1	1
[100 ‡]	Samuel Cox	2	2	1	2
[101 ‡]	John Murphy		1		1
[102 ‡]	John Boman	4	8	3	2
[103]	James McClane	3	1	2	1
[104 ‡]	James Pore		2	1	1
[105 ‡]	William Collins	4	10	2	2
[106 ‡]	John Reed	4	1	2	1
[107]	William Johnson	2	1		1
[108 ‡]	Simeon Shaver	1	1	1	1
[109*‡]	John Conyers	3	1		2
[110 ‡]	James Nelson	2	1	1	1
[111*‡]	Fitz Hutchins		1	1	1
[112 ‡]	George Hiet	5	1		1

ALEXANDER COUNTY (Continued)

No.	Heads of families	Males under 21	Of 21 & upwards	Females under 18	Females 18 & upwards
[113 ‡]	Mary Hollinshead	3		5	2
[114 ‡]	James Pringle		1		1
[115*‡]	Nicholas Wilson		1	5	2
[116*‡]	John Langham	3	2	4	2
[117*‡]	William Waughford		1	2	1
[118 ‡]	Henry Johnson	2	1		1
[119 ‡]	Joseph Brown	2	1	3	2
[120]	John Athernton	3	1	1	1
[121*‡]	Aron Atherton	2	1		3
[122*‡]	John Atherton		1		1
[123 ‡]	Thomas Royal	4	3	3	1
[124*‡]	William Biggerstaff	2	1	1	1
[125*‡]	Thomas Howard	1	1	1	1
[126*‡]	Moses Atherton	5	2	1	2
[127*‡]	Samuel Atherton	2	1	2	1

```
        Free White male under twenty one years of age      245
        Free White male of twenty one and upwards          179
        Free White female under Eighteen years of age      195
        Free White feemale of Eighteen and upwards         149
        Four female Slaves under Eighteen                    4
                                                           ___
                                                           772
```

Signed JOHN F SMITH, Com.
November 24th 1820

Corrected totals:
```
        Free white males under 21 years                    245
        Free white males of 21 years and upwards           180
        Free white females under 18 years                  195
        Free white females of 18 years and upwards         149
                                                           ___
                                                           769
    Slaves                                                   4
                                                           ___
                                              Total        773
```

CENSUS OF 1820

ALEXANDER COUNTY (Continued)

The federal and state censuses for Alexander County were both taken by John F. Smyth, who certified the state census on November 21 and the federal census on December 1 of 1820. The arrangement of names differs enough to prove that one census was not a copy of the other. Seven names appearing in the state census have been omitted from the federal census, two of which are probably repetitions. There are also minor variations in spelling, and in one case, Joshua Levingston (state census No. 80), the first name is changed to Elisha in the federal census. The county of Alexander was not organized until 1819, so its population statistics for 1818 are included in the census for Union County, taken by David and Jeremiah Brown. Discrepancies in the three enumerations are as follows:

1 Millikin, Alexander
   1818. Milligen, Alexandria
   F1820. Millekin, Alexander
3 McKinzie, Allen
   1818. McKinsy, Allen
   F1820. McKinzie, Allen
5 Harvell, Merrit
   1818. Harvel, Meret
   F1820. Harvell, Merrit
10 Baggs, Alexander
   1818. Beggs, Alexandria
   F1820. Baggs, Alexander
11 Oller, George, Sr.
   1818. Oller, George
   F1820. Oller, George, Sr.
13 Bradley, Charles
   1818. Bradley, Chals
   F1820. Bradley, Charles
15 Phillips, Samuel M.
   1818. Philips, Samuel
   F1820. Phillips, Samuel
16 Walker, William
   F1820. Welker, William
19 Graham, Levy
   1818. Grham, Levy
   F1820. Graham, Levi
24 Hughes, Levi
   1818. Huse, Levi
   F1820. Hughes, Levi
25 Provou, Mark
   1818. Pervo, Mark
   F1820. Provou, Mark
29 Murphey, James
   1818. Mu[r]phy, James
   F1820. Murphey, James
31 Gaston, Mathew
   1818. Gasten, Mathew
   F1820. Gastin, Mathew
34 McClane, James
   1818 and F1820. McClain, James
36 Fowler, Samuel
   1818. Fowuler, Samuel
37 Peyton, Thomas B.
   1818. Paten, Thomas B.
   F1820. Peyton, Thomas B.

42 Turpin, Nathan
   1818. Turpen, Nathen
   F1820. Turpin, Nathan
44 McKinzie, Stephen
   1818. McKinsy, Stephen
   F1820. McKinzie, Stephen
45 Brown, Green B.
   1818. Brown, Greenberry
   F1820. Brown, Green B.
47 Smyth, Maryann
   1818. Smith, Maryan
   F1820. Smyth, Maryann
48 Smyth, John F.
   1818. Smith, John
   F1820. Smyth, John F.
65 Rutherford, John
   F1820. Retherford, John
69 Phillips, James
   1818. Philips, James
   F1820. Phillips, James
71 Sutton, Edmond
   1818. Sutten, Edmond
   F1820. Sutton, Edmond
73 Alexander, William M.
   1818. Alexandria, William M.
   F1820. Alexander, William M.
76 Holly, William F.
   1818. Holley, William F.
   F1820. Holley, William F.
80 Levingston, Joshua
   F1820. Levingston, Elisha
81 Wilcox, Barbary
   F1820. Wilcx, Barbary
88 Daniel, William
   1818. Daniel, William
   F1820. Daniels, William
89 Allen, Nesbit
   1818. Allen, Nezebe
   F1820. Allen, Nesbit
107 Johnson, William
Probably a repetition of No. 53.
108 Shaver, Simeon
   F1820. Shaver, Simion
109 Conyers, John
   1818. Coniers, John
   F1820. Conyers, John

ALEXANDER COUNTY (Concluded)

111 Hutchins, Fitz
    1818 and F1820. Hutchings, Fitz
112 Hiet, George
    F1820. Hiet, John
116 Langham, John
    1818. Lanahan, John
    F1820. Langham, John
117 Waughford, William
    1818. Wafferd, William
    F1820. Waughford, William
121 Atherton, Aron
    1818. Etherton, Aron
    F1820. Atherton, Aron
122 Atherton, John
    1818. Etherton, John
    F1820. Atherton, John
123 Royal, Thomas
    F1820. Ryal, Thomas
124 Biggerstaff, William
    1818. Bigerstaff, William
    F1820. Biggerstaff, William
126 Atherton, Moses
    1818. Etherton, Moses
    F1820. Atherton, Moses
127 Atherton, Samuel
    1818. Etherton, Samuel
    F1820. Atherton, Samuel

The following names are found in the state census of 1820 but not in the federal census:

18 Braken, William
28 Smith, Nicholas
64 Oller, John, Sr.
66 Graves, Mary
103 McClane, James   Repetition of No. 34?
107 Johnson, William   Repetition of No. 53?
120 Athernton, John

CENSUS OF BOND COUNTY, 1820

The Number of persons within my Division Consisting of Bond County appears in a Schedule hereto annexed, Subscribed by me this 2d day of December 1820. Schedule of the whole Number of persons within Bond County.

Number of Families	Names of heads of Families	Free white Males		Free white Females	People of Color		Name of the Township where the Family resides	Number of Families in Each Township	Whole Population of Each Township
		Under Twenty-one years	Above the age of Twenty-one years		Free	Servants or Slaves			
1[‡]	Robert Huffman	1	1	1			Powers Township		
2[*‡]	James Blizzard	2	1	2					
3[‡]	John Hunt	5	1	5					
4[*‡]	William Brown	5	1	3					
5[*‡]	Bonham Harlan	3	1	3					
6[*‡]	Joseph Myers	2	1	4					
7[*‡]	Stephen Myers	1	1	4					
8[‡]	William Myers		2	1					
9[*‡]	William Dunn	1	1	5					
10[‡]	Samuel Duncan		1	1					
11[*‡]	Jesse Hanin	2	1	4					
12[‡]	Samuel Seward	2	1	1					
13[‡]	George Foss		2						
14[‡]	Hiram R. Hewley	1							
15[*‡]	Ignatius Anderson	6	1	3					
16[*‡]	James Hanin	2	1	4					
17[‡]	Frederick Berberick	3	1	4					
18[‡]	Joshua Babcock	2	1	3					
19[‡]	Benjamin Brazelton	2	1	1					
20[*‡]	Rufus Innman		4	2					
21[‡]	James Barns		1	2					
22[*‡]	Charles Revis	3	2	4					
23[‡]	Hubbard Short	3	2	3					
24[*‡]	Robert Baker	3	2	3					

The list of names for Bond County was numbered in the original, but the symbols have been supplied by the editor:
‡ Indicates name also in Federal Census for 1820.
* Indicates name also in State Census for 1818.

BOND COUNTY (*Continued*)

No.	Heads of families	Free white males		Free white females	People of color		Twp.	Families in twp.	Pop. of twp.
		under 21	21 & above		Free	Servants or slaves			
25[‡]	John Dimond	4	1	4					
26[‡]	Thomas Seers	2	1	2					
27[‡]	Thomas Aiken		2						
28[‡]	John Osmus	3	1	3					
29[‡]	William Stephenson	2	1	3					
30[*‡]	Even Hinton	5	1	2					
31[*‡]	Anne White	1		6					
32[*‡]	Benjamin Hinson	2	1	6					
33[*‡]	Joshua Barker		1	1					
34[*‡]	John Hinson	1	1	1					
35[‡]	Joseph Harness		1	1					
36[‡]	David Smith	5	1	4					
37[‡]	George Cole	2	1	5		1			
38[‡]	Robert Cole		1	1					
39[‡]	Samuel Smith		1	2					
40[‡]	George Green	2	3	3					
41[‡]	Syrus Kirby	1	1	6					
42[*‡]	James Green	4	1	2					
43[‡]	John Duncan		1	3					
44[‡]	Edmund Boez	2	2	5					
45[‡]	Aaron Smith		1	1					
46[‡]	John Nowlin	1	1	2					
47[*‡]	Fields Pruitt	2	1	5					
48[*‡]	Elijah Powers	4	1	3					
49[*‡]	John Powers		2	3					
50[‡]	George Taylor		1	3					
51[‡]	Robert Lorton, Sen.	1	1	3					
52[*‡]	James Boles	2	1	4					
53[‡]	Thomas Lorton	2	1	4					
54[‡]	Robert Lorton, Jur.	2	1	3					
55[‡]	Henry Curtis				14				
56[‡]	William Shean	1	1	1					
57[*‡]	Joseph Barber	5	1	2					
58[‡]	John Griggory	3	1	5					
59[‡]	Archibal Canady	2	1	2					
60[‡]	Isaac Reed		1	1					

CENSUS OF 1820

BOND COUNTY (*Continued*)

No.	Heads of families	Free white males		Free white females	People of color		Twp.	Families in twp.	Pop. of twp.
		under 21	21 & above		Free	Serv-ants or slaves			
61[*‡]	James Reed		1	3					
62[*‡]	Hugh Jackson	1	1	5					
63[*‡]	Alexander Orr	4	1	10					
64[*‡]	John King	4	2	3					
65[‡]	James Nantz		1	1					
66[*‡]	William Burges	4	1	2					
67[‡]	Henry Lorton		1	1					
68[‡]	James Karson	1	1	1					
69[*‡]	Philip Osmus		1	2					
70[‡]	John Taylor	5	1	4					
71[‡]	Isaac Renfrow	1	1	1					
72[‡]	Walter Taylor	1	1	5					
73[*‡]	Benjamin Bawlin		1	2					
74[‡]	Mary Braton	3		4					
75[‡]	William Samples	1	1	1					
76[*‡]	John Samples	2	1	2					
77[‡]	Joseph Bileyu	6	1	2					
78[*‡]	Philip Duff	4	1	6					
79[‡]	Peter Smith	1	1	1			Perryville Township		
80[‡]	Elizabeth Williams	2	2	2					
81[‡]	Henry Hall	2	1	2					
82[‡]	James Burnside, Jur	2	1	1					
83[‡]	Josiah Crawford	1		1					
84[‡]	John Burnside	1	1	2					
85[*‡]	James Burnside, Sen	1	1	4					
86[‡]	James Jack		1	1					
87[*‡]	Isaac Hill		2	3	1				
88[*‡]	John Lorton	1	2	3					
89[*‡]	John Hill	1	2	2					
90[‡]	Zachariah Morris	3	1	1					
91[‡]	Harmon Holt	3	2	7					
92[‡]	Hardy Foster	1	1	2					
93[*‡]	Henry Watley	3	1	1					
94[*‡]	Thomas Nicholas	6	1	4					
95[‡]	Samuel Lindley	3	1	4					
96[‡]	Andrew Bowman	6	1	3					

BOND COUNTY (*Continued*)

No.	Heads of families	Free white males		Free white females	People of color		Twp.	Families in twp.	Pop. of twp.
		under 21	21 & above		Free	Servants or slaves			
97[‡]	Burd E. Miles	1	1	1					
98[‡]	Nancy Duncan	4		4					
99[‡]	William Howard		1	1					
100[‡]	William Duncan		1	1					
101[*‡]	Abraham Bateman	5	1	5					
102[*‡]	Sarah Duncan	2		3					
103[‡]	Robert Duncan		1	1					
104[*‡]	John Whitley, Jur		1	3					
105[*‡]	Mills Whitley	2	1	2					
106[‡]	Henry McDaniel	1	1	2					
107[‡]	Samuel Little		2	1					
108[‡]	William Pursley	1	1	5					
109[‡]	James Hill		1	2					
110[*‡]	William Little	2	1	4					
111[*‡]	John Whitley, Sen	3	1	2					
112[‡]	Ishom Jackson	1		1					
113[‡]	Elisha Whitley	1		2					
114[‡]	Randle Whitley	2	1	2					
115[*‡]	John Huff	2	1	6					
116[*‡]	Martin Jones	1	2	3	1				
117[‡]	John Denton	1	1	1					
118[‡]	Jeremiah Evens	3	1	5			East fork Township		
119[‡]	Isaac Jones	1	1	4					
120[‡]	John Williams	2	1	4					
121[*‡]	Isham Revis	2	2	1					
122[‡]	Henry Lee	1	1	2					
123[*‡]	John Edington		1	4					
124[*‡]	William Nicholas	1	1	1	1				
125[‡]	John Warren	2	1	2					
126[*‡]	Zadock Phelps	3	1	5					
127[*‡]	John Phelps	1	1	1					
128[‡]	Frederick Phelps	1	1	1					
129[*‡]	Francis Harmon	2	1	1					
130[‡]	Benjamin Bishop	3	1	4					
131[*‡]	James Altom	5	1	1					
132[‡]	Robert Nicholas		1						

BOND COUNTY (*Continued*)

No.	Heads of families	Free white males		Free white females	People of color		Twp.	Families in twp.	Pop. of twp.
		under 21	21 & above		Free	Serv-ants or slaves			
133[‡]	Rosana Wright	2	3	2					
134[‡]	William Truskit	3	1	2					
135[‡]	Edward Code	1	1	5					
136[*‡]	John Smith	3	1	4			Vandalia Township		
137[*‡]	Henry Smith	4	1	2					
138[*‡]	Robert Daniel	1	1	2					
139[‡]	Adam Smith, Sen	1	2	1					
140[*‡]	William Howell	2	1	5					
141[*‡]	Loyd Lee	1	2	4					
142[*‡]	Martin Daniel	1	1	4					
143[‡]	Barton Daniel	2	1	4					
144[‡]	Jeremiah Daniel	1	1	1					
145[‡]	William Daniel		1	3					
146[‡]	Delila Daniel		1	6					
147[‡]	Archibal Ezell		4	4					
148[‡]	Whitmill Rial	2	1	6					
149[*‡]	Samuel Hanin	2	1	3					
150[*‡]	Francis Brown	4	2	2					
151[*‡]	Rufus Innman	1	2	2					
152[‡]	Philip Luster		1	1					
153[‡]	James Beal		1	1					
154[‡]	James Hooper	4	1	3					
155[*‡]	John A. Wakefield	1	2	1					
156[‡]	Joseph Hinds	3	2	5					
157[‡]	Adam Smith, Jur	5	1	2					
158[‡]	Elizabeth Hailey	2		2					
159[‡]	Edmund Taylor	2	1	3					
160[‡]	Andrew Milton		1	1					
161[‡]	John Evens		1	2					
162[*‡]	William L. Hickerson	3	1	3					
163[‡]	Elizabeth Thompson	3	2	2					
164[‡]	Abraham Sterns		1	1					
165[*‡]	Diana Wakefield	3		5					
166[‡]	Hiram Rountree		1	3					
167[‡]	Michael Dodd	4	2	2					
168[*‡]	John Hailey	1	1	4					

BOND COUNTY (Continued)

No.	Heads of families	Free white males		Free white females	People of color		Twp.	Families in twp.	Pop. of twp.
		under 21	21 & above		Free	Servants or slaves			
169[‡]	John Michad	1	1	2					
170[‡]	Henry Ledbetter		1	1					
171[‡]	Asa Ledbetter	3	2	3					
172[‡]	James Hailey	3	2	4					
173[‡]	G. W. Wood	3	1	2					
174[‡]	Arthur Berry		1	1					
175[‡]	George Scridmore		2						
176[‡]	Quinney		1		2				
177[‡]	Perregrin Patterson	1	1	4					
178[‡]	Rosanna Vineyard	1		1					
179[‡]	Henry Ginger		2	1					
180[‡]	Henry Luster	2	1	3					
181[‡]	David Luster	2	1	3					
182[‡]	John Baugh	5	7	6					
183[‡]	Daniel Bathrick		9	2					
184[‡]	Frederick Holman		4						
185[‡]	Edmund Tunstell	2	6	1					
186[‡]	Robert K. McLaughlin	1	2	1		6			
187[‡]	John Sheilds	1	1	3					
188[‡]	William Thacker	1	3	4					
189[‡]	John R. Harris		4						
190[‡]	Elijah C. Berry	5	3	4		4			
191[‡]	William Jordan	1	1						
192[‡]	Gerret Eoff	2	8	4					
193[‡]	James S. Dorris	2	1	2		1			
194[‡]	Robert Blackwell	1	1	2					
195[‡]	William Johnson	1	1	2					
196[‡]	Robert W. Randle	2	3	1					
197[‡]	John Warnick	1	3	4					
198[‡]	John Kerlogg		4	1					
199[‡]	Philip Martin		2	4					
200[‡]	Joseph Chaffin		1	2					
201[‡]	Joshua Barns	4	3	4					
202[‡]	A. G. Martin	1	1	5					
203[‡]	William Wallace		5	5					

CENSUS OF 1820

BOND COUNTY (Continued)

No.	Heads of families	Free white males		Free white females	People of color		Twp.	Families in twp.	Pop. of twp.
		under 21	21 & above		Free	Servants or slaves			
204[‡]	Archibal Luster	1	1	2					
205[‡]	Aaron Skeen	1	3	5					
206[‡]	Jacob Neely	2	1	5					
207[‡]	Richard Brazel	2	1	3					
208[‡]	Abraham Tettrick	1	1	2					
209[‡]	William Payton		1	2					
210[‡]	Michael Huffman	3	2	3					
211[‡]	Daniel Huffman	1	1	1					
212[‡]	John Hall	1	1	3					
213[‡]	Joseph Hall		2	1					
214[‡]	William Hall	2	2	3					
215[‡]	Henry Inmand	4	1	3					
216[‡]	Nancy Jurney	4	1	5					
217[‡]	John Thomas	1		1					
218[‡]	Thomas Higgins	2	1	3					
219[‡]	Jeremiah Riley		1						
220[‡]	Thomas Asher	1	1	1					
221[‡]	Robison Asher	1	1	5					
222[‡]	John O'Neill	1	1	2					
223[‡]	Hugh O'Neill	5	1	1					
224[‡]	Philip Moore	3	2	8					
225[‡]	David Waddle		1	1			Hurricane fork Township		
226[‡]	Charles Gillam, Jun	2	1	2					
227[‡]	Charles Gillam, Sen	3	1	2					
228[‡]	William Tilford	2	1	3					
229[*‡]	Levi Casey	1	2	3		1			
230[‡]	James Rolan	1	1	4					
231[‡]	James Lee	2		1					
232[‡]	Henry Lee		1	2					
233[‡]	James Little, Jur	1	1	2					
234[‡]	James Little, Sen	2	1	3					
235[‡]	Absolum Wadkins		1	2					
236[*‡]	Harris Revis	2	2	1					
237[‡]	Holle Prater	5	1	4					
238[‡]	Nathaniel Robins	2	1	2					
239[‡]	Marmeduke Robins	1	1	2					

BOND COUNTY (Continued)

No.	Heads of families	Free white males under 21	Free white males 21 & above	Free white females	People of color Free	People of color Servants or slaves	Twp.	Families in twp.	Pop. of twp.
240[‡]	Ambrose White	1	1	3					
241[‡]	John Blair	1	1	1					
242[‡]	Alexander McKinsey	1	1	5					
243[*‡]	Paul Beck	1	1	3					
244[‡]	Enos Blair	1	1	2					
245[*‡]	Colbert Blair	2	1	2					
246[*‡]	Newton Coffee	4	1	4					
247[‡]	John Beck	2	1	5					
248[*‡]	James Card	2	1	2					
249[‡]	John Russell	1	1	2					
250[‡]	George Davis	3	1	3					
251[‡]	Levi Verdan		1	2					
252[‡]	William Verdan		1	3					
253[‡]	Joshua Renfrow	1	1	4					
254[*‡]	Aaron Casey	1	2	2					
255[*‡]	John Lee	5	1	3					
256[*‡]	John Hill	1	2	3					
257[*‡]	Henry Hill	2	1	2					
258[‡]	Joseph Wright	4	1	1					
259[*‡]	Thomas Hill	1	1	1					
260[*‡]	Burwell Massie	4	1	2					
261[*‡]	Charles Stice	1	1	3					
262[*‡]	Henry Piatt	3	1	4					
263[‡]	William Hinton	1	1	2					
264[‡]	Easton Whiton	2	1	4	1				
265[‡]	William Freeman	1	1	3					
266[‡]	Simon Landes		1	1					
267[*‡]	Thomas Robison	2	1	3					
268[‡]	James Ward	1	1	2					
269[‡]	John Ward	3	1	4					
270[‡]	Mary Ward	3	1	3					
271[‡]	Elisha Freeman	1	2	2					
272[‡]	William McDavid	1	1	1				McCords Township	
273[‡]	David Bradford	1	1	4					
274[*‡]	Thomas Kirkpatrick		1	1					
275[‡]	Millo Wood	1	1	2					

BOND COUNTY (Continued)

No.	Heads of families	Free white males under 21	Free white males 21 & above	Free white females	People of color Free	People of color Serv-ants or slaves	Twp.	Families in twp.	Pop. of twp.
276[‡]	John Kirkpatrick	3	2	7					
277[‡]	Josiah Kirkpatrick	1	1	3					
278[‡]	Joseph Williams	5	1	3					
279[‡]	William M. Young	1	1	2					
280[‡]	Thomas Allison	2	1	1					
281[‡]	Samuel White	1	1	4					
282[‡]	James W. Willis		1	1					
283[‡]	William Steward		1	2					
284[‡]	Jesse Margrave	1	1	3					
285[‡]	John Margrave	1	1	2					
286[‡]	Jesse Jonston	3	1	5					
287[‡]	David D. Alexander	2	1	4					
288[‡]	Lydia Moore	1		2					
289[‡]	Edwin Meers	1	1	1					
290[*‡]	Robert McCord	4	1	7					
291[‡]	Alexander Holloday	3	1	5					
292[‡]	John White	2	1	6					
293[‡]	Thomas Wafer	1	1	2					
294[‡]	James Wafer		1	4					
295[‡]	Jonathan Glenn	1	1	2					
296[‡]	James Hill	1	1	3					
297[‡]	Robert Beaty	3	1	2					
298[*‡]	Zacariah Bridgewater	1	1	2					
299[‡]	James Denney	2	5	3					
300[‡]	John Troutman	1	1	1					
301[*‡]	Andrew Finley	3	1	1					
302[*‡]	Robert Briggs	2	2	5					
303[‡]	Isaac Cox		3	2					
304[‡]	James Black		5						
305[‡]	David McCord	3	1	2					
306[‡]	Jesse Townsend	2	4	5	2				
307[‡]	Jonathan Voiles		1	1					
308[‡]	Henry Brines	1	2	3					
309[‡]	William Cline	2	1	2					
310[‡]	Benjamin Anderson	1	1	2					
311[‡]	James Brines	1		2					

BOND COUNTY (*Continued*)

No.	Heads of families	Free white males under 21	Free white males 21 & above	Free white females	People of color Free	People of color Servants or slaves	Twp.	Families in twp.	Pop. of twp.
312[‡]	George Varner	2	1	3					
313[*‡]	Gurdon Crandle		2	2					
314[‡]	John J. Norton	3	2	5					
315[‡]	Jacob Cress	2	1	6					
316[‡]	Josiah Patton	1	1	2					
317[‡]	Gilford Parrish	2	1	3					
318[*‡]	James Street	5	1	4					
319[‡]	William Griffy	2	1	3					
320[*‡]	Jarvis Forehand	3	1	4					
321[‡]	John McFail	1	2	4					
322[‡]	John McAdams	3	1	2					
323[‡]	John C. Hays		1	1					
324[‡]	James Isaacs	2	1	2					
325[‡]	Joseph McAdams, Sen	6	1	2					
326[*‡]	William M. Crisp		1	5					
327[‡]	John Tilson		3						
328[‡]	Aaron Rule	2	1	1					
329[*‡]	John Yoekum	4	1	5					
330[‡]	David Kirkpatrick	3	1	7					
331[*‡]	Joel Smith	2	1	2					
332[*‡]	James Wilson	2	1	1					
333[‡]	Israel Seward	1	2	2	1				
334[‡]	Joseph McAdams, Jur		1	1					
335[‡]	Joshua C. Alexander	4	3	4					
336[‡]	James Wright	1	1	3					
337[*‡]	Alexander McWilliams	2	1	3					
338[*‡]	Robert Hill	4	1	2					
339[*‡]	Hugh Kirkpatrick	3	1			4			
340[‡]	John Elder		1	2					
341[‡]	Daniel Meredith	2	1	1					
342[‡]	Able Sparks	3	1	7					
343[‡]	Barnabas Mikael	4	1	1					
344[*‡]	William Pacely		1	3					

BOND COUNTY (*Continued*)

No.	Heads of families	Free white males under 21	Free white males 21 & above	Free white females	People of color Free	People of color Servants or slaves	Twp.	Families in twp.	Pop. of twp.
345[*‡]	Robert Pacely	1	1	5					
346[*‡]	Jonathan Berry	5	1	2					
347[*‡]	Samuel Dixon	4	1	5					
348[*‡]	Alexander Robison	3	1	3					
349[‡]	James McCord		1	1					
350[*‡]	John Leeper	6	1	3					
351[‡]	John Short		1	2			Ripley Township		
352[‡]	James Kirkpatrick	5	2	6					
353[‡]	William Russell	3	2	4					
354[‡]	Ishom Revis	3	1	5					
355[‡]	John Smith	2	1	3					
356[‡]	Thomas Long		1	3					
357[‡]	James Smith	2	1	3					
358[‡]	James McBride	3	2	2					
359[*‡]	John Lindley	4	1	4					
360[‡]	Francis Travis	1	1	2					
361[‡]	Samuel Eblin	1	1	3					
362[*‡]	William Young		1	1					
363[*‡]	William Scribner	2	1	7					
364[*‡]	Robert Dimond	4	2	4					
365[‡]	Barney Riley	1	1	1					
366[‡]	Tapley Young	1	3	4					
367[‡]	Samuel Powers	3	1	5					
368[‡]	Lot Litteral	1	1	2					
369[‡]	John McNeir	2	1	2					
370[‡]	Thomas Kirkpatrick	7	2	7					
371[*‡]	John Steel		2	3					
372[*‡]	Asahel Enloe	6	1	4					
373[‡]	John J. Walker		1	2					
374[‡]	Ira E. Hooker	3	1	2					
375[‡]	James B. Rutherford	2	1	1					
376[‡]	Seth Blanchard		3	1					
377[‡]	Enoch Sanford	4	2	4					
378[‡]	Samuel Whitcomb		1	1					
379[*‡]	James McKinney	2	1	2					
380[‡]	Green P. Rice	1	1	3		2			

BOND COUNTY (*Continued*)

No.	Heads of families	Free white males		Free white females	People of color		Twp.	Families in twp.	Pop. of twp.
		under 21	21 & above		Free	Servants or slaves			
381[*‡]	George Davidson	1	4	4					
382[*‡]	Wyatt Stubbl[ef]ield	2	4	3					
383[‡]	William Spratt		1	2					
384[‡]	Hugh Watson	3	1	5					
385[*‡]	Conrad Howsong		1	3					
386[*‡]	William Henderson	2	1	7					
387[*‡]	William Clark	2	1	2					
388[‡]	Andrew Moore	3	4	6					
389[*‡]	Peter Hubbard	5	2	1					
390[*‡]	Francis Kirkpatrick	1	1	6					
391[*‡]	John Kirkpatrick	8	1	6					
392[‡]	Hosea J. Camp	1	1	2					
393[*‡]	John Hopton	1	1	3					
394[*‡]	William Stubblfield	7	1	4					
395[‡]	George Shipman	1	1	4					
396[‡]	James Troutman		1	2					
397[‡]	Joseph Stoker	2	1	2					
398[‡]	Rhutia Durley	4	2	4	1				
399[*‡]	John Stubblefield	3	1	3					
400[*‡]	Abraham McGinnis	4	1	3					
401[‡]	James Barlow	3	1	2					
402[‡]	Spencer Clarey	1	1	2					
403[*‡]	Sarah Clarey	2		3					
404[‡]	William Hart		1	1					
405[*‡]	William Hunter	3	1	2					
406[‡]	Robert Stewart	1	1	3					
407[‡]	Edward Elam	1	1	1					
408[‡]	John Laughlin	3	2	6					
409[‡]	Hugh McReynolds	4	1	5					
410[*‡]	Robert G. White	4	1	2					
411[‡]	James G. Kirkpatrick	4	1	4					
412[*‡]	John Elles	1	1	7					
413[‡]	Thomas White, Jur		2	1					
414[‡]	Isaac White	1	2	4					
415[*‡]	Gideon Robison		1	3					
416[‡]	David Moffit	1	1	6					

CENSUS OF 1820

BOND COUNTY (Continued)

No.	Heads of families	Free white males under 21	Free white males 21 & above	Free white females	People of color Free	People of color Servants or slaves	Twp.	Families in twp.	Pop. of twp.
417[*‡]	William Robison	2	3	1					
418[‡]	Hugh Robison	2	1	3					
419[*‡]	John White		1	2					
420[*‡]	Thomas White, sen	3	3	3					
421[‡]	William Hasting	2	1	2					
422[‡]	John Huston	1	1	3	3				
423[*‡]	Richard White	2	5	3					
424[‡]	John Montgomery	3	2	1					
425[*‡]	Allen Comer	2	1	1					
426[‡]	Jane Nisbitt	2		4					
427[*‡]	Thomas Powers	2	1	2					
428[‡]	John Hunter, Jur	1	1	5					
429[‡]	Joseph Hunter	1	1	2					
430[*‡]	John Hunter, sen	1	1	1					
431[*‡]	Samuel Hunter	1	1	1					
432[*‡]	Hezekiah Archer	4	1	1					
433[‡]	Richmond Baker	2	1	2					
434[‡]	A. M. C. H. Nisbitt		1	2					
435[*‡]	Israel Archer	2	1	4					
436[‡]	Aquilla Suggs	4	2	3					
437[‡]	George Donald	2	1	1					
438[‡]	William Nelson	4	1	3					
439[‡]	Margaret Garrison	1		5					
440[‡]	Charles Baker	5	1	5					
441[*‡]	Elijah Estep	7	1	1					
442[‡]	Henry Williams	3	1	3					
443[*‡]	Robert Gillaspy	5	1	5					
444[‡]	Abednigo Baker	3	1	5					
445[‡]	Henry Files	5	2	4					
446[*‡]	Hardy Volintine		2	1		1			
447[*‡]	Austin Grissim	2	1	2					
448[‡]	Jacob Holbrook	7	1	4					
449[‡]	Benjamin Johnson		1	1					
450[*‡]	Charles Johnson	5	2	4					
451[‡]	Williamson Plant	2	2	4					
452[*‡]	E. L. R. Wheelock	1	4	1					

BOND COUNTY (Continued)

No.	Heads of families	Free white males under 21	Free white males 21 & above	Free white females	People of color Free	People of color Servants or slaves	Twp.	Families in twp.	Pop. of twp.
453[‡]	Leonard Goss	1	1	1					
454[‡]	John Jordan	2	1	2					
455[‡]	Silas Lee Wait	2	6	4					
456[*‡]	Jonathan Davis	5	1	2					
457[‡]	David Simmons		1	2					
458[*‡]	William Volintine	3	1	3		1			
459[‡]	John Wood	4	1	2					
460[*‡]	Benjamin James	1	1	3					
461[‡]	Zadock Smith	5	1	3					
462[‡]	Joseph Roberts		1	2					
463[*‡]	Samuel Lee	3	2	3					
464[‡]	Ralf Austin	2	1	1					
465[‡]	Ephraim Rosson	1		1					
466[‡]	Richard Worley	2	1	4					
467[‡]	John Lee	1	1	1					
468[‡]	John C. Vance		1	1					
469[‡]	Enoch Estep	1	1	1					
470[‡]	John Pricket	2	2	4					
471[*‡]	John Coil	4	2	5					
472[‡]	Rachel Barker	1		4					
473[*‡]	Samuel Hill	1	1	4		1			
474[‡]	Elias Baker	1	1	2					
475[‡]	James Baker	2	1	3					
476[*‡]	John Lewis	3	1	3					
477[‡]	William Gracy		4	4					
478[‡]	John Edwards	2	1	4					
479[‡]	Ransom Gaer	5	1	4					
480[*‡]	Andrew Moody	2	1	2					
481[*‡]	William Lindly	2		2					
482[*‡]	James Johnston	2	2	2					
483[‡]	McHenry Johnston		1	1					
484[‡]	John Gilmore	4	1	5					
	Ad	911	642	1334	22	27			

CENSUS OF 1820

BOND COUNTY (*Continued*)

There is of free white Males of Twenty-one years of age & upwards	642
Free white Males under Twenty-one years of age	906
Free white females	1334
Free people of Color	22
Servants or Slaves of Do	27
Total aggregate	2931

Signed, JOHN RUSSEL, Comr.

Corrected totals:

Free white males 21 years and upwards		641
Free white males under 21 years		906
Free white females		1335
		2882
Negroes		49
Free people of color	22	
Servants or slaves	27	
	49	
Total		2931

In the original manuscript the number 275 was omitted and the correction made at the end of the list by omitting a number for the last name, John Gilmore. In this reproduction the numbering has been corrected from this point on.

BOND COUNTY (Continued)

John Russell took both censuses for 1820, certifying the state census on the second and the federal census on the sixteenth of December. The state census for 1818 was taken by Martin Jones and dated May 14.

George W. Meguire, a "foreigner not naturalized," between the ages of 16 and 26, and with no family, is given in the federal census as residing between Andrew Bowman (96) and Burd E. Miles (97).

Discrepancies are as follows:

5 Harlan, Bonham
   1818. Harlin, Bonham
   F1820. Harlan, Bonham
6 Myers, Joseph
   1818. Mires, Joseph
   F1820. Myers, Joseph
7 Myers, Stephen
   1818. Mires, Stephen
   F1820. Myers, Stephen
11 Hanin, Jesse
   1818. Hanon, Jesse
   F1820. Hanin, Jesse
15 Anderson, Ignatius
   1818. Anderson, Ignatious
   F1820. Anderson, Ignatius
16 Hanin, James
   1818. Hanon, James
   F1820. Hanin, James
19 Brazelton, Benjamin
   F1820. Brazleton, Benjamin
20 Innman, Rufus
   1818. Inman, Rufus
   F1820. Innman, Rufus
22 Revis, Charles
   1818. Reavis, Charles
   F1820. Revis, Charles
29 Stephenson, William
   F1820. Stepheson, William
30 Hinton, Even
   1818. Hinton, Evans
   F1820. Hinton, Even
31 White, Anne
   Probably the widow of David White, 1818.
32 Hinson, Benjamin
   1818. Henson, Benjamin
   F1820. Hinson, Benjamin
34 Hinson, John
   1818. Henson, John
   F1820. Hinson, John
47 Pruitt, Fields
   1818. Prewit, Fields
   F1820. Pruitt, Fields
59 Canady, Archibal
   F1820. Canady, Archibald
66 Burges, William
   1818. Burgess, William
   F1820. Burges, William

69 Osmus, Philip
   1818. Osmus, Phillip
   F1820. Osmus, Philip
73 Bawlin, Benjamin
   1818. Bowling, Benjamin
   F1820. Bowlin, Benjamin
77 Bileyu, Joseph
   F1820. Bilyeu, Joseph
78 Duff, Philip
   1818. Duff, Phillip
   F1820. Duff, Philip
85 Burnside, James, Sen.
   1818. Burnside, James
   F1820. Burnside, James, Sen.
93 Watley, Henry
   1818. Whatley, Henry
   F1820. Watley, Henry
94 Nicholas, Thomas
   1818. Nichols, Thomas
   F1820. Nicholas, Thomas
111 Whitley, John, Sen.
   1818. Whitley, John
   F1820. Whitley, John, Sen.
121 Revis, Isham
   1818. Reavis, Isham
   F1820. Revis, Ishom
124 Nicholas, William
   1818. Nichols, William
   F1820. Nicholas, William
126 Phelps, Zadock
   1818. Felps, Zedoch
   F1820. Phelps, Zadock
127 Phelps, John
   1818. Felps, John
   F1820. Phelps, John
133 Wright, Rosana
   F1820. Wright, Rosanna
140 Howell, William
   1818. Howel, William
   F1820. Howell, William
149 Hanin, Samuel
   1818. Hanon, Samuel
   F1820. Hanin, Samuel
151 Innman, Rufus
   1818. Inman, Rufus
   F1820. Innman, Rufus

CENSUS OF 1820

BOND COUNTY (Continued)

162 Hickerson, William L.
    1818. Hickason, William
    F1820. Hickerson, William L.
165 Wakefield, Diana
    1818. Wakefield, Dianna
    F1820. Wakefield, Diana
168 Hailey, John
    1818. Haly, John
    F1820. Hailey, John
175 Scridmore, George
    F1820. Scridamore, George
201 Barns, Joshua
    F1820. Barnes, Joshua
236 Revis, Harris
    1818. Reavis, Harris
    F1820. Revis, Harris
245 Blair, Colbert
    1818. Blair, Colbin
    F1820. Blair, Colbert
246 Coffee, Newton
    1818. Coffe, Newton
    F1820. Coffee, Newton
260 Massie, Burwell
    1818. Massey, Burwell
    F1820. Massie, Burwell
262 Piatt, Henry
    1818. Pyatt, Henry
    F1820. Piatt, Henry
264 Whiton, Easton
    F1820. Whitton, Easton
267 Robison, Thomas
    1818. Robertson, Thomas
    F1820. Robison, Thomas
287 Alexander, David D.
    F1820. Alexander, John D.
289 Meers, Edwin
    F1820. Mears, Edwin
298 Bridgewater, Zacariah
    1818. Bridgwater, Zachariah
    F1820. Bridgewater, Zacariah
313 Crandle, Gurdon
    1818. Corrandle, Jordan B.
    F1820. Crandle, Gurdon
314 Norton, John J.
    F1820. Norton, John T.
320 Forehand, Jarvis
    1818. Forhand, Jarvis
    F1820. Forehand, Jarvis
326 Crisp, William M.
    1818. Crisp, William
    F1820. Crisp, William M.
329 Yoekum, John
    1818. Yokem, John
    F1820. Yoekum, John

344 Pacely, William
    1818. Pusley, William
    F1820. Pacely, William
345 Pacely, Robert
    1818. Parsley, Robert
    F1820. Pacely, Robert
347 Dixon, Samuel
    1818. Dickson, Samuel
    F1820. Dixon, Samuel
348 Robison, Alexander
    1818. Robertson, Alexander
    F1820. Robison, Alexander
364 Dimond, Robert
    1818. Diamond, Robert
    F1820. Dimond, Robert
365 Riley, Barney
    F1820. Riley, Barnebas
372 Enloe, Asahel
    1818. Enloe, Ashel
    F1820. Enloe, Asahel
381 Davidson, George
    1818. Davison, George
    F1820. Davidson, George
382 Stubbl[ef]ield, Wyatt
    1818. Stubblefield, Wyatt
    F1820. Stubblefield, Wyatt
385 Howsong, Conrad
    1818. Hussong, Conrad
    F1820. Howsong, Conrod
387 Clark, William
    1818. Clerk, William
    F1820. Clark, William
394 Stubblfield, William
    1818. Stubblefield, William
    F1820. Stubblefield, William
402 and
403 Clarey, Spencer & Sarah
    Evidently the son and widow of John Clary, 1818 (8).
410 White, Robert G.
    1818. White, Robert
    F1820. White, Robert G.
411 Kirkpatrick, James G.
    F1820. Kirkpatrick, James
412 Elles, John
    1818. Elles, John
    F1820. Ellis, John
415 Robison, Gideon
    1818. Robinson, Gideon
    F1820. Robison, Gideon
417 Robison, William
    1818. Robinson, William
    F1820. Robison, William

BOND COUNTY (*Concluded*)

- 420 White, Thomas, Sen.
  - 1818. White, Thomas
  - F1820. White, Thomas, Sen.
- 430 Hunter, John, Sen.
  - 1818. Hunter, John
  - F1820. Hunter, John, Sen.
- 436 Suggs, Aquilla
  - F1820. Sugg, Aquilla
- 443 Gillaspy, Robert
  - 1818. Gallispi, Robert
  - F1820. Gillaspy, Robert
- 447 Grissim, Austin
  - 1818. Grisham, Austin
  - F1820. Grissim, Austin
- 451 Plant, Williamson
  - F1820. Plant, William
- 461 Smith, Zadock
  - F1820. Smith, Zedock
- 464 Austin, Ralf
  - F1820. Austin, Ralph
- 471 Coil, John
  - 1818. Coyle, John
  - F1820. Coil, John
- 481 Lindly, William
  - 1818. Lindley, William
  - F1820. Lindly, William
- 482 Johnston, James
  - 1818. Johnson, James
  - F1820. Johnston, James

CENSUS OF CLARK COUNTY, 1820

I Charles Patrick of the County of Clark do Solemnly swear that I will well and truly make a correct enumeration of all persons resident within the County of Clark to the best of my abilety and returne the same to the Secretary of State on or before the first Monday of december in the year of eighteen hundred and twenty

CHARLES PATRICK

State of Illinois }
Clark County }

Be it remembered that on the first day of August came before me Charles Patrick and took the above Oath

JOHN BLACK
J P

CLARK COUNTY (*Continued*)

The whole number of Persons in Clark County appears in a schedule herto annexed (and subscribed by me) is nine hundred and thirty two.

Schedule of the whole number Persons in Clark County

Names of the County & Townships	Names of the Heads of Families	Free white males of twenty one years old & upwards	All other white Inhabitants	Free peopple of Color	Slaves
Clark County Wane Township	[1 ‡] Charleton Britton	1	2		
	[2*‡] James Johnston	1	8		
	[3*‡] Anthony Sanders	1	5		
	[4 ‡] Abner Fuller	2	2		
	[5 ‡] William Van Houter	3	6		
	[6 ‡] Lewis Murphey	1	4		
	[7*‡] Remember Blackman	2	4		
	[8 ‡] Jacob Jones	3	5		
	[9 ‡] Samuel Littlefield	1	3		
	[10*‡] Barnibald Runnolds	7	5		
	[11*‡] John Strutton	1	7		
	[12*‡] Johnathan Mayo	1	3		
	[13 ‡] Joseph Lowrie	1	5		
	[14 ‡] William Whitlesy	1	4		
	[15*‡] Alosyus Brown	1	4		
	[16*‡] Elijah Oston	2	9		
	[17 ‡] William Murphey	1	10		
	[18 ‡] Labin Burr	1	10		
	[19 ‡] Joseph Curtiss	1	2		
	[20 ‡] Samuel Williams	1	4		
	[21 ‡] David Boland	2	5		
	[22 ‡] Edward Wheeler	1	1		
	[23 ‡] Chansa Adkins	1	5		
	[24 ‡] Isaac Sandford	1	1		
	[25*‡] Edwin Persol	1	7		
	[26 ‡] James Farnum	1	1		
	[27*‡] Daniel Lane	2	7		
Pike Township	[28 ‡] Thomas Rodes	1	5		
	[29*‡] James Knight	3	6		
	[30*‡] David Caldwell	2	2		

Figures and symbols preceding names have been supplied by the editor:
‡ Indicates name also in Federal Census for 1820.
* Indicates name also in State Census for Crawford County, 1818.

CENSUS OF 1820

CLARK COUNTY (*Continued*)

County & township	No.	Heads of families	White males 21 & upwards	All other white	Free people of color	Slaves
	[31 ‡]	Thomas Foster	1	7		
	[32 ‡]	Elexander Ewing	1	2		
	[33 ‡]	James Eagleton	1	2		
	[34*‡]	James Martin	1	12		
	[35 ‡]	Martin Ray	1	2		
	[36*‡]	James M. Love	3	2		
	[37*‡]	Thomas Wilson	3	8		
	[38*‡]	William Lewis	1	3		
	[39 ‡]	Thomas Knight	1	2		
	[40*‡]	Mary Kilbourn		5		
	[41 ‡]	Eli Newel	1	5		
	[42 ‡]	John Ray	2	6		
Dubois Township	[43 ‡]	Cutler Leonard	4	2		
	[44*‡]	John Essrey	1	1		
	[45*‡]	John McClure	1	8		
	[46*‡]	James Cox	1	2		
	[47*‡]	Zacheas Hassle	1	4		
	[48*‡]	Charles Neely	1	8		
	[49*‡]	Moses Williams	1	5		
	[50*‡]	John Blake	1	9		
	[51*‡]	Enock Davis	1	4		
	[52*‡]	Zachariah Archer	1	7		
	[53*‡]	Charles K. Archer	1	4		
	[54 ‡]	Alden Winchester	1			
	[55 ‡]	Samuel Flemming	1	5		
	[56 ‡]	Jacob Poorman, Jr.	1	1		
	[57*‡]	Daniel Cornell	1	3		
	[58 ‡]	Sympson Morgan	1	6		
	[59 ‡]	Levi Sharp	1	5		
	[60 ‡]	Enock Davis	2	1		
	[61*‡]	William B. Archer	2	3		
	[62 ‡]	James Cantwell	1			
	[63*‡]	Abraham Snyder	2	7		
	[64*‡]	James Taylor	1	8		
	[65*‡]	William Lockard	2	8		
	[66*‡]	Joseph Dunlap	1	5		
	[67*‡]	John Chenoweth	2	5		

CLARK COUNTY (Continued)

County & township	No.	Heads of families	White males 21 & upwards	All other white	Free people of color	Slaves
	[68*‡]	Joseph Shaw	3	10		
	[69*‡]	John Welch	2	4		
	[70 ‡]	Jacob Poorman	1	7		
	[71*‡]	David Bright	1	6		
	[72 ‡]	John Stafford	1	5		
	[73*‡]	John Baker	1	7		
	[74*‡]	Lawrance Hollenback	1	10		
	[75 ‡]	Jeptha Baker	1	5		
	[76 ‡]	Jesse Eaton	1	3		
	[77*‡]	John Parker	3	4		
	[78*‡]	James W. Parker	1	3		
	[79*‡]	Daniel Parker	1	9		
	[80 ‡]	Thomas Brown	1	8		
	[81 ‡]	Elizabeth Bohn		7		
	[82*‡]	Heli Cornell	1	6		
Clark County Washington Township	[83*‡]	Amos Ashmore	1	10		
	[84 ‡]	William Black	1	9		
	[85 ‡]	Rebecca Black	2	1		
	[86 ‡]	William Black	1	2		1
	[87 ‡]	Richard Armstrong	1	9		
	[88 ‡]	John Black	2	5		
	[89*‡]	Jacob Long	1	4		
	[90*‡]	James Ashmore	2	2		
	[91*‡]	Peter Coykendoll	2	4		
	[92*‡]	Samuel Perry	3	10		
	[93 ‡]	Jacob Groves	1	1		
	[94*‡]	Samuel Ashmore	3	11		
	[95 ‡]	Thomas Black	1	7		
	[96 ‡]	Joseph Hawk	1			
	[97 ‡]	Isaac Hawk	1			
	[98 ‡]	Joel Cowan	1	5		
	[99*‡]	Hugh Henderson	1	11		
	[100 ‡]	Robert McCabe	1	4		
	[101*‡]	James McCabe	1	6		
	[102 ‡]	Jesse Essrey		3		
	[103 ‡]	Peggy Davis		6		

CLARK COUNTY (Continued)

County & township	No.	Heads of families	White males 21 & upwards	All other white	Free people of color	Slaves
Union Township	[104*‡]	Anthony Cox	1	6		
	[105*‡]	Resin Bell	1	3		
	[106 ‡]	Joseph Bell	1	4		
	[107*‡]	Samuel Prevo	1	9		
	[108*‡]	Joseph Owens	1	6		
	[109*‡]	James Cox	1	5		
	[110 ‡]	Thomas White	4	6		
	[111*‡]	David Hogue	1	7		
	[112 ‡]	Joseph Willard	1	9		
	[113 ‡]	Jacob Shetler	1			
	[114*‡]	Isaac Moore	2	6		
	[115*‡]	James B. Anderson	1	5		
	[116 ‡]	Cadwaleder Cooper	2	2		
	[117*‡]	James Bartlet	1	5		
	[118*‡]	Stephen Handy	1	4		
	[119 ‡]	William Martin	1	6		
	[120*‡]	Henory Harison	1	9		
	[121*‡]	John Handy	2	6		
	[122 ‡]	Moses McNeir	1	5		
	[123*‡]	Thomas Handy	5	6		
	[124 ‡]	Ezra Rowley	1	3		
	[125*‡]	Heugh Miller	3	2		
	[126 ‡]	Hugh Miller, Jr.	1	3		
	[127*‡]	Rheuben Crow	2	5		
	[128 ‡]	William Bartlet	1	5		
	[129 ‡]	Joshua Crow	1	2		
	[130*‡]	James McGath	3	6		
	[131*‡]	John Richardson	1	8		
	[132 ‡]	James C. Hilebart	2	1		
	[133*‡]	James Coneway	1	7		
	[134*‡]	Samuel Jemison	1	3		
	[135*‡]	Newil Leonard	1	3		
	[136 ‡]	Thomas Johnson	1	1		
	[137 ‡]	Thomas Laden	1	8		
	[138 ‡]	Samuel Handy	1	5		
	[139 ‡]	Aaron Hatfield	1	3		
	[140*‡]	Jacob Blaze	1	3		
	[141*‡]	Ezekiel Perdue	1	8		

CLARK COUNTY (Continued)

County & township	No.	Heads of families	White males 21 & upwards	All other white	Free people of color	Slaves
	[142*‡]	George W. Catron	1	4		
	[143*‡]	Syrus Sharp	1	8		
	[144 ‡]	Benj. Lamb	1	1		
	[145 ‡]	James Miller	1			
	[146 ‡]	Cornelius Lamb	2	1		
	[147 ‡]	Abner Lamb	1	4		
	[148 ‡]	Richard Robinson	1	4		
	[149*‡]	James E. Moore	1	2		
	[150 ‡]	Daniel Cortright	1	2		
			207	724		
		Whole number of Inhabitants		931		1

I do hereby certify the above to be a correct ennumeration of the Inhabitants of Clark County taken by me this 20th of November 1820

                        CHARLES PATRICK Commissioner C C

Totals:
    Free white males of 21 years and upwards   207
    All other white inhabitants   724
                                        931
    Slave   1
                          Total   932

CENSUS OF 1820

CLARK COUNTY (Continued)

Charles Patrick took both censuses for 1820, certifying the state census on November 20 and the federal census on November 25. Returns for 1818 are included in the 1818 census for Crawford County, from which Clark County was set off in 1819. Except for minor rearrangements of a few names and the variations in spelling noted below, the 1820 censuses are identical.

Discrepancies are as follows:

2 Johnston, James
   1818. Johnson, James
   F1820. Johnston, James
7 Blackman, Remember
   1818. Blackmon, Remember
   F1820. Blackman, Remember
10 Runnolds, Barnibald
   1818. Runnels, Barnabas
   F1820. Ronnalds, Barnibald
11 Strutton, John
   1818. Struton, John
   F1820. Strutton, John
14 Whitlesy, William
   F1820. Whitley, William
15 Brown, Alosyus
   1818. Brown, Aloscous
   F1820. Brown, Alosysus
16 Oston, Elijah
   1818. Auston, Eliga
   F1820. Osten, Elijah
19 Curtiss, Joseph
   F1820. Curtis, Joseph
23 Adkins, Chansa
   F1820. Adkins, Charles
25 Persol, Edwin
   1818. Purcell, Edward
   F1820. Persol, Edwin
26 Farnum, James
   F1820. Farnham, James
32 Ewing, Elexander
   F1820. Ewing, Alexander
40 Kilbourn, Mary
   1818. Cilbern, William D.
   F1820. Kilbourn, Mary
41 Newel, Eli
   F1820. Nuel, Eli
44 Essrey, John
   1818. Esry, John
   F1820. Essarey, John
45 McClure, John
   1818. M'Clewer, John
   F1820. McClure, John
46 Cox, James
   1818. Cocks, James
   F1820. Cox, James
47 Hassle, Zacheas
   1818. Hastel, Zachaus
   F1820. Hassle, Zacheus

48 Neely, Charles
   1818. Neely, Charles
   F1820. Neeley, Charles
49 Williams, Moses
   1818. Williams, Moses
   F1820. Williams, Mosis
51 Davis, Enock
   1818. Davis, Enoch
   F1820. Davis, Enoch
55 Flemming, Samuel
   F1820. Fleming, Samuel
57 Cornell, Daniel
   1818. Cornel, Daniel
   F1820. Cornell, Daniel
63 Snyder, Abraham
   1818. Snider, Abram
   F1820. Snyder, Abraham
67 Chenoweth, John
   1818. Chenowith, John
   F1820. Chenowith, John
71 Bright, David
   1818. Brite, Daniel
   F1820. Bright, David
74 Hollenback, Lawrance
   1818. Holanback, Laurence
   F1820. Hollenback, Lawrence
78 Parker, James W.
   1818. Parker, James
   F1820. Parker, James W.
81 Bohn, Elizabeth
   F1820. Bohan, Elizabeth
82 Cornell, Heli
   1818. Cornel, Heli
   F1820. Cornell, Heli
91 Coykendoll, Peter
   1818. Kaykendall, Peter
   F1820. Coykendoll, Peter
92 Perry, Samuel
   1818. Pery, Samuel
   F1820. Perry, Samuel
99 Henderson, Hugh
   1818. Henderson, Hew
   F1820. Henderson, Hugh
102 Essrey, Jesse
   F1820. Essarey, Jesse
104 Cox, Anthony
   1818. Cocks, Anthony
   F1820. Cox, Anthony

CLARK COUNTY (*Concluded*)

105 Bell, Resin
    1818. Ball, Risen
    F1820. Bell, Resin
108 Owens, Joseph
    1818. Oins, Joseph
    F1820. Owens, Joseph
109 Cox, James
    1818. Cocks, James
    F1820. Cox, James
114 Moore, Isaac
    1818. Moor, Isaac
    F1820. Moore, Isaac
115 Anderson, James B.
    1818. Anderson, James
    F1820. Anderson, James B.
116 Cooper, Cadwaleder
    F1820. Cooper, Cadwalider
120 Harison, Henory
    1818. Harrison, Henry
    F1820. Harison, Henry
122 McNeir, Moses
    F1820. McNeer, Moses
125 Miller, Heugh
    1818. Miller, Hew
    F1820. Miller, Hugh

127 Crow, Rheuben
    1818. Crow, Rubin
    F1820. Crow, Rheuben
130 McGath, James
    1818. McGerth, James
    F1820. McGath, James
132 Hilebart, James C.
    F1820. Hillebart, James C.
133 Coneway, James
    1818. Conaway, James
    F1820. Coneway, James
134 Jemison, Samuel
    1818. Jimerson, Samuel
    F1820. Jemison, Samuel
135 Leonard, Newil
    1818. Leonard, Newel
    F1820. Leonard, Nuel
137 Laden, Thomas
    F1820. Layton, Thomas
141 Perdue, Ezekiel
    1818. Perdew, Ezekel
    F1820. Perdue, Ezekiel
143 Sharp, Syrus
    1818. Sharp, Cyrus
    F1820. Sharp, Syrus
149 Moore, James E.
    1818. Moor, James
    F1820. Moore, James E.

CENSUS OF CRAWFORD COUNTY, 1820

State of Illinois Crawford County commissioners Court Special Term July 1820 Ordered

That Robert C. Ford be and he is hereby appointed commissioner to take the Census of this County agreeably to an act of the Legislator passed at their last session

Coppy Att

EDWARD H. PIPER Clk.
C C. C C

(A. true coppy)

Crawford
Census

Whites	3062
Blacks	95

I, Robert C. Ford of the County of Crawford do Solemnly Swear that I will well and truly make a correct enumeration of all persons resident within the County of Crawford to the best of my abillity and return the same to the Secretary of State on or before the first Monday in December in the year eighteen hundred and twenty.

ROBERT C. FORD

Sworn and Subscribed before me a Justice of the Peace in and for the said County of Crawford and State of Illinois this first day of August 1820

JAS. S. OTEY [Seal]
J.P.

CRAWFORD COUNTY (*Continued*)
Census of Crawford County Illins

Names of heads of Families	Free white males twenty one years old and upwards	All other White Inhabitants	Free people of Coulor	Servants or Slaves
[1*‡] David Stewart	3	4		
[2 ‡] James Wilson	5	5		
[3 ‡] George Calhound	4	3		
[4*‡] Edward H. Piper	1	2		
[5*‡] Edward N. Cullom	3	6		
[6 ‡] James S. Otey	2	2		
[7 ‡] Wickliff Kitchell	1	4		
[8*‡] Joseph Kitchell	2	7		
[9 ‡] Horrace E. Baker	1	2		
[10 ‡] John Shields	1	2		
[11*‡] William Wilson	1	4		
[12 ‡] Robert C. Ford	2	4		
[13 ‡] George W. Lindsay	1	1		
[14*‡] Abraham Taylor	2	5		
[15 ‡] Samuel Perkins	4	3		
[16 ‡] Lewis Perkins	2	2		
[17] Thomas Trimble	2	1		
[18*‡] Jonathan Purcell	1			
[19 ‡] Lawson Linton	1	2		
[20*‡] Joseph Fesler	1	3		
[21*‡] Job Harness	2	5		
[22 ‡] Wheeler Mallett	1	4		
[23*‡] Barnabas Marvel	1	2		
[24*‡] David Porter	1	6		
[25 ‡] Jesse Barlow	2	2		
[26*‡] Mathew Neely	1	1		
[27 ‡] Noah Biggs	1	2		
[28*‡] Elmond Goff	2	2		
[29*‡] Sarah Neely		7		
[30*‡] James Hungerford	3	4		
[31 ‡] Brice Purcell	1	1		
[32 ‡] Isaac Decker	2	7		
[33 ‡] James Moore	1	4		
[34*‡] John Moore	2	6		
[35*‡] Joseph Wells	2	4		
[36 ‡] Hezekiah Stratten	1	3		

Figures and symbols preceding names have been supplied by the editor:
‡ Indicates name also in Federal Census for 1820.
* Indicates name also in State Census for 1818.

CENSUS OF 1820

CRAWFORD COUNTY (Continued)

No.	Heads of families	White males 21 & upwards	All other white	Free people of color	Servants or slaves
[37*‡]	Abraham Bogard	1	9		
[38*‡]	Silas Harlen	1	2		
[39*‡]	Daniel Delap	1	9		
[40*‡]	James Caldwell	2	7		
[41*‡]	Thomas Gill	2	5		
[42*‡]	Andrew B. Rhea	2	5		
[43 ‡]	John McKinney	2	2		
[44 ‡]	James McKinney	1	3		
[45*‡]	Smith Shaw	2	10		
[46 ‡]	Wilson Lagow	2	5		3
[47*‡]	Jonas Butterfield	2	4		
[48*‡]	Israel Harris	3	3		
[49 ‡]	Ester Wells	1	4		
[50*‡]	Samuel Lindley	2	5		
[51*‡]	John W. Barlow	2	7		
[52*‡]	Marvel Marcum	1	10		
[53 ‡]	Samuel McDowell	1	2		
[54*‡]	Amos Phelps	2	5		
[55*‡]	George W. Bratten	1	7		
[56*‡]	John Waldrope	1	11		
[57 ‡]	Robert Porter	1	8		
[58 ‡]	John Wood	1	8		
[59*‡]	Mary Hutton	1	7		
[60*‡]	John Gill	1	5		
[61 ‡]	John Alexander	1	2		
[62 ‡]	William Chambers	1	4		
[63 ‡]	Jonas Painter	1	4		
[64*‡]	Isaac Lemasters	1	2		
[65 ‡]	Martha Hackett	1	7		
[66*]	Nancy Kitchell	1	1		
[67*‡]	Richard M. Highsmith	1	3		
[68 ‡]	Thomas Robinett	1	7		
[69 ‡]	Robert Miller	1	2		
[70*‡]	Samuel Drake	1	5		
[71*‡]	Rachel Miller	1	8		
[72 ‡]	Thomas Highsmith	1	1		
[73 ‡]	John Highsmith	1	3		
[74*‡]	William Highsmith	2	2		

CRAWFORD COUNTY (Continued)

No.	Heads of families	White males 21 & upwards	All other white	Free people of color	Servants or slaves
[75 ‡]	Ezra H. Allison	1	7		
[76 ‡]	Elijah Harper	1	3		
[77 ‡]	Henry Harper	1	3		
[78*]	Ezekiel Anderson			6	
[79 ‡]	Charles Emmons	2	10		
[80 ‡]	Andrew Pinkstaff	1	5		
[81 ‡]	John Pinkstaff	1	7		
[82 ‡]	Israel Price	1	4		
[83 ‡]	William Highsmith	1	3		
[84 ‡]	Michael Price	1	4		
[85 ‡]	Thomas Baggett	2	3		
[86*]	George Anderson			3	
[87]	Jasen Goen			5	
[88]	Austin Tann			3	
[89*]	Edy Cole			2	
[90*]	Enock Jones			3	
[91]	Joshua Anderson			4	
[92]	Betsey Anderson			6	
[93*]	John Porter			5	
[94]	Caleb Anderson			3	
[95 ‡]	Jacob Helverstine	1	4		
[96 ‡]	Amasa Vanmetre	1	1		
[97 ‡]	William Norris	1	2		
[98*]	Sian Morris			4	
[99*]	Edward Goen			2	
[100]	Nancy Morris			2	
[101]	John Evans			7	
[102*]	Isaac Goen			8	
[103 ‡]	David McCord	1	8		
[104 ‡]	Samuel H. McCord	1	2		
[105]	Robert McCord	2	7		
[106 ‡]	Adam Lackey, Jr.	1	2		
[107 ‡]	John Dollahan	1	4		
[108*‡]	Adam Lackey, Sr.	1	6		
[109*‡]	James Bryant	1	5		
[110 ‡]	Alexander Willber	1	4		
[111*‡]	Edward Mills	1	3		
[112 ‡]	William Childres	1	2		

CRAWFORD COUNTY (Continued)

No.	Heads of families	White males 21 & upwards	All other white	Free people of color	Servants or slaves
[113 ‡]	James Westfall	1	5		
[114 ‡]	Isaac Westfall	1	2		
[115 ‡]	James Whitton	1	4		
[116 ‡]	Nancy Pumphrey	1	3		
[117*‡]	Abraham Carnes	1	10		
[118 ‡]	John Watson	1	5		
[119*‡]	Lewis Goen	1	2		
[120*‡]	Barbary Lacey		4		
[121*‡]	Edman Rathbone	1	6		
[122 ‡]	John Wells	1	9		
[123 ‡]	Joseph Fail	1	3		
[124*‡]	William Westrope	2	7		
[125*‡]	George W. Kinkead	2	4		
[126 ‡]	Joshua Allender	2	5		
[127 ‡]	Diler Catterton	1	3		
[128*‡]	Francis Boggs	1	6		
[129 ‡]	Henry Wycoff	3	4		
[130*‡]	Cornelius Taylor	8	8		
[131 ‡]	William Brownfield	2	3		
[132 ‡]	John Glenn	3	2		
[133 ‡]	Isaac Taylor	2	4		
[134 ‡]	John Fail	1	4		
[135 ‡]	Olive Lorin		7		
[136 ‡]	William McClees	1	3		
[137 ‡]	William Mattingly	1	3		
[138 ‡]	Dickey Anderson	2	2		
[139]	Enock Bachus	1			
[140*]	Henry Johnston	1	8		
[141]	William Raggen	2	4		
[142]	Benjamin Arthur	1	7		
[143*‡]	Thomas Fife	1	7		
[144 ‡]	Washburn Blackmore	2	2		
[145 ‡]	Onatis Chafey	2	1		
[146 ‡]	James Barr	1	7		
[147 ‡]	John Benefield	1	4		
[148 ‡]	Robert Benefield	2	4		
[149 ‡]	Levi Frazey	1	3		
[150*‡]	John Brigman	2	5		

CRAWFORD COUNTY (*Continued*)

No.	Heads of families	White males 21 & upwards	All other white	Free people of color	Servants or slaves
[151 ‡]	James Y. Beard	1	1		
[152 ‡]	James Stewart	1	6		
[153 ‡]	Peter Shidler	1	7		
[154 ‡]	Jacob Quick	2	3		
[155*‡]	Michael Rollins	1	2		
[156 ‡]	Thaddeus Morehouse	2	6		
[157 ‡]	Robert Bartleys	1	4		
[158 ‡]	Peter Lewis	1	1		
[159 ‡]	George Goble	2	3		
[160*‡]	Jesse Spencer	3	2		
[161 ‡]	William C. Ashbrooke	2	2		
[162 ‡]	William Campbell	1	2		
[163]	James Orr	2	2		
[164 ‡]	Levi Ashbrooke	1	3		
[165 ‡]	John McBane	2	7		
[166*‡]	John Dunlap	2	7		1
[167*‡]	William Howard	1	7		2
[168 ‡]	William Wilkins	1	2		
[169 ‡]	Thomas Ashbrooke	1	1		
[170 ‡]	James McClure	1	4		
[171 ‡]	Jacob Goen	1	8		
[172]	Bennett Organ	1	3		
[173]	George Clevendure	2	6		
[174*‡]	John R. Adams	1	2		
[175*‡]	Samuel Leneur	1	7		
[176 ‡]	Patten Cuningham	1	5		
[177*‡]	George Ferris	2	4		
[178 ‡]	Benjamin Pettis	1	3		
[179 ‡]	John Robinson	2	6		
[180 ‡]	Samuel Norton	1	6		
[181*‡]	Andrew McClure	3	6		
[182 ‡]	John E. Stuffelbeam	1	3		
[183*‡]	Samuel Lemons	1	6		
[184 ‡]	Stephen Norton	1	1		
[185 ‡]	Calvin Trowbridge	2	7		
[186 ‡]	Thomas Evans	3	1		
[187*‡]	Daniel Travis	3	3		
[188 ‡]	Bazil Evans	1	7		

CRAWFORD COUNTY (Continued)

No.	Heads of families	White males 21 & upwards	All other white	Free people of color	Servants or slaves
[189*‡]	Joshua Gifford	1	4		
[190*‡]	David Ruby	1			
[191*‡]	Reuben Norton	2	6		
[192*‡]	Samuel Harris	2	5		4
[193 ‡]	Joseph Beard	1	9		
[194*‡]	John Laster	1	10		
[195*‡]	Benjamin McCrary	1	5		
[196*‡]	Daniel Allison	1	4		
[197 ‡]	Eli Harris	1	5		1
[198*‡]	Jonathan Allison	3	4		
[199*‡]	Edward Allison	1	4		
[200 ‡]	Charles Thompson	1	5		
[201*‡]	Ezekiel Turner	2	4		
[202*‡]	Thomas Anderson	2	6		
[203*‡]	Ruth Turner		5		
[204*‡]	Elizabeth Jones		6		
[205*‡]	William Adams	3	10		
[206]	Michael Shaver	2	2		
[207]	John B. Alexander	1	5		
[208*‡]	Alexander McDonald	1	2		
[209*‡]	John Berrey	1	5		
[210]	David Phelps	2	3		
[211*‡]	Scott Riggs	1	10		
[212*‡]	Samuel McClure	2	1		
[213 ‡]	Michael Stuffelbeam	1	2		
[214 ‡]	Sewel Goodridge	1	1		
[215*‡]	Aaron Ball	6	5		1
[216*‡]	William Everman	1	9		
[217*‡]	John Newland	1	5		
[218 ‡]	Thomas Newland	1	5		
[219*‡]	Jesse Page	1	5		
[220*‡]	Stephen Eaton	1	5		
[221 ‡]	Harmon Gregg	2			
[222 ‡]	Nathaniel Cochran	1	4		
[223 ‡]	Andrew Arnold	2	5		
[224*‡]	Benjamin Eaton	1	6		
[225*‡]	John Eaton	1	3		
[226*‡]	Richard Eaton	1	8		

CRAWFORD COUNTY (*Continued*)

No.	Heads of families	White males 21 & upwards	All other white	Free people of color	Servants or slaves
[227*‡]	Joseph Eaton	1	3		
[228 ‡]	John Gregg	2	3		
[229*‡]	Doctor Hill	1	5		
[230*‡]	Charles Hill	1	3		
[231*‡]	David Shook	1	6		
[232*‡]	George Miller	1	4		
[233 ‡]	John Boyd	1	9		
[234 ‡]	William Newland	1	2		
[235 ‡]	James Scoby	3			
[236 ‡]	John Newland	2	3		
[237*‡]	John Hill	1	7		
[238 ‡]	Elijah Kelog	2	2		
[239 ‡]	William Johnston	1	6		
[240 ‡]	Robert Johnston	1	8		
[241 ‡]	Nathaniel Newland	1	2		
[242 ‡]	Eli Newland	1	5		
[243 ‡]	Moses Murphey	1	4		
[244 ‡]	Jeremiah Murphey	1	8		
[245 ‡]	David Black	4	5		
[246*‡]	Philip Edwards	5	4		
[247 ‡]	William Mitchell	1			
[248 ‡]	Robert Mansell	1			
[249*‡]	William Bradbury	2	6		
[250*‡]	Jehu Hardin	1	3		
[251*‡]	Elisha Bradbury	1	3		
[252 ‡]	Fergus Hill	1	3		
[253*‡]	Thomas Hardin	1	3		
[254 ‡]	John Thompson	1	3		
[255*‡]	John Malcum	1	3		
[256*‡]	James Rhea	2	5		
[257 ‡]	John Greggs	1	2		
[258]	Stephen Hagar	1	2		
[259*‡]	Thomas Jones	1	8		
[260*‡]	Joseph P. Jones	1	2		
[261 ‡]	James Kennady	1	8		
[262*‡]	Isaac Brimberry	1	11		
[263*‡]	James Shaw	2	12		
[264 ‡]	William Mathews	1	9		

CENSUS OF 1820

CRAWFORD COUNTY (Continued)

No.	Heads of families	White males 21 & upwards	All other white	Free people of color	Servants or slaves
[265 ‡]	Francis Avaline	1	6		
[266 ‡]	Samuel Mathews	1	3		
[267*‡]	Joseph Shaw	2	6		
[268 ‡]	Richard Newport	1	2		
[269*‡]	William Waldrope	2	5		
[270*‡]	John Waldrope	1	4		
[271 ‡]	Greenberry Shaw	2	4		
[272 ‡]	Jefferson Morris	1	2		
[273 ‡]	Benoni Middleton	4	8		
[274 ‡]	Daniel Kinney	1	1		
[275*‡]	Thomas Patten	1	3		
[276 ‡]	Ithra Bashar	1	12		
[277 ‡]	Dennis Hearn	1	1		
[278*‡]	Mary Hearn		5		
[279*‡]	John Lamb	2	5		
[280*‡]	George Westnor	2	11		
[281*‡]	William Flippo	2	2		
[282*‡]	James Dial	1	2		
[283*‡]	George Smith	2	6		
[284*‡]	James Johnston	1	7		
[285 ‡]	James Bigs	1	9		
[286 ‡]	James Watts	4	5		
[287*‡]	Lewis Goodin	1	2		
[288 ‡]	Robert Watts	1	1		
[289*‡]	Lot Watts	1	3		
[290*‡]	Thomas Watts	1	5		
[291 ‡]	Ezekiel Watts	1	1		
[292*‡]	George Boher	1	5		
[293*‡]	Robert McDowell	2	5		
[294*‡]	Joseph Wood	1	3		
[295 ‡]	Wm. McDowell	1	9		
[296*‡]	Benjn. Wilson	1	1		
[297 ‡]	Elizabeth Ellis		3		
[298*‡]	William Barbie	1	1		
[299 ‡]	Joseph Little	1	3		
[300 ‡]	James Little	1	3		
[301 ‡]	Isaac Lewis	2	7		
[302 ‡]	John Siena	1	4		

CRAWFORD COUNTY (*Continued*)

No.	Heads of families	White males 21 & upwards	All other white	Free people of color	Servants or slaves
[303 ‡]	Benoni White	1	5		
[304*‡]	John Veach	1	8		
[305*‡]	David Reaville	1	3		
[306*‡]	Robert Montgomery	1	5		
[307 ‡]	John Hancock	8	3		
[308 ‡]	William James	1	7		
[309*‡]	William Parker	1	3		
[310 ‡]	Peter Peroginn	1	2		
[311*‡]	Nathan Rollins	3	2		
[312 ‡]	Province Rollins	1	1		
[313 ‡]	Joab Sexton	8			1
[314 ‡]	John Price	1	2		
[315 ‡]	John Flinn	1	3		
[316 ‡]	Elijah Gibbs	1	8		
[317 ‡]	Daniel Figgins	1	6		
[318 ‡]	John Peroginn	1	4		
[319 ‡]	Aaron Vanatta	2	7		
[320 ‡]	William Ellott	1	4		
[321 ‡]	James Ellott	2	2		
[322*‡]	George Parker	1	7		
[323 ‡]	George Nichols	1	7		
[324 ‡]	Jonathan Parker	1	8		
[325*‡]	John Asbell	1	5		
[326 ‡]	Robert Whitton	1	8		
[327*‡]	Samuel Henry	1	10		
[328 ‡]	Samuel Parker	1	8		
[329*‡]	James Spencer	1	1		
[330 ‡]	Levi Lee	2	4		
[331 ‡]	Seth H. Bates	1	11		
[332 ‡]	Pleasant Whitton		2		
[333 ‡]	James Parker, Jr.	1	5		
[334 ‡]	James Parker, Sr.	1	1		
[335 ‡]	Thomas H. McCorpin	1	4		
[336 ‡]	Nathan Cheek	1	4		
[337 ‡]	William Robbins	1	7		
[338*‡]	Thomas Low	2	3		
[339 ‡]	Benjamine Beckwith	1	4		
[340 ‡]	Silas Beckwith	1	1		

CRAWFORD COUNTY (Continued)

No.	Heads of families	White males 21 & upwards	All other white	Free people of color	Servants or slaves
[341 ‡]	Adam S. Hatfield	1	3		
[342 ‡]	William Flood	1	7		
[343*‡]	Samuel Shoulders	1	8		
[344*‡]	David Vanwinkle	1	10		
[345 ‡]	Mecum Main	1	1		
[346 ‡]	Greenbury Vanwinkle	1	3		
[347*‡]	Thomas Dunlap	1	3		
[348 ‡]	William Dunlap, Jun.	1	3		
[349*‡]	William Dunlap, Sen.	1	2		
[350*‡]	Joel Cheak	1	4		
[351 ‡]	William Grey	1	2		
[352*‡]	Jeremiah Hogue	1	4		
[353 ‡]	William Low	1	2		
[354 ‡]	Nathaniel Wayne	3	7		
[355 ‡]	James Bathe	1	6		
[356 ‡]	Joseph Kenedy	1	3		
[357*‡]	Andrew Montgomery	1	8		
[358*‡]	William Hearn	1	1		
[359*‡]	Benjamine Parker	1	7		
[360*‡]	John Jackson	1	6		
[361*‡]	William Ryan	1	2		
[362*‡]	Jonathan Wood	1	3		
[363*‡]	George Bathe	1	6		
[364*‡]	Isaac Parker	1	2		
[365*‡]	Frederck Merclay	1	5		
[366*‡]	Abraham Walters	1	5		
[367*‡]	Daniel Vanwinkle	1	7		
[368*‡]	Stephen Lee	1	3		
[369 ‡]	Nancy Burruss	1	3		
[370 ‡]	James Kidwell	1	3		
[371*‡]	James Lemasters	1	4		
[372 ‡]	John H. Jackson	1	3		
[373 ‡]	James Ryan	1	3		
[374 ‡]	Samuel Bedwell	1	2		
[375 ‡]	Lewis Little	1	4		
[376 ‡]	Briant Siena	1	4		
[377 ‡]	Hinson Bright	1	10		
[378*‡]	Edmon Hearn	1	4		

CRAWFORD COUNTY (*Continued*)

No.	Heads of families	White males 21 & upwards	All other white	Free people of color	Servants or slaves
[379*‡]	William Young	1	4		
[380*‡]	John S. Woodworth	1	2		
[381 ‡]	Isaac Walters	1	8		
[382*‡]	Jacob Walters	1	9		
[383*‡]	Joseph Person	3	7		
[384 ‡]	Nathan Mares	1	3		
[385*‡]	Thomas Young	1	5		
[386 ‡]	Enoch Willhoit	1	3		
[387 ‡]	Joshua Barbie	1	6		
[388*‡]	Benjamine Eaton	1	4		
[389*‡]	Jeffrey Salisbury	1	1		
[390 ‡]	Richard Lagow	2	10		
[391 ‡]	Thomas Jeffries	1	6		
[392 ‡]	William Delap	1	10		
[393 ‡]	Peter Barrik	2	8		
[394*‡]	Daniel Martin	2	5		
[395 ‡]	Richard Lemasters	2	1		
[396*‡]	John Martin	1	7		
[397*‡]	William Garritt, Junr.	1	2		
[398*‡]	William Garritt, Senr.	1	3		
[399*‡]	Jacob Garritt	2	5		
[400*‡]	David Magaha	3	6		
[401*‡]	Abraham Conrod	1	3		
[402 ‡]	William Granwell	1	5		1
[403*‡]	Francis Cullom	1	2		
[404*‡]	Hall Symes	1	5		
[405*‡]	Christopher Mais	2	7		
[406 ‡]	Rebeca Myres	2	7		
[407*‡]	Gabriel Funk	1	4		
[408*‡]	Daniel Funk	1	5		
[409 ‡]	John Fulton	1	3		
[410 ‡]	James Conrod	1	2		
[411 ‡]	Isaac Kinney	1	6		
[412*‡]	John Sackrider	2	5		
[413*‡]	John Funk	2	5		
[414 ‡]	Charles Lathop	3	5		
[415 ‡]	Bateman Ross	1	5		
[416*‡]	James Newland	1	7		

CENSUS OF 1820

CRAWFORD COUNTY (*Continued*)

No.	Heads of families	White males 21 & upwards	All other white	Free people of color	Servants or slaves
[417 ‡]	Ephraim Ross	3	4		
[418 ‡]	Tiba H. Wolcott	2	3		
[419 ‡]	Joshua Farnham	1	1		
[420 ‡]	Mary Parker	1	7		
[421*‡]	Elijah Spalding	2	2		
[422*‡]	Daniel Willard	1	7		
[423*‡]	Aaron Gire	1	4		
[424*‡]	Exum Gire	1	3		
[425 ‡]	Edward Legge	1	2		
[426*‡]	Shadrach B. A. Carter	1	5		
[427*‡]	Elias Driskill	1	5		
[428 ‡]	Alexander Brown	1	4		
[429*‡]	William Hicks	1	10		
[430 ‡]	John Thompson	2	8		
[431 ‡]	John Fox	1	7		
[432*‡]	John Crews	2	6		
[433*‡]	Samuel Brimbery	1	4		
[434 ‡]	Barnet Starr	1	3		
[435 ‡]	Absolom Starr	1	5		
[436*‡]	Richard Easton	2	9		
[437*‡]	Thomas Kenady	1	7		
[438 ‡]	John Starr	1	8		
[439 ‡]	David Baldy	2	3		
[440*‡]	Chakley Draper	1	8		
[441*‡]	Exum Spivy	1			
[442 ‡]	Eli Morris	1	5		
[443 ‡]	David Henderson	1	4		
[444 ‡]	Jesse Reynolds	1	6		
[445*‡]	Robert Holiday	1	3		
[446*‡]	John Evans	1	8		
[447 ‡]	Joseph Morrison	1	6		
[448*‡]	Jesse Gire	1	7		
[449*‡]	Esec Hecock	1	4		
[450*‡]	Henry Buckner	1	2		
[451*‡]	Benjamine Evans	1	11		
[452 ‡]	Anbrose Pease	4	4		
[453*‡]	Ralph Jeffers	4	8		
[454*‡]	Elisha Crocker	2	2		

CRAWFORD COUNTY (Continued)

No.	Heads of families	White males 21 & upwards	All other white	Free people of color	Servants or slaves
[455*‡]	Elisha Fitch	1	9		
[456*‡]	Elizabeth Bennett		7		
[457 ‡]	John Connaway	3	1		
[458 ‡]	Zepheniah Lewis	2	5		
[459 ‡]	Josiah Taylor	1	8		
[460 ‡]	James Garwood	1	4		
[461*‡]	Chester Fitch	1	4		
[462 ‡]	George Bennett	3	5		
[463*‡]	David Goss	1	4		
[464*‡]	John T. Snipes	1	4		
[465 ‡]	Mark Snipes	1	3		1
[466 ‡]	Jesse Snipes	1	4		
[467 ‡]	Stephen Norton, Sr.	1	1		
[468*‡]	Isaac Goen	1	3		
[469*‡]	William Houston	2	9		
[470 ‡]	James Benedict	1	5		
[471 ‡]	Aaron Benedict	1	2		
[472 ‡]	Jacob Deen	1	1		
[473 ‡]	Asa Norton	1	7		
[474*‡]	Robert Haskins	1	3		
[475]	James Morgan	3	6		
[476]	Ezekiel York	1	8		
[477]	David W. Stark	1	6		
[478 ‡]	Stephen Gaines	1	9		
[479 ‡]	Samuel Baker	3	7		
[480*‡]	Charles Sudriott	3	4		
[481*‡]	Louis Lavalette	1	7		
[482*‡]	John Johnston, Jr.	2	2		
[483*‡]	John Johnston, Sr.	3	5		
[484 ‡]	John Harriman	1	7		
[485*‡]	Elizabeth Stockwell	1	6		
[486*‡]	Thomas Mills	1	2		
[487*‡]	John Mills	1	4		
[488*‡]	Samuel Allison	2	2		
[489*‡]	Richard Allison	1	3		
[490*‡]	Daniel Kuykendal	2	3		
491 ‡]	Jerimiah Price	1	3		

CENSUS OF 1820

CRAWFORD COUNTY (Continued)

No.	Heads of families	White males 21 & upwards	All other white	Free people of color	Servants or slaves
[492*‡]	Asahel Haskins	1	4		
[493 ‡]	Elijah Lamphire	2	8		
[494*‡]	Henry Price	1	5		
[495 ‡]	David Price	1	2		
[496*‡]	Peter Price	1	4		
[497 ‡]	Jesse Slawson	2	7		
[498 ‡]	Joseph Wilber	1	5		
[499]	Jeremiah Hodgin	1	2		
[500 ‡]	Ambrose Whitlock	1	1		3
[501 ‡]	Daniel Herrington	3	5		
[502 ‡]	Alpheus Peckard	1			
[503 ‡]	Luke Matson	1	4		
[504 ‡]	John Long	2	5		
[505 ‡]	Thomas Edds	1	2		
[506*‡]	Jane Dubois	1	5		6
[507*‡]	Elizabeth Beard		4		
[508 ‡]	John Jackson	3	12		
[509 ‡]	John J. Jackson	1	4		
[510 ‡]	Richard Brawdy	2	12		
[511 ‡]	William Brawdy	1	3		
[512*]	James Butler			8	
[513*‡]	Jane Richardson	1	6		
[514*‡]	John Golaher	5	8		
[515 ‡]	Margaret Roberts	1	7		
[516 ‡]	Moses Roberts	4	3		
[517 ‡]	Walter Leonard	1	3		
[518*‡]	James Gibson	6	4		
[519 ‡]	John Pool	2	1		
[520 ‡]	James White	1	5		
[521*‡]	John Golaher, Jr.	1	2		
[522 ‡]	Henry Gillam	2	3		
[523 ‡]	Henry Matier	1	5		
[524*‡]	Peter Bono	3	2		
[525 ‡]	Tousaint Bayeau	1	6		
[526 ‡]	John Baptist Peleau	1	2		
[527 ‡]	Henry Lature	1	1		
[528*‡]	Frederick Allison	1	7		

CRAWFORD COUNTY (Continued)

No.	Heads of families	White males 21 & upwards	All other white	Free people of color	Servants or slaves
[529*‡]	Phebe Allison		7		
[530*‡]	Isaac Allison	1	4		
[531 ‡]	John Allison	1	6		
[532]	George Miller, Senr.	1	3		
[533]	Nimrod Plugh	1	7		

I certify the above to be a correct Schedule of the Census of Crawford County and State of Illinois.

ROBERT C. FORD
Commissioner C. C.

Corrected totals:

Free white males of 21 years and upwards		732
All other white inhabitants		2344
		3076
Negroes		95
Free persons of color	71	
Servants or slaves	24	
	95	
	Total	3171

CRAWFORD COUNTY (Continued)

Robert C. Ford took both the state and federal censuses for 1820; the state census is undated; the federal census was certified November 2, 1820. The 1818 census for Crawford County, which then included also the territory set aside as Clark County in 1819, was taken by William Cullom and certified May 15, 1818; an unsigned supplemental census, taken probably by the same man, was dated July 10 to 22, 1818.

The federal census lists four families not listed in the state census:

Jacob Brimberry	8 persons
Between Isaac Brimberry (262) and	
James Shaw (263).	
James Dalson	10 persons
Between Ephraim Ross (417) and	
Tiba H. Wolcott (418).	
In 1818 census as Dolson.	
Joseph Richardson	11 persons
Between Ralph Jeffers (453) and	
Elisha Crocker (454).	
In 1818 census.	
John White	3 persons
Between James Johnston (284) and	
James Watts (286).	
In 1818 census.	
Total	32 persons

Thirty-six names are listed in the state but not in the federal census for 1820. Of these, however, fifteen families are "free persons of color" of which there is no list in the federal census though the summary indicates a total of seventy-five such persons.

Discrepancies are as follows:

9 Baker, Horrace E.
    F1820. Baker, Horace E.
14 Taylor, Abraham
    1818. Taylor, Abram
    F1820. Taylor, Abraham
18 Purcell, Jonathan
    1818. Persell, Johnathan
    F1820. Purcell, Jonathan
20 Fesler, Joseph
    1818. Festler, Joseph
    F1820. Fesler, Joseph
21 Harness, Job
    1818. Harnis, Jobe
    F1820. Harness, Job
22 Mallett, Wheeler
    F1820. Mallott, Wheeler
23 Marvel, Barnabas
    1818. Mavern, Barnabas
    F1820. Marvell, Barnabas
26 Neely, Mathew
    1818. Nealy, Matthew
    F1820. Neely, Mathew
28 Goff, Elmond
    1818. Bernard and David Goff resided in this location.
    F1820. Goff, Elmond
29 Neely, Sarah
    1818. Nealy, John
    F1820. Neely, Sarah
34 Moore, John
    1818. Moor, John
    F1820. Moore, John
35 Wells, Joseph
    1818. Wels, Joseph
    F1820. Wells, Joseph
37 Bogard, Abraham
    1818. Bogard, Abram
    F1820. Bogard, Abraham
38 Harlen, Silas
    1818. Harlin, Silus
    F1820. Harlen, Silas
42 Rhea, Andrew B.
    1818. Rhea, Andrew
    F1820. Rhea, Andrew B.
48 Harris, Israel
    1818. Harris, Isral
    F1820. Harris, Israel
50 Lindley, Samuel
    1818. Lindly, Samuel
    F1820. Lindley, Samuel
51 Barlow, John W.
    1818. Barlow, John
    F1820. Barlow, John W.

CRAWFORD COUNTY (Continued)

52 Marcum, Marvel
    1818. Marcom, Marvel
    F1820. Marcum, Marvel
53 McDowell, Samuel
    F1820. McDowel, Samuel
55 Bratten, George W.
    1818. Bratton, George W.
    F1820. Bratten, George W.
56 Waldrope, John
    1818. Waldrop, John, Jr.
    F1820. Waldrope, John
59 Hutton, Mary
    1818. Hatton, Marthy
    F1820. Hutton, Mary
64 Lemasters, Isaac
    1818. Lamasters, Isaac
    F1820. Lemasters, Isaac
67 Highsmith, Richard M.
    1818. Hismith, Richard
    F1820. Highsmith, Richard M.
71 Miller, Rachel
    1818. Miller, William
    F1820. Miller, Rachel
74 Highsmith, William
    1818. Hesmith, William
    F1820. Highsmith, William
78 Anderson, Ezekiel
    1818. Anderson, Ezekel
83 Highsmith, William
    F1820. Highsmith, William, Jr.
89 Cole, Edy
    1818. Coal, Eady
90 Jones, Enock
    1818. Jones, Enoch
98 Morris, Sian
    1818. Moris, Sian
99 Goen, Edward
    1818. Goins, Edward
102 Goen, Isaac
    1818. Goins, Isaac
108 Lackey, Adam, Sr.
    1818. Lackey, Adam
    F1820. Lackey, Adam, Sr.
109 Bryant, James
    1818. Bryans, James
    F1820. Bryant, James
110 Willber, Alexander
    F1820. Wilber, Alexander
111 Mills, Edward
    1818. Mill, Edward
    F1820. Mills, Edward
117 Carnes, Abraham
    1818. Cairnes, Abram
    F1820. Carnes, Abraham

119 Goen, Lewis
    1818. Goin, Lewis
    F1820. Goen, Lewis
120 Lacey, Barbary
    1818. Lacy, Barbary
    F1820. Lacey, Barbary
121 Rathbone, Edman
    1818. Rathbourn, Camon
    F1820. Rathbone, Edman
125 Kinkead, George W.
    1818. Kinkade, George W.
    F1820. Kinkead, George W.
130 Taylor, Cornelius
    1818. Taylor, Cornelious
    F1820. Taylor, Cornelius
135 Lorin, Olive
    F1820. Lorin, Alive
137 Mattingly, William
    F1820. Mallingly, William
140 Johnston, Henry
    1818. Jonson, Henry
143 Fife, Thomas
    1818. Fiffe, Thomas
    F1820. Fife, Thomas
160 Spencer, Jesse
    1818. Sponsor, Jesse
    F1820. Spencer, Jesse
174 Adams, John R.
    1818. Addams, John R.
    F1820. Adams, John R.
175 Leneur, Samuel
    1818. Lanear, Samuel
    F1820. Leneur, Samuel
176 Cuningham, Patten
    F1820. Cunningham, Peter
177 Ferris, George
    1818. Pharris, George
    F1820. Ferris, George
181 McClure, Andrew
    1818. M Clewer, Andrew
    F1820. Mc Clure, Andrew
182 Stuffelbeam, John E.
    F1820. Stufelbeam, John E.
183 Lemons, Samuel
    1818. Lemmons, Samuel
    F1820. Lemons, Samuel
187 Travis, Daniel
    1818. Travers, Daniel
    F1820. Travis, Daniel
188 Evans, Bazil
    F1820. Evans, Bazal
189 Gifford, Joshua
    1818. Gilferd, Joshua
    F1820. Gifford, Joshua

CRAWFORD COUNTY (Continued)

191 Norton, Reuben
   1818. Norton, Rubin
   F1820. Norton, Reubin
194 Laster, John
   1818. Luster, John
   F1820. Laster, John
195 McCrary, Benjamin
   1818. Mcrary, Benjamin
   F1820. McCrary, Benjamin
196 Allison, Daniel
   1818. Alison, Daniel
   F1820. Allison, Daniel
198 Allison, Jonathan
   1818. Alison, Johnathan
   F1820. Allison, Jonathan
199 Allison, Edward
   1818. Alison, Edward
   F1820. Allison, Edward
201 Turner, Ezekiel
   1818. Terner, Ezekel
   F1820. Turner, Ezekiel
203 Turner, Ruth
   1818. Terner, Ruth
   F1820. Turner, Ruth
208 McDonald, Alexander
   1818. McDaniel, James
   F1820. McDonald, Alexander
209 Berrey, John
   1818. Berry, John
   F1820. Berry, John
211 Riggs, Scott
   1818. Riggs, Scot
   F1820. Riggs, Scott
212 McClure, Samuel
   1818. M Clewer, Samuel
   F1820. McClure, Samuel
213 Stuffelbeam, Michael
   F1820. Stuflebeam, Michael
215 Ball, Aaron
   1818. Ball, Aaron
   F1820. Ball, Aron
216 Everman, William
   1818. Evermon, William
   F1820. Everman, William
217 Newland, John
   1818. Newlin, John, Jr.
   F1820. Newland, John
221 Gregg, Harmon
   F1820. Greggs, Harmon
222 Cochran, Nathaniel
   F1820. Cochran, Nathaniel H.
228 Gregg, John
   F1820. Greggs, John

229 Hill, Doctor
   1818. Hill, Doctor
   F1820. Hill, Docter
231 Shook, David
   1818. Shook, Benjamin
   F1820. Shook, Daniel
232 Miller, George
   1818. Miller, George
   F1820. Miller, Nancy
238 Kelog, Elijah
   F1820. Kellog, Elijah
249 Bradbury, William
   1818. Bradburry, Wm.
   F1820. Bradbury, William
250 Hardin, Jehu
   1818. Harden, Jehu
   F1820. Hardin, Jehu
251 Bradbury, Elisha
   1818. Bradbury, Elisha
   F1820. Bradberry, Elisha
253 Hardin, Thomas
   1818. Harden, Thomas
   F1820. Hardin, Thomas
255 Malcum, John
   1818. Malcom, John
   F1820. Malcom, John
261 Kennady, James
   F1820. Kennedy, James
262 Brimberry, Isaac
   1818. Brimberry, Isaac
   F1820. Brimbery, Isaac
269 Waldrope, William
   1818. Waldrop, William
   F1820. Waldrope, William
270 Waldrope, John
   1818. Waldrop, John
   F1820. Waldrope, John
271 Shaw, Greenberry
   F1820. Shaw, Greenbery
273 Middleton, Benoni
   F1820. Middleton, Benjamin
275 Patten, Thomas
   1818. Patton, Thomas
   F1820. Patten, Thomas
276 Bashar, Ithra
   F1820. Brashar, Ithra
281 Flippo, William
   1818. Flipper, William
   F1820. Flippo, William
282 Dial, James
   1818. Deal, James
   F1820. Dial, James
284 Johnston, James
   1818. Johnson, James
   F1820. Johnston, James

CRAWFORD COUNTY (Continued)

285 Bigs, James
    F1820. Biggs, James
292 Boher, George
    1818. Baugher, George
    F1820. Boher, George
293 McDowell, Robert
    1818. McDowl, Robert
    F1820. McDowell, Robert
294 Wood, Joseph
    1818. Wood, Joseph, Sr.
    F1820. Wood, Joseph
298 Barbie, William
    1818. Barbee, William
    F1820. Barbie, William
299 Little, Joseph
    F1820. Little, Jasper
305 Reaville, David
    1818. Reavell, David
    F1820. Reaville, David
311 Rollins, Nathan
    1818. Rellens, Nathan
    F1820. Rollins, Nathan
325 Asbell, John
    1818. Asbel, John
    F1820. Asbell, John
329 Spencer, James
    1818. Spensor, James
    F1820. Spencer, James
339 Beckwith, Benjamine
    F1820. Beckwith, Benjamin
346 Vanwinkle, Greenbury
    F1820. Vanwinkle, Greenlee
349 Dunlap, William, Sr.
    1818. Dunlap, William
    F1820. Dunlap, William, Sr.
350 Cheak, Joel
    1818. Cheek, Joel
    F1820. Cheek, Joel
358 Hearn, William
    1818. Hern, William
    F1820. Hearn, William
359 Parker, Benjamin
    1818. Parker, Benjamin
    F1820. Parker, Benjamin
363 Bathe, George
    1818. Bayth, George
    F1820. Bathe, George
365 Merclay, Frederck
    1818. Markley, Frederick
    F1820. Merclay, Frederick
367 Vanwinkle, Daniel
    1818. Vanwikle, Daniel
    F1820. Vanwinkle, Daniel

371 Lemasters, James
    1818. Lasters, James
    F1820. Lemasters, James
376 Siena, Briant
    F1820. Siena, Bryant
378 Hearn, Edmon
    1818. Hearn, Edmond
    F1820. Hearn, Edman
380 Woodworth, John S.
    1818. Woodwourth, John S.
    F1820. Woodworth, John S.
388 Eaton, Benjamine
    1818. Eaton, Benjamin, Jr.
    F1820. Eaton, Benjamin
389 Salisbury, Jeffrey
    1818. Salsbury, Jefry
    F1820. Sallisbury, Jeffrey
397 Garritt, William, Jr.
    1818. Gerrard, William
    F1820. Garrett, William
398 Garritt, William, Sr.
    1818. Gerrard, William, Sr.
    F1820. Garrett, William, Sr.
399 Garritt, Jacob
    1818. Garrard, Jacob, Jr.
    F1820. Garrett, Jacob
400 Magaha, David
    1818. McGahey, David
    F1820. Magaha, David
401 Conrod, Abraham
    1818. Coonrod, Abram
    F1820. Conrod, Abraham
402 Granwell, William
    F1820. Greenwell, William
404 Symes, Hall
    1818. Sims, Hall
    F1820. Symmes, Hall
405 Mais, Christopher
    1818. Morrs, Cristopher
    F1820. Mais, Christopher
406 Myres, Rebeca
    F1820. Myers, Rebecca
407 Funk, Gabriel
    1818. Funk, Gabril
    F1820. Funk, Gabriel
413 Funk, John
    1818. Funk, John, Sr.
    F1820. Funk, John
414 Lathop, Charles
    F1820. Lathrop, Charles
416 Newland, James
    1818. Newlin, James
    F1820. Newland, James

CENSUS OF 1820

CRAWFORD COUNTY (Continued)

421 Spalding, Elijah
    1818. Spawling, Elezer
    F1820. Spaulding, Elijah
422 Willard, Daniel
    1818. Wilard, Daniel
    F1820. Willard, Daniel
423 Gire, Aaron
    1818. Guyer, Aaron
    F1820. Gire, Aaron
424 Gire, Exum
    1818. Guyer, Axim
    F1820. Gire, Exum
425 Legge, Edward
    F1820. Legg, Edward
426 Carter, Shadrach B.A.
    1818. Carter, S.B.A.
    F1820. Carter, Shadrach B.A.
427 Driskill, Elias
    1818. Driskell, Elias
    F1820. Dresskill, Elias
429 Hicks, William
    1818. Hix, William
    F1820. Hicks, William
433 Brimbery, Samuel
    1818. Brimberry, Samuel
    F1820. Brembery, Samuel
435 Starr, Absolom
    F1820. Starr, Absolem
437 Kenady, Thomas
    1818. Kenady, Thomas
    F1820. Kennedy, Thomas
440 Draper, Chakley
    1818. Draper, Chalkley
    F1820. Draper, Chalkley
441 Spivy, Exum
    1818. Spiqrey, Axim
    F1820. Spevy, Exum
445 Holiday, Robert
    1818. Holedy, Robert
    F1820. Holladay, Robert
446 Evans, John
    1818. Evens, John
    F1820. Evans, John
447 Morrison, Joseph
    F1820. Morrison, Joseph, Jr.
448 Gire, Jesse
    1818. Guyer, Jesse
    F1820. Gier, Jesse
449 Hecock, Esec
    1818. Heacock, Esir
    F1820. Heycock, Esok
451 Evans, Benjamine
    1818. Evins, Benjamin
    F1820. Evin, Benjamin
452 Pease, Anbrose
    F1820. Pease, Obrose
456 Bennett, Elizabeth
    1818. Bennet, James B.
    F1820. Bennett, Elizabeth
457 Connaway, John
    F1820. Conaway, John
458 Lewis, Zepheniah
    F1820. Lewis, Zephenah
460 Garwood, James
    F1820. Gorwood, James
464 Snipes, John T.
    1818. Snipes, John
    F1820. Snipes, John T.
468 Goen, Isaac
    1818. Goin, Isaac
    F1820. Goen, Isaac
474 Haskins, Robert
    1818. Haskin, Robert
    F1820. Haskins, Robert
478 Gaines, Stephen
    F1820. Gains, Stephen
480 Sudriott, Charles
    1818. Sudevoit, Charles
    F1820. Sudriott, Charles
481 Lavalette, Louis
    1818. Lavelit, Lewis
    F1820. Lavalette, Lois
482 Johnston, John, Jr.
    1818. Johnson, John, Jr.
    F1820. Johnson, John, Jr.
483 Johnston, John, Sr.
    1818. Johnson, John
    F1820. Johnson, John, Sr.
487 Mills, John
    1818. Mills, John W.
    F1820. Mills, John
488 Allison, Samuel
    1818. Alison, Samuel
    F1820. Allison, Samuel
489 Allison, Richard
    1818. Alison, Richard
    F1820. Allison, Richard
490 Kuykendal, Daniel
    1818. Kaykedall, Daniel
    F1820. Kuykendall, Daniel
491 Price, Jerimiah
    F1820. Price, Richard
492 Haskins, Asahel
    1818. Haskin, Ashers
    F1820. Haskins, Asahel
498 Wilber, Joseph
    F1820. Wilbre, Joseph

CRAWFORD COUNTY (*Concluded*)

502 Peckard, Alpheus
    F1820. Peckard, Alppeus
513 Richardson, Jane
    1818. Richardson, John B.
    F1820. Richardson, Jane
514 Golaher, John
    1818. Goliher, John
    F1820. Golahar, John
518 Gibson, James
    1818. Gipson, James
    F1820. Gibson, James
521 Golaher, John, Jr.
    1818. Goliher, John, Jr.
    F1820. Golaher, John

524 Bono, Peter
    1818. Boon, Peter
    F1820. Bono, Peter
525 Bayeau, Tousaint
    F1820. Boyeau, Tousaint
528 Allison, Frederick
    1818. Alison, Frederick
    F1820. Allison, Frederick
529 Allison, Phebe
    1818. Alison, Joseph
    F1820. Allison, Phebe
530 Allison, Isaac
    1818. Alison, Isaac
    F1820. Allison, Isaac

CENSUS OF EDWARDS COUNTY, 1820

Mount Carmel
Nover 17th 1820

Sir

Inclosed you will have the numbers of Inhabitance, of Different Classes resideing in Edwards County—Taken as accurately aposibel I have Spared no pains nessasary In obtaining them The County In many parts is thinly Setled I have in Sum instances rode 12 or 15 miles with out a hous or Eavin a path to Gide me But Bilive I have gethered up the fragments That there is none lost—

I am with Due respect
Your most obedent
SCOBY STEWART

To the Honorabel
The Secretary of State

Sensus of Edwards County For the State of Illenois—For the year of our Lord Ano Domina 1820—

Heads of Families With all other white Males of 21 years old and upwards	no. 775
All other white Inhabitance	no. 2570
Free peopel of Collor	no. 17
Servants or Slaves	no. 6
Total	3369

EDWARDS COUNTY (Continued)

Although Edwards County was created in 1815, there are no extant state census returns for that county prior to 1835. In 1818 Edwards County comprised all or parts of the present Jefferson, Wayne, Edwards, Wabash, Lawrence, Richland, Clay, and Marion counties. In 1819 Jefferson and Wayne had been created in the western two-thirds of that region, and are represented in the state census of 1820. For Edwards County itself there is only the summary given here. The federal census of 1820 lists 571 names of heads of families, and these are listed here for the sake of completeness in the list of names of Illinois pioneers of that date. Since this is a compilation of state and not of federal census returns the accompanying statistics await publication in United States Bureau of the Census compilations.

LIST OF NAMES IN FEDERAL CENSUS FOR EDWARDS COUNTY, 1820
Filed April 2, 1821
Census Taken by Guy W. Smith

1 Levi Joy
2 William A. Crowell
3 John Bte. L'Anglois
4 Francois L'Anglois
5 George Wheeler
6 John Holloway
7 Joseph Hoisington
8 Manlove Beauchamp
9 Arthur T. Vanderveer
10 Abner Armstrong
11 Alexander Z. Warner
12 August Lavoilete
13 Pierre Dubois
14 William Lavoilete
15 Joseph P. Bogard
16 Joshua Ewell
17 John Gray
18 James Gray
19 William Teasley
20 Eli Reed
21 John Neslor
22 John Stewart
23 Philip Plough
24 Mary Hall
25 John Groves
26 Neil Campbell
27 Reuben Jordan
28 Thomas Owens
29 James Jordan
30 John Painter
31 John Shives
32 Charles Burns
33 John Massie
34 Samuel Gransfield
35 Isaac Butler
36 Margaret Kershaw
37 John Mather
38 Samuel Cole
39 Lewis Dickerson
40 Lucy Tyner
41 Caleb Dickerson
42 Clem Martin
43 Thomas McKinney
44 Isham Rodgers
45 Joseph Rodgers
46 Thomas Smith
47 David Wright
48 James Vinson
49 Levi Compton
50 Ephraim Pharr
51 Asa Durley
52 John Blessenden
53 William Wood
54 Henry Cowling
55 George Walser
56 John Servington
57 Samuel Brown
58 Thomas Brown
59 John Thread
60 Jacob Penfold
61 William Simpkins
62 Charles Pugsley
63 Edward T. Hookham
64 James Olver
65 William White
66 Henry McCormac
67 John Dunn
68 John Collins
69 Henry Bowman
70 Philip Skidmore
71 Aaron Graham
72 Matthew Coombs
73 Captain Stone
74 Richard Flower
75 William Burton
76 George Flower
77 Alexander Grant
78 Thomas Shepperd
79 James Green
80 John Lewis
81 Robert Holiby
82 Malachi Hubbard

EDWARDS COUNTY (*Continued*)

83 John Brenchley
84 Joseph P. Haddock
85 Richard Birkbeck
86 Henry Kelley
87 Jonathan Lewis
88 Mary Bowman
89 Deborah Pritchard
90 Joseph Lazier
91 James Collier
92 William Clark
93 James Cooper
94 Emma Bennett
95 Edward Collier
96 Stephen Knight
97 George Woodham
98 Andro Languedoc
99 John Bte. Darus
100 Louis Languedoc
101 Pierre Pelletier
102 Thomas Buckhanan
103 Richard Freeman
104 Hezekiah Hardesty
105 Joseph Osbourne
106 John Powers
107 James Overstreet
108 Joshua Butler
109 Reuben Magoon
110 Thomas England
111 Elisha Warden
112 William Small
113 Samuel Brown
114 Jonathan Marney
115 Joseph Parish
116 William Blackburn
117 James Ryan
118 George Butler
119 Bernard McManus
120 Matthew Neeley
121 Moses Seeds
122 James Seeds
123 Tilman Melton
124 Henry Bennett
125 Robert Turner
126 Richard B. McCorkle
127 Elisha Spencer
128 Baldwin Clark
129 Jacob Shrader
130 John Currie
131 William Beauchamp
132 James Black
133 Nathan Fry
134 Sherman Prout
135 Aaron Gould
136 James Hutchins
137 William Simonds
138 John Tilton
139 Abijah Halley
140 William Stone
141 Joseph Jones
142 Beauchamp Hervey
143 Clarke Warden
144 Heman Barrough
145 Nancy Bennett
146 Mary Ano
147 Marvel S. Hicks
148 Cyrus Danforth
149 David McLaughlin
150 Joseph Ballard
151 Nancy Rawlings
152 William Leech
153 Charlo Moize
154 John L. Compton
155 Francis Arpant, Jr.
156 Francis Arpant
157 Joseph Arpant
158 Pierre Gramarr
159 Nicholas Bonneau
160 Joseph Dielle
161 Françoise Lavoilete
162 Charlo Languedoc
163 Abraham Penfold
164 Thomas Gill
165 George Wood
166 John Bonsley
167 John Jeffcoat
168 John Robinson
169 John Wood
170 John Hatfield
171 Morris Birkbeck
172 John Depew
173 Boswell Beasley
174 William Woodland
175 Ryal Emmerson
176 John Woodland
177 Noah Stepleford
178 Binus J. Wren
179 John Hall
180 Daniel Orange
181 John Burton
182 James Kennedy
183 William Everly
184 Thomas Sloan
185 Isaac Morris
186 Robert Anderson
187 John Hunt
188 Edward Bennett
189 John Bte. Momance
190 William Harn
191 Isaac Ellison
192 James Hunt

EDWARDS COUNTY (*Continued*)

193 Roland Lane
194 Sidney Spring
195 John Mann
196 Henry Hunt
197 Benjamin Skinner
198 John Buckles
199 David Bailey
200 Mary Mounce
201 James Edmondson
202 Benjamin Bogard
203 George Wilson
204 Thomas Thacker
205 Thomas Kearney
206 John Mitchell
207 Lott Sarns
208 Luke Tippet
209 Thomas Mason
210 Adrian Anglin
211 Mary Gallant
212 John Hughes
213 David Hughes
214 Randolph Clark
215 William Hughes
216 John Clark
217 William Wilson
218 Elisha Anglan
219 Thomas Dawson
220 David Locke
221 Adam Galloway
222 John Cunningham
223 Joe Pixley
224 William Hatch
225 John A. Bunting
226 Joseph Wright
227 Andrew F. Dyer
228 Thomas McClane
229 Richard Frear
230 James Lanterman
231 Alsey Miller
232 Gabriel Scott
233 James Clemmens
234 John Clemmens
235 John Hindman
236 Robert Denison
237 William Denison
238 John Clark
239 Benjamin Gibbs
240 Antoine Z. Chenet
241 Thomas Brooks
242 John Herring
243 James Johnston
244 Elijah Banks
245 Alexander Banks
246 Sarah Harness
247 Thomas Pulliam
248 Joseph R. Buckhanan
249 Francis Smith
250 Asa Hammond
251 Jacob Bright
252 John Anthis
253 Thomas Gould
254 Peter Keen
255 Robert Bell
256 Reuben T. Baker
257 Joshua Beall
258 Benjamin Peacock
259 Scoby Stewart
260 Francis Dixon
261 Robert Lucas
262 Thomas S. Hinde
263 Moses Laws
264 Araminta Dukes
265 Joseph Williams
266 William P. Blanchard
267 Joseph Glasscock
268 Alexander Turner
269 John Scott
270 Thomas Fish
271 John Martin
272 William Martin
273 Samuel H. Clubb
274 Thomas Blackburn
275 Isaac Higgins
276 Constantine McMahan
277 Joseph Lamott
278 Joseph Clayton
279 William Spencer
280 Jonathan Leech
281 Henry Fail
282 Sardis R. Chase
283 James Rankin
284 Henry Dubois
285 George Fail
286 Benjamin Matthews
287 William Rankin
288 Samuel Ramsey
289 Daniel Groves
290 Isaiah Lewis
291 Paul Lewis
292 Daniel Paine
293 William Bennett
294 Joseph Dixon
295 William Corie
296 Ephraim Wanzer
297 James Ockletree
298 Edward Mundy
299 Elijah Harris
300 Mary Brooks
301 Joseph Babcock
302 Charles Rigg

EDWARDS COUNTY (Continued)

303 Patience Brynes
304 John Ingersol
305 Polly Corter
306 George Anthis
307 Spencer Wood
308 John L. Hearndon
309 Thomas Webb
310 William Dummet
311 James Gilmore
312 Cornelius DeLong
313 Major Spencer
314 James Rollins
315 Thomas Turner
316 Samuel Mundy
317 George Barney
318 Arnold B. Dake
319 Guy W. Smith
320 John Snider
321 William McIntosh
322 Hugh Seeds
323 William Bogle
324 Cornelius Vanderhoof
325 Victor Buckhanan
326 John Buckhanan
327 Anthony Leech
328 James Whitlock
329 Benjamin Hulbert
330 Henry Leek
331 Peter Miller
332 David Jennings
333 Peter I. Davinport
334 John Armstrong
335 Joseph Vilnave
336 Charles Gardner
337 William Phipps
338 George Oman
339 Chauncey White
340 Solomon Kenneipp
341 John Brown
342 Jeremiah Wilson
343 William Brown
344 William Liddle
345 John Smith
346 Henry Young
347 Robert McNair
348 James Ruark
349 Hannah Osgood
350 Robert Higgins
351 Moses Petty
352 Samuel Stults
353 Benjamin Sumner
354 George Claypoole
355 Jeremiah Wood
356 James Campbell
357 John Craddock
358 Lemuel Barlow
359 William Binion
360 Dugal Campbell
361 Nathan Rollings
362 Ephraim Dunham
363 William P. Wilson
364 John Stilwell
365 Thomas Baird
366 John McClary
367 Benjamin Clark
368 William R. Baker
369 Abraham Jones
370 Smith Mounce
371 Joseph Lane
372 James W. D. Taylor
373 John Embree
374 William P. Hamilton
375 Joseph Hanks
376 James Jackson
377 Oswald Warrington
378 Nathaniel Tait
379 David Thompson
380 Joel Churchill
381 James Tyner
382 Thomas Tyner
383 Samuel Simco
384 Christian Earnst
385 Henry Fettinger
386 Jesse Bealls
387 Benjamin Reynolds
388 Daniel Williams
389 James Andrews
390 Zeba French
391 Coles Besley
392 John White, Jr.
393 Jairus Fordice
394 John Cortrecht
395 William Cunningham
396 James Adams
397 Richard Jackman
398 Daniel S. Churchill
399 Enoch Greathouse
400 Hugh Martin
401 James Lansdown
402 William Ridgley
403 John C. Ruark
404 Ephraim D. Armstrong
405 James Banks
406 Charles Hensley
407 Pierre Edline
408 James McMillen
409 William H. Sams
410 Ransalier N. Smith
411 Sparling Young
412 Joseph Bogart

EDWARDS COUNTY (Continued)

413 James Johnston
414 James Ellis
415 T. A. Lafond
416 John Proctor
417 Henry McGregor
418 George Field
419 Jervis Dale
420 Benjamin McLeef
421 John McLeef
422 Nathaniel Hendricks
423 John McNair
424 William Weirs
425 Samuel Rigg
426 Daniel Sheffield
427 Ebenezer Kelley
428 George Michaels, Jr.
429 Ebenezer Putnam
430 Archibald Melrose
431 Bryant Walker
432 James Cooper
433 William Melrose
434 Jonathan Shelby
435 Daniel Boltinghouse
436 James Collier
437 John Michaels
438 Elijah Pollard
439 Hezekiah Clark
440 Francois Vallie
441 James Rawlings
442 Elias Jordan
443 Cadwallader Jones
444 Henson Williams
445 James Huston
446 John Martin
447 John Stewart
448 William Deputy
449 John White
450 Joel Bliss
451 James Hensley
452 Daniel Greathouse
453 John Huston
454 William Jordan
455 William Lawson
456 John Bell
457 John Crawford
458 Tarlton Boran
459 John Ano
460 Rezin Ruark
461 William Ramsey
462 Stephen Bliss
463 George Knight
464 Samuel Putnam
465 Cornelius Cannon
466 Samuel Stilwell
467 Reuben Blackford
468 David Moss
469 William Saturly
470 James Majors
471 William Clark
472 John Phipps
473 Edward West
474 John Leech
475 James Dawson
476 John Arnold
477 Elias Brockway
478 Booker Shields
479 Daniel Keen
480 Joshua Jordan
481 William Wright
482 Edward Ulm
483 Jacob Arnold
484 Abraham Welsher
485 Cornelius Carpenter
486 Francis Lavoilette
487 John McIntosh
488 William Travis
489 Rezin Clubb
490 Thomas Banks
491 Joseph Gardner
492 Benjamin Smith
493 Robert Carpenter
494 William Spencer
495 Jacob Trout
496 John B. Griffeth
497 Henry Huston
498 Samuel Newell
499 Jeremiah Ballard
500 John Waggonner
501 Olney Payne
502 James Rollins
503 Larkin Anthis
504 John Andrew
505 William Johnston
506 George Pugh
507 George Letherlaird
508 James Martin
509 Elijah Compton
510 Caleb Jordan
511 William Arnold
512 Allen Emmerson
513 Asa Smith
514 William Smith
515 Abraham Morrill
516 James Parker
517 Joseph Selley
518 Robert Erwin
519 Samuel Cross
520 Joel Boyd
521 John Cross
522 Thomas Boyd

EDWARDS COUNTY (*Concluded*)

523 David Lewis
524 William Boyd
525 Thomas Leech
526 Isaac Harness
527 William Haney
528 John K. Arnold
529 Henry Utter
530 Levi Couch
531 Absalom Milton
532 Hugh Kincade
533 Thomas Gardner
534 John Harrison
535 Samuel N. Campbell
536 John L. Johnston
537 Moses Decker
538 David Hunt
539 Stephen Simmons
540 Moses Michaels
541 John Shadle
542 Robert Frazer
543 John Grayson
544 Philo Ingraham
545 William Barney
546 John Wood
547 Alexander Wood
548 Joseph Wood
549 Joseph Preston
550 William Higgins
551 George W. Higgins
552 William Pool
553 James Pool
554 Ransom Higgins
555 Benjamin Taylor
556 George Higgins
557 Zadochiah Winters
558 Gervase Heazleton
559 John Tome
560 Moses Bedell
561 John Compton
562 Henry J. Mills
563 Pelick Hull
564 Hugh Calhoun
565 Henry Cusick
566 Samuel Fettinger
567 William West
568 Lemuel Haskins
569 John Higgins
570 James Embree
571 Seth Gard

CENSUS OF FRANKLIN COUNTY, 1820

The names of The Heads of the Familes in this Collum	Free white males 21 years old and upwards in this Collum	All other white inhabitents in this Collum	Free people of Color in this Collum	Servants or Slaves in this Collum
[1 ‡] Edward Carter	1	7		
[2 ‡] Samuel Swafford	1	7		
[3 ‡] Shadrick Cheek	1	7		
[4] Randle Dye	1	1		
[5] Sary Owens		1		
[6*‡] Elijah Ewing	2	5		
[7 ‡] John Conger	1	9		
[8*‡] Thomas M. Dorris	1	2		
[9*‡] John Thompson	2	4		1
[10*‡] Robe[r]t M'Crary	1			
[11*‡] Aaron Youngblood	1	11		
[12 ‡] Robert More	1	2		
[13*‡] John More	1	6		
[14*‡] Joseph Thompson	1	7		
[15*‡] John Browning	2	8		
[16 ‡] Baly Adams	1	1		
[17 ‡] George Oldham	1	2		
[18*‡] William Farris	2	5		
[19 ‡] William B. Perry	3	1		
[20*‡] Elias Jourdan	1	7		
[21*‡] Rial Williams	1	3		
[22*‡] Andrew Crunk	1	7		
[23*‡] John Crawford	1	9		
[24*‡] Jabez Hooker	1	3		
[25 ‡] Sion H. Michel	1	3		
[26*‡] Thomas More	2	4		
[27*‡] John Farris	1	9		
[28 ‡] Thomas Owens	1	2		
[29*‡] Benjamin Rodgers	1	3		
[30 ‡] Enoch Thompson	1	3		
[31*‡] James Smith	1	6		
[32 ‡] Anderson More	1	2		

Figures and symbols preceding names have been supplied by the editor:
‡Indicates name also in Federal Census for 1820.
*Indicates name also in State Census for 1818.

FRANKLIN COUNTY (Continued)

No.	Heads of families	White males 21 & upwards	All other white	Free people of color	Servants or slaves
[33 ‡]	Moses Jones	1	5		
[34 ‡]	Wiley Jones	1	1		
[35 ‡]	Richard Cantrall	2	10		
[36 ‡]	John W. Swafford	1	3		
[37*‡]	William King	1	9		
[38*‡]	Thomas R. Roberts	1	3		
[39 ‡]	Willson Wray	1	11		
[40 ‡]	Nancy Little		8		
[41*‡]	Edward Sullivan	1	4		
[42*‡]	Thomas Smothers	1	3		
[43 ‡]	John Ellis	1	1		
[44*‡]	Fanny Odle	1	3		
[45 ‡]	John W. Waller	1	4		
[46*‡]	Richard Waller	1	9		
[47*‡]	Mason Crawford	1	11		5
[48 ‡]	Isaac Jackson	1	1		
[49*‡]	John Hawl	1	5		
[50 ‡]	Gideon Taylor	1	1		
[51 ‡]	Benjamin Jackson		2		
[52*‡]	Nancy Adams		4		
[53 ‡]	Henry Yost	2	9		
[54 ‡]	Benjamin Jones	1	3		
[55 ‡]	Sampson Harris	1	7		
[56 ‡]	Benjamin Shatzer	1	7		
[57*‡]	Alexandrew M'Crary	1	2		
[58 ‡]	Charles Shannon	1	9		
[59*‡]	John Williams	2	5		
[60 ‡]	Samuel Whitly	2	3		
[61*‡]	James Rodgers	2	2		
[62*‡]	William Rodgers	1	1		
[63 ‡]	Nathaniel Armstrong	1	6		
[64 ‡]	Rebecca Jones		2		
[65 ‡]	Nathaniel Jones		3		
[66 ‡]	Abraham Horsler	1	2		
[67*‡]	Thomas Lamply	1	6		
[68 ‡]	Joseph Plaster	2	4		
[69 ‡]	Richard Caldwell	1	3		
[70*‡]	Isaac Gaily	2	10		

FRANKLIN COUNTY (Continued)

No.	Heads of families	White males 21 & upwards	All other white	Free people of color	Servants or slaves
[71 ‡]	Robert M'Clane	1	6		
[72 ‡]	James Aken	1	5		
[73 ‡]	James Eubanks	1	1		
[74*‡]	Samuel Young	1	1		
[75*‡]	Elijah Tailor	1	2		
[76 ‡]	Aaron Tailor	2	7		
[77*‡]	Ely Webb	1	4		
[78 ‡]	Charles Miller	1	4		
[79 ‡]	Catherine Stilly		5		
[80 ‡]	Stephen Orsbern	1	6		
[81*‡]	Nathaniel Harmanson	1	3		
[82 ‡]	Joel Pace	1	10		
[83 ‡]	Riggs Penington	2	8		
[84 ‡]	Joseph Orsbern	1	8		
[85 ‡]	Peter Phillips	1	4		
[86 ‡]	Peter French	1	1		
[87 ‡]	Abraham Ervin	1	7		
[88 ‡]	Richard Ervin	1	5		
[89*‡]	Jacob Phillips	2	6		
[90*‡]	John Kirk	1	5		
[91*‡]	Lazeraus Webb	2	11		
[92 ‡]	Killion Sandusky	1	3		
[93*‡]	John Miller	1	11		
[94*‡]	Charles Miller	1	3		
[95 ‡]	James Neece	1	7		
[96 ‡]	William Miller	1	7		
[97 ‡]	John Richardson	1	9		
[98 ‡]	James Allen	2	3		
[99 ‡]	Daniel Ward	1	6		
[100*‡]	William Frizel	1	6		
[101 ‡]	John Sanders	1	2		
[102*‡]	Absolum Estis	1	9		
[103*‡]	John Cox	1	8		
[104 ‡]	George Joy	1	3		
[105*‡]	Joseph Estis	1	9		
[106 ‡]	Thomas M. Night	1	5		
[107 ‡]	Marada Robertson	1	7		
[108*‡]	John Sandusky	1	1		

CENSUS OF 1820

FRANKLIN COUNTY (Continued)

No.	Heads of families	White males 21 & upwards	All other white	Free people of color	Servants or slaves
[109*‡]	Chamlin Hutson	1	6		
[110 ‡]	Nevel Thompson	1	7		
[111*‡]	John Robertson	1	2		
[112*‡]	Kinchen Odum	1	2		
[113 ‡]	William Weekly	1	2		
[114 ‡]	Lemuel Harrison	1	3		
[115 ‡]	Andrew U. Harrisson	1	5		
[116*‡]	Reece Perkings	1	2		
[117*‡]	John K. Patrick	1	7		
[118*‡]	Charles Umphrais	1	6		
[119*‡]	Crawford Berns		1	9	
[120*‡]	James Armstrong	1	5		
[121 ‡]	John Nangle	1	5		
[122*‡]	John Waddle	1	2		
[123 ‡]	William Barker	1	4		
[124 ‡]	Thomas Willkisson	1			
[125*‡]	William Ewbanks	1	11		
[126 ‡]	Stephen Ammermon	1	9		
[127*‡]	Mical Rollens	1	9		
[128 ‡]	John Blankingship	1	11		
[129*‡]	William Neal	1	4		
[130*‡]	Welden Manen	1	7		
[131 ‡]	William Blankenship	1	2		
[132*‡]	John Lonis	1	3		
[133 ‡]	Nathan Clampet	1	8		
[134 ‡]	John Milegan	1	8		
[135*‡]	Nancy Neal		9		
[136*‡]	James Jordan	1	5		
[137*‡]	Edmond Baker	1	8		
[138 ‡]	Rauben allen	2	5		
[139*‡]	William Dunlap	1	5		
[140 ‡]	William Rice	1	13		
[141*‡]	John Hooker	1	4		
[142 ‡]	John Adams	1	6		
[143 ‡]	James How	1	2		
[144 ‡]	Fanny Aken		3		
[145*‡]	William Green	1	5		
[146 ‡]	William Hooker	1	5		

FRANKLIN COUNTY (Continued)

No.	Heads of families	White males 21 & upwards	All other white	Free people of color	Servants or slaves
[147 ‡]	Robert Worthen	1	1		
[148*‡]	William Berns		1	7	
[149*‡]	John Roberts	2	3		
[150 ‡]	James Stuard	1	6		
[151*‡]	Major Lockaleer	1		12	
[152*‡]	Richard Ratclift	1	3		
[153 ‡]	John Ivory			6	
[154 ‡]	Joseph Ivory			2	
[155*‡]	Elijah Berns	1		6	
[156 ‡]	Absolum H. Duel	1	3		
[157*‡]	Stephen Berns			11	
[158*‡]	Spencer Wadkins	1		4	
[159*‡]	John Damron	1	3		
[160*‡]	Hezekiah Garret	1	1		
[161*‡]	Soosan Shoults		1		
[162 ‡]	Dennis Dorety	2	8		
[163*‡]	David Shoults	1	2		
[164*‡]	Samuel Decen	3	5		
[165*‡]	John R. Shoults	1			
[166*‡]	John Shoults	2	4		
[167*‡]	Charles Shoults		2		
[168 ‡]	Margaret M'Clane		5		
[169*‡]	John Damron	3	7		
[170*‡]	Jessy Aplen	1	4		
[171*‡]	Phillip Tramell	1	3		
[172*‡]	Joseph Nuten	1	6		
[173 ‡]	Thomas Gillard	1	8		
[174 ‡]	Walter M'Daniel	1	9		
[175 ‡]	James Allen	1	6		
[176 ‡]	John Siratt	1	1		
[177*‡]	Joseph Siratt	1	8		
[178 ‡]	Lazeraus Turner	1	4		
[179 ‡]	Charles Damron		4		
[180 ‡]	David H. Corder	1	4		
[181 ‡]	George Davis	1	4		
[182 ‡]	Stephen Stilly	1	4		
[183*‡]	Henry Parsons	1	7		
[184 ‡]	Thomas Tramell	1	1		

FRANKLIN COUNTY (Continued)

No.	Heads of families	White males 21 & upwards	All other white	Free people of color	Servants or slaves
[185 ‡]	Elizabeth Tramell	1	1		
[186 ‡]	James Corder	1	2		
[187 ‡]	Samuel Parks	1	3		
[188 ‡]	Soloman Russle			2	
[189*‡]	Zachariah Wright	1	4		
[190*‡]	Demcy odum	2	3		
[191 ‡]	Richard Garret	1		2	
[192 ‡]	Edward Crouch	1	5		
[193*‡]	Richard Bankston	1	6		
[194 ‡]	Isaac Smith	1	3		
[195*‡]	Davis Stilly	1	9		
[196 ‡]	Jourdan Stilly	1	2		
[197*‡]	Mosses Garret	1	4		
[198 ‡]	John Pickford	1	5		
[199*‡]	Lasandrew Jones		9		
[200*‡]	Robert Armstrong	1	5		
[201 ‡]	Isaac Corban	1	3		
[202*‡]	Francis Jourdan	2	9		
[203*‡]	William MC.Elyea	2	8		
[204 ‡]	George Hill	1	1		
[205 ‡]	William Gazeway	1	1		
[206 ‡]	Helmer Vanwinkle	1	5		
[207 ‡]	John C. Baker	1	3		
[208*‡]	Simon M. Hubbard	2	6		
[209*‡]	Samuel Ford			2	
[210*‡]	Alizabeth Dement		8		
[211*‡]	Starling Hill	1	6		
[212 ‡]	James Trull	1	4		
[213 ‡]	Lemuel Crane	1	7		
[214 ‡]	Mathew Crane	1	1		
[215 ‡]	Fedrick Forster	1	4		
[216 ‡]	John H. Carter	1	1		
[217 ‡]	Henry Forster	1	2		
[218*‡]	John G. Simpkins	1	6		
[219*‡]	John Boles	1	4		
[220*‡]	Patsy Griffy		6		
[221 ‡]	William Ewbanks	1	1		
[222 ‡]	David Barnhill	1	6		

FRANKLIN COUNTY (Continued)

No.	Heads of families	White males 21 & upwards	All other white	Free people of color	Servants or slaves
[223*‡]	John Duncan	2	7		
[224*‡]	Elijah Spiller	1	7		
[225*‡]	Martin Duncan	2	3		
[226*‡]	Cudworth Harrisson	1	2		
[227*‡]	John Nelson	1	6		
[228 ‡]	Samuel L. Murphy	1	4		
[229 ‡]	William Spiller	1	13		
[230 ‡]	Joshua Tague	1	5		
[231*‡]	Elijah Flanery	1	6		
[232*‡]	Abraham Flanery	2	4		
[233 ‡]	Nicholas Parks	1	5		
[234*‡]	John Roland	1	6		
[235*‡]	John Tippy	1	4		
[236*‡]	Abraham Tippy	2	9		
[237 ‡]	Samuel Hendly	1	4		
[238 ‡]	John Phillips	1	2		
[239]	Louis Deratt	1	4		
[240 ‡]	Samuel Stags	1	3		
[241 ‡]	Benjamin Chitty	2	6		
[242 ‡]	James Neece	1	4		
[243 ‡]	Archabald Goodman	1	6		
[244 ‡]	William Norris	2	1		
[245 ‡]	Stephen Winchel	1	7		
[246 ‡]	John Norris	1	10		
[247*‡]	Jhasper Crane	1	8		
[248*‡]	Spencer Crane	1	10		
[249 ‡]	James Goodman	1	2		
[250*‡]	Ragsdale Roland	1	8		
[251*‡]	Solomon Snider	1	8		
[252 ‡]	Robert Cambell	1	3		
[253 ‡]	James MC. Daniel	1	6		
[254 ‡]	John Smith	1	4		
[255*‡]	William Cambell	1	7		
[256 ‡]	Henry Caggle	1	4		
[257 ‡]	Darneal Cambell	1	5		
[258 ‡]	Sary Chamlis		5		
[259*‡]	Nelson MC. Dowel	2	3		
[260*‡]	Phillip Russle	3	8		

CENSUS OF 1820

FRANKLIN COUNTY (Continued)

No.	Heads of families	White males 21 & upwards	All other white	Free people of color	Servants or slaves
[261 ‡]	Polly Parmer		2		
[262 ‡]	William Hickum	1	11		
[263 ‡]	Henry Hunter	1	5		
[264*‡]	Abraham Piatt	1	2		
[265 ‡]	John Arnet	1	3		
[266*‡]	Willis Tiner	1	4		
[267*‡]	Joshua Tiner	5	11		
[268 ‡]	Thomas C. Lowden	1	1		
[269 ‡]	John D. Reece	1	4		
[270*‡]	Nathan Arnet	1	6		
[271 ‡]	David Herring	1	4		
[272*‡]	Isaac Herring	1	5		
[273*‡]	Coonrad Baker	1	6		
[274 ‡]	James Herring	1	2		
[275 ‡]	John Lamn	1	7		
[276 ‡]	John Davis	1	5		
[277 ‡]	Roubin odle	1	2		
[278*‡]	Johnathan Herring	1	2		
[279 ‡]	William Baker	1	6		
[280 ‡]	John Hill	1	9		
[281 ‡]	William Pickford	1	7		
[282*‡]	William A. Roberts	1	1		
[283 ‡]	Benjamin Smith	1	5		
[284 ‡]	Hiram Cothern	1	6		
[285 ‡]	Equiller Wily	3	8		
[286 ‡]	Bland Murry	1	5		
[287 ‡]	John Jones	1	5		
[288*‡]	John Wren	1	1		
[289 ‡]	John Wren	2	4		1
[290*‡]	Isaac Mobly	1	6		
[291 ‡]	George P. Boyer	1	1		
[292 ‡]	Alexandrew MC. Ginty	1	2		
		314	1387	67	7
			314	7	
			1701	74	
			1775		

John Ewing

FRANKLIN COUNTY (Continued)

Corrected totals:

Free white males of 21 years and upwards		314
All other white inhabitants		1376
		1690
Negroes		70
Free persons of color	63	
Servants or slaves	7	
	70	
Total		1760

CENSUS OF 1820

FRANKLIN COUNTY (Continued)

The 1818 census taken by John Browning was certified July 11. John Ewing took both censuses for 1820, the federal census having been certified by him on December 22, and the state census approved by the county commissioners at their December term.

Both censuses for 1820 list 292 families, but of these each census lists three families not mentioned by the other. Those listed in the state census only are:

- 4 Dye, Randle
- 5 Owens, Sary
- 239 Deratt, Louis

Those listed in the federal census only are:

Baker, Benjamin
  A family of two residing next to William Baker (279). In the state census the total for William Baker is the same as that for both Benjamin and William Baker in the federal census.

Maddox, John P.
  A family of five. Data added in a note at the end of the list.

Youngblood, Isaiah
  Family of three residing next to Kinchen Odum (112) and William Baker (279).

Discrepancies are as follows:

- 8 Dorris, Thomas M.
  - 1818. Dorres, Thos.
  - F1820. Dorris, Thomas M.
- 9 Thompson, John
  - 1818. Tompson, John
  - F1820. Thompson, John
- 10 M'Crary, Robet
  - 1818. Mcreerey, Robert
  - F1820. McCrary, Robert
- 11 Youngblood, Aaron
  - 1818. Yongblood, Aaron
  - F1820. Youngblood, Aaron
- 12 More, Robert
  - F1820. Moor, Robert
- 13 More, John
  - 1818. Moore, John
  - F1820. More, John
- 16 Adams, Baly
  - F1820. Adams, Baily
- 18 Farris, William
  - 1818. Faris, Wm.
  - F1820. Farris, William
- 20 Jourdan, Elias
  - 1818. Jordan, Elias
  - F1820. Jourdan, Elias
- 22 Crunk, Andrew
  - 1818. Cronk, Andrew
  - F1820. Crunk, Andrew
- 25 Michel, Sion H.
  - F1820. Michiel, Sion H.
- 26 More, Thomas
  - 1818. Moore, Thos.
  - F1820. More, Thomas
- 29 Rodgers, Benjamin
  - 1818. Rogers, Benj.
  - F1820. Rodger, Benjamin
- 32 More, Anderson
  - F1820. Moore, Anderson
- 35 Cantrall, Richard
  - F1820. Cantrell, Richard
- 38 Roberts, Thomas R.
  - 1818. Roberts, Thos.
  - F1820. Roberts, Thomas R.
- 41 Sullivan, Edward
  - 1818. Suillevin, Edward
  - F1820. Soalivan, Edward
- 44 Odle, Fanny
  - 1818. Odle, Fanney
  - F1820. Odle, Fanny
- 46 Waller, Richard
  - 1818. Waler, Richard
  - F1820. Waller, Richard
- 49 Hawl, John
  - 1818. Hall, John
  - F1820. Hall, John
- 50 Taylor, Gideon
  - F1820. Tailor, Gidion
- 51 Jackson, Benjamin
  - F1820. Jackson, Bengamin
- 52 Adams, Nancy
  - 1818. Adams, Nancey
  - F1820. Adams, Nancy
- 57 M'Crary, Alexandrew
  - 1818. Mcreerey, Elexander
  - F1820. M'Crary, Alexandrew

FRANKLIN COUNTY (*Continued*)

61 Rodgers, James
    1818. Rogers, Jas.
    F1820. Rodgers, James
62 Rodgers, William
    1818. Rogers, Williams
    F1820. Rodgers, William
64 Jones, Rebecca
    F1820. Jones, Rebecka
66 Horsler, Abraham
    F1820. Harsler, Abraham
67 Lamply, Thomas
    1818. Lampley, Thos.
    F1820. Lamply, Thomas
69 Caldwell, Richard
    F1820. Caldwell, Robert
70 Gaily, Isaac
    1818. Galey, Isaac
    F1820. Gaily, Isaac
73 Eubanks, James
    F1820. Eubank, James
74 Young, Samuel
    1818. Yong, Saml.
    F1820. Young, Samuel
75 Tailor, Elijah
    1818. Taylor, Eljah
    F1820. Tailor, Elijah
77 Webb, Ely
    1818. Web, Eli
    F1820. Webb, Ely
79 Stilly, Catherine
    F1820. Stilly, Caty
81 Harmanson, Nathaniel
    1818. Hamerson, Nat.
    F1820. Harmanson, Nathaniel
82 Pace, Joel
    F1820. Page, Joel
88 Ervin, Richard
    F1820. Erwin, Richard
89 Phillips, Jacob
    1818. Philips, Jacob
    F1820. Phillips, Jacob
91 Webb, Lazeraus
    1818. Web, Lazerous
    F1820. Well, Lazarous
92 Sandusky, Killion
    F1820. Sanduskia, Kellion
95 Neece, James
    F1820. Nees, James
97 Richardson, John
    F1820. Richason, John
100 Frizel, William
    1818. Frizell, Wm.
    F1820. Frizzle, William

102 Estis, Absolum
    1818. Estes, Absalom
    F1820. Estes, Absolem
105 Estis, Joseph
    1818. Estes, Joseph
    F1820. Estes, Joseph
106 Night, Thomas M.
    F1820. McNight, Thomas
107 Robertson, Marada
    F1820. Roberson, Merriday
108 Sandusky, John
    1818. Sendusky, John
    F1820. Sanduskia, John
109 Hutson, Chamlin
    1818. Hutson, Chamberlin
    F1820. Hutson, Chamlin
110 Thompson, Nevel
    F1820. Thomas, Nevil
111 Robertson, John
    1818. Robinson, Jno.
    F1820. Robertson, John
112 Odum, Kinchen
    1818. Odam, Kinching
    F1820. Odam, Kinchen
113 Weekly, William
    F1820. Weakly, William D.
115 Harrisson, Andrew U.
    F1820. Harrison, Andrew U.
116 Perkings, Reece
    1818. Perkins, Isaac
    F1820. Pirkins, Rees
117 Patrick, John K.
    1818. Kirkpatrick, Jno.
    F1820. Kirkpatrick, John
118 Umphrais, Charles
    1818. Humphry, Charles
    F1820. Humphris, Charles
119 Berns, Crawford
    1818. Burnes, Crawford
    F1820. Berns, Crawford
124 Willkisson, Thomas
    F1820. Wilkison, Thomas
125 Ewbanks, William
    1818. Ewbanks, William
    F1820. Eubank, William
126 Ammermon, Stephen
    F1820. Amormon, Stephen
127 Rollens, Mical
    1818. Rollens, Mikel
    F1820. Rollens, Michill
128 Blankingship, John
    F1820. Blankenship, John
130 Manen, Welden
    1818. Manon, Welden
    F1820. Manon, Weldon

FRANKLIN COUNTY (Continued)

131 Blankenship, William
    F1820. Blankeship, William
132 Lonis, John
    1818. Lounius, John
    F1820. Lounis, John
134 Milegan, John
    F1820. Milligan, John
135 Neal, Nancy
    1818. Neal, Joseph
    F1820. Neal, Nancy
136 Jordan, James
    1818. Jordan, James
    F1820. Jourdan, James
137 Baker, Edmond
    1818. Baker, Edmond
    F1820. Baker, Edmund
138 Allen, Rauben
    F1820. Allen, Reuben
139 Dunlap, William
    1818. Dunlap, William
    F1820. Dunlapt, William
148 Berns, William
    1818. Burnes, Wm.
    F1820. Burns, William
150 Stuard, James
    F1820. Steward, James
151 Lockaleer, Major
    1818. Lockler, Magey
    F1820. Lockaleer, Major
152 Ratclift, Richard
    1818. Ratliff, Richard
    F1820. Ratliff, Richard
153 Ivory, John
    F1820. Ivy, John
154 Ivory, Joseph
    F1820. Ivy, Josepth
155 Berns, Elijah
    1818. Burnes, Elijah
    F1820. Burns, Elijah
156 Duel, Absolum H.
    F1820. Duel, Absolem H.
157 Berns, Stephen
    1818. Burnes, Stephen
    F1820. Burns, Steaphen
158 Wadkins, Spencer
    1818. Watkins, Speser
    F1820. Wadkens, Spencer
159 Damron, John
    1818. Dammern, John, Sr.
    F1820. Damron, John
160 Garret, Hezekiah
    1818. Garret, Hezekiah
    F1820. Garrett, Hisakiah

161 Shoults, Soosan
    1818. Shultz, Susannah
    F1820. Shoults, Susan
162 Dorety, Dennis
    F1820. Daugherty, Dennis
164 Decen, Samuel
    1818. Deeson, Samuel
    F1820. Decen, Samuel
165 Shoults, John R.
    1818. Shultz, John
    F1820. Shoults, John R.
166 Shoults, John
    1818. Shultz, John
    F1820. Shoults, John M.
167 Shoults, Charles
    1818. Shultz, Jacob
    F1820. Shoults, Charles
169 Damron, John
    1818. Damren, John, Jr.
    F1820. Damron, John
170 Aplen, Jessy
    1818. Aplen, Jesse
    F1820. Apling, Jessy
171 Tramell, Phillip
    1818. Trammel, David
    F1820. Trammel, Phillip
172 Nuten, Joseph
    1818. Newten, Joseph
    F1820. Newton, Joseph
176 Siratt, John
    F1820. Sirratt, John
177 Siratt, Joseph
    1818. Suratt, Joseph
    F1820. Sirratt, Joseph
178 Turner, Lazeraus
    F1820. Turner, Lazerous
182 Stilly, Stephen
    F1820. Stilly, Steaphen
183 Parsons, Henry
    1818. Parsons, Henrey
    F1820. Parsons, Henry
188 Russle, Soloman
    F1820. Rusle, Soloman
189 Wright, Zachariah
    1818. Wright, Zachariah
    F1820. Rite, Zachariah
190 Odum, Demcy
    1818. Odam, Dempsey
    F1820. Odem, Demcy
195 Stilly, Davis
    1818. Stilley, Davis
    F1820. Stilly, Davis
197 Garret, Mosses
    1818. Garret, Moses
    F1820. Garrett, Moses

ILLINOIS HISTORICAL COLLECTIONS

FRANKLIN COUNTY (Concluded)

199 Jones, Lasandrew
    1818. Jones, Cassandra
    F1820. Jones, Lasandrew
203 MC.Elyea, William
    1818. Mceya, Wm.
    F1820. McElyea, William
205 Gazeway, William
    F1820. Gasaway, William
209 Ford, Samuel
    1818. Froo, Samuel
    F1820. Ford, Samuel. The location is the same but the family of 1818 is listed as white. 1818 census (56).
210 Dement, Alizabeth
    1818. Diment, David
    F1820. Dement, Elizabeth
215 Forster, Fedrick
    F1820. Forster, Federic
216 Carter, John H.
    F1820. Parker, John H.
218 Simpkins, John G.
    1818. Simpkins, John G.
    F1820. Simkins, John G.
219 Boles, John
    1818. Boles, John
    F1820. Bolls, John
220 Griffy, Patsy
    1818. Griffeth, Thomas
    F1820. Grifeiths, Patsy
221 Ewbanks, William
    F1820. Ewbank, William
223 Duncan, John
    1818. Dunkin, John
    F1820. Duncan, John
224 Spiller, Elijah
    1818. Spiller, Elijah
    F1820. Spiller, Eligah
225 Duncan, Martin
    1818. Duncan, Martin A.
    F1820. Duncan, Martin
226 Harrisson, Cudworth
    1818. Harrison, Cudworth
    F1820. Harrison, Cudworth
231 Flanery, Elijah
    1818. Flanary, Elijah
    F1820. Flanery, Elijah
234 Roland, John
    1818. Roland, John
    F1820. Rolan, John
235 Tippy, John
    1818. Tippey, John
    F1820. Tippy, John
236 Tippy, Abraham
    1818. Tippey, Abraham
    F1820. Tippy, Abraham

240 Stags, Samuel
    F1820. Staggs, Samuel C.
247 Crane, Jhasper
    1818. Crain, Jesper
    F1820. Crane, Jhasper
248 Crane, Spencer
    1818. Crain, Spencer
    F1820. Crane, Spencer
250 Roland, Ragsdale
    1818. Roland, Ragsdale
    F1820. Rolan, Ragsdale
252 Cambell, Robert
    F1820. Campbell, Robert
255 Cambell, William
    1818. Campbell, Wm.
    F1820. Campbell, William
257 Cambell, Darneal
    F1820. Campbell, Darneal
260 Russle, Phillip
    1818. Russel, Philip
    F1820. Russle, Phillip
264 Piatt, Abraham
    1818. Pyott, Abraham
    F1820. Piatt, Abraham
265 Arnet, John
    F1820. Aarnet, John
266 Tiner, Willis
    1818. Tiner, Willes
    F1820. Tiner, Willis
270 Arnet, Nathan
    1818. Arnett, Nathan
    F1820. Arnet, Nathan
271 Herring, David
    F1820. Herren, David
272 Herring, Isaac
    1818. Herring, Isaac
    F1820. Herren, Isaac
273 Baker, Coonrad
    1818. Baker, Coonrad
    F1820. Baker, Coonrod
277 Odle, Roubin
    F1820. Odle, Rouban
278 Herring, Johnathan
    1818. Herring, Jonathan
    F1820. Herren, Jonathan
282 Roberts, William A.
    1818. Roberts, William
    F1820. Roberts, William A.
284 Cothern, Hiram
    F1820. Cathern, Hiram
290 Mobly, Isaac
    1818. Moberley, Isaac
    F1820. Mobley, Isaac
291 Boyer, George P.
    F1820. Bowyer, John B.

CENSUS OF 1820

CENSUS OF GALLATIN COUNTY, 1820

No.	Heads of families	Free white males 21 & upwards	All other white inhabitants	Free people of color	Servants or slaves
[1*‡]	Robert Peeples	3	7		
[2*‡]	Abraham T. McCooll	4	7		
[3*‡]	James Fields	1	3		
[4*‡]	John Robinson	1	4		
[5*‡]	William Ellis	1	7		1
[6 ‡]	Garner Moreland	1	2		
[7 ‡]	Thomas M. Robinson	1	3		
[8 ‡]	James Bell	3	4		
[9*‡]	Harrison Wilson	2	3		1
[10 ‡]	Roswell Macefield	3	2		
[11 ‡]	Cornelius Gryder	1	7		
[12*‡]	John Forister	3	7		3
[13*‡]	Joseph Clark	1	6		
[14*‡]	Joseph Cozad	1	6		
[15 ‡]	John Abar	1	3		
[16 ‡]	Arthur McCan	1	5		
[17 ‡]	Nathan Olney	1	6		
[18*‡]	John McGlaughlin	3	2		
[19 ‡]	David Fade	1	9		
[20 ‡]	Samuel Marshall	1	3		
[21*]	William Finch	1	4		
[22 ‡]	Zadock Aidelott	2	9		
[23 ‡]	Levi Aydelott	1	2		
[24 ‡]	Joseph Humes	2	10		
[25]	Joseph Robinet	1	6		
[26 ‡]	John C. Gilworth	1	2		
[27*‡]	Martin Hitchcock	2	10		
[28 ‡]	James McGehee	1	1		
[29 ‡]	Henry McGehee	1	2		
[30*‡]	John Frazer	2	5		
[31 ‡]	James P. Thompson	1	1		
[32*‡]	Hazle Moreland	1	6		
[33*‡]	Neal Thompson	1	5		

Figures and symbols preceding names have been supplied by the editor:
‡ Indicates name also in Federal Census for 1820.
* Indicates name also in State Census for 1818.
No headings for columns appear in manuscript for Gallatin County. Totals show that ones supplied are correct.

GALLATIN COUNTY (Continued)

No.	Heads of families	White males 21 & upwards	All other white	Free people of color	Servants or slaves
[34]	Obid Copeland			2	
[35*]	James Hood			5	
[36 ‡]	W. A. Docker	1	3		
[37*‡]	William McCoy	1	6		1
[38 ‡]	James W. Sinclare	7	4		
[39*‡]	Joseph Scott	1	4		
[40*]	Nimrod Scott	1	4		
[41*‡]	Samuel Clark	2	7		7
[42 ‡]	James Logan	2	3		
[43 ‡]	Adam Logan	1	1		
[44*‡]	Stephen Perkins	1	6		
[45*‡]	Thomas Dawson	3	6		
[46*‡]	William Moor	1	7		
[47*]	James Pantus	3	5		
[48*‡]	William Duvall	1	3		
[49*‡]	Green Powell	1	4		
[50*‡]	Nicholas Powell	1	2		
[51 ‡]	Noble Morrison	1	5		
[52 ‡]	Frederick Mattby	1	6		
[53]	Richard Hall	1	7		
[54*]	Edward Mobley	1	2		
[55*‡]	John Wilson, Sen.	1	9		
[56*‡]	John Wilson, Jr.	1	4		
[57*‡]	John Duvall	1	3		
[58*‡]	Humphrey Scroggin	1	8		
[59 ‡]	Carter Scroggin	1	2		
[60 ‡]	Barten Scroggin	1	2		
[61*]	Moses Odom	1	7		
[62*‡]	Harlin Carrol	1	4		
[63*]	Joseph McCool	1	4		
[64*]	Isaak L. Potts	1	2		2
[65 ‡]	Edward Sharewood	1	1		
[66*‡]	Moses Sharewood	2	6		
[67 ‡]	Alexander K. Boutwell	1	2		
[68*]	Stephen Boutwell	2	4		
[69*]	James Willis	2	3		
[70*]	James Dillard	1	8		
[71]	Austin Dillard	1	5		

CENSUS OF 1820

GALLATIN COUNTY (Continued)

No.	Heads of families	White males 21 & upwards	All other white	Free people of color	Servants or slaves
[72*‡]	Leony C. Boutwell	1	6		
[73]	Voluntine Tite	1	3		
[74*]	Nicholas Powell	1	6		
[75]	Jonathan Stout	1	8		
[76*‡]	Suddith Meeks	2	9		
[77*‡]	Armsted Smoot	2	8		
[78]	Joell Wells	1	5		
[79]	William Baldin	1	1		
[80]	Henry Just	1	1		
[81*]	Alexander Barnhill	1	6		
[82*‡]	James M. Peddigrew	1	5		
[83]	Charles Pettigrew	1	1		
[84*‡]	Phillip Hinson	1	9		
[85 ‡]	Jaramiah Vinsan	1			
[86*‡]	Michael Sprinkle	1	3		
[87]	Heny Boyer	1	3		
[88 ‡]	John Mills	2	7		
[89*‡]	Edward Mattingley	1	5		
[90 ‡]	Zacheriah Mattingley	1	4		
[91*‡]	Thornton Cummons	1	5		
[92*‡]	William Cummons	1	3		
[93 ‡]	Peter Gates	1	2		
[94*‡]	John Rieds	1	6		
[95*‡]	Thomas Thompson	4	7		
[96]	William Wilsher	1	1		
[97]	Edmund Stokes	2	5		
[98*‡]	Haley Ragland	1	4		
[99*‡]	George Ragland	2	2		
[100]	Thomas T. Tunstel	4	4		
[101]	Abram Levingston	1	1		
[102]	Nathaniel Chilson	1	7		
[103]	William Bates	1	2		1
[104*‡]	Samuel Turner	1	3		
[105]	John Smoot	1	8		
[106]	William Dail	1	6		
[107*‡]	Robert R. Funkhowser	9	6	2	23
[108]	William Goss	1	5		
[109*‡]	Ensley Clark	1	5		

GALLATIN COUNTY (Continued)

No.	Heads of families	White males 21 & upwards	All other white	Free people of color	Servants or slaves
[110 ‡]	Joseph Vanmeter	1	6		
[111]	Alexander McGoon	1	3		
[112*‡]	Michael Jones	2	2		4
[113]	Amos Garrason	1	1		
[114 ‡]	Joseph Demaret	1	4		
[115*‡]	Thomas Sloo	2	2		
[116*‡]	Boston Daimwood	2	2		
[117 ‡]	John Mauldin	1	3		
[118*‡]	John Hamilton	1	3		
[119*‡]	Joseph Reed	1	5		
[120 ‡]	Christopher H. Sharpe	2	6		
[121]	Abel Duey	2	2		
[122 ‡]	Morris Ocanrey	1	7		
[123 ‡]	Buckner Hatfield	1	1		
[124]	John Newby	1	1		
[125*‡]	William Darte	1	5		
[126 ‡]	Sarah Robinson		8		
[127*‡]	Hazel Moreland	4	3		2
[128]	John Brady	2	5		
[129*‡]	Thomas G. Wood	2	8		1
[130*‡]	John Campbell	1	4		
[131*]	Bazzle Dodge	1	5		
[132]	Patrick Davis	2	6		
[133*‡]	William Tommason	1	8		
[134]	Simmean Owens	1	1		
[135*‡]	Thomas Akers	2	2		
[136 ‡]	Henry Howard	1	2		
[137*‡]	Andrew Slack	1	4		1
[138*]	William Akers	1	5		
[139]	James C. Haskins	1	10		
[140*‡]	John Hubbard	2	4	2	3
[141 ‡]	Archibald Campbell	1	2		
[142*‡]	William Kelleay	2	4		
[143]	Merradith W. Fisher	1	3		1
[144]	Catharine Johnson		7		
[145 ‡]	William Caldwell	1	4		
[146 ‡]	Ralph Hall	1			
[147 ‡]	Samuel L. White	1	4		

GALLATIN COUNTY (Continued)

No.	Heads of families	White males 21 & upwards	All other white	Free people of color	Servants or slaves
[148]	Ira A. Hooker	2	5		
[149*]	John Carter	1	4		
[150*‡]	Jacob Sexton	1	6		
[151 ‡]	Alexander H. Clark	1	2		
[152*]	Isaac Reiley	1	2		
[153*‡]	Joseph Reiley	1	7		
[154*‡]	Henry Madlock	1	6		
[155]	Labon Robinson	1	4		
[156 ‡]	Elizabeth Thomas		2		
[157*‡]	Ephraim Hubbard	1	2		6
[158*‡]	Nicholas Casey	3	1		40
[159]	Moses Hayes	1	8		
[160 ‡]	Peyton Hunt	1	2		
[161 ‡]	Joseph Cane	10	2		
[162 ‡]	Benjamin White	1	7		2
[163]	Isaac Stutson	1	5		
[164*‡]	Moses M. Rowlings	2	3	1	3
[165]	George R. Walker	2	7		
[166*]	Obid Flinn	1	3		2
[167]	William Flinn	1	1		
[168 ‡]	William Flint	1	2		
[169]	John Hayes	1	2		
[170]	Joseph Hayes	1	3		
[171*]	John Brown	2	4		
[172*‡]	Hugh McConel	2	6		
[173]	Henry Willim	1	3		
[174 ‡]	Jacob Thorn	1	2		
[175*]	David Haney	1	4		
[176*]	Isaac Baldin	1	5		
[177*‡]	Joseph Ferdin	1	4		
[178]	John W. Greenwood	1	4		
[179]	Benjamine Straton			4	
[180*‡]	Hubbard Dar	1	4		
[181]	Richard Maxwell	1	1		
[182*‡]	John G. Daimwood	1	7		
[183 ‡]	William Forister	2	9		
[184*]	John Cook	1	8		
[185 ‡]	Richard McInder	3			

GALLATIN COUNTY (Continued)

No.	Heads of families	White males 21 & upwards	All other white	Free people of color	Servants or slaves
[186]	Henry Cryder	1	4		
[187 ‡]	Andrew Johnson	1	1		
[188*‡]	Andrew Wilkins	1	9		
[189 ‡]	James Carpenter	1	5		
[190*‡]	Isaac Hogan	3	7		
[191]	Peter Sanders	1	2		
[192*‡]	Lewis Kikendall	1	4		2
[193*]	James Willis	1	3		
[194]	Asel Dutton	1	6		
[195*‡]	Thomas Johnson	1	4		1
[196*‡]	Robert M. Tarlton	3	3		1
[197*‡]	Ezekiel Frazer	1	4		
[198*]	Willis Owens	1	1		
[199*‡]	Geter Baker	1	6		
[200 ‡]	Hardy Willis	1	1		
[201*]	William C. T. Peters	2	4		
[202 ‡]	Fatima McCleland	6	5		4
[203*‡]	Simon Cade			2	
[204 ‡]	Benjamine Harrison	3			
[205*‡]	James Cane	2	2		3
[206 ‡]	John Limrick	1	3		
[207 ‡]	Alexander H. Kane	2			
[208*‡]	O. C. Vanlandingham	2			
[209 ‡]	Jacob Barger	2	6		2
[210 ‡]	Christopher Hobson	13	8		
[211 ‡]	Joseph R. G. Pool	1	1	4	16
[212*‡]	John Marshall	1	6		1
[213 ‡]	James Coldwell	1	3		
[214*‡]	Charles Campbell	2	8		3
[215*‡]	Samuel R. Campbell	2	2		2
[216 ‡]	Robert D. Mclean	12	4		3
[217*]	Ann Weathero		3		
[218 ‡]	David P. Willis	1			
[219 ‡]	Luther Beal	1	4		
[220]	Tobias Feygabush	3	4		
[221]	Christian Hailman	1	3		
[222*]	John Rohrer	4	4		
[223]	John Newell	11	7		2

GALLATIN COUNTY (Continued)

No.	Heads of families	White males 21 & upwards	All other white	Free people of color	Servants or slaves
[224*]	Isham Cheek			8	
[225 ‡]	Paul Coburn	1	4		
[226 ‡]	Lemuel M. Wilson	1	4		
[227*‡]	John Caldwell	1	5		
[228*‡]	James Wilson	2	4		
[229]	Elizabeth Huse	1	5		
[230]	John Vickerey	1	5		
[231 ‡]	Cathorine Fuller	1	5		
[232 ‡]	Anthony Low	1	6		
[233 ‡]	Calvin Edwars	4	4		
[234 ‡]	Joseph Logsdon	4	1		
[235*‡]	Margarett Logsdon		5		
[236 ‡]	Amos Hodge	1	5		
[237*‡]	Abner Rowson	1	5		
[238 ‡]	John Cayton	1	2		
[239]	William Smith	2	5		
[240]	John Loller	2	3		
[241 ‡]	Thomas C. Browne	3	3		3
[242*‡]	Cornelius Lafferty	3	5		1
[243]	Mary Robinson	2	3		
[244*‡]	Benjamin Mosby	3	5		2
[245 ‡]	John Thompson	1	2		
[246*]	Isaac Hide	2	3		
[247 ‡]	John Willis	1	1		
[248*]	John Murphy	2	4		
[249*‡]	Joseph M. Street	2	10		2
[250]	John Browne	9	8		2
[251*‡]	Joel Martin	2	8		
[252]	John Gephart	1	1		
[253*]	Joshua Sexton	5	1		
[254*]	Malach C. Willis	1	3		
[255]	Daniel Marshall	1	3		
[256]	N. H. H. Hooler	1	7		
[257]	Michael Cain	1	5		
[258*‡]	Robert Watson	1	4		
[259]	Robert Christian	1	2		
[260 ‡]	James Greenwood	2	5		
[261 ‡]	William Wing	1	1		

GALLATIN COUNTY (Continued)

No.	Heads of families	White males 21 & upwards	All other white	Free people of color	Servants or slaves
[262]	Josiah Caswell	2	3		
[263 ‡]	Joseph Lowery	1	2		
[264]	Susanah Carter		1		
[265]	Alfred McIntire	1	5		
[266]	Lucy Wells		11		
[267*‡]	Robert Owens	1	11		
[268*]	Lewis Parris	2	2		
[269*]	Mason Woods	1	5		
[270*‡]	Robert Hardin	1	4		
[271*‡]	William Robinson	1	6		
[272]	Thomas Dotson	1	1		
[273]	Samuel Heddy	1	13		
[274]	Aaron Heddy	1	5		
[275]	John McCollister	1	3		
[276]	Robert McCollister	1	2		
[277 ‡]	Nathaniel Cox	1	4		
[278 ‡]	Alexander Cox	1	2		
[279*]	John Hutchcraft	1	8		
[280*‡]	Stephen Fields	1	5		
[281*‡]	James Drake	1	4		
[282 ‡]	Robert A. Denn	1	2		
[283]	Peter Westerfield	1	5		
[284*‡]	David Gill	1	4		
[285]	Sophia Norton		3		
[286 ‡]	George Harrison	1	4		
[287*‡]	James Calbert	1	7		
[288]	Thomas Just	1	3		
[289*]	Samuel Underwood	1	7		
[290]	Reuben Alphin	1	1		
[291]	Henry Just	1	1		
[292*]	Asa Ledbetter	2	5		
[293]	Henry Ledbetter	1	9		
[294*]	Chatten Scroggins	1	6		
[295]	Jacob Wallace	1	2		
[296*]	Rebakah Wammock	1	5		
[297*]	Green Wammock	1	4		
[298]	Benjamine Wammock	1	1		
[299*]	Henry Ledbetter	1	1		

GALLATIN COUNTY (Continued)

No.	Heads of families	White males 21 & upwards	All other white	Free people of color	Servants or slaves
[300]	John Michael	1	2		
[301*]	John Scroggin	1	4		
[302]	Walter Teadford	1	6		
[303]	William Kesterson	1	5		
[304*]	Samuel Morris	1	4		
[305]	Jaramiah Hubs	1	7		
[306]	Thomas Lanier	1	6		
[307*‡]	Warner Buck	3	2		
[308 ‡]	James Stinson	2	4		
[309]	John Smith	2	5		
[310*‡]	Emanuel Ensminger	14	8		5
[311*‡]	William Burnett	4	6		
[312 ‡]	Arthur G. Young	1	4		1
[313 ‡]	Thomas Graves	1	2		
[314*‡]	James McCastlin	2	4		
[315*‡]	Webster McCastlin	1	2		
[316 ‡]	Jaramiah Haws	1	2		
[317*‡]	Elias Chaffin	1	2		
[318*‡]	Richard Foley	1			
[319*‡]	Elijah Butler	1	7		
[320]	David Pantier	1	4		
[321]	Moses Hutson	2	6		
[322 ‡]	Charles Hill	4	1		1
[323*]	William Black	3	3		
[324 ‡]	John Needeham	1	1		
[325*‡]	William Daniel	1	5		
[326*]	Nancy Herrod		6		
[327*‡]	Alexander McCroy	1	8		
[328 ‡]	John Buckston	1			
[329]	Bethel Pew	1	4		
[330 ‡]	Liman Sabin	1			
[331]	Talton M. Caines	1	5		
[332]	Robert Cooper	1	5		
[333*‡]	Eli Gaston	1	8		
[334]	John Gaston	1	1		
[335]	Reubin Alton	1	1		
[336*‡]	James Aluin	3	5	1	
[337]	Daniel Reynolds	1	2		

GALLATIN COUNTY (Continued)

No.	Heads of families	White males 21 & upwards	All other white	Free people of color	Servants or slaves
[338]	Thomas Reed	1	2		
[339]	Samuel Jackson	1	6		
[340]	Joseph Jackson	1	1		
[341*]	Mary Hatsel		4		
[342]	Elizabeth Aanderson		3		
[343]	James Griggery	1	6		
[344]	Abraham Fuller	1	3		
[345]	William Keney	1	1		
[346*‡]	John Newell	3	7		
[347*]	William Young	1	5		
[348]	John Groves	1	4		
[349]	Joel Wells, Sen.	1	5		
[350]	Joel Wells, Junr.	1	1		
[351]	Michael Bartlett	1	1		
[352]	Lewis Howell	1	6		
[353*]	Sampson Dunn	1	7		
[354]	Jonathan Coburn	1	4		
[355]	James Dunn	1	2		
[356]	Novel Browne	1	4		
[357*‡]	Brice Hannah	3	2		
[358]	Houson Fletcher	1	1		
[359 ‡]	Joseph Warthon	2	7		
[360 ‡]	George Johnson	4	4		19
[361*]	Daniel Norington			9	
[362]	Lewis Smith			3	
[363*‡]	Samuel Caldwell			2	
[364 ‡]	David Dimmery			6	
[365]	Samuel Coldwell			5	
[366*]	Jeffery Dupriest			2	
[367]	Benjamine Coleman			2	
[368]	Jacob Shickle			7	
[369]	William Harsford			5	
[370]	Robert Spears	1	3		
[371]	Jarrl Davis			4	
[372*‡]	David Barnett	2	6		
[373*]	William Reynolds	1	6		
[374*]	Joseph Baker	1	10		
[375*]	Benjamine Waldin	1	10		1

GALLATIN COUNTY (Continued)

No.	Heads of families	White males 21 & upwards	All other white	Free people of color	Servants or slaves
[376*‡]	James C. Barnett	1	3		
[377 ‡]	Bazel Barnett	1	8		
[378]	John Barnett	[No	data giv	en]	
[379]	William Briggman	1	4		
[380*]	Jacob Baugher	1	6		
[381*]	James Ledbetter	1	8		
[382*]	John Smith	1	8		
[383]	Michael Browne	1	8		
[384]	Richard Buffington	1	1		
[385 ‡]	Berrimon Shumake	1	2		
[386 ‡]	Thomas Cummons	1	6		
[387 ‡]	John McSpanon	1	3		
[388]	James McSpanon	[1]	2		
[389*‡]	William Waggoner	1	5		
[390*‡]	Benjamin Cummons	1	7		
[391*‡]	George Tarlton	1	8		
[392]	Levi McGlaughlin	1	2		
[393*]	Robert Patton	1	8		
[394*‡]	John Kinsall	2	1		
[395]	Jarrett Garner	1			
[396 ‡]	Andrew Jammason	1	6		
[397*‡]	William Cummons	1	2		
[398]	William Cruson	1	6		
[399 ‡]	Curtis Johnson	2	6		
[400]	Mathew Gillospel	1	2		
[401*‡]	John Berry	1	9		
[402 ‡]	Melachi Harford	1	2		
[403 ‡]	Jessee Harford	1	7		
[404 ‡]	William Trasey	1	1		
[405 ‡]	John S. Young	1	5		
[406*‡]	Benjamin Bramlett	2	3		
[407 ‡]	David Crabell	1	2		
[408*‡]	Coleman Browne	2	4		
[409*‡]	Thomas Browne	2	3		
[410*]	Samuel Little	1	5		
[411]	Wright Little	1	3		
[412*]	Nathan Bridgeman	2	7		
[413 ‡]	Reuben Bramlett	1	3		

GALLATIN COUNTY (Continued)

No.	Heads of families	White males 21 & upwards	All other white	Free people of color	Servants or slaves
[414]	Nathan Bramlett	1	1		
[415*‡]	Henry Bramlett	1	3		
[416 ‡]	William Browne	1	5		
[417*‡]	John Browne	1	3		
[418*‡]	Simpson Newman	2	6		
[419*‡]	William Sutton	1	5		
[420*‡]	Mavil Browne	1	3		
[421 ‡]	Isaac Simpson	1	3		
[422 ‡]	Thomas Margraves	1	3		
[423]	Elias Chaffin Junr.	1	2		
[424*]	Joseph Owen	3			11
[425*‡]	Timothy Guard	4	7	5	34
[426]	William Polls	1	5		1
[427]	John Granger	3	10		
[428*‡]	Thomas Smith	1	6		2
[429 ‡]	David Grable	1	4		
[430*]	Daniel L. Miner	1	5		
[431 ‡]	Clinton Brigance	1	2		
[432 ‡]	Samuel Upchurch	3	5		
[433 ‡]	David Boyes	1	5		
[434*‡]	Joseph T. Atchison	1	3		
[435*‡]	John Gassaway	1	3		
[436 ‡]	John Karnes	1	9		
[437*]	John Martin	1	4		
[438 ‡]	Robert Moore	1	2		
[439*‡]	Eli Adams	1	5		
[440*‡]	John Williams	2	6		
[441*‡]	William Cox	1	2		
[442 ‡]	Richard Isom	1	6		
[443 ‡]	Jacob Feasle	1	4		
[444 ‡]	William Crafford	1	6		
[445*‡]	James Rieves	1	10		
[446*‡]	Chester Bethell	2	6		
[447*‡]	James Hampton	1	3		
[448*]	Isaac Hall	1	4		
[449]	George Anderson	1	2		
[450*‡]	Thomas Gassaway	2	5		
[451 ‡]	Elenor Tir		6		

CENSUS OF 1820

GALLATIN COUNTY (Continued)

No.	Heads of families	White males 21 & upwards	All other white	Free people of color	Servants or slaves
[452*‡]	George Bond	2	9		
[453 ‡]	Thomas Herrold	1	2		
[454*‡]	John Hall	3	2		
[455 ‡]	William Hall	1	5		
[456 ‡]	Mathew Hall	1	4		
[457 ‡]	John Williams	2	6		
[458*‡]	Henry Duncane	1	7		
[459]	Thomas Waller	1	5		
[460]	Benjamine Mobley	1			
[461 ‡]	John Odle	1	2		
[462 ‡]	Joseph Patterson	1	6		
[463*‡]	Parrott Pate	1	6		
[464*‡]	William Pate	1	7		
[465 ‡]	John McCrarey	2	6		
[466 ‡]	John Bagby	1	4		
[467 ‡]	George Parker	1	2		
[468 ‡]	John Garner	1	3		
[469*‡]	Absolem Abner	1	4		
[470 ‡]	Harmon Stricklin	1	3		
[471*]	William Abner	1	4		
[472*]	Joseph Taylor	1	3		
[473 ‡]	Urier Carson	1	6		
[474 ‡]	Sarah Taylor		4		
[475*‡]	Henry Cox	1	9		
[476 ‡]	Lytle Neal	1	2		
[477]	Stephen Burns			10	
[478*]	William Dillingham	1	6		
[479*]	Michael Dillingham	1	2		
[480*‡]	William Stricklin	2	7		
[481*‡]	Smith Hampton	1	10		
[482*‡]	Jonathan Stricklin	1	4		
[483 ‡]	Edmund Vinson	1	3		
[484*‡]	John Gaskins	2	5		
[485 ‡]	Turner Cook	2	3		
[486*‡]	Elish Cook	1	10		
[487 ‡]	James Sloan	1	6		
[488 ‡]	Jessee Stiff	1	1		
[489 ‡]	Thomas Kelton	2	2		

GALLATIN COUNTY (Continued)

No.	Heads of families	White males 21 & upwards	All other white	Free people of color	Servants or slaves
[490]	David B. Russell	1			
[491 ‡]	Thadah Gaskins	1	1		
[492 ‡]	Wiley Fleetewood	1	2		
[493 ‡]	Hatton Fleetewood	1	1		
[494 ‡]	William Derham	1	2		
[495 ‡]	William Holland	1	8		
[496 ‡]	Zimry Garrison	1	5		
[497*‡]	Isaac N. Barker	1	5		
[498 ‡]	Henry Bracken	1	7		
[499]	Vatchel Clarey	1	1		
[500 ‡]	James Furgason	1	9		
[501 ‡]	William Talbert	1	7		
[502 ‡]	Hugh Parks	1	3		
[503 ‡]	Charles Ervin	1	2		
[504*‡]	Amus Willey	1	5		
[505 ‡]	Elijah Harris	1	10		
[506*‡]	Jessee Mitchell			4	
[507 ‡]	Jessee Shaw	1	2		
[508 ‡]	Robert Mitchell	2	7		
[509*‡]	Reuben Burdin	1	2		
[510 ‡]	James Adams	1	4		
[511 ‡]	James Mcfarland	3	7		
[512*‡]	Hampton Pankee	1	8		
[513*‡]	Shaderick Dunn	1	11		
[514*]	John Adkison	1	4		
[515]	Edward Henderson	1			
[516]	Brient Wilkens	1	5		
[517]	Sherrod Henderson	1	6		
[518 ‡]	Wilson Henderson, Senr.	2	2		
[519]	Wilson Henderson, Junr.	1	5		
[520*‡]	James Henderson	1	1		
[521 ‡]	Robert Henderson	1	2		
[522 ‡]	Thomas Standley	1	2		
[523*]	Joseph Adkison	1	6		
[524*]	Charles McClain	1	13		
[525*]	Hugh Robinson	1	2		
[526]	Walter Mcdanold	1	6		
[527*‡]	Dowell Ressell	1	6		

GALLATIN COUNTY (Continued)

No.	Heads of families	White males 21 & upwards	All other white	Free people of color	Servants or slaves
[528]	John Tanner	1	6		
[529]	Willaby Wilkins	1	7		
[530]	Richard Harris	1	6		
[531]	William Brackman	1	9		
[532]	Marke Robinson	2	6		
[533]	Enenor Roach		3		
[534*‡]	Samuel Watkins	6		3	8
[535 ‡]	Richard Adams	1	3		
[536*]	Charles Mick	1	7		
[537*‡]	Hankerson Rood	4	4		
[538*‡]	Chism Estes	1	9		
[539]	John Parker	1	1		
[540*‡]	Bird Stafford	1	3		
[541*]	Richard Riddle	1	8		
[542]	William Taylor	1	5		
[543*]	Giles Taylor	2	5		
[544]	Abaham Granger	3	7		
[545*‡]	Jacob Pruett	1	9		
[546 ‡]	James Alvey	1	3		
[547*‡]	Thomas Barlow	1	8		
[548*]	Benjamin Tolley	1	5		
[549]	Samuel Kimmel	1	4		
[550*‡]	Marmaduk S. Davenport	3	6		2
[551*]	Henry Blalock	1	10		
[552*]	Charles Williams	1	6		
[553*‡]	Otho Davenport	2	5		
[554*‡]	Robert Keeth	1	3		
		784	2330	98	239
					98
					2330
					784
					3451

GALLATIN COUNTY (*Continued*)

I Doe certify the foregoing to be a correct innumeration of the inhabittance of the County of Gallatin State of Illinois

OTHO DAVENPORT Commitioner

Corrected totals:

Free white males 21 years and upwards		784
All other white inhabitants		2335
		3119
Negroes		337
Free persons of color	98	
Servants or slaves	239	
	337	
Total		3456

CENSUS OF 1820

GALLATIN COUNTY (*Continued*)

The census returns for Gallatin County were taken by three men—William McCoy took the two 1818 censuses, Otho Davenport the state census for 1820, and Richard T. Jones the federal census for 1820. There are wider discrepancies between the census tables for Gallatin than for any other county, so much so that it is impossible to accept any of the figures found as the accurate enumeration of the population for either 1818 or 1820. The 1818 census lists 542 families as of May 30; the additional census taken between June 1 and July 28, 1818, adds 74 families, a total of 616 families in Gallatin County in 1818 as against 554 listed in the state census (returned December 1, 1820) and 451 families listed in the federal census (certified January 27, 1821). The state census for 1820 lists 103 more families than the federal census, but the discrepancy is even greater than that as 224 families listed in the state census do not appear in the federal census, and 119 of those in the federal census are not in the state census. Seventy-seven families in the state but not in the federal census are found in 1818 census; 20 of those only in the federal census are in the 1818 census.

The larger population given for 1818 is partly accounted for by the fact that many families are apparently listed more than once in that census, indicating that they were still moving about and not yet located. The discrepancies between the two 1820 censuses would be somewhat reduced also if it could be shown that families with the same surname were always identical. Frequently brothers or several unrelated families residing together more or less temporarily would give in different names as head of the family. Where the size and location of the family seems to correspond definitely this is indicated in the notes, but in many cases such a relationship, though probably existing, cannot be established from such a comparison.

These discrepancies in the tables are due largely to the fact that the population of Gallatin County was more mobile than that of any other county. Shawneetown, its county seat, was the port of entry through which practically all immigrants came into the state and from which the roads led to all the other counties. Families sometimes settled in the county permanently, but more often stayed a short time and then settled elsewhere. Undoubtedly many transients were listed by the census takers as residents.

The following names appear in the federal census but not in the 1820 state census.

*Addison, Thomas	Cook, Margaret
Armstrong, John	*Cooper, Joseph
Bain, Moses	Cotton, Elias
Bamber, John	Cotton, Elihu
Barnett, Joseph	*Cowin, John
Berry, John	Cranshaw, E.
*Berry, William	Cranshaw, John
Biddle, Richard	*Cravins, Jesse
*Black, John	Crenshaw, Abraham
Bondter, John	Curry, William A.
Boughman, John	Davenport, James
Brown, Jesse	Dawsey, John
Buffington, Abraham	Dix, John
Buffington, Philip C.	*Eddy, Henry
Burnes, John	Elmore, William
Bushhart, George	Finley, William S.
Caithle, William	Fleming, William
Carnes, Jacob	Forrester, John, Jr.
Casewill, John	Ghaston, Robt.
Chaple, Solomon	Ghasting, Wilson
Chilson, Jesse	*Gillaspie, John
Christopher, John	Gittle, Saml.
Clayton, William	Hall, Achibald
Cochran, Andrew P.	Hall, John
Cochran, John	Hall, William
Connel, John M.	*Hardin, Jeptha

GALLATIN COUNTY (Continued)

Hastin, George
Hayes, Calvin
*Hayes, Samuel
Helmstutter, Christ
Hodge, John
Hodges, William
Holmes, Bryon
Jad, Timothy
Kinner, James
Latherham, James
Ledbetter, Sarah
Litener, Jacob
Loften, Samuel
Logan, Fleming
Logsdon, Joseph
Martin, A.
Maloney, David
McDaniel, Abraham
*McGehee, William
   1818. McGhee, Wm.
*McLean, John
   1818. M'Clane, John
Madison, James
Marimaid, Jesse
Martin, Robert
Michael, Mathew
Middleton, Henry
Minah, Lunah
Molany, Daniel
*Moody, William
Morgan, John
Murry, James
Owen, Robert
Paren, James M.
Philips, John
Philips, Sally
Purkins, Ephraim

*Reives, John C.
   1818. Rives, John C.
*Rice, B.
   1818. Rice, Benj.
Rieves, Gustavus
Rude, Elijah
Sands, John
*Seaton, Peter C.
Sherarer, John
Simpson, Daniel
Smith, Martin
Snell, Lewis
*Spance, John
   1818. Spencer, John
Steward, John
Stilley, Stephen
Stilson, Lara
Strader, Benjamin
Swaton, John
Talby, Pleasant
Tarlton, Charles
Thompson, James
Thompson, Thomas
*Thompson, William
Vance, Nicholas, Jr.
Vaught, Thomas F.
Wallingford, Joseph
Wary, Vachel G.
Waters, Hiram
*White, Samuel
*Wilhitt, Mathew
   1818. Willhite, Matthew
Willard, Harry
Williams, Jesse
Wilson, Russell F.
Wilton, Henry

Discrepancies are as follows:

1 Peeples, Robert
   1818. Peebles, Robert
   F1820. Peeples, Robert
2 McCooll, Abraham T.
   1818. M'Cool, Abriham
   F1820. McCoole, A.T.M.
6 Moreland, Garner
   F1820. Moreland, Gardner
8 Bell, James
   F1820. Beall, James
10 Macefield, Roswell
   F1820. Mansfield, Roswell
11 Gryder, Cornelius
   F1820. Grider, Cornelius
12 Forister, John
   1818. Forrester, John
   F1820. Forrester, John

13 Clark, Joseph
   1818. Clarke, Joseph
   F1820. Clark, Joseph
18 McGlaughlin, John
   1818. M'Lauflen, John
   F1820. McLaughlin, John
19 Fade, David
   F1820. Fall, David
22 Aidelott, Zadock
   F1820. Aydolett, Zadoc
23 Aydelott, Levi
   F1820. Aydolett, Levi
26 Gilworth, John C.
   F1820. Gilbrith, John
30 Frazer, John
   1818. Freazer, John
   F1820. Frazer, John

CENSUS OF 1820

GALLATIN COUNTY (Continued)

31 Thompson, James P.
    F1820. Thompson, James B.
32 Moreland, Hazle
    1818. Moreland, Hazel, [Jr. ?]
    F1820. Moreland, Hazel, Jr.
36 Docker, W. A.
    F1820. Docker, William A.
37 McCoy, William
    1818. M'Coy, Wm.
    F1820. McCoy, Will
38 Sinclare, James W.
    F1820. Sinclair, James M.
45 Dawson, Thomas
    1818. Dawsen, Thomas
    F1820. Dawson, Thomas
46 Moor, William
    1818. Moore, Wm.
    F1820. Moore, William
50 Powell, Nicholas
    1818. Powell, Nicholas
    F1820. Powell, Nicholas, Sr.
52 Mattby, Frederick
    F1820. Mantley, Frereck
55 Wilson, John, Sr.
    1818. Wilson, John
    F1820. Wilson, John
56 Wilson, John, Jr.
    1818. Wilson, John
    F1820. Wilton, John
58 Scroggin, Humphrey
    1818. Scroggins, Humphrey
    F1820. Scroggins, Humphrey
59 Scroggin, Carter
    F1820. Scroggins, Carter
60 Scroggin, Barten
    F1820. Scroggins, Barten
61 Odom, Moses
    1818. Odrien, Moses
62 Carrol, Harlin
    1818. Carrel, Harlande
    F1820. Carrel, Starling
64 Potts, Isaak L.
    1818. Potts, Isaac
65 Sharewood, Edward
    F1820. Sherwood, Edward
66 Sharewood, Moses
    1818. Sherewood, Moses
    F1820. Sharwood, Moses
72 Boutwell, Leony C.
    1818. Boutwell, Leony
    F1820. Boutwell, Loney
76 Meeks, Suddith
    1818. Meeks, Judey
    F1820. Meeks, Judith

77 Smoot, Armsted
    1818. Smoot, Armstord
    F1820. Smoot, Armsted
82 Peddigrew, James M.
    1818. Pettygrew, James M.
    F1820. Pettygrove, James M.
84 Hinson, Phillip
    1818. Henson, Phillip
    F1820. Hinson, Philip
85 Vinsan, Jaramiah
    F1820. Vinson, Jeremiah
89 Mattingley, Edward
    1818. Matney, Edward
    F1820. Mallinly, Edward
90 Mattingley, Zacheriah
    F1820. Mattoney, Zachariah
91 Cummons, Thornton
    1818. Cummins, Thornton
    F1820. Cummons, Thornton
92 Cummons, William
    1818. Cummins, Wm.
    F1820. Cummons, Will, Sr.
94 Rieds, John
    1818. Reed, John
    F1820. Reed, John
98 Ragland, Haley
    1818. Ragline, Haly
    F1820. Raglen, Haley
99 Ragland, George
    1818. Ragline, George
    F1820. Raglen, George
107 Funkhowser, Robert R.
    1818. Funkhouser, Robert
    F1820. Funkhouser, Robert M.
109 Clark, Ensley
    1818. Clarke, Anesly
    F1820. Clark, Ansley
114 Demaret, Joseph
    F1820. Demarris, Joseph
115 Sloo, Thomas
    1818. Sloo, Thomas, Sr.
    F1820. Sloo, Thomas, Sr.
117 Mauldin, John
    F1820. Maulding, John
118 Hamilton, John
    1818. Hambleton, John
    F1820. Hamilton, John
120 Sharpe, Christopher H.
    F1820. Sharp, Christopher H.
122 Ocanrey, Morris
    F1820. Connery, Maurice
125 Darte, William
    1818. Dart, Wm.
    F1820. Dart, Will

GALLATIN COUNTY (*Continued*)

126 Robinson, Sarah
    F1820. Robinson, Sally
127 Moreland, Hazel
    1818. Moreland, Hazel [Sr. ?]
    F1820. Moreland, Hazel
130 Campbell, John
    1818. Campbel, John
    F1820. Campbell, John
131 Dodge, Bazzle
    1818. Dodge, Bazel
133 Tommason, William
    1818. Thomason, William
    F1820. Thomson, William
142 Kelleay, William
    1818. Kelly, Wm.
    F1820. Kelley, William
145 Caldwell, William
    F1820. Caldwell, Will
151 Clark, Alexander H.
    F1820. Clark, Alexr.
152 Reiley, Isaac
    1818. Riley, Isaac
153 Reiley, Joseph
    1818. Reily, Joseph
    F1820. Riley, Joseph
154 Madlock, Henry
    1818. Medlock, Henry
    F1820. Medlock, Henry
157 Hubbard, Ephraim
    1818. Hubbard, Ephrim
    F1820. Hubbard, Ephraim
158 Casey, Nicholas
    1818. Cassy, Nicholas
    F1820. Casey, Nicholas
161 Cane, Joseph
    F1820. Cain, Joseph
162 White, Benjamine
    F1820. White, Benjamin
164 Rowlings, Moses M.
    1818. Rowlings, Moses M.
    F1820. Rawlings, Moses M.
166 Flinn, Obid
    1818. Flinn, Obadiah
172 McConel, Hugh
    1818. M'Connell, Hugh
    F1820. McConnell, Hugh
175 Haney, David
    1818. Hany, David
177 Ferdin, Joseph
    1818. Ferdin, Joseph
    F1820. Furden, Joseph
180 Dar, Hubbard
    1818. Dare, Hubbard
    F1820. Dare, Hubbard
182 Daimwood, John G.
    1818. Damewood, John
    F1820. Daimwood, John G.
183 Forister, William
    F1820. Forster, William
187 Johnson, Andrew
    F1820. Johnston, Andrew
192 Kikendall, Lewis
    1818. Kuykendoll, Lewis
    F1820. Kuykindall, Lewis
193 Willis, James
    1818. Willis, James, Jr.
195 Johnson, Thomas
    1818. Johnston, Thomas
    F1820. Johnston, Thomas
197 Frazer, Ezekiel
    1818. Freazer, Ezekiel
    F1820. Frazer, Ezekiel
198 Owens, Willis
    1818. Owen, Willis
199 Baker, Geter
    1818. Baker, Jeter
    F1820. Baker, Jeter
200 Willis, Hardy
    F1820. Willis, Archibald
201 Peters, William C. T.
    1818. Petters, Wm. C.
202 McCleland, Fatima
    F1820. McClernand, Fatina
204 Harrison, Benjamine
    F1820. Harrison, Benjamin
205 Cane, James
    1818. Cain, James
    F1820. Cane, James
206 Limrick, John
    F1820. Limerick, John
208 Vanlandingham, O. C.
    1818. Vanlandingham, ——
    F1820. Vanlandingham, O. C.
209 Barger, Jacob
    1818. Berger, Jacob
    F1820. Barger, Jacob
213 Coldwell, James
    F1820. Caldwell, James
214 Campbell, Charles
    1818. Cambple, Charles
    F1820. Campbell, Charles
215 Campbell, Samuel R.
    1818. Campble, Saml. R.
    F1820. Campbell, Saml. R.
216 Mclean, Robert D.
    F1820. McClean, R. D.
217 Weathero, Ann
    1818. Witherow, Nancy

GALLATIN COUNTY (Continued)

219 Beal, Luther
    F1820. Bell, Luther
224 Cheek, Isham
    1818. Cheach, Isem
225 Coburn, Paul
    F1820. Coalbourn, Paul
228 Wilson, James
    1818. Wilson, James
    F1820. Willson, James
231 Fuller, Cathorine
    F1820. Fuller, Catharine
232 Low, Anthony
    F1820. Law, Anthony
234 Logsdon, Joseph
    F1820. Logson, Joseph
235 Logsdon, Margarett
    1818. Logston, Peggy
    F1820. Logston, Margaret
236 Hodge, Amos
    F1820. Hodg, Amos
237 Rowson, Abner
    1818. Rosen, Abner
    F1820. Rawson, Abner
238 Cayton, John
    F1820. Caton, John
242 Lafferty, Cornelius
    1818. Lafferty, Cornelus
    F1820. Laffarty, Cornelius
244 Mosby, Benjamine
    1818. Moseby, Benjamin
    F1820. Mosbey, Benjamin
248 Murphy, John
    1818. Murphey, John
254 Willis, Malach C.
    1818. Willis, Malacah
258 Watson, Robert
    1818. Watson, Robt.
    F1820. Watston, Robt.
263 Lowery, Joseph
    F1820. Lowry, Joseph
267 Owens, Robert
    1818. Owens, Robert
    F1820. Owen, Robert
268 Parris, Lewis
    1818. Parris, Luess
269 Woods, Mason
    1818. Wood, Mason
279 Hutchcraft, John
    1818. Hutchcrafft, John
282 Denn, Robert A.
    F1820. Dean, Robert A.

287 Calbert, James
    1818. Colbert, James
    F1820. Colbert, James
294 Scroggins, Chatten
    1818. Croggins, Chattin
296 Wammock, Rebakah
    1818. Wormack, Wm.
297 Wammock, Green
    1818. Wormack, Green
301 Scroggin, John
    1818. Scroggins, John
304 Morris, Samuel
    1818. Morriss, Saml.
307 Buck, Warner
    1818. Buck, Warner
    F1820. Buck, Warner, Sr.
311 Burnett, William
    1818. Burnett, Will
    F1820. Burnett, Will
312 Young, Arthur G.
    F1820. Young, A. G.
314 McCastlin, James
    1818. M'Caslin, James
    F1820. McCastlins, James
315 McCastlin, Webster
    1818. MCassahan, Webster
    F1820. McCastlins, Webster
316 Haws, Jaramiah
    F1820. Hawes, J.
317 Chaffin, Elias
    1818. Chaffen, Elias
    F1820. Chaffin, Elias
318 Foley, Richard
    1818. Folly, Richard
    F1820. Folid, Richard
324 Needeham, John
    F1820. Needham, John
326 Herrod, Nancy
    1818. Herod, John
327 McCroy, Alexander
    1818. M'Koy, Alexander
    F1820. McCroy, Alexander
328 Buckston, John
    F1820. Buckstan, John
330 Sabin, Liman
    F1820. Sabin, Lyman
333 Gaston, Eli
    1818. Gaston, Eli
    F1820. Gaston, Elihu
336 Aluin, James
    1818. Albin, James
    F1820. Albin, James
341 Hatsel, Mary
    1818. Hatchel, Mary

GALLATIN COUNTY (*Continued*)

353 Dunn, Sampson
    1818. Dun, Sampson
359 Warthon, Joseph
    F1820. Wathen, Joseph
361 Norington, Daniel
    1818. Norante, Daniel
364 Dimmery, David
    F1820. Dimeral, David
366 Dupriest, Jeffery
    1818. Deprest, Jeffrey
373 Reynolds, William
    1818. Runnels, Wm.
375 Waldin, Benjamine
    1818. Walden, Benj.
376 Barnett, James C.
    1818. Barnett, James
    F1820. Barnett, James C.
380 Baugher, Jacob
    1818. Boier, Jacob
385 Shumake, Berrimon
    F1820. Shormac, John B.
386 Cummons, Thomas
    F1820. Cummings, Thomas
387 McSpanon, John
    F1820. M'Sparner, John
389 Waggoner, William
    1818. Wagner, Wm.
    F1820. Waggoner, Will
390 Cummons, Benjamine
    1818. Cummins, Benjamin
    F1820. Cummins, Benjamin
391 Tarlton, George
    1818. Tarlton, Townsen
    F1820. Talton, T.
396 Jammason, Andrew
    F1820. Jimason, Andrew
397 Cummons, William
    1818. Cummins, Wm.
    F1820. Cummins, William, Jr.
401 Berry, John
    1818. Bery, John
    F1820. Berry, John
402 Harford, Melachi
    F1820. Herefore, M.
403 Harford, Jessee
    F1820. Herefore, Jesse
404 Trasey, William
    F1820. Tracy, William
406 Bramlett, Benjamine
    1818. Bramlett, Benj.
    F1820. Bramblet, Benjamin
407 Crabell, David
    F1820. Grable, David A.

408 Browne, Coleman
    1818. Brown, Coleman
    F1820. Brown, Coalman
409 Browne, Thomas
    1818. Brown, Thomas
    F1820. Brown, Thomas
412 Bridgeman, Nathan
    1818. Bridgman, Nathan
413 Bramlett, Reuben
    F1820. Bramblett, Reubin
415 Bramlett, Henry
    1818. Bramlett, Henry
    F1820. Bramblet, Henry
416 Browne, William
    F1820. Brown, William
417 Browne, John
    1818. Brown, John
    F1820. Brown, John
420 Browne, Mavil
    1818. Brown, Marvel
    F1820. Brown, Marvel
421 Simpson, Isaac
    F1820. Simson, Isaac
422 Margraves, Thomas
    F1820. Margrave, Thos.
424 Owen, Joseph
    1818. Owens, Joseph
425 Guard, Timothy
    1818. Gaurd, Timothy
    F1820. Guard, Timothy
431 Brigance, Clinton
    F1820. Brigum, Clinton
432 Upchurch, Samuel
    F1820. Upchurch, John
433 Boyes, David
    F1820. Baze, David
434 Atchison, Joseph T.
    1818. Attchasen, Joseph T.
    F1820. Atchison, Joseph
435 Gassaway, John
    1818. Gassaway, John
    F1820. Gasaway, John
437 Martin, John
    1818. Marton, John
438 Moore, Robert
    F1820. More, Robert
442 Isom, Richard
    F1820. Isham, Richard
443 Feasle, Jacob
    F1820. Feezle, Jacob W.
444 Crafford, William
    F1820. Crofford, William
445 Rieves, James
    1818. Reives, James
    F1820. Rieves, James

GALLATIN COUNTY (Continued)

446 Bethell, Chester
    1818. Bethel, Chester
    F1820. Bethle, Chester
450 Gassaway, Thomas
    1818. Gassaway, Ths
    F1820. Gasaway, Thomas
451 Tir, Elenor
    F1820. Furr, Eliver
453 Herrold, Thomas
    F1820. Herrald, Thomas
458 Duncane, Henry
    1818. Dunkin, Henry
    F1820. Duncan, Henry
463 Pate, Parrott
    1818. Pate, Parrett
    F1820. Pate, Parrot
465 McCrarey, John
    F1820. McCreary, John
466 Bagby, John
    F1820. Bagbey, John
469 Abner, Absolem
    1818. Abney, Absolom
    F1820. Abney, Abner
470 Stricklin, Harmon
    F1820. Stricktin, Harmon
471 Abner, William
    1818. Abney, Wm.
472 Taylor, Joseph, or 474 Taylor, Sarah
    1818. Tayler, Joseph
    F1820. Taylor, Isaiah
473 Carson, Urier
    F1820. Crarson, Euriah
476 Neal, Lytle
    F1820. Kneel, Little
479 Dillingham, Michael
    1818. Dillingham, Mich.
480 Stricklin, William
    1818. Strickland, William
    F1820. Strickland, William
481 Hampton, Smith
    1818. Hampton, Smith
    F1820. Hamton, Smith
482 Stricklin, Jonathan
    1818. Strickland, Jonathan
    F1820. Strickland, Jonathan
483 Vinson, Edmund
    F1820. Vincen, Edmond
484 Gaskins, John
    1818. Gaskins, John
    F1820. Ghastings, John
486 Cook, Elish
    1818. Cooke, Elisha
    F1820. Cook, Elicia

488 Stiff, Jessee
    F1820. Stiff, Jesse
491 Gaskins, Thadah
    F1820. Ghastings, Thadius
492 Fleetewood, Wiley
    F1820. Fleetwood, Wiley
493 Fleetewood, Hatton
    F1820. Fleetwood, Haton
494 Derham, William
    F1820. Durham, William
496 Garrison, Zimry
    F1820. Garrison, Zemra
497 Barker, Isaac N.
    1818. Baker, Isaac N.
    F1820. Barker, Isaac M.
500 Furgason, James
    F1820. Ferguson, James
501 Talbert, William
    F1820. Tolbott, William
502 Parks, Hugh
    F1820. Parks, Hue
503 Ervin, Charles
    F1820. Irvin, Charles
504 Willey, Amus
    1818. Wiley, Ames
    F1820. Willey, Amos
506 Mitchell, Jessee
    1818. Michael, Jessee
    F1820. Mitchel, Jesse
507 Shaw, Jessee
    F1820. Shaw, Jesse
508 Mitchell, Robert
    F1820. Michel, Robert
509 Burdin, Reuben
    1818. Birdon, Reuben
    F1820. Burden, Reuben
511 Mcfarland, James
    F1820. McFarlen, James
512 Pankee, Hampton
    1818. Panky, Hamton
    F1820. Pankey, Hampton
513 Dunn, Shaderick
    1818. Dunn, Shadric
    F1820. Dunn, Shedrick
514 Adkison, John
    1818. Atkinson, John
518 Henderson, Wilson, Sr.
    F1820. Henderson, Wilson
522 Standley, Thomas
    F1820. Stanley, Thos.
523 Adkison, Joseph
    1818. Atkinson, Joseph
525 Robinson, Hugh
    1818. Robertson, Hugh

GALLATIN COUNTY (*Concluded*)

527 Ressell, Dowell
    1818. Russell, James M. D.
    F1820. Russel, James W.
536 Mick, Charles
    1818. Micks, Charles
537 Rood, Hankerson
    1818. Rude, Hankersen
    F1820. Rude, Hankerson
538 Estes, Chism
    1818. Este, Chism
    F1820. Estis, Chism
545 Pruett, Jacob
    1818. Prowitt, Jacob
    F1820. Pruit, Jacob

548 Tolley, Benjamin
    1818. Tolly, Benjamin
550 Davenport, Marmaduk S.
    1818. Devanpert, M.D.
    F1820. Davenport, M.S.
551 Blalock, Henry
    1818. Blalocke, Henry
553 Davenport, Otho
    1818. Devanport, Otho
    F1820. Devenport, Otho
554 Keeth, Robert
    1818. Koetah, Elizabeth
    F1820. Keeth, Elizabeth

CENSUS OF 1820

CENSUS OF JACKSON COUNTY, 1820
CENSUS

Of the Inhabitants of Jackson County in the State of Illinois, taken in conformity to the Act of Assembly of said state entitled "an act Providing for taking the Census of the state of Illinois," for 1820—Aproved March 23, 1819—

I Matthew Duncan of the County of Jackson do solemnly swear, that I will well and truly make a correct enumeration of all persons resident within the County of Jackson to the best of my ability, and return the same to the Secretary of State, on or before the first Monday in December in the year eighteen hundred and twenty.

MATTHEW DUNCAN

Sworn to and subscribed before me the Subscriber one of the Justices of the peace in and for the County of Jackson and state of Illinois this 1st day of August 1820—

J. S. DORRISS J P

CENSUS FOR JACKSON

	Names of Heads of Families	Free White Males					Free White Females					Foreigners not naturalized	No. of persons engaged in agriculture	No. of persons engaged in commerce	No. of persons engaged in manufactures
		Under 10 years old	Of 10 & under 16	Of 16 & under 26	Of 26 & under 45	Of 45 & upwards	Each column including the heads of families	Under 10 years of age	10 & under 16	16 & under 26	26 & under 45	45 & upwards			
[1*‡]	James S. Dorris	2			1					2						
[2 ‡]	James Gilles	1		6		1		2	2	1				1		
[3]	Samuel D. Dixon			1											1	
[4]	Jeptha Sweet				1										1	
[5]	Saml L. Burton				1											
[6*‡]	Geo. Creath	1	1	2		1		1	2	2	1			4		3
[7*‡]	Conrad Will			5	4			2			1					
[8*‡]	Charles Garner	2			1	1		1			1	1		1	2	2
[9*‡]	Ben. Henderson	2			1			1		1				1		7
[10 ‡]	Wm. Baker							4	3		1			1		
[11 ‡]	Ezekel Hennery	4	1		1			1	1		1			1		
[12*‡]	David Halladay	4	1	1	2					1		1	1	7		1
[13*‡]	James Hall, Ser					1										
[14 ‡]	James Nee			4				4	2		1			1	1	3
[15*‡]	James Hall, Jr.	1	2	2		1						1		6		
[16 ‡]	James Hall 3d			1					1							
[17]	David Marton				1			1		1						
[18 ‡]	William Martin				1			1		1						
[19*‡]	Robert Henderson	2			1			3		1				1		
[20 ‡]	Wm. Gill	3	3	1		1		1				1		6	1	
[21 ‡]	John Littlefield	1			2			2		1				1		1
[22*‡]	John Robinson	1		1	1			3		1				2		1
[23 ‡]	Robert Carden			1		1			2	1	1			2		1
[24*‡]	William McMillen	1			1			1		1				2		2
[25*‡]	Hugh McMillon			2		1						1		1		
[26 ‡]	Joseph McKinney	1		1				2		1				1		1
[27 ‡]	Preclla McCoupin										2					2
[28 ‡]	Francis Thornbury	2		1		1			1			1		2		
[29 ‡]	Nicholas Piles	1	1	1	1			2	2		1			2		
[30 ‡]	Saml. Smith				1			4			1			1		
[31 ‡]	Ezekel Tumbleson	1		1						1				1		

Figures and symbols preceding names have been supplied by the editor:
‡ Indicates name also in Federal Census for 1820.
* Indicates name also in State Census for 1818.
Writing is blurred for the subdivisions under "Free white Females." Probable ages have been supplied.

COUNTY FOR 1820

Slaves Males					Slaves Females					Free Coulered Persons Males				Free Coulered Persons Females				Total
Under 14	Of 14 & under 26 years old	Of 26 & under 45	Of 45 & upwards	Remarks	Under 14	Of 14 & under 26	Of 26 & under 45	45 & upwards	Total slaves Male & Female	Under 14 years old	14 & under 26 years old	26 & under 45 years old	45 & upwards	Under 14 years old	Of 14 & under 26	Of 26 & under 45 years old	45 & upwards	
	1																	6
																		13
																		[2]
																		[2]
																		1
																		1
																		11
												1						13
																		9
																		5
																		8
																		9
					1		1											10
																		5
1																		12
																		8
																		2
1																		3
																		3
1																		6
1																		3

JACKSON COUNTY (Continued)

	Names of Heads of Families	Free white males					
		Under 10 years old	Of 10 & under 16	between 16 & 18	of 16 & under 21	of 21 & under 45	of 45 & upwards each including heads of Fs.
[32 ‡]	Joseph T. Williams	1			1		1
[33*‡]	Terry Williams	4	2			1	
[34*‡]	William Garner					1	
[35]	John M. Campbell					1	
[36*‡]	James White		2			1	
[37*‡]	James West	1	1			1	
[38*‡]	William Davis	1				1	
[39 ‡]	John Campbell	3	1	1	1		1
[40*‡]	William Taylor	1				1	1
[41*‡]	Thomas Taylor	2	1	1	1		1
[42]	Hyram Root			1		2	1
[43 ‡]	Levy French					1	
[44*‡]	Robert M'Elvane	3	1			1	
[45*‡]	Lewis Wells				2		1
[46*‡]	Abner Pyle		1			1	
[47*‡]	Elijah Wells	4				1	
[48*‡]	Thomas Wells	1				1	
[49*‡]	Lewis Wells					1	
[50*‡]	John Pile	3	1			1	
[51 ‡]	William Pile	1	3				1
[52*‡]	Thomas Wadley					1	
[53*‡]	Jessy Rasco		1			1	
[54 ‡]	Hampton Reess	2	1		1	1	

JACKSON COUNTY (Continued)

Free white Females									Slaves						
								Males				Females			
Under 10 years of	of 10 & under 16	of 16 & under 21 including heads of Families	of 26 & under 45 includes Heads of F.	of 45 & upwards including Do.	No of persons engaged in agriculture	No of Do in Commerce	No of Do in Manufacturing	Under 14	of 14 & under 26	of 26 & under 45	of 45 and upwards	Under 14	of 14 & under 26	of 26 & under 45—	of 45 and upwards
		2		1	1										
2	1		1												
3		1													
1		1													
1			1												
1			1												
	1		1												
1	1	1		1											
		2		1											
			1												
				1											
5	1		1												
1			1												
2			1	1											
1	1		1												
	1		1												
3		1	1												
		1													
2	1	2	1												
2	1	1	1												

JACKSON COUNTY (*Continued*)

	Names of Heads of Families	Free White Males					Free	
		Under 10 years of age	of 10 & under 16 years of age	of 16 & under 21 including heads of families	of 21 & under 45 including heads of	of 45 & upwards including heads &c	Under 10 years of age—	of 10 & under 16 including heads &c
[55 ‡]	William Langly	1			1			
[56*‡]	James Wootan	2			1		1	
[57*‡]	Catherine Butcher			2			1	1
[58 ‡]	Jacob Hagler			1		1		
[59]	Thomas Smith			1				1
[60*‡]	Thomas Arnold	2		1	1			
[61 ‡]	John Bittle		1		1		2	
[62 ‡]	Walter Taylor				2		1	
[63 ‡]	John D. Winters			2				1
[64 ‡]	Henry Lype	1			1		2	
[65 ‡]	John Hagle	5		1	1		2	1
[66*‡]	Thomas Burns	6			1		1	
[67 ‡]	John Hopkins	2			1		1	
[68 ‡]	Joseph Welty			1	1			1
[69 ‡]	Phillip Hagle	3	1		1		3	1
[70 ‡]	Adam Vansee	1			1		1	
[71 ‡]	Sam Eatherton	1			1		4	
[72]	John Welty			1				
[73 ‡]	Peter Hagler	2			1			
[74*‡]	James Smith	2		1	1		2	2
[75 ‡]	George Lupe	1		1				
[76 ‡]	Washington Edward	2		1			2	
[77 ‡]	Danl. Dry	1		1			1	
[78*‡]	David Woods	1			1			
[79 ‡]	John Lype			4		1		

CENSUS OF 1820

JACKSON COUNTY (*Continued*)

White Females			Number of persons eng in agriculture	Slaves — Males				Slaves — Females				Total of Free whites	Total of Slaves	Total
of 16 & under 26 including heads &c	of 26 & under 45 including heads	of 45 & upwards including heads of Families		Under 14	of 14 & under 26 years of age	of 26 & under 45	of 45 & upwards	Under 14	of 14 & under 26	of 26 & under 45	of 45 and upwards			
	1		1											
1	1		1											
		1												
2														
	1													
	1													
1														
	1													
	2			1		1		1	1					
	1													
	1													
	1													
1														
	1													
	1													
1														
	1													
1														
	1													
		1												

JACKSON COUNTY (*Continued*)

	Names of Heads of Families	Free White Males					Free White		
		under 10	10 & under 16	16 & under 26	26 & under 45	45 & upward	[under 10]	[10 & under 16]	16-26
[80 ‡]	Leonard Lype	2		1	1	1		2	
[81]	Wm. Davis					1			
[82*‡]	Ben F. Connor	1		2	1		1		1
[83*‡]	James Quarles	1			1		2		1
[84*‡]	John Deason	5	1		1		1	1	
[85*‡]	Wm. D. Fuqua			1	1				1
[86 ‡]	Charles Swane	2	1	1	1		1	2	1
[87 ‡]	John Lype	1			1				1
[88 ‡]	Jonas Lype	1			1		3		
[89 ‡]	Jonas Vansel	3	2	1		1	1		1
[90 ‡]	Robert Rogers				1		2		1
[91 ‡]	Andrew Hopkins					1			
[92 ‡]	Jonus Acord	2			1		2		1
[93 ‡]	James Hopkins	2	1	1	1		1	1	
[94 ‡]	Simon Willard	4	1	4	1				
[95 ‡]	Adinegah Ball	1	1		1		2	1	
[96 ‡]	Harmon Leak	3	1	1	1				
[97 ‡]	Jonathan Bowerman			2			2		1
[98 ‡]	Wm. Thralkel	1			1		3		1
[99*‡]	Wm. Ausburn	1	2	1		1		1	2
[100*‡]	John Flacke	1	2	2		1		2	
[101*‡]	Green Henson	3			1		1		
[102*‡]	Benj. Walker		1	2		1			
[103 ‡]	Saml. Cochran	1		1		1			
[104*‡]	James Gill	2	1		1		2	1	
[105*‡]	Thomas Morrow	1			2				
[106*‡]	Joseph Goodbred			2			1		1
[107*‡]	William Gaston	2	3		1	1	4	3	1

CENSUS OF 1820

JACKSON COUNTY (Continued)

Females		Slaves					Free persons of Color					
		Males			Females		Males			Females		
26-45	45	under 10	10 & under 16	16 & under 26	under 10	& upwards	under 10	10 & under 16	16 & under 26			
	1											
1												
1												
1												
	1											
	1											
1												
1												
1												
1												
	1											
	1											
1												
	1											
	1	1			1	1						
1					1							
1												

ILLINOIS HISTORICAL COLLECTIONS

JACKSON COUNTY (Continued)

	Names of Heads of Families	Free White Males				Free White		
		under 10	10 & under 16	16 & under 26	26 & under 45	45 & upwards	under 10	10 & under 16	16 & under 26
[108*‡]	Aaron Davis	2		1		1	1	1	1
[109 ‡]	Matthias Davis					1			
[110*‡]	Wm. M. Bruer	4			1		1	2	
[111]	John Deeds			1					
[112*‡]	Chas. McKinney	3	1		1		1	1	
[113*‡]	John Morrow	3			1				
[114*‡]	Peter Hammond	1	2	1		1	1	1	
[115 ‡]	Suard Clayton			1			3		1
[116*‡]	James Davis		1	1		1		1	1
[117*‡]	Giles Henson	2	2			1	2		
[118*‡]	William McRoberts	1	1			1	2	1	
[119 ‡]	Danl. Nelson				1		2		
[120 ‡]	Marvelle Henson			1					1
[121*‡]	Allen Henson			2		1			
[122*‡]	John Aaron	2			1		1		
[123*‡]	Benjamin Henson	4	1	1	1			1	
[124*‡]	Jacob Lusadder	1	1	1			2	2	
[125 ‡]	George Imgram			1			2	1	
[126 ‡]	Lee Wood	1		1			1		2
[127 ‡]	Thos. East			1			1		
[128*‡]	Shadrach Massey	7	1	1			2		
[129*‡]	Isaac Jarrot	3	2			1	1	1	
[130*‡]	Rowland Glenn	2		2		1			2
[131*‡]	Thos. Glenn	1		1					1
[132*‡]	Isac Glenn	2				1			1
[133 ‡]	Alex. Cochran	1		1					1
[134*]	Geo. Ingram					1	2	2	
[135*‡]	Robt. Gilihan			1			1		1
[136*‡]	Squire Crane	1			1	1			
[137 ‡]	Adam Woldrich	1			1				1
[138 ‡]	James Ward	4				1			1
[139 ‡]	M. Albert				1				1

CENSUS OF 1820

JACKSON COUNTY (*Continued*)

Females		Slaves						Free persons of Colour			
		Males			Females			Males		Females	
26 & under 45	45 & upwards	under 14	14 & under 26	26 & under 45	under 14	14 & under 26	26 & under 45				
1	1										
1											
1											
1											
	1										
	1										
1											
1											
	1										
1											
1	1			1							
1											
1											
1											
1	1										
1											

JACKSON COUNTY (Continued)

Heads of families	Free white males					Free white		
	Under 10	10–16	16–26	26–45	45 & over	Under 10	10–16	16–26
[140 ‡] Mary Reynolds	1	1				1	1	
[141*‡] Val. Dillinger	4	2			1	1		1
[142*‡] Parker Grovner	1				1		1	
[143*‡] Geo. Cline			1	1				1
[144*‡] Z. Brooks	1				1	1		
[145*‡] John Roberts					1	1		
[146*‡] Wm. Roberts	1	1		1	1	1	1	
[147*‡] D. Bilderback	3	1		1	2	4		
[148 ‡] Peter Gallaher	1	1		1	1	1	1	1
[149 ‡] John Cline				1				
[150*‡] Wm. Boon	3	3		1	2	4		
[151*‡] Wm. Baker					1			
[152*‡] Stephen Jones	2			1	1	1	1	
[153 ‡] Simon Albert	3	3			1		1	1
[154 ‡] Abner Bryon				1				1
[155 ‡] Mary Woldrech	1		1					1
[156 ‡] Jacob Ankeny	2			2	1		1	
[157*‡] John Bowles	1			3	4	1	2	
[158*‡] Evan Thompson	2			1	1	2	2	
[159 ‡] Stephen Kelly	3	1			1			
[160*‡] Mary Span						5	2	
[161*‡] A. Chapman				1				
[162] John Thompson					1	1		1

CENSUS OF 1820

JACKSON COUNTY (*Continued*)

females		Slaves						Free persons of color					
		Males			Females			Males			Females		
26–45	45 & over	Under 14	14–26	26–45	Under 14	14–26	26–45						
	1												
	1												
1													
1													
	1												
1													
1													
1													
1		2		1			1						
1													
1													
	1												
1	1												
1													
1													
1													
1	1												
1	1												
	1												

JACKSON COUNTY (Continued)

	Names of Heads of Families	Free White Males		Free White Females		Male Slaves		Female Slaves	
		under 21	over 21	under 18	over 18	under 21	over 21	under 14	over 14
[163*‡]	Matthew Duncan	1	2		1	2	1		2
[164 ‡]	Jo. Duncan	1	4		1				1
[165*‡]	Wm. Grubb		1	1	1				
[166*‡]	Jacob Butcher	4	1	2	2				
[167 ‡]	Robert Marshall	4	1	3	2				
[168]	Jas. Werst	4	1	2	1				
[169 ‡]	H. Dillinger		5						
[170 ‡]	Jane Cox		2	2	2				
[171*‡]	John Byers	1	4	4	1				
[172*‡]	Thos. Jenkins	3	1	3	1				
[173*‡]	Alexr. Clark	2	2	3	2				
[174 ‡]	Robert Cochran		3	2	2				
[175 ‡]	Wm. Lindsey	1	2	1	2				
[176 ‡]	Richard Brown	1	1	1	1				
[177*‡]	Elias Ford	1	1		1				
[178*‡]	E. Pyatt		1		1				
[179*‡]	C. Swartz	1	3	2	1				
[180*‡]	H. Davis, Ser.	1	1	3	1				
[181*‡]	E. Davis	1	1	1	2				
[182*‡]	Adam Fifer	3	1	2					
[183*‡]	C. Davis	2	1		1	3	2		
[184 ‡]	Mary Phelps	3		2	1				
[185*‡]	John Glenn		1	6	1				
[186 ‡]	John Smith		1		1				
[187 ‡]	Wm. Brown	1	1		1				
[188*‡]	H. Noble, ser.	1	1		1				
[189*‡]	H. Noble, jun.		1	3	1				
[190*‡]	R. Brown, Ser.		1		1				
[191*‡]	John Phelps	2	1						
[192*‡]	Ben Ripley	2	1	1	1				
[193*‡]	Francis Garner	4	2	1	1				
[194*‡]	Danl. Duldumin	7	3	1	1				
[195*‡]	Drury Harrgton	3	1	4	1				
[196*‡]	Wateres Cochran		1	1	1				
[197*‡]	Nancey Wortham	1	2	1	1				
[198*‡]	K. Edwards	1	1	1	2				

CENSUS OF 1820

JACKSON COUNTY (*Continued*)

	Heads of families	Males under 21	Males over 21	Females under 18	Females over 18	Male slaves under 21	Male slaves over 21	Female slaves under 14	Female slaves over 14
[199*‡]	John Shannon	3	1	2	1				
[200*‡]	Joseph French	1	4	2	1				
[201 ‡]	T. French	1	1		1	5 slaves			
[202*‡]	Thos. Crane	3	1	2	1				
[203*‡]	Wm. Fox	3	1	4	1				
[204 ‡]	Henry Benson	2	1	3	1				
[205 ‡]	Wm. Akin	1	1	1	1				
[206 ‡]	Jesse Elmore	1	1		2				
[207]	R. Daily	1	1		1				
[208 ‡]	Danl. Doty	2	1	2	1				
[209*‡]	Wm. Doty	2	1	2	1				
[210*‡]	John Lucas	1	1		1				
[211]	John Deron	4	1		2				
[212*‡]	Marvin Fuller	4	3	3	1				
[213*‡]	Peter Kimmel	6	3	3	1				
[214*‡]	Jesse Griggs	5	4	3	2				
[215 ‡]	John Halderburn	1	1	1					
[216*‡]	James Herald		1	2					
[217 ‡]	C. Litebarger	1	1	1	1				
[218 ‡]	Q. L. Lennon	2	1		1				
[219 ‡]	John D. Rutan		2	2	1				
[220 ‡]	Geo. Powers		1		1				
[221 ‡]	D. H. Kelly		1	2	1				
[222 ‡]	W. O. Harrington	2	2	2	1				
[223*‡]	John Ankeny	4	7	1	2				
[224 ‡]	John Finnian	1	3	1	1	There is but one free person of color in this county a male over 21 years of age.			
[225 ‡]	R. Redfield	1	3		1				
[226 ‡]	Henry Woton	1	1		1				
[227*‡]	D. Woton	1	2	3	1				

JACKSON COUNTY (Continued)

	Names of heads of families	Free white males		Free white females		Male Slaves		Female Slaves	
		under 21	over 21	under 18	over 18	under 21	over 21	under 21	over 21
[228]	John S. Duncan		1	1	1				
[229 ‡]	David D. Holder	4	1						
[230*‡]	Elijah Wentworth	2	1	5	1				
[231]	Wm. Linn	1	1		1	1	1	1	
[232*‡]	Wm. Hyers	2	1	1	1				
[233*‡]	Richd. Sorrels	4	1	3	1				
[234*‡]	Saml. Pyatt	1	1	1	1				
[235*‡]	Ralph Davis	1	1	2	1				
[236]	—— Langleey	1	1	4	1				
[237 ‡]	Ben Brown	3	3	1	1				
[238 ‡]	Robert Crow	1	1		1				
[239*‡]	Robert B. Johnson	1	1	3	1				
[240*‡]	Wm. Johnson	1	1	1	1				
[241*‡]	Jno. Campbell, Ser	5	2	1	1				
[242]	Jno. Campbell, jr		1	1	1				
[243*‡]	John Hann	4	1		1				
[244 ‡]	Sam. Sorrels	1	1		1				
[245]	N. Conant		1						
[246 ‡]	—— Barrow	1	1		1				
[247]	John Guinn	4	1		1				
[248]	M. Cannada		1						
[249]	J. Oder	3	1	2	1				
[250]	Jos. Cross	4	1	1	1				
[251]	Mumford Williams		1						
[252]	Archd. M'Kinney		1						
[253]	Wm. Cochran		1						
[254]	Jas. Cochran		1						
[255]	Wm. Hutchinson		1						
[256]	Sam. Smith		1	4	1				
[257*]	[Pe]ter Woldrige	1	1	4	1				
[258 ‡]	Jesse Crow		1		2				
[259]	[J. ?] Robinson	1							
[260]	John Milligan	2	2	3	1				
[261]	Wm. Crow		1						
[262*‡]	Isaac Thompson	1	1	1	1				
[263]	[Huy?] Helm		1						

CENSUS OF 1820

JACKSON COUNTY (Continued)

	Heads of families	Males under 21	Males over 21	Females under 18	Females over 18	Male slaves under 21	Male slaves over 21	Female slaves under 21	Female slaves over 21
[264]	H. F. Snyder		1						
[265]	Saml. Myers		1						
[266 ‡]	Jos. Staton	2	1	6	1				
[267]	Isaaih Thompson, Ky.		1						
[268]	William Ripley		1						
[269*‡]	Saml. Neep		1		1				
[270]	John Ostrander		1						
[271]	Wm. Lindsey	1	1	1	1				
[272]	Wm. Campbell	2	1	2	1				
[273*]	John Lasley		1		1				
[274]	John Roper		1						
[275]	Tim. Nash		1						
[276*‡]	James Taylor		2						
[277]	J. Manning		1						
[278 ‡]	H. McMillen, jr.	1	1						
[279]	H. Sollemell					1			
[280]	J. Hooker		1						
[281]	John Githen		1						
		516	297	375	355	10	6	2	5

1 free person of color
sum total 1567

MATTHEW DUNCAN

Censor of Jackson County

JACKSON COUNTY (*Continued*)

Corrected totals:

Free white males		867
Free white females		666
		1533
Negroes		39
Free persons of color	1	
Servants or slaves	38	
	39	
	Total	1572

CENSUS OF 1820

JACKSON COUNTY (Continued)

The 1818 census was taken by Conrad Will. It is undated. The state census for 1820 was taken by Matthew Duncan sometime between August 1 and December 1. The federal census for 1820 was taken by Hugh Steel and certified November 29. Two hundred fifty-three families are given in the federal census and 281 families in the state census of 1820. Twenty-one families listed in the federal census are not listed in the state census; five of these families, however, appear in the 1818 census. Forty-nine families listed in the state census are not listed in the federal census; and of these, three families are in the 1818 census. The total discrepancy between the federal and state census is 70 families, 62 families appearing in one census only. Many of those listed in the state census, especially in the latter pages, were single men, presumably transients looking for a permanent location before bringing their families.

The following names are found in the federal census but not the state census:

Bradshaw, Elijah
Crane, James
Cravel, Allen
Cross, Arthur
*Davis, Hezekiah, Jr.
Davis, Jacob
*Davis, Jesse
*Davis, Sam'l.
Duncan, James M.
Green, Wm.
Henderson, John

Holliday, Elizabeth
Owens, Michael
Palmer, Solomon
Pyle, Thos.
Russel, John
Skinner, Ephraim
*Thompson, Abner
*Thornton, John
Vollwinder, Henry
White, Thomas, Jr.

Discrepancies are as follows:

1 Dorris, James S.
   1818. Dorris, James S.
   F1820. Dorriss, James S.
2 Gilles, James
   F1820. Gillis, James
8 Garner, Charles
   1818. Gernor, Charels
   F1820. Garnor, Charles
9 Henderson, Ben
   1818. Henderson, Benjamin
   F1820. Henderson, Benjamin
11 Hennery, Ezekel
   F1820. Hening, Ezekiel
12 Halladay, David
   1818. Holliday, David
   F1820. Holloday, David
14 Nee, James
   1820. Neel, James
24 McMillen, William
   1818. McMellen, William
   F1820. M'Millin, Wm.
25 McMillon, Hugh
   1818. McMillen, Hugh
   F1820. M'Millin, Hugh, Sr.
26 McKinney, Joseph
   F1820. M'Kinny, Joseph
27 McCoupin, Preclla
   F1820. M'Coppin, Priscilla

28 Thornbury, Francis
   F1820. Thornsbury, Francis
29 Piles, Nicholas
   F1820. Pyle, Nicholas
31 Tumbleson, Ezekel
   F1820. Tumbleston, Zekiah
34 Garner, William
   1818. Garner, William F.
   F1820. Garnor, Wm.
43 French, Levy
   F1820. French, Levi
44 M'Elvane, Robert
   1818. Muckelvane, Robt.
   F1820. M'Elvane, Robert
45 Wells, Lewis
   1818. Wells, Lewis, Sr.
   F1820. Wells, Lewis, Sr.
49 Wells, Lewis
   1818. Wells, Lewis, Jr.
   F1820. Wells, Lewis, Jr.
50 Pile, John
   1818. Pyle, John
   F1820. Pyle, John
51 Pile, William
   F1820. Pyle, William
53 Rasco, Jessy
   1818. Rasco, Jesse
   F1820. Rasco, Jesse

JACKSON COUNTY (Continued)

14 Reess, Hampton
    F1820. Reese, Edward H.
16 Wootan, James
    1818. Wooten, James
    F1820. Ooten, James
57 Butcher, Catherine
    1818. Butcher, George
    F1820. Butcher, George
61 Bittle, John
    F1820. Biddle, John
62 Taylor, Walter
    F1820. Taytor, Walter
65 Hagle, John
    F1820. Hagler, John
69 Hagle, Phillip
    F1820. Hagler, Phillip
70 Vansee, Adam
    F1820. Vansel, Adam
71 Eatherton, Sam
    F1820. Etherton, Samuel
73 Hagler, Peter
    F1820. Hagter, Peter
75 Lupe, George
    F1820. Lipe, Geo.
76 Edward, Washington
    F1820. Edwards, Washington
78 Woods, David
    1818. Woods, David
    F1820. Wood, Daniel
79 Lype, John
    F1820. Lipe, John, Sr.
80 Lype, Leonard
    F1820. Lipe, Leonard
82 Connor, Ben F.
    1818. Conner, Benjamin F.
    F1820. Conner, Benj. F.
84 Deason, John
    1818. Deason, John
    F1820. Deson, John
85 Fuqua, Wm. D.
    1818. Fuquay, William D.
    F1820. Fuquay, Wm. D.
87 Lype, John
    F1820. Lipe, John, Jr.
88 Lype, Jonas
    F1820. Lipe, Jonas
90 Rogers, Robert
    F1820. Rodgers, Robt.
92 Acord, Jonus
    F1820. Acard, Jonas
95 Ball, Adinegah
    F1820. Ball, Adonigah
96 Leak, Harmon
    F1820. Leek, Harmon

98 Thralkel, Wm.
    F1820. Thralkel, William
99 Ausburn, Wm.
    1818. Osburn, William
    F1820. Osburn, William
100 Flacke, John
    1818. Flack, John
    F1820. Flack, John
101 Henson, Green
    1818. Henson, Green
    F1820. Henson, G. W. G.
106 Goodbred, Joseph
    1818. Goodbread, Joseph
    F1820. Goodbread, Joseph
107 Gaston, William
    1818. Gastin, William
    F1820. Gaston, Wm.
110 Bruer, Wm. M.
    1818. Brewer, William
    F1820. Brewer, Wm. M.
112 McKinney, Chas.
    1818. McKinney, Charles
    F1820. M'Kenney, Charles
115 Clayton, Suard
    F1820. Clayton, Sword
120 Henson, Marvelle
    F1820. Henson, Marvill
124 Lusadder, Jacob
    1818. Lusadder, Jacob
    F1820. Luzaden, Jacob
125 Imgram, George
    F1820. Ingram, George
128 Massey, Shadrach
    1818. Massey, Shadrach
    F1820. Massy, Shedrick
129 Jarrot, Isaac
    1818. Jarret, Isaac
    F1820. Jarrot, Isaac
130 Glenn, Rowland
    1818. Glenn, Robt.
    F1820. Glenn, Robert
132 Glenn, Isac
    1818. Glenn, Isaac
    F1820. Glenn, Isaac
134 Ingram, Geo.
    1818. Ingrum, George
135 Gilihan, Robt.
    1818. Gilliham, Robert
    F1820. Gilihan, Robert
136 Crane, Squire
    1818. Crain, Squire
    F1820. Crane, Squire
137 Woldrich, Adam
    F1820. Wolrick, Adam

CENSUS OF 1820

JACKSON COUNTY (Continued)

139 Albert, M.
    F1820. Albert, Michial
140 Reynolds, Mary
    F1820. Raynolds, Mary
141 Dillinger, Val
    1818. Dillinger, Valentine
    F1820. Dillinger, Valantine
142 Grovner, Parker
    1818. Grovenor, Parker
    F1820. Grovener, Parker
144 Brooks, Z.
    1818. Brucks, ———
    F1820. Brooks, Zaphne
147 Bilderback, D.
    1818. Beldeback, Daniel
    F1820. Bilderback, Daniel
148 Gallaher, Peter
    F1820. Galaher, Peter
154 Bryon, Abner
    F1820. Brian, Abner
155 Woldrech, Mary
    F1820. Wolrick, Mary
158 Thompson, Evan
    1818. Thompson, Eden
    F1820. Thompson, Even
160 Span, Mary
    1818. Span, John
    F1820. Span, Mary Ann
161 Chapman, A.
    1818. Chapman, Mr.
    F1820. Chapman, Avery
164 Duncan, Jo
    F1820. Duncan, Joseph
165 Grubb, Wm.
    1818. Grubb, William
    F1820. Grub, William
167 Marshall, Robert
    F1820. Marshel, Robert
169 Dillinger, H.
    F1820. Dillinger, Henry
171 Byers, John
    1818. Byars, John
    F1820. Byers, John
172 Jenkins, Thos.
    1818. Jenkens, Thomas
    F1820. Jenkins, Thos.
174 Cochran, Robert
    F1820. Cothran, Robert
175 Lindsey, Wm.
    F1820. Linsey, Wm.
176 Brown, Richard
    F1820. Brown, Rich'd, Jr.
178 Pyatt, E.
    1818. Piatt, Ebenezer
    F1820. Pyatt, Ebenezer

179 Swartz, C.
    1818. Swartz, Catherine
    F1820. Schwartz, Catherine
180 Davis, H., Sr.
    1818. Davis, Hezekiah
    F1820. Davis, Hezekiah, Sr.
181 Davis, E.
    1818. Davis, Eliphaz
    F1820. Davis, Eliphus
183 Davis, C.
    1818. Davis, Clement
    F1820. Davis, Clement
188 Noble, H., Sr.
    1818. Noble, Henry, Sr.
    F1820. Noble, Henry, Sr.
189 Noble, H., Jr.
    1818. Noble, Henry, Jr.
    F1820. Noble, Henry, Jr.
190 Brown, R., Sr.
    1818. Brown, Richd, Sr.
    F1820. Brown, Richd, Sr.
192 Ripley, Ben
    1818. Ripley, Benjn.
    F1820. Richley, Benj.
193 Garner, Francis
    1818. Garner, Francis
    F1820. Garnor, Francis
194 Duldumin, Danl.
    1818. De Chein, Danl.
    F1820. Du Chemin, Daniel
195 Harrgton, Drury
    1818. Harrington, Drewry
    F1820. Harrington, Drury
196 Cochran, Wateres
    1818. Cocthrin, Waters
    F1820. Cotron, Waters
197 Wortham, Nancey
    1818. Worthen, Nancy
    F1820. Worthen, Nancy
198 Edwards, K.
    1818. Edwards, Kinian
    F1820. Edwards, Kinian
199 Shannon, John
    1818. Shannan, John
    F1820. Shannon, John
201 French, T.
    F1820. French, Samuel
202 Crane, Thos.
    1818. Crain, Thomas
    F1820. Crane, Thos.
205 Akin, Wm.
    F1820. Aekin, Wm.
206 Elmore, Jesse
    F1820. Elmoy, Jessee

JACKSON COUNTY (*Concluded*)

- 209 Doty, Wm.
  - 1818. Dotey, William
  - F1820. Doty, William
- 215 Halderburn, John
  - F1820. Holderbaum, John
- 216 Herald, James
  - 1818. Herreld, James
  - F1820. Herrald, James
- 217 Litebarger, C.
  - F1820. Leightebarger, Conrad
- 218 Lennon, Q. L.
  - F1820. Lennon, James L.
- 221 Kelly, D. H.
  - F1820. Kelly, David W.
- 222 Harrington, W. O.
  - F1820. Harrington, Wiley O.
- 223 Ankeny, John
  - 1818. Ankeney, John
  - F1820. Ankeny, John
- 224 Finnian, John
  - F1820. Fineren, John
- 225 Redfield, R.
  - F1820. Redfield, Rural
- 226 Woton, Henry
  - F1820. Ooten, Henry
- 227 Woton, D.
  - 1818. Wooten, Daniel
  - F1820. Oaoten, Daniel
- 230 Wentworth, Elijah
  - 1818. Witworth, Elijah
  - F1820. Wintworth, Elijah
- 232 Hyers, Wm.
  - 1818. Hiars, William
  - F1820. Hyers, William
- 234 Pyatt, Saml.
  - 1818. Piatt, Samuel
  - F1820. Pyatt, Saml.
- 238 Crow, Robert
  - F1820. Craw, Robet
- 239 Johnson, Robert B.
  - 1818. Johnston, Robert
  - F1820. Johnson, Robert
- 240 Johnson, Wm.
  - 1818. Johnston, William
  - F1820. Johnson, William
- 243 Hann, John
  - 1818. Henn, John
  - F1820. Hand, John
- 246 Barrow, ———
  - F1820. Barrow, John
- 257 Woldrige, Peter
  - 1818. Wolerick, Peter
- 258 Crow, Jesse
  - F1820. Crow, Mary
- 269 Neep, Saml.
  - 1818. Neip, S. & Co.
  - F1820. Neep, Samuel
- 273 Lasley, John
  - 1818. Lastley, John
- 278 McMillen, H., Jr.
  - F1820. M'Millin, Hugh

CENSUS OF JEFFERSON COUNTY, 1820

A Book containing the census of Jefferson County August the 1st 1820

Names of heads of families	Free white males twenty one years Old and upwards	All other white inhabitants	Servants or slaves	Free people of Colour			
				Names of heads of families	Males twenty one years Old and upward	All other free coloured inhabitants	Servants or Slaves
[1 ‡] Joseph Jordan	3	6					
[2 ‡] William Jordan	2	6					
[3 ‡] Nicholas Wren	1	4					
[4*‡] John Jordan	2	5					
[5 ‡] Thomas Jordan	1	4					
[6 ‡] William Hynes	1	9					
[7] John Vance	1	1					
[8 ‡] Thomas Jordan	2	8					
[9 ‡] William Maxwell	1	9					
[10*‡] Robert Maxwell	1	1					
[11 ‡] Hugh Maxwell		2					
[12 ‡] Zenas Herrington	1	2					
[13 ‡] John Going	1	3					
[14 ‡] Robert Snodgrass	1	2					
[15 ‡] James Piles	1	2					
[16 ‡] William Jimmison	1	2					
[17 ‡] Joshua Piles	2	8					
[18 ‡] Leonard Piles	1	11					
[19 ‡] James C. Smirl	2	5					
[20 ‡] James Roberts	1	9					
[21 ‡] John Walling	1	5					
[22 ‡] William Frost	1	1					
[23 ‡] Lemuel Lee	3	3					
[24] Aaron Hicks	2	5					
[25] Enos Silsbe	1	2					
[26 ‡] Abijah Lee	3	2					
[27 ‡] John Tolley	1	2					

Figures and symbols preceding names have been supplied by the editor:
‡ Indicates name also in Federal Census for 1820.
*Indicates name also in State Census for White County, 1818.

JEFFERSON COUNTY (Continued)

No.	Heads of families	White males 21 & upwards	All other white	Servants or slaves	Free people of color			Servants or slaves
					Heads of families	Males 21 & upwards	All other	
[28]	Jacob Fuller	1	2					
[29]	William Umprey	1	6					
[30]	William Ingrum	1	5					
[31 ‡]	Malichi Ware	1	7					
[32 ‡]	James Young	1	5					
[33 ‡]	William Albert	1	3					
[34 ‡]	Samuel Young	1	1					
[35 ‡]	Jacob Albert	1	3					
[36 ‡]	Joseph Hensley	3	6					
[37 ‡]	Robert Holt	1	3					
[38 ‡]	Samuel Eblin	2	8					
[39 ‡]	Rufus Ricker	2	3					
[40]	Isaac Allen	1	3					
[41 ‡]	Benjamin Vermillion	1	3					
[42 ‡]	Jeremiah McKinny	2	4					
[43 ‡]	Joseph McKinny	1	9					
[44 ‡]	Felix McBride	1	2	1				
[45 ‡]	Samuel Gaston	1	8					
[46 ‡]	Pleasant Going	3	3					
[47 ‡]	Dorcas Bunday	5	2					
[48 ‡]	Samuel Huff	1	10					
[49 ‡]	Nathanial S. Andrews	2	6					
[50 ‡]	Thomas Welch	1	8					
[51 ‡]	John McKinny	1	2					
[52]	Arba Andrews	1	1					
[53 ‡]	William Going	1	7					
[54]	Robert Hensley	1	1					
[55 ‡]	Leftridge Hensley	1	2					
[56]	John Wells	1	3					
[57 ‡]	Martin Maxwell	1	1					
[58*‡]	Samuel Martin	1	4					
[59 ‡]	James Dawson	1	4					
[60 ‡]	Harberd Avents	1	6					
[61 ‡]	Fleming Greenwood	2	7					
[62 ‡]	Garrison Greenwood	1	1					
[63*]	James Johnson	1	7					
[64*‡]	John Wilkerson	2	10					

CENSUS OF 1820   123

JEFFERSON COUNTY (Continued)

No.	Heads of families	White males 21 & upwards	All other white	Serv-ants or slaves	Free people of color			Serv-ants or slaves
					Heads of families	Males 21 & upwards	All other	
[65 ‡]	John Lee	1	4					
[66]	Edward Maxey	1	3					
[67*‡]	Hennery B. Maxey	1	3					
[68 ‡]	Thomas M. Casey		2					
[69]	Asail Baitman	1	2					
[70 ‡]	Nelson Fergurson	1	3					
[71 ‡]	James Abbet	1	8					
[72 ‡]	John Abbet	1	7					
[73 *]	Joel Pace	3						
[74 ‡]	Nathan Goodrich	1	3					
[75 ‡]	Lewis Watkins	3	9					
[76 ‡]	Hennery Watkins	1	5					
[77 ‡]	Moses Ham	1	9					
[78 ‡]	William Page	1	3					
[79 ‡]	Young Seemore	1	4					
[80*‡]	Dempsey Hood	2	2					
[81 ‡]	Robert Cook	1	3					
[82*‡]	Joseph Reed	1	3					
[83 ‡]	James E. Davis	1	6					
[84 ‡]	Hester Wilkey	2	3					
[85*‡]	Maxey Wilkey	1	5					
[86 ‡]	George Bradford	1	2					
[87*‡]	Abner Bradford	1	2					
[88*‡]	Samuel Bradford	1	5					
[89 ‡]	Thomas Hopper	1	10					
[90 ‡]	William Casey	2	6					
[91 ‡]	James Rollins	1	3					
[92 ‡]	James McNary	1	2					
[93]	Robert Sharp	1	1					
[94 ‡]	Abraham P. Casey	1	5					
[95 ‡]	Joshua Robinson	1	1					
[96*‡]	Lucy Robinson		3					
[97*‡]	Barton Atchison	1	6					
[98 ‡]	William Atchison	1	1					
[99 ‡]	John Harper	1	6					
[100 ‡]	James Chaffin	1	1					
[101 ‡]	Curtice Caldwell	1	1					

JEFFERSON COUNTY (*Continued*)

No.	Heads of families	White males 21 & upwards	All other white	Servants or slaves	Free people of color Heads of families	Males 21 & upwards	All other	Servants or slaves
[102]	William Jordan	1	1					
[103*‡]	Daniel Crenshaw	1	8					
[104 ‡]	Green P. Casey	1	1					
[105 ‡]	Iaac. Casey	1	4					
[106]	John Jackson	2	4					
[107 ‡]	John C. Casey	1	4					
[108 ‡]	William Wood	1	1					
[109]	Elihu Maxey	1	2					
[110 ‡]	Bennet N. Maxey	1	1					
[111*‡]	William Maxey	1	5					
[112 ‡]	John Tilor	1	6					
[113 ‡]	William Dupriest	1	4					
[114 ‡]	Archabald Harris	2	5					
[115 ‡]	Thomas D. Miner	1	8					
[116 ‡]	Elisha M. Purkins	1	3					
[117 ‡]	Overton Harlow	1	6					
[118 ‡]	Elijah Jolliff	1	2					
[119 ‡]	Alden Hany	1	1					
[120 ‡]	William Hicks	1	6					
[121 ‡]	John Utchler	1	3					
[122 ‡]	Nicholas Stull	1	6					
[123 ‡]	James Hicks	1	3					
[124]	Francis Hany	1	1					
[125 ‡]	William Hicks	1	5					
[126]	Lewis Johnson	1	8					
[127 ‡]	Lanslot Foster	1	1					
[128 ‡]	Isaac Hicks	1	4					
[129 ‡]	Alferd Wood	1	6					
[130]	Joseph Dods	1	5					
[131 ‡]	Reubin Jackson	1	2					
[132 ‡]	Zadoc Casey	1	4					
[133 ‡]	Rhody Allen	1	5					
[134]	Hennery Watkins	1	8					
[135 ‡]	Fredrich Felps	1	1					
[136 ‡]	Zadoc Felps	1	8					
[137 ‡]	John Felps	1	2					
[138]	Francis Harmon	1	3					

JEFFERSON COUNTY (Continued)

No.	Heads of families	White males 21 & upwards	All other white	Servants or slaves	Free people of color			Servants or slaves
					Heads of families	Males 21 & upwards	All other	
[139*]	Benjamin Bishop	1	7					
[140*‡]	Peter Fannon	1	4					
[141 ‡]	Peggy More		6					
[142]	Hal Hubberd	1						
[143]	Thomas Adams	2	11					
[144 ‡]	Oliver Morris	1	1					
	Total 144 Fam.	176	603	1				

I do hereby certify that the foregoing List is a correct enumeration of .... The whole number of souls in Jefferson County & the attached part thereof is 780 ....

Done by OLIVER MORRIS ....

JEFFERSON COUNTY (Continued)

Jefferson County was a part of Edwards and White counties until 1819. As there are no extant census returns for Edwards County in 1818 no comparison can be made with the 1820 schedules for that county. However, eighteen names found in the 1820 state census for Jefferson County are found in the White County census for 1818. The federal census for Jefferson County was taken by Lewis Watkins and certified November 13, 1820. The state census taken by Oliver Morris is dated August 1, 1820, this date probably being the date on which the enumeration was begun. The state census lists 144 families and the federal census 129 families. Twenty-six families appearing in the state census are omitted from the federal census and 11 families in the federal census are omitted from the state census.

Discrepancies are as follows:

2 Jordan, William
   F1820. Jordan, William, Sr.
4 Jordan, John
   1818. Jorden, John
   F1820. Jordan, John
8 Jordan, Thomas
   F1820. Jordan, Thomas, Jr.
12 Herrington, Zenas
   F1820. Harrington, Zenos
19 Smirl, James C.
   F1820. Smerls, James
27 Tolley, John
   F1820. Tully, John
33 Albert, William
   F1820. Ulbert, William
35 Albert, Jacob
   F1820. Ulbert, Jacob
42 McKinny, Jeremiah
   F1820. McKenny, Jeremiah
43 McKinny, Joseph
   F1820. McKenny, Joseph
44 McBride, Felix
   F1820. McBride, Felex
46 Going, Pleasant
   F1820. Goings, Pleasant
47 Bunday, Dorcas
   F1820. Bundy, Dorcus
49 Andrews, Nathanial S.
   F1820. Andress, Nathan
50 Welch, Thomas
   F1820. Welsh, Thomas
51 McKinny, John
   F1820. McKenny, John
60 Avents, Harberd
   F1820. Avant, Harbert
62 Greenwood, Garrison
   F1820. Greenwood, Garrelson
64 Wilkerson, John
   1818. Wilkerson, John
   F1820. Welkerson, John
67 Maxey, Hennery B.
   1818. Maxy, Henry B.
   F1820. Maxy, Henry B.

71 Abbet, James
   F1820. Abbot, James
72 Abbet, John
   F1820. Abbot, John
73 Pace, Joel
   1818. Page, Joel
76 Watkins, Hennery
   F1820. Watkins, Henry
79 Seemore, Young
   F1820. Semore, Young
80 Hood, Dempsey
   1818. Hood, Demps
   F1820. Hood, Demcy
82 Reed, Joseph
   1818. Read, Joseph
   F1820. Reed, Joseph
83 Davis, James E.
   F1820. Davies, James E.
84 Wilkey, Hester
   F1820. Wilky, Hester
85 Wilkey, Maxey
   1818. Wilkey, Maxwell
   F1820. Wilky, Mackeil
91 Rollins, James
   F1820. Rollings, James
96 Robinson, Lucy
   1818. Robertson, Lucy
   F1820. Robinson, Lucy
97 Atchison, Barton
   1818. Atcheson, Barton
   F1820. Atchisson, Barton
98 Atchison, William
   F1820. Atchisson, William
101 Caldwell, Curtice
   F1820. Caldwell, Curtis
105 Casey, Iaac.
   F1820. Casey, Isaac
110 Maxey, Bennet N.
   F1820. Maxy, Benet N.
111 Maxey, William
   1818. Maxy, William
   F1820. Maxy, William
112 Tilor, John
   F1820. Tyler, John

JEFFERSON COUNTY (Concluded)

115 Miner, Thomas D.
    F1820. Minor, Thos. D.
116 Purkins, Elisha M.
    F1820. Perkins, Elisha M.
118 Jolliff, Elijah
    F1820. Jolleff, Elijah
127 Foster, Lanslot
    F1820. Foster, Lancelot
129 Wood, Alferd
    F1820. Wood, Alfred

131 Jackson, Reubin
    F1820. Jackson, Reuben
132 Casey, Zadoc
    F1820. Casey, Zadok
133 Allen, Rhody
    F1820. Allen, Rody
135 Felps, Fredrich
    *F1820. [P]helps, Frede[rick]
136 Felps, Zadoc
    *F1820. F[el?]ps, Zadoc

Families listed in the federal census but not in the state:

Bowling, James
Byrons, Samuel
Casey, Abraham T.
Fansherp, Isaac
Fulfer, Jessee
Fulfer, Isaac

Howel, William L.
Norton, Jacob
Pace, Spencer
Tully, Dorcus
Wallen, James

*MS. torn.

CENSUS OF JOHNSON COUNTY, 1820

State of Illinois Johnson County

This day personaly appeard before me William Mcfatridge an acting Justice of the peace in and for said County Joseph Kuykendall after being duly appointed by the County Commissioners Court and took the oath prescribed by law for taking the Census or enumeration for Johnson County Illinois State
Given under my hand and seal this 9th day of September 1820

                    WILLIAM MCFATRIDGE   Seal
                    J.P. J.C.

CENSUS OF 1820

JOHNSON COUNTY (Continued)

The whole number of Persons in the county Johnson State of Illinois appears in a Schedule hereto annexed by Joseph Kuykendall who being appointed by the County commissioners court to take in the Census for the State of Illinois for the county of Johnson and have taken the oath according to Law

Names of heads of Famielies in Johnson County Ill.	Free white Males under 21 years	Free white Males of 21 years & upwards	Free white Feemales under 21 years of age	Free white Females of 21 years of age & upwards	Slaves Males	Slaves Females	Free Blacks
1[*‡] John Bridges	4	3	4	1			
2[*‡] Joshua Gore	2	1	1				
3[*‡] John McGinness	2	1	1	1			
4[‡] Samuel McGinness		1		1			
5[‡] Wm McGinness	1	1		1			
6[*‡] Richard McGinness	3	1	3	1			
7[*‡] Milton Smith	6	1	3	1			
8[‡] Aaron McIntosh	1	1		2			
9[‡] Nathan Baker	3	1		1			
10[*‡] John Oliver	1	2	1	2			
11[‡] Levi Buzbe		1	1	1			
12[‡] Lewis Worrel	3	1		1			
13[*‡] Rex Carter	2	1	4	1			
14[‡] Moreton Carter	2	1	2	2			
15[‡] Thomas Standard	1	1		1			
16[*‡] Wm. Stanard	1	1	3	2			
17[‡] Thomas Dunsworth	4	1	3	1			
18[‡] Richard Elkin		1	1	1			
19[*‡] Wm. Elkin	2	1		1			
20[*‡] Bennet Handcock	2	1	1	2			

Names for Johnson County were numbered in the original. Symbols preceding names have been supplied by the editor:
  ‡ Indicates name also in Federal Census for 1820.
  * Indicates name also in State Census for 1818.

JOHNSON COUNTY (*Continued*)

No.	Heads of families	White males under 21	White males 21 & upwards	White females under 21	White females 21 & upwards	Slaves Males	Slaves Females	Free Blacks
21[‡]	Etheldred Peacock	2	1	1	1			
22[*‡]	John Elkin	3	2	2	2			
23[*‡]	Benjamin Gurley		1		1			
24[*‡]	James Sitton	1	1	2	1			
25[‡]	John Weaver	1	1		1			
26[‡]	Jacob Canada	1	2	2	1			
27[‡]	Jesse Canada	2	1	1	1			
28[*‡]	Adam Harvic	2	1	3	1			
29[*‡]	James Crunk		1	1	1			
30[‡]	James Taylor	1	1	1	1			
31[‡]	Hardy Cooper	2	2	3	2			
32[*‡]	Jeptha Wise	5	1	1	1			
33[‡]	Anson Gurley	3	1	2	1			
34[‡]	John Ross	1	1	1	1			
35[*‡]	Matthew Johnson	1	1	4	2			
36[‡]	Joseph Wright	1	2	2	2			
37[‡]	Charles Huddleston		1	2				
38[‡]	Frances Johnson	2		2	1			
39[‡]	Caleb Hayward		1	2	1			
40[*‡]	Squire Choat	5	2	3	1			
41[‡]	Reuben Wright		1	2	1			
42[*‡]	David Elms	6	1	4	1			
43[*‡]	William Shelby	1	1	2	1			
44[*‡]	Joel Johnson	3	1	2	1			
45[*‡]	David Shearer	2	2	4				
46[*‡]	Elizabeth Mount	3	1	3	1			
47[‡]	John Standard		1	1	1			
48[‡]	Harvey Crosswite	3	2	2	1			
49[‡]	Mary Delaney	2	2	1	2			
50[*‡]	Hezekiah West	2	2	5	1			
51[*‡]	Willis Borin	2	2	4	1			
52[‡]	Richard Messer	1	1	5	1			
53[‡]	Elisha H Coleman	1						
54[*‡]	Samuel Reed		1					

CENSUS OF 1820

JOHNSON COUNTY (Continued)

No.	Heads of families	White males under 21	White males 21 & upwards	White females under 21	White females 21 & upwards	Slaves Males	Slaves Females	Free Blacks
55[‡]	Abram Shelby		1	2	1			
56[*‡]	Samuel S. Simpson	2	1		1			
57[‡]	John Hawkins	2	1	3	1			
58[*‡]	Henry Mangrem	3	2	4	1			
59[*‡]	Thomas Doyl		1		1			
60[‡]	Samuel Mathis	3	1	1	1			
61[*‡]	William McNorton	1	1					
62[*‡]	William Russel		1					
63	John McGowen		1					
64[*‡]	William Copland		1	1	1			
65[*‡]	Jesse Fane	1	1		1			
66[*‡]	John Gore	2	1	3	1			
67[‡]	Elisha Browning		1	3	1			
68[*‡]	Robert Little	2	1	6	1			
69[*‡]	John L. Cooper	1	1	3				
70[‡]	James Jones	7	2	2	1			
71[*‡]	Matthew Mathis	3	1	3	1			
72[*‡]	James Bane	4	1	2	1			
73[‡]	John Hendrixon	1	1	1				
74[‡]	James White	2	1	3	1			
75[‡]	William Gouge	1	1		1			
76[*‡]	James Lisenby	1	1	2				
77[*‡]	Isaac Worley	3	2	1	1			
78[*‡]	John S. Graves	2	1	2	1			
79[*‡]	Andrew Cochran	4	1	4	1			
80[‡]	Mary Cochran	1	1	1	1			
81[‡]	Betsy Cochran	5		3	1			
82[*‡]	Frederic Graves	1	1		1			
83[*‡]	Randolph Casey	2	1	1	1			
84[*‡]	William Gothard	2	1	2	1			
85[*‡]	Joshua Elkin	1	1	4	2			
86[‡]	Whitney Elkin	1		1				
87[*‡]	Alexander McGowen	3	1	4	1			
88[‡]	Champion Wilson		1	2				

JOHNSON COUNTY (Continued)

No.	Heads of families	White males under 21	White males 21 & upwards	White females under 21	White females 21 & upwards	Slaves Males	Slaves Females	Free Blacks
89[‡]	James Westbrook	4	1	2	1			
90[‡]	Samuel Langdon	2	1	5	1			
91[*‡]	Samuel McGowen	3	1	1	1			
92[*‡]	Spencer Grogan	7	1	2	1			
93[‡]	John Bane	2	1	5	1			
94[‡]	Samuel J. Chapman	2	2	2	1			
95[‡]	Samuel Lathem	1	1	2	1			
96[*‡]	Reuben Wilson	3	1	3	2			
97[‡]	Henry Osburn	3	1	2	1			
98[‡]	Abner Cox	1	2	5	1			
99[‡]	John Veach	1	2	2	2			
100[‡]	Elias Herral	2	2	2	1			
101[*‡]	Hardy Johnson	3	1	4	1			
102[*‡]	Levi Casey	1	1	4	1			
103[*‡]	Jeremiah Lisenby	1	1	1	2			
104[*‡]	John Reaves		1	2	1			
105[*‡]	John Peterson	3	1	4	1			
106[*‡]	George Brazil	3	2	4	1			
107[*‡]	John C. Smith	4	1		1			
108[‡]	James H. Martin		3	1	2			
109[*‡]	John Heater	2	1		1			
110[*‡]	Moses Cochran	3	1	2	1			
111[‡]	Lawrence Beaver	1	1		1			
112[*‡]	Wheeler Bivens	2	1		1			
113[‡]	Mark Renfro	3	1		1			
114[*‡]	John Grishum	7	1	5	1			
115[*‡]	Aaron B. Brown	2	1	1	1		1	
116[‡]	William Phelps	4	1	1	1			
117[*‡]	Isaac D. Willcox	1	2	1	1	1	3	
118[*‡]	Abraham Russel	1	1	1	1			
119[*‡]	John Russel	3	1	3	1			
120[*‡]	John Copland	6	1	1	1	5	2	
121[‡]	James Copland		1		1			
122[‡]	Andrew Wolf	1	1	2				
123[*‡]	James Hawkins	1	1		1			1
124[‡]	Milton Ladd	2	2	2	1			

JOHNSON COUNTY (Continued)

No.	Heads of families	White males under 21	White males 21 & upwards	White females under 21	White females 21 & upwards	Slaves Males	Slaves Females	Free Blacks
125[*‡]	James Finney		3	1	1		1	
126	Caleb Irvin	3	1		1			
127[*‡]	Jacob Harvic		2	1	2			
128[‡]	Joseph McCorkle	1	3	1	2			
129	Abraham Hendry	2	1	2	1			
130[‡]	William Allard		1	1	2			
131[*‡]	William Simpson	2	2	1	1			
132[‡]	William Simpson	2	1	1	1			
133[‡]	George Lysles	1	1	1	1			
134[‡]	William Damron		1	2				
135[‡]	Henry Slankard	3	1	1	1			
136[*‡]	William Mcfatridge	3	4	5	1			
137[*‡]	Samuel Wyatt		1	1	1			
138[*‡]	Jesse Allen	2	1	3	1			
139[‡]	Rowland Gray	4	2	3	1			
140[‡]	Edward Harris	2	1		1			
141	Samuel Volner	3	2	2	1			
142[*‡]	Lewis J. Simpson	2	4	1	2			

JOHNSON COUNTY (*Continued*)

Agregate of the number of personsons in Johnson County

275	177	261	146	6	7	1
Free white Males under 21 years	Free white Males of 21 years & upwards	Free white females under 21 years of age	Free white females of 21 years & upwards	Slaves, Males	Females	Free people of colour

Sum total of the number of souls within Johnson County, Ill, the Division alloted me Joseph Kuykendall, is 873

JOHNSON COUNTY (*Continued*)

Hezekiah West took the 1818 census for Johnson County, certifying the returns on May 26. Joseph Kuykendall took both the state and the federal census for 1820, the federal census evidently being a copy of the state census. Four names were omitted from the federal census, probably due to carelessness in transcribing. They are:

    63 McGowen, John
    126 Irvin, Caleb
    129 Hendry, Abraham
    141 Volner, Samuel

One name, Wheeler Bivens, appears twice in the federal census.

Of the 174 families listed in 1818, seventy-five were still in the county in 1820.

The variations in spelling are minor:

2 Gore, Joshua
    1818. Gore, Joshua, Sr.
    F1820. Gore, Joshua
3 McGinness, John
    1818. Meginness, John
    F1820. McGinness, John
7 Smith, Milton
    1818. Smith, Milliton
    F1820. Smith, Milton
8 McIntosh, Aaron
    F1820. McErtosh, Aaron
9 Baker, Nathan
    F1820. Baker, Nathen
10 Oliver, John
    1818. Olever, John
    F1820. Oliver, John
11 Buzbe, Levi
    F1820. Busby, Levi
12 Worrel, Lewis
    F1820. Worrell, Lewis
13 Carter, Rex
    1818. Carter, Ricks
    F1820. Carter, Rex
14 Carter, Moreton
    F1820. Carter, Morten
16 Stanard, Wm.
    1818. Standard, Wm.
    F1820. Standard, William
19 Elkin, Wm.
    1818. Elkins, Wm.
    F1820. Elkin, William
20 Handcock, Bennet
    1818. Hancock, Bennet
    F1820. Handcock, Bennet
22 Elkin, John
    1818. Elkins, John
    F1820. Elkin, John
24 Sitton, James
    1818. Sutton, James
    F1820. Sitton, James
28 Harvic, Adam
    1818. Harvick, Adam
    F1820. Harvick, Adam

42 Elms, David
    1818. Elems, David
    F1820. Elms, David
49 Delaney, Mary
    F1820. Delany, Mary
51 Borin, Willis
    1818. Boren, Willis
    F1820. Boren, Willis
53 Coleman, Elisha H.
    F1820. Coleman, Elisha F.
58 Mangrem, Henry
    1818. Mangram, Henry
    F1820. Mangum, Henry
59 Doyl, Thomas
    1818. Doyle, Thomas
    F1820. Doyal, Thomas
60 Mathis, Samuel
    F1820. Matthews, Samuel
61 McNorton, William
    1818. McNorten, Wm.
    F1820. McNorton, William
64 Copland, William
    1818. Copeland, Wm.
    F1820. Copland, William
65 Fane, Jesse
    1818. Fane, Jesse
    F1820. Fain, Jesse
66 Gore, John
    1818. Gore, John W.
    F1820. Gore, John
71 Mathis, Matthew
    1818. Matthews, Matthew
    F1820. Matthews, Matthew
72 Bane, James
    1818. Bain, James
    F1820. Bane, James
73 Hendrixon, John
    F1820. Hendrixson, John
76 Lisenby, James
    1818. Lizenby, James
    F1820. Lisenby, James

JOHNSON COUNTY (*Concluded*)

77 Worley, Isaac
   1818. Worldley, Isaac
   F1820. Worley, Isaac
78 Graves, John S.
   1818. Graves, John S.
   F1820. Graves, John
79 Cochran, Andrew
   1818. Coghren, Andrew
   F1820. Cochran, Andrew
82 Graves, Frederic
   1818. Graves, Fredrick
   F1820. Gravis, Frederic
83 Casey, Randolph
   1818. Kasey, Randolph
   F1820. Casey, Randolph
84 Gothard, William
   1818. Godthard, Wm.
   F1820. Gothard, William
85 Elkin, Joshua
   1818. Elkins, Joshua
   F1820. Elkin, Joshua
87 McGowen, Alexander
   1818. Megowen, Alexander
   F1820. McGowen, Alexander
89 Westbrook, James
   F1820. Westbrooke, James
91 McGowen, Samuel
   1818. Megowen, Samuel
   F1820. McGowan, Samuel
96 Wilson, Reuben
   1818. Wilson, Reubin
   F1820. Wilson, Reubin
102 Casey, Levi
   1818. Kasey, Levi
   F1820. Casy, Levi
103 Lisenby Jeremiah
   1818. Lizenby, Jeremiah
   F1820. Lisenby, Jeremiah

104 Reaves, John
   1818. Reaves, John
   F1820. Reeves, John
106 Brazil, George
   1818. Brasele, George
   F1820. Brazil, George
109 Heater, John
   1818. Heeter, John
   F1820. Heater, John
114 Grishum, John
   1818. Gressham, John
   F1820. Grishum, John
115 Brown, Aaron B.
   1818. Brown, Aron B.
   F1820. Brown, Aaron B.
117 Willcox, Isaac D.
   1818. Wilcox, Isaac D.
   F1820. Willcox, Isaac D.
119 Russel, John
   1818. Russel, John O.
   F1820. Russel, John
120 Copland, John
   1818. Copeland, John
   F1820. Copland, John
127 Harvic, Jacob
   1818. Harvick, Jacob
   F1820. Harvick, Jacob
131 Simpson, William
   1818. Simpson, Wm., Sr.
   F1820. Simpson, William
137 Wyatt, Samuel
   1818. Wiot, Samuel
   F1820. Wyatt, Samuel
142 Simpson, Lewis J.
   1818. Simpson, Lewis
   F1820. Simpson, Lewis J.

CENSUS OF MADISON COUNTY, 1820

An annumeration of the Inhabitance of Madison County State of Illinois August 1820.

	Names of Heads of Families	Free white males over 21 years of age	All other free white Inhabitance	Free people of Colour	Servants or Slaves	Total
[1*‡]	John Springer	2	6			8
[2 ‡]	William Sage	1	4			5
[3*‡]	Low Jackson	2	7		1	10
[4*‡]	Thomas Smith	3	11			14
[5*‡]	William Rines	1	4			5
[6*‡]	John Gillham	3	3			6
[7*‡]	Ann Dunigan		7			7
[8*‡]	Thomas Cox	2	4			6
[9*‡]	Thomas Davidson	2	9			11
[10 ‡]	David Gillham	1	3			4
[11*‡]	John Stout	2	8			10
[12 ‡]	Richard Gibbs	2	8			10
[13*‡]	Benjamin Wood	1	5			6
[14 ‡]	Edward Prater	4	1			5
[15 ‡]	Robert Pulham	3	8			11
[16*‡]	Christley Stout	1	5			6
[17*‡]	Matthew Cowin	1	4			5
[18 ‡]	Robert Sinclair	4				4
[19 ‡]	Dempsey Swanson	1	1			2
[20 ‡]	Polly Swanson	1	2			3
[21*‡]	Samuel Gillham	1	9			10
[22 ‡]	Prissilly Denny		2			2
[23 ‡]	Thomas Davice	3	3			6
[24*‡]	John Lewis	3	6			9
[25 ‡]	Thomas Bergess	2	2			4
[26 ‡]	William G. Pinkard	1	3			4
[27 ‡]	Nathaniel Pinkard	8	4			12
[28 ‡]	Daniel Croom	1	3			4
[29 ‡]	Susannah Smith	2	4			6
[30 ‡]	Claiton Tiffin	3	4	1	3	11
[31 ‡]	Benjamin Root	3	3			6
[32*‡]	Clade Brown	1				1

Figures and symbols preceding names have been supplied by the editor:
‡ Indicates name also in Federal Census for 1820.
* Indicates name also in State Census for 1818.

138   ILLINOIS HISTORICAL COLLECTIONS

MADISON COUNTY (*Continued*)

No.	Heads of families	White males 21 & over	All other white	Free people of color	Servants or slaves	Total
[33 ‡]	Charles Gear	5	4			9
[34 ‡]	Armstead Tailor	1	4			5
[35*‡]	William Morris	1	6			7
[36*]	Rodolphus Langworthy	1				1
[37]	James W. Whitney	1				1
[38 ‡]	Edward Bishop	2	3			5
[39 ‡]	John Rian	1	3			4
[40 ‡]	David Bishop	2	4			6
[41*‡]	Charles Davis	1	4			5
[42 ‡]	Joel Finch	2	8			10
[43 ‡]	Alexandria Hart	3	3			6
[44 ‡]	Robert A. Bany	3	4			7
[45]	Israel Oterbury	1	1			2
[46*‡]	Samuel Delaplane	1	7			8
[47 ‡]	Isaac Waters	1	7			8
[48 ‡]	Joshua Hanks	1	2			3
[49 ‡]	John R. Whiswell	1	1			2
[50 ‡]	Buennet Maxey	4	2			6
[51]	Oliver Foster	1	7			8
[52*‡]	Ebenezer Hodges	4	9			13
[53 ‡]	Benjamin Smith	2	1			3
[54 ‡]	Mary Mcaester		5			5
[55*‡]	Jonithan Brown	1	7			8
[56 ‡]	Francis Spencer	1	1			2
[57 ‡]	Isaac Woodbourn	2	3			5
[58 ‡]	Erastus Brown	1	6			7
[59 ‡]	William Speaks	5	4			9
[60]	Hezakiah Gridley	2				2
[61 ‡]	Benjamin Spencer	1	4			5
[62*]	James Carlin	1	2			3
[63*‡]	Joseph Vaughn	2	7			9
[64 ‡]	James Breden	1	6			7
[65*‡]	Abraham Pruitt	1	8			9
[66*‡]	James Stockton	4	3			7
[67*]	William Pruitt	2	6			8
[68*‡]	James G. Swinington	2	6			8
[69]	James White	3	5			8
[70 ‡]	Mary Dickson	1	1			2

CENSUS OF 1820

MADISON COUNTY (Continued)

No.	Heads of families	White males 21 & over	All other white	Free people of color	Servants or slaves	Total
[71 ‡]	Thomas Lipincott	2	2			4
[72 ‡]	Joel Bacon	2	5			7
[73]	Henry Blanford	2	1			3
[74*‡]	John Wallis	3	3			6
[75 ‡]	John S. Stutson	1	4			5
[76 ‡]	Martin Rose	1	1			2
[77]	Ephraem Harper	1				1
[78*‡]	Samuel Caiman	1	3			4
[79 ‡]	Daniel Johnson	1	4			5
[80 ‡]	Hezekiah Crosby	3	6			9
[81*‡]	Adit Meacham	1	2			3
[82*‡]	Edward Fountain	2	7			9
[83 ‡]	Agustus Langworthy	4	4			8
[84*‡]	Isham Gillham	2	7		1	10
[85 ‡]	Henry Hopkison	12	5			17
[86]	Enos Pembrook	7	12			19
[87]	Abner Young	1	4			5
[88*‡]	Ormon Beamon	1	4			5
[89*‡]	Aaron Suton	3	6			9
[90 ‡]	Robert Coalman	3	1			4
[91*‡]	John Rattan	3	4			7
[92*]	Nancy Barrow		5			5
[93*‡]	Elizabeth Higgins	1	2			3
[94*‡]	Soloman Pruitt	2	6			8
[95 ‡]	Dorotha Pruitt		3			3
[96 ‡]	Emanual West	3	11		2	16
[97 ‡]	John Russel	1	1			2
[98 ‡]	Benjamin Wright			9		9
[99*‡]	Jesse Starky	1	10		2	13
[100*‡]	John Starky	1	3			4
[101 ‡]	Jeremiah Wright			3		3
[102 ‡]	John Young	1	8			9
[103*‡]	Jacob Deades	1	6			7
[104*‡]	George Hunter	1	4			5
[105]	Joseph Hardican	1				1
[106 ‡]	William Wiat	1	4			5
[107*‡]	William Write	1	2			3
[108*]	John Hunter	1	4			5

MADISON COUNTY (*Continued*)

No.	Heads of families	White males 21 & over	All other white	Free people of color	Servants or slaves	Total
[109*‡]	William Watson	1	7			8
[110]	James Huston	1	5			6
[111 ‡]	William Cawley	1	4			5
[112*‡]	William Wiatt	1	3			4
[113 ‡]	Absolem Woolams	2	2			4
[114*]	William Yorke	1	3			4
[115 ‡]	Edward Clanton	1	7			8
[116*‡]	William Wiatt	1	2			3
[117 ‡]	John Wiatt	1	3			4
[118*‡]	Peter Waggoner	1	8			9
[119*‡]	Abel Moore	4	7			11
[120*‡]	William Moore	5	5			10
[121*‡]	John Rows	1	7			8
[122*‡]	Samuel Williams	1	5			6
[123 ‡]	Squire Harvel	1	12			13
[124 ‡]	Cavel Archer	1	5			6
[125 ‡]	Charles Harrel	1	3			4
[126*‡]	Isaac Chandler	1	3			4
[127*‡]	Thomas Chandler	1	2			3
[128*‡]	Kerenhappuch Mcafee		3			3
[129*‡]	Martin Jones	1	4			5
[130 ‡]	Larkin Thaxton	1	6			7
[131 ‡]	Green W. Short	1	2			3
[132*‡]	George Moore	1	3			4
[133]	Thomas Tidinas	1	2			3
[134]	Daniel A. Lanterman	1	2			3
[135 ‡]	Moses Parker	2	1			3
[136 ‡]	Samuel Davis	1	2			3
[137 ‡]	Henery Head	5	4			9
[138*‡]	Joshua Delaplane	1	12			13
[139*‡]	John Robertson	1	4			5
[140 ‡]	William Sharoon	2	3			5
[141*‡]	James Robertson	1	8			9
[142 ‡]	Hugh S. Corhern	1	9			10
[143 ‡]	Aaron Hood	1	7			8
[144*‡]	James Willson	1	8			9
[145]	Robert Morse	1	4			5
[146 ‡]	James Wilder	2	6			8

MADISON COUNTY (Continued)

No.	Heads of families	White males 21 & over	All other white	Free people of color	Servants or slaves	Total
[147*‡]	William Gillham	2	10			12
[148*‡]	Joshua Atwaters	9	6			15
[149*‡]	Walter J. Sealy	8	3	2	1	14
[150 ‡]	Thomas Tindal	1	5			6
[151*‡]	Jesse Bell	1	8			9
[152*‡]	Isaac Gillham	2	5			7
[153]	Samuel Gray	2	3			5
[154*‡]	John T. Luske	5	4			9
[155*‡]	Jacob Snider	1	5			6
[156*‡]	George Kinder	3	6			9
[157]	James Monday	2	4			6
[158 ‡]	Scene Roy	1	3			4
[159*‡]	James Wright	2	4			6
[160*]	Cleavland Hageler	1	7			8
[161*‡]	John Delaplane	1	2			3
[162 ‡]	George Coldwell	3	1			4
[163*‡]	William Lollis	1	1			2
[164*‡]	Henery Bonner	1	6			7
[165]	James Hassley	1				1
[166]	William Newman	1	1			2
[167 ‡]	George Shane	5	1			6
[168 ‡]	David Wright	1	3			4
[169*‡]	John Vicary	1	6			7
[170*‡]	William Jones	2	7			9
[171 ‡]	John Arnet	1	5			6
[172]	Ira Kelly	1	6			7
[173*‡]	Denny Davis	1	4			5
[174 ‡]	Ira W Bacon	1	1			2
[175 ‡]	Willaby Adams	1	5			6
[176*‡]	John Jones	1	3			4
[177 ‡]	James Whitlock	1	3			4
[178*‡]	Alexandria S. Biram	2	3			5
[179 ‡]	Isaac Wood	1	3			4
[180 ‡]	John Newman	1	7			8
[181*‡]	Zadok Newman	1	5			6
[182]	Alfred Jackson	1	2			3
[183*‡]	Shadrach Jackson	1	1			2
[184*‡]	William Ogle	1	5			6

MADISON COUNTY (Continued)

No.	Heads of families	White males 21 & over	All other white	Free people of color	Servants or slaves	Total
[185 ‡]	William Montgomery	3	5		1	9
[186*‡]	William Jones	1	8	2		11
[187 ‡]	Henery Whitlock	1	1			2
[188 ‡]	Richard Smith	1	2			3
[189 ‡]	Samuel Mahurin	2	4			6
[190 ‡]	William Ennis	1	1			2
[191 ‡]	Stepen Shorte	1	4			5
[192 ‡]	Joseph Wise	1	3			4
[193*‡]	William Scott	2	11			13
[194 ‡]	William M, Clarke	1	6			7
[195 ‡]	James S. Pearce	1	3			4
[196*‡]	James Parke	1				1
[197*]	Alexandria Boner	2	2			4
[198*‡]	James Bace	1	6			7
[199*‡]	Henery Cook	1	6		1	8
[200*‡]	David Akeman	1	6			7
[201*‡]	William Hocksey	3	11		1	15
[202 ‡]	William Good	1	3			4
[203*‡]	John Good	1	3			4
[204*‡]	Abraham Hayter	2	5			7
[205 ‡]	Mathias Handlon	1	1			2
[206*]	Joel Whiteside	3	9			12
[207*‡]	Henery Reviss	1	1			2
[208*‡]	Jacob Gunterman	1	10			11
[209 ‡]	Thomas Smith	1	3			4
[210 ‡]	Caleb Gunterman	1	2			3
[211 ‡]	Richard Knight	1	2			3
[212*‡]	Joseph Bartlet	3	6			9
[213*‡]	Joseph Snodgrass	1	7			8
[214*‡]	Edward Tailor	3	5			8
[215]	Osin M. Ross	1	4			5
[216 ‡]	Jesse Starke	1	7			8
[217*‡]	Edward Fruit	1	8			9
[218]	John Newman	1	1			2
[219*‡]	James Gillham	1	3			4
[220*‡]	Hanner Sanders	2	6			8
[221*‡]	William Tompson	1	5			6
[222*‡]	Obediah Waddle	2	2			4

MADISON COUNTY (Continued)

No.	Heads of families	White males 21 & over	All other white	Free people of color	Servants or slaves	Total
[223*‡]	James Tompson	2	2			4
[224 ‡]	Theopholus W. Smith	1	9			10
[225*‡]	John Todd	1	4		2	7
[226*‡]	James Metty	1	2			3
[227 ‡]	Joseph L. Barton	2	3			5
[228*]	Samuel Wood	2	8			10
[229]	George D. Barnet	1	8			9
[230]	Abbias Worthbacor	1	3			4
[231*‡]	Robert Whiteside	1	8			9
[232]	Marke Ragan	1	3			4
[233]	James Hoosong	1	1			2
[234*‡]	George Bridgers	2	3			5
[235]	Jacob Casteel	1	2			3
[236*‡]	David Hendershot	2	10			12
[237 ‡]	Watel Denny	1	7			8
[238]	Chiles W. Hagelar	1	6			7
[239]	Isaac Hagelar	2	8			10
[240*‡]	John Herren	1	9			10
[241]	Joseph Smith	2	10			12
[242*‡]	Matthew Holland	1				1
[243 ‡]	Caleb Odle	1	9			10
[244*‡]	Jonithan L. Harrass	2	6			8
[245*‡]	Adley Harrass	1	2			3
[246 ‡]	Edwin Harrass	1	2			3
[247 ‡]	Elizabeth Gingles	1	4		1	6
[248 ‡]	John Harrass	1	2		1	4
[249]	Matthew Holland	1	4			5
[250 ‡]	Robert W. Harrass	1	1			2
[251*‡]	Ebeniah Gullet	1	3			4
[252*‡]	Gilbert Watson	3	9			12
[253 ‡]	John H. Spencer	3	6	1	2	12
[254 ‡]	John Gullet	1	1			2
[255 ‡]	Ira Gullet	1	2			3
[256*‡]	James Ramsey	2	2			4
[257 ‡]	William Ramsey	1	1			2
[258*‡]	Robert Craigg	1	6			7
[259*‡]	John M. Berry	1	2			3
[260*‡]	James Good	1	3			4

MADISON COUNTY (*Continued*)

No.	Heads of families	White males 21 & over	All other white	Free people of color	Servants or slaves	Total
[261*‡]	Joseph Dunkin	1	7			8
[262 ‡]	Joseph Grace	1	2			3
[263 ‡]	John Gear	1	6			7
[264 ‡]	Elizabeth Hunter	1	7			8
[265*‡]	William Parkison	3	6			9
[266 ‡]	Nancy Whiteside	2	4			6
[267 ‡]	Robert Pogue	1	7		2	10
[268*‡]	Robert G. Anderson	1	7			8
[269 ‡]	Daniel Tollman	9	3			12
[270*‡]	Jacob Deck	1	2			3
[271 ‡]	Adam Miller	1	7			8
[272 ‡]	John Deck	1	1			2
[273*‡]	William Quigley	2	4			6
[274*‡]	Joseph Reynolds	1	4			5
[275 ‡]	James Dabbs	1	11			12
[276 ‡]	Robert Hill	1	8			9
[277*‡]	Edward Larkin	3	6			9
[278 ‡]	William Ambrose	1	9			10
[279*‡]	David Stockton	2	10			12
[280*‡]	James Gribbins	1	2			3
[281]	James Johnson	2	2			4
[282*‡]	George Coonrod	2	9			11
[283*‡]	James Stean	3	2			5
[284]	Robert Morgan	1	1			2
[285*‡]	Charles Desherly	2	1			3
[286 ‡]	Daniel Neles	1	1			2
[287*‡]	Louis Mar	1	9			10
[288]	Joke Barbee	1	4			5
[289*‡]	Rachael Royboalt		3			3
[290 ‡]	Francis Dieumy	1	8			9
[291 ‡]	John Borney	1	1			2
[292 ‡]	Robert S. Walker	7				7
[293*‡]	William Aston	3	3			6
[294*‡]	Daniel Patongill	1	1			2
[295 ‡]	Patsey Vickmore	3	7			10
[296 ‡]	John Fortner	1	6			7
[297*‡]	Samuel Stallians	1	4			5
[298*‡]	John Stallians	1	2			3

MADISON COUNTY (Continued)

No.	Heads of families	White males 21 & over	All other white	Free people of color	Servants or slaves	Total
[299 ‡]	William Stallians	1	1			2
[300*‡]	Jacob Segar	1	3			4
[301 ‡]	Francis Diou	1	8			9
[302*‡]	Blackston Howard	1	8			9
[303*‡]	George Richardson	1	7			8
[304]	Elisha Macry	1				1
[305 ‡]	George Grayham	1	2			3
[306*‡]	Henery Emerich	1	2			3
[307]	Thomas Seward	1	3			4
[308*‡]	Joseph Buck	2	6			8
[309 ‡]	William Buck	1	2			3
[310*‡]	John Adkins	2	4			6
[311*‡]	Joseph Williams	1	4			5
[312 ‡]	Elisha Cadwell	1	4			5
[313*‡]	George Cadwell	1	7			8
[314]	James Walker	1	7			8
[315 ‡]	James Berry	1	9			10
[316]	Daniel Fowler	2	1			3
[317 ‡]	Partrach Labour	2	1			3
[318*‡]	Benjamin Merit	6	6			12
[319]	Denison Kingsbury	3				3
[320 ‡]	John Movill			3		3
[321 ‡]	William Court	1	6			7
[322]	William Hawkins	5	5			10
[323 ‡]	George Wimon	1	5			6
[324 ‡]	John Hanner	5	1			6
[325 ‡]	Philip Cobic	2	6			8
[326 ‡]	James Robertson	1	6			7
[327*‡]	Charles Shin	2	5			7
[328 ‡]	Benjamin Merit	2	6			8
[329]	James Kingsbury	3				3
[330*‡]	Reuben Walker	1	7			8
[331*‡]	George Hewitt	1	2			3
[332*‡]	John Clarke	2	6			8
[333 ‡]	Voluntine Kinder	2	6			8
[334*‡]	Jacob Kinder	2	5			7
[335*‡]	John Davidson	3	4			7
[336*‡]	James Gillham	1	3			4

MADISON COUNTY (*Continued*)

No.	Heads of families	White males 21 & over	All other white	Free people of color	Servants or slaves	Total
[337 ‡]	John Young	1	1			2
[338 ‡]	Thomas Rice	1	9		1	11
[339 ‡]	Robert Joab	1	3			4
[340*‡]	Alexandria Laughlin	3	7			10
[341*‡]	Thomas Gillham	2	5			7
[342*‡]	Isaac Gillham	1	4			5
[343*‡]	William Gillham	3	5			8
[344*‡]	John Hawk	3	6			9
[345*‡]	Philip Hawk	2	5			7
[346*]	Amos Squires	1	10			11
[347 ‡]	William Wadle	1	2			3
[348]	Moses Eedes	2	4			6
[349*‡]	William Adkins	2	4			6
[350*‡]	Thomas Johnson	1	3			4
[351 ‡]	John Adkins	1	1			2
[352*‡]	Matthew Dare	1	3			4
[353]	Charles Purse	2	11			13
[354]	Jacob Bradley	1	4			5
[355]	Thomas Norris	1	3			4
[356]	John Waddle	1	1			2
[357*‡]	Andrew Emiett	1	7			8
[358*‡]	John Singleton	2	4		6	12
[359 ‡]	Robert Garret	2	2			4
[360]	Henry harriss	5	13		2	17
[361]	John Hickey	2	9			11
[362 ‡]	Marget Miller		6			6
[363*‡]	William Gooen	1	2			3
[364*‡]	Abraham Sippy	1	4			5
[365*]	Nathan Carpenter	3	3			6
[366]	Nancey griffin		2			2
[367*‡]	William griffin	1	4			5
[368*‡]	Rodah Bishop		6			6
[369*]	Jesse Waddle	1	6			7
[370 ‡]	Daniel McDonel	1	2			3
[371]	Philip hains	1	6			7
[372 ‡]	James H gilham	2	3			5
[373*]	Clamons gilham	1	6			7
[374]	thomas Smith	1	3			4

CENSUS OF 1820

MADISON COUNTY (Continued)

No.	Heads of families	White males 21 & over	All other white	Free people of color	Servants or slaves	Total
[375*‡]	Samuel Brown	1	12			13
[376]	William Mallors	1	9			10
[377 ‡]	Nathaniel Morison	1	7			8
[378 ‡]	Sally Coventry	1	5			6
[379 ‡]	David Robertson	1	9			10
[380 ‡]	Stephen Langworthy	2	12			14
[381*‡]	Benjamin Diliplane	1	4			5
[382 ‡]	Daniel Hoosong	3	7			10
[383*‡]	William Otwell	3	6			9
[384 ‡]	William Robertson	1	2			3
[385*‡]	John Diliplane	1	4			5
[386*‡]	Jonas Bradshaw	1	2			3
[387*‡]	Nancy Bradshaw	1	2			3
[388*‡]	David Nix	1	3		1	5
[389]	Isaac Hauskins	1	6			7
[390*‡]	William B Whiteside	2	9			11
[391*‡]	Thomas Reynolds	2	6		3	11
[392*‡]	Robert Reynolds	2	3		1	6
[393*‡]	William Whitehead	1	3			4
[394*‡]	Robert Reynolds	2	4		4	10
[395*‡]	James Reynolds	2	2		1	5
[396*‡]	John Nix	1	3			4
[397*‡]	Ambrose Nix	1	3			4
[398*‡]	Micajah Cox	2	6			8
[399*‡]	John Barnet	1	9			10
[400*‡]	Nelson Alexandria	1	4			5
[401*‡]	Samuel Judy	1	8		2	11
[402 ‡]	Lewis Sherman	2	3			5
[403 ‡]	Joab Sherman	1	5			6
[404 ‡]	Lemmons Hauskins	1	4			5
[405 ‡]	Sarah Vaughn	1	7		1	9
[406]	Charles Mcines	1	2			3
[407]	John Mcines	1	1			2
[408]	Elias Mcines	1	2			3
[409]	William Mcines	1	2			3
[410*‡]	Francis Colene	1	5			6
[411]	George Tompson	1	2			3
[412 ‡]	Isaac Chandler	6	3			9

MADISON COUNTY (Continued)

No.	Heads of families	White males 21 & over	All other white	Free people of color	Servants or slaves	Total
[413]	George Chandlar	1	3			4
[414 ‡]	William Chandler	1	3			4
[415*‡]	Sarah Grots		8			8
[416*‡]	Thomas Moore	1	1			2
[417*‡]	William Carnes	2	3			5
[418 ‡]	William Adkins	2	7			9
[419]	William Laong	1	1			2
[420*‡]	Peter Marter	1	9			10
[421 ‡]	Peter Mares	1	9			10
[422*‡]	Batist Joneroy	1	6			7
[423]	Batest Deboc	1	9			10
[424]	Peter King	1	1			2
[425 ‡]	Me Me	1	5			6
[426 ‡]	William Cooper	2	2			4
[427 ‡]	Abraham Claypole	3	1			4
[428*‡]	Elijah Mathers	3	5			8
[429 ‡]	Thomas Foster	2	5			7
[430*‡]	John Waggoner	1	3			4
[431*‡]	Jonithan Casslin	1	7			8
[432*‡]	Hanna Smith	2	5			7
[433 ‡]	Nathan Morgan	1	1			2
[434*‡]	Thomas Manan	1	8			9
[435 ‡]	George Harland	1	4			5
[436*‡]	Michael Squirs	2	4			6
[437 ‡]	Isaac McMahen	1	3			4
[438*‡]	Elisha Pritchit	1	2			3
[439 ‡]	Richard Moorehead	1	7			8
[440 ‡]	William Buennet	1	3		5	9
[441*‡]	Abner Wright	3	2			5
[442]	William Penny	1	4			5
[443*‡]	George Armstrong	1	6			7
[444]	William Brewin	1	5			6
[445 ‡]	James Read	1	2			3
[446 ‡]	Anson Collins	3	2			5
[447*]	Henry Beag	1	2			3
[448*‡]	John Williamson	1	4			5
[449 ‡]	William B. Penny	2	4			6
[450]	Abner Wright	1	3			4

CENSUS OF 1820

MADISON COUNTY (Continued)

No.	Heads of families	White males 21 & over	All other white	Free people of color	Servants or slaves	Total
[451*‡]	Philip Teter	1	4			5
[452 ‡]	Gideon Scantlin	1	8			9
[453*‡]	George Debond	1	8			9
[454*‡]	Robert McMahan	1	2			3
[455]	Isaac McMahan	1	4			5
[456*‡]	Jesse Coneway	2	4			6
[457 ‡]	Benjamin Johnson	2	4			6
[458 ‡]	James McFearson	1	1			2
[459 ‡]	Royal Tifft	3	8			11
[460*‡]	Abner O. Kelly	1	7			8
[461*]	Henry Tailor	1	6			7
[462*]	Jubilee Pozia	2	3			5
[463]	Isham Ramsey	1	3			4
[464*‡]	Beverley Guthery	1	8			9
[465*‡]	Dempsey Guthery	3	9			12
[466 ‡]	William Guthery	1	2			3
[467*‡]	Amos Batterton	3	8			11
[468 ‡]	John Hadely	1	9			10
[469*‡]	Benjamin Eves	1	4			5
[470*‡]	John Haker	1	1			2
[471*‡]	Cornelius Tolly	1	2			3
[472*‡]	Joel Whitsid	3	9			12
[473*‡]	Aaron Armstrong	1	11			12
[474*‡]	Sasanah Aarstrong		3			3
[475*‡]	David Roach	1	3			4
[476]	William Linton	1	2			3
[477*‡]	Gorge Barnesback	2	8			10
[478]	John Minter	1	3			4
[479 ‡]	thomas gilerland	1	2			3
[480*]	Misalent holady	1	1			2
[481*‡]	John Barber	1	6			7
[482*‡]	thomas good	2	2		2	6
[483 ‡]	Josiah Write	3	2			5
[484]	Rheubin hopkins	9	6		2	17
[485 ‡]	harris Coffin	1	5			6
[486*‡]	John Blacburn	1	4			5
[487 ‡]	hugh Conaway	3	4			7
[488*‡]	Benjamin Stephenson	2	4	2	8	16

MADISON COUNTY (Continued)

No.	Heads of families	White males 21 & over	All other white	Free people of color	Servants or slaves	Total
[489*‡]	Joseph Borow	2	3			5
[490*‡]	Jeptha Lampkins	7	4		2	13
[491]	Samuel Denton	1	2			3
[492]	Edmon Conley	1	3			4
[493 ‡]	Samuel Johnson	1	7			8
[494 ‡]	Samuel owens	1	5			6
[495 ‡]	Jesey Larrence	1	2			3
[496*‡]	thomas Walls	1	8			9
[497*‡]	Charles Tindol	1	3			4
[498*‡]	James Wright	3	2			5
[499*‡]	William Hinch	1	5			6
[500 ‡]	Samuel Hammont	1	1			2
[501 ‡]	Niclis Rushes	1	2			3
[502 ‡]	Ishom Dalton	3	4			7
[503*‡]	John Owins	4	1			5
[504 ‡]	Jephe Winser	6	3			9
[505*‡]	John McKee	1	2			3
[506*‡]	William L. May	2	5		1	8
[507*‡]	James Pharris	1	1			2
[508*‡]	John Herington	1	6			7
[509 ‡]	Samuel Read	2	2			4
[510*‡]	Robert Sibool	2	3			5
[511*‡]	Samuel Sibool	1	2			3
[512*‡]	William Pervines	2	5			7
[513 ‡]	William Harman	2	3			5
[514]	Ebenser Provins	1	2			3
[515*‡]	S. T. Venas Gaskil	1	8			9
[516]	James Crowel	1	4			5
[517 ‡]	Lewis Kermack	1	8			9
[518*‡]	David Gaskil	1	10			11
[519*‡]	Robert McMahan	1	8			9
[520 ‡]	Easther Hall	1	2			3
[521*‡]	William Beard	1	10			11
[522 ‡]	Limon Gillet	1	2			3
[523*‡]	Elijah Renshaw	1	8			9
[524 ‡]	Abraham Renshaw	1	3			4
[525*‡]	Margaret Renfrow	1	5			6
[526 ‡]	Joseph Renfrow	1	2			3

CENSUS OF 1820 151

MADISON COUNTY (Continued)

No.	Heads of families	White males 21 & over	All other white	Free people of color	Servants or slaves	Total
[527 ‡]	Jesse Yates	1	6			7
[528 ‡]	Abraham Smith	1	6			7
[529*‡]	Andrew Turner	1	4			5
[530 ‡]	John Roach	1	1			2
[531*‡]	John Turner	2	5			7
[532 ‡]	John Logsdon	2	4			6
[533*‡]	John Hall	2	9			11
[534*‡]	Anderson Smith	1	12			13
[535*‡]	William Hall	1	3			4
[536*‡]	John Cook	1	5			6
[537 ‡]	George Matice	1	5			6
[538 ‡]	Warde Eldrid	3	2			5
[539 ‡]	William Eldrid	1	4			5
[540*‡]	James Downing	1	13			14
[541]	Thomas Muns	2	1			3
[542*‡]	David Moore	1	5			6
[543]	William Downing	1	6			7
[544*‡]	Isaac Clarke	1	5			6
[545 ‡]	Jehosifat Eldrid	3	6			7
[546*]	Seth Hodge	1	5			6
[547]	John Lawrison	1	4			5
[548]	John Pompter	3	8			11
[549 ‡]	Lucy Clarke	1	4			5
[550 ‡]	William Hall	1	1			2
[551*‡]	Abraham Vanhoser	1	10			11
[552 ‡]	Joab Robertson	2	8			10
[553 ‡]	Peter Etter	1	4			5
[554 ‡]	Daniel D. Rice	1	5			6
[555 ‡]	Isaac Reaves	1	4			5
[556 ‡]	Richard Atison	1	2			3
[557*‡]	James Wats	1	4			5
[558 ‡]	Jonithan Denton	2	12			14
[559*‡]	Alexandria Conley	2	5			7
[560*‡]	Isaac Conley	1	4			5
[561*‡]	Hesley Conley		7			7
[562]	Francis Pearce	2	4			5
[563 ‡]	Nancy Stice		5			5
[564 ‡]	Rice Dunkin	1	7			8

MADISON COUNTY (Continued)

No.	Heads of families	White males 21 & over	All other white	Free people of color	Servants or slaves	Total
[565]	William Hars	1	8			9
[566]	Daniel Pearce	1	7			8
[567 ‡]	William Robertson	1	10			11
[568*‡]	Joseph Everman	3	5			8
[569 ‡]	Henery Rigin	3	1			4
[570]	John Essey	3	2			5
[571 ‡]	Thomas Baker	2	3			5
[572 ‡]	Calvin Mcrey	3	1			4
[573]	Thomas C. Caret	1	5			6
[574 ‡]	William Sealy	1	5			6
[575 ‡]	Archer G. Hardin	1	3			4
[576 ‡]	Hiram Chappin	1	2			3
[577 ‡]	Morgan Tompson	1	1			2
[578 ‡]	Edward Day	3	4			7
[579 ‡]	Walker Nealous	1	3			4
[580*‡]	John Gearvis	1	6			7
[581]	Olif Smith		3			3
[582*‡]	Isaac West	2	8			10
[583*‡]	James Parmer	2	9			11
[584*]	John C. Wood	3	5			8
[585*‡]	George Tase	2	10			12
[586*‡]	Henry Kelly	3	5			8
[587*‡]	Jonithan Starke	1	9			10
[588]	Emely Bales	2	4			6
[589 ‡]	Elizabeth Randol	2	4			6
[590 ‡]	Payton Randol	1	1			2
[591]	Agnes P. Kay		3			3
[592 ‡]	Thomas Magirer	1	2			3
[593 ‡]	William Skiner	1	8			9
[594*‡]	Whitmell Herington	1	7			8
[595 ‡]	Jacob Jackson	3	5			8
[596 ‡]	Hessel North	1	2			3
[597 ‡]	Timothy Lad	1	2			3
[598*‡]	Simeon Owins	1	6			7
[599*‡]	Parseal P Enos	1	2			3
[600 ‡]	Gaaius Padock	4	3			7
[601*‡]	Lewis Deads	1	6			7
[602 ‡]	Harles Walker	1				1

MADISON COUNTY (Continued)

No.	Heads of families	White males 21 & over	All other white	Free people of color	Servants or slaves	Total
[603 ‡]	Prier Scrgins	1	1			2
[604*‡]	Samuel A Walker	1	7			8
[605 ‡]	Joseph Slatten	1	10			11
[606 ‡]	Jesse Belemon	1	2			3
[607 ‡]	George Fanon	1	7			8
[608 ‡]	Joseph Fanon	1	3			4
[609 ‡]	John Story	1	2			3
[610]	Samuel B Jones	1	6			7
[611 ‡]	John Tompson	1	2			3
[612 ‡]	Amos Reader	1	7			8
[613 ‡]	William C Wigins	7	6			13
[614]	Mary Mekel		8	1		9
[615*‡]	Paris Mayson	3	3	2		8
[616*‡]	Josiah Armstrong	1	3			4
[617]	William Hinton	1	2			3
[618 ‡]	Charles Brown	1	1			2
[619*‡]	Daniel Brown	1	5			6
[620 ‡]	Jesse B. Thomas	2	3		5	10
[621 ‡]	James Mayson	4	4		2	10
[622]	Robert Crofferd			7		7
[623*‡]	Austin Sims	1	4			5
[624 ‡]	John Ivins	1	3			4
[625 ‡]	Stephen Jones	2	9			11
[626 ‡]	James Beas	1	6			7
[627 ‡]	Thomas Rhea	1	5			6
[628 ‡]	Alexandria Thompson	1	2			3
[629 ‡]	Richard Knight	1	2			3
[630 ‡]	Smith Pharis	1	5			6
[631*‡]	George Pharis	1	2			3
[632]	James Manuel	1	2			3
[633*‡]	Netter Piper	1	9			10
[634 ‡]	John Piper	1	2			3
[635 ‡]	John Haxy	1	2			3
[636*‡]	Philip Penn	1	4			5
[637 ‡]	James Pearce	1	6			7
[638 ‡]	Thomas Johnson	2	2			4
[639*‡]	Richard Wood	1	6			7
[640 ‡]	Polly Johnson		3			3

MADISON COUNTY (Continued)

No.	Heads of families	White males 21 & over	All other white	Free people of color	Servants or slaves	Total
[641*‡]	Robert Coatter	2	10			12
[642*‡]	Henry East	1	6			7
[643*‡]	James East	1	11			12
[644 ‡]	William D. Rice	1	5			6
[645*‡]	James Pearce	2	3			5
[646 ‡]	Samuel Mcalee	1	3			4
[647 ‡]	Joseph Howard	1	1			2
[648 ‡]	Samuel Mcalee	1	2			3
[649 ‡]	John Macalle	2	3			5
[650*‡]	John Larde	1	3			4
[651 ‡]	Andrew Lawel	1	3			4
[652*‡]	Jacob Landers	1	6			7
[653*‡]	Henry Landers	1	3			4
[654 ‡]	Washington Parkison	1	5			6
[655]	Anderson Riley	1	5			6
[656 ‡]	Nancey Lee	1	4			5
[657*‡]	Willey Dugger	1	3			4
[658*‡]	Robert hines	1	3			4
[659*‡]	William Mcadams	2	5			7
[660*‡]	Jurden ussel	2	7	1		10
[661 ‡]	Henry fannon	1	1			2
[662*‡]	Jeret dugger	1	6			7
[663*]	Aaron Rule	1	4			5
[664 ‡]	Joseph May	1	9			10
[665 ‡]	John S. talor	1	3			4
[666*‡]	John Howard	1	10			11
[667 ‡]	James Newles	2	8			10
[668]	Stephen Kirkindoll	1	2			3
[669 ‡]	Benjamin Harrass	2	10			12
[670]	James Lowly	1	4			5
[671*‡]	John Linnley	1	3			4
[672*‡]	Mathias Shelton	2	4			6
[673*‡]	John Read	1	2			3
[674 ‡]	John Steal	1	5			6
[675 ‡]	David S. White	1	7			8
[676*‡]	Robert Brazel	1	7			8
[677*‡]	Robert White	1	5			6
[678*‡]	Thomas Flanigan	1	1			2

CENSUS OF 1820   155

MADISON COUNTY (*Continued*)

No.	Heads of families	White males 21 & over	All other white	Free people of color	Servants or slaves	Total
[679*‡]	Andrew St. John	1	10			11
[680*‡]	John White	1	10			11
[681 ‡]	Joseph Jones	2	8			10
[682]	Marke Ragin	1	2			3
[683 ‡]	Daniel Funderburk	1	3			4
[684 ‡]	George Boulton	1	5			6
[685*‡]	John Ragin	1	6			7
[686*]	William Armstrong	1	3			4
[687*‡]	Robert Armstrong	1	7			8
[688]	James Severs	1	2			3
[689 ‡]	Jacob Brown	2	2			4
[690 ‡]	Andrew Armstrong	1	3			4
[691 ‡]	William Kingston	1				1
[692*‡]	Thomas Armstrong	1	1			2
[693*‡]	Reard Kingston	1	2			3
[694]	Thomas Pilkinton	1	8			9
[695 ‡]	Voluntine Vanhooser	1	10			11
[696*‡]	Abraham Vanhooser	1	2			3
[697*]	John McKee	1	2			3
[698*‡]	Harden Warrin	1	7			8
[699*‡]	David Samples	2	7			9
[700]	Johnsem Shelton	1	5			6
[701 ‡]	James Dowdy	1	5			6
[702*‡]	Benjamin J. Hageler	1	4			5
[703*‡]	Jacob Hagler	2	5			7
[704 ‡]	William Vineyard	1	4			5
[705*‡]	William R. Hageler	1	5			6
[706*‡]	Jesse Renfrow	1	3			4
[707]	Joseph Renfrow	1	2			3
[708*‡]	Jesse Patree	2	7			9
[709 ‡]	James Hoosong	1	1			2
[710*‡]	Jacob Hoosong	1	5			6
[711 ‡]	Peter Smarte	1	6			7
[712 ‡]	Francis Griffin	1	1			2
[713 ‡]	David Anderson	1	6			7
[714*‡]	John Shinn	2	7			9
[715*‡]	Caleb Shinn	1	2			3
[716 ‡]	John Giger	2	6			8

MADISON COUNTY (*Continued*)

No.	Heads of families	White males 21 & over	All other white	Free people of color	Servants or slaves	Total
[717]	John C. Alley	1	1			2
[718 ‡]	Elijah P. Blakeman	2	8			10
[719 ‡]	Andrew Mathis	1	8			9
[720 ‡]	James Finch	1	2			3
[721 ‡]	Lephod Finch	1	2			3
[722*‡]	Isaac Ferguson	1	9	1		11
[723 ‡]	John Barbarah	1	3			4
[724 ‡]	Samuel Lawrance	1	6			7
[725]	Martin Bourt	1	13			14
[726]	Berthena Orcut		3			3
[727 ‡]	Curtis Blakeman	4	9			13
[728 ‡]	Justice Alburt	1	2			3
[729*‡]	Cristopher Pane	1	4			5
[730 ‡]	John Churlin	1	7			8
[731*‡]	Adams Chiles	2	4			6
[732*‡]	Hiram Robins	1	3			4
[733 ‡]	Elijah E. Beason	2	6			8
[734*]	Jacob Varner	1	3			4
[735 ‡]	George C. Allin	7	8			15
[736 ‡]	James Ground	1	6			7
[737 ‡]	Heney Peck	1	4			5
[738 ‡]	James Hall	3	4			7
[739 ‡]	Ebian Twist	1	4			5
[740 ‡]	Moses Twist	2	8			10
[741 ‡]	Elizeph Judd	2	4			6
[742]	Oliver Scutton	1	1			2
[743]	George Simes	1	7			8
[744]	Dempsey Swanson	1	2			3
[745 ‡]	Joshua Hankes	1	2			3
[746]	William B. Lair	1	7			8
[747]	Simeon Willcock	1	4			5
[748 ‡]	John Swidden	1	2			3
[749]	Thomas Permeture	1	2			3
[750 ‡]	John Lewis	1	6		1	8
[751 ‡]	George Blair	1	3			4
[752 ‡]	John Sulivan	1	2			3
[753]	Catharine Mcfaddin	1	2			3
[754]	Alexandria Moore	1	7			8

CENSUS OF 1820   157

MADISON COUNTY (Continued)

No.	Heads of families	White males 21 & over	All other white	Free people of color	Servants or slaves	Total
[755]	Nathaniel Rowden	1	6			7
[756 ‡]	James L. Whiteside	1	5			6
[757 ‡]	James Sulivan	1	3			4
[758*‡]	Thomas Piper	2	5			7
[759]	George Hutton	2	3			5
[760 ‡]	William Beatis	1	4			5
[761*‡]	Andrew Dunigan	1	7			8
[762 ‡]	Martin Feehans	3	9			12
[763 ‡]	James Moffet	3	3			6
[764 ‡]	Edward Caral	4	4			8
[765 ‡]	Thomas Lofton	2	2			4
[766*‡]	John Lofton	2	8			10
[767]	Matthew Davidson	2	3			5
[768]	William Gillham	1	2			3
[769*‡]	William Davidson	1	2			3
[770*‡]	John Gillham	1	4			5
[771*]	Charles Gillham	1	4			5
[772*‡]	William Gillham	1	5			6
[773*‡]	John Findley	1	6			7
[774*‡]	Samuel Kinkade	1	6			7
[775 ‡]	William Rogers	1	3			4
[776]	James Andrews	1	5			6
[777*]	Joseph White	1	10			11
[778 ‡]	Thomas Linn	3	3			6
[779 ‡]	Joshua Patterson	2	1		1	4
[780 ‡]	David Stout	2	3			5
[781 ‡]	John Brown	2	5			7
[782 ‡]	John Cran	1	8			9
[783 ‡]	Jehugh Brown	1	10			11
[784 ‡]	William Robins	1	5			6
[785]	Jacob bowyer	2	4			6
[786*‡]	William Rowden	2	5			7
[787*‡]	Danel Allen	4	3			7
[788 ‡]	Lius Robertes	1	2			3
[789*‡]	James Pruitt	2	1			3
[790 ‡]	Salley King		4			4
[791*‡]	Vines Hix	1	2			3
[792 ‡]	Thomas Crain	2	5			7

MADISON COUNTY (Continued)

No.	Heads of families	White males 21 & over	All other white	Free people of color	Servants or slaves	Total
[793 ‡]	Middleton Crain	1	3			4
[794*‡]	Thomas Carlen	1	5			6
[795*‡]	William Savag	1	2			3
[796 ‡]	Jacob Wagner	2	2			4
[797*‡]	William Web	1	2			3
[798*‡]	Isaac Pruitt	2	6			8
[799 ‡]	Benjamin ogle	1	5			6
[800*‡]	Calvin Tunell	1	4			5
[801*‡]	William hoskins	1	4			5
[802*‡]	Walker danel	1	6			7
[803*‡]	William Costley	1	10			11
[804*]	Fillemen higgins	1	6			7
[805*‡]	Thomas Daniel	1	2			3
[806 ‡]	Thomas Hill	1	1			2
[807*‡]	Wiley Green	1	3			4
[808*‡]	William Green	1	4			5
[809*‡]	Robert Means	1	6			7
[810*‡]	John Hewitt	1	2			3
[811 ‡]	William Johnson	1	5			6
[812*‡]	William Vaughn	2	6			8
[813 ‡]	George Lewis	1	3			4
[814*‡]	Philip Grimes	1	6			7
[815*‡]	Austin Gibbs	1	2			3
[816*‡]	John Johnson	1	6			7
[817 ‡]	Christain Link	1	6			7
[818 ‡]	David Hudson	1	5			6
[819 ‡]	James Davidson	1	1			2
[820 ‡]	John Frazier	1	5			6
[821*‡]	Hail Mason	1	4			5
[822 ‡]	Matthew Hacock	2	2			4
[823]	Peter Warrin	1	2			3
[824*‡]	James Gray	3	11		5	19
[825*‡]	Isham Vinson	1	6			7
[826*‡]	Wiley Smarte	1	5			6
[827*‡]	Samuel Viles	1	9			10
[828]	David Gilgasper	1	3			4
[829 ‡]	Thomas Slocham	1	1			2
[830 ‡]	Ebenezar Wead	1	2			3

MADISON COUNTY (Continued)

No.	Heads of families	White males 21 & over	All other white	Free people of color	Servants or slaves	Total
[831*‡]	Maryann Black	2	3			5
[832 ‡]	Huston Reynolds	1	8			9
[833 ‡]	James Breath	1	9			10
[834*‡]	John McCullum	1	3			4
[835*‡]	Abraham Howard	1	10			11
[836*‡]	Rowlen P. Allen	12	5			17
[837 ‡]	Oliver Kelly	3	5			8
[838*‡]	Matthew Tarence	2	8			10
[839*‡]	Joseph Robertson	1	5			6
[840*‡]	Isham Randol	1	2			3
[841 ‡]	Josiah Randol	4	7			11
[842*‡]	Samuel Whiteside	1	9			10
[843 ‡]	Samuel Hambleten	1	1			2
[844*‡]	John McKinney	2	7			9
[845*‡]	John Findley	2	5			7
[846]	Howard Findley	1	1			2
[847]	Levi Reynolds	1				1
[848 ‡]	Abraham Leggit	1	3			4
[849*‡]	Samuel Scott	3	6			9
[850 ‡]	John Bradshaw	1	7			8
[851 ‡]	James Redding	2	5			7
[852*‡]	Andrew Lockheart	1	7			8
[853 ‡]	Isaac Carret	1				1
[854*‡]	Martin Wood	1	7			8
[855*‡]	William Barton			8		8
[856]	William Findley	1	7			8
[857*]	David Coop	2	5			7
[858*‡]	John Powel	1	1			2
[859 ‡]	John Robertson	2	4			6
[860 ‡]	William Drunnian	2	9			11
[861 ‡]	Alexandria Pichy	1	3	1		5
[862 ‡]	Joab Fletcher	1	2			3
[863]	James Cassner	2	1			3
[864*‡]	William Wood	2	4			6
[865 ‡]	Joseph Dodds	1	7			8
[866 ‡]	Edward Tailor	1	6			7
[867*‡]	James Simms	2	9			11
[868 ‡]	James Black	1	3			4

MADISON COUNTY (Continued)

No.	Heads of families	White males 21 & over	All other white	Free people of color	Servants or slaves	Total
[869 ‡]	Adam Hambleton	1	7			8
[870*‡]	Samuel Vance	1	3			4
[871 ‡]	Gideon Vance	1	1			2
[872 ‡]	Eldrid White	1	7			8
[873 ‡]	John Davis	1	7			8
[874*‡]	John Davis	1	1			2
[875 ‡]	George Lotti	2	4			6
[876 ‡]	Benjamin Million	1	6			7
[877 ‡]	Thomas Davis	1	3			4
[878 ‡]	Jesse Davis	1	1			2
[879 ‡]	David Davis	1	11			12
[880*‡]	Peter Yorker	2	5			7
[881 ‡]	Josiah Simes	1	1			2
[882 ‡]	Morris Davis	1	6			7
[883 ‡]	Jesse Willson	1	8			9
[884 ‡]	Joseph Thomas	1	6			7
[885 ‡]	Elizabeth Cox		5			5
[886 ‡]	Bowling Cox	1	1			2
[887 ‡]	Thomas Black	2	8			10
[888*‡]	William Johnson	1	3			4
[889 ‡]	Joshua Harley	1	6			7
[890*‡]	John Tailor	1	6			7
[891*‡]	Jahue George	1	5			6
[892 ‡]	Joseph Drunnion	1	8			9
[893*‡]	John Smith	1	6			7
[894 ‡]	Headley Smith	1	2			3
[895 ‡]	David Mils	1	8			9
[896 ‡]	Marget Stallions		3			3
[897 ‡]	Thomas Nots	1	10			11
[898 ‡]	John Bell	1	6			7
[899 ‡]	Zachariah Peters	1	6			7
[900*‡]	Ivin Smith	1	2			3
[901 ‡]	Isaac Kees	4	5			9
[902 ‡]	Norris A Thomas	1	2			3
[903 ‡]	George Hayworth	2	8			10
[904 ‡]	Jonithan Piper	1	3			4
[905 ‡]	Isaac Kees	2	4			6
[906*‡]	John Wood	1	7			8

MADISON COUNTY (Continued)

No.	Heads of families	White males 21 & over	All other white	Free people of color	Servants or slaves	Total
[907]	Joab Burden	1	1			2
[908*‡]	James Shelton	3	2	1	1	7
[909 ‡]	Jonithan Willcocks	2	7			9
[910 ‡]	Mathias Edes	1	3			4
[911]	Robert Gipson	1	5			6
[912 ‡]	Stephen French	1	3			4
[913 ‡]	George Kingston	2				2
[914 ‡]	Robert Gipson	1	5			6
[915 ‡]	William Fagan	1	4			5
[916 ‡]	Samuel Danley	1	6			7
[917 ‡]	Isaac Mires	1	3			4
[918 ‡]	John Cottonbarger	1	2			3
[919 ‡]	Charles Moore	1	6			7
[920 ‡]	William Cammore	1	2			3
[921]	John Smith	1	8			9
[922 ‡]	Isaac Congor	1	6			7
[923 ‡]	Daniel Harper	1	3			4
[924 ‡]	Jacob Dean	1	6			7
[925 ‡]	William Britan	1	4			5
[926 ‡]	Henry Cooper	1	2			3
[927*‡]	Joshua Dean	1	11			12
[928 ‡]	William Lofton	1	4			5
[929 ‡]	Fielden Delany	1	6		1	8
[930 ‡]	James W. Chapman	1	5			6
[931 ‡]	James Latham	6	9			15
[932 ‡]	James Tailor	4	7			11
[933]	John Porter	1	2			3
[934 ‡]	James Sales	1	3			4
[935 ‡]	Philip Smith	1	5			6
[936 ‡]	William Capture	2	3			5
[937 ‡]	Caleb Gill	1	4			5
[938]	John Bogard	1	4			5
[939 ‡]	Larry Husk	1	3			4
[940 ‡]	Elijah Hust	1	2			3
[941 ‡]	John Davidson	1	4			5
[942 ‡]	Matthew Huberd	1	6			7
[943 ‡]	James Stewart	1	7			8
[944 ‡]	Stephen Tollman	2	4			6

ILLINOIS HISTORICAL COLLECTIONS

MADISON COUNTY (Continued)

No.	Heads of families	White males 21 & over	All other white	Free people of color	Servants or slaves	Total
[945 ‡]	Abraham Hutchens [?]	1	6			7
[946 ‡]	Nathaniel Huzzer	1	6			7
[947]	David Porter	1				1
[948 ‡]	Chapter Oarinduff	2	11			13
[949 ‡]	John Cammon	1	6			7
[950 ‡]	Jeramah Smith	1	5			6
[951 ‡]	Hardin Counsel	2	1			3
[952 ‡]	Robert Mcalean	1	4			5
[953]	James Ruben	1				1
[954 ‡]	John Cline	1	2			3
[955 ‡]	Jacob Lanton	1	6			7
[956 ‡]	Jonithan Hog	1	4			5
[957 ‡]	Stephen England	1	7			8
[958 ‡]	John Cline	1	2			3
[959 ‡]	Ivins E Britain	2	2			4
[960 ‡]	Delphus Nelson		8			8
[961 ‡]	William Higins	1	8			9
[962 ‡]	Wiett Tenton	1	4			5
[963]	Asa Clinelow	1	3			4
[964 ‡]	Levi Clanterman	2	7			9
[965 ‡]	Jacob Bower	3	5			8
[966]	James Matis	1	7			8
[967]	Robert Clain	4	2			6
[968 ‡]	Alexandria Crofford	1	5			6
[969 ‡]	John Prim	1	5			6
[970 ‡]	Isaac Huffard	2	3			5
[971]	William Higins	2	2			4
[972 ‡]	Mathew Rogers	1	5			6
[973 ‡]	Mathew Rogers	1	2			3
[974 ‡]	David onstot	1	3			4
[975 ‡]	Benjamin Day	1	4			5
[976 ‡]	Wilim Short	1	3			4
[977 ‡]	William White	1	6			7
[978 ‡]	Oshel Willcox	1	6			7
[979 ‡]	William holland	1	5			6
[980*‡]	Joseph Smith	1	7			8
[981*‡]	James hains	1	3			4
[982 ‡]	Andrew girner	2	5			7

CENSUS OF 1820   163

MADISON COUNTY (*Continued*)

No.	Heads of families	White males 21 & over	All other white	Free people of color	Servants or slaves	Total
[983 ‡]	Martin higgains	2	2			4
[984 ‡]	William Macneal	1	2			3
[985*‡]	William Blain	2	2			4
[986 ‡]	John Hill	2				2
[987 ‡]	John Anderson	1	5			6
[988 ‡]	William Anderson	3	1			4
[989 ‡]	Eli Scott	1	3			4
[990 ‡]	John Scott	1	8			9
[991 ‡]	Ebenezar Barnes	1	4			5
[992*‡]	James Larde	1	5			6
[993 ‡]	William Juney	1	3			4
[994*‡]	Thomas Shelton	1	2			3
[995 ‡]	Jeremiah bery	1	1			2
[996 ‡]	Elijah Slator	4	3			7
[997 ‡]	John Driar	1	4			5
[998 ‡]	William Sealy	3	3			6
[999 ‡]	Jesse Southwick	3	7			10
[1000 ‡]	Pretree Hinch	1	3			4
[1001 ‡]	Abraham Peas	1	2			3
[1002 ‡]	Joseph Enesley	1	1			2
[1003 ‡]	George Stout	1	8			9
[1004 ‡]	Thomas Vandagriff	1	6			7
[1005]	Stephen Peril	1	9			10
[1006 ‡]	Buennet Burge	2	3			5
[1007 ‡]	James White	1	3			4
[1008 ‡]	Buennet Burge Jr.	2	7			9
[1009 ‡]	Pheneas Hill	1	7			8
[1010 ‡]	Barten Daroneal	1	6			7
[1011 ‡]	John Daroneal	1	5			6
[1012 ‡]	John Wisecoff	1	5			6
[1013*‡]	John Campbell	1	2			3
[1014 ‡]	Jacob Simes	1	6			7
[1015*‡]	Simon Lindley	2	4			6
[1016*‡]	John Briscow	1	8			9
[1017*‡]	Henry Brown	2	2			4
[1018 ‡]	Levi Harber	1	2			3
[1019*‡]	Daniel Dunesmore	3	4			7
[1020 ‡]	Sefus Dunsmore	1	1			2

MADISON COUNTY (Continued)

No.	Heads of families	White males 21 & over	All other white	Free people of color	Servants or slaves	Total
[1021*‡]	Absolem Baker	3	6			9
[1022]	William Penny	1	5			6
[1023 ‡]	Robert Penny	1	6			7
[1024 ‡]	John Penny	1	6			7
[1025 ‡]	James Ratliff	1	7			8
[1026 ‡]	James Fisher	1	3			4
[1027 ‡]	Henry Keltner	1	6			7
[1028*‡]	Solomon Keltner	1	3			4
[1029 ‡]	William Ratliff	1	2			3
[1030 ‡]	John Ratliff	1	3			4
[1031 ‡]	William Yocam	1	5			6
[1032 ‡]	Joshua Fisher	1	3			4
[1033 ‡]	Thomas Melton	1	1			2
[1034 ‡]	Joseph Fisher	1	4			5
[1035 ‡]	George Dammel	1	3			4
[1036 ‡]	James Fisher	2	3			5
[1037 ‡]	Tompson Ratliff	1	1			2
[1038 ‡]	Joab Ratliff	1	6			7
[1039 ‡]	Strauder Ball	1	6			7
[1040 ‡]	William Croy	1	2			3
[1041 ‡]	Joshua Croy	3	5			8
[1042 ‡]	Abner Enard	1	3			4
[1043*‡]	Allen Bridges	1	2			3
[1044 ‡]	Rowlin Shepherd	1	13			14
[1045]	Peter Shepherd	1	1			2
[1046 ‡]	Samuel Larn	1	13			14
[1047 ‡]	John Broad	1	3			4
[1048 ‡]	Moses Broad	2	5			7
[1049 ‡]	Dallis Scott	1	3			4
[1050 ‡]	William Davis	1	2			3
[1051 ‡]	Alexandria Pervines	1	2			3
[1052 ‡]	John Pervines	2	3			5
[1053 ‡]	Robert Willbern	1	8			9
[1054]	Henry Tenegar	1	5			6
[1055 ‡]	Daniel Mathis	1	2			3
[1056 ‡]	Absolem Mathis	1	6			7
[1057 ‡]	William Neal	1	6			7
[1058 ‡]	Robert Plant	1	2			3

MADISON COUNTY (Continued)

No.	Heads of families	White males 21 & over	All other white	Free people of color	Servants or slaves	Total
[1059 ‡]	John Clary	1	1			2
[1060 ‡]	William Clary	1	2			3
[1061 ‡]	John Clary	2	4			6
[1062 ‡]	Jesse Armstrong	1	5			6
[1063 ‡]	William Sampson	1				1
[1064]	Rhereh Clary	1	5			6
[1065]	George Harmon	1				1
[1066 ‡]	Robert Armstrong	3	5			8
[1067 ‡]	William Vermetre	1	8			9
[1068 ‡]	Joseph Lakons	1	1			2
[1069 ‡]	Soloman Pruitt	1	8			9
[1070 ‡]	Rial Potter	1	13			14
[1071*‡]	David Miller	2	3			5
[1072*‡]	Moses Miller	1	7			8
[1073 ‡]	Jacob Miller	1	5			6
[1074 ‡]	Solomon Miller	1	7			8
[1075 ‡]	James Miller	1	3			4
[1076 ‡]	John Raily	1	3			4
[1077 ‡]	William Walter	1	4			5
[1078]	Jesse Silvely	3	2			5
[1079 ‡]	John Penny	1	6			7
[1080*‡]	William Penny	2	4			6
[1081 ‡]	Robert Penny	1	6			7
[1082 ‡]	David Smith	1	4			5
[1083 ‡]	Abraham Sinard	1	6			7
[1084 ‡]	John Comeins	1	4			5
[1085 ‡]	Alexandria Reavis	1	4			5
[1086*‡]	Solomon Pearce	1	6			7
[1087 ‡]	Robert A. Pearce	2	11			13
[1088 ‡]	Edward Perkins	2	5			7
[1089 ‡]	Jeramiah Pearcifield	1	2			3
[1090 ‡]	William Kirkpartrack	1	5			6
[1091 ‡]	David Coy	1	2		1	4
[1092 ‡]	Abraham Carlock	1	10			11
[1093 ‡]	Isaac Carlock	1	4			5
[1094 ‡]	Margaret Kelloms		4			4
[1095 ‡]	Joseph Isbal	1	5			6
[1096 ‡]	Thomas Isbal	1	1			2

MADISON COUNTY (Continued)

No.	Heads of families	White males 21 & over	All other white	Free people of color	Servants or slaves	Total
[1097 ‡]	Elijah Putman	1	3			4
[1098 ‡]	Peter Lanterman	3	5			8
[1099 ‡]	John Lanterman	2	4			6
[1100 ‡]	Richard Dogit	1	5			6
[1101 ‡]	Henry Kelly	3	1			4
]1102 ‡]	John Kelly	1	5			6
]1103*‡]	Elijah Kelly	1	3			4
]1104 ‡]	William Kelly	1	9			10
[1105 ‡]	Andrew Elliott	1	3			4
[1106 ‡]	Jacob Ellis	1	9			10
[1107 ‡]	Levi Ellis	1	6			7
[1108 ‡]	John Linsey	1	8			9
[1109 ‡]	Samuel Little	2	7			9
[1110 ‡]	Archibald Turner	1	5			6
[1111*‡]	Stephen Pool	1	9			10
[1112 ‡]	John Glexen [?]	2	4			6
[1113 ‡]	John Pillars	1	6			7
[1114 ‡]	Joshua Brown	1	6			7
[1115]	Jonithan Emthan	1	9			10
[1116 ‡]	Shelton Alton	1	5			6
[1117]	David Scroxtable	1	4			5
[1118]	William Cahe	1				1
[1119*‡]	Moses Archer	1	3			4
[1120 ‡]	William Archer	2	6		1	9
[1121]	John Sims	1	2			3
[1122]	Abraham Duff	1	9			10
[1123*‡]	James Johnson	1	4			5
[1124 ‡]	William Vinson	1	3			4
[1125 ‡]	George Devenporte	1	7			8
[1126 ‡]	Isaac Parker	2	4			6
[1127]	David Ditson	1	4			5
[1128 ‡]	Jesse Ditson	1	4			5
[1129]	Jacob Kinney	2	10			12
[1130 ‡]	John Roberts	2	5			7
[1131 ‡]	Ansel Cox	2	3			5
[1132 ‡]	Joseph Buckhanon	1	10			11
[1133 ‡]	Michael Antle	1	9			10
[1134]	Semore Calogue	1	9			10

CENSUS OF 1820

MADISON COUNTY (Continued)

No.	Heads of families	White males 21 & over	All other white	Free people of color	Servants or slaves	Total
[1135]	Elisha Calogue	3	6			9
[1136 ‡]	James Card	1	3			4
[1137 ‡]	Samuel Shepherd	1	2			3
[1138 ‡]	Thomas Bristow	1	6			7
[1139 ‡]	Zechariah Keagmen	2	3			5
[1140 ‡]	Joseph Porter	2	2			4
[1141]	Reder Porter	1				1
[1142 ‡]	Guin Porter	1	6			7
[1143 ‡]	Thomas Arnet	1	4			5
[1144*‡]	Christopher Stubbins	2	6			8
[1145 ‡]	Aaron Willson	3	7			10
[1146]	Isaac Smith	1	2			3
[1147]	Moses Nash	1	4			5
[1148]	Joseph Cuddeting	2				2
[1149 ‡]	Isaac Reavis	1	8			9
[1150 ‡]	James Crain	2	2			4
[1151]	Ira Heady	1	3			4
[1152*‡]	Thomas Cowwich	1	8			9
[1153]	Samuel Mogget	2	1			3
[1154]	Stephen Umstead	2	3			5
[1155]	John Adams	2				2
[1156 ‡]	Abraham Williams	1	7			8
[1157 ‡]	Quillar Low	1	3			4
[1158 ‡]	Asa Smith	2	3			5
[1159 ‡]	Abraham Collins	3	5			8
[1160*]	Thomas Hambleton	1	3			4
[1161 ‡]	James Wood	1	8			9
[1162 ‡]	Jacob Baker	1	1			2
[1163]	Alfred Miller	1	8			9
[1164*‡]	John Thomas	1	3			4
[1165 ‡]	Jacob Anderson	2	8			10
[1166 ‡]	Jahue Shelly	2	7			9
[1167]	George Shills	1	1			2
[1168 ‡]	John Hatchison	1	3			4
[1169 ‡]	Samuel Hatchison	1	3			4
[1170]	Drury Rawlin	1	5			6
[1171 ‡]	John Fornestake	4	9			13
[1172]	Thomas Craly	1	3			4

MADISON COUNTY (*Continued*)

No.	Heads of families	White males 21 & over	All other white	Free people of color	Servants or slaves	Total
[1173 ‡]	John Pearcy	1	6			7
[1174 ‡]	Alexandria Wells	1	5			6
[1175]	Abbert Brown	1				1
[1176 ‡]	James Bruce	1	4			5
[1177 ‡]	Nathaniel Winters	1	3			4
[1178*‡]	Thomas Allen	1	7			8
[1179*‡]	Samuel Allen	1	5			6
[1180 ‡]	John Scott	2	8			10
[1181 ‡]	Michael Asherst	1	3			4
[1182 ‡]	James Tailor	1	3			4
[1183*‡]	David Barrow	1	8			9
[1184*‡]	John Barrow	1	4			5
[1185*‡]	Bekey Wason	2	2			4
[1186*‡]	John Allen	1	3			4
[1187*‡]	Richard Rattan	1	9			10
[1188 ‡]	Daniel Duvall	2	4			6
[1189*‡]	Isaac More	2	3			5
[1190 ‡]	Jacob Moore	1	2			3
[1191 ‡]	Clarke Beebe	3	2			5
[1192*‡]	James Pruitt	2	7			9
[1193*‡]	Francis Bell	1	8			9
[1194*‡]	William Morrow	2	7			9
[1195 ‡]	James Allen	1	1			2
[1196*‡]	Zachariah Allen	4	11		2	17
[1197]	David Markes	2	3			5
[1198]	Alven Case	1	1			2
[1199]	James Henderson	1	7			8
[1200 ‡]	William Thaxton	2	3			5
[1201]	Simeon Whitney	2	3			5
[1202 ‡]	John Stokes	1	3			4
[1203 ‡]	James Powel	1	7			8
[1204 ‡]	John Peake	1	2			3
[1205]	Jiles Carel	2	6			8
[1206 ‡]	James Mcnary	1	2			3
[1207 ‡]	James Rowlin	1	3			4
[1208]	Luke Waltrip	2	6			8
[1209 ‡]	William Waltrip	1	8			9
[1210 ‡]	Robert Whitiker	1	7			8

CENSUS OF 1820

MADISON COUNTY (Continued)

No.	Heads of families	White males 21 & over	All other white	Free people of color	Servants or slaves	Total
[1211 ‡]	Andrew Headen	1	7			8
[1212*‡]	Thomas Rattan	4	8		3	15
[1213*‡]	John Allen	1	4			5
[1214]	Isaac Stephens	2	2			4
[1215 ‡]	Thomas Allen	4	3			7
[1216]	John Hill	1	9			10
[1217 ‡]	Philip Fry	2	3			5
[1218 ‡]	John Cooper	1	5			6
[1219*‡]	John Drum	1	5			6
[1220 ‡]	John Blany	1	4			5
[1221 ‡]	Thomas Findley	1	4			5
[1222 ‡]	James Miller	2	7			9
[1223*]	Isaac Tailor	1	5			6
[1224*]	Benjamin Allen	1	3			4
[1225 ‡]	Robert Jackson	1	11			12
[1226]	John Thomas	1	11			12
[1227*]	James Dunn	1	2			3
[1228 ‡]	Thomas Lunley	1	7			8
[1229]	David Rodden	1	2			3
[1230 ‡]	James Nelson	1	6			7
[1231 ‡]	James Pinkerton	1	9			10
[1232 ‡]	Michael Headick	1	6			7
[1233*‡]	Alcey Pullham	1	9		3	13
[1234]	Abraham Cells	1	6			7
[1235 ‡]	Abraham Rush	1	3			4
[1236 ‡]	Joseph Reynolds	1	5			6
[1237*‡]	Watty Mcfarlin	1	3			4
[1238 ‡]	Buennet White	2	7			9
[1239*‡]	John Moore	1	9			10
[1240 ‡]	James Hambleton	1	5			6
[1241]	John Hill	1	2			3
[1242*]	Thomas Hall	1	2			3
[1243*]	John Stone	1	6			7
[1244*‡]	Charles Kitchins	1	5			6
[1245*‡]	John Collins	2	5			7
[1246*‡]	Samuel Thomas	1	3			4
[1247 ‡]	Absolem Clark	2	8			10
[1248*]	James Coldwell	2	7			9

MADISON COUNTY (*Continued*)

No.	Heads of families	White males 21 & over	All other white	Free people of color	Servants or slaves	Total
[1249]	Constantine Clarkson	1	5			6
[1250]	David Brazel	1	3			4
[1251*‡]	Arthel Honeycutt	1	12			13
[1252*‡]	Davis Carter	1	4			5
[1253*‡]	John Wilkins	1	4			5
[1254*‡]	Jacob Lerton	2	9		3	14
[1255*‡]	Daniel Parkison	1	6			7
[1256*‡]	John Cooper	1	8			9
[1257 ‡]	William Brag	1	3			4
[1258 ‡]	Jacob Cooper	1	1			2
[1259*‡]	Bennet Nowlin	1	5			6
[1260 ‡]	Justus Hinkle	2	15			17
[1261]	Elijah Hinkle	1	1			2
[1262 ‡]	Robert Davis	1	3			4
[1263 ‡]	David Cannon	1	6			7
[1264 ‡]	Henry Nelly	1	1			2
[1265 ‡]	Martin Baker	1	3			4
[1266 ‡]	Joseph Nelly	1	7			8
[1267 ‡]	William Baker	1	2			3
[1268 ‡]	William Nelson	1	7			8
[1269 ‡]	Henry Funderburth	2	7			9
[1270 ‡]	Daniel Liles	1	7			8
[1271 ‡]	James Toddle	1	3			4
[1272 ‡]	William Scott	1	4			5
[1273 ‡]	Jacob Rape	1	3			4
[1274 ‡]	Peter Rape	1	3			4
[1275 ‡]	Joseph Firguson	1	3			4
[1276*‡]	John Firguson	1	6			7
[1277 ‡]	William Firguson	2	2			4
[1278*‡]	Alston Firguson	1	3			4
[1279 ‡]	Joseph Dickson	1	9			10
[1280 ‡]	Mason Lowrler	2	9			11
[1281]	Federic Wise	1	1			2
[1282 ‡]	John Rutherford	1	3			4
[1283 ‡]	Henry Goodon	1	4			5
[1284]	Elihu Dalen	2	2			4
[1285*‡]	James Snodgrass	1	4			5
[1286*‡]	James Snodgrass	1	7			8

CENSUS OF 1820   171

MADISON COUNTY (Continued)

No.	Heads of families	White males 21 & over	All other white	Free people of color	Servants or slaves	Total
[1287*‡]	Ribers Carmel	2	7			9
[1288*‡]	James Simmons	2	5			7
[1289*‡]	Israel Turner	1	3			4
[1290*‡]	Robert Stice	1	4			5
[1291]	Rebecca Vinny		9			9
[1292*‡]	Daniel Moore	2	4			6
[1293 ‡]	Jacob Grage	1	5			6
[1294 ‡]	Daniel Good	1	2			3
[1295]	Hardin Patterson	1	2			3
[1296 ‡]	Isaac Perkins	1	3			4
[1297 ‡]	Martin Hennis	1	3			4
[1298 ‡]	John Sinnet	1	2			3
[1299 ‡]	Flebin Mattis	1	6			7
[1300*‡]	Titus Grage	2	9			11
[1301 ‡]	William Montgomery	1	6			7
[1302 ‡]	Aaron Holey	1	3			4
[1303]	Olaver Stotton	1	4			5
[1304]	John Morice	3	5			8
[1305 ‡]	James McCoy	1	4			5
[1306 ‡]	Readman Striman	1	3			4
[1307 ‡]	Henry Giger	1	1			2
[1308 ‡]	Benjamin Campbell	1	1			2
[1309 ‡]	Benjamin Cherry	1	1			2
[1310 ‡]	Witte Stritlen	1	3			4
[1311 ‡]	Asa Scroud	1	7			8
[1312]	Simeon Scroud	1				1
[1313 ‡]	Philip Clarke	5				5
[1314]	Charles Mcnut	1				1
[1315 ‡]	William Roberts	1	5			6
[1316 ‡]	Joseph Lorton	1	2			3
[1317 ‡]	Robert Satley	1	2			3
[1318 ‡]	Solomon Francis	1	2			3
[1319 ‡]	Isaac Parker	2	4			6
[1320 ‡]	Reubin Berdin	3	5			8
[1321*‡]	John Warrick	3	5			8
[1322*]	William Shelton	4	7			11
[1323 ‡]	Andrew Roberts	1	2			3
[1324 ‡]	James Bowlen	1	3			4

MADISON COUNTY (Continued)

No.	Heads of families	White males 21 & over	All other white	Free people of color	Servants or slaves	Total
[1325 ‡]	John Gragg	1	1			2
[1326 ‡]	Ansel Hubbard	1	8			9
[1327*‡]	Josiah Comins	2	6			8
[1328]	Biram Kinney	1	5			6
[1329 ‡]	Peter Gunterman	1	3			4
[1330 ‡]	Daniel Mcfamd	1	4			5
[1331 ‡]	John Smith	1	3			4
[1332]	John Powel	2	8			10
[1333*‡]	John Medford	2	7			9
[1334*‡]	Thomas Firguson	1	1			2
[1335 ‡]	John Gunterman	1	1			2
[1336 ‡]	John Gunterman	1	2			3
[1337*]	Moses Evlin	1	6			7
[1338*‡]	Levi Roberts	2	3			5
[1339]	Samuel Mcdurum	1	1			2
[1340 ‡]	Mason Cockram	1	1			2
[1341*‡]	John Evlin	3	10			13
[1342 ‡]	Ebenezer Smith	1	5			6
[1343]	David Lindley	1	3			4
[1344 ‡]	Samuel Gates	1	6			7
[1345 ‡]	David Dutton	1	3			4
[1346 ‡]	Daniel Church	1	6			7
[1347 ‡]	John M. Smith	1				1
[1348*]	John Shaw	1				1
[1349 ‡]	Nathaniel Shaw	1	1			2
[1350]	Hiram Warde	1	3			4
[1351 ‡]	William Mattis	1	6			7
[1352 ‡]	John Mattis	1	3			4
[1353 ‡]	John Curtis	1	4			5
[1354]	Silas Westfield	2				2
[1355]	Elizabeth Morin		5			5
[1356 ‡]	Richard Diley	1	5			6
[1357]	John Battel	1	3			4
[1358]	Lewis Battel	1	2			3
[1359*‡]	Antwine Desily	1	6			7
[1360 ‡]	John Richy	1	5			6
[1361]	John Pickly	1				1
[1362 ‡]	Richard Dickison	1				1

MADISON COUNTY (Continued)

No.	Heads of families	White males 21 & over	All other white	Free people of color	Servants or slaves	Total
[1363]	James Titball	1				1
[1364]	James Hill	1				1
[1365 ‡]	Ephraim Egerster	2	6			8
[1366]	James Moore	1				1
[1367]	James Crandal	1				1
[1368]	James Vancraft	1				1
[1369 ‡]	Martin Linsley	3	3			6
[1370*‡]	James Smith	2	1			3
[1371]	Polite Moze	1	5			6
[1372]	Francis Roy	1	6			7
[1373 ‡]	David Gilbert	1	3			4
[1374 ‡]	David Criswell	4	5			9
[1375]	Daniel Hayns	1	4			5
[1376]	Rachel Wardsworth		5			5
[1377]	William Nash	1	2			3
[1378 ‡]	John Boalter	1	3			4
[1379]	John Buoyar	1	8			9
[1380 ‡]	Benjamin Mcentire	1	5			6
[1381 ‡]	Thomas Little	1	8			9
[1382 ‡]	William Read	2	3			5
[1383 ‡]	Jonithan Mayland	1				1
[1384*‡]	Levi Scott	1	4			5
[1385*‡]	Jesse Enness	1	3			4
[1386*‡]	John Quigley	1	4			5
[1387 ‡]	Luther Calvin	2	8			10
[1388]	Hugh Miller	2	1			3
[1389]	John Simons	1	6			7
[1390]	John Cain	1				1
[1391*‡]	James Beaman	3	8		1	12
[1392*]	Andrew Paton	1	4			5
[1393]	George Allen	1	1			2
[1394 ‡]	Henry B Ragan	1				1
[1395*‡]	Benjamin Sidman	2	9			11
[1396]	Aden E Mitchum	1	1			2
[1397]	John Ruthorford	1	4			5
[1398]	William B. Crowder	1	6			7
[1399 ‡]	Daniel Wise	1	1			2
[1400*‡]	John Green	2	4			6

MADISON COUNTY (Continued)

No.	Heads of families	White males 21 & over	All other white	Free people of color	Servants or slaves	Total
[1401*‡]	Moses Findley	1	2			3
[1402 ‡]	John Huitt	4	4			8
[1403 ‡]	Tempel Nick	1	2			3
[1404*‡]	Nellis Cheak	1	5			6
[1405*‡]	John Franklin	1	5			6
[1406 ‡]	Margaret Lions		6			6
[1407]	Matthew Moss	1	2			3
[1408 ‡]	Samuel Hill	1	2			3
[1409*‡]	Ephraim Wood	1	8			9
[1410*‡]	James Tunnell	2	2			4
[1411*]	Jacob Linder	1	8			9
[1412*‡]	Sampson Wood	1	1			2
[1413 ‡]	Robert Cottet	18	3		3	24
[1414*‡]	Young Wood	1	3			4
		2070	6338	45	96	8549

YOUNG WOOD Com

Corrected totals:

    Free white males of 21 years and upwards   2064

    All other white inhabitants   6317

         8381

    Negroes   141

        Free persons of color   45

        Servants or slaves   96

         141

    Total   8522

CENSUS OF 1820

MADISON COUNTY (Continued)

Madison County was the largest county of Illinois in 1820, comprising all the territory north of St. Clair County and west of Bond, with the most densely populated part of the state in the present county of Madison, and the rest of its population widely scattered in small settlements reaching as far north as the present Springfield. It is hardly surprising then, to find that the state census taken by Young Wood and the federal census taken by Thomas Reynolds differ considerably. The state census reports a total of 1,414 families with a total population of 8,522, while the federal census reports 2,021 families with a total population of 13,550. However, the federal census figures are undoubtedly padded, three pages with a total of 76 names being repeated with minor variations as to spelling and the population data; many other names appear two or three times and some of these are undoubtedly repetitions; furthermore, where names correspond in the two schedules, the federal census usually shows larger families than the state (6.7 per family in federal—6.03 per family in state). It is probably safe to deduct at least 100 families and 500 persons from the federal census figures for repetitions alone. However, the federal enumerator did visit many localities which were missed by the state enumerator. Among the townships where a large percentage of the population was missed by Wood are: Goshen, Bounty Land, Springfield, Six Mile Prairie, Edwardsville, Ridge Prairie, Greenfield, and Fork Prairie. In other words, he confined himself to the more densely populated regions. Wood, on the other hand, lists 254 names which have not been identified with names in the federal census. Of these, forty appear in the 1818 census. Forty-four names from the 1818 census are found only in the federal census. Except for a small group of names beginning with No. 1354, however, these names are interlarded between those found in both enumerations, indicating that he probably did not visit any localities not visited by Reynolds. Furthermore, Reynolds was evidently more familiar with the names than Wood, who spelled phonetically, and in places where both men visited neighborhoods in somewhat the same order it is nearly always possible to make the names, even though spelled differently or even at first thought different names, coincide. These differences are pointed out in the notes. With these discrepancies it is difficult to estimate the actual population of Madison County for 1820, but it seems likely that it was not over 1,900 families with a total population of about 11,000 to 11,500.

Discrepancies are as follows:

5 Rines, William
   1818. Ryan, William
   F1820. Ryans, William
6 Gillham, John
   1818. Gilham, John
   F1820. Gillham, John
7 Dunigan, Ann
   1818. Dunagan, Ann
   F1820. Danogin, Anne
   This name is given twice in the federal census, first as a resident of Ridge Prairie and second as a resident of Greenfield. Probably the same woman.
9 Davidson, Thomas
   1818. Davidson, Thomas
   F1820. Davidson, Thomas G.
10 Gillham, David
   F1820. Gilham, David M.
15 Pulham, Robert
   F1820. Pullem and Pullam, Robert
   Name repeated.
16 Stout, Christley
   1818. Stout, Christopher
   F1820. Stout, Christopher

17 Cowin, Matthew
   1818. Cowen, Matthew
   F1820. Cowan, Matthew
18 Sinclair, Robert
   F1820. St. Clair, Robert
21 Gillham, Samuel
   1818. Gilham, Samuel
   F1820. Gillham, Samuel
22 Denny, Prissilly
   F1820. Dennis, Priscilly and Dennis, Pricilia. Name repeated.
23 Davice, Thomas
   F1820. Davis, Thomas
24 Lewis, John
   1818. Louis, John
   F1820. Louis, John
25 Bergess, Thomas
   F1820. Burgess, Thomas
28 Croom, Daniel
   F1820. Crum, Daniel
30 Tiffin, Claiton
   F1820. Tiffin, Clayton
31 Root, Benjamin
   F1820. Root, Benjamine

MADISON COUNTY (Continued)

32 Brown, Clade
    1818. Brown, Chad
    F1820. Brown, Chad
34 Tailor, Armstead
    F1820. Taylor, Amsterd
36 Langworthy, Rodolphus
    1818. Langworthy, Reodolphus
39 Rian, John
    F1820. Ryan, John
43 Hart, Alexandria
    F1820. Hart, Alexander
44 Bany, Robert A.
    F1820. Bane, Robert A.
46 Delaplane, Samuel
    1818. Delaplane, Samuel
    F1820. Deleplain, Samuel
49 Whiswell, John R.
    F1820. Wiswall, John R.
50 Maxey, Buennet
    F1820. Maxey, Bennett
52 Hodges, Ebenezer
    1818. Hodges, Ebenezer
    F1820. Hodge, Ebenezer
54 Mcaester, Mary
    F1820. McCaster, Mary
55 Brown, Jonithan
    1818. Brown, Jonathan
    F1820. Brown, Jonathan
57 Woodbourn, Isaac
    F1820. Woodburn, Isaac
62 Carlin, James
    1818. Carland, James
63 Vaughn, Joseph
    1818. Vaughn, Josiah
    F1820. Vaughn, Josiah
64 Breden, James
    F1820. Breton, James
65 Pruitt, Abraham
    1818. Pruitt, Abram
    F1820. Pruitt, Abraham
68 Swinington, James G.
    1818. Swinerton, James G.
    F1820. Swenerton, James G.
74 Wallis, John
    1818. Wallace, John
    F1820. Wallace, John
78 Caiman, Samuel
    1818. Beeman, Samuel
    F1820. Beeman, Samuel
79 Johnson, Daniel
    F1820. Johnston, Daniel
83 Langworthy, Agustus
    F1820. Langworthy, Augustus

84 Gillham, Isham
    1818. Gilham, Isham
    F1820. Gilham, Isom
85 Hopkison, Henry
    F1820. Hopkinson, Henry
88 Beamon, Ormon
    1818. Beeman, Orman
    F1820. Beeman, Orman
89 Suton, Aaron
    1818. Sutton, Aaron
    F1820. Sutton, Aaron
90 Coalman, Robert
    F1820. Coleman, Robert
94 Pruitt, Soloman
    1818. Pruitt, Solomon
    F1820. Pruitt, Solomon
95 Pruitt, Dorotha
    F1820. Pruitt, Dolley
96 West, Emanual
    F1820. West, Emanuel J.
    The name appears twice in the federal census, first in Wood River and then in Six Mile Prairie. Probably the same man.
97 Russel, John
    F1820. Russell, John
98 and 101 Wright, Benjamin and Jeremiah
    In the federal census in the same locality two Wrights were listed, Ison and George. Though the numbers do not correspond the families are probably the same.
99 Starky, Jesse
    1818. Starky, Jessee
    F1820. Starky, Jessee
100 Starky, John
    1818. Starky, John
    F1820. Starkey, John
103 Deades, Jacob
    1818. Deeds, Jacob
    F1820. Deeds, Jacob
107 Write, William
    1818. Right, William
    F1820. Wright, William
111 Cawley, William
    F1820. Calvey, William W.
113 Woolams, Absolem
    F1820. Woolens, Absalon
114 Yorke, William
    1818. York, William
117 Wiatt, John
    F1820. Wyatt, John
118 Waggoner, Peter
    1818. Waggoner, Petter
    F1820. Waggoner, Peter

CENSUS OF 1820

MADISON COUNTY (Continued)

121 Rows, John
    1818. Rose, John
    F1820. Rose, John
123 Harvel, Squire
    F1820. Horvell, Squire
124 Archer, Cavel
    F1820. Archer, Covill
125 Harrel, Charles
    F1820. Harrel, Charles W.
126 Chandler, Isaac
    1818. Chandler, Isaac
    F1820. Chanler, Isaac
128 Mcafee, Kerenhappuch
    1818. McAfee, Carry Happy
    F1820. McKee, Happa
130 Thaxton, Larkin
    F1820. Thockson, Larkin
132 Moore, George
    1818. Moore, George
    F1820. Moor, George
137 Head, Henery
    F1820. Head, Henry
138 Delaplane, Joshua
    1818. Delaplane, Joshua
    F1820. Deleplain, Joshua
139 Robertson, John
    1818. Robinson, John
    F1820. Robertson, John
141 Robertson, James
    1818. Robinson, John
    F1820. Robinson, John
142 Corhern, Hugh S.
    F1820. Cochrane, Hugh S.
147 Gillham, William
    1818. Gilham, William
    F1820. Gilham, William
148 Atwaters, Joshua
    1818. Atwater, Joshua
    F1820. Atwater, Joshua
149 Sealy, Walter J.
    1818. Seely, Walter J.
    F1820. Seely, Walter J.
151 Bell, Jesse
    1818. Belle, Jessee
    F1820. Bell, Jessee
152 Gillham, Isaac
    1818. Gilham, Isaac
    F1820. Gilham, Isaac
154 Luske, John T.
    1818. Lusk, John T.
    F1820. Lusk, John T.
158 Roy, Scene
    F1820. Roy, Charles

159 Wright, James
    1818. Right, James
    F1820. Wright, James
160 Hageler, Cleavland
    1818. Hagler, Cleveland
161 Delaplane, John
    1818. Delaplane, John
    F1820. Deleplain, John
162 Coldwell, George
    F1820. Caldwell, George
163 Lollis, William
    1818. Lawless, William
    F1820. Lawless, William
164 Bonner, Henery
    1818. Bonner, Henry
    F1820. Bonner, Henry
169 Vicary, John
    1818. Vickory, John
    F1820. Vickery, John
171 Arnet, John
    F1820. Arnett, John
173 Davis, Denny
    1818. Davis, Dennis
    F1820. Davis, Dennis
174 Bacon, Ira W.
    F1820. Bacon, Ira
175 Adams, Willaby
    F1820. Adams, William
178 Biram, Alexandria S.
    1818. Byran, Alexnr
    F1820. Byrum, Alexander
179 Wood, Isaac
    F1820. Woods, Isaac
181 Newman, Zadok
    1818. Newman, Zadock
    F1820. Newman, Zedock
183 Jackson, Shadrach
    F1820. Jackson, Shade
187 Whitlock, Henery
    F1820. Whitlock, Henry
189 Mahurin, Samuel
    F1820. Mahuel, Samuel
190 Ennis, William
    F1820. Enes, William
191 Shorte, Stepen
    F1820. Short, Stephen
195 Pearce, James S.
    F1820. Pierce, James
196 Parke, James
    1818. Parks, James
    F1820. Park, James
197 Boner, Alexandria
    1818. Bonner, Alexander

MADISON COUNTY (Continued)

198 Bace, James
    1818. Bates, James
    F1820. Bates, James
199 Cook, Henery
    1818. Cook, Henry
    F1820. Cook, Henry
200 Akeman, David
    1818. Aikman, David
    F1820. Aikman, David
201 Hocksey, William
    1818. Hocksey, William
    F1820. Hoxey, William
204 Hayter, Abraham
    1818. Hayter, Abraham
    F1820. Hiter, Abraham
205 Handlon, Mathias
    F1820. Hanley, Nathias
206 Whiteside, Joel
    1818. Whitesides, Uel
207 Reviss, Henery
    1818. Reavis, Henry
    F1820. Revis, Henry
208 Gunterman, Jacob
    1818. Guntryman, Jacob
    F1820. Gunterman, Jacob
212 Bartlet, Joseph
    1818. Bartlett, Joseph
    F1820. Bartlett, Joseph
213 Snodgrass, Joseph
    1818. Snotgrass, Joseph
    F1820. Snodgrass, Joseph
214 Tailor, Edward
    1818. Taylor, Edward
    F1820. Taylor, Edward
216 Starke, Jesse
    F1820. Stark, Jesse
217 Fruit, Edward
    1818. Fruitt, Edmund
    F1820. Fruit, Edmond
219 Gillham, James
    1818. Gilham, James
    F1820. Gilham, James
220 Sanders, Hanner
    1818. Saunders, George
    F1820. Sandress, Hannah and Sanders, Hanna. Name repeated.
221 Tompson, William
    1818. Thompson, William
    F1820. Thompson, William
222 Waddle, Obediah
    1818 and F1820. Waddle, Obadiah
223 Tompson, James
    1818. Thompson, James
    F1820. Thompson, James
224 Smith, Theopholus W.
    F1820. Smith, Theopholas
226 Metty, James
    1818. Metta, James
    F1820. Mettee, Jacques
228 Wood, Samuel
    1818. Woods, Samuel
231 Whiteside, Robert
    1818. Whitesides, Robert
    F1820. Whitesides, Robert
234 Bridgers, George
    1818. Bridges, George
    F1820. Bridges, George
236 Hendershot, David
    1818. Hendershot, David
    F1820. Hendershott, David
237 Denny, Watel
    F1820. Daney, Walter
240 Herren, John
    1818. Herron, John
    F1820. Herron, John
243 Odle, Caleb
    F1820. Odell, Calot
244 Harrass, Jonithan L.
    1818. Harris, Jonathan L.
    F1820. Harris, Jonathan L.
245 Harrass, Adley
    1818. Harris, Adley
    F1820. Harris, Adloc
246 Harrass, Edwin
    F1820. Harris, Ervin
247 Gingles, Elizabeth
    1818. Jingles, Elizabeth
    F1820. Ingles, Elizabeth
248 Harrass, John
    F1820. Harris, John
250 Harrass, Robert W.
    F1820. Harris, Robert W.
251 Gullet, Ebeniah
    1818. Gullick, Beniah
    F1820. Gullick, Beniah
254 Gullet, John
    F1820. Gullick, John
255 Gullet, Ira
    F1820. Gullick, Ira
256 Ramsey, James
    1818. Ramsey, James
    F1820. Ransey, James
257 Ramsey, William
    F1820. Ranscy, James
258 Craigg, Robert
    1818. Craig, Robert
    F1820. Craig, Robert

CENSUS OF 1820 179

MADISON COUNTY (*Continued*)

259 Berry, John M.
    1818. Berry, John
    F1820. Berry, John
260 Good, James
    1818. Good, James
    F1820. Good, Jonas
261 Dunkin, Joseph
    1818. Duncan, Joseph
    F1820. Duncan, Joseph
262 Grace, Joseph
    F1820. Gracia, Joseph
263 Gear, John
    F1820. Gracie, John
264 Hunter, Elizabeth
    F1820. Hunter, Elisabeth
265 Parkison, William
    1818. Parkerson, William
    F1820. Parkison, William
266 Whiteside, Nancy
    F1820. Whitesides, Nancy
269 Tollman, Daniel
    F1820. Tolman, Daniel
277 Larkin, Edward
    1818. Larkins, Edward
    F1820. Larkins, Edward
279 Stockton, David
    1818. Stockton, Davis
    F1820. Stocton, Davis
280 Gribbins, James
    1818. Gribbin, James
    F1820. Griblens, James
282 Coonrod, George
    1818. Coonrad, George
    F1820. Coonrad, George
283 Stean, James
    1818. Steen, James
    F1820. Steen, James
285 Desherly, Charles
    1818. Dezurley, Charles
    F1820. Desherley, Charles
286 Neles, Daniel
    F1820. Daniel, Nicholas
287 Mar, Louis
    1818. Mars, Louis
    F1820. Lamorse, Lewis, Sr.
289 Royboalt, Rachael
    1818. Runbolt, Rachel
    F1820. Rybolt, Richard
290 Dieumy, Francis
    F1820. Dio, Pierre
291 Borney, John
    F1820. Borna, Jacob
293 Aston, William
    1818. Astin, William
    F1820. Asten, William

294 Patongill, Daniel
    1818. Petingill, Daniel
    F1820. Patengale, Daniel
295 Vickmore, Patsey
    F1820. Beckmore, Martha
297 Stallians, Samuel
    1818. Stallings, Samuel
    F1820. Stallion, Samuel
298 Stallians, John
    1818. Stallings, John
    F1820. Stallians, John
299 Stallians, William
    F1820. Stallion, William
301 Diou, Francis
    F1820. Dira, Francis
305 Grayham, George
    F1820. Graham, George
306 Emerich, Henery
    1818. Emmertt, Henry
    F1820. Emeret, Henry
310 Adkins, John
    1818. Adkins, John
    F1820. Atkins, John, Sr.
312 Cadwell, Elisha
    F1820. Cadwell, Abijah
317 Labour, Partrach
    F1820. Lawler, Patrick
318 Merit, Benjamin
    1818. Merritt, Benj.
    F1820. Merritt, Benjamin
320 Movill, John
    F1820. Movell, John
321 Court, William
    F1820. Cort, William
323 Wimon, George
    F1820. Wineman, George
325 Cobic, Philip
    F1820. Carloo, Philip
327 Shin, Charles
    1818. Simms, Charles
    F1820. Simms, Charles
328 Merit, Benjamin
    F1820. Merett, Benjamin
332 Clarke, John
    1818. Clark, John
    F1820. Clark, John
333 Kinder, Voluntine
    F1820. Kinder, Volentine
335 Davidson, John
    1818. Davidson, John
    F1820. Davidson, John, Sr.
336 Gillham, James
    1818. Gilham, James
    F1820. Gilham, James

MADISON COUNTY (Continued)

338 Rice, Thomas
    F1820. Rice, Thomas K.
339 Joab, Robert
    F1820. Jobe, Robert
340 Laughlin, Alexandria
    1818. Laughlin, Alexn
    F1820. Laughlin, Alexander
341 Gillham, Thomas
    1818. Gilham, Thomas
    F1820. Gilham, Thomas
342 Gillham, Isaac
    1818. Gilham, Isaac
    F1820. Gilham, Isaac
343 Gillham, William
    1818. Gilham, William
    F1820. Gilham, William
344 Hawk, John
    1818. Hawks, John
    F1820. Hawk, John
345 Hawk, Philip
    1818. Hawks, Philip
    F1820. Hawk, Philip
347 Wadle, William
    F1820. Woodall, William
349 Adkins, William
    1818. Adkin, William
    F1820. Atkins, William
350 Johnson, Thomas
    1818. Johnson, Thomas
    F1820. Johnston, Thomas
351 Adkins, John
    F1820. Atkins, John, Jr.
352 Dare, Matthew
    1818. Dair, Matthew
    F1820. Dar, Mathew
357 Emiett, Andrew
    1818. Emmett, Andrew
    F1820. Emret, Andrew
361 Hickey, John
    F1820. Hickle, John
362 Miller, Marget
    F1820. Miller, Margaretta
363 Gooen, William
    1818. Goings, William
    F1820. Going, William
364 Sippy, Abraham
    1818. Sippi, Abraham
    F1820. Sippe, Abraham
368 Bishop, Rodah
    1818. Bishop, Rhody
    F1820. Bishop, Rhody
369 Waddle, Jesse
    1818. Waddle, Jessee
370 McDonel, Daniel
    F1820. McDaniel, Daniel

373 Gilham, Clamons
    1818. Gilham, Clement
377 Morison, Nathaniel
    F1820. Morrison, Nathaniel
381 Diliplane, Benjamin
    1818. Delaplane, Benj.
    F1820. Deleplain and Diliplane (name repeated), Benjamin
382 Hoosong, Daniel
    F1820. Husong, Daniel
383 Otwell, William
    1818. Ottwell, William
    F1820. Otwell, William
385 Diliplane, John
    1818. Delaplane, John
    F1820. Deleplain, John
387 Bradshaw, Nancy
    1818. Bradshaw, Ann
    F1820. Bradshaw, Anne
388 Nix, David
    1818. Nix, David
    F1820. Nix, Davis
390 Whiteside, William B.
    1818. Whitesides, William B.
    F1820. Whitesides, William B.
392 Reynolds, Robert
    1818. Reynold, Robert
    F1820. Reynolds, Robert, Jr.
394 Reynolds, Robert
    1818. Reynolds, Robert, Sr.
    F1820. Reynolds, Robert, Sr.
399 Barnet, John
    1818. Barnett, John
    F1820. Barnett, John C.
400 Alexandria, Nelson
    1818. Alexander, Nelson
    F1820. Alexander, Nelson
402 Sherman, Lewis
    F1820. Shearman, Lurana
403 Sherman, Joab
    F1820. Shearman, Job J.
404 Hauskins, Lemmons
    F1820. Haskin, Samuel
405 Vaughn, Sarah
    F1820. Vaughn, Sally
410 Colene, Francis
    1818. Coleen, Francis
    F1820. Colene, Francis
412 Chandler, Isaac
    F1820. Chandlier, Isaac
415 Grots, Sarah
    1818. Groats, Sarah
    F1820. Grafts, Sally

MADISON COUNTY (Continued)

416 Moore, Thomas
    1818. More, Thomas
    F1820. Moore, Thomas
417 Carnes, William
    1818. Kerns, William
    F1820. Carnes, William
418 Adkins, William
    F1820. Atkins, William, Jr.
420 Marter, Peter
    1818. Martin, Peter
    F1820. Martin, Pierre
421 Mares, Peter
    F1820. Marso, Pierre
422 Joneroy, Batist
    1818. Janderow, Baptiste
    F1820. Jondra, Baptiste
425 Me Me
    F1820. Meme, Baptiste
428 Mathers, Elijah
    1818. Matthers, Elihue
    F1820. Mather, Elihu
431 Casslin, Jonithan
    1818. Casterline, Jonathan
    F1820. Casterlan, Jonathan
432 Smith, Hanna
    1818. Smith, Hanna
    F1820. Smith, Hannah
434 Manan, Thomas
    1818. Mannen, Thomas
    F1820. Mamnon, Thomas
435 Harland, George
    F1820. Harlin, George
436 Squirs, Michael
    1818. Squires, Michael
    F1820. Squires, Michael
438 Pritchit, Elisha
    1818. Pritchard, Abisha
    F1820. Prichard, Abisha
439 Moorehead, Richard
    F1820. Morehead, Richard
440 Buennet, William
    F1820. Bennett, William
441 Wright, Abner
    1818. Right, Abner
    F1820. Wright, Abner
445 Read, James
    F1820. Reed, James
447 Beag, Henry
    1818. Beck, Henry
451 Teter, Philip
    1818. Teeter, Philip
    F1820. Teters, Philip
452 Scantlin, Gideon
    F1820. Scandland, Gideon

453 Debond, George
    1818. Debond, George
    F1820. De Bom, George
456 Coneway, Jesse
    1818. Conoway, Jessee
    F1820. Conoway, Jesse
457 Johnson, Benjamin
    F1820. Johnston, Benjamin
458 McFearson, James
    F1820. McPhearson, James
460 Kelly, Abner O.
    1818. Kelly, Abnor O.
    F1820. Kelly, Abner O.
461 Tailor, Henry
    1818. Taylor, Henry
462 Pozia, Jubilee
    1818. Posey, Jubilee
464 Guthery, Beverley
    1818. Guthrie, Beverly
    F1820. Guthrie, Beverly
465 Guthery, Dempsey
    1818. Guthrie, Dempsey
    F1820. Guthrie, Demcy
466 Guthery, William
    F1820. Guthrie, William
467 Batterton, Amos
    1818. Batterton, Moses
    F1820. Battelton, Amos
468 Hadely, John
    F1820. Hadley, John
469 Eves, Benjamin
    1818. Eves, Benj.
    F1820. Eaves, Benjamin
470 Haker, John
    1818. Hawker, John
    F1820. Hawker, John
472 Whitsid, Joel
    1818. Whitesides, Joel
    F1820. Whiteside, Joel
473 Armstrong, Aaron
    1818. Armstrong, Aron
    F1820. Armstrong, Aaron
474 Aarstrong, Sasanah
    1818. Armstrong, Susanah
    F1820. Armstrong, Susannah
477 Barnesback, Gorge
    1818. Barnsback, George
    F1820. Barnsback, George
479 Gilerland, Thomas
    F1820. Gillerland, Thomas
480 Holady, Misalent
    1818. Holliday, Milicent
481 Barber, John
    1818. Barbour, John
    F1820. Barber, John

MADISON COUNTY (*Continued*)

483 Write, Josiah
    F1820. Wright, Josias
485 Coffin, Harris
    F1820. Coffman, Harris
486 Blacburn, John
    1818. Blackburn, John
    F1820. Blackburn, John
489 Borow, Joseph
    1818. Borough, Joseph
    F1820. Borough, Joseph
490 Lampkins, Jeptha
    1818. Lampkins, Jopthah
    F1820. Lampkins, Jeptha
493 Johnson, Samuel
    F1820. Johnston, Samuel
495 Larrence, Jesey
    F1820. Lawrence, Jessee
496 Walls, Thomas
    1818. Wall, Thomas
    F1820. Walls, Thomas
497 Tindol, Charles
    1818. Tindal, Charles
    F1820. Tindle, Charles
498 Wright, James
    1818. Right, James
    F1820. Wright, James, Jr.
500 Hammont, Samuel
    F1820. Hamilton, Samuel
501 Rushes, Niclis
    F1820. Russel, Nicholas
502 Dalton, Ishom
    F1820. Dalton, Isham
503 Owins, John
    1818. Owings, John
    F1820. Owens, John
504 Winser, Jephe
    F1820. Windsor, Jeptha
507 Pharris, James
    1818. Pharis, James
    F1820. Farris, James, Jr.
508 Herington, John
    1818. Herrington, John
    F1820. Herrington, John
509 Read, Samuel
    F1820. Reed, Samuel
510 Sibool, Robert
    1818. Seybold, Robert
    F1820. Sybold, Robert
511 Sibool, Samuel
    1818. Seybold, Samuel
    F1820. Sybold, Samuel
512 Pervines, William
    1818. Parviance, William
    F1820. Purvines, William

513 Harman, William
    F1820. Harmon, William
515 Gaskil, S. T. Venas
    1818. Gaskill, Sylvanus
    F1820. Gaskill, Sylvenus
517 Kermack, Lewis
    F1820. Cormack, Lewis
518 Gaskil, David
    1818. Gaskill, David
    F1820. Gaskill, David
519 McMahan, Robert
    1818. McMahan, Robert
    F1820. McMahan, Robert, Jr.
520 Hall, Easther
    F1820. Hall, Eastor
521 Beard, William
    1818. Baird, William
    F1820. Beaird, William
522 Gillet, Limon
    F1820. Jillet, Lemon
524 Renshaw, Abraham
    F1820. Renshaw, Absalom
525 Renfrow, Margaret
    1818. Renfro, Margerett
    F1820. Rentfrew, Margaret
526 Renfrow, Joseph
    F1820. Rentfrow, Joseph
527 Yates, Jesse
    F1820. Yates, Jessee
535 Hall, William
    1818. Hall, William
    F1820. Hall, William, Sr.
537 Matice, George
    F1820. Mathis, George
538 Eldrid, Warde
    F1820. Eldrid, Ward
539 Eldrid, William
    F1820. Eldred, William
542 Moore, David
    1818. Moore, David
    F1820. Moor, David
544 Clarke, Isaac
    1818. Clark, Isaac
    F1820. Clark, Isaac
545 Eldrid, Jehosifat
    F1820. Eldred, Jehoshephat
546 Hodge, Seth
    1818. Hodges, Seth
549 Clarke, Lucy
    F1820. Clarke, William
550 Hall, William
    F1820. Hall, William, Jr.
551 Vanhoser, Abraham
    1818. Vanhooser, Abraham, Sr.
    F1820. Van Hooser, Abraham

MADISON COUNTY (*Continued*)

552 Robertson, Joab
    F1820. Robertson, Job
553 Etter, Peter
    F1820. Eter, Peter
554 Rice, Daniel D.
    F1820. Dedricks, Daniel
555 Reaves, Isaac
    F1820. Rieves, Isaac
556 Atison, Richard
    F1820. Haduson, Richard
557 Wats, James
    1818. Watt, James
    F1820. Watts, James
558 Denton, Jonithan
    F1820. Denton, Jonathan
559 Conley, Alexandria
    1818. Conly, Alexander
    F1820. Conley, Alexander
561 Conley, Hesley
    1818. Conley, Hesse
    F1820. Conley, Hesey
564 Dunkin, Rice
    F1820. Duncan, Rice
568 Everman, Joseph
    1818. Everman, Joseph
    F1820. Eberman, Joseph
569 Rigin, Henery
    F1820. Riggins, Henry
572 Mcrey, Calvin
    F1820. McCrary, Horatio
    Probably the same family, from the location.
575 Hardin, Archer G.
    F1820. Herrington, Archery G.
576 Chappin, Hiram
    F1820. Chapley, Hiram
577 Tompson, Morgan
    F1820. Thompson, Morgan
579 Nealous, Walker
    F1820. Nichols, Walker
580 Gearvis, John
    1818. Jarvice, John
    F1820. Jarvis, John
583 Parmer, James
    1818. Palmer, James
    F1820. Palmer, James
585 Tase, George
    1818. Teas, George
    F1820. Teas, George
587 Starke, Jonithan
    1818. Stark, Jonathan
    F1820. Stark, Jonathan
589 Randol, Elizabeth
    F1820. Randle, Elizabeth
590 Randol, Payton
    F1820. Randol, Payton and Peyton. Name repeated.
592 Magirer, Thomas
    F1820. McGuire, Thomas J.
593 Skiner, William
    F1820. Skinner, William
594 Herington, Whitmell
    1818. Herrington, Whitmill
    F1820. Herington, Whitmill
596 North, Hessel
    F1820. Noah, Asa
597 Lad, Timothy
    F1820. Ladd, Timothy
598 Owins, Simeon
    1818. Owings, Simms
    F1820. Owins, Simion
599 Enos, Parseal P.
    1818. Enos, Pascal P.
    F1820. Ennes, Pascoll P.
600 Padock, Gaaius
    F1820. Paddock, Gaines
601 Deads, Lewis
    1818. Deeze, Levi
    F1820. Dees, Levy
602 Walker, Harles
    F1820. Walker, Archer
603 Scrgins, Prier
    F1820. Scraggins, Prier
604 Walker, Samuel A.
    1818. Walker, Samuel A.
    F1820. Walker, Samuel
605 Slatten, Joseph
    F1820. Slater, Joseph
606 Belemon, Jesse
    F1820. Bellemey, Jessee
607 Fanon, George
    F1820. Fannon, George
608 Fanon, Joseph
    F1820. Fannon, Joseph
609 Story, John
    F1820. Stove, John
611 Tompson, John
    F1820. Thompson, John
612 Reader, Amos
    F1820. Reeder, Amos
613 Wigins, William C.
    F1820. Wiggins, William C.
615 Mayson, Paris
    1818. Mason, Paris
    F1820. Mason, Paris
616 Armstrong, Josiah
    1818. Armstrong, Joshua
    F1820. Armstrong, Joshua

MADISON COUNTY (Continued)

621 Mayson, James
    F1820. Mason, James
623 Sims, Austin
    1818. Simms, Augustin
    F1820. Simmons, Augustus
624 Ivins, John
    F1820. Evens, John
626 Beas, James
    F1820. Best, James
627 Rhea, Thomas
    F1820. Ray, Thomas
628 Thompson, Alexandria
    F1820. Thompson, Alexander
630 Pharis, Smith
    F1820. Farris, Smith
631 Pharis, George
    1818. Pharis, George W.
    F1820. Farris, George
633 Piper, Netter
    F1820. Piper, Nutter
635 Haxy, John
    F1820. Hoxey, John
638 Johnson, Thomas
    F1820. Johnston, Thomas
640 Johnson, Polly
    F1820. Johnston, Milley
641 Coatter, Robert
    1818. Coulter, Robert
    F1820. Catter, Robert
644 Rice, William D.
    F1820. Rice, William
645 Pearce, James
    1818. Pearce, James
    F1820. Pierce, James
646 Mcalee, Samuel
    F1820. McLilley, Samuel, Sr.
648 Mcalee, Samuel
    F1820. McLilley, Samuel, Jr.
649 Macalle, John
    F1820. McLilley, John
650 Larde, John
    1818. Lard, John
    F1820. Laird, John
651 Lawel, Andrew
    F1820. Lisle, Andrew
654 Parkison, Washington
    F1820. Parkenson, Washington
656 Lee, Nancey
    F1820. Lee, Elizabeth
657 Dugger, Willey
    1818. Dugger, Wesley
    F1820. Dugger, Westley
660 Ussel, Jurden
    1818. Uzzel, Jordan
    F1820. Uzzell, Jorden
661 Fannon, Henry
    F1820. Faning, Henry
662 Dugger, Jeret
    1818. Dugger, Jarrot
    F1820. Dugger, Jarrott
665 Talor, John S.
    F1820. Taylor, John
667 Newles, James
    F1820. Nuel, James
669 Harrass, Benjamin
    F1820. Harris, Benjamin
671 Linnley, John
    1818. Lindley, John
    F1820. Lindley, John
672 Shelton, Mathias
    1818. Shelton, Matthias
    F1820. Shelton, Nathius
673 Read, John
    1818. Reed, John
    F1820. Reed, John
674 Steal, John
    F1820. Steel, John
676 Brazel, Robert
    1818. Brassell, Robert
    F1820. Brasele, Robert
678 Flanigan, Thomas
    1818. Flanigin, Thomas
    F1820. Flanigan, Thomas
681 Jones, Joseph
    F1820. Jones, Josiah
683 Funderburk, Daniel
    F1820. Funderburgh, Daniel
684 Boulton, George
    F1820. Bolton, Charles
685 Ragin, John
    1818. Riggin, John
    F1820. Riggin, John
693 Kingston, Reard
    1818. Kingston, Richard
    F1820. Kingston, Richard
695 Vanhooser, Voluntine
    F1820. Van Hooser, Valentine
696 Vanhooser, Abraham
    1818. Vanhooser, Abraham, Jr.
    F1820. Van Hooser, Abraham
698 Warrin, Harden
    1818. Warren, Harden
    F1820. Warren, Hardy
702 Hageler, Benjamin J.
    1818. Hagler, Benj. J.
    F1820. Hagler, Benjamin
704 Vineyard, William
    F1820. Vinard, William
705 Hageler, William R.
    1818. Hagler, William R.
    F1820. Hagler, William

MADISON COUNTY (Continued)

706 Renfrow, Jesse
    1818. Renfrow, Jesse
    F1820. Renfro, Jesse
708 Patree, Jesse
    1818. Rountree, Jessee
    F1820. Roundtree, Jesse
709 Hoosong, James
    F1820. Husong, James
710 Hoosong, Jacob
    1818. Hoosong, Jacob
    F1820. Husong, Jacob
711 Smarte, Peter
    F1820. Smart, Peter
712 Griffin, Francis
    F1820. Griffin, William W.
714 Shinn, John
    1818. Shinn, John, Jr.
    F1820. Shinn, John
718 Blakeman, Elijah P.
    F1820. Blackman, Elijah
719 Mathis, Andrew
    F1820. Mathus, Andrew
720 Finch, James
    F1820. French, James
721 Finch, Lephod
    F1820. Finch, Leford
722 Ferguson, Isaac
    1818. Furguson, Isaac
    F1820. Ferguson, Isaac
723 Barbarah, John
    F1820. Barnaba, John
724 Lawrance, Samuel
    F1820. Lawrence, Samuel
728 Alburt, Justice
    F1820. Gives Justice Desiles (5 persons) and Miran Allcut (4 persons) as living side by side in this locality.
729 Pane, Cristopher
    1818. Paine, Christopher
    F1820. Payne, Christopher
730 Churlin, John
    F1820. Cleveland, John
731 Chiles, Adams
    1818. Kile, Adam
    F1820. Kile, Adam
732 Robins, Hiram
    1818. Robbins, Hiram
    F1820. Robins, Hiram
733 Beason, Elijah E.
    F1820. Cleson, Elijah
735 Allin, George C.
    F1820. Allen, George C.
737 Peck, Heney
    F1820. Peck, Henry

739 Twist, Ebian
    F1820. Twist, Eddey
741 Judd, Elizeph
    F1820. Judd, Eleazer
745 Hankes, Joshua
    F1820. Hanks, Joshua
748 Swidden, John
    F1820. Swicher, John
752 Sulivan, John
    F1820. Sullivan, John
756 Whiteside, James L.
    F1820. Whitesides, James
757 Sulivan, James
    F1820. Sulliven, James
760 Beatis, William
    F1820. Bols, William
761 Dunigan, Andrew
    1818. Dunagun, Andrew
    F1820. Dunagin, Andrew
762 Feehans, Martin
    F1820. Fuan, Martin
763 Moffet, James
    F1820. Moffitt, James
764 Caral, Edward
    F1820. Carrel, Edward
766 Lofton, John
    1818. Lofton, John G.
    F1820. Lofton, John G.
770 Gillham, John
    1818. Gilham, John
    F1820. Gilham, John D.
771 Gillham, Charles
    1818. Gilham, Charles
772 Gillham, William
    1818. Gilham, William
    F1820. Gillham, William
773 Findley, John
    1818. Findley, John
    F1820. Finley, John
774 Kinkade, Samuel
    1818. Kinkaid, Saml
    F1820. Kinkade, Samuel J.
775 Rogers, William
    F1820. Rodgers, William
778 Linn, Thomas
    F1820. Lynn, Thomas
780 Stout, David
    F1820. Stout, John
783 Brown, Jehugh
    F1820. Brown, John
787 Allen, Danel
    1818. Allen, Daniel
    F1820. Allen, Daniel
788 Robertes, Lius
    F1820. Roberts, Elias

MADISON COUNTY (*Continued*)

791 Hix, Vines
    1818. Hicks, Vynes
    F1820. Hicks, Barnes
792 Crain, Thomas
    F1820. Crane, Thomas
793 Crain, Middleton
    F1820. Crane, Philo M.
794 Carlen, Thomas
    1818. Carland, Thomas
    F1820. Carlen, Thomas
795 Savag, William
    1818. Savage, William
    F1820. Savage, William
796 Wagner, Jacob
    F1820. Waggoner, Jacob
797 Web, William
    1818. Webb, William
    F1820. Webb, William
800 Tunell, Calvin
    1818. Tunnell, Calvin
    F1820. Tunnel, Calvin
801 Hoskins, William
    1818. Haskins, William
    F1820. Haskins, William
802 Danel, Walker
    1818. Daund, Walker
    F1820. Daniel, Walker
803 Costley, William
    1818. Costly, William
    F1820. Costley, William
804 Higgins, Fillemen
    1818. Higgins, Philemon
    F1820. Higgins, Fill
805 Daniel, Thomas
    1818. Dannel, Thomas
    F1820. Daniel, Thomas
807 Green, Wiley
    1818. Green, Willy
    F1820. Green, Wiley
810 Hewitt, John
    1818. Hewit, John
    F1820. Hewitt, John
811 Johnson, William
    F1820. Johnston, William
814 Grimes, Philip
    1818. Grimes, Philip
    F1820. Grines, Philip
815 Gibbs, Austin
    1818. Gibbs, Hauston V.
    F1820. Gibbs, Orton
820 Frazier, John
    F1820. Frasure, Lydia
822 Hacock, Matthew
    F1820. Hecock, Matthew

825 Vinson, Isham
    1818. Vincent, Isham
    F1820. Vincent, Isom
826 Smarte, Wiley
    1818. Smart, Wiley
    F1820. Smart, Wiley
827 Viles, Samuel
    1818. Vials, Samuel
    F1820. Voiles, Samuel
829 Slocham, Thomas
    F1820. Slokum, Thomas
830 Wead, Ebenezar
    F1820. Weed, Edward G.
831 Black, Maryann
    1818. Black, Marian
    F1820. Black, Mary Ann
832 Reynolds, Huston
    F1820. Reynolds, Husten
833 Breath, James
    F1820. Breach, James
834 McCullum, John
    1818. McCullum, John
    F1820. McCullom, John T.
836 Allen, Rowlen P.
    1818. Allen, Rowland P.
    F1820. Allen, Rowland P.
837 Kelly, Oliver
    F1820. Kelly, Oliver L.
838 Tarence, Matthew
    1818. Torance, Matthew
    F1820. Torrence, Matthew
839 Robertson, Joseph
    1818. Robinson, Joseph
    F1820. Robertson, Joseph
840 Randol, Isham
    1818. Randle, Isham
    F1820. Randle, Isham
841 Randol, Josiah
    F1820. Randol, Josias
843 Hambleten, Samuel
    F1820. Hamilton, Samuel
844 McKinney, John
    1818. McKinny, John
    F1820. McKinney, John
845 Findley, John
    1818. Findley, John
    F1820. Finley, John
848 Leggit, Abraham
    F1820. Leggitt, Abraham A.
852 Lockheart, Andrew
    1818 and F1820. Lockhart, Andrew
853 Carret, Isaac
    F1820. Scarrett, Isaac

CENSUS OF 1820

MADISON COUNTY (*Continued*)

854 Wood, Martin
    1818. Wood, Martin
    F1820. Woods, Morton
855 Barton, William
    S1820. Gives as "free persons of colour"; F1820 as whites.
858 Powel, John
    1818. Powel, John
    F1820. Powell, John
860 Drunnian, William
    F1820. Drennon, William
861 Pichy, Alexandria
    F1820. Richey, Alexander
862 Fletcher, Joab
    F1820. Fletcher, Job
864 Wood, William
    1818. Woods, William
    F1820. Woods, William
866 Tailor, Edward
    F1820. Taylor, Edmond
869 Hambleton, Adam
    F1820. Hamilton, Adam
870 Vance, Samuel
    1818. Vann, Saml.
    F1820. Vancel, Samuel
871 Vance, Gideon
    F1820. Vancel, Gideon
872 White, Eldrid
    F1820. White, Edward
874 Davis, John
    1818. Davis, John E.
    F1820. Davis, John, Jr.
875 Lotti, George
    F1820. Lott, George
878 Davis, Jesse
    F1820. Davis, Joshua
880 Yorker, Peter
    1818. Yoakum, Peter
    F1820. Yokum, Peter
881 Simes, Josiah
    F1820. Simmons, Josias
885 Cox, Elizabeth
    F1820. Cox, Jessee
886 Cox, Bowling
    F1820. Cox, Bolen
888 Johnson, William
    1818. Johnson, William
    F1820. Johnston, William
889 Harley, Joshua
    F1820. Durley, Jehu
890 Tailor, John
    1818. Taylor, John
    F1820. Taylor, John
891 George, Jahue
    1818. George, Jehue
    F1820. George, Jehue

892 Drunnion, Joseph
    F1820. Drummon, Joseph
893 Smith, John
    F1820. Smith, Rutha
894 Smith, Headley
    F1820. Smith, Hadly
895 Mils, David
    F1820. Mise, Aaron
896 Stallions, Marget
    F1820. Stallians, Margaret
897 Nots, Thomas
    F1820. Knotts, Thomas
899 Peters, Zachariah
    F1820. Peter, Zacheriah
900 Smith, Ivin
    1818. Smith, Evan
    F1820. Smith, Even
901 Kees, Isaac
    F1820. Keys, Isaac, Sr.
905 Kees, Isaac
    F1820. Keys, Isaac, Jr.
906 Wood, John
    1818. Wood, John
    F1820. Woods, John
909 Willcocks, Jonithan
    F1820. Wilcocks, John
910 Edes, Mathias
    F1820. Eads, Matthew
914 Gipson, Robert
    F1820. Gripeson, Robert
917 Mires, Isaac
    F1820. Myres, Isaac
918 Cottonbarger, John
    F1820. Coppinberger, John
919 Moore, Charles
    F1820. More, Charles
920 Cammore, William
    F1820. More, William C.
922 Congor, Isaac
    F1820. Conger, Isaac
925 Britan, William
    F1820. Breton, William
927 Dean, Joshua
    1818. Deen, Joshua
    F1820. Dean, Joshua
929 Delany, Fielden
    F1820. Delany, Fielding
930 Chapman, James W.
    F1820. Chapman, James
931 Latham, James
    F1820. Laitham, John
934 Sales, James
    F1820. Sayles, James
936 Capture, William
    F1820. Carpenter, William

MADISON COUNTY (*Continued*)

937 Gill, Caleb
    F1820. Crill, Caloss
939 Husk, Larry
    F1820. Husk, Lany
940 Hust, Elijah
    F1820. Hurst, Elijah
941 Davidson, John
    F1820. Davidson, John, Jr.
942 Huberd, Matthew
    F1820. Hurlburt, Matthew
943 Stewart, James
    F1820. Steward, James
944 Tollman, Stephen
    F1820. Stillman, Stephen
945 Hutchens[?], Abraham
    F1820. Hutchinson, Abraham
946 Huzzer, Nathaniel
    F1820. Husey, Nathan
948 Oarinduff, Chapter
    F1820. Orindorff, Christopher
949 Cammon, John
    F1820. Campbell, John
950 Smith, Jeramah
    F1820. Smith, Jeremiah
951 Counsel, Hardin
    F1820. Council, Hardy
952 Mcalean, Robert
    F1820. McClenham, Robert
954 Cline, John
    F1820. Elins, John
955 Lanton, Jacob
    F1820. Larton, Jacob
956 Hog, Jonithan
    F1820. Hodge, Jonathan
958 Cline, John
    F1820. Cline, Andrew
959 Britain, Ivins E.
    F1820. Britton, Evens E.
960 Nelson, Delphus
    F1820. Nelson, Delphy S.
961 Higins, William
    F1820. Higgins, William
962 Tenton, Wiett
    F1820. Cantrill, Wyatt
964 Clanterman, Levi
    F1820. Cantrel, Levi
968 Crofford, Alexandria
    F1820. Crawford, Alexander
970 Huffard, Isaac
    F1820. Halfacre, Isaac
972 and
973 Rogers, Mathew
    F1820. Rodgers, Matthew
976 Short, Wilim
    F1820. Short, William

977 White, William
    F1820. White, Robert
978 Willcox, Oshel
    F1820. Wilcoks, Ossian
981 Hains, James
    1818. Haines, James
    F1820. Hanes, James
982 Girner, Andrew
    F1820. Gardner, Andrew
983 Higgains, Martin
    F1820. Higgins, Marten
984 Macneal, William
    F1820. McNabb, William
985 Blain, William
    1818. Blair, William
    F1820. Blair, William
991 Barnes, Ebenezar
    F1820. Barnes, Ebenezer
992 Larde, James
    1818. Lard, James
    F1820. Laird and Lard (name repeated), James
993 Juney, William
    F1820. Journey, William
995 Bery, Jeremiah
    F1820. Berry, Fortnates
996 Slator, Elijah
    F1820. Slater, Elijah
997 Driar, John
    F1820. Dryer, John
999 Southwick, Jesse
    F1820. Southwick, Jessee
1000 Hinch, Pretree
    F1820. Hinch, Peter
1001 Peas, Abraham
    F1820. Pease, Abraham
1002 Enesley, Joseph
    F1820. Insley, Joseph
1004 Vandagriff, Thomas
    F1820. Vandergrifft, Thomas
1006 Burge, Buennet
    F1820. Burge, Bennet
1008 Burge, Buennet, Jr.
    F1820. Byrum, Buennet, Jr.
1009 Hill, Pheneas
    F1820. Hill, Phineas
1010 Daroneal, Barten
    F1820. Darneal, Barton
1011 Daroneal, John
    F1820. Daniel, John
1012 Wisecoff, John
    F1820. Wycock, John
1014 Simes, Jacob
    F1820. Crimes, Jacob

MADISON COUNTY (*Continued*)

1016 Briscow, John
    1818. Brisco, John
    F1820. Brosco, John
1018 Harber, Levi
    F1820. Harbin, Levy
1019 Dunesmore, Daniel
    1818. Dunsmore, Daniel
    F1820. Dunesmore, David
1020 Dunsmore, Sefus
    F1820. Dunsmore, Joseph
1021 Baker, Absolem
    1818. Baker, Absolam
    F1820. Baker, Absolum
1023 Penny, Robert
    F1820. Penney, Robert
1024 Penny, John
    F1820. Penney, John
1025 Ratliff, James
    F1820. Ratcliff, James
1027 Keltner, Henry
    F1820. Rittiner, Henry
1028 Keltner, Solomon
    1818. Keltner, Solomon
    F1820. Rettener, Solomon
1029 Ratliff, William
    F1820. Ratcliff, William
1030 Ratliff, John
    F1820. Ratcliff, John
1031 Yocam, William
    F1820. Yoakum, William
1032 Fisher, Joshua
    F1820. Fisher, Joseph
1033 Melton, Thomas
    F1820. Milton, Thomas
1035 Dammel, George
    F1820. Domran, George
1037 Ratliff, Tompson
    F1820. Ratcliff, Thomas
1038 Ratliff, Joab
    F1820. Ratcliff, James
1039 Ball, Strauder
    F1820. Ball, Strother
1040 Croy, William
    F1820. Crow, William
1042 Enard, Abner
    F1820. Inard, Abner
1044 Shepherd, Rowlin
    F1820. Shepherd, Robert
1046 Larn, Samuel
    F1820. Lairs, Samuel
1047 Broad, John
    F1820. Broad, John B.
1049 Scott, Dallis
    F1820. Scott, Dalis

1051 Pervines, Alexandria
    F1820. Pervunce, Alexander
1053 Willbern, Robert
    F1820. Willbur, Robert
1055 Mathis, Daniel
    F1820. Matthews, Daniel
1056 Mathis, Absolem
    F1820. Matthews, Absalom
1059 Clary, John
    F1820. Clary, John, Sr.
1061 Clary, John
    F1820. Clary, John, Jr.
1062 Armstrong, Jesse
    F1820. Armstrong, Jessee
1067 Vermetre, William
    F1820. Van Metre, William
1068 Lakons, Joseph
    F1820. Lakins, Joseph
1069 Pruitt, Soloman
    F1820. Pruett, Solomon
1070 Potter, Rial
    F1820. Potter, Royal
1076 Raily, John
    F1820. Richey, John
1077 Walter, William
    F1820. Waters, William
1079 Penny, John
    F1820. Penney, John
1080 Penny, William
    F1820. Penney, William
1081 Penny, Robert
    F1820. Penney, Robert
1083 Sinard, Abraham
    F1820. Sinnard, Abraham
1084 Comeins, John
    F1820. Cummins, William
1085 Reavis, Alexandria
    F1820. Revise, Alexander
1086 Pearce, Solomon
    1818. Pearce, Solomon
    F1820. Pierce, Solomon
1087 Pearce, Robert A.
    F1820. Pierce, Robert
1089 Pearcifield, Jeramiah
    F1820. Purcefield, Jeremiah
1090 Kirkpartrack, William
    F1820. Kirkpatrick, William
1091 Coy, David
    F1820. McCoy, David
1094 Kelloms, Margaret
    F1820. Cellums, Peggy C.
1095 Isbal, Joseph
    F1820. Isbell, Joseph
1096 Isbal, Thomas
    F1820. Isbell, Thomas

MADISON COUNTY (Continued)

1100 Dogit, Richard
    F1820. Dodge, Richard
1102 Kelly, John
    F1820. Kelley, John
1105 Elliott, Andrew
    F1820. Eliott, Andrew
1108 Linsey, John
    F1820. Lindsley, John
1112 Glexen[?], John
    F1820. Glenn, John
1113 Pillars, John
    F1820. Spellers, John
1116 Alton, Shelton
    F1820. Olfan, Shelton
1123 Johnson, James
    1818. Johnson, James
    F1820. Johnston, James
1124 Vinson, William
    F1820. Vincent, William
1125 Devenporte, George
    F1820. Devenport, George
1128 Ditson, Jesse
    F1820. Delson, Jesse
1132 Buckhanon, Joseph
    F1820. Buchannon, John
1136 Card, James
    F1820. Carr, James
1138 Bristow, Thomas
    F1820. Bristo, Thomas
1139 Keagmen, Zechariah
    F1820. Eckburn, Zecheriah
1143 Arnet, Thomas
    F1820. Arnett, Thomas, Sr.
1144 Stubbins, Christopher
    1818. Stubbins, Christopher
    F1820. Stubbins, Christopher B.
1145 Willson, Aaron
    F1820. Wilson, Aaron
1149 Reavis, Isaac
    F1820. Rieves, Isaac
1150 Crain, James
    F1820. Crane, James
1152 Cowwich, Thomas
    1818. Cowhill, Thomas
    F1820. Cowhick, Thomas
1157 Low, Quillar
    F1820. Low, Aquilla
1159 Collins, Abraham
    F1820. Collens, Ambrose
1160 Hambleton, Thomas
    1818. Hamilton, Thomas
1161 Wood, James
    F1820. Woods, James
1166 Shelly, Jahue
    F1820. Shelly, John
1168 Hatchison, John
    F1820. Atchison, John
1169 Hatchison, Samuel
    F1820. Atchison, Samuel
1171 Fornestake, John
    F1820. Fornostock, Jacob
1173 Pearcy, John
    F1820. Piercy, John
1174 Wells, Alexandria
    F1820. Wells, Alexander
1176 Bruce, James
    F1820. Brook, James
1177 Winters, Nathaniel
    F1820. Winters, Nathan
1181 Asherst, Michael
    F1820. Aster, Michael
1185 Wason, Bekey
    1818. Wauson, Rebecca
    F1820. Wasen, James
1189 More, Isaac
    1818. Moore, Isaac
    F1820. Moore, Isaac
1191 Beebe, Clarke
    F1820. Bebee, Charles, Babee, Charles Repeated.
1193 Bell, Francis
    1818. Belle, Francis
    F1820. Bell, Francis
1195 Allen, James
    F1820. Allen, James M.
1200 Thaxton, William
    F1820. Thackston, William
1203 Powel, James
    F1820. Powell, James
1204 Peake, John
    F1820. Pike, John
1207 Rowlin, James
    F1820. Rollings, James
1210 Whitiker, Robert
    F1820. Whitacre, Robert
1211 Headen, Andrew
    F1820. Hendricks, Andrew
1217 Fry, Philip
    F1820. Frye, Philip
1219 Drum, John
    1818. Drumm, John
    F1820. Drum, John
1220 Blany, John
    F1820. Blaney, John
1221 Findley, Thomas
    F1820. Finley, Thomas
1223 Tailor, Isaac
    1818. Taylor, Isaac
1228 Lunley, Thomas
    F1820. Lumley, Thomas

MADISON COUNTY (Continued)

1231 Pinkerton, James
    F1820. Binkerton, James
1232 Headick, Michael
    F1820. Hendricks, Michael
1233 Pullham, Alcey
    1818. Pulliem, Alsa
    F1820. Pulliam, Alsey
1235 Rush, Abraham
    F1820. Bush, Abraham
1237 Mcfarlin, Watty
    1818. McFarland, Walter
    F1820. McFarlin, Walter
1238 White, Buennet
    F1820. White, Banard
1240 Hambleton, James
    F1820. Hamilton, James
1244 Kitchins, Charles
    1818. Kitchens, Charles
    F1820. Kichens, Charles
1245 Collins, John
    1818. Collins, John
    F1820. Collians, John
1247 Clark, Absolem
    F1820. Clark, Absalum
1248 Coldwell, James
    1818. Caldwell, James
1251 Honeycutt, Arthel
    1818. Honeycut, Hartwell
    F1820. Honeycutt, Hartwell
1254 Lerton, Jacob
    1818. Lurton, Jacob
1255 Parkison, Daniel
    1818. Parkison, Daniel
    F1820. Parkinson, Daniel
1257 Brag, William
    F1820. Bragg, William
1259 Nowlin, Bennet
    1818. Nowling, Bennett
    F1820. Noland, Bennett and Nowland Name repeated.
1260 Hinkle, Justus
    F1820. Hincle, Justus
1263 Cannon, David
    F1820. Cowan, David
1264 Nelly, Henry
    F1820. Neeley, Henry
1266 Nelly, Joseph
    F1820. Neely, Joseph
1269 Funderburth, Henry
    F1820. Funderburgh, Henry
1270 Liles, Daniel
    F1820. Lisle, Daniel
1271 Toddle, James
    F1820. Twadley, James

1275 Firguson, Joseph
    F1820. Ferguson, Joseph
1276 Firguson, John
    1818. Furguson, John
    F1820. Ferguson, John
1277 Firguson, William
    F1820. Furgeson, William
1278 Firguson, Alston
    1818. Furguson, Alston
    F1820. Furguson, Alston
1280 Lowrler, Mason
    F1820. Lawland, Morris
1283 Goodon, Henry
    F1820. Gordon, Henry T. and Garden, Henry T. Name repeated.
1285 Snodgrass, James
    1818. Snotgrass, James
    F1820. Snodgrass, James, Sr.
1286 Snodgrass, James
    1818. Snotgrass, James
    F1820. Snodgrass, James, Jr.
1287 Carmel, Ribers
    1818. Cormack, Rivers
    F1820. Cormack, Rivers
1292 Moore, Daniel
    1818. Moore, Daniel G.
    F1820. Moore, Daniel G.
1293 Grage, Jacob
    F1820. Graig, Jacob
1297 Hennis, Martin
    F1820. Hinnon, Sarah
1299 Mattis, Flebin
    F1820. Mathis, Clibon
1300 Grage, Titus
    1818. Gregg, Titus
    F1820. Gragg, Titus
1302 Holey, Aaron
    F1820. Hawley, Aaron
1306 Striman, Readman
    F1820. Strickland, Redman
1310 Stritlen, Witte
    F1820. Strickland, Wiatt
1311 Scroud, Asa
    F1820. Stroud, Asa
1313 Clarke, Philip
    F1820. Clark, Philip
1317 Satley, Robert
    F1820. Sattirly, Robert
1320 Berdin, Reubin
    F1820. Burden, Reubin
1321 Warrick, John
    1818. Warwick, John
    F1820. Warrick, John

MADISON COUNTY (Continued)

1324 Bowlen, James
    F1820. Bolen, James
1325 Gragg, John
    F1820. Graig, John
1326 Hubbard, Ansel
    F1820. Hubbart, Ansel
1327 Comins, Josiah
    1818. Cummons, Josiah
    F1820. Cummins, Josias
1330 Mcfamd, David
    F1820. McFane, David
1334 Firguson, Thomas
    1818. Furguson, Thomas
    F1820. Ferguson, Thomas
1335 and 1336 Gunterman, John
    F1820. Gunterman, John, Sr. and Jr.
1337 Evlin, Moses
    1818. Evelin, Moses
1340 Cockram, Mason
    F1820. Cackson, Mason
1341 Evlin, John
    1818. Evelin, John
    F1820. Eveland, John
1344 Gates, Samuel
    F1820. Grafts, Samuel
1346 Church, Daniel
    F1820. Church, Daniel, Sr.
1351 Mattis, William
    F1820. Metts, William
1352 Mattis, John
    F1820. Metts, John
1353 Curtis, John
    F1820. Curtis, John G.
1359 Desily, Antwine
    1818. Dezurley, Antoine
    F1820. Desherley, Antonio
1360 Richy, John
    F1820. Richey, John
1369 Linsley, Martin
    F1820. Lindsley, Martin L.
1373 Gilbert, David
    F1820. Gillbert, David
1374 Criswell, David
    F1820. Cresswell, Walter J.
1378 Boalter, John
    F1820. Bolton, John

1380 Mcentire, Benjamin
    F1820. McIntire, Benjamin
1382 Read, William
    F1820. Reed, William
1383 Mayland, Jonithan
    F1820. Malone, Jonithan
1385 Enness, Jesse
    1818. Ennis, Jessee
    F1820. Enes, Jessee
1391 Beaman, James
    1818. Beeman, James
    F1820. Beman, James
1392 Paton, Andrew
    1818. Patton, Andrew V.
1394 Ragan, Henry B.
    F1820. Rager, Henry B.
1395 Sidman, Benjamin
    1818. Stedman, Benj.
    F1820. Steadman, Benjamin
1397 Ruthorford, John
    F1820. Rutherford, John
1401 Findley, Moses
    1818. Findley, Moses
    F1820. Finley, Moses
1403 Nick, Tempel
    F1820. Nix, Temple
1404 Cheak, Nellis
    1818. Cheek, Willis
    F1820. Cheek, Willis
1406 Lions, Margaret
    F1820. Lyons, James
1409 Wood, Ephraim
    1818. Wood, Ephraim
    F1820. Woods, Ephraim
1410 Tunnell, James
    1818. Tunnel, James
    F1820. Tunnel, James, Sr.
1412 Wood, Sampson
    1818. Wood, Sampson
    F1820. Woods, Sampson
1413 Cottet, Robert
    F1820. Collett, Robert
1414 Wood, Young
    1818. Wood, Young
    F1820. Woods, Young

MADISON COUNTY (*Continued*)

The following names were omitted from the state census (exclusive of those in the federal census which were obviously padding):

Ridge Prairie
  Tifft, David
  Wise, Jacob
Goshen
  Prat, Nathaniel
  Ransom, Merritt
  Whitehead, James
  Slater, Samuel
  Dillen, Waller
  Brock, Solomon
  Woollen, John
  Johnston, Andrew
  Porter, James
  Hill, Robert
  *Gilham, Rydus C.
  Owsey, William
  Philips, Peasley
  Benett, John R.
  Stupp, James
  Whitmore, George
  Crawford, Samuel
  Crawford, William
  Cottle, David
  Cottle, William
  *Watson, James
  Ross, Ethan E.
  Petit, Henry
  Bradley, James
  Harmon, John W.
  Steward, James
  Ingland, John M.
  Bird, John J.
  Dodge, Peter
  Cox, Abicha
  Wiley, John
  Shutwell, George
  Chenney, Robert
  Love, John
  Crip, Jacob
  Finley, James
  Ward, Joshua
  Wier, Joseph
  Prow, Reuben
  Jones, Thomas
  Britton, David L.
  Rangerton, Thomas
  Rentfrow, James
  Blaney, Robert
  Leonard, John
  Romey, Nancey
  Boyd, George
  Barrow, John

Wood River
  *Jones, William
Goshen
  McCants, John
  McCants, Thompson
  Painter, Joseph
Greenfield
  Nuckles, James
  Hicks, Job
  Lindley, Joseph
  Morton, Oliver
  Carick, Thomas
Silver Creek
  *Harris, Eli G.
  Kilbourn, Mary
  Hobbs, John
  Gracia, Joseph
  *Davis, John
    1818. Davis, John E.
  Parish, Joseph
  Walters, Isaiah
  Hunter, Elizabeth
  Banes, Robert
  Thorp, Henry B.
  Goodsel, Jacob
  Catter, James
  Cleveland, John
  Dotchin, John
  Meeks, Thomas
  Coil, Nicholas
  Dugger, John
  Burt, Morton
  Aikles, William
Goshen
  Anderson, John
  Walker, Jacob W.
  Walker, John
  Stork, Jonathan
  *Clark, William
  Bartlett, Wm. B.
  Yaples, Jacob
  Bates, Thomas
  Nevins, John
  Simmons, George
  Benston, Oliver
  Hinch, William
  *Farris, James, Sr.
    1818. Pharis, James
  Hoxey, John
  Thompson, John, Sr.
  Sackett, Simon
  Woods, William C.

MADISON COUNTY (Continued)

Wilcox, Eli
Chapman, Richard
Camp, Telemanchus
Cormack, John
*Williams, Richard
  1818. William, Richard
Chapman, John
Casteel, John
*Jones, Bennet
  1818. Jones, Benett
Thompson, John, Jr.
Belemor, Isaac
Kelly, Henry
Wait, Thomas B.
*Barnett, Thomas
Morgan, William H.
Petite, David M.
Van Pelt, Darick
Gray, William
Wood River
  Culliam, John, Jr.
Alton
  Ross, Leonard
  Ross, Harrington
  Ross, Henry J.
  Ross, William
  Spigue, William
  Canel, Lawrence
Piasas
  Carvel, John
  Halton, James
  Wadley, Jacob
  *Gilham, Jane
  *Richardson, John
  Roberts, Thomas
  Moor, Alliot
  Huse, Sanford
  Helterbran, David
  Henry, James
Bounty Land
  Pettet, Solomon
  Go, Joseph
  Jervy, Joseph
  Hanes, Aaron
  Rayboy, John Baptise
  Dickson, James
  Twasure, Thomas
  Crosieure, Simeon
  Broadwell, Backster
  Troy, Charles
  Taylor, Rachel
  Maning, Mary
  Chense, Daniel, Jr.
  Tupper, Henry

Hinkley, Nathaniel
Fry, William
Whipple, Daniel
Janes, Belus
Leven, James
Franklin, Ebenezer
Shane, Daniel
Davis, Samuel
Moyers, Isaac
Loup, Henry
Keys, Willard
Befra, John Baptist
Pettett, John R.
Lemain [?], Andrew
Pelkey, Baptiste
*Tebeau, John B.
  1818. Teoboc, John B.
Adams, Joseph
Chermont, Pierre
Lacroy, Baptiste
Hanes, Barnabus
Barcroft, Aaron
Ward, William
Long, Christopher
Massey, William
Kelly, George
Eveland, Isaac
Ward, William
Boroff, John
Apple Creek
  Inkland, Nicholas
  Smith, Benjamin
  Taylor, William
  Horton, Daniel
  Miller, John
  Miller, Uriah
  Brush, Alkenerey
  Spencer, Stephen W.
  Lemington, John
  Reeder, Levy
  Hiticks, William
  Casebry, John
  Taylor, George
  Spencer, Francis
Springfield
  Miller, Adam
  McCrana, Thomas
  Laby, Simeon
  Jordon, James
  Pierce, Stephen
  Cape, Jabese
  Shelton, James
  Linch, Patrick

CENSUS OF 1820

MADISON COUNTY (Continued)

Fork Prairie
  Knotts, Thomas
  Potter, James
  Milton, Lazerous
  Farris, John
  Williams, William
  Husbands, Thomas
  Husbands, Flour
  Husbands, William
  Weatherman, John
  Vancell, Adam
  Green, Robert
  Jones, Clayborn
  Davis, William
  Vancil, Penrod
  Lee, Samuel
  Crawford, Abel
  Hodge, William
  Terrell, Stephen
Springfield
  Knight, James
  Pain, Olaney
  Crimes, Jacob
  Wycock, John
  Riggins, Morth
  Coleman, Abigal
  Davis, Oliver
  Enocks, John
  Barton, Elihu
  Nixson, William
  Smith, Enoch
  Hance, John
  Allen, William
  Kings, Rufus
  Hodge, James
  Winters, James
  Winsor, John
  Coleans, Abijah
  Coons, Edward
  Smith, William
  Lealer, Thomas
  Salems, Daniel
  Cormock, David
  Jones, Thomas
  Gilmore, Ephraim
  Hewitt, Timothy
  Lilburn, George
  Denton, Jessee
  Hanson, Jacob
  Piper, Robert
  May, Joseph
  Halfoway, Isaac
  Carrel, Josias
  Pierce, Philip
  Dees, Caleb

Wood River
  Whitlock, James
  Gillerland, Martin
  Springer, Nathaniel
  Donelson, William
  Hogan, Daniel
  Parks, Francis
  *Newman, Joseph
  *Cox, John
  Easterbrook, John
  Lawrance, William
  Wise, Joseph
  Lawrence, Solomon
  Watts, Thomas
  Crawder, Charles
  Pruitt, Solomon
  Higgins, Hiram
  West, Emanuel J.
  Wise, Henry
  Calvy, Richard
  Heady, Sally
  Wright, Isom
  Parker, William
  Rhoads, George
  Varick, Nancy
  Norman, John
  New, John
  Harlen, Charles W.
  Reddon, James
  Leonard, Polly
  Sells, Jacob
  Rodden, Robert
  Bacon, Oran
  French, Joseph
  Cox, Bolen
  Bark, William
  Shadwick, Iram
  Carter, John
  Huntington, Ebenezer
  Bissell, Jerajah
  Shaw, Luthern
  Fay, Jonathan B.
  Bane, Robert
  Rhodes, Clayburn
  Brown, Joseph
  Blackshire, Luke
  Slokeham, Jacob
Edwardsville
  Gibson, William
  Horsler, James
Ridge Prairie
  Lahone, Pierre
  Lahone, John Baptiste
  Allery, Baptiste
  Jandra, Papu

MADISON COUNTY (Continued)

Six Mile Prairie (Most of these names were repeated under the following township, Edwardsville.)
  Cox, Daniel
  Cox, Jarrot
  Burgum, Joseph
  Askins, Philoman
  Gordon, William
  Berry, Samuel
  Walker, Benjamin
  Newal, Thomas
  McDiarman, George
  Lawler, Patrick
  Cadwell, Abijah
  Williams, Elizabeth
  Emret, Sally
  *Lofton, Easter
    1818. Lofton, Esther
  Mallory, Eleson
  Stucer, Thomas
  Borna, Jacob
  Labarb, Baptiste
  Dio, Pierre
  Lewis, Nicholas
  Leonard, Frances, Jr.
  Barb Barb, Lewis
  Baismauve, Jacob
  Doneo, Laurence
  Allexander, Rewben
  Weathers, Enoch
  Gibbins, James
  Elidge, William
  West, Emanuel J.
  Juntum, Tuson
  Wise, Joseph
  Herron, William
  McAlley, David
Edwardsville
  *Edwards, Ninian
  Sur Petite, Antonio
  LeRoy, Simon
  LeRoy, Semore
  Canada, Edmond
  Winchester, Palemon H.
  Kerr, James
  Gilham, Erades
  Welch, Rufus
  Whitesides, William H.
Piassas
  Ryans, Henry
Alton
  Welch, William
  Rutherford, Richard
  Neil, John O.
  Pigott, John
  Daley, Michael
Edwardsville
  DeCamp, Samuel G. J.
  Moor, Hardin
Six Mile Prairie
  *Hays, Henry
    1818. Haze, Henry
Bounty Land
  Tesson, Albert
  Hade, William
  Valentine, Jacob
  Brown, James P.
  Hale, Benjamin
Goshen
  *Belska, George
    1818. Belsha, George
  Ferris, James
  *McKee, Robert
  Nimon, Jacob
  Biss, James
  Farmings, George
  Aikman, David
  Starkey, Jesse
  *McKinney, Hampton
    1818. McKeney, Hampton
  Kelly, Hezekiah L.
  Hicks, Henry
  Doliens, Charles
  Haskin, Samuel
  Leonard, Lawrence
  Bruer, John
  Thompson, James
Greenfield
  Meeker, Daniel
  Judy, Samuel
  Huse, Charles M.
  Brush, William
  Conway, Joseph
  Hickle, John
  Bevens, Charles
  Court, William
  Davidson, Ephraim
  McCants, Elias
  Chase, Ashur
  Stephenson, Thomas B.
  Ray, Thomas
  Jones, Stephen
  Owens, Simeon
  Baker, Alsworth
  McKee, Mary
  *Wheelock, Simon
  Swader, John
  Van Metre, Thomas
  Meacham, Eathan
  Stockton, Rura

MADISON COUNTY (*Continued*)

Milton
  Smith, Peter
  Reichercker, John
  Davis, Peter
  Ronderman, Adam
Greenfield
  Norman, John
  Nix, Ephraim
  Boyd, Jonathan
  Cavanah, Charles
  Wiley, John
  Ramis, William
  Pipp, Patrick
  Slokeum, Samuel
  Wetmore, Hartshorn
  Graves, John
  Thompson, Samuel
  Shotwell, Henry
  Harden, John
  Rants, Robert
  Silkwood, Solomon
  Gilham, J. C.
Edwardsville
  Johnston, Jarvis
  Gilham, Ezekiel
  Hamilton, Samuel
  Gillerland, Thomas
Ridge Prairie
  Stephenson, Ruff
  Rhodes, Claybourn
  McCarter, Mary
  *Gillham, John, Sr.
    1818. **Gilham, John**
  McCants, Elias
  Carry, James
  Brady, Thomas
  Christy, William
  Denney, William W.
  Massock, David
  Hall, Harry
  Barker, Joseph
  Bradburn, James
  Tennelly, Hugh
  Lalar, Jacob
  Crasley, Samuel
  Bell, John S.
  Burk, James
  Fellows, Willis
  Gates, Hiram
  Griffeith, Joshua
  Fulton, Aaron
  Ferris, Robert
  Furlong, John
  Reed, Jacob
  Darby, John F.

Piasaw
  Jefferson, Luke
  Kinsay, Nietry
  Wells, John
  Brown, Henry
  Lambert, Elisha
  Humphreys, James
Greenfield
  Handy, James
  Wilkins, Susan
  Leak, Richard
  Cramwell, John
  Comwell, Titus
  Bentson, William
  Duleu, Elijah
  Fryer, Thomas
  Latter, Joseph
  Reeder, Philip
  Pleasants, Thomas
  Flagg, Nathaniel
  Ripley, Arnold
  Adams, Henry
  Sidney, Samuel
  Nangle, Daniel
  Golder, Jacob
  Golder, John R.
  Dayless, John W.
  Nevens, John
  Akens, Christain
  Galaton, Solomon
  McKinney, Owen
  Furlong, John
  Hines, William
  Hines, John
  Daniels, Aaron
  Rasons, Joseph
  Rolls, Daniel
  Dereckson, John
  Vanbuskurk, Larence
  Rowlings, Ecker
  Lavety, Russell
  Earles, James
  Black, David R.
  Arcana, Joseph
  Ireland, Samuel
  Woodard, Joseph L.
  Kunland, David
  Yald, Henry
  Wilkins, David
  Byrd, John
  Griffin, Peggy
  Carpenter, Ephraim
  *Taylor, John
  Hamilton, James
  Barnett, Henry

MADISON COUNTY (Continued)

Greenwood, James
Conly, Willis
Foster, Daniel
Six Mile Prairie
Gray, Joseph
Davis, Othencall
McCants, John
Johnson, John
Lear, Samuel
Nowland, Bennett
Barnaba, John
Morgan, Jonathan
Paul, Stephen
Niles, Henry
Twadey, James
Gingles, Samuel
Vinyard, William
Waddle, James
West, Isaac
Dunn, Jacob
Daniel, John
Esbill, Henry
Wood, Richard
Cowen, William
Willis, John
Headrick, Charles
Decamp, Jacob
Decamp, Charles
Dreine, Benjamine
Grigery, Charles
Eveland, Frederick
Skidmore, John W. L.
Vinyard, William
Linn, Aneas
Marr, Alexander
Allen, James
Cawerly, James F.
Sydner, Washington
Griswood, Cyrus
Eddor, Samuel
Betwood, Edmond F.
Twitty, Russel
Redman, Abraham
Demon, Robert
Pleasants, Thomas
Kingston, David
Young, Benjamine
Linsly, Jacob
McKnight, Robert
Aples, Samuel
Hamer, James
Hanill, James
Twist, Solomon
Jacaway, Jane
Reynolds, Joseph L.
Reynolds, Samuel
Harden, Alfred
Harden, James
Mason, Robert
Yaple, David
Darr, William
Salter, Joseph
Rolls, Daniel
Dicron, Robert E.
Geory, John
Conner, James
Priestly, James
Richardson, James
Hayes, Solomon
Doane, Henry
Foster, Robert M.
Lawless, Samuel
Dereckson, John
Lawland, Morris
Roan, James
Roan, Thomas
Guy, Francis
Ransom, Thomas
Scranton, James
McKee, Benjamine
Davis, Rowland
Jones, Enoch
Lavine, James
Chouven, Lopenne
Faris, Alexan
Stone, David
Haden, James
Canady, William
Howel, Wallace
Shanan, Mary
Valliant, Antoin
Hobb, Victor
Smith, Christain
Spens, George
Martin, Adam
Lefavre, Francis
Crawford, John
Miller, John
Marten, James
Duce, Augustus
Brady, Peter
Payne, Nathaniel
Valain, Francis
Lang, Francis
McConel, Mary
Hawdsheall, Jacob
Hadsheall, Samuel
Arnold, James
McGowen, James

MADISON COUNTY (Continued)

Bess, David H.
Deane, William
Bissniss, Joseph
Lecuras, Amos
Roach, David
Randle, Josias, Jr.
Whitmore, Solomon
Nixon, David
Welch, Enoch
Hodge, Erastes
Davis, James
Davis, Thomas
Davis, Samuel
Hance, Jacob
Hance, John
Ingrum, Peter
Jones, James M.
McKinny, James
Davidson, William
Boice, John
Hoxcy, John
Waller, Thomas
Moore, William
Davis, Denis
Harben, George
*Squires, Michael
Green, Wiley
Stephenson, Ruff
Smith, Hanah
Sanders, Hanah
Dunegan, Ann
Greenfield
  Roads, Clayburn
  Larkins, Edward
Six Mile Prairie
  Crown, Davis
  Mathes, Edward
  Dayle, Thomas
  Redfield, Amos
  Evins, Lewis
  Davidson, William M.
  Pleasants, Thomas R.
  Hoskins, Isaac
  Squires, Michael
  Buckley, Peter
  Hempstead, Stephen
  Hamilton, Hedman
  Brockway, Jonathan Niles
  Kellogg, Lymon
  Kellogg, Elisha
  Boggard, Samuel
  Eddy, Horatice
  Dayal, Isaac
  Shepherd, Samuel
  Roe, Isaac F.

Webster, Judiah
Nash, Stephen
Abrahams, Lewis
Arnett, Thomas, Jr.
Boll, Stephen
Stratton, Joseph
Hodge, Joseph
Miller, John
Colt, Anson
Shelton, James
Coventry, John C.
Andrews, Amos
Hodge, David
Smart, Bennet
Whitley, Samuel
Carvel, John
Stephens, John
Griffen, Jacob
McNary, James
Apple Creek
  Ruble, Jesse
  Bowman, Abraham
  White, Samuel
  Lepherd, Nicholas
  Killwell, James
  Thornton, John
  Smith, Aaron
  Finley, John
  Potter, Andrew
  Thornton, John
  Leggitt, Abraham A.
  Scarrett, Nathan
  Waggoner, John
  Hagar, John, Sr.
  Scott, William
Ridge Prairie
  *Painter, John
    1818. Paint, John
  Hall, James
  Russell, Nicholas
  Woods, Richard
  Stovell, Elizabeth
  Samples, David
  Sawyer, James
  Kingston, Abraham
  *Norman, William
  Day, William
  Kendall, Stephen
  *Milton, Ranson
    1818. Milan, Ransom
  Black, Andrew
  *Kown, James
    1818. Keown, James
  Hays, William
  McCrary, Horatio

MADISON COUNTY (Concluded)

Morse, Samuel
Troy Vil.
  Eberman, John
  Yaple, John
  Fray, Daniel
  Ripper, John
  Ellison, Andrew
  *Randle, Thomas
Ridge Prairie
  Courtney, William
Silver Creek
  Lowell, Daniel
Sangamo
  Laitham, Richard
  Norman, Isaac G.
  Morehead, Elickander
Ridge Prairie
  Allen, Ira
  Allen, James
  *Randle, Pyram
  1818. Randle, Parham
  Vanstuter, Adam
  Vanstuter, Peter
Fork Prairie
  Williams, Andrew
  Fowler, Mason
  Williams, Elias
  Twadley, James
  Robertson, Hardy
  Ferguson, John
  Goodin, Levi
  Shaw, Smith
  Vina, Abraham
  Berly, Thomas
  Brents, Joshua
  Carter, Oliver
  McConnel, William
  Needle, James
  Cass, Lewis
  Benson, William
  Laughlin, Michael
  Amalin, Alexi
  Inglis, Boon
  Miles, Josias
  Burn, Lewis
Edwardsville
  Hopkins, William H.
Fork Prairie
  Wallace, William
  Wallace, James
  Hawley, Isaac
  Chilton, William
  Burden, Julie

Satterly, Archibald
Coper, John
Coppenborger, Jacob
Hurst, James
Wakefield, George
Lugart, Nathan
Millagan, Ferguson
Sangamo
  Davis, John
  Davis, Henry
  Davis, Joel
  Strickland, Joseph
  Davis, John
  Brock, John
  Copfil, James
  Baird, Charles
  Phelps, Elias
  Atkins, Robert
  Hubert, Baley
  Stroud, John
  Wenkfield, James
  Lankeston, Jaconeas
  Parks, Matthew
Springfield
  Prim, Thomas
Sangamo
  Musick, Robert
  Hopkins, Ezekiel
  Hill, Jeremiah
  Blany, Robert
Springfield
  Medows, James
  Philips, William
  Wadkins, Joseph
  Green, George
  Kirby, Cirus
  Neal, Jessee
  Spicers, Solomon
  Yoakum, James
  Penney, Solomon
  Irvin, Samuel
  Smith, David
  Percyfield, Henry
  Morgan, William
  Stewart, Ephraim
  Carlock, George
  Arnett, Jacob
  Trockwell, David
  Catherington, Jonathan
  Lindley, Mark
  Scimmus, John
Fork Prairie
  Newhouse, Samuel

CENSUS OF 1820

CENSUS OF MONROE COUNTY, 1820

Page 1st. Schedule of the whole number of Inhabita in the County of Monroe, agreeably to the act of the General assembly of the State of Illinois for taking the census in 1820

	Names of hads of Families	Free white persons		People of Color			
		Males 21 years of age & upwards	All other white inhabitance	Free	Servants	Slaves	Aggregate
[1*‡]	Joseph A. Beaird	1	6			8	15
[2*‡]	Philip Rader	1	4		2		7
[3*‡]	Joseph Hogan	1	2		5		8
[4*‡]	Solomon Shook	5	4	1	2		12
[5*‡]	Jacob Trout	1	4		1		6
[6 ‡]	James B. Moore	3	8		4		15
[7 ‡]	George Ramey	3	9				12
[8 ‡]	Seth Coleman	2	6	6	1		15
[9*‡]	John Divers	1	3			5	9
[10*‡]	Robert Hawk	2	4				6
[11*‡]	Richard Mattingly	2	4		2		8
[12 ‡]	John D. Whiteside	1	4	1	2		8
[13*‡]	John Modglin	1	8				9
[14*‡]	Henry Modglin	2	5				7
[15*‡]	Mary Amos	1	5	1			7
[16 ‡]	John B. Wyzer		3	1			4
[17*‡]	James McRoberts	2	6		1		9
[18*‡]	John Cooper	2	2				4
[19 ‡]	Solomon Dixon	1	8				9
[20*‡]	Thomas Tolbott	2	2				4
[21 ‡]	Edward Garrish	1	2				3
[22*‡]	Elisha Axley	1	6				7
[23 ‡]	Daniel Gregg	2	1				3
[24 ‡]	Hugh Ralston	1	3				4
[25 ‡]	Henry Dixon	1	2				3
[26 ‡]	Samuel Dixon	1	1				2
[27 ‡]	Nathan Dixon	2	1				3
[28 ‡]	Abraham Dixon	2	5				7

Figures and symbols preceding names have been supplied by the editor:
‡ Indicates name also in Federal Census for 1820.
* Indicates name also in State Census for 1818.

MONROE COUNTY (Continued)

No.	Heads of families	Free white persons		People of color			Aggregate
		Males 21 & upwards	All other white	Free	Servants	Slaves	
[29 ‡]	Norman Scovil	1	3				4
[30 ‡]	Isaac J. Baily	1	1				2
[31 ‡]	Robert Baily	1					1
[32*‡]	John McDavid	1	8				9
[33*‡]	Ellis Chalpin	2	3				5
[34 ‡]	Elisha Starr	1	3				4
[35*‡]	Seth Chalpen	2	5				7
[36 ‡]	Daniel Hull	2	1				3
[37*‡]	Solomon Goss	1	4				5
[38 ‡]	Samuel Powel	1	8				9
[39*‡]	Absolum Bradshaw	1	8				9
[40*‡]	William Everitt	1	6				7
[41 ‡]	Jacob Fultze	1	3				4
[42*‡]	Robert Kidd	1	9				10
[43 ‡]	James Leper	2	5				7
[44*‡]	Joseph Worley	2	4				6
[45 ‡]	Ira Scovil	2	2				4
[46*‡]	Ezekiel Preston	2	9				11
[47*‡]	William Alexander	2	4				6
[48 ‡]	John Drody	2	1				3
[49*‡]	William Worley	2	4				6
[50*‡]	John Worley	1	4				5
[51*‡]	James Henderson	2	8				10
[52*‡]	Isaiah Levins	4	5				9
[53 ‡]	John Dunn	2	2				4
[54*‡]	George Wallis	1	4				5
[55*‡]	Andy Kinney	4	5				9
[56*‡]	David Bagley	2	8				10
[57 ‡]	Hambleton Smith	1	5				6
[58 ‡]	David Lavisee	1	3				4
[59*‡]	Adam Smith	1	8				9
[60 ‡]	Ebenezer Coleman	1	2				3
[61 ‡]	Henry C. Mizner	3					3
[62 ‡]	Samuel Mooney	1					1
[63 ‡]	William Goldsmith	1	5				6
[64 ‡]	William F. Roberts	3	2				5
[65 ‡]	David Ditch	4	8				12

MONROE COUNTY (Continued)

No.	Heads of families	Free white persons		People of color			Aggregate
		Males 21 & upwards	All other white	Free	Servants	Slaves	
[66 ‡]	Asa Hussey	1	2				3
[67 ‡]	Adney Hussey	1	2				3
[68*‡]	John C. James	4	8				12
[69*‡]	Thomas Marrs	1	6				7
[70*‡]	Coldwell Cairns	2	5		1		8
[71*‡]	James R. Sheppard	1	2				3
[72*‡]	Alexander Jameson	5	6				11
[73*‡]	James & Saml. Turner	2					2
[74*‡]	William Lemon	3	4				7
[75 ‡]	Samuel Baily	1	1				2
[76*‡]	Charlotte Chalfin	1	4				5
[77*‡]	Edward Clark	1	6				7
[78*‡]	Rubin Miller	1	5				6
[79 ‡]	Robert Miller	1	2				3
[80*‡]	William Chalfin	1	2				3
[81 ‡]	Jacob Stong	1	4				5
[82*‡]	Michael Miller	2	5				7
[83 ‡]	Susan Clark	1	2				3
[84*‡]	Felix Clark	3	5				8
[85*‡]	James McDonald	1	7				8
[86*‡]	Jacob Eastwood	1	5				6
[87*‡]	Daniel H. Hambleton	1	3				4
[88 ‡]	Fredreck Varnum	1	3				4
[89*‡]	Joseph Kinney	1	3				4
[90*‡]	Jacob Clark	3	9				12
[91*‡]	George McMuthey	1	7				8
[92 ‡]	Hilyard Hix	1	4				5
[93*‡]	John Tolin	1	6				7
[94*‡]	Thomas M. Hambleton	1	3				4
[95*‡]	Isaac Tolin	1	2				3
[96*‡]	Joshua Cary	1	3				4
[97*‡]	Nethaniel Hambleton	1	1				2
[98*‡]	Moses Vernum	4	3				7
[99*‡]	Daniel Barker	1	4				5
[100*‡]	Zopher Williams	1	9				10
[101 ‡]	Zacariah Norton	1	6				7

MONROE COUNTY (Continued)

No.	Heads of families	Free white persons		People of color			Aggregate
		Males 21 & upwards	All other white	Free	Servants	Slaves	
[102*‡]	Josiah Lemen	1	6				7
[103*‡]	William Lemen	1	5				6
[104*‡]	Henry Miller	2	7				9
[105 ‡]	Sarah Hogan		7				7
[106*‡]	Jesse W. Cooper	2	1				3
[107 ‡]	Burdet Green	1	1				2
[108*‡]	Daniel Rapert	1	4				5
[109 ‡]	Nicholas Grote	3	2				5
[110 ‡]	Freeman Kelley	1	6				7
[111 ‡]	John Kelley	1	2				3
[112*‡]	Benjamin Scovil	1	4				5
[113*‡]	John Miller	2	3				5
[114*‡]	Samuel Nowlin	2	5				7
[115 ‡]	Daniel Winn	1	3				4
[116*‡]	Alexander McNabb	1	9				10
[117*‡]	Raphael Drury	2	3				5
[118 ‡]	Jesse Boggs	1	2				3
[119*‡]	Francis Baldwin	1	4				5
[120*‡]	Adams Payne	3	3				6
[121 ‡]	Denis Dace	1	1				2
[122*‡]	Mary Dace		5				5
[123 ‡]	Andrew Hilton	3	6				9
[124*‡]	John McClure	2	1				3
[125 ‡]	Billington Taylor	1	9				10
[126 ‡]	Samuel Dunn	1	4				5
[127*‡]	John Hogan	2	5				7
[128 ‡]	Benonia Clark	2	3				5
[129 ‡]	William Foster	1	7				8
[130 ‡]	Philip Danford	1	2				3
[131*‡]	James Lemen	1	1				2
[132*‡]	Moses Lemen	1	4				5
[133 ‡]	Isaac J. Hatch	3	2				5
[134*‡]	Susanna Barker	2	2				4
[135 ‡]	Daniel Hilton	2	10				12
[136 ‡]	James Bartlet	1	3				4
[137 ‡]	Levi Dains	2	10				12
[138*‡]	Thomas James	6	3				9

CENSUS OF 1820

MONROE COUNTY (*Continued*)

No.	Heads of families	Free white persons		People of color			Aggregate
		Males 21 & upwards	All other white	Free	Servants	Slaves	
[139 ‡]	David Burk	1	6				7
[140 ‡]	Stephen Dolson	1	1				2
[141 ‡]	William Bryan	1	3				4
[142 ‡]	Peter Adlesperger	1	8				9
[143*‡]	John Moredock	3	6				9
[144*‡]	William Arundle	2	1				3
[145 ‡]	Moses Lock	1	2				3
[146 ‡]	John Lock	1	1				2
[147 ‡]	Samuel Lock	1	1				2
[148*‡]	Geradis Lock	1	6				7
[149 ‡]	James A. James	1	1				2
[150*‡]	William Chance	1	3				4
[151*‡]	Theron Brownfield	1	5				6
[152*‡]	Thomas Lusby	1	2				3
[153*‡]	Francis Osborn	2	3				5
[154*]	Thomas Nelson	4	4				8
[155*‡]	John Jameson	1	6				7
[156*‡]	Ichebod Valuntine	1	6				7
[157*‡]	George Atcheson	1	4				5
[158*‡]	Enoch Moore	2	6				8
[159*‡]	Henry Warderman	1	1				2
[160 ‡]	John Shahan Junr	1	1				2
[161*‡]	Daniel Sink	2	11				13
[162*‡]	Solomon Story	3	4				7
[163*‡]	Daniel Starr	4	7				11
[164*‡]	J. Milton Moore	2	4				6
[165*‡]	William B. Whaley	1	5				6
[166 ‡]	Seth Converse	2					2
[167*‡]	Luke Patterson	1	6				7
[168 ‡]	James Evins	3	4				7
[169*‡]	Levi Piggot	1	7				8
[170*‡]	Michael Crosson	1	2				3
[171*‡]	John Shahan Senr	1					1
[172*‡]	John Roach	2	9				11
[173*‡]	William Howard	2	6				8
[174*‡]	Jehu Scott	1	9				10
[175 ‡]	Rubin Gore	1	1				2

MONROE COUNTY (*Continued*)

No.	Heads of families	Free white persons		People of color			Aggregate
		Males 21 & upwards	All other white	Free	Servants	Slaves	
[176*‡]	John Mitchell	1	7				8
[177*‡]	Leonard Carr	1	10				11
[178*‡]	William Hogan	2	7				9
[179*‡]	John Moore	1	11				12
[180*‡]	Riding B. Herring	1	5				6
[181*‡]	Francis Kirkpattrick	1	4				5
[182*‡]	William Grate	1	3				4
[183 ‡]	William Bishop	1	3				4
[184*‡]	Rubin Bradly	1	2				3
[185*‡]	William Barrick	2	1				3
[186*‡]	George Estis	1	5				6
[187*‡]	Mary Garritson	1	10				11
[188*‡]	John Robins	1	3				4
[189 ‡]	Elisha Fowler	1	5				6
[190*‡]	Daniel Shook	2	4				6
[191 ‡]	John Smith	2	1				3
[192 ‡]	Ambrose Pamer	1	2				3
[193 ‡]	Robert Haskins	3	6				9
[194 ‡]	Alexander dye	2	5				7
[195*‡]	James Fowler	2	1				3
[196*‡]	John Alexander	1	7				8
[197 ‡]	David Greaton	1	6				7
[198*‡]	Nancy Whaley	2	7				9
[199 ‡]	Richard Ackless	3	5				8
[200*‡]	Thomas Pourter	2	2				4
[201 ‡]	William Griffin	2	2				4
[202 ‡]	Nimrod Triplet	1	1				2
[203 ‡]	Elizabeth Triplet	2	4				6
[204 ‡]	Leonard Nelton	1	1				2
[205 ‡]	Harrison Dye	1	2				3
[206 ‡]	Labin Eals	1					1
[207*‡]	Jacob Clover	1	7				8
[208*‡]	Joshua Talbott	2	8				10
[209*‡]	Jonathan Sheppard	1	2				3
[210*‡]	David Robison	2	9				11
[211 ‡]	Pattrick McGrew	1	7				8
[212 ‡]	Lewis Nowlin	1	3				4

CENSUS OF 1820

MONROE COUNTY (Continued)

No.	Heads of families	Free white persons		People of color			Aggregate
		Males 21 & upwards	All other white	Free	Servants	Slaves	
[213*‡]	Davis Whiteside	2	8				10
[214*‡]	Elijah Talbott	1	6				7
[215 ‡]	John Brownfield	2	8				10
[216*‡]	William Woodrome	1	5				6
[217 ‡]	Henry Isler	1	5				6
[218 ‡]	Albert Huit	1	3				4
[219*‡]	Daniel Vaughn	1	5				6
[220 ‡]	Henry Naff	1	7				8
[221*‡]	Christian Holderman	1	5				6
[222*‡]	William Riggs	1	3				4
[223*‡]	Ishmael Dillard	1	6				7
[224*‡]	William Sterret	1	2				3
[225*‡]	Thomas Sterret	2	3				5
[226*‡]	James Taylor	2	5				7
[227*‡]	Thomas Taylor Junr	1	3				4
[228*‡]	Tabitha Johnston		9				9
[229*‡]	Benjamin Marney	2	4				6
[230 ‡]	Markus Pelham	1	4				5
[231*‡]	James Woodrome	1	4				5
[232*‡]	Joel Woodrome	1	6				7
[233 ‡]	Elijah Axly	1	2				3
[234*‡]	Auther Eberman	1	4				5
[235 ‡]	Hutchison & Stewart	7					7
[236*‡]	James Bradshaw	1	7				8
[237*‡]	Thomas Taylor Senr.	1	6				7
[238 ‡]	Ruth Cormac		2				2
[239*‡]	Joseph McMeans	1	5				6
[240*‡]	Richard Brownfield	2	2				4
[241 ‡]	Jacob Finatia	1	1				2
[242 ‡]	Rubin May	1	1				2
[243*‡]	Linvil McDaniel	1	8				9
[244 ‡]	James McDaniel	1	1				2
[245*‡]	David Woodrome	1	3				4
[246*‡]	Charles Patterson	1	2				3
[247 ‡]	Solomon Patterson	1	5				6
[248 ‡]	William Right	1	5		.		6
[249*‡]	William Forquer	2	5				7

MONROE COUNTY (*Continued*)

No.	Heads of families	Free white persons		People of color			Aggregate
		Males 21 & upwards	All other white	Free	Servants	Slaves	
[250 ‡]	Gardner Stone	2	3				5
[251*‡]	Elizabeth Ford		3				3
[252 ‡]	David Scott	1	9				10
[253 ‡]	Jesse Miller	1	1				2
[254 ‡]	John McCormac	1	4				5
[255*‡]	Daniel Bryan	1	3				4
[256*‡]	Henry Field	1	3				4
[257 ‡]	Charles Read	1	5				6
[258*‡]	Mary Dickerson		6				6
[259*‡]	Michael Hammond	1	6				7
[260 ‡]	Jesse McKane	1					1
[261*‡]	Prince Bryant	3	6				7

MONROE COUNTY (*Continued*)

Recapitulation of the foregoing schedule containing the whole number of inhabitance in the County of Monroe.

Pages	Free white inhabitance		People of color			
	Males 21 years old & upwards	All other white inhabitance	Free	Servants	Slaves	Aggregate
total	393	1111	10	21	13	1548
	1111					
	393					
	————					
	1504 [Whites]					

I certify that the foregoing Schedule Containing one thousand five hundred & forty six persons is the whole number of Inhabitance in the County of Monroe State of Illinois, taken agreeably to the act of the General Assembly of said State for taking the Census in the year 1820

PRINCE BRYANT. Commissioner

Monroe County }
November 2nd 1820 }

As the pages do not correspond with the pages of this volume the totals for each page as given in the manuscript have been omitted here and totals only given.

MONROE COUNTY (Continued)

John Moore took the census for Monroe County in 1818 and Prince Bryant took both the state and the federal census for 1820. The state census was certified November 2 and the federal census December 4, 1820.

One name found in the state census for 1820 is not found in the federal census though the family is listed in the 1818 census:

154 Nelson, Thomas

Ninety-six families are listed in the federal but not in the state census for 1820. These are interspersed throughout the list, and as the federal census is otherwise more detailed than the state census the one list is probably not a copy of the other but a new enumeration in spite of the fact that they are dated only a month apart. The state census was perhaps taken in the early autumn before the annual post-harvest immigration. The additional names found in the federal census are as follows:

Finley, John
Lee, ———
Barritt, William
Bushnel, Lyman
Bushnel, Solomon
Hurley, Priastly
Frost, Epraim P.
Miles, Stephen
Parker, James
Scott, Benjamin
Greenleaf, Mayo
Stevenson, William
Scott, George
Humphress, Pendleton
Blodgett, Amesa
Drew, Charles
Johnston, Charles
Evins, Samuel
*Summers, John
*Sherrill, Aventon
  1818. Sherill, Avington
Dixon, Amos
McDavid, Anthony
Barmore, William
Gordon, Redman
Hull, James
Hardin, Sarah
McCallum, Edward
*Rainor, Samuel
  1818. Raner, Samuel
Wyot, William
Masterson, Benjamin
Jewit, Gilmon
Beers, Moses
Stephens, James
Scoby, John
Coleborn, Thomas
Lathrop, Fayette
Jeffers, Joseph
Welch, Thomas
Smith, Elias
Leathers, Charles

Phillips, John
Lawrence, John B.
Francis, John
Shear, William
Wilson, Henry
Cissel, Edward
Wilcox, Gad
Axley, James
McKee, Samuel
McKee, Stewart
Moulinaix, James
Dougin, James
Fisher, Francis
McDonald, William
Bapest, Daniel
Lashway, John B.
*Thompson, William
Elliott, Jacob
Monholand, John
*Fry, Joseph
  1818. Try, Joseph
Steward, John
Thompson, John
Spriggins, Thomas
Evins, Joseph
Webster, Elijah
Dace, Harmon
Dimmie, Samuel
Naff, Jacob
Carlile, James
Cook, Elias R.
Beaumont, James S.
Roberts, Isaiah
Forquer, George
Leeper, John
Marsh, Shewbell
Garvis, Moses
*Todd, Susanna
  1818. Todd, Widow
May, Samuel
Lawrence, Richard
Gosner, Peter

MONROE COUNTY (Continued)

Agin, John
Miller, James
Oliver, James
Wiswell, Jesse
Atkinson, Mahlon
Trask, Marvin
Trask, Joseph
Miller, Richard

Boother, John
Thompson, H. O.
Gifford, Abraham
Danes, Benjamin
Scott, John
Ward, Solomon
Pourter, Andrew
Smith, Nancy

Discrepancies are as follows:

13 Modglin, John
    1818. Modglin, John, Sr.
    F1820. Modglin, John
15 Amos, Mary
    1818. Amos, Abraham
    F1820. Amos, Mary
20 Tolbott, Thomas
    1818. Talbott, Thomas
    F1820. Talbott, Thomas
33 Chalpin, Ellis
    1818. Chalfin, Elis
    F1820. Chalfin, Ellis
35 Chalpen, Seth
    1818. Chalfin, Seth
    F1820. Chalfin, Seth
39 Bradshaw, Absolum
    1818. Bradshaw, Absalum
    F1820. Bradshaw, Absolum
43 Leper, James
    F1820. Leeper, James
52 Levins, Isaiah
    1818. Levens, Isaiah
    F1820. Levins, Isaiah
55 Kinney, Andy
    1818. Kinney, Andey
    F1820. Kinney, Andy
58 Lavisee, David
    F1820. Lavisse, David
60 Coleman, Ebenezer
    F1820. Colborne, Ebenezer
62 Mooney, Samuel
    F1820. Money, Samuel
65 Ditch, David
    F1820. Dilch, David
68 James, John C.
    1818. James, John
    F1820. James, John C.
70 Cairns, Coldwell
    1818. Cairns, Caldwell
    F1820. Cairns, Coldwell
71 Sheppard, James R.
    1818. Sheepherd, James
    F1820. Sheppard, James R.

73 Turner, James & Saml.
    1818. Turner, Samuel
    F1820. Turner, James & Samuel
74 Lemon, William
    1818. Lemen, William
    F1820. Lemon, William
75 Baily, Samuel
    F1820. Bailey, Samuel
76 Chalfin, Charlotte
    1818. Chalfin, Amos
    F1820. Chalfin, Charlotte
78 Miller, Rubin
    1818. Miller, Reuben
    F1820. Miller, Rubin
85 McDonald, James
    1818. McDonald, James
    F1820. McDonold, James
88 Varnum, Fredreck
    F1820. Vernum, Frederick
91 McMuthey, George
    1818. McMurtry, George
    F1820. McMuttrey, George
97 Hambleton, Nethaniel
    1818. Hambleton, Nat.
    F1820. Hambleton, Nethniel
98 Vernum, Moses
    1818. Varnum, Moses
    F1820. Vernum, Moses
103 Lemen, William
    1818. Lemmon, William
    F1820. Lemen, William
107 Green, Burdet
    F1820. Green, Burdit
108 Rapert, Daniel
    1818. Raport, Daniel
    F1820. Rapert, Daniel
109 Grote, Nicholas
    F1820. Grate, Nicholas
112 Scovil, Benjamin
    1818. Scovel, Benjamin
    F1820. Scovil, Benjamin
114 Nowlin, Samuel
    1818. Nolin, Samuel
    F1820. Nowlin, Samuel

MONROE COUNTY (Continued)

121 Dace, Denis
    F1820. Dace, Dennis
122 Dace, Mary
    1818. Dace, Michael
    F1820. Dace, Mary
124 McClure, John
    1818. McClure, John
    F1820. McCluer, John
128 Clark, Benonia
    F1820. Clark, Benona
134 Barker, Susanna
    1818. Barker, Zebediah
    F1820. Barker, Susanna
144 Arundle, William
    1818. Arundel, William
    F1820. Arundle, William
148 Lock, Geradis
    1818. Lock, Gerardis
    F1820. Lock, Gerades
153 Osborn, Francis
    1818. Orsborn, Francis
    F1820. Osbourn, Frances
155 Jameson, John
    1818. Jameson, John
    F1820. Jamison, John
156 Valuntine, Ichebod
    1818. Volentine, Ichabod
    F1820. Valuntine, Ichebod
159 Wardenman, Henry
    1818. Wadderman, Henry
    F1820. Waderman, Henry
160 Shahan, John, Jr.
    F1820. Shahan, John
162 Story, Solomon
    1818. Stong, Solomon
    F1820. Story, Solomon
165 Whaley, William B.
    1818. Whaley, Baker
    F1820. Whaley, William B.
169 Piggot, Levi
    1818. Piggott, Levi
    F1820. Piggot, Levi
170 Crosson, Michael
    1818. Crossen, Michael
    F1820. Croson, Michael
171 Shahan, John, Sr.
    1818. Sheehen, John
    F1820. Shahan, John
176 Mitchell, John
    1818. Mitchel, John
    F1820. Mitchell, John
180 Herring, Riding B.
    1818. Herren, ——
    F1820. Herring, Redding B.
181 Kirkpattrick, Francis
    1818. Kirkpatrick, Francis
    F1820. Kirkpattrick, Francis
182 Grate, William
    1818. Grote, William
    F1820. Grate, William
184 Bradly, Rubin
    1818. Bradley, Reuben
    F1820. Bradly, Rubin
186 Estis, George
    1818. Estes, George
    F1820. Estis, George
187 Garritson, Mary
    1818. Garetson, James
    F1820. Garretson, Mary
192 Pamer, Ambrose
    F1820. Pammer, Ambrose
198 Whaley, Nancy
    1818. Whaley, James
    F1820. Whaley, Nancy
200 Pourter, Thomas
    1818. Porter, Thomas
    F1820. Pourter, Thomas
202 Triplet, Nimrod
    F1820. Triplett, Minrod
203 Triplet, Elizabeth
    F1820. Triplet, Elizebeth
209 Sheppard, Jonathan
    1818. Shepherd, Jonathan
    F1820. Sheppard, Jonathan
218 Huit, Albert
    F1820. Huitt, Albertt
219 Vaughn, Daniel
    1818. Vaughan, Daniel
    F1820. Vaughn, Daniel
221 Holderman, Christian
    1818. Halderman, Christian
    F1820. Holderman, Christian
223 Dillard, Ishmael
    1818. Dillard, Ishmael
    F1820. Dillard, Ishmail
224 Sterret, William
    1818. Sterrett, William
    F1820. Sterrett, William
225 Sterret, Thomas
    1818. Sterrit, Thomas
    F1820. Sterrett, Thomas
228 Johnston, Tabitha
    1818. Johnson, Wm.
    F1820. Johnston, Tabitha
230 Pelham, Markus
    F1820. Pelham, Marcus
233 Axly, Elijah
    F1820. Axley, Elijah

MONROE COUNTY (Concluded)

234 Eberman, Auther
    1818. Eberman, Arthur
    F1820. Eberman, Auther
235 Hutchison & Stewart
    F1820. Hutcheson & Stewart
238 Cormac, Ruth
    F1820. McCormick, Ruth
239 McMeans, Joseph
    1818. McMeen, Joseph
    F1820. McMeans, Joseph
241 Finatia, Jacob
    F1820. Fenatia, Jacob

243 McDaniel, Linvil
    1818. McDanold, Linville
    F1820. McDaniel, Lenvil
254 McCormac, John
    F1820. McCormick, John
256 Field, Henry
    1818. Fields, Henry
    F1820. Field, Henry
258 Dickerson, Mary
    1818. Dickason, George
    F1820. Dickerson, Mary
259 Hammond, Michael
    1818. Hammon, Michael
    F1820. Hammond, Michael

CENSUS OF POPE COUNTY, 1820

Schedule of the whole number of Inhabitants in the County of Pope in conformity to the act of the General assembly of the state of Illinois for taking the Census for the year *1820*.

Names of Heads of Families	Free white persons		People of Colour			Aggregate
	Males 21 years of age and upwards	All other white Inhabitants	Free	Servants	Slaves	
[1*‡] John Steel	2	8				10
[2*‡] Saml. Omelveny	2	6				8
[3*‡] Thos. Wallace	1	8				9
[4*‡] Lincy Madlin	1	5				6
[5*‡] Hugh Robinson	4	3				7
[6 ‡] Asa Foster	1	3				4
[7*‡] Isam Clay	4	4				8
[8 ‡] Jasper Simmons	1	6				7
[9*‡] Geo Jackson	1	5				6
[10 ‡] S. Soward	2	4				6
[11 ‡] James Williams	1	3				4
[12*‡] Alx: Blair	3	5				8
[13*‡] Coleman Haws	1	5				6
[14*‡] Thos. Cowsart	1	5				6
[15*‡] Saml. M. Morrow	1	6				7
[16 ‡] Elisha Mills	2	3				5
[17*‡] Alx: Parkison	1	6				7
[18*‡] James Cowsart	1	9				10
[19] Benjn. Peninton			2			2
[20*‡] Geo. Vinard	1	5				6
[21 ‡] Geo. Roper	1	5				6
[22 ‡] Roswell Chancey	2	3				5
[23 ‡] Saml. Brown	1	3				4
[24 ‡] Widow Brown	2	3				5
[25 ‡] William Sellers	1	8				9
[26*‡] Robt. Cowsert	1	3				4
[27*‡] John Mattison	1	2				3

Figures and symbols preceding names have been supplied by the editor:
‡ Indicates name also in Federal Census for 1820.
* Indicates name also in State Census for 1818.

CENSUS OF 1820

POPE COUNTY (Continued)

No.	Heads of families	Free white persons		People of color			Aggregate
		Males 21 & upwards	All other white	Free	Servants	Slaves	
[28*‡]	Widow Johnson	1	1				2
[29 ‡]	Henry Mott	2	10				12
[30 ‡]	Barny McCan	1	3				4
[31*‡]	Geo: Hamilton	1	2		1		3
[32*‡]	Strongman Mogelon	1	7				8
[33*‡]	John Coliar	1	8				9
[34*‡]	Abm. Joiner	1	2				3
[35*‡]	Henry Skinner	1	2				3
[36 ‡]	Andw. Skinner	1	1				2
[37*‡]	John Hawes	2	7				9
[38*‡]	Wm. Modglin	1	4				5
[39 ‡]	Widow Hawes	1					1
[40*‡]	Rees Shelby	1	5				6
[41*‡]	N. Story	1	2				3
[42 ‡]	Hickman Joiner	1	1				2
[43*‡]	Frs. Hogg	1	7				8
[44*‡]	John Storey	1	2				3
[45*‡]	Mark Whiticker	4	6				10
[46 ‡]	Widow Buckner	2	1				3
[47*‡]	James Buckner	1	3				4
[48 ‡]	John Williams	1	6				7
[49*‡]	Thos. Rose	1	8				9
[50*‡]	Wm. Hays	1	3				4
[51*‡]	Abel Richison	2	7				9
[52 ‡]	Randall Towns	1	5				6
[53 ‡]	Jno. Hence	2	4				6
[54 ‡]	Wm. Latham	1	5				6
[55 ‡]	Elbert Rose	3	8				11
[56 ‡]	Geo. Rightnour	1	6				7
[57 ‡]	Greggs Clary	1	1				2
[58*‡]	Danl. Watkins	2	6				8
[59*‡]	John Redford	1	1				2
[60*‡]	Jacob Shelby	2	6	1			8
[61*‡]	Even Shilby	1	3				4
[62*‡]	John Bradner	1	2				3
[63]	Lincey Modlin	1	4				5

POPE COUNTY (*Continued*)

No.	Heads of families	Free white persons		People of color			Aggregate
		Males 21 & upwards	All other white	Free	Servants	Slaves	
[64 ‡]	Levi Joiner	1	3				4
[65*‡]	John Joiner	1	2				3
[66 ‡]	Pleasant Rose	1	4				5
[67 ‡]	Sharon Rose	1	2				3
[68*‡]	Jesse Green	1	2				3
[69*‡]	John Turner	1	5				6
[70*‡]	Reuben Green	1	3				4
[71 ‡]	Widow Joiner		5				5
[72 ‡]	Cage Joiner	1	2				3
[73*‡]	Wm. Joiner Jnr.	1	5				6
[74*‡]	Wm. Joiner Snr.	1	1				2
[75 ‡]	Jonn. Jackson	1	1				2
[76*‡]	Lot Joiner	1	5				6
[77 ‡]	Wm. Gibson	1	7				8
[78*‡]	Achilles McFarlin	1	5				6
[79*‡]	Molton Eubanks	1	1				2
[80 ‡]	John Lovetetty	1	1				2
[81*‡]	John Armstrong	1	4				5
[82 ‡]	John McLean	1	4				5
[83 ‡]	Lawdy King	1	7				8
[84 ‡]	Dd. McMurphy	1	9				10
[85*‡]	Richd. Lee	1	9				10
[86*‡]	Isaac Pettette	1	5				6
[87*‡]	John Howard	3	5				8
[88*‡]	Ezekiel McCoy	3	9				12
[89*‡]	Jonas Ingraham	1	5				6
[90*‡]	Danl. Vinyard	2	7				9
[91*‡]	John Gingor	1	2				3
[92 ‡]	Isaac Reeder	1	9				10
[93*‡]	Nathan Warnick	2	4				6
[94*‡]	Nathan Warnick	1	3				4
[95 ‡]	Wm. Jones	1	3				4
[96 ‡]	Richd. Lee	1	3				4
[97 ‡]	Simon Womel	1	11				12
[98 ‡]	Morace Relay	1	2				3
[99*‡]	Widow Lisenby		9				9

CENSUS OF 1820 217

POPE COUNTY (Continued)

No.	Heads of families	Free white persons		People of color			Aggregate
		Males 21 & upwards	All other white	Free	Servants	Slaves	
[100 ‡]	Betsy Lisenby		3				3
[101 ‡]	Thos. Dryton	1	1				2
[102*‡]	Spires Singleton	1	7				8
[103 ‡]	Isaac Hide	2	3				5
[104 ‡]	James Hale	1	3				4
[105*‡]	Jesse Green	1	10				11
[106*‡]	Wm. Huston	1	8				9
[107 ‡]	Widow Ross	1					1
[108 ‡]	Danl. Chanler	1	1				2
[109 ‡]	Ely Chandler	1	1				2
[110 ‡]	Thos. Chandler	1	1				2
[111*‡]	R. C. Atkinson	1	5				6
[112*‡]	Richd Bennett	1	6				7
[113 ‡]	Widow Hathaway	1	2				3
[114*‡]	Geo. Leaky	1	7				8
[115 ‡]	Moses Twitchell	4	7				11
[116 ‡]	Andw. Chancy	4	1				5
[117 ‡]	Joseph Conway	1	1				2
[118 ‡]	Saml. Hafsey	1	8				9
[119 ‡]	Benjn. Wilson	2	5				7
[120 ‡]	Platt Mott	1	2				3
[121 ‡]	Jas. P. Mott	2	5				7
[122 ‡]	Israel Chancey	1	6				7
[123 ‡]	Widow Joiner	1	4				5
[124 ‡]	Lemuel Overby	2	9				11
[125 ‡]	Mathew Turner	1	5				6
[126*‡]	Jas. Hill	2	7				9
[127*‡]	J. D. Scott	1					1
[128 ‡]	Henry Leytell	2	1				3
[129 ‡]	Thos Kennedy	1	4				5
[130 ‡]	Isaac Grizell	1	3				4
[131 ‡]	Judithan Dimy	1	4				5
[132 ‡]	Z. Hallock	1	2				3
[133*‡]	John Morris	2	9				11
[134*‡]	John Jackson	1	4				5
[135*‡]	Beno. Lee	2	10				12

POPE COUNTY (*Continued*)

No.	Heads of families	Free white persons		People of color			Aggregate
		Males 21 & upwards	All other white	Free	Servants	Slaves	
[136 ‡]	H W Gibson	1	10				11
[137*‡]	James Lee	1	3				4
[138 ‡]	David Gillett	1	1				2
[139*‡]	Lewis Pankey	2	2				4
[140 ‡]	Josh. Bassitt	2	2				4
[141 ‡]	Chas. Smith	1	4				5
[142 ‡]	Ery Bassett	1	2				3
[143 ‡]	Andw. Jackson	1	5				6
[144*‡]	Thos. Brown	1	4				5
[145 ‡]	John Stevens	1	3				4
[146*‡]	John Daniel	1	2				3
[147*‡]	John Leiper	1	4				5
[148*‡]	Larken Keistirson	2	2				2
[149*‡]	Lewis Barker	3	5				8
[150 ‡]	Widow McKillen		6				6
[151 ‡]	William Kullison	1	6	1			8
[152*‡]	David Dees	1	8				9
[153 ‡]	Robert Field	1	4				5
[154*‡]	James Hull	1	1				2
[155 ‡]	Jno. Wilkinson	1	9				10
[156*‡]	Jno. Vaughan	2	3				5
[157 ‡]	Luke Tichet	1	4				5
[158 ‡]	Pliny Barnum	2	6				8
[159*‡]	Robt. Keisterson	1	2				3
[160 ‡]	Peter Keistirson	1	3				4
[161 ‡]	B. Coffin	1	2				3
[162*‡]	Widow Palmer	3	7				10
[163 ‡]	Joseph Baldwin	3	7	1			10
[164 ‡]	Mr. Meason	1	5				6
[165*‡]	Widow Smock	6	9				15
[166 ‡]	David Hurr	1	7				8
[167 ‡]	Allen Hill	1	1				2
[168 ‡]	Dickson Scott	2			1		2
[169*‡]	Wm. Pankey	1	6				7
[170 ‡]	John Midelton	1	2				3
[171*‡]	Henry Rose	2	2				4

POPE COUNTY (*Continued*)

No.	Heads of families	Free white persons		People of color			Aggregate
		Males 21 & upwards	All other white	Free	Servants	Slaves	
[172 ‡]	Barney Hungerford	1	2				3
[173 ‡]	Wm. Jones	1					1
[174 ‡]	John Cole	1	1				2
[175*‡]	John Glass	1	3				4
[176*‡]	Dudley Glass	1	9				10
[177 ‡]	Joshua Ross	1	2				3
[178*‡]	John Wilson	1	6				7
[179 ‡]	Philo Averill	1	6				7
[180 ‡]	Joseph Neill	1	3				4
[181*‡]	Jacob Ralsion	3	6		4		9
[182*‡]	Geo: Storey	2	7				9
[183*‡]	Geoe Vaughan	3	8				11
[184*‡]	Jess :e McCool	1	5				6
[185 ‡]	Wm˙ Dearman	3	6				9
[186 ‡]	John Owens	1	7				8
[187 ‡]	Jacob Shuffelberger	1	9				10
[188 ‡]	Abm. Schuffelberger	1	3				4
[189 ‡]	Abm. Roads	2	3				5
[190 ‡]	John Curtis	3	5				8
[191 ‡]	Betsey Johnson	1	6				7
[192 ‡]	Chas. Johnston	1	9				10
[193 ‡]	James Snow	2	4				6
[194*‡]	James A. Whitesides	1	9		5		10
[195 ‡]	Martin Brown	1	3				4
[196 ‡]	John Morse	1	7				8
[197*‡]	Lincoln Harper	1	8				9
[198 ‡]	Jacob Carrell	1	2				3
[199 ‡]	Abm. Hudleton	2	7				9
[200 ‡]	John Whitside	1	4		1		5
[201 ‡]	Joel Williams	1	6				7
[202 ‡]	Mathew Jenkins	1	2				3
[203 ‡]	David Thomas	1	4				5
[204 ‡]	Jacob Kennedy	1	4				5
[205 ‡]	Geo. Abbett	1	4				5
[206 ‡]	Jacob Kennedy	2	3				5
[207*‡]	Wm. Modgelon	1	1				2

POPE COUNTY (*Continued*)

No.	Heads of families	Free white persons		People of color			Aggregate
		Males 21 & upwards	All other white	Free	Servants	Slaves	
[208*‡]	Jacob McCollum	1	2				3
[209*‡]	Jno. Bruington	1	7				8
[210 ‡]	Nefel Leech	1	5				6
[211*‡]	Joseph McHenry	2	4				6
[212*‡]	Wm. Wilson	1	3				4
[213*‡]	Benjn. Bowman	1	5				6
[214 ‡]	James McKee	1	7				8
[215*‡]	Herman Slankard	1	4				5
[216 ‡]	Rachal Hethcot	1					1
[217*‡]	Isiah Leech	1	6				7
[218 ‡]	Robt. Devise	1	1				2
[219*‡]	John Witt	5	9				14
[220 ‡]	Lugar Wright	1	6				7
[221 ‡]	Jacob Sivey	1	4				5
[222 ‡]	Samuel Meredith	1	9				10
[223 ‡]	Saml Bailey	1	5				6
[224 ‡]	Jas. Ellis	3	7				10
[225*‡]	Jos. Dillard	2	4				6
[226*‡]	Thos. Reed	2	5				7
[227*‡]	John McHenry	1	5				6
[228 ‡]	Polly Simson	1	3				4
[229*‡]	Benjn. McCool	1	4				5
[230 ‡]	Joel Williams	1	6				7
[231*‡]	Hiram Pehny	2	4				6
[232 ‡]	Wm. Pringall	1	2				3
[233 ‡]	James Murphy	1	2				3
[234 ‡]	Luke Vaughan	3	6				9
[235 ‡]	M B Hill	3	6				9
[236 ‡]	Andre Reed	1	4				5
[237 ‡]	Israel Bozarth	2	7				9
[238 ‡]	J. Cotton	1	8				9
[239*‡]	Franklin Perry	2	9				11
[240 ‡]	Jos. Wilson	1	7				8
[241 ‡]	Henry Bogus	1	7				8
[242 ‡]	Lewis Johnson	1	5				6
[243 ‡]	Jas. Robinson	2	3				5

CENSUS OF 1820

POPE COUNTY (Continued)

No.	Heads of families	Free white persons — Males 21 & upwards	Free white persons — All other white	People of color — Free	People of color — Servants	Slaves	Aggregate
[244 ‡]	Edw. Robinson	1	7				8
[245 ‡]	Saml. Hazell	1	4				5
[246 ‡]	Jos. Wilson	1	9				10
[247 ‡]	Travis Morris	2	3				5
[248 ‡]	Wylie James	1	4				5
[249 ‡]	John Holmes	1					1
[250 ‡]	Red:ng Wright	1	2				3
[251*‡]	King Hazele	1	6				7
[252*‡]	Danl Hazele	2	2				4
[253*‡]	John Hayes	1	4				5
[254*‡]	Isaac Rolston	1	3				4
[255*‡]	Robt. Hays	2	5			4	7
[256*‡]	Geo. Slankard	1	5				6
[257 ‡]	Jeremiah Jones	1	5				6
[258 ‡]	Thos. Waters	1	7				8
[259*‡]	Geo. Slankard	1	5				6
[260*‡]	Joshua Slankard	1	3				4
[261*‡]	Hezek: Hill	2	8				10
[262 ‡]	B F Gavott	1	3				4
[263 ‡]	Saml. Pomely	1	6				7
[264 ‡]	Jas. Crawford	1	3				4
[265 ‡]	Geo: Hanna	1	3				4
[266*‡]	Wm. Hannah	1	3				4
[267 ‡]	Geo: Hodge	1	5				6
[268*‡]	Jonas Ethridge	1	6				7
[269*‡]	Alx: Murphy	1	8				9
[270 ‡]	Joseph Lewis	2	6				8
[271 ‡]	Richd. Chuning	2	7				9
[272 ‡]	Widow Goodall	1	2				3
[273*‡]	Robt. Hamilton	3	8				11
[274*‡]	Jas. Craford	1	2				3
[275 ‡]	Saml. Alexander	2	7				9
[276 ‡]	John Rush	2	7				9
[277 ‡]	Davis Stucker	1	1				2
[278 ‡]	Z Blackford	1	4				5
[279 ‡]	Geo: Dougherty	2	5				7

POPE COUNTY (Continued)

No.	Heads of families	Free white persons		People of color			Aggregate
		Males 21 & upwards	All other white	Free	Servants	Slaves	
[280 ‡]	N. Hooker	1	3				4
[281*‡]	James King	1	4				5
[282 ‡]	Arthur Storm	2	3				5
[283 ‡]	J Hamilton	1	1				2
[284 ‡]	S Hocum	1	3				4
[285 ‡]	R. Fulherson	1	6				7
[286 ‡]	S Simmons	2	2				4
[287*‡]	B Belford	2	4				6
[288*‡]	I Harper	2	10				12
[289*‡]	Wm. Belford	1	6				7
[290 ‡]	Wm. Leland	1	7				8
[291*‡]	Jacob Storm	1	8				9
[292 ‡]	J Montgomery	1	7				8
[293*‡]	W. Stucker	1	7				8
[294 ‡]	Wm. Cowan	2	2				4
[295 ‡]	Jas. Pettilla	2	4				6
[296 ‡]	Thos. Watters	1	2				3
[297 ‡]	Ely Casteel	1	6				7
[298*‡]	J. Calvert	2	4				6
[299 ‡]	J Hannah	1	6				7
[300*‡]	James Hannah	1	3				4
[301*‡]	J Calvert	1	1				2
[302 ‡]	W. Lampins	1	6				7
[303*‡]	F Gloss	1	6				7
[304 ‡]	J Gloss	1	1				2
[305*‡]	Jon. Gloss	1	6				7
[306 ‡]	J Shaw	2	7				9
[307 ‡]	E Allen	1	2				3
[308 ‡]	Dd Shockney	1	2				3
[309 ‡]	J Scott	1	3			2	4
[310 ‡]	S Turner	2	6				8
[311 ‡]	F McLinden	1	9				10
[312*‡]	J Williams	1	8				9
[313 ‡]	Wm. Manning	1	4				5
[314]	Asa Gallamon	1					1
[315*‡]	Jno. Modglin	1	3				4

CENSUS OF 1820

POPE COUNTY (Continued)

No.	Heads of families	Free white persons		People of color			Aggregate
		Males 21 & upwards	All other white	Free	Servants	Slaves	
[316 ‡]	J. Williamson	1	4				5
[317*‡]	R Ferris	1	5				6
[318 ‡]	S Atterberry	1	5				6
[319 ‡]	C King	1	6				7
[320*‡]	C Shelby	1	2				3
[321*‡]	J Richie	1	8				9
[322 ‡]	S. Ditterline	1	1				2
[323*‡]	R Roberts	3	6				9
[324*‡]	J Ditterline	2	6				8
[325 ‡]	T Campbell	1	7				8
[326 ‡]	Jno. Cook	1	5				6
[327 ‡]	R Potter	1	2				3
[328 ‡]	Wm. Griffith	1	1				2
[329 ‡]	S Campbell	4	7				11
[330*‡]	E Flannery	1	4				5
[331 ‡]	Wm. Caswell	1	2				3
[332*‡]	L Drewry	2	5				7
[333 ‡]	I Rowse	1	6				7
[334 ‡]	B F. Odle	1	3				4
[335 ‡]	L. Curtis	1	6				7
[336 ‡]	L Rouse	2	11				13
[337 ‡]	J Snider	1	2				3
[338 ‡]	T Webster	1	5				6
[339 ‡]	S Rathbone	1	3				4
[340 ‡]	Wm. Cook	1	7				8
[341 ‡]	A Croft	2	7				9
[342 ‡]	P Vance	1	3				4
[343*‡]	J Lard	1	3				4
[344 ‡]	Abm. Griffith	1	5				6
[345 ‡]	Jno Simmons	1	4				5
[346 ‡]	M Burbank	1	2				3
[347*‡]	R Fisk	2	3				5
[348*‡]	A. F. Fisk	3	5				8
[349 ‡]	Mrs Pitt	1	4				5
[350 ‡]	J. C Kidd	3	2				5
[351 ‡]	Jas. Lean	1	5				6

POPE COUNTY (Continued)

No.	Heads of families	Free white persons		People of color			Aggregate
		Males 21 & upwards	All other white	Free	Servants	Slaves	
[352*‡]	W. Bartlett			3			3
[353 ‡]	J Bartlett			6			6
[354 ‡]	J Turner	1	4	1			6
[355 ‡]	R. Douglass	1	4				5
[356*‡]	Jno Stubbs	2	6				8
[357 ‡]	R Stubbs	1	2				3
[358 ‡]	Geo McCormick	1	1				2
[359 ‡]	Jno. McCormick	1	8				9
[360 ‡]	Wm. McCormick	1	5				6
[361 ‡]	S Carpenter	1	4				5
[362 ‡]	J Bennett	1	6				7
[363*‡]	R Robinson			1			1
[364 ‡]	D Jackson	1	3				4
[365 ‡]	J Nelly	1	4				5
[366 ‡]	Widow Saunders	1	4				5
[367 ‡]	Wm Young	2	5				7
[368 ‡]	R Joiner	1	9				10
[369*‡]	J L. Warnick	1	3				4
[370 ‡]	J. Mc Carty	1	2				3
[371*‡]	M. Stubbs	1	6				7
[372 ‡]	Wm. Glover	1	3				4
[373*‡]	R. Geving	1	1				2
[374*‡]	J. Manning	1	1				2
[375*‡]	B Titsworth	1	2				3
[376 ‡]	Widow Simpson	1	6				7
[377 ‡]	J Parrott	1	1				2
[378 ‡]	A Hunter	1	6				7
[379*‡]	B Thompson	1	2				3
[380*‡]	Wm Neely	1	2				3
[381 ‡]	J. Glover	2	5				7
[382*‡]	H Lewis	1	3				4
[383*‡]	Geo Lewis	2	6				8
[384*‡]	O. S Clark	1	2				3
[385*‡]	Thos. Thompson	1	8				9
[386*‡]	James Neely	1	1				2
[387 ‡]	J. Crouse	1	4				5

POPE COUNTY (*Continued*)

No.	Heads of families	Free white persons		People of color			Aggregate
		Males 21 & upwards	All other white	Free	Servants	Slaves	
[388 ‡]	Jos Cross	1	4				5
[389 ‡]	Ab: Ladison	2	3				5
[390 ‡]	T. T. Farris	1	1				2
[391 ‡]	Jno Montgomery	2	2				4
[392 ‡]	C Ferguson	1	3		1		5
[393 ‡]	J H Smith	1	5				6
[394 ‡]	J Parker	3	4				7
[395 ‡]	J. Parrott	1	1				2
[396 ‡]	Jno Fartner	1	3				4
[397 ‡]	Geo Hoage	1	6				7
[398 ‡]	And: Lewis	1	3				4
[399 ‡]	Wm. Glover	1	3				4
[400*‡]	W H. Williams	2	5				7
[401*‡]	J. P. Gillispie	1	6				7
[402 ‡]	H Bennett	1	3				4
[403*‡]	J Brown	1	8				9
[404*‡]	Jno Edwards	1	6				7
[405 ‡]	J. Lewis	1	5				6
[406 ‡]	Jacob Lewis	1	5				6
[407 ‡]	Abm Lashang	1	1				2
[408*‡]	Widow Frost	2	6				8
[409*‡]	Jno Wood	1	6				7
[410 ‡]	Geo Wood	1	2				3
[411*‡]	Reuben Glover	2	3				5
[412*‡]	Jno Glover	1	3				4
[413*‡]	Jno Henly	1	7				8
[414 ‡]	H Bennett	1	3				4
[415*‡]	Jas N. Fox	2	5				7
[416 ‡]	Wd. Dooms	2	5				7
[417 ‡]	Jos. Cross	1	4				5
[418*‡]	Jno Cross	1	4				5
[419*‡]	Geo Simpkins	1	6				7
[420 ‡]	P. Fox	1	2				3
[421*‡]	S. Lemnor	1	1				2
[422*‡]	J Young Blood	1	6				7
[423 ‡]	Jno Henly	2	6				8

POPE COUNTY (Continued)

No.	Heads of families	Free white persons		People of color			Aggre-gate
		Males 21 & upwards	All other white	Free	Servants	Slaves	
[424 ‡]	A Mahan	1	3				4
[425*‡]	Wm Redkin	1	3				4
[426*‡]	D. S. Taylor	1	6				7
[427*‡]	Chs Deyer	3	8				11
[428*‡]	Ab: Dyer	2	5				7
[429*‡]	Wm Dyer	2	4				6
[430 ‡]	B. Hyfell	3	3				6
[431*‡]	Isaac B Scott	1	3				4
[432*‡]	Robt. Scott	2	9				11
[433*‡]	Dd. Cowan	1	2				3
[434 ‡]	Jas. Crochett	1	3				4
[435*‡]	Jno. Crochett	1	3				4
[436*‡]	A Robinson	3	8				11
[437 ‡]	J Falkner	1	3				4
[438*‡]	S Smith	1	4				5
[439 ‡]	Jno Hamilton	2	6				8
[440*‡]	D B Gloss	1	3				4
[441 ‡]	C C. Burns	1	5				6
[442*‡]	S Waters	1	5				6
[443 ‡]	Jno. L. Bogardus	2	4				6
[444 ‡]	Jno. Leonard	1	11				12
[445 ‡]	J Beyard	1	3				4
[446 ‡]	J. C. Nichols	1	3				4
[447*‡]	A Chipps	3	1		1		4
[448*‡]	J. E. Willis	3	6				9
[449 ‡]	Wm. Sim	1					1
[450 ‡]	Laben Payne	2	8				10
[451 ‡]	Polly Porter	1	5				6
[452 ‡]	Abm. Moore	1	7				8
[453 ‡]	Mrs. Mattox		4				4
[454*‡]	Jno Roberts	1	3				4
[455 ‡]	Jos: E. Pryor	3	4				7
[456 ‡]	C. Tull	3	6				9
[457 ‡]	R Hancock	2	5				7
[458*‡]	D Fields	2	5				7
[459 ‡]	S Haymon	1	2				3

POPE COUNTY (Continued)

No.	Heads of families	Free white persons		People of color			Aggregate
		Males 21 & upwards	All other white	Free	Servants	Slaves	
[460 ‡]	E. Church	1	5				6
[461 ‡]	S Burnett	3	7		1		10
[462 ‡]	C. P. Aester	2	2				4
[463 ‡]	Jas. Falkner	1	5				6
[464 ‡]	B Stevens	1	4				5
[465*‡]	F Moore	1	5				6
[466 ‡]	A Innman	1	3				4
[467 ‡]	Jno Ellis	2	4				6
[468 ‡]	Wm. Rondo	1	7				8
[469 ‡]	Hugh McNulty	3					3
[470 ‡]	Thos. Ferguson	1	4				5
[471*‡]	Jno. Crawford	2	8				10
[472 ‡]	Geo. Crawford	1	1				2
[473]	Job Clevenger	1					1

POPE COUNTY (*Continued*)

White males 21 years & upwards	636
All other white inhabitants	2080
Free people of colour	14
Servants	20
	2750

SAMUL OMELVENY Comr.
State of Illinois
Census for
1820.
Pope County
S. OMELVANY

White		2716
Free		14
Serv.		20
	Total	2750

Corrected totals:

Free white males of 21 years and upwards		635
All other white inhabitants		2083
		2718
Negroes		37
Free persons of color	16	
Servants	21	
	37	
	Total	2755

POPE COUNTY (Continued)

Samuel Omelveny took all three censuses of Pope County. The state census of 1820 is evidently a copy of the federal census, with the data as to ages, etc., condensed into four columns. One family was omitted in copying:

Ezekiel Clay, residing between Isam Clay (7) and Jasper Simmons (8). His family is listed as follows:

1 free white male 16-26 yr.
4 free white females under 10 yr.
1 free white female 16-26 yr.

This name appears in the 1818 census under the spelling Ezekel Clay. Four names appear in the state census which are not in the federal census: Benjn. Peninton (19), Lincey Modlin (63—a repetition of 4?), Asa Gallamon (314) and Job Clevenger (473).

Discrepancies are as follows:

1 Steel, John
   1818. Steel, James
   F1820. Steel, James
4 Madlin, Lincy
   1818. Modglen, Linsey
   F1820. Madglen, Linsey
5 Robinson, Hugh
   1818. Robison, Hugh
   F1820. Robison, Hugh
6 Foster, Asa
   F1820. Foster, Asey
7 Clay, Isam
   1818. Clay, Isam
   F1820. Clay, Isom
8 Simmons, Jasper
   F1820. Simons, Jasper
10 Soward, S.
   F1820. Soward, Charels
13 Haws, Coleman
   1818. Haws, Colman
   F1820. Haws, Colman
14 Cowsart, Thos.
   1818. Cousart, Thomas
   F1820. Cousart, Thomas
15 Morrow, Saml. M.
   1818. Morow, Samuel M.
   F1820. Morow, Samuel Mills
18 Cowsart, James
   1818. Cousart, James
   F1820. Cousart, James
20 Vinard, Geo.
   1818. Vinyard, George
   F1820. Vinyard, George
22 Chancey, Roswell
   F1820. Chancy, Raswell
25 Sellers, William
   F1820. Sellars, William
26 Cowsert, Robt.
   1818. Cousart, Robart
   F1820. Cousart, Robart

28 Johnson, Widow
   1818. Jonston, Widow
   F1820. Jonston, Widow
29 Mott, Henry
   F1820. Mott, Henery
30 McCan, Barny
   F1820. McCan, Barney
31 Hamilton, Geo.
   1818. Hamilton, George
   F1820. Hamelton, George
32 Mogelon, Strongman
   1818. Modglen, Straingman
   F1820. Modglen, Straingman
33 Coliar, John
   1818. Colier, John
   F1820. Colier, John
34 Joiner, Abm.
   1818. Joiner, Abram
   F1820. Joiner, Abram
35 Skinner, Henry
   1818. Skinner, Henery
   F1820. Skinner, Henry
37 Hawes, John
   1818. Haws, John
   F1820. Haws, John
38 Modglin, Wm.
   1818. Modglen, William
   F1820. Modglen, William
39 Hawes, Widow
   F1820. Haws, Widow
40 Shelby, Rees
   1818. Shelvey, Reece
   F1820. Shelbey, Rees
41 Story, N.
   1818. Storey, Nethan
   F1820. Storey, Nethan
43 Hogg, Frs.
   1818. Hogg, Frances
   F1820. Hogg, Frances

POPE COUNTY (*Continued*)

45 Whiticker, Mark
    1818. Whitiker, Mark
    F1820. Whitiker, Mark
49 Rose, Thos.
    1818. Roas, Thomas
    F1820. Roas, Thomas
51 Richison, Abel
    1818. Richison, Abel
    F1820. Richison, Able
52 Towns, Randall
    F1820. Towns, Randel
54 Latham, Wm.
    F1820. Lethem, William
55 Rose, Elbert
    F1820. Roas, Elbert
56 Rightnour, Geo.
    F1820. Rightenour, George
57 Clary, Greggs
    F1820. Clery, Veach
58 Watkins, Danl
    1818. Wadkens, Daniel
    F1820. Wadkens, Daniel
59 Redford, John
    1818. Redfern, John
    F1820. Redfern, John
60 Shelby, Jacob
    1818. Shelvery, Jacob
    F1820. Shelveny, Jacob
61 Shilby, Even
    1818. Shelvey, Even
    F1820. Shelvey, Even
62 Bradner, John
    1818. Braner, John
    F1820. Braner, John
64 Joiner, Levi
    F1820. Joiner, Levy
66 Rose, Pleasant
    F1820. Roas, Pleasant
67 Rose, Sharon
    F1820. Roas, Sherman
68 Green, Jesse
    1818. Green, Jessey
    F1820. Green, Jessey
69 Turner, John
    1818. Turnar, John
    F1820. Turner, John
70 Green, Reuben
    1818. Green, Ruben
    F1820. Green, Ruben
73 Joiner, Wm., Jr.
    1818. Joiner, William, Jr.
    F1820. Joiner, William
74 Joiner, Wm., Sr.
    1818. Joiner, William, Sr.
    F1820. Joiner, William

75 Jackson, Jonn
    F1820. Jackson, Jonathan
78 McFarlin, Achilles
    1818. McFarlen, Achilles
    F1820. McFarlen, Achilles
79 Eubanks, Molton
    1818. Eubanks, Molten
    F1820. Eubanks, Molten
80 Lovetetty, John
    F1820. Lovlety, John
82 McLean, John
    F1820. McClean, John
83 King, Lawdy
    F1820. King, Lowdy
86 Pettette, Isaac
    1818. Peteet, Isaac
    F1820. Peteet, Isaac
88 McCoy, Ezekiel
    1818. McCoy, Ezekel
    F1820. McCoy, Ezekel
89 Ingraham, Jonas
    1818. Ingram, Jonas
    F1820. Ingram, Jonas
91 Gingor, John
    1818. Ginger, John
    F1820. Ginger, John
93 and 94 Warnick, Nathan
    1818. Warnick, Nethan and
        Warnick, Abram
    F1820. Warnick, Nethan
96 Lee, Richd
    F1820. Lee, Rebecka
98 Relay, Morace
    F1820. Reley, Morice
99 Lisenby, Widow
    1818. Lisenbay, Widow
    F1820. Lisenbay, Widow
100 Lisenby, Betsy
    F1820. Lisenbay, Betsy
101 Dryton, Thos.
    F1820. Dryton, Thomas B.
102 Singleton, Spires
    1818. Shingelton, Squire
    F1820. Singilton, Spyres
104 Hale, James
    F1820. Hail, James
105 Green, Jesse
    1818. Green, Jessey
    F1820. Green, Jessey
106 Huston, Wm.
    1818. Huston, William
    F1820. Hutson, William
108 Chanler, Danl
    F1820. Chandler, Daniel

CENSUS OF 1820

POPE COUNTY (Continued)

- 109 Chandler, Ely
  - F1820. Chandler, Eli
- 111 Atkinson, R. C.
  - 1818. Adkison, Robert
  - F1820. Adkison, Robert C.
- 112 Bennett, Richd
  - 1818. Bennett, Richard
  - F1820. Bennet, Richard
- 114 Leaky, Geo.
  - 1818. Lackey, George
  - F1820. Lecky, George
- 117 Conway, Joseph
  - F1820. Conaway, Joseph
- 118 Hafsey, Saml.
  - F1820. Hufsey, Samuel
- 119 Wilson, Benjn.
  - F1820. Wilson, Bengeman
- 122 Chancey, Israel
  - F1820. Chancey, Izrel
- 124 Overby, Lemuel
  - F1820. Overbay, Lemuel
- 127 Scott, J. D.
  - 1818. Scott, James D.
  - F1820. Scott, James D.
- 128 Leytell, Henry
  - F1820. Lytle, Henry
- 129 Kennedy, Thos.
  - F1820. Kenedy, Thomas
- 130 Grizell, Isaac
  - F1820. Grizel, Isaac
- 131 Dimy, Judithan
  - F1820. Demick, Judthan
- 132 Hallock, Z.
  - F1820. Hallick, Zeblen
- 133 Morris, John
  - 1818. Morice, John
  - F1820. Morice, John
- 135 Lee, Beno
  - 1818. Lee, Benoni
  - F1820. Lee, Benony
- 136 Gibson, H. W.
  - F1820. Gillem, William H.
- 137 Lee, James
  - 1818. Lee, James, Sr.
  - F1820. Lee, James
- 138 Gillett, David
  - F1820. Gillet, David
- 139 Pankey, Lewis
  - 1818. Pankey, Lues
  - F1820. Pankey, Lues
- 140 Bassitt, Josh.
  - F1820. Bassitt, Josia
- 141 Smith, Chas.
  - F1820. Smyth, Charels
- 142 Bassett, Ery
  - F1820. Basset, Irie
- 147 Leiper, John
  - 1818. Leeper, John
  - F1820. Leeper, John
- 148 Keistirson, Larken
  - 1818. Kesterson, Larken
  - F1820. Kesterson, Larken
- 149 Barker, Lewis
  - 1818. Barker, Lues
  - F1820. Barker, Lues
- 151 Kullison, William
  - F1820. Cullison, William
- 153 Field, Robert
  - F1820. Fields, Robert
- 155 Wilkinson, Jno.
  - F1820. Wilkinson, James
- 156 Vaughan, Jno.
  - 1818. Von, John
  - F1820. Von, John
- 157 Tichet, Luke
  - F1820. Tacket, Lues
- 159 Keisterson, Robt.
  - 1818. Kesterson, Robert
  - F1820. Kesterson, Robert
- 160 Keistirson, Peter
  - F1820. Kesterson, Peter
- 161 Coffin, B.
  - F1820. Cafen, Barnabus
- 162 Palmer, Widow
  - 1818. Palmor, John
  - F1820. Palmon, Widow
- 163 Baldwin, Joseph
  - F1820. Balden, Joseph
- 164 Meason, Mr.
  - F1820. Meson, John
- 168 Scott, Dickson
  - F1820. Scott, Dixon
- 169 Pankey, Wm.
  - 1818. Pankey, William
  - F1820. Panky, William
- 171 Rose, Henry
  - 1818. Roas, Henery
  - F1820. Roas, Henery
- 173 Jones, Wm.
  - F1820. Jons, William
- 176 Glass, Dudley
  - 1818. Glass, Dudly
  - F1820. Glass, Dudly
- 177 Ross, Joshua
  - F1820. Ross, John
- 179 Averill, Philo
  - F1820. Aurel, Philo
- 180 Neill, Joseph
  - F1820. Neel, Joseph

POPE COUNTY (Continued)

181 Ralsion, Jacob
    1818. Robison, Jacob
    F1820. Robison, Jacob
183 Vaughan, Geo.
    1818. Von, George
    F1820. Von, George
184 McCool, Jessee
    1818. McCool, Jessey, Sr.
    F1820. McCool, Jessey
185 Dearman, Wm.
    F1820. Dorman, William
186 Owens, John
    F1820. Owens, James
187 Shuffelberger, Jacob
    F1820. Shufelbarger, Jacob
188 Schuffelberger, Abm.
    F1820. Shufelbargr, Absolem
189 Roads, Abm.
    F1820. Roads, Absalem
190 Curtis, John
    F1820. Curtice, John
191 Johnson, Betsey
    F1820. Jonston, Betsy
192 Johnston, Chas.
    F1820. Jonston, Charels
194 Whitesides, James A.
    1818. Whitsids, James A.
    F1820. Whitsid, James A.
195 Brown, Martin
    F1820. Brown, Mertain
196 Morse, John
    F1820. Mors, John
197 Harper, Lincoln
    1818. Harper, Lincolen
    F1820. Harpr, Lincolen
198 Carrell, Jacob
    F1820. Carvel, Jacob
199 Hudleton, Abm.
    F1820. Hudelston, Abram
202 Jenkins, Mathew
    F1820. Jinkens, Matha
204 Kennedy, Jacob
    F1820. Kenedy, Jacob
205 Abbett, Geo.
    F1820. Abbet, George
206 Kennedy, Jacob
    F1820. Kenedy, Jacob
207 Modgelon, Wm.
    1818. Modglen, William
    F1820. Modglen, William
208 McCollum, Jacob
    1818. McColam, Jacob
    F1820. McColem, Jacob
210 Leech, Nefel
    F1820. Leach, Nefel

211 McHenry, Joseph
    1818. McHenery, Joseph
    F1820. McHenery, Joseph
213 Bowman, Benjn.
    1818. Bowman, Bengeman
    F1820. Boman, Bengman
215 Slankard, Herman
    1818. Slankard, Herman
    F1820. Slankard, Hickman
216 Hethcot, Rachal
    F1820. Hethcock, Rachel
217 Leech, Isiah
    1818. Leech, Josia
    F1820. Leach, Josia
218 Devise, Robt.
    F1820. Davice, Robart
220 Wright, Lugar
    F1820. Right, Lugar
222 Meredith, Samuel
    F1820. Merideth, Samuel
223 Bailey, Saml
    F1820. Balies, Samuel
224 Ellis, Jas.
    F1820. Ellice, James
225 Dillard, Jos.
    1818. Dilard, Josaph
    F1820. Dillard, Joseph
227 McHenry, John
    1818. McHenery, John
    F1820. McHenry, John
228 Simson, Polly
    F1820. Simpson, Mary
229 McCool, Benjn.
    1818. McCool, Bengman
    F1820. McCool, Benjamin
231 Pehny, Hiram
    1818. Penny, Hiram
    F1820. Penney, Hiram
232 Pringall, Wm.
    F1820. Prengel, William
233 Murphy, James
    F1820. Murphey, James
235 Hill, M. B.
    F1820. Hill, Widow B.
236 Reed, Andre
    F1820. Reed, Andrew
237 Bozarth, Israel
    F1820. Bozier, Israel
238 Cotton, J.
    F1820. Cotton, John
239 Perry, Franklin
    1818. Penny, Frenklen
    F1820. Perry, Franklin
240 Wilson, Jos.
    F1820. Williams, James

POPE COUNTY (Continued)

241 Bogus, Henry
    F1820. Boges, Henry
242 Johnson, Lewis
    F1820. Johnston, Lewis
245 Hazell, Saml.
    F1820. Hazzel, Samuel
247 Morris, Travis
    F1820. Morris, Treves
248 James, Wylie
    F1820. Jones, Whyley
249 Holmes, John
    F1820. Homes, John
251 Hazele, King
    1818. Hazel, King
    F1820. Hazel, King
252 Hazele, Danl.
    1818. Hazel, Daniel
    F1820. Hazel, Daniel
253 Hayes, John
    1818. Hays, John
    F1820. Hayes, John
254 Rolston, Isaac
    1818. Ralston, Isaac
    F1820. Ralston, Isaac
255 Hays, Robt.
    1818. Hays, Robart
    F1820. Hayes, Robert
    S1820. Gives Hays "4 slaves."
    F1820. Lists them separately as
        follows:
    Hays Negroes
        3 males under 10
        1 male 10-16
        "Louis is about 22 yrs. old,
        Jane about 27"
256 Slankard, Geo.
    1818. Slankard, George, Sr.
    F1820. Slankard, George
259 Slankard, Geo.
    1818. Slankard, Georg, Jr.
    F1820. Slankford, George
261 Hill, Hezek.
    1818. Hail, Hizekia
    F1820. Hail, Hezakiah
262 Gavott, B. F.
    F1820. Gavt, Benjamin F.
264 Crawford, Jas.
    F1820. Crawford, James L.
265 Hanna, Geo.
    F1820. Hannah, George
268 Ethridge, Jonas
    1818. Ethridge, Jonathan
    F1820. Ethrige, Jonathan

269 Murphy, Alx.
    1818. Murphy, Alexander
    F1820. Murphey, Alexander
271 Chuning, Richd.
    F1820. Chuing, Richard
273 Hamilton, Robt.
    1818. Hamilton, Robart
    F1820. Hamelton, Robert
274 Craford, Jas.
    1818. Craford, James
    F1820. Crawford, James
277 Stucker, Davis
    F1820. Stucker, Davies
278 Blackford, Z.
    F1820. Blackford, Zefenia
279 Dougherty, Geo.
    F1820. Daugherty, George
280 Hooker, N.
    F1820. Hocker, Neman
282 Storm, Arthur
    F1820. Stow, Arthur
283 Hamilton, J.
    F1820. Hamilton, John
284 Hocum, S.
    F1820. Hockam, Silas
285 Fulherson, R.
    F1820. Fulkison, Richard
286 Simmons, S.
    F1820. Simmons, Samuel
287 Belford, B.
    1818. Belford, Benjamin
    F1820. Belford, Benjamin
288 Harper, I.
    1818. Harper, Isaac
    F1820. Harper, Isaac
289 Belford, Wm.
    1818. Belford, William
    F1820. Belford, William
292 Montgomery, J.
    F1820. Montgomery, James
293 Stucker, W.
    1818. Stucker, Willice
    F1820. Stucker, Willis
294 Cowan, Wm.
    F1820. Cowen, William
295 Pettilla, Jas.
    F1820. Pitilla, James
296 Watters, Thos.
    F1820. Waters, Thomas
297 Casteel, Ely
    F1820. Casteel, Eli
298 Calvert, J.
    1818. Clavert, John, Sr.
    F1820. Calvert, John

POPE COUNTY (Continued)

299 Hannah, J.
    F1820. Hannah, John
301 Calvert, J.
    1818. Clavert, John, Jr.
    F1820. Calvert, John
302 Lampins, W.
    F1820. Lampens, Wood
303 Gloss, F.
    1818. Glass, Frances
    F1820. Gless, Francis
304 Gloss, J.
    F1820. Glass, Joseph
305 Gloss, Jon.
    1818. Glass, John
    F1820. Glass, John
306 Shaw, J.
    F1820. Shaw, James
307 Allen, E.
    F1820. Allen, Edward
308 Shockney, Dd.
    F1820. Shokney, David
309 Scott, J.
    F1820. Scott, Joshua
310 Turner, S.
    F1820. Turner, Samuel
311 McLinden, F.
    F1820. McClendon, Frederick
312 Williams, J.
    1818. Williams, Joshua
    F1820. Williams, Joshua
315 Modglin, Jno.
    1818. Modglen, John
    F1820. Modglen, John
316 Williamson, J.
    F1820. Williamson, John
317 Ferris, R.
    1818. Faires, Robert
    F1820. Ferris, Robert
318 Atterberry, S.
    F1820. Armstrong, Simon
319 King, C.
    F1820. King, Charles
320 Shelby, C.
    1818. Shelvey, Charels
    F1820. Shelby, Charles
321 Richie, J.
    1818. Richey, James
    F1820. Rechey, James
322 Ditterline, S.
    F1820. Diterline, Samuel
323 Roberts, R.
    1818. Robenet, Richart
    F1820. Robenet, Richard

324 Ditterline, J.
    1818. Diterline, John
    F1820. Diterline, John
325 Campbell, T.
    F1820. Campbell, Thomas
327 Potter, R.
    F1820. Potter, Reuben
329 Campbell, S.
    F1820. Campbell, Stephen
330 Flannery, E.
    1818. Flanery, Eliga
    F1820. Flannery, Elijha
332 Drewry, L.
    1818. Drurey, Lues
    F1820. Drewry, Louis
333 Rowse, I.
    F1820. Rouse, Isaac
335 Curtis, L.
    F1820. Curtis, Lewis
336 Rouse, L.
    F1820. Rouse, Lewis
337 Snider, J.
    F1820. Snider, John
341 Croft, A.
    F1820. Crofts, A.
343 Lard, J.
    1818. Lard, James
    F1820. Lard, J.
344 Griffith, Abm.
    F1820. Griffith, A.
345 Simmons, Jno.
    F1820. Simmons, J.
347 Fisk, R.
    1818. Fisk, Robart
    F1820. Fisk, R.
348 Fisk, A. F.
    1818. Fisk, Abram G.
    F1820. Fisk, A. J.
350 Kidd, J. C.
    F1820. Kidd, J.
351 Lean, Jas.
    F1820. Lane, J.
352 Bartlett, W.
    1818. Barklet, Willice
    F1820. Bartlett, Wm.
354 Turner, J.
    F1820. Tiner, J.
356 Stubbs, Jno.
    1818. Stubs, John
    F1820. Stubbs, J.
358 McCormick, Geo.
    F1820. McCormick, G.
361 Carpenter, S.
    F1820. Cavender, S.

CENSUS OF 1820

POPE COUNTY (Continued)

363 Robinson, R.
    1818. Robison, Richard D.
    F1820. Rollinson, R.
365 Nelly, J.
    F1820. Kneely, J.
369 Warnick, J. L.
    1818. Warick, Julies
    F1820. Warlock, J. L.
370 McCarty, J.
    F1820. McCarty, John
371 Stubbs, M.
    1818. Stubs, Moses
    F1820. Stubb, M.
373 Geving, R.
    1818. Green, Richard
    F1820. Green, R.
374 Manning, J.
    1818. Maning, John
    F1820. Manning, J.
375 Titsworth, B.
    1818. Titsworth, Bengeman
    F1820. Titsworth, B.
379 Thompson, B.
    1818. Thompson, Benegar
    F1820. Thompson, B.
381 Glover, J.
    F1820. Glover, Joseph
382 Lewis, H.
    1818. Lues, Henery
    F1820. Lewis, H.
383 Lewis, Geo.
    1818. Lues, George
    F1820. Lewis, G.
384 Clark, O. S.
    1818. Clark, Owen S.
    F1820. Clark, O. S.
385 Thompson, Thos.
    1818. Thompson, Thomas
    F1820. Thompson, T.
386 Neely, James
    1818. Neely, John
    F1820. Neely, J.
387 Crouse, J.
    F1820. Cross, J.
389 Ladison, Ab.
    F1820. Larrison, A.
390 Farris, T. T.
    F1820. Ferris, T. T.
391 Montgomery, Jno.
    F1820. Montgomery, J.
392 Ferguson, C.
    F1820. Ferguson, K.
393 Smith, J. H.
    F1820. Storry, J. H.

395 Parrott, J.
    F1820. Parrett, J.
396 Fartner, Jno.
    F1820. Falkner, J.
397 Hoage, Geo.
    F1820. Hoag, G.
398 Lewis, And.
    F1820. Lewis, A.
400 Williams, W. H.
    1818. Wilson, William
    F1820. Wilson, Wm. H.
401 Gillispie, J. P.
    1818. Gelespy, John P.
    F1820. Gillaspie, J. P.
402 Bennett, H.
    F1820. Bennet, Aard
403 Brown, J.
    1818. Brown, Joseph
    F1820. Brown, J.
404 Edwards, Jno.
    1818. Edwards, John
    F1820. Edwards, J.
406 Lewis, Jacob
    F1820. Lewis, J.
407 Lashang, Abm.
    F1820. Lewis, A.
409 Wood, Jno.
    1818. Wood, John
    F1820. Wood, J.
410 Wood, Geo.
    F1820. Wood, G.
411 Glover, Reuben
    1818. Glover, Ruben
    F1820. Glover, R.
412 Glover, Jno.
    1818. Glover, John
    F1820. Glover, J.
413 Henly, Jno.
    1818. Henley, John
    F1820. Henly, J.
415 Fox, Jas. N.
    1818. Fox, James N.
    F1820. Fox, J. N.
416 Dooms, Wd.
    F1820. Dames, W.
417 Cross, Jos.
    F1820. Cross, J.
418 Cross, Jno.
    1818. Cross, John
    F1820. Cross, J.
419 Simpkins, Geo.
    1818. Simkens, George
    F1820. Simpkins, G.

POPE COUNTY (*Concluded*)

421 Lemnor, S.
    1818. Lamar, Solomon
    F1820. Lemar, J.
422 Young Blood, J.
    1818. Young Blood, James
    F1820. Youngblood, J.
423 Henly, Jno.
    F1820. Henly, J.
425 Redkin, Wm.
    1818. Redkin, William S.
    F1820. Redkins, Wm.
426 Taylor, D. S.
    1818. Taylor, David S.
    F1820. Taylor, D. S.
427 Deyer, Chs.
    1818. Dyer, Charels
    F1820. Dyer, C.
428 Dyer, Ab
    1818. Dyer, Abiga
    F1820. Dyer, A.
430 Hyfell, B.
    F1820. Hyfall, B.
431 Scott, Isaac B.
    1818. Scott, Isaac B.
    F1820. Scott, I. B.
432 Scott, Robt.
    1818. Scott, Robert
    F1820. Scott, R.
433 Cowan, Dd.
    1818. Cowan, David
    F1820. Cawan, D.
434 Crochett, Jas.
    F1820. Crochett, J.
435 Crochett, Jno.
    1818. Crocket, John
    F1820. Crochitt, Jno.
436 Robinson, A.
    1818. Robison, Allen
    F1820. Robinson, A.
438 Smith, S.
    1818. Smyth, Samuel
    F1820. Smith, S.
440 Gloss, D. B.
    1818. Glass, David
    F1820. Glass, D. B.
442 Waters, S.
    1818. Waters, Shedrick
    F1820. Waters, S.

443 Bogardus, Jno. L.
    F1820. Bogardus, J. S.
444 Leonard, Jno.
    F1820. Leonard, J.
445 Beyard, J.
    F1820. Beard, J.
446 Nichols, J. C.
    F1820. Nichold, J. C.
447 Chipps, A.
    1818. Chipps, Amos
    F1820. Chipps, A.
448 Willis, J. E.
    1818. Willis, James E.
    F1820. Willis, J. E.
449 Sim, Wm.
    F1820. Sin, Wm.
450 Payne, Laben
    F1820. Payne, L.
452 Moore, Abm.
    F1820. Moore, A.
454 Roberts, Jno.
    1818. Robarts, John
    F1820. Roberts, J.
455 Pryor, Jos. E.
    F1820. Pryor, J.
458 Fields, D.
    1818. Fields, Daniel
    F1820. Field, D.
459 Haymon, S.
    F1820. Haymour, S.
462 Aester, C. P.
    F1820. Herte, C. P.
463 Falkner, Jas.
    F1820. Falkner, J.
465 Moore, F.
    1818. Moor, Frances
    F1820. Moore, F.
467 Ellis, Jno.
    F1820. Ellis, J.
468 Rondo, Wm.
    F1820. Rondeau, Wm.
470 Ferguson, Thos.
    F1820. Ferguson, T.
471 Crawford, Jno.
    1818. Crawford, John
    F1820. Crawford, J.

CENSUS OF RANDOLPH COUNTY, 1820

A Book containing the number of the Inhabitants of Randolph County, as directed by the Legislature of the State of Illinois.

August 1st 1820   JAMES THOMPSON.

Names of heads of families	Free white males 21 years old & upwards	All other white Inhabitants	Free people of color Servants or Slaves	Total
[1 ‡] John M'Ferron	3	9		12
[2 ‡] Wm. C. Greenup	3	4		7
[3 ‡] Miles Hotchkiss	1	8		9
[4] James Atkins	2	7	4	13
[5 ‡] James Conner	1	5		6
[6 ‡] Chauncey S. Burr	15	5	1	21
[7 ‡] Edmund Roberts	1	3	1	5
[8 ‡] Michael Jones	1	6	1	8
[9 ‡] Henry S. Dodge	1	5	1	7
[10 ‡] Francis Walker	2			2
[11 ‡] John Edgar	5	1	19	25
[12] Francis Brown	2	11		13
[13 ‡] Elizabeth Chapell	2	10		12
[14 ‡] Terrace Novall	1	8		9
[15 ‡] Warren Brown	1	1		2
[16] Gague Roderick	1	10		11
[17 ‡] Peter Roderick	1	2		3
[18] Abram Pascal	1	5		6
[19 ‡] Geo. Stamm Jr.	1	3		4
[20 ‡] Smith Daggot	1	1		2
[21 ‡] Henry Woodworth	1	5		6
[22 ‡] Robert Morrison	3	4	5	12
[23 ‡] Nathaniel Pope	2	7	7	16
[24 ‡] Philip Fouke	9	8	1	18
[25] Wm. Oby	2		1	3
[26 ‡] Danl. Coffman	1	3		4
[27 ‡] Calvin Larrens	4	3	2	9
[28 ‡] John Jaundron	2	3	4	9
[29 ‡] Wm. L. Reynolds	1	2	1	4
[30 ‡] Wm. Simonton	2	4	5	11

Figures and symbols preceding names have been supplied by the editor:
‡ Indicates name also in Federal Census for 1820.
* Indicates name also in State Census for 1818.

RANDOLPH COUNTY (Continued)

No.	Heads of families	White males 21 & upwards	All other white	Free people of color servants or slaves	Total
[31*‡]	Edward Cowles	4		2	6
[32 ‡]	Elias K. Kane	3	5	5	13
[33 ‡]	Michel Dannie	2	3		5
[34 ‡]	Wm. Morrison	5	10	20	35
[35 ‡]	Josiah Betts	1	1	1	3
[36 ‡]	Shadrach Bond	2	5	14	21
[37 ‡]	Joseph Pasia	2	5		7
[38 ‡]	John Morris	3		2	5
[39]	Camila Toulouce	1		5	6
[40 ‡]	Antoine Chamberlain	1	4		5
[41 ‡]	Batiste Reum	1	4		5
[42 ‡]	Louis Lameur	2	4		6
[43 ‡]	John Bacchus			8	8
[44]	Mary St. Piere	2			2
[45]	Joseph St. Piere	1	5		6
[46 ‡]	Wm. G. Hizer	2	1		3
[47 ‡]	Michel Dannie	1	1		2
[48 ‡]	Clement C. Conway	4	6		10
[49 ‡]	Antoine Cato			3	3
[50 ‡]	Battiste Dannie	1	4		5
[51 ‡]	Mary Chamberlain	1	5		6
[52 ‡]	Raphael Widen	1	3		4
[53]	Joseph St. Piere	3	6		9
[54 ‡]	Thomas Deruse	3	5		8
[55 ‡]	Madame Bevanue		1	7	8
[56 ‡]	Antoine Dannie	1	5		6
[57 ‡]	Michel B. Dannie	1	5		6
[58 ‡]	Terrace Ternour		7		7
[59]	Sillis Edgar			7	7
[60 ‡]	Samuel Lybarger	2	4		6
[61 ‡]	Ferrander Terrango			4	4
[62 ‡]	Batiste Sagan	2	5		7
[63 ‡]	Enoch Paine	3	4		7
[64 ‡]	William Christy	1	5		6
[65*‡]	Wm. Berry	1	3		4
[66 ‡]	Robert Blackwell	1	2		3
[67 ‡]	Geo Stamm Senr	3	5		8
[68]	Arthur Berry	1	1		2

RANDOLPH COUNTY (*Continued*)

No.	Heads of families	White males 21 & upwards	All other white	Free people of color servants or slaves	Total
[69 ‡]	Antoine Autire	1	2		3
[70]	John Maxell	1	3		4
[71 ‡]	Stephen Paver	1	2		3
[72 ‡]	Madame Pera		6		6
[73 ‡]	George A. Tifney	1	6	1	8
[74 ‡]	Joseph Ar. Chambo	2	1	3	6
[75 ‡]	Henry Bevanue	3	8	6	17
[76 ‡]	Hugh H. Maxell	1	7	5	13
[77 ‡]	David Hathorn	1	7		8
[78 ‡]	James Lindsey	3	2		5
[79 ‡]	James Hathorn	1	7		8
[80 ‡]	James Wilson	1	5		6
[81 ‡]	Joseph Orr	1	2		3
[82 ‡]	Enos Christy	2	3		5
[83 ‡]	John Maxell	1	3		4
[84 ‡]	John Adams	1	10		11
[85 ‡]	Thomas Orr	1	3		4
[86 ‡]	Wm. H. Hays	1	6		7
[87 ‡]	Ezra Owen	1	6		7
[88 ‡]	Alexr. Wilson	1	4		5
[89 ‡]	Lemuel Owen	1			1
[90*‡]	Nortan Hull	1	4		5
[91 ‡]	Abram Horine	2	7		9
[92*‡]	Joseph Sprigg	1	9		10
[93 ‡]	David Blackwell	1	2	1	4
[94 ‡]	James Atkins	2	5	4	11
[95 ‡]	Thomas Vance	1	8		9
[96 ‡]	Jacob Fisher	2	3		5
[97 ‡]	Henry Royer	2	3		5
[98 ‡]	Henry Will	1	8		9
[99 ‡]	Antoine Dannie	1	5		6
[100 ‡]	Louis Chambelain	1	2		3
[101 ‡]	Pierre Levery	2	6		8
[102 ‡]	Alexy Bovy	1	6	1	8
[103 ‡]	Henry Kimbell	4	8		12
[104 ‡]	John Carpenter	1	5		6
[105]	Nathan Cloyes	2	3		5
[106 ‡]	Joseph Barton	2	9	5	16

RANDOLPH COUNTY (Continued)

No.	Heads of families	White males 21 & upwards	All other white	Free people of color servants or slaves	Total
[107 ‡]	Joseph Johnson	1	4		5
[108 ‡]	Wm. Wigger	1	10		11
[109 ‡]	David Winfield	1	8		9
[110 ‡]	Danl. Ferguson	1	5		6
[111 ‡]	Jacob Woolsey	1	12		13
[112 ‡]	Saml. Abbot	1	5		6
[113 ‡]	Thurston Thomas	1	3		4
[114 ‡]	David Page	1	1		2
[115 ‡]	Spencer Atkins	4	4		8
[116 ‡]	Adam Youngman	1	2		3
[117 ‡]	David Husband	2	3	1	6
[118 ‡]	Shelton Evans	3	4		7
[119 ‡]	James Chenny	1	6		7
[120 ‡]	Blan Ballard	1	7		8
[121 ‡]	Louis Beatt	1	5		6
[122 ‡]	Charles Dannie	1	9		10
[123 ‡]	Batiste Chamberlain	1	9		10
[124 ‡]	John Menard	2	9	1	12
[125 ‡]	Michel Autire	1	2		3
[126 ‡]	Daniel Buel	1	2		3
[127 ‡]	Wm. Hamilton	1	9		10
[128 ‡]	Henry Conner	2	7	6	15
[129]	James Conner	2	4		6
[130 ‡]	John McFarlin	3	1		4
[131 ‡]	James Mud	1	4		5
[132 ‡]	Thomas Mud	3	6		9
[133 ‡]	Benedict Horrel	2	3		5
[134 ‡]	Wm. Steel	1	4		5
[135 ‡]	Amos Paxton	3	1		4
[136 ‡]	Richard Brewer	1	2		3
[137 ‡]	Henry Oharrah	1	8		9
[138 ‡]	James Whaling	2	7		9
[139 ‡]	Hannah Kenedy	1	5		6
[140 ‡]	Saml. Hill	1	3		4
[141 ‡]	Wm. Nelson	3	10		13
[142 ‡]	Prudy Wilson	1	3		4
[143 ‡]	Michael Dillen	1	9		10
[144 ‡]	Edmund Faherty	1	9		10

CENSUS OF 1820

RANDOLPH COUNTY (*Continued*)

No.	Heads of families	White males 21 & upwards	All other white	Free people of color servants or slaves	Total
[145]	Patrick Faherty	1	7		8
[146 ‡]	Franklin Owen	1	6		7
[147 ‡]	Robt. Wilson	1	3		4
[148 ‡]	John C. Crozier	1	1		2
[149 ‡]	Preston Bricky	1	3		4
[150 ‡]	Wm. Peach	1	8		9
[151 ‡]	Nancy Guthrie	2	7		9
[152 ‡]	Henry Nooe	4	3		7
[153 ‡]	David Fulton	1	8		9
[154 ‡]	Susannah Allen	2	4		6
[155 ‡]	Edward Ralls	1	5		6
[156 ‡]	Wm. Been	1	2		3
[157 ‡]	Robert Smith	1	4		5
[158 ‡]	George Reel	2	5		7
[159 ‡]	John Frankfort	1	4		5
[160 ‡]	David Simonton	3	2	4	9
[161 ‡]	Othiel Levens	1	6		7
[162 ‡]	Paul Harlston	1	5	1	7
[163 ‡]	Rosannah Fulton		1	2	3
[164 ‡]	George Glen	2	2		4
[165 ‡]	Joseph Griffin	2	6		8
[166 ‡]	Thomas Levens	1	7	2	10
[167 ‡]	David Lawson	1	10		11
[168 ‡]	Susannah Lecompt	1	3	11	15
[169 ‡]	Henry Karr	1	1		2
[170 ‡]	Thomas Wyet	3			3
[171 ‡]	Batiste LaCavy	2	1		3
[172 ‡]	John Marray	1	4		5
[173 ‡]	Henry Teebo	1	3		4
[174 ‡]	Joseph Ponner	1	5		6
[175 ‡]	Mary Cochenny	1	4		5
[176 ‡]	Batiste Oliver	1	1		2
[177 ‡]	Izado Punner	1	4		5
[178 ‡]	Madame Nicholas	2	3		5
[179 ‡]	Joseph Gran Louis	1	5		6
[180 ‡]	Antoine Blay	2	6	2	10
[181 ‡]	Madame Damore		1	2	3
[182 ‡]	Joseph Blay	3	7		10

RANDOLPH COUNTY (Continued)

No.	Heads of families	White males 21 & upwards	All other white	Free people of color servants or slaves	Total
[183 ‡]	Madame Degannie		3		3
[184 ‡]	Michel Declue	2	2		4
[185 ‡]	Charles Blay	1	7		8
[186 ‡]	Alexy Ponner	1			1
[187 ‡]	Antoine Ruvia	2	6	6	14
[188 ‡]	Madame Drury	2	3		5
[189 ‡]	Madame Pelky	1	3		4
[190 ‡]	Madame Larsoan		4	2	6
[191 ‡]	Madame Charlo Teebo		4		4
[192 ‡]	Joseph LaToural	1	2		3
[193 ‡]	Madame LaChance		5	7	12
[194 ‡]	Joseph Dorvan	2	2		4
[195 ‡]	Jacco Chein	1	2		3
[196 ‡]	Joseph Trucky	1	2		3
[197 ‡]	Madame Pachon Nicholas		2		2
[198 ‡]	Francis Teebo	1	8	1	10
[199 ‡]	Henry Barbeau	1	2	4	7
[200 ‡]	Antoine Blay	1	2	1	4
[201 ‡]	Stephen Langloy	1	7		8
[202 ‡]	August Allard	1	3	3	7
[203 ‡]	John Batiste Roy	1	1		2
[204 ‡]	Yasaint LaToural	2	2		4
[205 ‡]	Aaron Droddy	1	3		4
[206 ‡]	Francis Tangua	2	8	3	13
[207 ‡]	Archibald McNabb	2	6	4	12
[208 ‡]	Joseph Buttilet	1	1		2
[209 ‡]	Andrew Roy	1	4		5
[210 ‡]	John Batiste Godair	2	8	2	12
[211 ‡]	Francis Langloy	4	8		12
[212 ‡]	Andrew Barbeau	1	9	7	17
[213 ‡]	Antoine Barbeau	1	1	4	6
[214 ‡]	Batiste Barbeau	1	2	4	7
[215 ‡]	Francis Brown	2	9		11
[216 ‡]	Mrs. Learner	1	3		4
[217 ‡]	Charles Cavenah	1	6		7
[218 ‡]	Thomas Philips	2	1		3
[219 ‡]	Reuben Sacket	1	7		8
[220 ‡]	Michael Smith	1	7		8

CENSUS OF 1820

RANDOLPH COUNTY (Continued)

No.	Heads of families	White males 21 & upwards	All other white	Free people of color servants or slaves	Total
[221 ‡]	Saml. Taylor	2	4		6
[222 ‡]	James Taylor	1	4		5
[223 ‡]	George Day	4	8		12
[224 ‡]	Danl. Roderick	3	6		9
[225]	Peter Roderick	1	2		3
[226 ‡]	Nicholas Paschal	1	2		3
[227 ‡]	Theodore Burr	1	2		3
[228 ‡]	James Turner	2	3		5
[229 ‡]	Francis Menard	1		8	9
[230 ‡]	Pascal LaSource	1	7		8
[231 ‡]	Alexander Nooe	1	2		3
[232 ‡]	Patrick Cavenah	1	2		3
[233 ‡]	Isaac Hall	1	4		5
[234 ‡]	Silas Leeland	2	5		7
[235 ‡]	Terrace Terongy		1	6	7
[236 ‡]	Antoine Beuatt	1	5		6
[237 ‡]	Joseph Teulia	1	7		8
[238 ‡]	Louis Fortune	1	4		5
[239 ‡]	Pierre Coleen	1	1		2
[240 ‡]	Ursula LaFlue	1	6		7
[241 ‡]	Pierre Deruse	1	4		5
[242 ‡]	Joseph Beuatt	1	3		4
[243 ‡]	Michel Beuatt	1	3		4
[244 ‡]	Louis Sagan	1	2		3
[245 ‡]	Batiste Sagan	1	3		4
[246 ‡]	Benjamin Beuatt	1	4		5
[247 ‡]	Zenia Beuatt	1	2		3
[248 ‡]	Tropa Manuel	1	3		4
[249 ‡]	Joseph Toulouce	2	7		9
[250 ‡]	Louis Sagan	1	3		4
[251 ‡]	Antoine Chenny	2	7		9
[252 ‡]	Alexander Nicholas	1	4		5
[253 ‡]	Silas Skellinger	1	7		8
[254 ‡]	Andrew Charleville	2	5	1	8
[255 ‡]	Joseph Jaundron	1	1		2
[256 ‡]	Antoine Bevanue	1	1		2
[257 ‡]	Joseph Barrettel	2	4		6
[258 ‡]	Akan Deruse	1	4		5

RANDOLPH COUNTY (*Continued*)

No.	Heads of families	White males 21 & upwards	All other white	Free people of color servants or slaves	Total
[259 ‡]	Michel Margoto			4	4
[260 ‡]	Thomas Reynolds	1	4	1	6
[261 ‡]	Jackson Taylor	2	10		12
[262 ‡]	Batiste Charleville	1	2		3
[263 ‡]	Pierre Boneau	1	5		6
[264 ‡]	John Clement	1	1		2
[265 ‡]	Antoine Du Cleau	1	6	2	9
[266 ‡]	Isaac Rust	3			3
	N. B. To this place contains the number of inhabitants living on the West side of the Kaskaskia River and in Randolph County.				
[267 ‡]	George Steele	3	4		7
[268 ‡]	Jacob Bowerman	2	4		6
[269]	John Barrow	1	5		6
[270 ‡]	Arthur Cross	1	3		4
[271 ‡]	William Gwin	2	4		6
[272 ‡]	Malchi Holloman	1	8		9
[273 ‡]	Cornelius Adkins	1	7		8
[274 ‡]	John Steele Snr.	2	2		4
[275 ‡]	John Steele Jnr.	1	1		2
[276 ‡]	John Steele	1	9		10
[277 ‡]	James Steele	1	2		3
[278 ‡]	John Layne	4	6		10
[279 ‡]	Caleb Pedrick	1	6		7
[280 ‡]	Denard Short	1	2		3
[281 ‡]	Shadrach Lively	1	2		3
[282 ‡]	John Fursea	1	10		11
[283 ‡]	Archibald Snodgrass	1	7		8
[284 ‡]	Archibald Steele	2	4		6
[285 ‡]	Stepen Gaston	1	7		8
[286 ‡]	James McDonough	1	2		3
[287 ‡]	James Lock	1	1		2
[288 ‡]	David Looney	2	8		10
[289 ‡]	Samuel Crawford	1	4		5
[290 ‡]	John Pillars	1	6		7

RANDOLPH COUNTY (*Continued*)

No.	Heads of families	White males 21 & upwards	All other white	Free people of color servants or slaves	Total
[291 ‡]	James McFarlin	1	9		10
[292 ‡]	Charles C Glover	1	3		4
[293 ‡]	Solomon Fursea	1	3		4
[294 ‡]	Solomon Baker	1	7		8
[295 ‡]	William Robertson	1	2		3
[296 ‡]	Jessee Bowerman	1	3		4
[297 ‡]	Joseph Robertson	1	4		5
[298 ‡]	Richard Robertson	2	5		7
[299 ‡]	James Robertson	1	3		4
[300 ‡]	Henry House	1	2		3
[301 ‡]	Micajah House	1	11		12
[302 ‡]	John Murphrey Sen	3	7		10
[303 ‡]	James Murphry	1	6		7
[304 ‡]	John Murphry Jnr.	1	3		4
[305 ‡]	Frances Davis		5		5
[306 ‡]	Robert Huggans	1	11		12
[307 ‡]	William Wiley	1	6		7
[308 ‡]	John Wiley	1	5		6
[309 ‡]	James Baird	1	10		11
[310 ‡]	Arthur Parks	1	9		10
[311 ‡]	James Patterson	2	6		8
[312 ‡]	John Lively	2	5		7
[313 ‡]	Joseph Weir	1	4		5
[314 ‡]	William Elliott	1	11		12
[315 ‡]	Larkin Dial	1	7		8
[316 ‡]	Thomas Blair	1	1		2
[317 ‡]	Patrick Ranes	1	4		5
[318 ‡]	Nathaniel Davis	1	5	1	7
[319 ‡]	John Mordock	1	1		2
[320 ‡]	Andrew Borders	2	3	3	8
[321 ‡]	Alexander Hodge	1	3		4
[322 ‡]	Sarah Clark		1	1	2
[323 ‡]	Isaac Raney	1	3		4
[324 ‡]	Samuel Little	1	7		8
[325 ‡]	William Edgar	2	5		7
[326 ‡]	Washington C Ballard	1	9		10
[327 ‡]	Samuel Y Henry	1	2		3
[328 ‡]	James Clark	1	7	2	10

RANDOLPH COUNTY (*Continued*)

No.	Heads of families	White males 21 & upwards	All other white	Free people of color servants or slaves	Total
[329 ‡]	John McDill	2	2	1	5
[330 ‡]	David Kithcart	2	2		4
[331 ‡]	William Campbell	1	2		3
[332 ‡]	Alexander Alexander	2	4		6
[333 ‡]	Thomas Swanwick	8	12		20
[334 ‡]	James McMurdo	1	2		3
[335 ‡]	John Raney	1	2		3
[336 ‡]	James Munford	1	5		6
[337 ‡]	John Dicky	1	4		5
[338 ‡]	Samuel Nisbet	1	7		8
[339 ‡]	James Huggans	1	2		3
[340 ‡]	John McMillin	1	5		6
[341 ‡]	William Gordin	2	3		5
[342 ‡]	Robert Moore	1	1		2
[343 ‡]	Jacob Van	3	8		11
[344 ‡]	Stephen Tildon	1	7		8
[345 ‡]	John Mahan	2	4		6
[346 ‡]	Reuben Tindle	2	2		4
[347 ‡]	Robert Tindle	2	6		8
[348 ‡]	John Lacey	1	3		4
[349 ‡]	James Gaston	2		5	7
[350 ‡]	James Black	2	5		7
[351 ‡]	Robert Hindman	2	8		10
[352 ‡]	Benjamin Crane	1	7	5	13
[353 ‡]	Isaak Vineyard	1	2		3
[354 ‡]	William Bilderback	2	4		6
[355 ‡]	James Bilderback	1	1		2
[356 ‡]	Harvey Clendenan	1	2		3
[357 ‡]	Charles Bilderback	1	2		3
[358 ‡]	Samuel Mansco	2	3		5
[359 ‡]	Leonard Carter	1	7		8
[360 ‡]	Joel Crane	2	6		8
[361 ‡]	William Mansco	1	1		2
[362 ‡]	Samuel Johnston	1	2		3
[363 ‡]	William Payne	1	4		5
[364 ‡]	John Crane	1	4		5
[365 ‡]	Samuel Parks	1	4		5
[366 ‡]	Aseab Smith	1	5		6

CENSUS OF 1820

RANDOLPH COUNTY (*Continued*)

No.	Heads of families	White males 21 & upwards	All other white	Free people of color servants or slaves	Total
[367 ‡]	William Smith	1	6		7
[368]	John Griffith	1	6		7
[369]	Jane Winter		5		5
[370 ‡]	Benjamin A Porter	16	9		25
[371 ‡]	Nathaniel J Divine	1	2		3
[372]	Adanijah Ball	1	6		7
[373 ‡]	Timothy Dustin	1	8		9
[374 ‡]	William Cochran	2	4		6
[375 ‡]	Obadeah Fields	1	3		4
[376*‡]	Curtis Conn	2	6	1	9
[377]	Alexander Nooe	1	2		3
[378 ‡]	James Johnston	1	10		11
[379 ‡]	Nicholas Beat	1	9		10
[380 ‡]	James Sterrel	1	1		2
[381 ‡]	Alexander Beat	2	5		7
[382 ‡]	Mitchael Shalovel	1	1		2
[383]	Baptiste Icondro	1	3		4
[384 ‡]	Antwine Raviel	1	5		6
[385 ‡]	Antwine Montroy	1	5		6
[386 ‡]	Baptiste Montroy	1	6		7
[387 ‡]	Henry Petit	1	3		4
[388 ‡]	John Clendenan	1	4		5
[389 ‡]	Peter Paul	1	5		6
[390 ‡]	Joseph Curry	1	3		4
[391 ‡]	James Clendenon	1	4		5
[392 ‡]	Martha Hurd	2	2		4
[393 ‡]	George Franklin	1	8	1	10
[394 ‡]	Joseph Harmon	1	4		5
[395 ‡]	Samuel Weir	1	4		5
[396 ‡]	John Taggart	1	5		6
[397 ‡]	Eli Short	1	6		7
[398 ‡]	Amos Anderson	1	9		10
[399 ‡]	John Young	1	1		2
[400 ‡]	Joseph Joy	1	2	3	6
[401 ‡]	John F Berry	1	2		3
[402 ‡]	Silas Cristlar	1	6		7
[403 ‡]	David Petit	1	4		5
[404 ‡]	James Richardson	2	4		6

RANDOLPH COUNTY (*Continued*)

No.	Heads of families	White males 21 & upwards	All other white	Free people of color servants or slaves	Total
[405 ‡]	Abijah Leavitt	1	11		12
[406 ‡]	Peter Menard	5	7	11	23
[407 ‡]	Daniel Taggart	1	2		3
[408 ‡]	Alexander Barbour	1	9		10
[409]	Elijah Allcorn	2	6		8
[410 ‡]	James Lee	1	12		13
[411 ‡]	Racheal Hughes		8		8
[412 ‡]	Jonathan Ditch	5	8		13
[413 ‡]	Stace McDonough	5	7		12
[414 ‡]	Amos Lively	2	4		6
[415 ‡]	Margaretta Gaston		3		3
[416 ‡]	James Slater	1	9		10
[417]	Reddick Council	1	4		5
[418]	Sion Smith	1	8		9
[419]	Thomas Marsh	2			2
[420]	John Baccus			8	8
[421 ‡]	Louis Demars			5	5
[422 ‡]	Antwine Recaw	1		6	7
[423 ‡]	Antwine Labrea	1	7		8
[424 ‡]	Ellison Tolbert	1	3		4
[425 ‡]	William Tolbert	1	4		5
[426 ‡]	Joseph Lively	2	5		7
[427 ‡]	William Turner	1	7		8
[428 ‡]	William Fowler	1	4		5
[429 ‡]	James Fowler	1	2		3
[430 ‡]	William Morris	1	6		7
[431 ‡]	James McNulty	1	7		8
[432 ‡]	John Baird	1	6		7
[433 ‡]	James McClerkin	1	5		6
[434 ‡]	James Lively	1	8	1	10
[435 ‡]	Richard Busely	2	2		4
[436 ‡]	Hugh Lastly	1	4		5
[437 ‡]	Archibald Thompson	1	3		4
[438 ‡]	William Gaston	1	5		6
[439 ‡]	Reuben Lively	2	5		7
[440 ‡]	John Anderson Jnr	1	5		6
[441 ‡]	Thomas Wilson	1	3		4
[442 ‡]	George W Hickcox	2	3	3	8

RANDOLPH COUNTY (*Continued*)

No.	Heads of families	White males 21 & upwards	All other white	Free people of color servants or slaves	Total
[443 ‡]	John McMillin	1	3		4
[444 ‡]	Thomas Crawford	1	6		7
[445 ‡]	Thomas McBride	2	7		9
[446 ‡]	Elijah Nobles	1	8		9
[447 ‡]	John McBride	1	6		7
[448 ‡]	Robert McDaniel Jnr	1			1
[449 ‡]	George Wilson	1	10		11
[450 ‡]	Cloe Danes		4		4
[451 ‡]	Samuel Douglas	1	3		4
[452 ‡]	Absolom Cox	2	8		10
[453 ‡]	George Bags	1	6		7
[454 ‡]	Samuel Gladney	1			1
[455 ‡]	Ann McMillin		4		4
[456 ‡]	Leonard Stephens	2	8		10
[457 ‡]	Ralph Scudder	1	4		5
[458 ‡]	Isaac Scudder	2	4		6
[459 ‡]	Howel Beesely	1	6		7
[460 ‡]	Thomas Fulton	2	5	1	8
[461 ‡]	John Bags	1	2		3
[462 ‡]	Robert McDaniel Snr	1	5		6
[463 ‡]	William McBride Snr	1	2		3
[464 ‡]	John S Davis	1	2		3
[465 ‡]	John Baty Snr	2	7		9
[466 ‡]	Andrew McFerron	1	5		6
[467 ‡]	Robert McFerron	1	2		3
[468 ‡]	John Baty Jnr	1	2		3
[469 ‡]	James Couch	2	7		9
[470 ‡]	Moses Wilson	3	6		9
[471 ‡]	Robert Bratney	2		1	3
[472 ‡]	Robert Man	1	6		7
[473 ‡]	William Man	1	1		2
[474 ‡]	Gabriel Jones	1	5		6
[475 ‡]	Charles Owens	1	3		4
[476 ‡]	Richard Green	1	5		6
[477 ‡]	John Vineyard	2	2		4
[478 ‡]	Shadrach Lively	1	9		10
[479]	Charles Stratton	3	7	4	14
[480 ‡]	Sammuel Barker	1	5		6

RANDOLPH COUNTY (Continued)

No.	Heads of families	White males 21 & upwards	All other white	Free people of color servants or slaves	Total
[481 ‡]	Thomas Roberts	1	6		7
[482 ‡]	John Bilderback	3	7		10
[483 ‡]	Sylvanus Harlow	1	9		10
[484]	John Young	1	5		6
[485 ‡]	Crispen Wright	1	2		3
[486 ‡]	Jacob Harmon	1	5		6
[487 ‡]	Daniel Porter			9	9
[488 ‡]	Ephraizm Bilderback	1	6		7
[489 ‡]	Aquilla Brown	1	3		4
[490 ‡]	William Haydon	1	7		8
[491 ‡]	John Perry	2	1		3
[492 ‡]	William Fisher	2	4	1	7
[493 ‡]	James Bradley	1			1
[494 ‡]	Barnet Gray	4	5		9
[495 ‡]	Caleb Hart	1	5		6
[496 ‡]	James Gray	1	2		3
[497 ‡]	Jonathan Petit	2	7		9
[498 ‡]	James Thompson Snr	2	3		5
[499 ‡]	Josiah Allcorn	1	8		9
[500 ‡]	Martha Curry		4		4
[501 ‡]	James Foster	1	7		8
[502 ‡]	Sammuel Lard	1	4		5
[503 ‡]	John Campbell	2	6		8
[504 ‡]	William Thompson	1	5		6
[505 ‡]	Samuel Lard Snr	1	4		5
[506 ‡]	James Wilson	2	8		10
[507 ‡]	William Barnet	1	1	8	10
[508 ‡]	Archibald Thompson	2	4		6
[509 ‡]	Robert Thompson Jnr	1	6		7
[510 ‡]	John Cochran	1	4	1	6
[511 ‡]	Samuel Hathorn	1	3		4
[512 ‡]	John Barnet	1	4		5
[513 ‡]	John Allen	1	7		8
[514 ‡]	Samuel Crozier	1	7		8
[515 ‡]	Alexander Lastley	1	2		3
[516 ‡]	Alexander McKelvy	1	6		7
[517 ‡]	William Allen	1	4		5
[518 ‡]	William McBride Jnr	1	3		4

CENSUS OF 1820

RANDOLPH COUNTY (*Continued*)

No.	Heads of families	White males 21 & upwards	All other white	Free people of color servants or slaves	Total
[519 ‡]	Robert Foster	2	7		9
[520 ‡]	John Hill	1			1
[521 ‡]	Isabella English		3		3
[522 ‡]	Samuel McClinton	1			1
[523 ‡]	John McClinton	1			1
[524 ‡]	James Anderson	1	2		3
[525 ‡]	William Riche	1	4		5
[526 ‡]	David Anderson	2	5		7
[527 ‡]	Robert Hill	1	8		9
[528 ‡]	John Anderson Snr	1	3		4
[529 ‡]	Alexander Campbell	1	10		11
[530 ‡]	Robert Thompson Snr	1	5		6
[531 ‡]	Samuel Thompson	1	2		3
[532 ‡]	Moses Thompson	1	4		5
[533 ‡]	John Irwin	1	8		9
[534 ‡]	Andrew McCormac	2	7		9
[535]	Robert Conn	1			1
[536 ‡]	James Stratian	1	7		8
[537 ‡]	John Miller	3	4		7
[538 ‡]	Richard Robertson Jnr	1	4		5
[539 ‡]	Robert McCrackin	3	3	1	7
[540 ‡]	Francis Montroy	1	5		6
[541 ‡]	James Thompson Jr	1	3		4

N.B. To this place contains the number of inhabitants on the East side of the Kaskaskia River, and in Randolph County.

Total 3531

RANDOLPH COUNTY (Continued)

November 27th, 1820

I do hereby certify that the number of inhabitants in Randolph County have been taken according to law, which are as follow (viz) 774 free white males 21 years old and upwards.—2415 other white inhabitants.—342 free people of color Servants and Slaves making in all 3531 inhabitants of all ages, Sexes and color contained in Randolph County.

JAMES THOMPSON

Corrected totals:

Free white males of 21 years and upwards	776
All other white inhabitants	2415
	3191
Free people of color	342
Total	3533

CENSUS OF 1820

RANDOLPH COUNTY (Continued)

The 1818 census for Randolph County is missing, probably lost in the fire which scorched and partially destroyed the 1818 census for St. Clair County. A one page "return of the additional census," bound out of place in the volume, appears to be a fragment of the supplemental census for Randolph County. James Thompson took both the state and federal census for 1820, certifying the state enumeration on November 27, 1820, and the federal enumeration January 6, 1821. The two lists are not identical, however, the state list containing 541 families and the federal list containing 547 families. Thirty families named in the state census are not found in the federal census, and thirty-six named in the federal census are not found in the state census, in addition to which one name in the federal census is illegible.

Those families appearing only in the federal census are as follows:

Barbo, Silas
Barrettel, Francis
Bradley, Joshua
Cassey, Antoine
Clark, Robert
Coddle, William
Colbert, Harrison
*Davis, Joshua
Depue, Mary
Deruse, Joseph (Appears twice.)
Ferrander, Mary
Fulton, Harriet
Godair, Zemry
Hanly, Frances
Harmon, Catharine
Harnet, Hiram
Jelly, Andrew
Man, Frederick

McDill, Thomas
McFeron, John
McKelvy, Hugh
McMillin, James
Morrison, Phoebe
Murphrey, Jeremiah
Onjer, Ferdinand
Rockwell, Jay T.
Ross, Thomas
Sikes, John
Stoker, James
Stuart, William
Stublefield, Lemuel
Taylor, John
Van, Matthew
Wilkerson, Jacceard
Willis, Sam'l.

Discrepancies are as follows:

13 Chapell, Elizabeth
   F1820. Chapelle, Elizabeth
19 Stamm, Geo., Jr.
   F1820. Stamm, George
28 Jaundron, John
   F1820. Jeondro, Baptiste
29 Reynolds, Wm. L.
   F1820. Reynolds, Wm.
38 Morris, John
   F1820. Morris, Batisted
40 Chamberlain, Antoine
   F1820. Chamberla, Antoine
41 Reum, Batiste
   F1820. Reau, Baptiste
42 Lameur, Louis
   F1820. Lamure, Francis
43 Bacchus, John
   F1820. Bachus, John
46 Hizer, Wm. G.
   F1820. Hizer, Wm.
49 Cato, Antoine
   F1820. Catto, Antoine
51 Chamberlain, Mary
   F1820. Chamberla, Mary

55 Bevanue, Madame
   F1820. Bevanue, Modlen
57 Dannie, Michel B.
   F1820. Dannie, Michel
58 Ternour, Terrace
   F1820. Tonish, Terrace
61 Terrango, Ferrander
   F1820. Terrongy, Besons
62 Sagan, Batiste
   F1820. Segan, Batiste
67 Stamm, Geo., Sr.
   F1820. Stamm, Geo.
71 Paver, Stephen
   F1820. Pavo, Akan
72 Pera, Madame
   F1820. Pero, Peter
74 Chambo, Joseph Ar.
   F1820. Chamberla, Joseph
90 Hull, Nortan
   1818. Hull, Norton
   F1820. Hull, Norton
100 Chambelain, Louis
   F1820. Chamberlan, Louis

RANDOLPH COUNTY (Continued)

113 Thomas, Thurston
 F1820. Thomas, Thruston
121 Beatt, Louis
 F1820. Beauatt, Louis
123 Chamberlain, Batiste
 F1820. Chamberla, Batiste
126 Buel, Daniel
 F1820. Buell, Dan'l
137 Oharrah, Henry
 F1820. Oharra, Henry
138 Whaling, James
 F1820. Whalin, James
170 Wyet, Thomas
 F1820. Wiyet, Thomas
173 Teebo, Henry
 F1820. Tebo, Henry
177 Punner, Izado
 F1820. Ponner, Izedo
184 Declue, Michel
 F1820. De Clue, Michel
191 Teebo, Madame Charlo
 F1820. Tebo, Madame Charlo
197 Nicholas, Madame Pachon
 F1820. Nicholas, Madame Pacho
198 Teebo, Francis
 F1820. Tebo, Francis
202 Allard, August
 F1820. Allard, Agust
204 La Toural, Yasaint
 F1820. La Toural, Yosaint
205 Droddy, Aaron
 F1820. Droddy, Aron
210 Godair, John Batiste
 F1820. Godair, John B.
213 Barbeau, Antoine
 F1820. Barbo, Antoine
214 Barbeau, Batiste
 F1820. Barbo, Batiste
226 Paschal, Nicholas
 F1820. Pascal, Nicholas
228 Turner, James
 F1820. Turney, James
232 Cavenah, Patrick
 F1820. Cavenaugh, Patrick
234 Leeland, Silas
 F1820. Leland, Silas
239 Coleen, Pierre
 F1820. Colien, Pierre
240 La Flue, Ursula
 F1820. La Fleau, Ursula
242 Beuatt, Joseph
 F1820. Beauatt, Joseph
243 Beuatt, Michel
 F1820. Beauatt, Michel
244 Sagan, Louis
 F1820. Segan, Louis

245 Sagan, Batiste
 F1820. Segan, Batiste
246 Beuatt, Benjamin
 F1820. Beatt, Benjamin
247 Beuatt, Zenia
 F1820. Beatt, Zenia
250 Sagan, Louis
 F1820. Segan, Louis
272 Holloman, Malchi
 F1820. Holloman, Maleki
279 Pedrick, Caleb
 F1820. Padrick, Caleb
281 Lively, Shadrach
 F1820. Lively, Shadrach, Sr.
285 Gaston, Stepen
 F1820. Gaston, Stephen
298 Robertson, Richard
 F1820. Robertson, Richard, Sr.
317 Ranes, Patrick
 F1820. Ranes, Partrick
326 Ballard, Washington C.
 F1820. Ballard, Washington
327 Henry, Samuel Y.
 F1820. Henry, Samuel
343 Van, Jacob
 F1820. Von, Jacob
346 Tindle, Reuben
 F1820. Tindle, Reuben W.
351 Hindman, Robert
 F1820. Hindman, John
358 Mansco, Samuel
 F1820. Mansker, Samuel
361 Mansco, William
 F1820. Mansker, Samuel
363 Payne, William
 F1820. Pane, William
370 Porter, Benjamin A.
 F1820. Porter, Benjamin
371 Divine, Nathaniel J.
 F1820. Divine, Nathaniel
375 Fields, Obadeah
 F1820. Fields, Obediah
376 Conn, Curtis
 1818. Conn, Curtis
 F1820. Conn, Curtus
380 Sterrel, James
 F1820. Stull, James
382 Shalovel, Mitchael
 F1820. Shalovel, Mitchall
384 Raviel, Antwine
 F1820. Raviel, Anthony
386 Montroy, Baptiste
 F1820. Montroy, John B.
391 Clendenon, James
 F1820. Clendenan, James

RANDOLPH COUNTY (*Concluded*)

402 Cristlar, Silas
    F1820. Cristler, Silas
403 Petit, David
    F1820. Petet, David
405 Leavitt, Abijah
    F1820. Leaviett, Abijah
411 Hughes, Racheal
    F1820. Hughes, Rachael
412 Ditch, Jonathan
    F1820. Ditch, Jonathan M.
421 Demars, Louis
    F1820. Demars, Lewis
424 Tolbert, Ellison
    F1820. Tolbert, Elison
433 McClerkin, James
    F1820. McClarkin, James
435 Busely, Richard
    F1820. Busly, Richard
437 Thompson, Archibald
    F1820. Thompson, Archibald, Jr.
442 Hickcox, George W.
    F1820. Hickcox, George
452 Cox, Absolom
    F1820. Cox, Absalom
459 Beesely, Howel
    F1820. Buseby, Howel
462 McDaniel, Robert, Sr.
    F1820. McDonul, Robert, Sr.
468 Baty, John, Jr.
    F1820. Baty, John
472 Man, Robert
    F1820. Mann, Robert
473 Man, William
    F1820. Mann, William
478 Lively, Shadrach
    F1820. Lively, Shadrach, Jr.
480 Barker, Sammuel
    F1820. Barker, Lemuel
483 Harlow, Sylvanus
    F1820. Harlow, Silvanus
485 Wright, Crispen
    F1820. Wright, Crispin
490 Haydon, William
    F1820. Hadon, William
499 Allcorn, Josiah
    F1820. Alcorn, Josiah
502 Lard, Sammuel
    F1820. Lard, Samuel, Jr.
508 Thompson, Archibald
    F1820. Thompson, Archibald, Sr.
514 Crozier, Samuel
    F1820. Crosier, Samuel
533 Irwin, John
    F1820. Irvin, John
536 Stratian, James
    F1820. Strahan, James
541 Thompson, James, Jr.
    F1820. Thomason, John

CENSUS OF ST. CLAIR COUNTY, 1820

Names of heads of families in St Clair County	Free White males under twenty one	Free White males of twenty one & under forty five	Free White males of forty five & upwards	Free White females under eighteen	Free White females of eighteen & under forty five	Free White females of forty-five & upwards	Free people of color	Slaves or Servants
[1*‡] Cornelius Gooding			1	2				
[2*‡] Robert Gooding	1	1		3	1			
[3 ‡] Isaac Gooding		1		1	1			
[4*‡] James Glass	2	2		2	1			
[5 ‡] Arthur Patterson	2	1		3	1			
[6*‡] Stephen Lacey	1	1		2	1			
[7 ‡] John Ross		1		2	1			
[8 ‡] Thomas Jarrot	3		1	5	1	1		
[9 ‡] John Lacey		1			2			
[10*‡] Thomas Harrison	4	1		3	1			
[11 ‡] Thomas Cox	4	1	1	3	1			
[12*‡] Samuel Hinton	2		1		1	1		
[13 ‡] Vachel Hinton		1		1				
[14 ‡] William Hinton	1	1		1	1			
[15*‡] Mathew Roach	3		1	3		1		
[16 ‡] John Roach	1		1					
[17 ‡] Joseph Primm	1	1			1			
[18*‡] John Primm		2	2			1		
[19*‡] Daniel Stookey	5	1	1	2		1		
[20 ‡] Simon Stookey	1	1			1			
[21 ‡] Abraham Eyman	3	3	1	2	2	1		
[22*‡] Coonrod Goodner	2	1	1	1	1	1		
[23 ‡] John Bloom		1		1	1			
[24 ‡] Benjamin Davis	3	1		2	1			
[25*‡] Henry Randleman		1			1			
[26 ‡] John Arthurloney	1	1		3	1			
[27 ‡] Charles Jones	2		1	3	1			
[28 ‡] William Morgan	5	1		3	1			

Figures and symbols preceding names have been supplied by the editor:
‡ Indicates name also in Federal Census for 1820.
* Indicates name also in State Census for 1818.

CENSUS OF 1820

ST. CLAIR COUNTY (Continued)

No.	Heads of families	Males under 21	Males 21–45	Males 45 & upwards	Females under 18	Females 18–45	Females 45 & upwards	Free people of color	Slaves or servants
[29*‡]	Arthur Morgan	4		2	6	1			
[30 ‡]	Edward Wilson	1	1		2	1			
[31 ‡]	William Biggs, Jnr	3	2		2	2			
[32 ‡]	James Nowlin	4	1		1	1	1		
[33 ‡]	William Wilson	1	1			1	1		
[34 ‡]	Otho Wilson	2	1		4	2			
[35 ‡]	Samuel Hill	2	2		1	1			1
[36*‡]	Jacob Lunceford	1	3		1	1			
[37*‡]	Isaac Reed		1		5	1			
[38*‡]	John L. Whiteside		1	1	1	1			
[39 ‡]	James Shepherd	2	1		1	1	1		
[40 ‡]	John Morgan	4	1		1	1			
[41 ‡]	John Johnston	2		1	3		1		
[42 ‡]	John W. Johnson		1		3	1			
[43*‡]	William Ryan	2	1		1	2			
[44 ‡]	John Byrns	3	1			1			
[45*‡]	John Teeter			2	2	3	1		
[46*‡]	Samuel Henry		1			1			
[47 ‡]	Caleb Lacey		1		1	1			
[48*‡]	Jacob Randleman		2		3	1			
[49*‡]	Silas Mauzy	1	1		1	1			
[50 ‡]	Micajah Wyatt	1	1			1			
[51 ‡]	Andrew McCorkle		1			1			
[52 ‡]	John A. Mauzy	3	2		1	1			
[53 ‡]	Fransess Gooding	2			3	1			
[54 ‡]	Thomas Henry		1		5	1			
[55 ‡]	James Makemson	3		1	1	1			
[56 ‡]	Jacob Hopkins	2	1		2	1			
[57*‡]	Henry Taylor	2	1		3	1			
[58 ‡]	Shelten Allfin	2	1		2	1			
[59 ‡]	James Smith		2		1	1			
[60 ‡]	Roland Grant	1	1		4	1			
[61 ‡]	Daniel Bonham		1		1	1	1		
[62 *]	John Robertson	3	1		1	1			
[63*‡]	Benjamin Goodner	2	1		1	2			
[64 ‡]	Benjamin Brownin		1		1	1			
[65*‡]	Ann Lacey	3	1				1		

ST. CLAIR COUNTY (Continued)

No.	Heads of families	Males under 21	Males 21-45	Males 45 & upwards	Females under 18	Females 18-45	Females 45 & upwards	Free people of color	Slaves or servants
[66*‡]	James Tanahill	1	2		3	1			
[67 ‡]	Zachariah Stephenson		1			1			
[68 ‡]	Clement Bostwick		2		2	1			
[69 ‡]	Hannah Potter	2	1		1		1		
[70*‡]	Jeremiah Phillips	2	2		1	1			
[71 ‡]	Henry Carr	3		1	2	1	1		
[72 ‡]	Alexander Barnet	1	1			1			
[73 ‡]	Timothy Higgins	3	3		2	1			
[74]	Timothy Hinckley	1	1			1			
[75]	John Smith	6		1	3	1			
[76]	Solomon Lamb	2	1		1	1			
[77]	Wolcot Lewis	1	1			1			
[78*‡]	Charles P. Walker	3	2		1	1			
[79 ‡]	John Byrd		1		4	1			
[80 ‡]	Lester Smith	1	1						
[81 ‡]	Thomas Winstanly	1	1	1		1			
[82 ‡]	Edward Newsham		2			1			
[83 ‡]	William Threlfall	5	1	1	4	1	1		
[84*‡]	Abraham McMurtry	5		1	2	1			
[85 ‡]	Henry McKee	2	1		2	1			
[86 ‡]	Chesley Allen	4	3	1	1	1			
[87]	John Gregson	2	1			1			
[88 ‡]	John Watson		1			1			
[89 ‡]	William Allen, Sen	1		1	1	1			
[90 ‡]	Pattrick Flauharty	7		1	2	1			
[91 ‡]	Stanly Dodge		1		3	1			
[92 ‡]	William Allen, Jun	2	1			1			
[93 ‡]	Hubbard Brewer	3		1			1		
[94*‡]	Henry Nulle	1	2			1			
[95 ‡]	Henry Brewer	4	1		1	1			
[96 ‡]	Arthur Murry	1	1			1			
[97 ‡]	Jarrot Brickey	2		1			1		
[98*‡]	Rawleigh Ralls	1		1	2	1	1		
[99 ‡]	John Brunt	2		1		1			
[100 ‡]	Nancy Guthrie	3				1	1		
[101 ‡]	John Morrison		3						3
[102 ‡]	Stephen Brewer		1			1			

ST. CLAIR COUNTY (Continued)

No.	Heads of families	Males under 21	Males 21-45	Males 45 & upwards	Females under 18	Females 18-45	Females 45 & upwards	Free people of color	Slaves or servants
[103 ‡]	James Smith	4		1	3	1			
[104 ‡]	James S Robertson		1		1	1			
[105*‡]	Robert Smith	4	2	1	3		1		
[106 ‡]	Elijah Camron	4	1	1	2	1			
[107 ‡]	Gorge Hickman		1		1	1			
[108*‡]	Charles Ratcliff	1	1		1	1			
[109 ‡]	Ransom Coddle		1		5	1			
[110*‡]	William Gilar	1	1			1			1
[111*‡]	Mark Ward	2		1	2	1	1		
[112 ‡]	Bennet Mason		1		1	1			
[113*‡]	Michael Ratcliff	3	1			1	1		
[114 ‡]	Henry Darter	2	1	1	4	1			
[115*‡]	Isrual Strait	3	1		3	1			
[116*‡]	David Pulliam		1		2	1			
[117*‡]	Paul McMillian	3		1	3	2			
[118]	Betsey Smith	1				1			
[119]	Isaac Hayle		1						
[120 ‡]	Phillip Land	3	1		3	1			
[121 ‡]	Jacob Lunce	1	1		1	1			
[122*‡]	Isaac Griffen	4	1		2	1			
[123*‡]	Andrew Free	6		1	1	1			
[124*‡]	Isaac Hickman	3	1		1	1			
[125*‡]	Bolsor Null	1	1		3	1	1		
[126*‡]	John Scott		1		1				
[127]	William L Hawley		1						
[128 ‡]	Thomas Pulliam	1	2		2	1			1
[129 ‡]	Henry Johnson	2	2	1	4	1			
[130 ‡]	William D Noble	1	1						
[131 ‡]	William Vestal		1		2	1			
[132 ‡]	John Boucher	1	1			1			
[133 ‡]	John Glover		1		3	1			
[134*‡]	Henry Walker	2	1		1	1			
[135 ‡]	David R Chance	1	1		2	1			
[136*‡]	Samuel Shook	3	2		1	1			
[137 ‡]	Gorge Mitchel	1	1		1				
[138*‡]	Pattrick Huggins	2	1		2	1			
[139*‡]	Robart Stockton	2	1		5	1			

ST. CLAIR COUNTY (Continued)

No.	Heads of families	Males under 21	Males 21–45	Males 45 & upwards	Females under 18	Females 18–45	Females 45 & upwards	Free people of color	Slaves or servants
[140*‡]	John H McLamore		1			1			
[141*‡]	David Walker	2	1		5	2			
[142 ‡]	Elijah Davis	3		1	1				
[143*‡]	Stephen Whiteside	2	1		3	1			
[144 ‡]	Edward Clark	1	1		1	1			
[145 ‡]	Willis Bracket		1			1			
[146 ‡]	Mary Hobson	1			3	1			
[147 ‡]	John Hobson	3	1	1	2	1	1		
[148*]	Hugh Smiley	1	1		1	1			
[149 ‡]	John Fraker		1			1			
[150*‡]	Edward Summers			1	1	1			
[151 ‡]	John M Wilson	3	1	1	1	1			
[152 ‡]	Joseph Miller	2	2			1			
[153*‡]	David Hill	1	1		1	1			
[154 ‡]	Ruth Hill	2					1		
[155*‡]	Samuel Scott	4		1	3	1	1		
[156*‡]	Thomas Talbot	2	1		1	2			
[157 ‡]	Henry Carr	2	1		3	2			
[158 ‡]	Abner Carr	4	2			1			
[159 ‡]	Samuel Smith	1	2	1	4		1		
[160 ‡]	Caleb Barker	2	1		4	1			
[161*‡]	William Fowler	1	1		1	1			
[162 ‡]	Coonrad Carr	7	1		3	1			
[163 ‡]	Ritchard Temple	1	1		1	1			
[164 ‡]	Greenbury Patterson	2	1		4	1			
[165 ‡]	Joseph McClintick	3	1		5	1			
[166 ‡]	James C Glasgow		2		1	1			
[167 ‡]	Washenton West	2	1	1	2	1	1		11
[168*‡]	William Miller	2	2	2	4	1	1		
[169 ‡]	William Graves	1	2		1	1			2
[170 ‡]	John Middlecoff	2	2		2	1			
[171 ‡]	John B Robertson		1			1			1
[172 ‡]	James Mitchel	2	1		2	1			1
[173]	Thomas Vaughn		1			1			
[174 ‡]	William Gillaspie	2	1		2	1			
[175*‡]	Jacob Short	5	1		2	1			
[176 ‡]	Richard Raper	1	1			1			

ST. CLAIR COUNTY (Continued)

No.	Heads of families	Males under 21	Males 21–45	Males 45 & upwards	Females under 18	Females 18–45	Females 45 & upwards	Free people of color	Slaves or servants
[177*‡]	William Rittenhouse	3	1		1	2			
[178 ‡]	George Jack		1			1			
[179 ‡]	John Rengold	1	1						
[180 ‡]	Moss K Botsford	3	16	1	3	1			2
[181 ‡]	Ann Bennet	1			1	1			
[182 ‡]	Nancy Russel	3			3	2			
[183 ‡]	William Small	2	1		1	1			
[184*‡]	William Holcomb	3	1	1	2	2	1		
[185 ‡]	John H Dennis		4		1	1			6
[186*‡]	Daniel Stout	1	1		1	1			
[187 ‡]	Francis T Crabb	1	3			1			
[188*‡]	Lewis W Myers	1	4		3	2	1		
[189*‡]	William Mears	2	1		1	1			2
[190 ‡]	Reuben Anderson	3	4	1	1	1			1
[191 ‡]	Thomas Cowhen	1	2		3	1			
[192*‡]	William Heath	2		1	1	1	1		
[193 ‡]	William Glasgow	1	3			1			
[194 ‡]	Rachel Murry	3			5	1			
[195 ‡]	James Adams	3		1	2	3			
[196 ‡]	Elijah Rittinghouse	[3?]	1	1	4	1	1		
[197 ‡]	Sally Sparks	2			3	2			
[198 ‡]	Robert Carns	2	1		2	1			
[199 ‡]	Edmond P Wilkeson	1	1		1	1		1	1
[200*‡]	William Hook	3	1	1	1	1			
[201 ‡]	William G Goforth		1			1			
[202 ‡]	Robert Taft		3						
[203 ‡]	Ephrefram Harris		1			1			
[204*‡]	James Hoggshead	1	2		1	1			
[205 ‡]	Joseph Green	3	3		1	1	1		
[206 ‡]	Richard W Chandler	1	2			1		1	
[207 ‡]	Vaulentine Gates		1			1			
[208]	Daniel Bean	4	1			1			
[209 ‡]	John Vaughn			1			1		
[210*‡]	John Glass	2	1		3	1			
[211*‡]	Thomas Primm	5	1		1	1			
[212 ‡]	James McLane	3		1	3		1		
[213 ‡]	Christopher Eyman	4	2	1	3	1	1		

ST. CLAIR COUNTY (Continued)

No.	Heads of families	Males under 21	Males 21-45	Males 45 & upwards	Females under 18	Females 18-45	Females 45 & upwards	Free people of color	Slaves or servants
[214 ‡]	William Sample	1	1		1	1	1		
[215 ‡]	Smith Crane	2	4		2	2		1	
[216 ‡]	Elisha Fish	1	3		2	1			
[217*‡]	John Stanly	5	1		2	1	1		
[218 ‡]	Joseph Bear	3	2		2	1			
[219 ‡]	John P Anderson	1	3	1	3		1		
[220 ‡]	John McCullough		1			1			
[221*‡]	William Phillips	5	1		1	1			
[222 ‡]	Daniel Phillips	3	2		2	1			
[223 ‡]	Henry Beare		1		1	1			
[224*‡]	James Marney	2	1		4	1			
[225 ‡]	Gorge Blair			1	1		1		
[226 ‡]	Joel Holkomb		1			1			
[227 ‡]	James Blair		1			1			
[228 ‡]	Samuel Ogle	5	2	1	1	1	1		
[229*‡]	Joseph Walton	4	1		1	1			
[230*‡]	John Hendrix	5		1	1		1		
[231 ‡]	John D Rush	3	4		2	1			
[232]	John P Robertson		3				1		
[233 ‡]	Samuel Beadle	3	2		3	1		1	
[234 ‡]	Levi Day	3	2		1	1			
[235 ‡]	Thomas Moore		1		2	1			
[236 ‡]	Anthony Badgley	2	2	1	3		1		
[237 ‡]	Hiram Badgley		1			1			
[238 ‡]	William Beare	1	2	1	1	1			
[239 ‡]	James Pettet		1			1			
[240 ‡]	Thomas Ervine	3	1			1			
[241 ‡]	James Simpson		1		7	1			
[242 ‡]	Aaron Badgley	4		1	3		1		
[243 ‡]	Jobe Badgley	6	3		1	1			
[244*‡]	William Stout	1	1		3	1			
[245 ‡]	William Bonham	2	1		1	1			
[246 ‡]	Mallakiah Bonham		1	1			1		
[247]	Samuel Bonham	1	1		3	1			
[248]	Peter Bear	5		1	2	2			
[249*‡]	Aaron Shook	3	1		2	1			

CENSUS OF 1820

ST. CLAIR COUNTY (Continued)

No.	Heads of families	Males under 21	Males 21–45	Males 45 & upwards	Females under 18	Females 18–45	Females 45 & upwards	Free people of color	Slaves or servants
[250*‡]	William T Kinkaid	2	1		1	1			
[251 ‡]	Daniel Berkey	3	1		2	1			
[252 ‡]	William S Colbreath		2		1	1			
[253*‡]	Jonas Shook		2	1		1	1		
[254 ‡]	James Kincaid	1	1		1	1			
[255 ‡]	Andrew Kincaid	1		1		3	1		
[256*‡]	Jeremiah Hand	2		1	4	1			
[257 ‡]	Abraham Badgley	2	1	1	2	1	1		
[258 ‡]	Joab Hayden	2	1		5	1			
[259 ‡]	Ichabod Badgley	2	1		5	1			
[260*‡]	Solomon Teter		3			2			
[261 ‡]	William M Brewer	2	1		2	1			
[262*‡]	John Messenger	4	1	2	2	1	1		
[263 ‡]	Elizabeth Prichard	1			1	1			
[264 ‡]	Peter Stroad	2	1		1	1			
[265 ‡]	Isaac Badgley		1		1	1			
[266*‡]	Daniel Million	3	1		4	1			
[267*‡]	Thomas Gillam	2	2	1	3	1			
[268 ‡]	Elizabeth Sales	1			5	1			
[269 ‡]	John J Whiteside	1	1	1	2		1		
[270*‡]	James Pulliam	2	1		2	1			
[271 ‡]	Edmond Weed	2	4		2	1			
[272 ‡]	John Cotton	3		1	2	2			
[273 ‡]	Peter Sprinkle	3		1	3	1			
[274 ‡]	John Pulliam	4	1			1			
[275 ‡]	Stephen Cooper	1	2		2	1			
[276*‡]	Anthony M Thomas	2	1		4	1			
[277*‡]	Jacob Whiteside	3	1		1	1			
[278*‡]	Hosea Rigg	2		1		1	1		
[279*‡]	Clement Rigg	1	2		1	1			
[280*‡]	Aaron Quick	6	2		2	1			
[281 ‡]	John H Gay	1	2		2	2			1
[282*‡]	Peter Hill	7	1	1	3	1			
[283*‡]	John Rider	2	2		3	2			
[284 ‡]	Joseph Goddard	1	1			1			
[285 ‡]	Ruben Goddard	1	1		2	1	1		
[286 ‡]	John Severo		1		1	1			

ST. CLAIR COUNTY (Continued)

No.	Heads of families	Males under 21	Males 21–45	Males 45 & upwards	Females under 18	Females 18–45	Females 45 & upwards	Free people of color	Slaves or servants
[287*‡]	Samuel Shook	5	3	1	1		1		
[288*‡]	John Stuntz	4	2		4	1			
[289]	Allen Smith	1	1		1	1			
[290*‡]	Gorge Wilderman	4	3		2	1			
[291*‡]	Peter Osamus	5	1		3	1			
[292]	Henry Brown		1		1	1			
[293 ‡]	Jacob Wilderman		1		1	1			
[294*‡]	James Wilderman	1	1		4	1			
[295 ‡]	Byrd Eastas	4	1		2	1			
[296*‡]	Jacob Hoosar	3	1		2	1			
[297 ‡]	Benjamin Phillips		2		3	1			
[298*‡]	Dorsey Wilderman	2	1		2	1			
[299 ‡]	Jacob Carr	1	1		5	1			
[300 ‡]	Elijah Smith	1	1		7	1			
[301 ‡]	Luke Barnet	1	3		2	1	1		
[302 ‡]	Thomas McGuire	3	1		5	1			
[303*‡]	John Woods	5	1		1	1			
[304 ‡]	Benjamin Angelo	2	1			1			
[305 ‡]	John Angelo		1			1			
[306*‡]	Lewis Larama	1	1		1	1			
[307*‡]	Peter Rettenghouse	1	1	1	2	1			
[308*‡]	Silvester Merrell	3	1		1	1			
[309*‡]	William D Moore	3	1			1			1
[310 ‡]	John Calbreath		1		.	1			
[311*‡]	Alexander Scott	2	1		6	1		1	
[312 ‡]	Elijah Charles Sen			1	1	1	1		
[313 ‡]	Peter Mitchel	6	1	1	5	1			
[314 ‡]	Edward Mitchel	1	1	1	2		1	2	
[315]	Joseph Phillips	3			1	1			
[316*‡]	Parker Jarvis	1	2			1			
[317]	Henry Jones		3						
[318 ‡]	Ruth Pentecost	4			3	2			
[319 ‡]	Alexander Nash		1			1			
[320 ‡]	Calvin Day	1	6		2	1	1		
[321 ‡]	John Jackson	2	2	1					
[322]	Mary Ann White	1			1		1		
[323*‡]	Francis Maxant	4	1		2	1			

ST. CLAIR COUNTY (Continued)

No.	Heads of families	Males under 21	Males 21–45	Males 45 & upwards	Females under 18	Females 18–45	Females 45 & upwards	Free people of color	Slaves or servants
[324*‡]	Risden Moore, Ser	3		1	2	2	1	5	
[325*‡]	Benjimin Watts	3		1	2		1		
[326 ‡]	Loyd Belt	1		1	1		1	2	1
[327*‡]	Benjamin Woods	4	1	1	1	1			
[328*‡]	Joseph Ogle, Jn	1	1			1			
[329 ‡]	Robert Leman	5	1		4	1			
[330*‡]	Paul Kingston	3	2		1	2			
[331*‡]	William Rutherford	4	1		1	1			
[332*‡]	William Moore, Ser	2	1		1	1		1	
[333 ‡]	Walter Westfield	2	2		1	1		1	
[334*‡]	Richard Wright		1			1			
[335*‡]	William Scott	4	2	1	2	1			
[336*‡]	Joseph Scott	5	1		3	1			
[337 ‡]	Carter Anderson	3	2		3	1			
[338 ‡]	Sarah Scott	5		1	1	2			
[339 ‡]	Hannah Adams	5	1		2	2			
[340*‡]	Charles R Matheny	3	1		3	1			
[341*‡]	Samuel Scott	3	1		2	2			
[342 ‡]	Mathew T Cox	1	2		4	2			
[343 ‡]	Josiah Patterson	1	1		1	1			
[344 ‡]	William Biggs Ser	3		1	3		1		
[345 ‡]	Able Fike	6	1		3	1			
[346*‡]	John Ward	1	1			1			
[347 ‡]	Gorge Lowe		1		2	1			
[348 ‡]	Joseph Pate	1	1	1	2		1		
[349 ‡]	William Pate		1		1	1			
[350 ‡]	Able Ward	1	1			1			
[351*‡]	William Kinney	3	3		4	1		2	1
[352 ‡]	Samuel Horney	1	1			2			
[353 ‡]	John Were	2	1		1	1			
[354*‡]	William L Whiteside	4		1	3	1			
[355*‡]	David Knight			1			1		
[356 ‡]	Peter Wright		1		1	1			
[357*‡]	Abraham Varner	2		1	1		1		
[358*‡]	Malkem Johnson	7	1		1	1			
[359]	John McCan		1		1	1			
[360]	James Sammons		1		1	1			

ST. CLAIR COUNTY (Continued)

No.	Heads of families	Males under 21	Males 21-45	Males 45 & upwards	Females under 18	Females 18-45	Females 45 & upwards	Free people of color	Slaves or servants
[361*‡]	Jacob Ogle Jur	3	1		4	1			
[362*‡]	Noah Matheney		1		2	1			
[363*‡]	Thornton Peoples	1	1		3	1			
[364 ‡]	Joseph Wilbanks		1			1			
[365 ‡]	Miles Abbernathar	2	1		2	1			
[366 ‡]	Robert McClure	1	1			1			
[367*‡]	Paul Gaskill	5	2	1	6	1			
[368 ‡]	Nathan Jones	2	1		2	1			
[369*‡]	James Walker	2	1			1			
[370*‡]	John Kingston		1	1				1	
[371 ‡]	James Anderson	3		1	1	1			
[372 ‡]	Joseph Padfield	2	1		1	1			
[373 ‡]	Moses Short	2	1	1	1	2			
[374 ‡]	Jacob Rayhill		1						
[375*‡]	William Walker	1	2		4	1			
[376]	Aaron Quigley		1						
[377 ‡]	Stephen Ballard	3	1		1	1			
[378 ‡]	Ezekel Jones	1	1			1			
[379 ‡]	William Hart	1	1			1			
[380*‡]	William Penn		1		1	1			
[381*‡]	William McNail	2	2		2	1			
[382 ‡]	Robert Farrer	2			4	1			
[383 ‡]	Aaron Land	4	1		3	1			
[384*‡]	Ephran Pirkins	2	1			1			
[385 ‡]	Josiah Crocker	6	1	1	1	1			
[386 ‡]	Christopher Folks	2	2	1	2		1		
[387*‡]	Henry Stout	1	1	1	1	1			
[388 ‡]	Joseph Smith	3	1		1	1			
[389*‡]	David Phillips	2		1	1	1			
[390*‡]	John Steel	1	2	1	2		1		
[391*‡]	Jesse Perkins	1	1		1	1			
[392*‡]	James Hart	2	1			1			
[393 ‡]	David B. Driskill	3	1		2	1			
[394*‡]	William King	2	1		6	1			
[395*‡]	John Leach	5	1		1	1			
[396 ‡]	Archabald Allen	1	1		2	1			
[397 ‡]	Levi Wells		2						

CENSUS OF 1820 267

ST. CLAIR COUNTY (*Continued*)

No.	Heads of families	Males under 21	Males 21–45	Males 45 & upwards	Females under 18	Females 18–45	Females 45 & upwards	Free people of color	Slaves or servants
[398 ‡]	James Silkwood	3	1		2	1			
[399 ‡]	James Northcraft	3	1		1	1			
[400*‡]	William Virgin	1	1			1			
[401*‡]	Enoch Hayle		2		1	1			
[402 ‡]	Joshua Clark	3	1		2	1			
[403*‡]	Thomas Howel	1	1		1	1			
[404*‡]	Robart Hayle	1	1		1	1			
[405 ‡]	Ichabod Allen		2	1	1	1			
[406*‡]	James Phillips	4	1		1	1			
[407*‡]	Elijah Rittenhouse	1	1		1	1			
[408*‡]	Joshua Perkins	1	3	1	1		1		
[409 ‡]	William Wright		1		4	1			
[410*‡]	Burrel Hill	4	1		2	1			
[411*‡]	John D Thomas	4	1		3	1			
[412 ‡]	William Atcheson	4		1	2	1			
[413 ‡]	Peter Malcom		1		1	1			
[414 ‡]	Samuel Steel		1		1	1			
[415*‡]	Daniel Pierce	2	4	1	3	1			
[416 ‡]	John Helm	2	1		1	1			
[417*‡]	Gorge Jimmeson			1			1		
[418*‡]	Eli Ward	5	1		1	1			
[419 ‡]	Robert Abenathy	1	1	1	2		1		
[420 ‡]	Isaa Basey	5	1		1	1			
[421*‡]	Benjamin Ogle		1	1	3				
[422 ‡]	William McMurry	1	3		1	1			
[423*‡]	Henry Mace	2	2		4	1			
[424]	William Hilt		1			1			
[425*‡]	James Moore	3	1		2	1			
[426*‡]	James Watts		1		2	1			
[427 ‡]	John Crocker	3	1		1	1			
[428 ‡]	Hugh Alexander	3	6	1	2	2	1		
[429 ‡]	David Alexander	4	1	1	1	2	1		
[430*‡]	John Scott	7	1			2			
[431*‡]	Joshua Oglesby	3	1	1	2	1			
[432*]	Robert K McLaughlin		1			1			7
[433]	William A Beard		1						
[434*‡]	Nathan Titus							9	

ST. CLAIR COUNTY (Continued)

No.	Heads of families	Males under 21	Males 21-45	Males 45 & upwards	Females under 18	Females 18-45	Females 45 & upwards	Free people of color	Slaves or servants
[435*‡]	Josep Land	2	1		4	1			
[436 ‡]	John Deaton	3	1		4	1			
[437 ‡]	Daniel Wilbanks	5	1	1	2		1		
[438 ‡]	John H Wood	3	1		2	1			
[439 ‡]	William G Brown	3	2		5	2			
[440 ‡]	Aaron Robertson	2	1		1	1			
[441 ‡]	John Jarvis		1		4	1			
[442 ‡]	Obediah Silkwood		1		4	1			
[443 ‡]	John Padon	1	1		1	1			
[444*‡]	Robert Thomas	1	1		5	1			
[445*‡]	Theophilus M Nicklas		3		2	1			
[446 ‡]	Isabella Driskell				1	1			
[447 ‡]	Jacob Smith		1	2		1	1		
[448*‡]	Job Vanwinkel	5	1		2	1			
[449 ‡]	Robert Chesney	1	1	1	6		1		
[450*‡]	Thomas Stubelfield	1		1	3	1			
[451 ‡]	Moses Land	1	1		1	1			
[452 ‡]	Alexander Cuberson		2			1		1	
[453*‡]	Moses Herring	2	1		4	1			
[454*‡]	William Hill		1		1	1			
[455 ‡]	John Whiteside		1			1			
[456 ‡]	Joseph Chance	4		1	5	1			
[457]	Joseph Abbernatha	4	1		4	1			
[458 ‡]	Gorge Bridges		1		2	1			
[459*‡]	James D Thomas	3	1		1	1			
[460*‡]	Brice Virgin	2	1	1	2	1	1		
[461 ‡]	Tobias Bright	1	1		1	1			
[462 ‡]	James W Davidson	4	1		1	2			
[463 ‡]	Bennet Stiner	1	1	1					
[464 ‡]	Jacob Hardy	1	2	1	2		1		
[465 ‡]	Randolph Boman		1			1			
[466 ‡]	Levi Simmon	5	1		3	2			
[467 ‡]	Randolph Weldney	4		1	3		1		
[468*‡]	Ira Manville		1	1	2	1	2		
[469*‡]	Nathaniel Hill	2	1		1	2			
[470 ‡]	James Redpath	2		1	3	1			
[471 ‡]	Merreness Loveland	1	1			1			

ST. CLAIR COUNTY (Continued)

No.	Heads of families	Males under 21	Males 21–45	Males 45 & upwards	Females under 18	Females 18–45	Females 45 & upwards	Free people of color	Slaves or servants
[472*‡]	John Liveley	2	2		3	1			
[473*‡]	William James	5	1		2	1			
[474 ‡]	Jane Mason	1			4		1		
[475 ‡]	Seth Catline		2						
[476 ‡]	Roswel Sturdevan	2	2			1			
[477 ‡]	William Hill		2			2			
[478 ‡]	Adam Henderson	2	1	1	4	1			
[479 ‡]	William Nichols		2	1		1			
[480 ‡]	Adam McDaniel		1			1			
[481*‡]	Absolom Penington	1		1			1		
[482*‡]	Absolom P Free	1	1			1			
[483*‡]	Able McNail	1	1		3	1			
[484 ‡]	James Dupuy	4	1		4	1			
[485*‡]	John Walker	2	1		1	2			
[486*‡]	Robert Middleton	3	1		2	1			
[487 ‡]	Herman Leck	1		1			1		
[488 ‡]	Elizabeth Morriss	5			1	1			
[489 ‡]	Joseph Dupuy	4	1		4	1			
[490 ‡]	William Dupuy	2			1				
[491*‡]	Levi Stroad	4	1		1	1			
[492 ‡]	Joseph Millsted			1	1	1			
[493*‡]	Abraham Johnson	4	1		4	1			
[494 ‡]	John Marloe	5	1		2	1			
[495 ‡]	Samuel Dickson	3	1		1	1			
[496*‡]	Joel Jackson	6	1	1	2				
[497 ‡]	James Deaton	6	2		2		1		
[498*‡]	Jonathan Gaskell	3	1		3	2			
[499 ‡]	Robert Duncain	1	1	1	1	1			
[500*‡]	Peter Teterick	3	1			1			
[501 ‡]	James Robertson	2	1		1	1			
[502 ‡]	John Colbreath	1		1			1		
[503*‡]	Robert Hughes	3	1		1	1			
[504*‡]	Risdon Moore, Jnr	4	1	1	2		1		2
[505 ‡]	Thriston Adams	2		1	3	1			
[506]	George Harris	1	1	1	2	3			
[507 ‡]	Tilghiman H West	4	1		4	1			8
[508 ‡]	James C Davis	1		1		1			

ST. CLAIR COUNTY (Continued)

No.	Heads of families	Males under 21	Males 21–45	Males 45 & upwards	Females under 18	Females 18–45	Females 45 & upwards	Free people of color	Slaves or servants
[509 ‡]	William Henderlight		1		1	1			
[510*‡]	Samuel Mitchel	2		1	4	1			
[511 ‡]	Elijah Charles jun		1		2	1			
[512 ‡]	James Craford	1	1		2	1			
[513*‡]	Marshal Hawkins	1	1		1	1			
[514*‡]	John Pea	2	2		2	1			
[515 ‡]	Isaah Hawkins	1		1			1		
[516 ‡]	Mercy Wells	5	1		1		1		
[517]	Catharine Vineyard	3			1	1	1		
[518*‡]	Jessey Waker			1			1		
[519 ‡]	David Evret	5	1		2	1			
[520 ‡]	William Alexander	1	3			1			
[521*‡]	William Moore		1		2	1			
[522 ‡]	Jerrimiah Simpkins	2	1		3	1			
[523 ‡]	Silas Crane	1		1	1		1		
[524*‡]	James McCann	2		1	5		1		
[525 ‡]	Meredith Cooper	1	1		3	1			
[526 ‡]	William Adair	2	1		3	1			
[527 ‡]	Samuel Allen	2	3		1	1			
[528 ‡]	Samuel Tosier	1	3		1	1			
[529 ‡]	John Thomas	7		1	2	1	1		
[530]	William Rowe	1	1		1	1			
[531*‡]	Zachariah Hays	3	1	2	2	1			
[532 ‡]	Andrew Fergeson	1	1		3	2			
[533 ‡]	William Bridges	4	1		1	1			
[534 ‡]	Edward Foxwell	2	2	1	3	1	1		
[535*‡]	David L West	3	1		1	1			
[536 ‡]	Alexander Anderson	3		1	5	1			
[537 ‡]	John Tallant	2		1	1		1		
[538 ‡]	Nathaniel Bell	1		1	1		1		
[539*‡]	Isreal Robertson		1		1	1	1		
[540 ‡]	Joseph Ogle	2	1			1			
[541 *]	James Tolly	1				1			
[542 ‡]	Solomon Perkins	1	1			1			
[543]	Zepheniah Ames	3		1	3		1		
[544 ‡]	Gorge Dickson	1		1	1		1		
[545*‡]	Stephen T Terry	3		1		1	1		

CENSUS OF 1820   271

ST. CLAIR COUNTY (Continued)

No.	Heads of families	Males under 21	Males 21-45	Males 45 & upwards	Females under 18	Females 18-45	Females 45 & upwards	Free people of color	Slaves or servants
[546 ‡]	Gideon Simpson		2			1	1	1	
[547 ‡]	John Hart	4	1			1			
[548 ‡]	Sarah Enochs	1	1	1	2		1		
[549 ‡]	Charles Rubey	1	2	1		1	1		
[550 ‡]	Thomas Hall		1		2	1			
[551*‡]	Jane Moore	1			1	1	1		
[552 ‡]	William Simpson	2	2		1	1			
[553 ‡]	John Byrd	9	1	1	3	3			
[554 ‡]	Pattrick Hogan	2	1		1	1			
[555]	John Thuston	2	1		1	1			
[556 ‡]	Isham Tolly	2		1	1		1		
[557 ‡]	Joseph Leman	4	2		2	1			
[558*‡]	Gorge Pricket	3	1	1	1		1		
[559 ‡]	Jonah Pierceau	3		1	1	2	1		
[560*‡]	Samuel Winson							5	
[561 ‡]	Benjamin Herron		2						
[562]	James Singleton							6	
[563 ‡]	Samuel Eldrige	3		1	2	1			
[564*‡]	Jacob Ogle sen	3	1	1	1	1			
[565 ‡]	Elijah Lewis	1	1			1			
[566 ‡]	Stephen Box		2		2	1			
[567 ‡]	Joab Jenkins		1	1		1	1		
[568 ‡]	Abraham Bunker		1		2	1			
[569*‡]	Joseph Ogle, Ser			1	1		1		
[570 ‡]	John Porter	1	1			1			
[571 ‡]	Gorge Davis	1	1			1			
[572*‡]	David Sparks	3	1	1	1	2			
[573*‡]	Rebecah Porter	3			3	1			
[574*‡]	Samuel Redman	1		1			1		
[575 ‡]	John Lee	2	1	1	5	1			
[576 ‡]	Anthony Pate	6	1	1	1	2			
[577*‡]	Elizabeth Jorney	5	4	1	2	1			
[578*‡]	Henry Walker	2		1	1	2			
[579 ‡]	Gorge McDaniel	6	1		3	2	1		
[580 ‡]	Dorsey Boring	1	2			1			
[581 ‡]	Adam Vineyard	3	1		3	1			
[582*‡]	Thomas Ray	3	3		1	2		1	

ST. CLAIR COUNTY (*Continued*)

No.	Heads of families	Males under 21	Males 21–45	Males 45 & upwards	Females under 18	Females 18–45	Females 45 & upwards	Free people of color	Slaves or servants
[583 ‡]	John Handcock		1		1	1			
[584 ‡]	Elizabeth Postelwyt	3			2	1			
[585 ‡]	Andrew Welch	1	1		1	1			
[586*‡]	Nathan Horner		1		2	1			
[587 ‡]	Temprence Stanphell	1				1			
[588 ‡]	James Magill	3	1		3	2			
[589 ‡]	Catharine Hutcheson	4			4	1			
[590 ‡]	Eleezer Hathaway	2		1		1			
[591 ‡]	Thomas T. Gasler		1			1			
[592 ‡]	William Mayhoe	3	2		1	2			
[593 ‡]	Daniel Matheney	1	1		3	1			
[594*‡]	Joseph Penn, sr	1	1	1	1		1		
[595 ‡]	Joseph Penn, jur		1			1			
[596 ‡]	Brian Mooney	1	1	1	5		1		
[597]	John Crocker	3	1		1	1			
[598*‡]	John Higgins		1	1		1	2		
[599 ‡]	Samuel Hall	3	1		3	1			
[600 ‡]	Joseph Duglass	1	1		1	1			
[601*‡]	Paul Wilks		1			1			
[602*‡]	Whitfield Townsend	2	1		2	1			
[603 ‡]	William Brazule	2		1	2	3			
[604 ‡]	James Taylor	2	1		2	1			
[605 ‡]	Neal Keneday	2	1		1	1			
[606 ‡]	Mary Bradsby	1	2		1	1	1		
[607 ‡]	Mary Brock	2	1			1	1		
[608 ‡]	Nichlas Horner	2		1		1	1		
[609 ‡]	James Smith		1		2	1			
[610 ‡]	William Cheeves							7	
[611*]	Phillip Smith	4	1	1	1	1			
[612 ‡]	Richard Lyons							7	
[613 ‡]	George Coppenbrger	1	1		4	1			
[614 ‡]	William Tille	1	1			1			
[615 ‡]	John Tille		1			1			
[616 ‡]	William Padfield, sr	3	1	1	1		1		
[617*‡]	David Lowe	4		2			1		
[618 ‡]	Mathew Pate	2	1		1	1			
[619 ‡]	John Barton		1		1	1			

CENSUS OF 1820   273

ST. CLAIR COUNTY (Continued)

No.	Heads of families	Males under 21	Males 21–45	Males 45 & upwards	Females under 18	Females 18–45	Females 45 & upwards	Free people of color	Slaves or servants
[620*‡]	Samuel McDaniel	3	1		5	1			
[621*‡]	Richard Vanansdol	4	1		4	1			
[622 ‡]	William Barton	2	2	1	4	1			
[623]	Easther Nichlas	2			1	1			
[624 ‡]	Christopher Carpenter	4	1		1	1	1		
[625 ‡]	Henry Rule			1		1			
[626 ‡]	Joel Beaver	5	1	1	1	1			
[627 ‡]	Joseph Devenport	2	2		1	1			
[628 ‡]	John Saler		1		1	1			
[629 ‡]	Charles Lowry		1			1			
[630*‡]	Francis Swann	3	1		3	1			
[631 ‡]	William Robans		1			1			
[632 ‡]	John Dew		1			2		4	
[633 ‡]	Zepheniah Lenard	5		1	5	1	1		
[634 ‡]	Jules Nichlas	5	1		3	1			
[635 ‡]	Sarah Nichlas	2			1	1	1		
[636 ‡]	Sally Chambers	1			1		1		
[637 ‡]	Moses Carrick	6		1					
[638*‡]	John Simmons	1	2		1	1			
[639 ‡]	William Padfield, sr	3	3	1	3		1	6	
[640 ‡]	David Sharp		1						
[641 ‡]	Samuel H. Thomson		1		2	1			
[642 ‡]	Peter L. Limmerick	1	1		1	1			
[643*‡]	Samuel Piles	2	2		1	1		1	
[644 ‡]	John Broom	3	1		2	1			
[645]	Henry Marllo	2	1			1			
[646 ‡]	Robert Abenerthy		1		1	1			
[647*‡]	Solomon Linch	3	1	1	1		1		
[648]	Isaac Linch	1	1		1	1			
[649*‡]	William Padfield, jr	1	1		3	1			
[650*‡]	George Slaton	4	1		2	2	1		
[651*‡]	Henry Hutton	4	1		3	1			
[652 ‡]	Anthony W. Casad	2	2		1	1			
[653]	Battee Abenerthy		1	1	1		1		
[654*‡]	Robert Moore	2	1		2	1			
[655*‡]	James Walker	6		1	2	1			
[656 ‡]	James Crocker	2		1	3	3	1		

ST. CLAIR COUNTY (Continued)

No.	Heads of families	Males under 21	Males 21-45	Males 45 & upwards	Females under 18	Females 18-45	Females 45 & upwards	Free people of color	Slaves or servants
[657 ‡]	John Coone	5	1		3	1			
[658 ‡]	John Cooksey	4		1	1	1			
[659*‡]	Benjamin Moody	6		1	4	1			
[660 ‡]	Harmon Hatfield	2	1		2	1			
[661 ‡]	William Cox	3	1		5	1	1		
[662*‡]	Thomas Knighton	1		1			1		
[663 ‡]	Moses Land jn		1		1	1			
[664]	Peggy Carns	2				1			
[665 ‡]	Martain Deal	4	1		3	1			
[666 ‡]	Delilah Smith	3			3	1			
[667 ‡]	George Harrison	2	1		1	1			
[668*‡]	Isaac Quick	1		1	2	1			
[669]	William Hill	1	1		2	1			
[670*]	Hugh Gilbreath	2	1		3	1			
[671*‡]	William Ritheghouse sr			1	1		1		
[672 ‡]	Elijah Rittenghouse	1	1		1	1			
[673 ‡]	James Pea		1		1	1			
[674*‡]	Lewis Herron	2	1			1			
[675*‡]	David Howel	1	2		3	1			
[676 ‡]	William Whitchurch	8	1		2	1			
[677 ‡]	Samuel McLane	3	1		2	1			
[678*‡]	Daniel Griffeth	2	1		2	1			
[679*‡]	Phillip Vineyard	1	3		1	1	1		
[680 ‡]	James Estep	2	1			1			
[681]	Vanwincle Varner		1		2	1			
[682*]	Bennet Million	3	1	1	5	1			
[683*‡]	Benjamin Million	1		1	1		1		
[684 ‡]	John Newcomb	3	1		1	1			
[685*‡]	Mary Rittenhouse	4			3	1			
[686 ‡]	Gorge Tenant							8	
[687]	Joseph Cornelius	5	3	1				2	
[688*‡]	Eli Hart	3	1		1	1			
[689]	John Glice	2	1			1			
[690 ‡]	Jonas Swagart	3	2		4	2	1		
[691 ‡]	Samuel Holts	2	2		2	1			
[692*‡]	Gorge F. Keneday	1	2		3	1			

CENSUS OF 1820

ST. CLAIR COUNTY (Continued)

No.	Heads of families	Males under 21	Males 21-45	Males 45 & upwards	Females under 18	Females 18-45	Females 45 & upwards	Free people of color	Slaves or servants
[693*‡]	William Thomson	2	1			1			
[694 ‡]	John Eckerd	2	2			1			
[695 ‡]	Mary Williams	3			3	1			
[696*‡]	James Hart		1		1	1			
[697 ‡]	John Grist	2	1			1			
[698*‡]	Gorge Swaggart	4	3	1	1	1			
[699 ‡]	Edward Thomas		1	1					
[700 ‡]	Richard Stillwell	1	2		1	1			
[701 ‡]	John Maning		1						
[702 ‡]	Joseph Gunvill	4	2		1	1			
[703 ‡]	Hugh Larama	1	2			1			
[704 ‡]	Thomas Eads	3	1		2	1			
[705*‡]	John Shinberger	2	2		5	1			
[706*‡]	Lewis Garvy	2	2		1	1			
[707*‡]	Enos Garvy	1		1	2				
[708*‡]	Battice Lacounts, Ser	1	1		1	1		1	
[709*‡]	Augustice Trotier		1		1	1			
[710 ‡]	John Boveneau	2	1		1	1			
[711*‡]	Nichlas Trusoe	2	2	1	2	1			
[712 ‡]	Paul Larama	2		1	2	2			
[713 ‡]	Joseph Boneue	2	2		2	1			
[714*‡]	Francis Trotier	2	1	1	1	1			
[715 ‡]	Joseph Lapaugh		2			1		1	
[716 ‡]	Nichlas Bosso	3	1		3	1			
[717*‡]	Gabriel Marlo	1	4	1	1		1		
[718*‡]	Simon Vanarsdol	3	9	1	1	1			
[719 ‡]	Phillip Laplumb			2			1		
[720 ‡]	Joseph Greennah	2	1		2	1			
[721*‡]	Lewis Pensono	6	3	1	2		1	1	
[722 ‡]	Jack Burdauk	1	1	1	3				
[723 ‡]	Henry Brusko		1		1	1			
[724 ‡]	Antoine Renneo	2	1	1	2	1	1		
[725 ‡]	John Bullard		10	1	1	2			
[726 ‡]	Elisha Smith		3						
[727 ‡]	John Waggoner		3		1	1			
[728 ‡]	Epharim Town	4	4		2	1			3
[729 ‡]	Obediah Coburn	4	1	1	2		1		

ST. CLAIR COUNTY (Continued)

No.	Heads of families	Males under 21	Males 21-45	Males 45 & upwards	Females under 18	Females 18-45	Females 45 & upwards	Free people of color	Slaves or servants
[730 ‡]	Eli Wyatt		1			1			
[731 ‡]	John Farley	3	1	1	2	2			
[732 ‡]	Elijah Adkinson		1			1			
[733 ‡]	Thomas Dowler		3			1			
[734*‡]	Thomas Roach			1	1	1	1		
[735]	Nathaniel Davis	1	1			1			
[736 ‡]	Samuel Wigans		6						
[737]	Jesse Lambert		1						
[738 ‡]	David Howard	1	2			1			
[739 ‡]	Eli Savage	1	1	1	2		1		1
[740 ‡]	Nichlas St Anthony	2		2	3	1			
[741 ‡]	John Hammond	4	1			1			
[742 ‡]	William Bridges	3		1	2	1			
[743 ‡]	James Savage		1			1			
[744 ‡]	Joseph Nevet	1	1			1	1		
[745 ‡]	David Coone		3			1			
[746]	James Savage		4		2	1			1
[747*‡]	William Ratcliff	2	4						
[748 ‡]	Thomas Osbourn	4	1			1	1		
[749 ‡]	William Lee		1				1		
[750 ‡]	John Simkye	2	1				1		
[751 ‡]	Alansen Mead		1				1		
[752 ‡]	Jacob Snider	1	4				1		
[753 ‡]	Peter Johetee		1				1		
[754 ‡]	Joseph Darby	2	1			3	1		
[755 ‡]	Joseph Lechanoe, Ser		1	1		2			
[756 ‡]	Joseph Lechanoe Jur	1	1			2	1		
[757 ‡]	Andrew Tolly	2	1			1	1		
[758 ‡]	Thomas Mason	1	1			1	1		
[759 ‡]	Lewis Gandrow	1	1	1	1	1			
[760 ‡]	Peter Shuckey	1	1	1	1	1			
[761*‡]	Michael Souldan	2	1			2	1		
[762 ‡]	Nichles Bovneu	1	1			1	1		1
[763 ‡]	Anthony Potts	3		1	2	1	1		
[764*‡]	John Lafumba	1	1	2	3	2			
[765*‡]	Lewis Goodeau		1			1			
[766*‡]	Battice Perredu	1	1			1			

CENSUS OF 1820

ST. CLAIR COUNTY (Continued)

No.	Heads of families	Males under 21	Males 21–45	Males 45 & upwards	Females under 18	Females 18–45	Females 45 & upwards	Free people of color	Slaves or servants
[767 ‡]	John Christmas	2	1		1				
[768 ‡]	Lewis Parrish		1		5	1			
[769*‡]	Lewis Pensono	3	3	1	5	1			
[770 ‡]	Ames Trumbeau		2	1	1				
[771 ‡]	Francis Savern		1						
[772 ‡]	Francis Dement	2		1	4	1	1		
[773*‡]	Joseph Trotier	2	3		1				3
[774 ‡]	Simon Bartrau	1	7	1	2	1	1		
[775*‡]	Battice Lacoumpt	4	1		2	1			
[776 ‡]	Joseph Lamarsh		1	1	1		1		
[777*‡]	Basel Lacoumpt		2		1				
[778 ‡]	John B Blundau	1		2	1				
[779 ‡]	Battice Lalong	2	1		2	1			1
[780*‡]	Juliann Lacoumpt	3		1	1	1			
[781 ‡]	Battice Shatrau		1		3		1		1
[782 ‡]	Joseph Delong	4		1	1	1	1		1
[783 ‡]	Joseph Decompt	1	1			1			
[784 ‡]	Gebriel Dacator	2	1		1	1			
[785 ‡]	Lewis Pereau	6	1	1	5	1	1		
[786]	Joseph Pealet	5	1		1	1			
[787*‡]	Lewis Pealet	1	1			1			
[788 ‡]	Joseph Rale	5	1		1	1			
[789*‡]	Francis Farraer	2	5	1	2	1			
[790 ‡]	Anthony Rock	1	1			1			
[791*‡]	Francis Turcothe	2		2	5	1			
[792 ‡]	John B Carron			1	2	1			
[793 ‡]	Francis Pensano	3	1		2	1			
[794 ‡]	James Martain	2	1		1	1			
[795 ‡]	John de Laygest		1			1			
[796*‡]	Nickles Jarrot	1		1	3	1	1		12
[797 ‡]	Joseph Lapage		1			1			
[798 ‡]	John Bovoneau	3	3		2	1			
[799*‡]	Guy Morrison		1						1
[800 ‡]	Michael Vincant	1	2	1	1	2	1		
[801*‡]	Olive Updyke					2			
[802 ‡]	Francis Voodry		4						
[803 ‡]	Charles Bobo	1	1		3	1			

ST. CLAIR COUNTY (Continued)

No.	Heads of families	Males under 21	Males 21–45	Males 45 & upwards	Females under 18	Females 18–45	Females 45 & upwards	Free people of color	Slaves or servants
[804 ‡]	Madam Lapage	2							
[805 ‡]	Josef Manville	1	2		1	2			
[806 ‡]	Joseph Lataue	3	1		4	1			
[807 ‡]	Battece Marshal	1	1		1	1			
[808 ‡]	Joseph Bully	4		1	1	1			
[809*‡]	Lewis Labasha	5		1	2	1			
[810*‡]	Francis Lapois	3	1			1			
[811 ‡]	Root Novet	1	1			1			
[812*‡]	Lewis Larama s [r?]			1	1				
[813*‡]	Mashec Gamlau	2	1			2			
[814 ‡]	Thomas Terveya				1				
[815 ‡]	Anthony Lapoxey		1		2	2			
[816*‡]	Peter Gamlah	7	7	1	1	1			
[817 ‡]	James Voodry	1	2		1	1			
[818*‡]	John Rannals		1		1	2			
[819 ‡]	Samuel Bates							6	
[820 ‡]	Joseph Evans	1	2		2	1			
[821 ‡]	Margaret Goddard						1		
[822*‡]	John Hay	5		1	6	1			
[823*‡]	Lewis St John	2	1		4	1			
[824 ‡]	Joseph Lapaugh	1		1	1		1		
[825 ‡]	Edward Neal	7	2		1	1			
[826*‡]	Lewis Lacoumpt		1	1	1	2			
[827*‡]	Paul Paupau	4	2		1	1			
[828 ‡]	Lewis Amley, Ser	1	1		2	1			
[829 ‡]	Battece Dacoto		1			1			
[830 ‡]	Peter Lapaugh	2	2		2	1			
[831 ‡]	Lewis Amley	1	1						
[832*‡]	Joseph Paupaugh	4	1	1	2	1			
[833 ‡]	Michael Burnaugh		1	1	3	1			
[834*‡]	Michael Pelate	1	1			1			
[835 ‡]	Johaim Lamatte	4	2			1			
[836*‡]	John Hays		1		4	2			
[837 ‡]	Joseph Barbary	1	2		1	1	1		
[838 ‡]	Towe Sheretau	1	1	1	6	1	1		
[839 ‡]	Lewis Ragar	1	2	1	2		1		1
[840 ‡]	Bartholemew Provo		1	1		1			

ST. CLAIR COUNTY (Continued)

No.	Heads of families	Males under 21	Males 21–45	Males 45 & upwards	Females under 18	Females 18–45	Females 45 & upwards	Free people of color	Slaves or servants
[841 ‡]	Margaret Compass		1		1	2	1		
[842 ‡]	Joseph Bohanan		1			1			
[843 ‡]	Peter Roch	1		1					
[844*‡]	James Rose	1	2		1	1			
[845 ‡]	Tocan Trobley	1	1		1	2			
[846 ‡]	Tadale Pensono	1		3	4	2	1		
[847 ‡]	Antwine Lacoumpt		2						
[848 ‡]	Battece Allery	3	1		1		1		
[849 ‡]	Thomas Shautaue		1	1					
[850*‡]	Peter Goodane	3	2	1	1	1	1		
[851*‡]	Lewis Voodree	2	2		1	1			
[852 ‡]	Francis Voodree		3						
[853 ‡]	David Blackwel	1	1			1			
[854 ‡]	Charles Woodworth		2			2			
[855*‡]	John O Prentice	3	1		3	1			
[856 ‡]	James Duncan		1			1			
[857 ‡]	Frank Plasant							5	
[858 ‡]	Teague Desheat							5	
[859*‡]	Warrick Moore							8	
[860]	Samuel Turus							5	
[861 ‡]	John P Cremer	2	2	1	3	1			
		1569	1007	264	1329	763	165	98	76

ST. CLAIR COUNTY (*Continued*)

Whole number of free white males under twenty one	1569
Number of free white males of twenty one and under forty five	1007
Number of free white males of forty five & upwards	264
Whole number of free white males	2840
Number of free white females	2257
Whole number of free white persons	5097
Number of free people of color	98
Number of slaves or servants or slaves	76
Whole number	5271

I hereby certify that the foregoing enumeration is correct to the best of my knowledge as made by me for the County of St. Clair, agreeable to an Act providing for taking the Census of the Inhabitants of the State of Illinois

Given under my hand as Commissioner for the County of St. Clair the 30th of November 1820.

Quallified Voters 1271   CORNELIUS GOODING
Errors Excepted

Corrected totals:

Free white males under 21 years of age		1590
Free white males 21 years and under 45 years		997
Free white males 45 years and upwards		264
Free white females under 18 years of age		1332
Free white females 18 years and under 45 years		793
Free white females 45 years and upwards		165
		5141
Negroes		188
Free persons of color	108	
Servants or slaves	80	
	188	
Total		5329

CENSUS OF 1820

ST. CLAIR COUNTY (*Continued*)

The 1818 census of St. Clair County was taken by William Moore and is dated June 1. Cornelius Gooding took the state census for 1820, certifying the returns on November 30, 1820. Robert Lemon took the federal census for 1820, but no date for certification appears. There are 861 names in the state and 878 names in the federal census. Of these, fifty-two names are found in the state but not in the federal census and seventy-two names in the federal but not in the state census.

The following names found in the federal census do not appear in the state census for 1820:

Belleville Township
  Brigam, Ebenezer
  Ransam, Amherst
  Wark, James
  Harris, William
  Deuvcelbliss, William
  Kinney, William
  Smith, Jacob
  Barret, John
  Miller, Patcy
  [*Illegible name*]
Ogle Township
  Lemen, James
  *Moore, Curtis
  Cowles, Alfred
  *Holcomb, Zachariah
    1818. Halcomb, Zacabiah
  Webster, Samuel
  Cannon, Thomas
  Pate, Anthony
  Collier, Stephen
  Hodges, Seth
  Quick, Thomas
  *Jarvis, Fanlin
    1818. Jarvis, Franklin
  Fisher, Comfort
  Woods, Louis
  Ramsey, Samuel
  Roberts, John T.
Chambers Township
  Fellows, Joseph
  Chaffin, Joseph
  Padfield, Joseph
  Samuels, Reuben
  *Walker, William
  Journey, John
  Padon, William
Silver Creek Township
  Shepherd, Elihu H.
  Bridgeman, Joseph
  Commerce, Rickets
  Hail, Thomas
  Padfield, Thomas

  Rayhill, George
  Brewer, Peggy
  Isom, George W.
Turkey Hill Township
  Buzan, Jesse
  Freeman, Richman
  John   1 free colored
  Parker 1 free colored
  *Taylor, Joseph
Scott Township
  Atcheson, Matthew
  Drakes, John
Spring Township
  Preston, Ann
  Nowland, Louis
  *Walker, Jesse, Jr.
    1818. Walker, Jessee, Jr.
  Parker, John
  Casteel, Abraham
Cahokia Township
  Antwine
  Penvine, Francis
  Mary 1 free colored
  Flaery, Louis
  Voodra, Peter
  Livinston, John P.
Illinois Township
  Davidson, Samuel
  Gorden, William
  Johnson, Pedrick
  Sullivan, James
  Mattheis
  Bowls, Mary
  Thomas, Edmond
  *Shinbarger, Lawrence
    1818. Schenbarger, Lawrence
  Trotier, August, Jr.
  Yonar, John B.
  Bruyatt, Joseph
  Bice, Samuel
  Kelley, Zebedee
Manville Township
  Steward, Joshua

Discrepancies are as follows:

1 Gooding, Cornelius
    1818. Goodner, Cornelius
    F1820. Gooding, Cornelius

2 Gooding, Robert
    1818. Goodin, Robert
    F1820. Gooding, Robert

ST. CLAIR COUNTY (Continued)

- 8 Jarrot, Thomas
  - F1820. Jarrard, Thomas
- 15 Roach, Mathew
  - 1818. Roach, Mathew
  - F1820. Roach, Matthew
- 16 Roach, John
  - F1820. Roach, John D.
- 19 Stookey, Daniel
  - 1818. Stookey, Daniel
  - F1820. Stokey, Daniel
- 22 Goodner, Coonrod
  - 1818. Goodner, Conrad
  - F1820. Goodner, Conrad
- 26 Arthurloney, John
  - F1820. Arthurlana, John
- 27 Jones, Charles
  - F1820. Janes, Charles
- 36 Lunceford, Jacob
  - 1818. Luncford, Jacob
  - F1820. Lunceford, Jacob
- 37 Reed, Isaac
  - 1818. Reeder, Isaac
  - F1820. Reed, Isaac
- 38 Whiteside, John L.
  - 1818. Whitesides, John L.
  - F1820. Whitesides, John L.
- 41 Johnston, John
  - F1820. Johnson, John
- 43 Ryan, William
  - 1818. Rian, William
  - F1820. Ryan, William
- 44 Byrns, John
  - F1820. Burns, John
- 45 Teeter, John
  - 1818. Teter, John
  - F1820. Teter, John
- 50 Wyatt, Micajah
  - F1820. Wiatt, Micajah
- 51 McCorkle, Andrew
  - F1820. McCorcle, Andrew
- 53 Gooding, Fransess
  - F1820. Gooding, Francis
- 55 Makemson, James
  - F1820. Macomson, Janes
- 58 Allfin, Shelten
  - F1820. Alphin, Sheton
- 60 Grant, Roland
  - F1820. Grant, Rowland
- 61 Bonham, Daniel
  - F1820. Bohham, Daniel
- 64 Brownin, Benjamin
  - F1820. Browen, Benjamin
- 66 Tanahill, James
  - 1818. Tannehill, James
  - F1820. TannyHill, James
- 71 Carr, Henry
  - F1820. Carr, Henry, Sr.
- 72 Barnet, Alexander
  - F1820. Burnet, Alexander
- 78 Walker, Charles P.
  - 1818. Walker, Charles
  - F1820. Walker, Charles P.
- 80 Smith, Lester
  - F1820. Smith, Leister
- 82 Newsham, Edward
  - F1820. Nawsham, Edward
- 84 McMurtry, Abraham
  - 1818. McMurtry, Abraham
  - F1820. McMurtry, Abram
- 86 Allen, Chesley
  - F1820. Allen, Chesly
- 90 Flauharty, Pattrick
  - F1820. Faherty, Patrick
- 92 Allen, William, Jr.
  - F1820. Allen, William
- 94 Nulle, Henry
  - 1818. Null, Henry, Jr.
  - F1820. Null, Henry
- 97 Brickey, Jarrot
  - F1820. Bricky, Jarrot
- 98 Ralls, Rawleigh
  - 1818. Rawles, Raleigh
  - F1820. Rolls, Rolly
- 100 Guthrie, Nancy
  - F1820. Gutry, Nancy
- 102 Brewer, Stephen
  - F1820. Brewer, Henry
- 104 Robertson, James S.
  - F1820. Robinson, James
- 105 Smith, Robert
  - 1818. Smith, Robert
  - F1820. Smith, Mary
- 106 Camron, Elijah
  - F1820. Carmen, Elijah
- 107 Hickman, Gorge
  - F1820. Hickman, George
- 109 Coddle, Ransom
  - F1820. Caudle, Ransom
- 110 Gilar, William
  - 1818. Guiler, William
  - F1820. Guyler, William
- 112 Mason, Bennet
  - F1820. Mason, Bennit
- 113 Ratcliff, Michael
  - 1818. Ratcliff, Michel
  - F1820. Ratcliff, Michael
- 115 Strait, Isrual
  - 1818. Straigh, Israel
  - F1820. Straight, Israel

ST. CLAIR COUNTY (Continued)

116 Pulliam, David
    1818. Pulham, David
    F1820. Pulliam, Davis
117 McMillian, Paul
    1818. McMilliom, Paul
    F1820. McMillion, Paul
120 Land, Phillip
    F1820. Land, Philip
122 Griffen, Isaac
    1818. Griffin, Isaac
    F1820. Griffin, Isaac
123 Free, Andrew
    1818. Free, Andrew
    F1820. Tree, Andrew
124 Hickman, Isaac
    1818. Hicman, Is[aac]
    F1820. Hickman, Isaac
125 Null, Bolsor
    1818. Null, Bolser
    F1820. Null, Bolsam
126 Scott, John
    1818. Scott, John, Sr.
    F1820. Scott, John, Sr.
131 Vestal, William
    F1820. Vastal, William
135 Chance, David R.
    F1820. Chance, David
136 Shook, Samuel
    1818. Shook, Samuel, Jr.
    F1820. Shook, Samuel
138 Huggins, Pattrick
    1818. Huggins, Patrick
    F1820. Huggins, Patrick
139 Stockton, Robart
    1818. Stogdon, Robert
    F1820. Stockton, Robert
140 McLamore, John H.
    1818. McLamore, John H.
    F1820. McLimore, John H.
148 Smiley, Hugh
    1818. Smily, Hugh
150 Summers, Edward
    1818. Summers, Edward D.
    F1820. Summers, Edward
155 Scott, Samuel
    1818. Scott, Samuel
    F1820. Scott, Samuel, Sr.
156 Talbot, Thomas
    1818. Talbott, Thomas W.
    F1820. Talbott, Thomas W.
157 Carr, Henry
    F1820. Carr, Henry, Jr.
162 Carr, Coonrad
    F1820. Carr, Conrod

163 Temple, Ritchard
    F1820. Temple, Richard
164 Patterson, Greenbury
    F1820. Patterson, Green B.
165 McClintick, Joseph
    F1820. McClintic, Joseph
166 Glasgow, James C.
    F1820. Glasgow, James
167 West, Washenton
    F1820. West, Washington
170 Middlecoff, John
    F1820. Middlecough, John
171 Robertson, John B.
    F1820. Robinson, John B.
177 Rittenhouse, William
    1818. Rettenhouse, William
    F1820. Rittenhouse, William, Sr.
179 Rengold, John
    F1820. Ringgold, John
180 Botsford, Moss K.
    F1820. Bottsford, Moss K.
181 Bennet, Ann
    F1820. Bennit, Anna
182 Russel, Nancy
    F1820. Russell, Anna
184 Holcomb, William
    1818. Halcomb, William
    F1820. Holcomb, William
188 Myers, Lewis W.
    1818. Myre, Louis W.
    F1820. Myers, Louis W.
191 Cowhen, Thomas
    F1820. Cowan, Thomas
193 Glasgow, William
    F1820. Glagow, William
196 Rittinghouse, Elijah
    F1820. Rittenhouse, Elijah, Sr.
199 Wilkeson, Edmond P.
    F1820. Wilkison, Edmond P.
201 Goforth, William G.
    F1820. Goforth, William P.
203 Harris, Ephrefram
    F1820. Harris, Ephraim
204 Hoggshead, James
    1818. Hogshead, James
    F1820. Hoggshed, James
206 Chandler, Richard W.
    F1820. Chanler, Richard W.
207 Gates, Vaulentine
    F1820. Gates, Valentine
212 McLane, James
    F1820. McClain, James
213 Eyman, Christopher
    F1820. Eyman, Henry

ST. CLAIR COUNTY (*Continued*)

215 Crane, Smith
    F1820. Crane, Samuel
217 Stanly, John
    1818. Stanley, John
    F1820. Stanlay, John
218 Bear, Joseph
    F1820. Beer, Josep
219 Anderson, John P.
    F1820. Anderson, John M.
220 McCullough, John
    F1820. McCully, John
221 Phillips, William
    1818. Philips, William
    F1820. Philips, William
222 Phillips, Daniel
    F1820. Philips, Daniel
223 Beare, Henry
    F1820. Beer, Henry
225 Blair, Gorge
    F1820. Blair, George
226 Holkomb, Joel
    F1820. Holcomb, Joel
230 Hendrix, John
    1818. Hendricks, John
    F1820. Hendricks, John
231 Rush, John D.
    F1820. Derush, John
233 Beadle, Samuel
    F1820. Beedle, Samuel
236 Badgley, Anthony
    F1820. Badley, Anthony
238 Beare, William
    F1820. Beer, William
239 Pettet, James
    F1820. Pettit, James
240 Ervine, Thomas
    F1820. Irvin, Thomas
243 Badgley, Jobe
    F1820. Badgley, Job
245 Bonham, William
    F1820. Banham, William
246 Bonham, Mallakiah
    F1820. Bonham, Malachiah
250 Kinkaid, William T.
    1818. Kinkand, William T.
    F1820. Kindead, William T.
251 Berkey, Daniel
    F1820. Berky, Daniel
252 Colbreath, William S.
    F1820. Calbreath, William S.
254 Kincaid, James
    F1820. Kinkead, James
255 Kincaid, Andrew
    F1820. Kinkead, Andrew

258 Hayden, Joab
    F1820. Hayden, Jacob
263 Prichard, Elizabeth
    F1820. Prichard, Mrs.
264 Stroad, Peter
    F1820. Stroud, Peter
266 Million, Daniel
    1818. Million, Daniel
    F1820. Millian, Daniel
267 Gillam, Thomas
    1818. Gilham, Thomas
    F1820. Gillham, Thomas
270 Pulliam, James
    1818. Pulham, James
    F1820. Pulliam, James
277 Whiteside, Jacob
    1818. Whitesides, Jacob
    F1820. Whiteside, Jacob
278 Rigg, Hosea
    1818. Riggs, Hosea
    F1820. Rigg, Hosea
279 Rigg, Clement
    1818. Riggs, Clemment
    F1820. Rigg, Clement
283 Rider, John
    1818. Rider, John
    F1820. Ryder, John
284 Goddard, Joseph
    F1820. Godric, Joseph
285 Goddard, Ruben
    F1820. Godric, Reuben
286 Severo, John
    F1820. Seever, John
287 Shook, Samuel
    1818. Shook, Samuel, Sr.
    F1820. Shook, Samuel, Sr.
290 Wilderman, Gorge
    1818. Wilderman, George
    F1820. Wilderman, George
291 Osamus, Peter
    1818. Osmus, Peter
    F1820. Osymus, Peter
295 Eastas, Byrd
    F1820. Eastess, Bird
296 Hoosar, Jacob
    1818. Howzer, Jacob, Sr.
    F1820. Hoozer, Jacob
297 Phillips, Benjamin
    F1820. Philips, Benjamin
298 Wilderman, Dorsey
    1818. Wilderman, Dossey
    F1820. Wilderman, Dossey
301 Barnet, Luke
    F1820. Barret, Luke

ST. CLAIR COUNTY (*Continued*)

- 306 Larama, Lewis
  - 1818. Laremore, Louis
  - F1820. Larimy, Louis
- 307 Rettenghouse, Peter
  - 1818. Rettonhouse, Peter
  - F1820. Rettenhouse, Peter
- 308 Merrell, Silvester
  - 1818. Merril, Sylvester
  - F1820. Merrylls, Sylvester
- 310 Calbreath, John
  - F1820. Colbreath, John
- 312 Charles, Elijah, Sr.
  - F1820. Chales, Elijah, Sr.
- 314 Mitchel, Edward
  - F1820. Mitchell, Edward
- 323 Maxant, Francis
  - 1818. Maxey, Francis
  - F1820. Maxaw, Francis
- 324 Moore, Risden, Sr.
  - 1818. Moore, Risdon, Sr.
  - F1820. Moore, Risdon
- 326 Belt, Loyd
  - F1820. Belt, Lloyd
- 329 Leman, Robert
  - F1820. Lemen, Robert
- 335 Scott, William
  - 1818. Scott, William, Sr.
  - F1820. Scott, William
- 340 Matheny, Charles R.
  - 1818. Matheny, Charls R.
  - F1820. Matheny, Charles R.
- 342 Cox, Mathew T.
  - F1820. Cox, Matthew
- 344 Biggs, William, Sr.
  - F1820. Biggs, William
- 345 Fike, Able
  - F1820. Fyke, Abel
- 347 Lowe, Gorge
  - F1820. Lowe, George, Jr.
- 350 Ward, Able
  - F1820. Ward, Abel
- 352 Horney, Samuel
  - F1820. Harney, Samuel
- 353 Were, John
  - F1820. Ware, John
- 354 Whiteside, William L.
  - 1818. Whitesides, William L.
  - F1820. Whiteside, William L.
- 355 Knight, David
  - 1818. Knight, David
  - F1820. Night, David
- 357 Varner, Abraham
  - 1818. Varner, Abraham
  - F1820. Varnen, Abraham
- 358 Johnson, Malkem
  - 1818. Johnson, Malcomb
  - F1820. Johnson, Malcom
- 362 Matheney, Noah
  - 1818. Matheny, Noah
  - F1820. Matheny, Noah
- 363 Peoples, Thornton
  - 1818. Peoples, Thorton
  - F1820. Peoples, Thornton
- 364 Wilbanks, Joseph
  - F1820. Willbanks, Josph
- 365 Abbernathar, Miles
  - F1820. Abernatha, Miles
- 367 Gaskill, Paul
  - 1818. Gaskill, Paul
  - F1820. Gascal, Paul
- 368 Jones, Nathan
  - F1820. Jones, Naathan
- 369 Walker, James
  - 1818. Walker, James, Jr.
  - F1820. Walker, James
- 378 Jones, Ezekel
  - F1820. Jones, Ezekiel
- 381 McNail, William
  - 1818. McNail, William
  - F1820. McNail, William B.
- 382 Farrer, Robert
  - F1820. Farrar, Robert
- 384 Pirkins, Ephran
  - 1818. Perkens, Ephraim
  - F1820. Perkins, Ephraim
- 386 Folks, Christopher
  - F1820. Foulks, Christopher
- 388 Smith, Joseph
  - F1820. Smith, Josep
- 389 Phillips, David
  - 1818. Philips, David
  - F1820. Philips, David
- 391 Perkins, Jesse
  - 1818. Perkins, Jessee
  - F1820. Perkins, Jesse
- 393 Driskill, David B.
  - F1820. Driskel, Beechem
- 395 Leach, John
  - 1818. Leach, John
  - F1820. Leech, John
- 396 Allen, Archabald
  - F1820. Allen, Archibald
- 399 Northcraft, James
  - F1820. Northcroft, James F.

ST. CLAIR COUNTY (Continued)

401 Hayle, Enoch
    1818. Hale, Enoch
    F1820. Hayle, Enoch
404 Hayle, Robart
    1818. Hale, [Robert?]
    F1820. Hayl, Robert
406 Phillips, James
    1818. Philips, James
    F1820. Philips, James
407 Rittenhouse, Elijah
    1818. Rittenhouse, Eligah
    F1820. Rittenhouse, Elijah
410 Hill, Burrel
    1818. Hill, Burrell
    F1820. Hill, Burrel
413 Malcom, Peter
    F1820. Macom, Peter
415 Pierce, Daniel
    1818. Peirce, Daniel
    F1820. Pierce, Daniel
417 Jimmeson, Gorge
    1818. Jamesson, George
    F1820. Jamison, George
419 Abenathy, Robert
    F1820. Abernatha, Robert
420 Basey, Isaa
    F1820. Basye, Isaac
430 Scott, John
    1818. Scott, John, Jr.
    F1820. Scott, John, Jr.
432 McLaughlin, Robert K.
    1818. McLaughlin, R. K.
434 Titus, Nathan
    1818. Titus, Nan (a black)
    F1820. Titus, Naathan
435 Land, Josep
    1818. Land, Joseph
    F1820. Land, Joseph
437 Wilbanks, Daniel
    F1820. Willbanks, Daniel
440 Robertson, Aaron
    F1820. Robinson, Aaron
442 Silkwood, Obediah
    F1820. Silkwood, Obadiah
445 Nicklas, Theophilus M.
    1818. Nichols, Theophilus M.
    F1820. Nicols, Theophilus M.
446 Driskell, Isabella
    F1820. Drikel, Isabella
448 Vanwinkel, Job
    1818. Vanwinkle, Job
    F1820. Vanwinkle, Job
450 Stubelfield, Thomas
    1818. Stubblefield, Thomas
    F1820. Ftubblefield, Thomas

452 Cuberson, Alexander
    F1820. Culbertson, Alexande
453 Herring, Moses
    1818. Herin, Moses
    F1820. Herrin, Moses
458 Bridges, Gorge
    F1820. Bridges, George
463 Stiner, Bennet
    F1820. Styner, Bennit
464 Hardy, Jacob
    F1820. Hardey, Jacob
465 Boman, Randolph
    F1820. Bomon, Randolph
466 Simmon, Levi
    F1820. Simmons, Levi
467 Weldney, Randolph
    F1820. Wilder, Randolph
468 Manville, Ira
    1818. Manvill, Ira
    F1820. Manville, Ira
470 Redpath, James
    F1820. Redpeth, James
471 Loveland, Merreness
    F1820. Lovelands, Merriness W.
472 Liveley, John
    1818. Lively, John
    F1820. Lively, John
475 Catline, Seth
    F1820. Cottand, Seth
476 Sturdevan, Roswel
    F1820. Sturdevan, Roswell
479 Nichols, William
    F1820. Nicols, William
480 McDaniel, Adam
    F1820. McDonald, Adam
481 Penington, Absolom
    1818. Pennington, Absolom
    F1820. Pennington, Absalom
482 Free, Absolom P.
    1818. Free, Absolam P.
    F1820. Free, Absalom P.
483 McNail, Able
    1818. McNail, Abel A.
    F1820. McNail, Abel
484 Dupuy, James
    F1820. Dupey, James
487 Leck, Herman
    F1820. Lick, Herman
488 Morriss, Elizabeth
    F1820. Morris, Elizabeth
489 Dupuy, Joseph
    F1820. Dupey, Joseph
490 Dupuy, William
    F1820. Dupey, William

ST. CLAIR COUNTY (Continued)

491 Stroad, Levi
    1818. Stroud, Levi
    F1820. Stroud, Levi
492 Millsted, Joseph
    F1820. Milstead, Joseph
494 Marloe, John
    F1820. Marlow, John
498 Gaskell, Jonathan
    1818. Gaskill, Jonathan
    F1820. Gascal, Jonathan
499 Duncain, Robert
    F1820. Duncan, Robert
500 Teterick, Peter
    1818. Tetricks, Peter
    F1820. Tetrick, Peter
501 Robertson, James
    F1820. Robinson, James
502 Colbreath, John
    F1820. Colbreath, John H.
503 Hughes, Robert
    1818. Hughes, Robert
    F1820. Hughs, Robert
505 Adams, Thriston
    F1820. Adams, Tressy
509 Henderlight, William
    F1820. Hinderlite, William
510 Mitchel, Samuel
    1818. Mitchell, Samuel
    F1820. Mitchell, Samuel
512 Craford, James
    F1820. Crawford, James
513 Hawkins, Marshal
    1818. Hawkins, Marshal
    F1820. Hawkins, Marshal D.
515 Hawkins, Isaah
    F1820. Hawkins, Josiah
516 Wells, Mercy
    F1820. Wells, Mary
518 Waker, Jessey
    1818. Walker, Jessee, Sr.
    F1820. Walker, Jesse
519 Evret, David
    F1820. Everitt, David
521 Moore, William
    1818. Moore, William, Jr.
    F1820. Moore, William, Jr.
522 Simpkins, Jerrimiah
    F1820. Simpkin, Jeremiah
525 Cooper, Meredith
    F1820. Cooper, Merideth
528 Tosier, Samuel
    F1820. Tozier, Samuel
532 Fergeson, Andrew
    F1820. Ferguson, Andrew

537 Tallant, John
    F1820. Talent, John
538 Bell, Nathaniel
    F1820. Belle, Nathaniel
539 Robertson, Isreal
    1818. Robinson, Israel
    F1820. Robinson, Israel
544 Dickson, Gorge
    F1820. Dickson, George
545 Terry, Stephen T.
    1818. Terry, Stephen
    F1820. Terry, Stephen
549 Rubey, Charles
    F1820. Ruby, Charles
554 Hogan, Pattrick
    F1820. Hogan, Patrick
556 Tolly, Isham
    F1820. Tolly, Isom
557 Leman, Joseph
    F1820. Lemen, Joseph
558 Pricket, Gorge
    1818. [Prickett?], George
    F1820. Pricket, George
559 Pierceau, Jonah
    F1820. Pierson, Josiah
561 Herron, Benjamin
    F1820. Herrin, Benjamin
563 Eldrige, Samuel
    F1820. Eldridge, Samuel
565 Lewis, Elijah
    F1820. Louis, Elijah
567 Jenkins, Joab
    F1820. Jenkins, Job
568 Bunker, Abraham
    F1820. Bunker, Abram
573 Porter, Rebecah
    1818. Porter, Rebecca
    F1820. Porter, Rebecka
574 Redman, Samuel
    1818. Redmond, Samuel
    F1820. Readman, Samuel
577 Jorney, Elizabeth
    1818. Journey, Elizabeth
    F1820. Journey, John
579 McDaniel, Gorge
    F1820. McDonald, George
580 Boring, Dorsey
    F1820. Boring, Dossy
583 Handcock, John
    F1820. Hancock, John O.
584 Postelwyt, Elizabeth
    F1820. Postleweight, John
586 Horner, Nathan
    1818. Horner, Nathan
    F1820. Horner, Naathan

288   *ILLINOIS HISTORICAL COLLECTIONS*

ST. CLAIR COUNTY (*Continued*)

587 Stanphell, Temprence
    F1820. Stanfield, Temperance
590 Hathaway, Eleezer
    F1820. Hathaway, Eleazer
591 Gasler, Thomas T.
    F1820. Gazley, Thomas T.
592 Mayhoe, William
    F1820. Mahu, William
593 Matheney, Daniel
    F1820. Matheny, Samuel
594 Penn, Joseph, Sr.
    1818. Penn, Joseph
    F1820. Penn, Josep, Sr.
596 Mooney, Brian
    F1820. Mooney, Bryant
600 Duglass, Joseph
    F1820. Dougless, Joseph
602 Townsend, Whitfield
    1818. Townzen, Whitfield
    F1820. Townzen, Whitfield
603 Brazule, William
    F1820. Brazel, William
605 Keneday, Neal
    F1820. Canada, Neill
606 Bradsby, Mary
    F1820. Bradsby, James
607 Brock, Mary
    F1820. Brock, Oliver
609 Smith, James
    F1820. Smith, James H.
610 Cheeves, William
    F1820. Chavis, William
611 Smith, Phillip
    1818. Smith, Philip
613 Coppenbrger, George
    F1820. Copperbarger, George
614 Tille, William
    F1820. Tilly, William
615 Tille, John
    F1820. Tilly, John
616 Padfield, William, Sr.
    F1820. Padfield, William
617 Lowe, David
    1818. Low, David
    F1820. Lowe, David, Sr.
618 Pate, Mathew
    F1820. Pate, Matthew
620 McDaniel, Samuel
    1818. McDonald, Samuel
    F1820. McDonold, Samuel
621 Vanansdol, Richard
    1818. Vanosdole, Richard
    F1820. Vanasdal, Richard
627 Devenport, Joseph
    F1820. Devinport, Joseph

628 Saler, John
    F1820. Saylor, John
629 Lowry, Charles
    F1820. Lowrie, Charles
630 Swann, Francis
    1818. Swan, Frances
    F1820. Swan, Francis
631 Robans, William
    F1820. Robins, William
633 Lenard, Zepheniah
    F1820. Leonard, Zephaniah
634 Nichlas, Jules
    F1820. Nicols, James
635 Nichlas, Sarah
    F1820. Nicols, Sarah
636 Chambers, Sally
    F1820. Chambers, Sarah
639 Padfield, William, Sr.
    F1820. Padfield, William
641 Thomson, Samuel H.
    F1820. Thompson, Samuel H.
642 Limmerick, Peter L.
    F1820. Nimrick, Peter L.
643 Piles, Samuel
    1818. Pyle, Samuel
    F1820. Pyle, Samuel
646 Abenerthy, Robert
    F1820. Abernatha, Robert, Jr.
647 Linch, Solomon
    1818. Linck, Solomon
    F1820. Lynch, Solomon
649 Padfield, William, Jr.
    1818. Padfeld, William, Jr.
    F1820. Padfield, William, Jr.
650 Slaton, George
    1818. Slaton, George
    F1820. Slayton, George
652 Casad, Anthony W.
    F1820. Cazad, Anthony W.
655 Walker, James
    1818. [Walker], James, Sr.
    F1820. Walker, James
657 Coone, John
    F1820. Koon, John
658 Cooksey, John
    F1820. Kooksey, John M.
660 Hatfield, Harmon
    F1820. Hatfield, Herman
662 Knighton, Thomas
    1818. Knighton, Thomas
    F1820. Nighting, Thomas
665 Deal, Martain
    F1820. Dyal, Martin
666 Smith, Delilah
    F1820. Smith, Delila

CENSUS OF 1820

ST. CLAIR COUNTY (Continued)

671 Ritheghouse, William, Sr.
    1818. Rittenhouse, William
    F1820. Rittenhouse, William, Sr.
672 Rittenghouse, Elijah
    F1820. Rittenhouse, Elijah, Sr.
674 Herron, Lewis
    1818. Herren, Lewis
    F1820. Herrin, Louis
677 McLane, Samuel
    F1820. McClain, Samuel
678 Griffeth, Daniel
    1818. Griffith, Daniel
    F1820. Griffith, Daniel
679 Vineyard, Phillip
    1818. Vineyard, Philip
    F1820. Vineyard, Philip
680 Estep, James
    F1820. Eastep, James
682 Million, Bennet
    1818. Million, Bennett
683 Million, Benjamin
    1818. Million, Benjamin
    F1820. Millian, Benjamin
684 Newcomb, John
    F1820. Newcom, John
690 Swagart, Jonas
    F1820. Swaggard, Elizabeth
692 Keneday, Gorge F.
    1818. Kenada, George F.
    F1820. Canada, George F.
693 Thomson, William
    1818. Thompson, William
    F1820. Thompson, William
694 Eckerd, John
    F1820. Eckard, John
697 Grist, John
    F1820. Griste, John
698 Swaggart, Gorge
    1818. Swaggert, George
    F1820. Swaggard, Goorge
701 Maning, John
    F1820. Mannan, John
702 Gunvill, Joseph
    F1820. Gunville, Joseph
703 Larama, Hugh
    F1820. Laurum, Hubert
704 Eads, Thomas
    F1820. Edes, Thomas
705 Shinberger, John
    1818. Schenbarger, Batise
    F1820. Shinbarger, Baptiest
706 Garvy, Lewis
    1818. Jarver, Lous
    F1820. Jarvis, Louis
707 Garvy, Enos
    1818. Jarver, Enos
    F1820. Jarvis, Aneas
708 Lacounts, Battice, Sr.
    1818. Lacours, Batise
    F1820. Lecourse, Baptist
709 Trotier, Augustice
    1818. Trotier, Augestine
    F1820. Trotier, August, Sr.
710 Boveneau, John
    F1820. Bovinu, John
711 Trusoe, Nichlas
    1818. Trusoo, Nicholas
    F1820. Tuzer, Nichlas
712 Larama, Paul
    F1820. Loise, Paul
713 Boneue, Joseph
    F1820. Bono, Joseph
715 Lapaugh, Joseph
    F1820. Lapolh, Joseph
716 Bosso, Nichlas
    F1820. Bozenu, Nicholas
717 Marlo, Gabriel
    1818. Marlo, Gabrele
    F1820. Marlow, Gabriel
718 Vanarsdol, Simon
    1818. Vanosdol, Simon
    F1820. Vanasdol, Simon
719 Laplumb, Phillip
    F1820. Laflam, Philip
720 Greennah, Joseph
    F1820. Greenye, Josep
721 Pensono, Lewis
    1818. Pincinneau, Louis
    F1820. Pensino, Louis
722 Burdauk, Jack
    F1820. Burdo, John
723 Brusko, Henry
    F1820. Bruzeer, Henry
724 Renneo, Antoine
    F1820. Rieno, Antwine
728 Town, Epharim
    F1820. Town, Ephraim
729 Coburn, Obediah
    F1820. Ausburn, Obadiah
730 Wyatt, Eli
    F1820. Wight, Ailsy
732 Adkinson, Elijah
    F1820. Adkison, Elijah
736 Wigans, Samuel
    F1820. Wiggins, Samuel
740 St. Anthony, Nichlas
    F1820. St. Andre, Nicholas
741 Hammond, John
    F1820. Hammons, John

ST. CLAIR COUNTY (Continued)

742 Bridges, William
    F1820. Bridger, William
743 Savage, James
    F1820. Savage, William
744 Nevet, Joseph
    F1820. Nevit, Joseph
745 Coone, David
    F1820. Coons, David F.
748 Osbourn, Thomas
    F1820. Ausburn, Thomas
750 Simkye, John
    F1820. Sippy, John
751 Mead, Alansen
    F1820. Mede, Alanson
752 Snider, Jacob
    F1820. Snyder, Jacob
753 Johetee, Peter
    F1820. Johntee, Peter
754 Darby, Joseph
    F1820. Darbe, Joseph
755 Lechanoe, Joseph, Sr.
    F1820. Lechance, Joseph, Sr.
756 Lechanoe, Joseph, Jr.
    F1820. Lesance, Joseph, Jr.
757 Tolly, Andrew
    F1820. Tilly, Andrew
758 Mason, Thomas
    F1820. Mason, Tomas
759 Gandrow, Lewis
    F1820. Jandro, Louis
760 Shuckey, Peter
    F1820. Shirkee, Peter
761 Souldan, Michael
    1818. Sosha, Michael
    F1820. Socia, Michael
762 Bovneu, Nichles
    F1820. Bovinu, Nicholas
764 Lafumba, John
    1818. Lafranbroo, John B.
    F1820. Lafromba, John
765 Goodeau, Lewis
    1818. Godan, Louis
    F1820. Ganda, Louis
766 Perredu, Battice
    1818. Peradee, Batese
    F1820. Paridee, Baptiest
768 Parrish, Lewis
    F1820. Pash, Louis
769 Pensono, Lewis
    1818. Pincinnsau, Louision
    F1820. Pesano, Louis
770 Trumbeau, Ames
    F1820. Tromble, Amal
771 Savern, Francis
    F1820. Saven, Francis

774 Bartrau, Simon
    F1820. Barton, Simon
775 Lacoumpt, Battice
    1818. Lacounpt, Batise
    F1820. Lecomptre, Baptiest
776 Lamarsh, Joseph
    F1820. Lemarche, Josett
777 Lacoumpt, Basel
    1818. Lacompt, Brazil
    F1820. Lecomptre, Bazil
778 Blundau, John B.
    F1820. Blodeau, John B.
779 Lalong, Battice
    F1820. Lolande, Baptieste
780 Lacoumpt, Juliann
    1818. Lacompt, Julian
    F1820. Lecomptre, Julian
781 Shatrau, Battice
    F1820. Shatre, Baptieste
782 Delong, Joseph
    F1820. Delodge, Joseph
783 Decompt, Joseph
    F1820. Dechamp, Joseph
784 Dacator, Gebriel
    F1820. Decocashe, Gabriel
785 Pereau, Lewis
    F1820. Pereu, Louis
787 Pealet, Lewis
    1818. Petitte, Louis
    F1820. Pelette, Louis
788 Rale, Joseph
    F1820. Ruelle, Joseph
789 Farraer, Francis
    1818. Farriree, Franey
    F1820. Ferrierd, Francis
790 Rock, Anthony
    F1820. Rock, Antwine Couin
791 Turcothe, Francis
    1818. Tarcourt, Francis
    F1820. Turcotte, Francis
792 Carron, John B.
    F1820. Caron, John B.
794 Martain, James
    F1820. Martin, James
795 De Laygest, John
    F1820. Legyster, John B.
796 Jarrot, Nickles
    1818. Jarrot, Nicholas
    F1820. Jarrot, Nicholas
798 Bovoneau, John
    F1820. Bovinu, John
799 Morrison, Guy
    1818. Moreson, Guy
    F1820. Marrison, Guy

ST. CLAIR COUNTY (*Continued*)

800 Vincant, Michael
    F1820. Vincent, Mitchell
801 Updyke, Olive
    1818. Updike, Gilbert
    F1820. Abdik, Olive
802 Voodry, Francis
    F1820. Voodra, Francis
803 Bobo, Charles
    F1820. Beron, Charles
804 Lapage, Madam
    F1820. Lapage, Terrage
805 Manville, Josef
    F1820. Manville, Joseph
806 Lataue, Joseph
    F1820. Latau, Joseph
807 Marshal, Battece
    F1820. Marshau, Baptiest
808 Bully, Joseph
    F1820. Buya, Joseph
809 Labasha, Lewis
    1818. Labasere, Louis
    F1820. Labisya, Louis
810 Lapois, Francis
    1818. Laparsu, Francis
    F1820. Lapasse, Francis
811 Novet, Root
    F1820. Novall, Roseat
812 Larama, Lewis, S[r.?]
    1818. Laremire, Louis
    The federal census gives in this location:
    F1820. St. Jeremy, Louis
    1818. St. Garnaw, Louis
813 Gamlau, Mashec
    1818. Gambla, Michael
    F1820. Gumlah, Michael
814 Terveya, Thomas
    F1820. Tara, Thomas
815 Lapoxey, Anthony
    F1820. Lapansa, Antwine
816 Gamlah, Peter
    1818. Gambla, Pear
    F1820. Gamlah, Peter
817 Voodry, James
    F1820. Vodra, Yeyum
818 Rannals, John
    1818. Reynoalds, John
    F1820. Runnels, John
821 Goddard, Margaret
    F1820. Gorda, Margaret
823 St. John, Lewis
    1818. St. John, Louis
    F1820. St. John, Louis
824 Lapaugh, Joseph
    F1820. Pupah, Joseph
825 Neal, Edward
    F1820. Nail, Edward
826 Lacoumpt, Lewis
    1818. Lacompt, Louis
    F1820. Lacont, Louis
827 Paupau, Paul
    1818. Paupa, Paul
    F1820. Pupah, Paul
828 Amley, Lewis, Sr.
    F1820. Amlah, Louis, Sr.
829 Dacoto, Battece
    F1820. Dacuto, [J.?] Baptiest
830 Lapaugh, Peter
    F1820. Lapash, Peter
831 Amley, Lewis
    F1820. Amlah, Louis, Jr.
832 Paupaugh, Joseph
    1818. Paupa, Joseph
    F1820. Pupah, Joseph
833 Burnaugh, Michael
    F1820. Bernash, Michael
834 Pelate, Michael
    1818. Petitte, Michael
    F1820. Pelate, Michael
835 Lamatte, Johaim
    F1820. Lemette, Joachim
838 Sheretau, Towe
    F1820. Shartrau, Toashez
839 Ragar, Lewis
    F1820. Ruyar, Louis
840 Provo, Bartholemew
    F1820. Provo, Bartholmew
841 Compass, Margaret
    F1820. Compnio, Margaret
842 Bohanan, Joseph
    F1820. Buckana, Joseph
843 Roch, Peter
    F1820. Rock, Peter
844 Rose, James
    1818. Rows, James
    F1820. Rose, James
845 Trobley, Tocan
    F1820. Trombley, Isom
846 Pensono, Tadale
    F1820. Pensono, Hideal
847 Lacoumpt, Antwine
    F1820. Lacourse, Antwine
848 Allery, Battece
    F1820. Allery, Baptiest
849 Shautaue, Thomas
    F1820. Sharto, Thomas

ST. CLAIR COUNTY (Concluded)

850 Goodane, Peter
   1818. Goda, Pear
   F1820. Gouda, Peter
851 Voodree, Lewis
   1818. Vaudry, Louis
   F1820. Voodra, Louis
852 Voodree, Francis
   F1820. Voodra, Francis
853 Blackwel, David
   F1820. Blackwell, David

857 Plasant, Frank
   F1820. Pleasant, Frank
858 Desheat, Teague
   F1820. Deshiels, Tague
859 Moore, Warrick
   1818. Worrick (a black)
   F1820. Warrick, Moore
861 Cremer, John P.
   F1820. Creamer, Philip

CENSUS OF UNION COUNTY, 1820

Names of Heads of Families	Free white males twenty one years old and upwards	all other White Inhabitance	Free people of Collour	Servants or Slaves
[1*‡] Joshuay Morgan	1	6		
[2*‡] Lenard Morgan	2	5		
[3*‡] Jerremiah Brown	1	6		
[4*‡] David Brown	1	7		
[5*‡] David Cotner	3	6		
[6*‡] James Brown	1	5		
[7*‡] James Ellis	1	7		
[8*‡] Daniel Cimmel	2	4		
[9 ‡] John Duit	2	1		
[10 ‡] Abraham Anson	1	1		
[11] Peter Lingle	1	1		
[12*‡] John Barker	1	8		
[13 ‡] Joseph Hunsaker Junr	2	1		
[14*‡] Samuel Hunsaker Senr	1	13		
[15*‡] Jacob Wagoner	1	7		
[16 ‡] Daniel Spence	1	5		
[17*‡] George Brown Junr	1	5		
[18*‡] Christopher Houser	1	3		
[19 ‡] Michael Colier	2	4		
[20 ‡] Richard M Young	2	1		1
[21*‡] George Hunsaker Senr	2	4		
[22*‡] John Grammer	1	10		
[23*‡] David Hunsaker	2	3		
[24 ‡] Francis Parker	3	3		
[25*‡] John Thornton	4	8		
[26 ‡] Jacob Hibarger	2	5		
[27*‡] John S Hacker	6	3		
[28 ‡] William Gray	4	7		
[29 ‡] Edmund W. B. Jones	4	2		
[30 ‡] John Bailey	4	5		1
[31*‡] William Thornton Jur	3	2		
[32] William Gearling	2			
[33*‡] Daniel T Coleman	1	8		

Figures and symbols preceding names have been supplied by the editor:
‡ Indicates name also in Federal Census for 1820.
* Indicates name also in State Census for 1818.

UNION COUNTY (*Continued*)

No.	Heads of families	White males 21 & upwards	All other white	Free people of color	Servants or slaves
[34 ‡]	Elijah Carter	3	7		
[35*]	Isaac Williams	2	7		
[36*‡]	William Shelton	1	6		
[37*‡]	Henry Barrener Senr	2	6		
[38 ‡]	Armstead H Brown	1	4		
[39*‡]	Francis Murphey	1	6		
[40*‡]	John Bradshaw	1	10		3
[41*]	William Parker	1	8		
[42*‡]	Benjamin Mineace	1	4		
[43]	Constantine Kesler	1			
[44 ‡]	John Woory	1	7		
[45*‡]	Joel Boggess	1	8		
[46 ‡]	Adam Cruse	1	4		
[47*‡]	Hiley Murphey		10		
[48*‡]	John Jinkens	1	3		
[49*‡]	John Burden	1	6		
[50 ‡]	Marget Ellams		2		
[51*‡]	Elijah Bryan	1	4		
[52]	Abner Bryan	1	1		
[53]	Thomas Snodgrass	1	2		
[54]	James Howerton	1	3		
[55*‡]	James Ellams	1	6		
[56*‡]	Bazel Billingsley	2	3		
[57*‡]	Andy Trip	1	5		
[58 ‡]	Marget Cochran		1		
[59*‡]	John Trip	1	10		
[60*‡]	William Davison	1	5		
[61 ‡]	Andrew Steal	1	1		
[62*‡]	Walter Tetford	1	8		
[63 ‡]	Milleton Reynolds	1	7		
[64 ‡]	John Finney	1	9		
[65*‡]	William Welch	1	2		
[66 ‡]	David Reynolds	1	4		
[67*‡]	Hugh Craig	1	12		
[68]	Bazel Craig	1	1		
[69 ‡]	Sarah Craig		6		
[70*‡]	Oen Evans	2	8		1
[71*‡]	George Evans	3	4		1

CENSUS OF 1820

UNION COUNTY (Continued)

No.	Heads of families	White males 21 & upwards	All other white	Free people of color	Servants or slaves
[72 ‡]	Young F Stokes	1	3		
[73*‡]	John Stokes	2	9		
[74*‡]	Elijah Evans	2	2		
[75*‡]	William Durram	1	8		
[76*‡]	Msiah Davison	2	9		
[77*‡]	Joshuay Throgmorton	2	3		
[78*‡]	Patrick Maginnis	1	1		
[79*‡]	William Maginnis	1	5		
[80*‡]	William Barton	1	7		
[81*‡]	Thomas Standerd	1	8		
[82 ‡]	Willis Standerd	1	3		
[83 ‡]	Daniel Gore	1	3		
[84 ‡]	Isaac Bizel	2	4		
[85*‡]	Joshuay Gore	1	5		
[86*‡]	Thomas Gore	1	7		
[87 ‡]	Josiah Paterson	1	3		
[88 ‡]	Barney Smyth	1	9		
[89*‡]	James Robertson	1	3		
[90 ‡]	Patience Delaney		7		
[91 ‡]	William Delaney	1	4		
[92 ‡]	Molton Carter	1	9		
[93*‡]	John West	2	6		
[94 ‡]	Asa West	2	5		
[95]	Samuel Maginnes	1	1		
[96 ‡]	Mary Anyan		8		
[97*‡]	Isaac Beggs	1	8		
[98 ‡]	Zacheriah Walker	1	3		
[99*]	Alexander Beggs	2	5		
[100*‡]	Levy Paterson	1	8		
[101 ‡]	John Beggs	1	1		
[102*‡]	Archabel Beggs	1	8		
[103 ‡]	Jonathan Hugs	1	2		
[104 ‡]	Joseph Walker	1	3		
[105*‡]	Hozea Boren	2	7		
[106*‡]	Daniel Lingle	1	4		
[107*‡]	Thomas Macintorsh	1	5		
[108*‡]	Lewis Penrod	1	6		
[109 ‡]	Green House	1	3		

UNION COUNTY (Continued)

No.	Heads of families	White males 21 & upwards	All other white	Free people of color	Servants or slaves
[110 ‡]	John Cope	1	10		
[111 ‡]	Yost Cope	1	3		
[112 ‡]	Joseph Barber	1	5		
[113 ‡]	Michael Smyth	1	2		
[114*‡]	George Vineyard	1	4		
[115 ‡]	David Vineyard	1	2		
[116*‡]	John Vinyard	2	8		
[117*‡]	Jessee Suttle	1	8		
[118*‡]	Thomas Adams	1	4		
[119*‡]	Charles Makintorsh	1	1		
[120 ‡]	Bazel Boren	1	3		
[121*‡]	Thomas Cox	2	4		4
[122*‡]	John Boren	1	8		2
[123*‡]	Lee Cuday	1	5		
[124 ‡]	Daniel Carker	1	2		
[125 ‡]	Moses Micenhimer	1	3		
[126 ‡]	Marten Hofner	1	3		
[127*‡]	Robert Beggs	1	6		
[128*]	George Brown Senr	1	2		
[129*‡]	James Worthington Jr.	1	2		
[130*‡]	William Thornton	1	7		
[131*‡]	George Hunsaker Junr	1	4		
[132*‡]	John Hunsaker Senr	1	5		
[133*‡]	Samuel Hunsaker Jur	1	3		
[134*‡]	John Chrice	1	11		
[135*‡]	Jasiel Echols	1	6		
[136]	Henry Barriner Jun	7	2		
[137 ‡]	George Hartline	2	11		
[138*‡]	Christian Miller	2	8		
[139*‡]	Zacheriah MacDaniel	2	12		
[140*‡]	Robert Axley	1	8		
[141 ‡]	Stephen Crocker	1	2		
[142*‡]	Joseph Hunsaker Sen	1	4		
[143 ‡]	Jacob Hileman	3	5		
[144 ‡]	Peter Lence	2	5		
[145 ‡]	John Hofner	1	2		
[146 ‡]	Jacob Misenhimer	1	1		
[147*‡]	Thomas Sames	2	8		

CENSUS OF 1820

UNION COUNTY (Continued)

No.	Heads of families	White males 21 & upwards	All other white	Free people of color	Servants or slaves
[148*‡]	William Hutson	1	3		
[149*‡]	Michael Dillow	1	6		
[150 ‡]	Peter Barriner	1	7		
[151*‡]	William Worthington	1	4		
[152 ‡]	David Micenhimer	1	1		
[153 ‡]	Peter Powles	1	2		
[154 ‡]	John Dillow	1	2		
[155 ‡]	Jacob Carker	1	4		
[156*‡]	Wilkison Gadwin	1	7		
[157 ‡]	Peter Micenhimer	1	1		
[158*‡]	Cliff Hazlewood	1	12		
[159 ‡]	James Hazlewood	1	3		
[160*‡]	George Smiley	2	4		
[161*]	Robert Hargrave	1	5		
[162 ‡]	James Hairston	1	7		
[163*‡]	John Hairston	1	5		
[164 ‡]	George Hileman Jun	1	4		
[165*‡]	John Rupe	1	4		
[166 ‡]	George Lence Jr	1	2		
[167*‡]	Henry Cluts	1	5		
[168*‡]	Samuel Sprouce	1	8		
[169*‡]	John Garner	1	6		
[170 ‡]	Wesley G Nemo	1	4		
[171 ‡]	David Arnold	1	3		
[172*‡]	John B Murray	2	8		
[173]	Daniel Hinup	1	3		
[174 ‡]	Evin Henry	1	5		
[175*‡]	John Landers	1	6		
[176*‡]	Adam Clap Senr	2	6		
[177 ‡]	Benjamin Worthington	1	5		
[178*‡]	Nathaniel Hughs	1	10		
[179]	Samuel Hartline		2		
[180 ‡]	Michael Holshouser	1	4		
[181*‡]	Ester Lawrence	1	7		
[182 ‡]	Asa Chapman	3	7		
[183 ‡]	Samuel Drake	1	2		
[184 ‡]	Joseph Haukes	1	6		
[185*‡]	John Whitaker	1	4		

UNION COUNTY (Continued)

No.	Heads of families	White males 21 & upwards	All other white	Free people of color	Servants or slaves
[186*‡]	John Mowry	1	8		
[187*‡]	John Cimmel	1	6		
[188 ‡]	Richard Sumner	1	2		
[189 ‡]	Henry Noble	1	2		
[190 ‡]	Andrew Smyth	1	8		
[191]	David Thornton		2		
[192]	John Cervil	1	10		
[193 ‡]	Peter Miller	1	6		
[194*‡]	James Right	1	6		
[195*‡]	John Brown	1	11		
[196*‡]	Sollomon Penrod	1	2		
[197*‡]	Emanuel Penrod	1	1		
[198*‡]	John Penrod	1	3		
[199*‡]	Jacob Willis	1	9		
[200*‡]	George Davis	1	8		
[201 ‡]	Henry Lierly	1	8		
[202*‡]	John Lence	1	2		
[203*‡]	John Huskey	1	4		
[204 ‡]	William Sumner	1	4		
[205 ‡]	William Homes	1	2		
[206 ‡]	Abraham Brown	1	6		
[207*‡]	William Hughs	1	4		
[208]	John Crowl	1	1		
[209 ‡]	David Chrice	1	1		
[210*‡]	Fedrick Tope, Senr	1	6		
[211*‡]	Michael Linbeau	1	4		
[212*‡]	William Dod	2	6		
[213 ‡]	Russel E. Hecock	2	9		
[214*‡]	Jacob Rentleman	1	8		6
[215*‡]	Edmon Vancil	1	6		
[216 ‡]	Hiram Trip	1	3		
[217*‡]	John langley	1	6		
[218 ‡]	Jonston Summers	1	1		
[219*‡]	Antoney Lingle	1	4		
[220*‡]	Daniel Riter	1	4		
[221*‡]	Robert Crafton	1	7		1
[222*‡]	Jacob Treace	1	7		
[223*‡]	Joseph Palmer	2	4		

CENSUS OF 1820

UNION COUNTY (Continued)

No.	Heads of families	White males 21 & upwards	All other white	Free people of color	Servants or slaves
[224*‡]	Rice Sames	2	5		
[225]	Henry Culp	1	9		
[226*‡]	Jacob Littleton	2	5		
[227 ‡]	Abraham Bowman	1	4		
[228*‡]	Elijah Woodall	1	1		
[229 ‡]	John Redell	2	5		
[230]	Thomas Barker	1	4		
[231 ‡]	Henry Cruse	2	1		
[232 ‡]	Mathias Simerman Sen	1	2		
[233*‡]	Benjamin Hall	1	7		
[234 ‡]	Allin Penrod	2	7		
[235 ‡]	John Lingle	1	4		
[236*‡]	Jacob Wolf	1	7		
[237*‡]	Isaac Vancil	1	5		
[238 ‡]	Jacob Shepherd	2	3		
[239 ‡]	John Vancil Sen	1	9		
[240*‡]	Jonathan Huskey	1	5		2
[241*]	John Wigle	1	12		
[242 ‡]	John Minneace	1	2		
[243*‡]	Joseph Mucklehany	2	2		
[244*‡]	John Mackentorsh	1	6		
[245]	Jacob Lingle Jun	1	3		
[246 ‡]	John Hughs	1	3		
[247 ‡]	George James	1	6		
[248 ‡]	Marget Bennit		7		
[249*‡]	Hugh Irwin	1	7		
[250*‡]	Leven L. Holland	1	3		
[251*‡]	William Grammer	1	7		
[252*‡]	Samuel Lewis	1	8		
[253*‡]	Squire Bone	1	6		
[254*‡]	Abner Keith	1	8		
[255 ‡]	George Faggot	1	4		
[256*‡]	Aron Howard	1	4		
[257*‡]	Andrew Irwin	2	3		
[258*‡]	John Hargrave	2	2		
[259 ‡]	Jacob Millegin	1	3		
[260*‡]	Alexander Whitaker	1	4		
[261*‡]	Samuel Penrod Jur	1	6		

UNION COUNTY (*Continued*)

No.	Heads of families	White males 21 & upwards	All other white	Free people of color	Servants or slaves
[262*]	Thomas Green	3	9		
[263*‡]	James Willis	1	3		
[264*‡]	Giles Parmeley	1	9		
[265*‡]	Samuel Butsher	1	4		
[266*‡]	Robert Casey	1	6		
[267 ‡]	Anderson Standiver	1	5		
[268*‡]	James M. Abenathey	1	5		
[269*‡]	John Tweedy	1	5		
[270 ‡]	Adam Corble	1	7		
[271*‡]	Robert H. Loid	1	3		
[272 ‡]	William Trip	1	2		
[273*‡]	John Dailey	1	6		
[274 ‡]	Jacob Isenackle	1	9		
[275*‡]	Robert W. Crafton	1	3		
[276*‡]	Antoney Morgan	1	4		
[277]	Isaac Tinsley	1	1		
[278*‡]	Abraham Hunsaker Sen.	1	5		
[279*‡]	Oen Hughes	1	5		
[280 ‡]	Thomas Fisher	1	9		
[281*‡]	John Hargrave Jun.	1	4		
[282 ‡]	John Baltzele	1	3		
[283*‡]	William Craglole	2	7		
[284*‡]	Samuel Penrod Sen	1	9		
[285 ‡]	Ely Litleton	1	3		
[286 ‡]	Thomas Ferrel	1	2		
[287*‡]	Andy Penrod	1	3		
[288*‡]	John Tope	1	2		
[289 ‡]	Fedrick Tope Jun		3		
[290*‡]	Jacob Tope	1	2		
[291*‡]	Joseph Lamer	1	3		
[292 ‡]	Jacob Cluts	1	4		
[293 ‡]	Philip Cluts	1	1		
[294*‡]	David Penrod	1	5		
[295 ‡]	John Hill	1	2		
[296 ‡]	John Litleton	2	4		
[297 ‡]	Peter Dillow Sen	1	8		
[298]	Coonrad Siter	1	5		
[299 ‡]	Peter Casper	1	7		

UNION COUNTY (Continued)

No.	Heads of families	White males 21 & upwards	All other white	Free people of color	Servants or slaves
[300*‡]	John Hunsaker Jur	1	2		
[301 ‡]	Paul Lingle	1	7		
[302 ‡]	Benedick Mull	1	7		
[303 ‡]	Peter Sifford	1	2		
[304 ‡]	Israel Thompson	2	11		
[305*‡]	Thomas Summers	1	7		
[306 ‡]	Jacob Lingle Senr	1	9		
[307 ‡]	John Vancil Jun	1	4		
[308*‡]	John Lence Junr	1	4		
[309*‡]	Boston Lence	1	3		
[310*‡]	Davolt Lence	1	4		
[311]	Edmon Vancil Jur	1	3		
[312*‡]	Jonas Vancil	1	3		
[313]	John Grigery	1	2		
[314*‡]	Henry Lamer	1	7		
[315]	James Oldridge	2			
[316 ‡]	Ambros Sherril	1	7		
[317*‡]	John Hopkins	1	2		
[318 ‡]	Thomas Smyth	1	1		
[319*‡]	Peter Potmess	1	3		
[320]	Abraham Kokenower	1	4		
[321]	Abraham Morgan	1	1		
[322 ‡]	Joseph Hambrick	1	2		
[323*‡]	William Morgan	1	9		
[324]	Lewis Mishaw	1	1		
[325 ‡]	Mary Dewral		7		
[326 ‡]	Benjamin May	1	3		
[327*‡]	Joseph Waller	1	4		
[328*‡]	John Crips	1	6		
[329 ‡]	Jacob Craft	1	4		
[330 ‡]	Grammer Fisher	1	2		
[331*‡]	Thomas Craft	1	4		
[332*‡]	Sarah Robertson	1	6		
[333 ‡]	Christopher Elmore	1	6		
[334*‡]	George Lemmons	1	6		
[335*‡]	Robert Friet	1			
[336*‡]	Jane Fisher	1	2		
[337 ‡]	Richard Whitaker	1	2		

UNION COUNTY (Continued)

No.	Heads of families	White males 21 & upwards	All other white	Free people of color	Servants or slaves
[338 ‡]	John May	1	7		
[339*]	Patrick Corgin	1	7		
[340 ‡]	Robert Sammons	1	5		
[341 ‡]	Thomas Redell	1	10		
[342 ‡]	Vincent Robertson	1	3		
[343*‡]	Thomas Cox Jun	1	3		
[344*‡]	Jacob Wigle	1	5		
[345]	Sollomon Rogers	1			
[346 ‡]	Nancy Willard		3		
[347 ‡]	Hugh Cook	1	7		
[348 ‡]	John Eaton	1	4		
[349*‡]	Mary Bone		3		
[350 ‡]	Samuel Waldrup	1	4		
[351*‡]	Ephragn Noel	1	5		
[352 ‡]	Fedrick Cook	1	3		
[353*‡]	Ezechael Staton	1	5		
[354 ‡]	Jacob lierley	2	7		
[355 ‡]	Alizebeth Shepherd		4		
[356*‡]	Jacob Hunsaker Senr	1	2		
[357 ‡]	Abraham Hunsaker Jun	1	1		
[358]	Alizabeth Hackerty	1	4		
[359]	Susanna Wooten		5		
[360*‡]	George Wolf	1	6		
[361 ‡]	Nat Davis	1	6		
[362 ‡]	James U. Pecock	1	7		
[363 ‡]	John Bruce	1	3		
[364*‡]	James Tinsley	1	5		
[365*‡]	Fedrick Tolbert	1	3		
[366*‡]	John B. Roberts	1	3		
[367*‡]	Jacob Snider	2	5		
[368 ‡]	Benjamin West	1	5		
[369*‡]	David Miller	2	7		
[370]	Giles Turmon	1	2		
[371 ‡]	Peter Dillow Jun	1	2		
[372*‡]	Jacob Brown	1	4		
[373 ‡]	Jacob Dillow	2	6		
[374*‡]	Adam Clap Jun	1	5		
[375*‡]	Thomas Deen	1	3		

UNION COUNTY (Continued)

No.	Heads of families	White males 21 & upwards	All other white	Free people of color	Servants or slaves
[376*‡]	David Sames	1	4		
[377 ‡]	Calven Price	1	1		
[378]	John Kesler	1	6		
[379 ‡]	John Hess	1	7		
[380 ‡]	Mathias Simerman Jun	1	2		
[381*‡]	Jacob Hunsaker Jun	1	6		
[382]	Henry Cruse Jun	1	2		
[383*‡]	Jane Graham	1	3		
[384*‡]	Benjamin Mcraven	1	6		
[385*‡]	William Echols	1	5		
[386 ‡]	James Whitaker	1	2		
[387*‡]	George Cright	2	6		
[388 ‡]	John Micenhimer	1	1		
[389 ‡]	Pheby Worhengton		1		
[390*‡]	John Smyth	1	1		
[391]	George H. Brown	1	4		
[392]	John Treace	1	13		
[393 ‡]	Edward Davis	2	10		
[394 ‡]	Christian Flach	3	1		

UNION COUNTY (*Continued*)

Jonesborough Union County Illinois

A. D. 1820.

I do hereby certify that the foregoing list contains a true statement of the number of Inhabitants in Union County Illinois—taken down by me as the law directs—

WILLIAM ECHOLS C C
U C

[Free white males of 21 years and upwards][1]	1908
[All other white inhabitants]	461
[Servants or slaves]	19
[Free white males of 21 years and upwards]	7
[All other white inhabitants]	28
Total	2423

Corrected totals:

Free white males of 21 years and upwards	474
All other white inhabitants	1888
	2362
Servants or slaves	22
Total	2384

[1] The figures are not explained in the original, but the notations supplied correspond with the table headings. The last two items included in the total are from a page supplemental to the census proper.

CENSUS OF 1820

UNION COUNTY (Continued)

The census for Union County for 1818 was taken by David and Jeremiah Brown and is dated April 10, probably the date on which he commenced the work. The federal census for 1820 was taken by William Bartlett and the state census by William Echols, neither giving the month or day on which they were certified. The federal census is arranged in alphabetical order and lists 389 families as compared to 394 listed by the state census. The 1818 census includes also the names of residents of Alexander County, which was set off from Union County in 1819.

The federal census contains the following names not found in the 1820 state census:

Borin, John, Jr.
Citter, Coonrod
Clapp, William
Cruce, Peter
Crips, John (Repetition of No. 328?)
*Daugherty, Elizabeth
    1818. Doerty, Elizabeth
Dean, John
Donley, Jacob
Dougherty, George
Echols, John
Ellis, Jonathan
Gregory, Christian

Gregory, Jacob
Hileman, George, Sr.
*Johnson, Peter
Lence, Michael
Lially, Henry
Light, John
McBride, Hannah
*Miller, John
Price, John
Thompson, Jonas
*Youst, John
    1818. Yost, John

Discrepancies are as follows:

1 Morgan, Joshuay
    1818. Morgain, Joshua
    F1820. Morgan, Joshua
2 Morgan, Lenard
    1818. Morgen, Leonard
    F1820. Morgan, Leonard
3 Brown, Jerremiah
    1818. Brown, Jeremiah
    F1820. Brown, Jeremiah
7 Ellis, James
    1818. Ells, James
    F1820. Ellis, James
8 Cimmel, Daniel
    1818. Kimmel, Daniel
    F1820. Kimmel, David
9 Duit, John
    F1820. Duitt, John
10 Anson, Abraham
    F1820. Anson, Abraham W.
15 Wagoner, Jacob
    1818. Wagner, Jacob
    F1820. Waggener, Jacob
17 Brown, George, Jr.
    1818. Brown, George, Jr.
    F1820. Brown, George, 3d
19 Colier, Michael
    F1820. Colliers, Michael
21 Hunsaker, George, Sr.
    1818. Hunsaker, George, Sr.
    F1820. Hunsaker, George

22 Grammer, John
    1818. Grammer, John
    F1820. Grammar, John
26 Hibarger, Jacob
    F1820. Hybarger, Jacob
27 Hacker, John S.
    1818. Hacker, John
    F1820. Hacker, John S.
29 Jones, Edmund W. B.
    F1820. Jones, Edmund B. W.
31 Thornton, William, Jr.
    1818. Thornto[n], William, Jr.
    F1820. Thornton, William, 2d
37 Barrener, Henry, Sr.
    1818. Baringer, Henry
    F1820. Barringer, Henry
38 Brown, Armstead H.
    F1820. Brown, Armstead
39 Murphey, Francis
    1818. Furphy, Francies
    F1820. Murphey, Francies
42 Mineace, Benjamin
    1818. Menees, Benjamin
    F1820. Menece, Benjamin
44 Woory, John
    F1820. Ury, John
45 Boggess, Joel
    1818. Boges, Joel
    F1820. Bogus, Joel

UNION COUNTY (Continued)

46 Cruse, Adam
    F1820. Cruce, Adam
47 Murphey, Hiley
    1818. Murphy, Hyly
    F1820. Murphey, Hila
48 Jinkens, John
    1818. Jinkens, John
    F1820. Jenkins, John
49 Burden, John
    1818. Burden, John
    F1820. Burdon, John
50 Ellams, Marget
    F1820. Elms, Margret
51 Bryan, Elijah
    1818. Bryant, Elijah
    F1820. Bryant, Elijah
55 Ellams, James
    1818. Ellems, James
    F1820. Elms, James
56 Billingsley, Bazel
    1818. Billingsly, Bazzel
    F1820. Billingsley, Bazzel
57 Trip, Andy
    1818. Tripe, Jinny
    F1820. Tripp, Jenny
58 Cochran, Marget
    F1820. Cochran, Peggy
59 Trip, John
    1818. Trip, John
    F1820. Tripp, John
60 Davison, William
    1818. Davidson, William
    F1820. Davidson, William
61 Steal, Andrew
    F1820. Steele, Andrew C.
62 Tetford, Walter
    1818. Tedford, Walter
    F1820. Tedford, Walter
63 Reynolds, Milleton
    F1820. Reynolds, Milikin
67 Craig, Hugh
    1818. Crag, Hugh
    F1820. Craig, Hugh
70 Evans, Oen
    1818. Evenas, Oen
    F1820. Evans, Owen
71 Evans, George
    1818. Evens, George
    F1820. Evans, George
72 Stokes, Young F.
    F1820. Stokes, Young
74 Evans, Elijah
    1818. Evans, Elijha
    F1820. Evans, Elijah

75 Durram, William
    1818. Durham, William
    F1820. Durham, William
76 Davison, Msiah
    1818. Davidson, Masias
    F1820. Davidson, Masias
77 Throgmorton, Joshuay
    1818. Throgmorton, Joshua
    F1820. Throgmorton, Joshua
78 Maginnis, Patrick
    1818. McGines, Patrick
    F1820. McGinnes, Patrick
79 Maginnis, William
    1818. McGines, William
    F1820. McGinnes, William
80 Barton, William
    1818. Barten, William
    F1820. Barton, William
81 Standerd, Thomas
    1818. Standerd, Thomas
    F1820. Standard, Thomas
82 Standerd, Willis
    F1820. Standard, Willis
84 Bizel, Isaac
    F1820. Bizzel, Isaac
85 Gore, Joshuay
    1818. Gore, Joshua
    F1820. Gore, Joshua
87 Paterson, Josiah
    F1820. Patterson, Josiah
88 Smyth, Barney
    F1820. Smith, Barney
89 Robertson, James
    1818. Roberson, James
    F1820. Robertson, James
90 Delaney, Patience
    F1820. Delany, Patience
91 Delaney, William
    F1820. Delany, William
92 Carter, Molton
    F1820. Carter, Nancy
97 Beggs, Isaac
    1818. Beggs, Isaac
    F1820. Baggs, Isaac
98 Walker, Zacheriah
    F1820. Walker, Zachariah
99 Beggs, Alexander
    1818. Beggs, Alexandria
100 Paterson, Levy
    1818. Paterson, Levy
    F1820. Patterson, Levi
101 Beggs, John
    F1820. Baggs, John

CENSUS OF 1820

UNION COUNTY (*Continued*)

102 Beggs, Archabel
    1818. Beggs, Arichibel
    F1820. Baggs, Archabald
103 Hugs, Jonathan
    F1820. Hughes, Jonathan
105 Boren, Hozea
    1818. Boren, Hoza
    F1820. Borin, Hosea
107 Macintorsh, Thomas
    1818. Mcintosh, Thomas
    F1820. McIntosh, Thomas
108 Penrod, Lewis
    1818. Penrod, Louis
    F1820. Penrod, Lewis
109 Green House
    F1820. Greenhouse, Renfrew
111 Cope, Yost
    F1820. Cope, Youst
113 Smyth, Michael
    F1820. Smith, Michael
114 Vineyard, George
    1818. Vinyard, George
    F1820. Vinyard, George
115 Vineyard, David
    F1820. Vinyard, David
117 Suttle, Jessee
    1818. Suttler, Jesse
    F1820. Suttle, Jesse
119 Makintorsh, Charles
    1818. McIntosh, Charles
    F1820. McIntosh, Charles
120 Boren, Bazel
    F1820. Borin, Bazel
121 Cox, Thomas
    1818. Cox, Thomas, Sr.
    F1820. Cox, Thomas
122 Boren, John
    1818. Boren, John
    F1820. Borin, John
123 Cuday, Lee
    1818. Cude, Lee
    F1820. Cuddy, Lee
124 Carker, Daniel
    F1820. Carraker, Daniel
125 Micenhimer, Moses
    F1820. Micenhamer, Moses
126 Hofner, Marten
    F1820. Hofner, Martin
127 Beggs, Robert
    1818. Beggs, Robert
    F1820. Baggs, Robert
129 Worthington, James, Jr.
    1818. Worthington, James, Sr.
    F1820. Worthington, James

130 Thornton, William
    1818. Thornton, William, Sr.
    F1820. Thornton, William, Sr.
132 Hunsaker, John, Sr.
    1818. Hunsaker, John
    F1820. Hunsaker, John
133 Hunsaker, Samuel, Jr.
    1818. Hunsak, Samuel, Jr.
    F1820. Hunsaker, Samuel, Jr.
134 Chrice, John
    1818. Crise, John
    F1820. Crise, John
135 Echols, Jasiel
    1818. Eachols, Jesse
    F1820. Echols, Jesse
139 MacDaniel, Zacheriah
    1818. McDaniel, Zachariah
    F1820. McDaniel, Zachariah
141 Crocker, Stephen
    F1820. Croker, Stephen
142 Hunsaker, Joseph, Sr.
    1818. Hunsaker, Joseph
    F1820. Hunsaker, Joseph, Sr.
146 Misenhimer, Jacob
    F1820. Micenhamer, Jacob
147 Sames, Thomas
    1818. Sams, Thomas
    F1820. Sames, Thomas
148 Hutson, William
    1818. Hudson, William
    F1820. Hudson, William
149 Dillow, Michael
    1818. Delo, Michel
    F1820. Delo, Michael
150 Barriner, Peter
    F1820. Barringer, Peter
152 Micenhimer, David
    F1820. Micenhamer, David
153 Powles, Peter
    F1820. Powlas, Peter
154 Dillow, John
    F1820. Delo, John
155 Carker, Jacob
    F1820. Karraker, Jacob
156 Gadwin, Wilkison
    1818. Godwin, Wilkson
    F1820. Godwin, Wilkinson
157 Micenhimer, Peter
    F1820. Micenhamer, Peter
158 Hazlewood, Cliff
    1818. Hazzelwood, Clif
    F1820. Hazlewood, Cliff
160 Smiley, George
    1818. Smily, George
    F1820. Smiley, George

UNION COUNTY (Continued)

162 Hairston, James
    F1820. Hurston, James
163 Hairston, John
    1818. Harsten, John
    F1820. Hairston, John
166 Lence, George, Jr.
    F1820. Lence, George
168 Sprouce, Samuel
    1818. Sprous, Samuel
    F1820. Sprouce, Samuel
170 Nemo, Wesley G.
    F1820. Nimmo, Wesley G.
172 Murray, John B.
    1818. Murray, John B.
    F1820. Murry, John B.
174 Henry, Evin
    F1820. Henry, Evan
176 Clap, Adam, Sr.
    1818. Clap, Adam, Sr.
    F1820. Clapp, Adam
178 Hughs, Nathaniel
    1818. Huse, Nathaniel
    F1820. Hughes, Nathaniel
180 Holshouser, Michael
    F1820. Holeshouser, Michael
181 Lawrence, Ester
    1818. Leawrance, Easter
    F1820. Lawrance, Esther
184 Haukes, Joseph
    F1820. Hawks, Joseph
187 Cimmel, John
    1818. Kimmel, John
    F1820. Kimmell, John
190 Smyth, Andrew
    F1820. Smith, Andrew
193 Miller, Peter
    F1820. Miller, Peter, Sr.
194 Right, James
    1818. Write, James
    F1820. Wright, James
196 Penrod, Sollomon
    1818. Penrod, Solomon
    F1820. Penrod, Soloman
199 Willis, Jacob
    1818. Willes, Jacob
    F1820. Willis, Jacob
201 Lierly, Henry
    F1820. Leyrle, Henry
202 Lence, John
    1818. Lense, John, Sr.
    F1820. Lence, John, Sr.
203 Huskey, John
    1818. Husky, John
    F1820. Huskey, John

205 Homes, William
    F1820. Holmes, William
207 Hughs, William
    1818. Huse, William
    F1820. Hughes, William
209 Chrice, David
    F1820. Crise, David
210 Tope, Fedrick, Sr.
    1818. Tope, Fedrick
    F1820. Tope, Fredrick, Sr.
211 Linbeau, Michael
    1818. Limbaugh, Michel
    F1820. Limboch, Michael
212 Dod, William
    1818. Dod, William
    F1820. Dodd, William
213 Hecock, Russel E.
    F1820. Heacock, Russell E.
214 Rentleman, Jacob
    1818. Rentelman, Jacob
    F1820. Rentleman, Jacob
215 Vancil, Edmon
    1818. Vancel, Edmond
    F1820. Vancill, Edmund
216 Trip, Hiram
    F1820. Tripp, Hiram
217 Langley, John
    1818. Langly, John
    F1820. Langley, John
218 Summers, Jonston
    F1820. Summers, Johnson
219 Lingle, Antoney
    1818. Lingle, Anthony
    F1820. Lingle, Anthony
220 Riter, Daniel
    1818. Ritter, Daniel
    F1820. Ritter, Daniel
221 Crafton, Robert
    1818. Craften, Robert
    F1820. Crafton, Robert
222 Treace, Jacob
    1818. Trees, Jacob
    F1820. Treece, Jacob
224 Sames, Rice
    1818. Sams, Rice
    F1820. Sames, Riece
228 Woodall, Elijah
    1818. Woodoll, Elijha P.
    F1820. Woodall, Elijah
229 Redell, John
    F1820. Riddle, John
231 Cruse, Henry
    F1820. Cruce, Henry
232 Simerman, Mathias, Sr.
    F1820. Zimmerman, Mathias, Sr.

CENSUS OF 1820

UNION COUNTY (Continued)

234 Penrod, Allin
    F1820. Penrod, Allen
236 Wolf, Jacob
    1818. Wolf, Jacob
    F1820. Woolf, Jacob
237 Vancil, Isaac
    1818. Vancel, Isaac
    F1820. Vancill, Isaac
238 Shepherd, Jacob
    F1820. Shephard, Jacob
239 Vancil, John Sr.
    F1820. Vancill, John, Sr.
240 Huskey, Jonathan
    1818. Husky, Jonathan
    F1820. Huskey, Jonathan
242 Minneace, John
    F1820. Menece, John
243 Mucklehany, Joseph
    1818. Mclehanny, Joseph
    F1820. McElhany, Joseph
244 Mackentorsh, John
    1818. Mcintosh, John
    F1820. McIntosh, John
246 Hughs, John
    1818. Huse, John
    F1820. Hughes, John
248 Bennit, Marget
    F1820. Bennet, Margret
249 Irwin, Hugh
    1818. Irvin, Hugh
    F1820. Ervin, Hugh
250 Holland, Leven L.
    1818. Hollen, Leven L.
    F1820. Holland, Edmund
251 Grammer, William
    1818. Grammer, William
    F1820. Grammar, William
253 Bone, Squire
    1818. Boon, Squire
    F1820. Bone, Square
256 Howard, Aron
    1818. Howard, Aron
    F1820. Howard, Aaron
257 Irwin, Andrew
    1818. Irvin, Andrew
    F1820. Ervin, Andrew
258 Hargrave, John
    1818. Hargrave, John, Sr.
    F1820. Hartgrave, John, Sr.
259 Millegin, Jacob
    F1820. Milikin, Jacob
260 Whitaker, Alexander
    1818. Whitaker, Alexandria
    F1820. Whitaker, Alexander

263 Willis, James
    1818. Willes, James
    F1820. Willis, James
264 Parmeley, Giles
    1818. Parmerly, Gils
    F1820. Parmley, Jiles
265 Butsher, Samuel
    1818. Butcher, Samuel
    F1820. Butcher, Samuel
266 Casey, Robert
    1818. Casa, Robert
    F1820. Casey, Robert
267 Standiver, Anderson
    F1820. Standerford, Anderson
268 Abenathey, James M.
    1818. Abernathy, James
    F1820. Abanatha, James
269 Tweedy, John
    1818. Twedy, John
    F1820. Twiddy, John
270 Corble, Adam
    F1820. Cobble, Adam
271 Loid, Robert H.
    1818. Lloyd, Robert H.
    F1820. Lloyd, Robert H.
272 Trip, William
    F1820. Tripp, William
273 Dailey, John
    1818. Daly, John
    F1820. Daly, John
274 Isenackle, Jacob
    F1820. Icenoggle, Jacob
275 Crafton, Robert W.
    1818. Craften, Robert W.
    F1820. Crafton, Robert
276 Morgan, Antoney
    1818. Morgan, Anthony
    F1820. Morgan, Anthony
278 Hunsaker, Abraham, Sr.
    1818. Hunsaker, Abraham
    F1820. Hunsaker, Abraham, Sr.
279 Hughes, Oen
    1818. Huse, Oen
    F1820. Hughes, Owen
282 Baltzele, John
    F1820. Baltzell, John
283 Craglole, William
    1818. Craglo, William
    F1820. Cragloe, William
285 Litleton, Ely
    F1820. Littleton, Eli
286 Ferrel, Thomas
    F1820. Ferrill, Thomas

UNION COUNTY (Continued)

287 Penrod, Andy
    1818. Penrod, Andrew
    F1820. Penrod, Andrew
289 Tope, Fedrick, Jr.
    F1820. Tope, Fredrick, Jr.
291 Lamer, Joseph
    1818. Lamer, Joseph
    F1820. Lamour, Joseph
292 Cluts, Jacob
    F1820. Clutts, Jacob
296 Litleton, John
    F1820. Littleton, John
297 Dillow, Peter, Sr.
    F1820. Delo, Peter, 2nd
300 Hunsaker, John, Jr.
    1818. Hunsaker, John, Jr.
    F1820. Hunsaker, John, 2d
305 Summers, Thomas
    1818. Sumers, Thomas
    F1820. Summers, Thomas
306 Lingle, Jacob, Sr.
    F1820. Lingle, Jacob
307 Vancil, John, Jr.
    F1820. Vancill, John, Jr.
308 Lence, John, Jr.
    1818. Lense, John, Jr.
    F1820. Lence, John, Jr.
309 Lence, Boston
    1818. Lense, Boysten
    F1820. Lence, Boston
310 Lence, Davolt
    1818. Lense, Davoult
    F1820. Lence, Davault
312 Vancil, Jonas
    1818. Vancel, Jonas
    F1820. Vancill, Jonas P.
314 Lamer, Henry
    1818. Lamer, Henry
    F1820. Lamore, Henry
316 Sherril, Ambros
    F1820. Sherrill, Ambrose
318 Smyth, Thomas
    F1820. Smith, Thomas
319 Potmess, Peter
    1818. Portmess, Peter
    F1820. Potmicer, Peter
322 Hambrick, Joseph
    F1820. Hemrick, Joseph
323 Morgan, William
    1818. Morgen, William, Sr.
    F1820. Morgan, William
325 Dewral, Mary
    F1820. Durall, Ephraigm

328 Crips, John
    1818. Crips, John
    F1820. Cripps, John
330 Fisher, Grammer
    F1820. Fisher, Grammar
332 Robertson, Sarah
    1818. Roberson, John
    F1820. Robertson, John
334 Lemmons, George
    1818. Lemmons, George
    F1820. Lemons, George
335 Friet, Robert
    1818. Fryatt, Robert
    F1820. Fiatt, Robert
339 Corgin, Patrick
    1818. Corgen, Patrick
341 Redell, Thomas
    F1820. Riddle, Thomas
343 Cox, Thomas, Jr.
    1818. Cox, Thomas, Jr.
    F1820. Cox, Thomas S.
346 Willard, Nancy
    F1820. Williard, Nancy
349 Bone, Mary
    1818. Boon, Mary
    F1820. Bone, Mary
350 Waldrup, Samuel
    F1820. Walldrupe, Samuel
351 Noel, Ephragn
    1818. Noel, Ephrem
    F1820. Noel, Ephraigm
352 Cook, Fedrick
    F1820. Cook, Fredrick
353 Staton, Ezechael
    1818. Staten, Ezekel
    F1820. Statton, Ezekiel
354 Lierley, Jacob
    F1820. Lially, Jacob
355 Shepherd, Alizebeth
    F1820. Shephard, Elizabeth
360 Wolf, George
    1818. Woolf, George
    F1820. Woolf, George
361 Davis, Nat
    F1820. Davis, Nathaniel
362 Pecock, James U.
    F1820. Peacock, James U.
364 Tinsley, James
    1818. Tingly, James
    F1820. Tinsley, James
365 Tolbert, Fedrick
    1818. Tolbert, Fedrick
    F1820. Talbot, Fredrick

UNION COUNTY (Concluded)

366 Roberts, John B.
    1818. Roberds, John B.
    F1820. Roberts, John B.
371 Dillow, Peter, Jr.
    F1820. Delo, Peter
373 Dillow, Jacob
    F1820. Delo, Jacob
374 Clap, Adam, Jr.
    1818. Clap, Adam, Jr.
    F1820. Clapp, Adam, Jr.
375 Deen, Thomas
    1818. Deen, Thomas
    F1820. Dean, Thomas
376 Sames, David
    1818. Sams, David
    F1820. Sames, David
377 Price, Calven
    F1820. Price, Calvin
380 Simerman, Mathias, Jr.
    F1820. Simmerman, Mathias
383 Graham, Jane
    1818. Graham, Jinny
    F1820. Graham, Jane
384 Mcraven, Benjamin
    1818. McCravens, Benjamin
    F1820. McCraven, Benjamin
385 Echols, William
    1818. Eachols, William
    F1820. Echols, William
387 Cright, George
    1818. Crite, George
    F1820. Crite, George
388 Micenhimer, John
    F1820. Micenhamer, John
389 Worhengton, Pheby
    F1820. Worthington, Phebe
390 Smyth, John
    1818. Smith, John
    F1820. Smith, John
394 Flach, Christian
    F1820. Flock, Christian

CENSUS OF WASHINGTON COUNTY, 1820

A Schedule of the whole number of persons in the County of Washington State of Illinois as taking by Harry Wilton agreeable to a Law of said State passed the 23d March 1819—and taken in the month of August 1820.

Names of Heads of Families	Free white males under 21 years	Free white males 21 years and over	Females	Blacks
1[‡] Nathaniel Nowlen	1	1	2	
2[*‡] Leaiden Posey	3	1	1	
3[*‡] Archabald Andrews	4	1	5	
4[‡] John Bradford	2	1	3	
5[*‡] John Carrigan	2	2	2	2
6[‡] James Carrigan	2	1	4	
7[*‡] Wingate Maddox	3	1	4	
8[‡] Samuel McKeever	2	1	5	
9[*‡] John Wardsworth	1	1	6	1
10[*‡] Haden Watts	4	1	3	
11[*‡] Thomas Wardsworth	4	1	1	
12[‡] Gibeon Burton	1	1	4	
13[‡] Frederick Berry		1	1	
14[‡] Jesse Griffin	1	1	2	
15[‡] Isaac Huston	1	3	5	
16[*‡] Edward Cole	3	5	3	1
17[‡] Richard Cole	1	1	1	
18[‡] John Adams	1	4	2	
19[‡] Joseph White	3	1	3	
20 Amos Low		1	3	
21[*‡] John L Laughlin	3	1	3	
22[*‡] Robert McKeever	4	1	2	
23 Salmon Sherwood	4	3	7	
24[‡] Thomas Neal	1	1	3	
25[*‡] Richard Carter	3	1	4	
26 James Burrows		1	1	
27[‡] Samuel Chaping	3	2	3	
28[‡] Lorenzo Chaping	3	1	2	

The first 42 names in this census list were numbered in the original. The symbols as well as the later numbering have been supplied by the editor:
‡ Indicates name also in Federal Census for 1820.
*Indicates name also in State Census for 1818.

CENSUS OF 1820

WASHINGTON COUNTY (Continued)

No.	Heads of families	Males under 21	Males 21 & over	Females	Blacks
29[‡]	Stephen Hitchcock	2	1	3	
30	Peter Beach	1	1	2	
31[*‡]	Elizabeth Allen	1	2	[4]	
32[‡]	Edward McCart	3	3	3	1
33[*‡]	Gilleous Maddux	3	1	5	
34[‡]	Stewart Slavings	1	1	2	
35[*‡]	William Taylor	3	1	2	
36[‡]	David Roper	4	2	2	
37[‡]	Wm Vandergriff	1	1	1	
38[*‡]	Jacob Crocker		1	2	
39[‡]	Elizabeth Crocker	1	1	4	
40[*‡]	Arthur Crocker	2	2	3	
41[‡]	Jacob Brewer	2	1	2	
42[‡]	Daniel Strong	3	1	1	
[43 ‡]	John Brake	1	1	1	
[44 ‡]	William Lewis	2	1	1	
[45 ‡]	James Cockrum		1	4	
[46*‡]	Hugh Johnston		1	1	
[47*‡]	Daniel Simons	4	1	4	
[48*‡]	William Johnston	1	2	2	
[49*‡]	John Johnston Jr	3	1	2	
[50*‡]	James McCracken	2	1		
[51*‡]	William Johnston	3	1	4	
[52*]	Hosea Rawlins	3	1	2	
[53*‡]	John M. T. Ortin		1	1	
[54*‡]	James Ortin	3	1	3	
[55*‡]	John Welsh	3	1	3	
[56 ‡]	Robert Callahan	2	1	2	
[57 ‡]	Edmond Townsend	2	1	1	
[58*‡]	Collins Matheny	4	2	1	
[59*‡]	William Roundtree	4	1	6	
[60]	Daniel White	5	1	5	
[61*‡]	Thomas Hughey	1	2	2	
[62*‡]	Theopolis Herrald	1	1	1	
[63*‡]	John Johnston	1	1	2	
[64*‡]	John Hughey	1	1	2	
[65 ‡]	Peter Outhouse	2	2	3	
[66*‡]	John A. Evans	2	1	1	
[67 ‡]	John Outhouse	2	2	1	

WASHINGTON COUNTY (Continued)

No.	Heads of families	Males under 21	Males 21 & over	Females	Blacks
[68*‡]	James Eaden	4	1	1	
[69*‡]	Archabald Traylor	5	5	1	
[70*‡]	John Batteau	2	2	2	
[71 ‡]	Hardy Outhouse		1	1	
[72 ‡]	Meredy Outhouse		1	2	
[73*‡]	William Crocker	3	1	1	
[74*‡]	Daniel S. Swearingen	2	2	3	
[75 ‡]	Francis Webster	6	1	2	
[76*‡]	[Ch]arles Cox	[1]	1	[5]	
[77 ‡]	John Rowe	4	1	4	
[78 ‡]	James Carr		2		
[79*‡]	Benjamin Jones	2	1	4	
[80 ‡]	Peter Woollum		1	1	
[81 ‡]	William Blackman		1	2	
[82 ‡]	James J. Ryan	1	1	2	
[83 ‡]	Thomas L. Moore	3	1	3	
[84 ‡]	Jesse Moore	3	1	4	
[85 ‡]	David Johnston	2	1	3	
[86*‡]	Brazilla Silkwood		1	1	
[87 ‡]	John Reed		1	2	
[88 ‡]	David Thacker	2	1	3	
[89*‡]	Benjamin Cox	4	2	3	
[90*‡]	William Middleton	1	1	3	
[91*‡]	Solomon Silkwood	2	2	3	
[92 ‡]	Peter Stewart	3	1	4	
[93]	Absalom Perkins	1	1	1	
[94 ‡]	Brazilla Silkwood		1	3	
[95*]	Charles Butler	4	1	4	
[96*‡]	John Woodrum	3	1	3	
[97*‡]	Joseph Kenyon	4	1	1	
[98*‡]	Benjamin Hagerman	2	1	1	
[99 ‡]	Samuel Sharp	1	1	3	
[100 ‡]	James Buck		1	3	
[101 ‡]	Elizabeth Baker	5		3	
[102*‡]	John Nicholas	1	1	5	
[103 ‡]	Jonathan Sharp	1	1	1	
[104 ‡]	William Walker	1	1	1	
[105*‡]	Patsey Short	3		3	
[106*‡]	Alexander Maddux	4	1	3	

CENSUS OF 1820 315

WASHINGTON COUNTY (Continued)

No.	Heads of families	Males under 21	Males 21 & over	Females	Blacks
[107 ‡]	Nancy Berry	2		1	
[108 ‡]	John Molthrop	1	1	1	
[109 ‡]	John A. Molthrop	1	1	2	
[110]	Emma Hawkey	4		2	
[111 ‡]	William Scott		7		
[112*‡]	Philip Martin		2	5	
[113 ‡]	Hetty Posey	3		3	
[114 ‡]	Henry Sharp	6	1	4	
[115*‡]	Leonard Maddux	6	1	4	
[116*‡]	Lewis Maddux	6	1	2	
[117 ‡]	John Gilmore	5	1	1	
[118 ‡]	George Russel		2	2	
[119*‡]	Bowling Green	3	4	1	
[120*‡]	Charles Stevens	3	1	3	
[121*‡]	Zachariah Maddux	4	2	4	
[122*‡]	Jacob Terman	2	1	3	
[123 ‡]	William H Berry	5	1	3	
[124 ‡]	William Wall	1	2	2	
[125*‡]	Jonathan Hill	6	1	1	
[126*‡]	Andrew Bankston	3	1	4	
[127*‡]	William Symmes	6	1	3	
[128*‡]	William Steel	3	2	3	
[129 ‡]	Joseph Morton		1	1	
[130 ‡]	Henry Atkinson	2	2	4	
[131*‡]	Colyer Brown	1	1	2	
[132 ‡]	David Riddle	3	1	4	
[133 ‡]	William Orenduff	1	2	4	
[134*‡]	Samuel Brown		1	2	
[135*‡]	John Brown		1	2	
[136*‡]	Caton Usher	1	1	1	
[137*‡]	Alexander Chesney	2	1	1	
[138 ‡]	Benjamin Chesney	1	1	1	
[139*‡]	George Brown	3	1	1	10
[140]	Richard				
[141*‡]	Samuel Stewart	1	1	2	
[142*‡]	Britton Jorden		1	1	
[143 ‡]	James Gilbreath	3	7	2	5
[144*‡]	John Handy	3	3	2	
[145 ‡]	John Woodrome Jr	5	1	3	

WASHINGTON COUNTY (Continued)

No.	Heads of families	Males under 21	Males 21 & over	Females	Blacks
[146 ‡]	John Abbott	2	2	2	
[147 ‡]	Christopher Abbott	2	2	2	
[148 ‡]	John Foss		7	5	1
[149 ‡]	Charles Slade	2	1	3	4
[150 ‡]	Martha French	5		4	
[151*‡]	Lemuel Hawkins		1	4	
[152*‡]	John Carter		1	3	
[153 ‡]	Aliece Carter	1		2	
[154*‡]	Isaac Darneal	3	1	3	
[155*‡]	William Darneal	1	1	2	
[156*‡]	David White	4	1	3	
[157 ‡]	Meredith Castlebury	1	1	1	
[158 ‡]	James Anderson		1	1	
[159 ‡]	Elijah Peirce	5	1	4	
[160]	Susanah Anderson	1		3	
[161 ‡]	Anderson Chandler	3	1	1	
[162 ‡]	Isaac Anderson		1	2	
[163 ‡]	Biram Ray	3	1	2	
[164*‡]	Thomas Watkins	1	1	3	
[165*‡]	John Smith	6	1	5	1
[166*‡]	Christopher Rickafuse	1	2	3	
[167*]	David Peirce	1	2		
[168 ‡]	Elijah Bailes	2	1	4	
[169 ‡]	Elijah Lincoln		2	2	
[170 ‡]	Joseph Johnston	4	2	7	
[171*‡]	Jonathan Browder	1	3	4	
[172 ‡]	Hanson Godfrey		1	2	
[173 ‡]	Martha Townsend	3		2	
[174 ‡]	Edward Warren	2	2	3	
[175 ‡]	Hezekiah Rowe		1	1	
[176 ‡]	Susan Miller	1		5	
[177 ‡]	Stephen Rowe	2	1	1	
[178 ‡]	Lydia Savage	3		2	
[179*‡]	Beverly Watkins	2	1	6	
[180 ‡]	John H. Morgan	1	2	2	
[181 ‡]	John Ramsay	3	3	3	
[182 ‡]	John H Ramsay	1	2	1	
[183 ‡]	Thomas Gilliland	2	1	2	
[184 ‡]	Samuel Carr	1	1	2	

CENSUS OF 1820

WASHINGTON COUNTY (Continued)

No.	Heads of families	Males under 21	Males 21 & over	Females	Blacks
[185 ‡]	John Winters	1	1	3	
[186*‡]	Robert Davis	2	1	3	
[187*]	Joseph Robbins	3	1	1	
[188]	Solomon Eades	5	1	3	
[189]	John Alexander		1	2	
[190 ‡]	Nicholas Piles	2	1	1	
[191 ‡]	Joel Medley	2	1	1	
[192*‡]	Reuben Middleton	2	1	2	
[193*‡]	Ruth Washburn	2		1	
[194]	James Thompson	3	1	2	
[195*‡]	Pleasant Appling	2	1	3	
[196 ‡]	Simon Herron	2	1	6	
[197 ‡]	William Craten	1	1	4	
[198 ‡]	Hiram Virgin	1	1	1	
[199 ‡]	Major Herron	4	1	4	
[200]	Polly Allen	4	1	1	
[201 ‡]	John Evans	1	1	2	
[202 ‡]	William Ayers	3	1	5	
[203 ‡]	Russel Ayres		1	2	
[204 ‡]	Sarah Weeless	2		1	3
[205 ‡]	Susanah Edwards	2		3	
[206 ‡]	Elizabeth Weeless	3		1	
[207*‡]	William Weeless		1	2	
[208*‡]	Aaron Williams	4	1	3	
[209 ‡]	William Thompson	3	1	2	
[210 ‡]	Elihu Bandy	1	1	4	
[211*‡]	David J. McCord	1	1	1	
[212 ‡]	Charles McCord	5	1	3	1
[213*‡]	John R Hutchins		1	1	
[214*‡]	Absalem Minson	2	1	7	
[215 ‡]	James Gorden	1	1	3	
[216*‡]	John Dees	3	1	2	
[217*‡]	John Lard		1	3	
[218]	William Dees		1	3	
[219*‡]	Alexander White	4	1	1	
[220 ‡]	John Philips	1	1	1	
[221 ‡]	Joseph Whitenburg	1	1	2	
[222 ‡]	Samuel Whitenburg	1	1	1	

WASHINGTON COUNTY (Continued)

No.	Heads of families	Males under 21	Males 21 & over	Females	Blacks
[223]	John Low	2	1	4	
[224*‡]	Lewis Huggins		1	2	
[225*‡]	[David Huggins]	2	2	2	
[226*‡]	William Huggins	1	1	3	
[227 ‡]	Henry Boswell	1	1	1	
[228]	Zephaniah Nobles	1	2	1	
[229*‡]	William Johnston	1	1	1	
[230 ‡]	John Tilton	1	1	1	
[231 ‡]	Enoch Tilton		2	1	
[232 ‡]	William Carrigan	2	1	2	
[233 ‡]	Nathan Fatman	5	1	7	
[234 ‡]	William Thompson Jr.	1	1	2	
[235 ‡]	John Thompson		1	2	
[236 ‡]	Charles Harriman		2	4	
[237]	Amos Chandler		1	3	
[238 ‡]	Joshua Harriman		1	6	
[239 ‡]	John Thompson Jr.	1	2	2	
[240*‡]	James Thompson	1	1	2	
[241*‡]	Richard Thompson	7	1	4	
[242 ‡]	William Smith	2	2	4	
[243 ‡]	John Cooper	4	1	2	
[244*‡]	Absalom Yarbough	3	2	2	
[245*‡]	John Creal	3	2	5	
[246]	Zimriah Jentry		1	2	
[247*‡]	Alexander Maddux	6	1	1	
[248*‡]	Thomas F. Herbert		1		2
[249 ‡]	John Kain	1	1	1	
[250 ‡]	Samuel Arthur		1	1	
[251 ‡]	Mary Oates	3		4	
[252 ‡]	Seth Hilton		3	1	
[253 ‡]	James Manning	2	1	1	
[254 ‡]	Thomas Lyon	1	3	1	1
[255 ‡]	Richard Tilton	3	1	3	
[256 ‡]	Thomas Tilton		1	3	
[257*‡]	William H. Bradsby		1	2	
[258 ‡]	Demsey Kennedy		1	2	
[259 ‡]	Leonard Price	3	1	4	
[260*‡]	John Starnater	2	1	5	

CENSUS OF 1820

WASHINGTON COUNTY (*Continued*)

No.	Heads of families	Males under 21	Males 21 & over	Females	Blacks
[261*‡]	Ellis Chafin		1	2	
[262]	David Dow		3		
[263 ‡]	Erasmus Elliott	1	1	3	
[264]	John Champion	1	1	3	
		520	336	658	33

Aggregate 1547 persons

I do certify that the above list composes the number of inhabitants in Washington County.

This 6th Decr 1820.   HARRY WILTON

WASHINGTON COUNTY (Continued)

The Washington County census, dated June 1, 1818, was taken by John K. Maugham; the federal census, dated December 18, 1820, was taken by Calvin Barns; and the state census, "taken in the month of August 1820," was taken by Harry Wilton. Twenty-eight names appear in the federal census which are not found in the state census:

Shoal Creek
  Louzader, Isaac
  Slade, Charles
Crooked Creek
  *Wilten, Harry
    1818. Wilton, Harry
  Lee, Harvey
  Easen, Pomeroy
Covington
  Walker, James
  Scott, Isaac
  *White, Hartshorn
  Black, C. P.
  Rogers, Elisha B.
  Iric, William
  Temple, James
Carlyle
  Cooper, Harmon
  *Smith, Asahel
  Short, Bennet
  Newton, Charles
  Clark, John
  Hockin, Amy
  *Braselton, Benjamin
    1818. Brasilton, Benjamin
Sugar Creek
  Boyd, Joseph
  Begold, Joshua
  Reed, Charles
  *Silkwood, Hyram
Carington
  Bates, Thomas
  McIntyre, Hugh
  Jones, Jesse
  Hillhouse, William
  Nelson, John
Discrepancies are as follows:
1 Nowlen, Nathaniel
  F1820. Knowlan, Nathaniel
2 Posey, Leaiden
  1818. Posey, Leeaiden
  F1820. Posey, Leaiden
3 Andrews, Archabald
  1818. Andrus, Archabald
  F1820. Andrus, Archibal
5 Carrigan, John
  1818. Carigan, John
  F1820. Carrigan, John
7 Maddox, Wingate
  1818. Maddux, Wingate
  F1820. Maddux, Wingate

8 McKeever, Samuel
  F1820. McCiver, Samuel
9 Wardsworth, John
  1818. Wadsworth, John
  F1820. Wadsworth, John
10 Watts, Haden
  1818. Watts, Haden
  F1820. Wats, Haden
11 Wardsworth, Thomas
  1818. Wadsworth, Thomas
  F1820. Wadsworth, Thomas
12 Burton, Gibeon
  F1820. Burton, Gideon
14 Griffin, Jesse
  F1820. Griffin, Jessy
15 Huston, Isaac
  F1820. Hughson, Isaac
21 Laughlin, John L.
  1818. Laughlin, John Lewis
  F1820. Laughlin, Lewis
22 McKeever, Robert
  1818. McIver, Robert
  F1820. McCiver, Robert
25 Carter, Richard
  1818. Carter, Richard
  F1820. Carter, Richard P.
27 Chaping, Samuel
  F1820. Chapin, Samuel
28 Chaping, Lorenzo
  F1820. Chapin, Lorenzo
29 Hitchcock, Stephen
  F1820. Hitchcox, Stephen
33 Maddux, Gilleous
  1818. Maddux, Gilless
  F1820. Haddox, Gillis
34 Slavings, Stewart
  F1820. Slavens, Steward
37 Vandergriff, Wm.
  F1820. Vandegriff, Wm.
42 Strong, Daniel
  F1820. Strang, Daniel
45 Cockrum, James
  F1820. Cockrem, James
46 Johnston, Hugh
  1818. Johnston, Hugh
  F1820. Johnsen, Hugh
47 Simons, Daniel
  1818. Cymons, Daniel
  F1820. Simons, Daniel

CENSUS OF 1820

WASHINGTON COUNTY (Continued)

48 Johnston, William
    1818. Johnston, William
    F1820. Johnsen, William
49 Johnston, John, Jr.
    1818. Johnston, John S.
    F1820. Johnsen, John, Jr.
50 McCracken, James
    1818. McReaken, James
    F1820. McCrackin, James
51 Johnston, William
    1818. Johnston, William
    F1820. Johnsen, Wm., Sr.
52 Rawlins, Hosea
    1818. Rollins, Hosea
53 Ortin, John M. T.
    1818. Orton, John
    F1820. Orton, John
54 Ortin, James
    1818. Orton, James
    F1820. Orton, James
55 Welsh, John
    1818. Welch, John
    F1820. Welch, John
57 Townsend, Edmond
    F1820. Townsen, Edmun
58 Matheny, Collins
    1818. Matheny, Collins
    F1820. Mattheney, Collins
61 Hughey, Thomas
    1818. Huey, Thomas
    F1820. Hewey, Thomas
62 Herrald, Theopolis
    1818. Harrel, Theophilus
    F1820. Herril, Theophilus
63 Johnston, John
    1818. Johnston, John
    F1820. Johnsen, John, Sr.
64 Hughey, John
    1818. Huey, John
    F1820. Hewey, John
66 Evans, John A.
    F1820. Evans, John, Jr.
68 Eaden, James
    1818. Edon, James
    F1820. Eden, James
69 Traylor, Archabald
    1818. Taylor, Archibald
    F1820. Traylor, Archibal
70 Batteau, John
    1818. Bitto, John
    F1820. Batto, John
72 Outhouse, Meredy
    F1820. Outhouse, Meredith
80 Woollum, Peter
    F1820. Hulm, Peter

83 Moore, Thomas L.
    F1820. More, Thomas
84 Moore, Jesse
    F1820. More, Jessy
85 Johnston, David
    F1820. Johnson, David
88 Thacker, David
    F1820. Thacher, David
92 Stewart, Peter
    F1820. Steward, Peter
94 Silkwood, Brazilla
    F1820. Silkwood, Basil
96 Woodrum, John
    1818. Woodrum, John
    F1820. Woodrom, James
97 Kenyon, Joseph
    1818. Kinyon, Joseph
    F1820. Kinyon, Joseph
102 Nicholas, John
    1818. Nichols, John
    F1820. Nichols, Nohn
106 Maddux, Alexander
    1818. Maddux, Alexander, Jr.
    F1820. Maddox, Alexander
109 Molthrop, John A.
    F1820. Malthrop, John A.
113 Posey, Hetty
    F1820. Posey, Hester
115 Maddux, Leonard
    1818. Maddux, Leonard
    F1820. Maddox, Leonard
116 Maddux, Lewis
    1818. Maddux, Leven
    F1820. Maddox, Levin
119 Green, Bowling
    1818. Green, Bowling
    F1820. Green, Bolin
120 Stevens, Charles
    1818. Stephens, Charles
    F1820. Stevens, Charles
121 Maddux, Zachariah
    1818. Maddux, Zachariah
    F1820. Maddox, Zachariah
122 Terman, Jacob
    1818. Turman, Jacob
    F1820. Turman, Jacob
126 Bankston, Andrew
    1818. Bankson, Andrew
    F1820. Bankson, Andrew
127 Symmes, William
    1818. Sims, William
    F1820. Syms, William
130 Atkinson, Henry
    F1820. Atkins, Henry

WASHINGTON COUNTY (Continued)

131 Brown, Colyer
    1818. Brown, Colier
    F1820. Brown, Collier
133 Orenduff, William
    F1820. Orendorf, William
140 Richard ———
    No data given.
141 Stewart, Samuel
    1818. Stewart, Samuel
    F1820. Steward, Samuel
142 Jorden, Britton
    1818. Jordan, Briton
    F1820. Jordan, Britton
143 Gilbreath, James
    F1820. Gilbreth, James
145 Woodrome, John, Jr.
    F1820. Woodrum, John, Jr.
146 Abbott, John
    F1820. Abbot, John
147 Abbott, Christopher
    F1820. Abbot, Christopher
149 Slade, Charles
    F1820. Slade, Charles, Sr.
151 Hawkins, Lemuel
    1818. Hackins, Lemuel
    F1820. Hawkins, Lemuel
153 Carter, Aliece
    F1820. Carter, Ledsey
154 Darneal, Isaac
    1818. Darnal, Isaac
    F1820. Darnell, Isaac
155 Darneal, William
    1818. Darnall, William
    F1820. Darnell, William
159 Peirce, Elijah
    F1820. Pierce, Elijah
163 Ray, Biram
    F1820. Ray, Abiram
164 Watkins, Thomas
    1818. Wadkins, Thomas
    F1820. Watkins, Thomas
166 Rickafuse, Christopher
    1818. Richerfuse, Christopher
    F1820. Rickafoos, Christopher
167 Peirce, David
    1818. Peirce, David and Caleb
    F1820. Pierce, Caleb
168 Bailes, Elijah
    F1820. Bales, Elijah
170 Johnston, Joseph
    F1820. Johnson, Joseph
176 Miller, Susan
    F1820. Miller, Sarah
179 Watkins, Beverly
    1818. Wadkins, Beverly
    F1820. Watkins, Beverly
180 Morgan, John H.
    F1820. Morgan, John
181 Ramsay, John
    F1820. Ramsey, John
182 Ramsay, John H.
    F1820. Ramsey, John H.
183 Gilliland, Thomas
    F1820. Gillehan, Thomas
185 Winters, John
    F1820. Kinters, John
190 Piles, Nicholas
    F1820. Pyle, Nicholas
192 Middleton, Reuben
    1818. Middleton, Reuben
    F1820. Middleton, Rueben
195 Appling, Pleasant
    1818. Apling, Pleasant
    F1820. Aplin, Pleasant
196 Herron, Simon
    F1820. Herrin, Simon
197 Craten, William
    F1820. Crayton, William
198 Virgin, Hiram
    F1820. Virgin, Hyram
199 Herron, Major
    F1820. Herrin, Majer
201 Evans, John
    F1820. Evans, John, Jr.
203 Ayres, Russel
    F1820. Ayers, Russel
204 Weeless, Sarah
    F1820. Wheelis, Sarah
205 Edwards, Susanah
    F1820. Edwards, Susanna
206 Weeless, Elizabeth
    F1820. Wheelis, Elizabeth
207 Weeless, William
    1818. Wheeless, William
    F1820. Wheelis, William
208 Williams, Aaron
    1818. Williams, Aron
    F1820. Wms, Aaron
209 Thompson, William
    F1820. Thompsen, Wm.
210 Bandy, Elihu
    F1820. Bandy, Ellihu
211 McCord, David J.
    1818. McCord, David
    F1820. McCord, David
213 Hutchins, John R.
    1818. Hutchings, John
    F1820. Hutchins, John R.

WASHINGTON COUNTY (Concluded)

214 Minson, Absalem
    1818. Minson, Abraham
    F1820. Minsen, Abraham
216 Dees, John
    1818. Deas, John
    F1820. Dees, John
220 Philips, John
    F1820. Phillips, John
221 Whitenburg, Joseph
    F1820. Whittenburg, Joseph
222 Whitenburg, Samuel
    F1820. Whittenburg, Daniel
227 Boswell, Henry
    F1820. Baswell, Henry
229 Johnston, William
    1818. Johnston, William, Jr.
    F1820. Johnsen, William, Jr.
231 Tilton, Enoch
    F1820. Telton, Enoch
234 Thompson, William, Jr.
    F1820. Thompsen, Wm., Jr.
235 Thompson, John
    F1820. Thompsen, John
236 Harriman, Charles
    F1820. Harryman, Charles
238 Harriman, Joshua
    F1820. Harryman, Joshua

239 Thompson, John, Jr.
    F1820. Thompsen, John, Jr.
241 Thompson, Richard
    1818. Thomason, Richard
    F1820. Thomsen, Richard
244 Yarbough, Absalom
    1818. Yarbrough, Absalem
    F1820. Yarbor, Absalom
245 Creal, John
    1818. Creal, John
    F1820. Kreel, John
247 Maddux, Alexander
    1818. Maddux, Alexander
    F1820. Maddox, Alexander
251 Oates, Mary
    F1820. Oats, Mary
252 Hilton, Seth
    F1820. Hilten, Seth
255 Tilton, Richard
    F1820. Tilten, Richard
260 Starnater, John
    1818. Starnatur, John
    F1820. Starnater, John
261 Chafin, Ellis
    1818. Chaffin, Ellis
    F1820. Chaffin, Ellis

CENSUS OF WAYNE COUNTY, 1820

Wayne County State of Illenois	Free white Males under 21 to 21	Free white Males of 21 & upwards 21 & C.	Free white females under 21 to 21	Free white females of 21 & upwards 21 & C.	Slaves Males	Females of Slaves	Free Males of Colour	Free Females of Colour
[1 ‡] Mrs Anna Blesset	6	2		1				
[2 ‡] George Close	3	2	4	1				
[3 ‡] William Watkins	5	1	3	1				
[4 ‡] Michael Turney	1	3	1	1				
[5 ‡] Isaiah Turney	1		1					
[6 ‡] Isaac pickering	3	2	2	1				
[7 ‡] Daniel T. Gray	1	2	5	1				
[8 ‡] Solomon Stone	1	1	2	1				
[9 ‡] Archable Roberts	3	3	2	1				
[10 ‡] John Coonrod	1	1	1	1				
[11 ‡] James Taylor	6	1	2	1				
[12 ‡] James Gash		1	1	1				
[13 ‡] John Slocumb	1	1	1	1				
[14 ‡] Samuel Slocumb	5	3	3	2				
[15 ‡] Clariden Hoopper	1	2	1	1				
[16 ‡] Ephraim Merrit	3	2	5	1				
[17 ‡] William Simson Snr	1		1	1				
[18 ‡] Tolliver Simson	2	1	1	1				
[19 ‡] Rober Gray	1	1	1					
[20 ‡] William Simson Snr	1	1	1	1				
[21 ‡] Carmi Wells	2	1	2	1				
[22 ‡] Hatch & McCawley	1	4						
[23 ‡] John Dorrity	1	1	1					
[24 ‡] James Turner	3	1	4	1				
[25 ‡] Nathan Harris	2	1		2				
[26 ‡] Eligah Harris	2	1	3	1				
[27 ‡] Robert Jones	2	4	2	2				
[28 ‡] John Walker	3	1	5	1				
[29 ‡] Samuel T. Lock		1	1	1				

Figures and symbols preceding names have been supplied by the editor:
‡Indicates name also in Federal Census for 1820.

CENSUS OF 1820

WAYNE COUNTY (Continued)

No.	Names of heads of families	White males under 21	White males 21 & upwards	White females under 21	White females 21 & upwards	Male slaves	Female slaves	Free males of color	Free females of color
[30 ‡]	Richard Lock	3	1	3	1				
[31 ‡]	William Green	2	1	1	1				
[32 ‡]	James Lock		1		1				
[33 ‡]	Jobe Chapman		1		1				
[34 ‡]	George W Faris	2	2	3	1				
[35 ‡]	James Bird	2	1	5	1				
[36 ‡]	James Fitchgerral	2	1						
[37 ‡]	thomas Flutcher	2	1	1	1				
[38 ‡]	Samuel McNeil		1		1				
[39 ‡]	George Borah	3	2	1	1				
[40 ‡]	Enoch Nevils	1	1	3	1				
[41 ‡]	Richard Berks	6	2	2	1				
[42 ‡]	Harmon Horn	1	1	3	1				
[43 ‡]	Hiram Shores		1		1				
[44 ‡]	Reuben Shores	1	1	1	1				
[45 ‡]	Aquilla McCracken	6	2	2	1				
[46 ‡]	Pullem Hickenbottom	1	1	1	1				
[47 ‡]	John Hunt		1	1	1				
[48 ‡]	Jesse Johnson	5	1	2	1				
[49 ‡]	William Jones	1	1	2					
[50 ‡]	John Brown	1	1		1				
[51 ‡]	William Batson	1	1	2					
[52 ‡]	Walter Owen	2	2	2	2				
[53 ‡]	Nathan Owen		1	1					
[54 ‡]	Andrew Crews	2	2	1	1				
[55 ‡]	Joseph Martin		1	1					
[56 ‡]	Thomas Ellet		1	1	1				
[57 ‡]	James B. Martin	5	2	2	1				
[58 ‡]	James Ramsey	2	1	3	1				
[59 ‡]	James Stephenson	4	1	2	1				
[60 ‡]	Martin Cantwell	1	1	1	2				
[61 ‡]	James Butler	2	1	1	1				
[62 ‡]	Robert Gaston		1	2	1				
[63 ‡]	John Carson	3	2	3	1				
[64 ‡]	James Shaw	4	1	2	1				

WAYNE COUNTY (Continued)

No.	Names of heads of families	White males under 21	White males 21 & upwards	White females under 21	White females 21 & upwards	Male slaves	Female slaves	Free males of color	Free females of color
[65 ‡]	David Wright	2	1	1	1				
[66 ‡]	Jonathan Wright	1	1	2	1				
[67 ‡]	Andrew Wright	2	1		1				
[68 ‡]	George Turner	3	1	4	1				
[69 ‡]	William B. Davis		1	4	1				
[70 ‡]	Mrs Anna Barnhill	5	4		2				
[71 ‡]	Charles Hartgroves		1	2	1				
[72 ‡]	Joseph Hefferd	1	1		1				
[73 ‡]	James & George Jesseps		2						
[74 ‡]	A. Sanfrey & Graham		3	1	1				
[75 ‡]	William Elledge	2	1	1	1				
[76 ‡]	Drewery Young	1	1		1				
[77 ‡]	Daniel Elledge		1		1				
[78 ‡]	Isaac Elledge		3	3	1				
[79 ‡]	John Yong	1	1	4	1				
[80 ‡]	Hew Steward	1	1	1	1				
[81 ‡]	William Warren		1	4	1				
[82 ‡]	James Warren	1	1	6	1				
[83 ‡]	John Livergood	2	3		1				
[84 ‡]	Elliot Lacy		1	1	1				
[85 ‡]	John Bovee	2	1	4	1				
[86 ‡]	Charles W. Harrington		1	3	1				
[87 ‡]	John Elledge	1	2		1				
[88 ‡]	Walton & White	1	2	1	1				
[89 ‡]	John S. Huse Snr		2	1	1				
[90 ‡]	Daniel Bain Snr	3	3	4					
[91 ‡]	Benjamin Sumpter	1	1	2	1				
[92 ‡]	Robert H. Morris	1	2	2	1				
[93 ‡]	Unnah Wells	5	2	3	2				
[94 ‡]	Joseph Danforth	1	1	2					
[95 ‡]	George Burns		1	2	1				
[96 ‡]	Tiry Roberson	1	1		1				
[97 ‡]	John Taylor	3	1	2	1				
[98 ‡]	Alexander Clark	2	1	2	1				
[99 ‡]	Isaac Harris	3	1	5	1				
[100 ‡]	James Clark		1		2				

CENSUS OF 1820

WAYNE COUNTY (Continued)

No.	Names of heads of families	White males under 21	White males 21 & upwards	White females under 21	White females 21 & upwards	Male slaves	Female slaves	Free males of color	Free females of color
[101 ‡]	James Gaston	4	2	2	2				
[102 ‡]	Ruben Melton		1		1				
[103 ‡]	Robert R. Gaston	2	1	1	1				
[104 ‡]	John Hall	2	1	1	1				
[105 ‡]	Andrew Hall		1	2	1				
[106 ‡]	Henry Hall	5	1	1	1				
[107 ‡]	Seth Cason	2	1	2	2				
[108 ‡]	Henry Tilor	2	2	3	1				
[109 ‡]	John Johnson	3	1	1	1				
[110 ‡]	Ruben S. Spencer	1	2		1				
[111 ‡]	George T. Blesset	2	3	3	1				
[112 ‡]	Elkanah Bramlet	1	1	2					
[113 ‡]	Anthoney B. Turney	1	1	3	1				
[114 ‡]	James Clark snr	1	2	1					
[115 ‡]	Thomas Lee	2	1	2	1				
[116 ‡]	Stephen Coonrod		1	2					
[117 ‡]	James Ewing		1	1	1				
[118 ‡]	Henry Martin	1	2	1	1				
[119 ‡]	George Baugh	2	1		1				
[120 ‡]	Joseph Martin	4	1	4	1				
[121 ‡]	Owen Martin	2	1	1	1				
[122 ‡]	John B. Gash	3	1	2	1				
[123 ‡]	John Owen		1	1					
[124]	thomas Bradshaw	5	1	3	1				
[125 ‡]	John Pritchet	1	1	3	1				
[126 ‡]	Enoch Beech	3	2	1	1				
[127 ‡]	Richard Hall	2	1	1	1				
[128 ‡]	Mrs Susannah King	2		3	1				
[129 ‡]	William Russell	2	1	1	1				
[130 ‡]	Andrew Carson	2	2		1				
[131 ‡]	Nediam Hilliard		2		1				
[132 ‡]	William Clark		1	1	1				
[133 ‡]	Solomon Clark	1	1	3					
[134 ‡]	John Clark	2	1	2	1				
[135 ‡]	Andrew Clark	2	1	2	1				
[136 ‡]	Alferd Hall	1	1	1					

WAYNE COUNTY (Continued)

No.	Names of heads of families	White males under 21	White males 21 & upwards	White females under 21	White females 21 & upwards	Male slaves	Female slaves	Free males of color	Free females of color
[137 ‡]	David Hall	3	1	1	1				
[138 ‡]	John Lofton	1	1	1	1				
[139 ‡]	Caleb Ridgeway	5	2	3	2				
[140 ‡]	John Borah	2	1	1	1				
[141 ‡]	William Farley	4	1	1	1				
[142 ‡]	William Whitford		1	4	1				
[143 ‡]	Samuel Davison	2	2	5	2				
[144 ‡]	William Miller		1	1	1				
[145 ‡]	Issebell thrasher	3	1	4	2				2
[146 ‡]	Elexander Ramsey	2	1	2	1				
[147 ‡]	Elexander Neesbt	2	1	2	1				
[148 ‡]	Sarah Mcquorter	2		3	1				
[149 ‡]	Anthoney Street	4	1	3	2				
[150 ‡]	Samuel McCracken	3	3	6	3				
[151 ‡]	James Sanders	1	1		1				
[152 ‡]	John McCracken		1	1	1				
[153 ‡]	Daniel Brumley	4	1	2	1				
[154 ‡]	phillip Devore		1	3	2				
[155 ‡]	Sebaston Catt	2	1	4	1				
[156 ‡]	Aron Evins	2	1	1	3				
[157 ‡]	phillip Gatewood	3	1	3	1				
[158 ‡]	Richard Lewis		1	2	1				
[159 ‡]	John McCawley	2	1	3	1	3			
[160 ‡]	Daniel May		1	1	1				
[161 ‡]	John Melton	3	1		1				
[162 ‡]	George Sirkle	1	1	1					
[163 ‡]	thomas Elliot	2	1	3	1				
[164 ‡]	Mathias Misenhammer		3	1	1				
[165 ‡]	John G. Fitch	1	1	2	1				
[166 ‡]	Absolum Mounce	3	3	5	1				
[167 ‡]	William Lewis	3	2	1	1				
[168 ‡]	John Reatherford		2		1				
[169 ‡]	Joseph Clark		2	3	2				
[170 ‡]	Jesse Watson	6	1	4	1				
[171 ‡]	William Clark		1		1				
[172 ‡]	Andrew Bratton		2		1				

WAYNE COUNTY (Continued)

No.	Names of heads of families	White males under 21	White males 21 & upwards	White females under 21	White females 21 & upwards	Male slaves	Female slaves	Free males of color	Free females of color
[173 ‡]	Elsberry Armstrong	2	1	2	1				
[174 ‡]	Peter Staton	3	1	3	1				
[175 ‡]	Eligah Harland	3	1	1	1				
[176 ‡]	David Conner	1	1	3	1				
[177 ‡]	John Drew	2	1	2	1				
[178 ‡]	Edward Flatt	4	1	2	1				
[179 ‡]	Daniel Doddy	2	1	2	1				
[180 ‡]	Samuel Garrison	1	1	1	1				
[181 ‡]	David Garrison	2	1		1				
[182 ‡]	John Taylor	4	1	2	1				
[183 ‡]	Alanson doddy	5	1	2	1				
[184 ‡]	Elisha Esstes		1	1	1				
[185 ‡]	Robert D. Cates	3	1	1	1				
[186 ‡]	James Stanley	1	1	1	1				
[187 ‡]	Ignatious Jones	1	1	2	1				
[188 ‡]	George Russell	1	1	1	1				
[189 ‡]	thomas Cox	4	1	1	1				
[190 ‡]	Daniel Kenchalow	2	1	3	1				
[191 ‡]	Alex. Campbell	3	2	1	2				
[192 ‡]	John Turney	3	1	1	2				
	Total Amount 1144	353	253	343	195		3		2

November 28 1820   1144

ENOCH WILCOX

Corrected totals:

Free white males under 21 years	349
Free white males of 21 years and upwards	254
Free white females under 21 years	344
Free white females of 21 years and upwards	195
	1142
Negroes	5

Female slaves 3
Free persons of color 2
                        —
                        5

Total 1147

WAYNE COUNTY (Concluded)

Wayne County was a part of Edwards County until 1819 so the first census returns are those for 1820. Enoch Wilcox took both the state and federal census for 1820, dating both November 28. Aside from minor variations of spelling the only difference between the names is that Benjamin Phillpott, a free white male between the ages of 26 and 45, is given in place of Thomas Bradshaw (124) with his family of ten.

Discrepancies are as follows:

13 Slocumb, John
   F1820. Slocumb, John S.
16 Merrit, Ephraim
   F1820. Meret, Ephraim
17 Simson, William, Sr.
   F1820. Simpson, William, Sr.
18 Simson, Tolliver
   F1820. Simson, Toliver
19 Gray, Rober
   F1820. Gray, Robert S.
20 Simson, William, Sr.
   F1820. Simpson, William, Sr.
38 McNeil, Samuel
   F1820. McNeel, Samuel
40 Nevils, Enoch
   F1820. Neavel, Enoch
44 Shores, Reuben
   F1820. Shores, Ruben
55 Martin, Joseph
   F1820. Martin, Joseph, Sr.
56 Ellet, Thomas
   F1820. Elliot, Thomas
59 Stephenson, James
   F1820. Stepheson, James

74 Sanfrey, A. & Graham
   F1820. Sanfrey & Graham
79 Yong, John,
   F1820. Young, John
85 Bovee, John
   F1820. Bove, John
89 Huse, John S., Sr.
   F1820. Huse, John S.
98 Clark, Alexander
   F1820. Clark, Elexander
116 Coonrod, Stephen
   F1820. Coon Red, Stephen
120 Martin, Joseph
   F1820. Martin, Joseph, Sr.
131 Hilliard, Nediam
   F1820. Hillard, Nedian
147 Neesbt, Elexander
   F1820. Neesbet, Elexander
164 Misenhammer, Mathias
   F1820. Misen Hammer
184 Esstes, Elisha
   F1820. Estes, Elisha
191 Campbell, Alex.
   F1820. Cambbell, Alexander

CENSUS OF WHITE COUNTY, 1820

A list of all citizens of all ages and sexes and color in the County of White in the State of Illinois Taken by Jesse C Lockwood commissioner appointed by the county commissioners court of White County In pursuance of an Act of the Legislature of this State entitled an act providing for Taking the census of the Inhabitants of the State of Illenois November 22d 1820.

Jesse C. Lockwood, Commissioner

White County Name of the Township		Names of Heads of Families	Free White Males 21 years & upwards	All other White Inhabitants	Free people of Colour	Servants or Slaves
Township of West	[1 ‡]	Jesse C. Lockwood	2	3		
	[2 ‡]	Alexander Hosick	1	1		
	[3*‡]	Seth Hargrave	1	3		1
	[4*‡]	William Hosick	2	3		
	[5*‡]	Akillis Pierson	1	6		
	[6*‡]	Peter Miller	2	9		
	[7 ‡]	Robert Miller	1	2		
	[8 ‡]	Thomas Fields	1	4		
	[9*‡]	James Rutledge	1	8		
	[10 ‡]	Henry Davis	1	4		
	[11*‡]	William Rutledge	1	6		
	[12*‡]	Alexander Mahan	1	5		
	[13*‡]	Robert Story	1	9		
	[14*‡]	George Story Senr.	1	1		
	[15 ‡]	John Story	1	4		
	[16*‡]	John McLallan	1	5		
	[17 ‡]	Samuel McLallan	2	3		
	[18 ‡]	William McLallan	1	2		
	[19 ‡]	Andrew Nation	1	1		
	[20 ‡]	John Nation	1	1		
	[21*‡]	Andrew Story	1	6		
	[22 ‡]	Thomas Right	1	8		
	[23*‡]	George Story Junr.	1	4		
	[24 ‡]	Robert Wilson	1	6		
	[25 ‡]	Abel Rice	1	4		
	[26 ‡]	William Emmerson	1	8		

Figures and symbols preceding names have been supplied by the editor:
‡ Indicates name also in Federal Census for 1820.
* Indicates name also in State Census for 1818.

WHITE COUNTY (*Continued*)

Township	No.	Heads of families	White males 21 & upwards	All other white	Free people of color	Servants or slaves
	[27 ‡]	Ransom Hall	2	6		
	[28 ‡]	Jacob Davis	2	3		
	[29 ‡]	Resin Hall	1	2		
	[30 ‡]	Loch Phipps	1	7		
	[31 ‡]	John Bruce	1	2		
	[32 ‡]	Fielding Snider	1	6		
	[33*‡]	John Snider	2	8		
	[34 ‡]	John Gott	2	9		2
	[35 ‡]	William Rhodes	1	4		
	[36*‡]	Samuel Spillman	1	3		
	[37 ‡]	Richard Collard	2	11		
	[38 ‡]	Jacob Riley	1	4		
	[39 ‡]	John Morse	1	1		
	[40*‡]	James Martin	1	7		
	[41*‡]	Josiah Carter	1	8		
	[42 ‡]	Henry Bugg	1	1		
	[43*‡]	Henry Morgan	1	7		
	[44*‡]	Isaac Blag	1	4		
	[45 ‡]	Moses B Garner	1	3		
	[46 ‡]	Benjamin Brockett	1	9		
	[47 ‡]	Elisha White	1	2		
	[48 ‡]	Jonathan Parker	1	8		
	[49 ‡]	John Martin	2	6		
	[50*‡]	Isaac Shelby	1	7		
	[51*‡]	Francis Smith	1	2		
	[52 ‡]	George King	1	1		
	[53 ‡]	Thomas Brockett	1	4		
	[54 ‡]	Henry Wakefield	1	3		1
	[55*‡]	Green Baker	1	6		
	[56 ‡]	Polly McIntyre		7		
	[57*‡]	Peter Steel	1	8		
	[58 ‡]	Joseph Welsh	1	5		
	[59*‡]	John Funkhouser	2	6	1	3
	[60*‡]	Young Funkhouser	1	4		
	[61 ‡]	Jonathan Rose	1	2		
	[62*‡]	James Grey	4	5		3
	[63 ‡]	John H Jones	1			
	[64*‡]	Willis Hargrave	3	8		10

WHITE COUNTY (Continued)

Township	No.	Heads of families	White males 21 & upwards	All other white	Free people of color	Servants or slaves
	[65*‡]	James Ratcliff	3	5		5
	[66 ‡]	Josiah Stewart	1	3		
	[67 ‡]	John Grant	1	13		
	[68 ‡]	Hugh W Weed	9	7		
	[69 ‡]	Richard Graham	1	1		1
	[70 ‡]	John Smith	1			
	[71 ‡]	John B Paillie	2	2		
	[72 ‡]	Simeon Smith	1	1		
	[73 ‡]	Joseph Jackson	1	1		
	[74 ‡]	William B. McClean	9	3		2
	[75 ‡]	Jarvis Pierce	1	8		
	[76*‡]	John Ridgway	1	8		
	[77 ‡]	William Rearden	1	1		
	[78 ‡]	James Foley	2	6		
	[79 ‡]	John Lee	1	3		
	[80 ‡]	Samuel C Knapp	3	1		
	[81*‡]	John Craw	9	6		
	[82 ‡]	Josiah Fulford	1	7		
	[83*‡]	Daniel Hay	2	7		
	[84 ‡]	Francis Duffey	2			
	[85 ‡]	Andrew Eply	1	1		
	[86 ‡]	John Collins	1	4		
	[87*‡]	Samuel Hargrave	1	5		
	[88*‡]	Isaac Veatch	1	5		
	[89*‡]	Matthew Parks	1	3		
	[90 ‡]	Joshua Fields	1	7		
	[91*‡]	Elias Veatch	1	6		
	[92*‡]	John Forgison	1	4		
	[93 ‡]	Sidney North	1	6		
	[94*‡]	William Fields	1	4		
	[95*‡]	William Davidson	1	7		
	[96*‡]	Thomas Rutledge	2	9		
	[97 ‡]	James S. McLin	1	3		
	[98*‡]	James Miller	1	7		
	[99 ‡]	David W McLin	1	5		
	[100*‡]	James Mayes	1	3		
	[101*‡]	James Veatch	1	3		
	[102*‡]	John Veatch	1	3		

WHITE COUNTY (Continued)

Township	No.	Heads of families	White males 21 & upwards	All other white	Free people of color	Servants or slaves
	[103*‡]	Christopher Nation	1	10		
	[104*‡]	Isaac Logan	1	4		
	[105 ‡]	Robert Gowdy	1	9		
	[106*‡]	Thomas Garrison	1	4		
	[107 ‡]	Elizabeth Ramsey		6		
	[108*‡]	Matthew Wilson	2	7		
	[109*‡]	John B Wilson	1	5		
	[110 ‡]	Joel Herald	2	7		
	[111*‡]	Thomas Cameron	2	8		
	[112*‡]	Robert Hawthorn	2	2		
	[113 ‡]	Bartholomew McCan	1	7		
	[114 ‡]	John Montgomery	1	3		
	[115 ‡]	William Glasgow	1	5		
	[116 ‡]	Benjamin Cannon	1	3		
	[117 ‡]	Daniel Alexander	1	2		
	[118*‡]	Joshua Riggin	1	5		
	[119*‡]	James Shipley	1	7		
	[120 ‡]	Thomas R Ezell	1	7		
	[121 ‡]	William Hauze	1	2		
	[122 ‡]	John Ooley	1	5		
	[123*‡]	Henry Ooley	1	2		
	[124*‡]	George Berry	1	6		
	[125 ‡]	Heny Sumpter	1	1		
	[126*‡]	John Graham	1	7		
	[127*‡]	Adam Dosher	1	4		
	[128*‡]	Canaba Stevens	2	5		
	[129 ‡]	William Stevens	1	2		
	[130*‡]	Noah Stevens	1	3		
	[131 ‡]	Edmond Roberts	1	4		
	[132*‡]	John Hanes	1	7		
	[133 ‡]	Elizabeth Dosher		3		
	[134*‡]	John Barber	1	4		
	[135 ‡]	Jacob Denahoo	1	2		
	[136 ‡]	Susanna Cary		7		
	[137 ‡]	Adam Dosher	1	6		
	[138 ‡]	Michael Row	1	4		
	[139*‡]	Simon Newman	3	3		
	[140*‡]	Samuel Craig	2	10		3

CENSUS OF 1820

WHITE COUNTY (Continued)

Township	No.	Heads of families	White males 21 & upwards	All other white	Free people of color	Servants or slaves
	[141 ‡]	Samuel Bigerstaff	1	8		
	[142 ‡]	John Smith	1	2		
	[143 ‡]	Martin Jackson	1	8		
	[144*‡]	Asa Ross	2	4		
	[145*‡]	Joel Berry	1	2		
	[146 ‡]	David Burrell	1	3		
	[147*‡]	Thomas Forsythe	1	5		
	[148*‡]	Enoch Berry	2	8		
	[149*‡]	Jeremiah Hargrave	1	2		
	[150*‡]	David Shelby	1	1		2
	[151 ‡]	Solomon Bleu	4	5		1
	[152*‡]	Mordica S. Hamilton	1	6		
	[153 ‡]	Leonard White	3	3		2
	[154 ‡]	James Wilson	4	4		1
	[155 ‡]	George Walts	3	4		
	[156 ‡]	James Hobbs	1	2		
	[157 ‡]	William Hobbs	1	1		
	[158 ‡]	William Brown	1	2		
	[159 ‡]	John Vanzant	1	3		
	[160*‡]	John Lane	1	4		
	[161*‡]	John Starkey	1	6		
	[162 ‡]	Absolem Sawyer	1	7		
	[163 ‡]	Casada B. Williams	1	1		
	[164 ‡]	John Husk	1	4		
	[165 ‡]	Archibald Satterlee	1	2		
	[166 ‡]	Robert Satterlee	1	2		
	[167*‡]	Pierce Hawley	2	4		
	[168 ‡]	Oliver Stafford	1	5		
	[169 ‡]	John Patten	1	1		
	[170*‡]	David Upton	1	9		
	[171 ‡]	William Ferrel	3	3		
	[172 ‡]	Isaac McBroom	2	6		
	[173 ‡]	James Lassater	1	5		
	[174 ‡]	Lemuel Miller	1	2		
	[175*‡]	Francis Miller	2	2		
	[176 ‡]	William Miller	1	4		
	[177 ‡]	Nancy Lee		5		
	[178 ‡]	Lemuel Kennel	1			

WHITE COUNTY (Continued)

Township	No.	Heads of families	White males 21 & upwards	All other white	Free people of color	Servants or slaves
	[179 ‡]	Robert Wilson	1	2		
	[180 ‡]	Claton Fuller	1	8		
	[181 ‡]	Robin Porter	1	6		
	[182 ‡]	John D Calvert	1	3		
	[183*‡]	James Garrison	1	6		
	[184*‡]	Frederick Parmer	1	6		2
	[185 ‡]	William Foley	1	3		
	[186*‡]	William Parmer	1	4		
	[187*‡]	Absolem Garrison	1	8		
	[188 ‡]	William Husk	1	4		
	[189 ‡]	Robert Smith	1	2		
	[190*‡]	Walter Garner	5	4		
	[191 ‡]	Phillip J Halman	4	3		1
	[192*‡]	William Barns	1	5		
	[193 ‡]	Cornelius Vanzant	1	2		
	[194 ‡]	John Holiby	1	6		
	[195*‡]	Charles Cato	1	4		1
	[196 ‡]	James H Drew	2	1		
	[197 ‡]	Samuel Bozeman	2	5		
	[198 ‡]	George Newman	1	1		
	[199*‡]	William Caine	2	5		
	[200 ‡]	Thomas Hopson	2	4		
	[201 ‡]	Samuel Sexton	1	7		
	[202 ‡]	Robert Tinsley	2	5		
	[203 ‡]	William Dukes	1	2		
	[204*‡]	Edmond W Badger	1	5		
	[205*‡]	David Calvert	1	6		
	[206 ‡]	John Upton	1	11		
	[207*‡]	John Armstrong	1	11		
	[208*‡]	Moses Carlock	1	5		
	[209 ‡]	Joseph Bosarth	1	3		
	[210 ‡]	Elizabeth Jackson		4		
	[211*‡]	Lewis Green	1	1		
	[212*‡]	Charles Williams	1	2		
	[213 ‡]	David Shelby	1	3		
	[214*‡]	Thomas Wicker	1	8		
	[215 ‡]	Phillip Bartlet	1	4		
	[216*‡]	William Hunt	6			

CENSUS OF 1820

WHITE COUNTY (Continued)

Township	No.	Heads of families	White males 21 & upwards	All other white	Free people of color	Servants or slaves
Township North of West	[217*‡]	Elisha Gorden	1	3		
	[218 ‡]	David Procter	2	7		
	[219*‡]	George Cricel	1	9		
	[220*‡]	Isaac Hill	2	6		
	[221 ‡]	Benjamin Auxer	1	2		
	[222*‡]	Joseph Waller	1	8		
	[223*‡]	Charles Heard	1	5		
	[224 ‡]	Moses Bond	1	2		
	[225 ‡]	Moses Shearley	2	11		
	[226*‡]	Ennis Malden	3	5		
	[227 ‡]	Andrew Boyd	1	5		
	[228 ‡]	Henry Boyd	1	8		
	[229 ‡]	Hannah Garvin		3		
	[230*‡]	Nimrod Shearly	1	6		
	[231*‡]	John Gore	2	4		
	[232*‡]	William Hungate	1	7		
	[233 ‡]	Jacob Coffman	1	9		
	[234 ‡]	John Flint	1	2		
	[235*‡]	Jordan Vance	1	6		
	[236*‡]	Hiram Hodges	1	7		
	[237*‡]	Thomas Thompson	1	5		
	[238*‡]	John Minnus	1	4		
	[239 ‡]	Chester Carpenter	1	2		
	[240 ‡]	Jesse Balze	1			
	[241 ‡]	John Vance	1	1		
	[242*‡]	Andrew Vance	1	8		
	[243 ‡]	James More	1	2		
	[244 ‡]	John More	1	3		
	[245 ‡]	James Gibson	4	3		
	[246*‡]	Charles Hurd	1	5		
	[247*‡]	John Hardister	3	5		
	[248 ‡]	John Burton	1	1		
	[249*‡]	John Bishop	1	8		
	[250*‡]	John Townsend	1	4		
	[251 ‡]	Stephen Hurd	1	6		
	[252*‡]	Thomas Smith	1	3		
	[253 ‡]	Redman Perrey	1	9		
	[254*‡]	Elijah Parker	2	4		

WHITE COUNTY (Continued)

Township	No.	Heads of families	White males 21 & upwards	All other white	Free people of color	Servants or slaves
	[255 ‡]	Samuel Smith	1	12		
	[256*‡]	Robert More	1	2		
	[257*‡]	Jeremiah More	1	13		
	[258 ‡]	Samuel Vance	1	9		
	[259 ‡]	Lee Malden	1	3		
	[260*‡]	William Veatch	1	1		
	[261*‡]	Ambrose Malden	1	10		1
	[262*‡]	John Dale	1	7		
	[263*‡]	James Malden	1	5		
	[264 ‡]	Samuel Deats	1	3		
	[265 ‡]	Ralph Hatch	2			
	[266 ‡]	John Carter	1	5		
	[267 ‡]	Henry Webb	1	8		
	[268 ‡]	Henry Christle	2	8		
	[269 ‡]	Richard W Smith	1	5		
	[270*‡]	John Anderson	1	6		
	[271 ‡]	Richard Lock	1	6		
	[272 ‡]	Jonas Lock	1	1		
	[273*‡]	John Griffeth	1	5		
	[274 ‡]	Maston Bond	1	8		
	[275 ‡]	Thomas Sloo Jur.	3	2		2
	[276 ‡]	Daniel Burbanks	1	7		
	[277 ‡]	John Daly	1	11		
	[278 ‡]	John Warfield	1	3		
	[279*‡]	Gerrard Trammel	2	12		1
	[280*‡]	John B Cumpton	1	10		
	[281 ‡]	Mary Green	2	2		
	[282*‡]	James Flemming	1	3		
	[283*‡]	Elijah Kimzey	1	2		
	[284 ‡]	David Kimzey	1	5		
	[285 ‡]	Littlepage Procter	1	5		
	[286 ‡]	Fanny Stevens	1	6		
	[287 ‡]	John Procter	1	1		
	[288*‡]	William Wheeler Senr.	1	10		
	[289 ‡]	Abner Pierce	1	2		
	[290 ‡]	Merril Willis	1	5		
	[291 ‡]	Lewis Lane	2	4		
	[292 ‡]	Henry Wheeler	1	1		

WHITE COUNTY (Continued)

Township	No.	Heads of families	White males 21 & upwards	All other white	Free people of color	Servants or slaves
	[293 ‡]	Adam Richey	1	2		
	[294*‡]	Jesse Hyatt	1	6		
	[295*‡]	James Phipps	1	3		
	[296*‡]	William Wheeler Jur.	4	7		
	[297 ‡]	James Hall	1	1		
	[298 ‡]	William Hall	1	7		
	[299 ‡]	Townsend Talton	1	4		
	[300 ‡]	Sally Gatlin	1	3		
	[301*‡]	Edward Gatlin	1	3		
	[302 ‡]	Robert Anderson	1	2		
	[303 ‡]	James Lane	1	7		
	[304 ‡]	Jeremiah McNemar	1	5		
	[305 ‡]	Joseph Procter	1	2		
Township	[306*‡]	Samuel Hog	1	4		
South of	[307 ‡]	Stephen Parker	1	2		
West	[308 ‡]	Joseph Sweet	2	3		
	[309 ‡]	Theophilus Sweet	2	7		
	[310 ‡]	Benjamin Phipps	1	8		
	[311*‡]	Isaac Johnson	1	7		
	[312 ‡]	Jacob Brady	1	1		
	[313 ‡]	John Johnson	2	6		
	[314 ‡]	Drewry Thompson	1	3		
	[315 ‡]	William Sweeten	2	7		
	[316 ‡]	Robert Sweet	1	6		
	[317 ‡]	Pelick Sweet	1	7		
	[318 ‡]	Gilbert Grizzel	1	4		
	[319*‡]	Randolph Smith	1	7		
	[320 ‡]	James Henceson	1	7		
	[321 ‡]	Isaac Baits	1	4		
	[322*‡]	John Wilson	1	5		
	[323*‡]	Jacob Barker	2	8		
	[324 ‡]	Isaac Jewett	1	5		
	[325*‡]	William Hardister	2	5		
Moved out of the County Since the 1st day of August	[326*‡]	Elijah Mayfield	2	6		
	[327 ‡]	Michael Crose	1	2		
	[328 ‡]	James Crose	1	2		
	[329 ‡]	John Crose	1	3		
	[330 ‡]	Phillip Crose	1	6		

WHITE COUNTY (Continued)

Township	No.	Heads of families	White males 21 & upwards	All other white	Free people of color	Servants or slaves
Could not find him no Road	[331 ‡]	Isaac Mayfield	1	1		
	[332 ‡]	Nathaniel Gholtson	1	5		
I could not find him no Road	[333*‡]	George Nichols	1	7		
	[334 ‡]	Adonjah Grinds	1	2		
	[335 ‡]	Daniel Scott	1	3		
	[336 ‡]	Thomas Holaway	1	5		
	[337 ‡]	John Dragoo	1	10		
	[338*‡]	George McKenzie	1	6		
	[339 ‡]	Lewis Howell	1	7		
	[340 ‡]	George Hand	1	9		
	[341*‡]	William Watson	1	7		
	[342*‡]	James Watson	1	4		
	[343*‡]	Robert Watson	1	4		
	[344 ‡]	Hiram Greathouse	1	2		
	[345 ‡]	John Cook	1	2		
	[346 ‡]	Daniel Powell	1	3		
	[347*‡]	John Stone	2	4		
	[348 ‡]	Rebecca Grose		4		
	[349 ‡]	Frederick Maberry Senr.	1	11		
	[350*‡]	Jesse Maberry	1	3		
	[351*‡]	Willis Wheeler	2	6		
	[352*‡]	Solomon Maberry	1	5		
	[353 ‡]	Frederick Maberry Jur.	1	1		
	[354*‡]	David Maberry	1	6		
	[355*‡]	Frederick Maberry	1	8		

WHITE COUNTY (Continued)

Township	No.	Heads of families	White males 21 & upwards	All other white	Free people of color	Servants or slaves
Mantua	[356 ‡]	Solomon Crose	1	8		
	[357 ‡]	Zacheriah Cook	1	2		
	[358 ‡]	Edward Ferris	1	5		
	[359 ‡]	Samuel Barker	1	1		
	[360 ‡]	Alexander Douglas	1	9		
	[361 ‡]	Stephen McGeehee	1	4		
	[362*‡]	Charles Cook	1	6		
	[363*‡]	Walter McCoy	1	2		
	[364*‡]	Robert Davis	1	6		
	[365 ‡]	Bennet Hargrave	1	4		
	[366 ‡]	John Boler Jack	1	3		
	[367 ‡]	Joel Boler Jack	1	3		
	[368 ‡]	William Forrister	1	5		
	[369 ‡]	William Debord	1	6		
	[370 ‡]	Robert Yates	1	9		
	[371*‡]	Robert Bruce	1	5		
	[372 ‡]	Thomas Johnson	1	5		
	[373 ‡]	Samuel Hill	1	6		
	[374*‡]	Jacob Forrister	1	2		
	[375 ‡]	John Forrister	1	4		
	[376 ‡]	Cader Herald	1	3		
	[377*‡]	John McMurty	1	5		
	[378*‡]	Henry McMurty	1	5		
	[379 ‡]	William Eubanks	2	4		
	[380 ‡]	Reubin Bellaugh	1	6		
	[381 ‡]	Robert Davis	1	6		
	[382*‡]	John Vineyard	1	4		
	[383 ‡]	Solomon Debord	1	3		
	[384 ‡]	Wiley Trusty	1	1		
	[385*‡]	William Jordan	1	6		
	[386*‡]	William Davis	1	7		
	[387 ‡]	Thomas Toberry	1	4		
	[388*‡]	John Lamb	3	5		
	[389*‡]	Solomon Brill	1	7		
	[390*‡]	William McGehee Senr	1	3		
	[391*‡]	Isaac Satterfield	1	5		
	[392*‡]	William McGeehee Junr	1	7		

WHITE COUNTY (Continued)

Township	No.	Heads of families	White males 21 & upwards	All other white	Free people of color	Servants or slaves
	[393 ‡]	Jacob Phelps	1	5		
	[394 ‡]	James Archer	1	6		
	[395 ‡]	William H Smith	2	2		
	[396 ‡]	John Archer	1	5		
	[397*‡]	George Satterfield	1	4		
	[398*‡]	George Satterfield, Junr.	1	5		
	[399 ‡]	Elisha McGeehee	1	7		
	[400*‡]	Alexander Trousdell	1	11		
	[401*‡]	James Trousdell	1	2		
	[402 ‡]	David Pierce	1	7		
	[403 ‡]	Charles Edwards	1	9		
	[404 ‡]	Jesse Mitchell	1	5		
	[405 ‡]	Susanna Walden		5		
	[406 ‡]	John Underwood	2	4		
	[407*‡]	Evens Johns	1	3		
	[408*‡]	Zepheniah Johns	1	5		
	[409 ‡]	Reubin Nelson	1	3		
	[410*‡]	Jesse Pierce	1	8		
	[411 ‡]	Moses Pierce Junr.	1	1		
	[412*‡]	Moses Pierce Senr.	1	2		
	[413*‡]	John S Patillo	1	6		
	[414 ‡]	James R Abner	2	4		
	[415*‡]	Elisha Hall	2	4		
	[416 ‡]	Abner More	1	3		
	[417 ‡]	Isaac Mason	1	8		
	[418 ‡]	Nathan Nall	1	3		
	[419 ‡]	Thomas Rossin	1	5		
	[420 ‡]	Richard Harris	1	2		
	[421 ‡]	Joseph Taylor	1	4		
	[422 ‡]	Robert Harris	1	4		
	[423 ‡]	James Trousdell	1	8		
	[424*‡]	Thomas Dagley	2	1		
	[425 ‡]	George Roderick	1	3		
	[426 ‡]	Isaac Johnson	1	8		
	[427 ‡]	Jonathan Hull	2	1		
	[428*‡]	Samuel Dagley	1	4		
	[429 ‡]	Isaac Alvin	1	3		
	[430*‡]	Joshua Alvin	1	3		

WHITE COUNTY (Continued)

Township	No.	Heads of families	White males 21 & upwards	All other white	Free people of color	Servants or slaves
	[431 ‡]	Beder Wood	1	6		
	[432 ‡]	William Culbreath	1	9		
	[433 ‡]	Joel Wells	1	1		
	[434*‡]	Merrit Tayler	1	4		
	[435 ‡]	Darius North	8	2		1
	[436*‡]	William Witherow	1	5		
	[437*‡]	William Harget	1	4		
	[438*‡]	Joshua Dewey	1	2		
	[439*‡]	William Tombs	2	4		
	[440 ‡]	George Logan	1	7		
	[441 ‡]	Adam Thompson	1	5		
	[442 ‡]	Thomas White	1	5		
	[443 ‡]	James Briant	1	2		
	[444*‡]	Samuel Chapman	2	6		
	[445 ‡]	Daniel Briant	1	7		
	[446 ‡]	Charles Lee	1	5		
	[447*‡]	George Long	2	3		
	[448 ‡]	William Willis	1	6		
	[449*‡]	John Carter	1	4		
	[450 ‡]	Richard Frier	1	4		
	[451 ‡]	Peter Oneal	1	1		
	[452*‡]	John Langford	1	7		
	[453 ‡]	Phillip Owens	1	1		
	[454 ‡]	William Nevit	1	10		
	[455 ‡]	Clemont Edlin	1	2		
	[456 ‡]	Joseph More	1	2		
	[457 ‡]	John C Trousdell	1	4		
	[458 ‡]	Jacob Heck	1	10		
	[459 ‡]	William Singleton	1	9		
	[460*‡]	George Naught	1	1		
	[461 ‡]	Francis Goltson	2	4		
	[462 ‡]	James Rensaw	1	1		
	[463 ‡]	Benjamin Goltson	1	3		
	[464*‡]	Isaac Naught	1	6		
	[465 ‡]	John Goltson	1	6		
	[466*‡]	Hezekiah Oneal	1	4		
	[467 ‡]	William Walker	1	6		
	[468*‡]	Hosey Pierce	1	3		

WHITE COUNTY (Continued)

Township	No.	Heads of families	White males 21 & upwards	All other white	Free people of color	Servants or slaves
	[469 ‡]	William Thompson	2	9		
	[470 ‡]	Robert Moody	1	6		
	[471 ‡]	Sarah Heady		5		
	[472*‡]	Benjamin Smith	1	7		
	[473 ‡]	Thomas Heady	1	1		
Waconteby	[474*‡]	John Sumpter	1	3		
	[475 ‡]	Wallis Brown	1	1		
	[476*‡]	Manuel Madcalf	1	7		
	[477 ‡]	Isaac Schoolcraft	2	4		
	[478*‡]	Joseph Patten	2	4		
	[479 ‡]	Walter Times	1	2		
	[480*‡]	Isaac Funkhouser	2	8		
	[481*‡]	Christopher Young	1	8		
	[482*‡]	Christopher Funkhouser	2	3		
	[483 ‡]	John Shives	1	6		
	[484*‡]	John Gillison	2	7		
	[485 ‡]	Alexander Stewart	1	5		
	[486 ‡]	John Wiltsey	1	9		
	[487 ‡]	Frederick Wilmans	1	11		
	[488 ‡]	John Files Junr.	1	5		
	[489*‡]	John Files	1	5		
	[490 ‡]	Jesse Cravens	1	3		
	[491*‡]	Vincent Moreland	1	7		
	[492*‡]	Morgan Wallis	1	5		
	[493 ‡]	Thomas Hart	1	3		
	[494 ‡]	Jesse B. Day	1	2		
	[495*‡]	Henry Grimes	3	5		
	[496*‡]	William Files	1	4		
	[497*‡]	Peter Widows	3	10		
	[498 ‡]	Richard Arterbury	1	6		
	[499 ‡]	Elijah Harland	1	5		
	[500 ‡]	David W Ridgway	8			
	[501 ‡]	Green Lee	1	6		
	[502*‡]	William Ellis	1	5		
	[503 ‡]	William Green	2	10		
	[504*‡]	Henry Myers	1	6		
	[505 ‡]	Elizabeth Myers	1	4		1

WHITE COUNTY (Continued)

Township	No.	Heads of families	White males 21 & upwards	All other white	Free people of color	Servants or slaves
Priary	[506*‡]	Adam Crouch	5	2		
	[507 ‡]	James Clark	1	1		
	[508 ‡]	Benjamin Ellis	1	3	1	
	[509*‡]	Archibald Standifer	2	10		
	[510*‡]	John Myers	1	3		
	[511*‡]	Griffin Swords	1	7		
	[512*‡]	Robin Carlisle	1	3		
	[513 ‡]	John Edwards	1	6		
	[514 ‡]	Eli Waller	1	2		
	[515 ‡]	James Cann	1	3	1	
	[516*‡]	Abraham Auxer	1	6		
	[517 ‡]	Joseph Shelton	1	2		
	[518*‡]	Daniel McHenry	2	8		
	[519 ‡]	William Read	1	2		
	[520*‡]	Henry Jones	1	6		
	[521*‡]	Levi Morgan			2	
	[522 ‡]	Neptune Calvin			3	
	[523 ‡]	John H Courtney	1	4		
	[524*‡]	William McHenry	4	7		
	[525 ‡]	Ahira Jones	1	3		
	[526*‡]	Noah Kickendall	1	6		
	[527 ‡]	Matthew Jones			5	
	[528*‡]	George McCown Junr.	1	9		
	[529*‡]	George McCown	1	2		
	[530*‡]	Jesse Hubbard	2	5		
	[531 ‡]	John C Barnet	1	4		
	[532*‡]	Mulekiah Hubbard	1	3		
	[533*‡]	Archibald Farr	1	6		
	[534*‡]	Mary Blackford		6		
	[535*‡]	Nathaniel Blackford	2	4		
	[536 ‡]	George Hargrave	1	3		1
	[537 ‡]	Robert Buckels	2	2		
	[538*‡]	Aaron Williams	1	10		
	[539*‡]	Roly Williams	1	3		
	[540*‡]	Thomas Williams	1	5		
	[541 ‡]	John Elder	1	5		
	[542*‡]	Sarah Hood		6		
	[543*‡]	John Clark	1	9		

WHITE COUNTY (Continued)

Township	No.	Heads of families	White males 21 & upwards	All other white	Free people of color	Servants or slaves
	[544*‡]	James Hanna	2	1		
	[545*‡]	William B Allen	2	6		
	[546*‡]	Aaron Williams	1	4		
	[547 ‡]	John Colwell	2	10		
	[548*‡]	Joseph Pomroy	1	7		
	[549 ‡]	Robert Land	1	5		
	[550*‡]	William Vine	1	7		
	[551*‡]	Charles Mobly	1	4		
	[552 ‡]	John Madcalf	1	1		
	[553*‡]	John Hanna Senr.	1	8		
	[554*‡]	Alexander Hamilton	1	5		
	[555 ‡]	Benjamin Hauze	1	8		
	[556 ‡]	Benjamin Harvey	1	2		
	[557 ‡]	Benjamin R Smith	1	1		
	[558 ‡]	Hazzard Wilcox	2	5		
	[559*‡]	Thomas Maze	2	6		
	[560 ‡]	Harvey P Davison	1	4		
	[561 ‡]	William Childers	1	9		
	[562 ‡]	Alfred May	1	2		
	[563*‡]	James McCoy	2	8		
	[564*‡]	John E Anderson	1	5		
	[565*‡]	Thomas Logan	1	4		
	[566*‡]	Balem May	2	7		
	[567*‡]	Ann Bowye		1		
	[568*‡]	Benjamin Bryant	1	7		
	[569*‡]	William Robinson	1	9		
	[570 ‡]	Elijah Turner	1	8		
	[571*‡]	Willim Brown	1	6		
	[572 ‡]	John G Anderson	1	2		
	[573*‡]	William Merril	3	6		
	[574 ‡]	George Logan	1	6		
	[575*‡]	Alexander Logan	1	5		
	[576*‡]	James Garrison	1	9		
	[577*‡]	Edward D Hart	1	3		
	[578 ‡]	John Eastwood	1	4		
	[579 ‡]	David Eastwood	1	6		
	[580*‡]	William McKee	1	5		
	[581 ‡]	John Beck	1	4		

WHITE COUNTY (Continued)

Township	No.	Heads of families	White males 21 & upwards	All other white	Free people of color	Servants or slaves
	[582 ‡]	Frederick Cottenner	1	3		
	[583*‡]	Robert Shipley	1	6		
	[584 ‡]	John Shipley	1	1		
	[585 ‡]	Thomas Davis	1	2		
	[586 ‡]	Benjamin Beckus	2	5		
	[587 ‡]	Henry Hopewell	1	3		
	[588 ‡]	James Cliff	1	3		
	[589*‡]	Thomas McCollister	1	2		
	[590*‡]	Thomas Ezell	1	3		
	[591*‡]	John C Slocum	1	3		
	[592 ‡]	Stephen Beck	2	3		
	[593*‡]	Samuel Slocum	1	6		
	[594 ‡]	Gilbert Burcess			2	
	[595 ‡]	Charles Slocum	1	3		
	[596*‡]	John Baker	1	3		
	[597 ‡]	James Read	1	4		
	[598*‡]	Jacob Baker	1	3		
	[599*‡]	Thomas Thornbury	1	7		
	[600*‡]	Halbert Dosey	1	2		
	[601 ‡]	John Kiger	1	1		
	[602 ‡]	John Kiger Junr.	1	1		
	[603 ‡]	Elizabeth Stevens	1	5		
	[604 ‡]	Peter Vodris	1	4		
	[605*‡]	James Vodris	1	6		
	[606*‡]	John Read	4	7		
	[607*‡]	Cumstock Chapel	1			
	[608*‡]	Absolem Hurt	1	9		
	[609 ‡]	Abner Eastwood	2	2		
	[610 ‡]	John McCollister	1	2		
	[611*‡]	Ruth Smith		4		
	[612 ‡]	Adam Farley	1	7		
	[613*‡]	Carter Smith	1	2		
	[614*‡]	Edward McCollister	1	4		
	[615*‡]	Simon McCollister	2	3		
	[616*‡]	James McCollister	1	6		
	[617*‡]	Edward Farley	4	6		
	[618 ‡]	John Shinalt	1	3		
	[619 ‡]	Samuel McMullin	2	9		

WHITE COUNTY (Continued)

Township	No.	Heads of families	White males 21 & upwards	All other white	Free people of color	Servants or slaves
	[620 ‡]	Francis Farley	1	2		
	[621*‡]	John C. Craig	1	5		
	[622*‡]	John J Wilson	3	2		
	[623*‡]	Ervin Wilson	1	7		
	[624*‡]	Mary Walbert		3		
	[625*‡]	John Stevens	1	10		
	[626*‡]	Elam Stewart	2			
	[627*‡]	Thomas Southart	1	4		
	[628*‡]	Joseph Culberson	1	6		
	[629*‡]	Joseph Goodwin	1	1		
	[630*‡]	Elijah Goodwin	2	11		
	[631 ‡]	John Lesley	2	11		
	[632 ‡]	John Camel	1	5		
	[633*‡]	Joseph Burrel	2	6		
	[634*‡]	John Matthews	1	7		
	[635 ‡]	Abraham Richardson	1	1		
	[636*‡]	Adam Miller	1	6		
	[637 ‡]	Henry Miller	1	5		
	[638 ‡]	David Douthit	1	3		
	[639 ‡]	Cassandra Callahan		2		
	[640*‡]	Michael C Collins	1	5		
	[641*‡]	Jacob Bozeman	1	7		
	[642 ‡]	Samuel Long	2	2		
	[643 ‡]	Levi Williams	1	1		
	[644 ‡]	Prier Cottrell	1	5		
	[645*‡]	William Hood	2	5		
	[646*‡]	John Holland	1	3		
	[647 ‡]	Augustus Snider	1	6		
	[648 ‡]	Frederick Ruth	1			
	[649*‡]	Henry Sturn	3	3		
	[650*‡]	James Finley	1	3		
	[651 ‡]	William Pool	1	5		
	[652 ‡]	Phillip Sturn	1	3		
	[653*‡]	Arter Pool	1	7		
	[654*‡]	John Dennis	1	6		
	[655 ‡]	William Wilkins	1	2		
	[656 ‡]	Charles Sights	1			
	[657 ‡]	Thomas Robertson	1	3		

CENSUS OF 1820

WHITE COUNTY (Continued)

Township	No.	Heads of families	White males 21 & upwards	All other white	Free people of color	Servants or slaves
Fox River	[658*‡]	John McIntyre	1	2		
	[659 ‡]	Isaac Martin	2	3		
	[660*‡]	Abraham Griffith	1	2		
	[661 ‡]	William Grey	2	3		
	[662*‡]	Phillip Patten	1	7		
	[663*‡]	George Morris	1	3		
	[664*‡]	John Brown	1	3		
	[665*‡]	Daniel Brown	1	4		
	[666 ‡]	Stephen Colwell	1	4		
	[667 ‡]	Samuel T. Council	1	5		
	[668*‡]	Thomas Pool	1	1		
	[669*‡]	John Lucas	1	8		
	[670*‡]	Richard Graves	1	5		
	[671 ‡]	Nelson Graves	1	1		
	[672 ‡]	Samuel Hughs	1	4		
	[673*‡]	Jonathan Williams	1	7		
	[674*‡]	Isaac Drigger	1	2		
	[675 ‡]	Mark Stanley		4		
	[676*‡]	Samuel Hencely	1	7		
	[677 ‡]	Matthew Dockery	2	10		
	[678 ‡]	Joseph Craton	1	4		
	[679 ‡]	Reubin McHauz	1	6		
	[680*‡]	Absolem Driggers	2	4		
	[681*‡]	William Stanley	1	2		
	[682 ‡]	Benjamin Elliott	3	3		
	[683*‡]	Alexander Phillips	1	7		
	[684*‡]	Jesse Herring	1	4		
	[685 ‡]	Jonathan Stewart	1	7		
	[686 ‡]	James Higginson	2	3		
	[687*‡]	Phillip Underwood	1	6		
	[688 ‡]	John E. Vaught	1	1		
	[689 ‡]	Elijah Randolph	1	2		
	[690 ‡]	Auther Williams	1	3		
	[691*‡]	John Chism	1	5		1
	[692 ‡]	Daniel Bidwell	1	4		
	[693*‡]	Eli Stewart	1	8		
	[694*‡]	Daniel Brown	1	4		
	[695 ‡]	Robert Graham	1	4		

WHITE COUNTY (Continued)

Township	No.	Heads of families	White males 21 & upwards	All other white	Free people of color	Servants or slaves
	[696*‡]	James Hodkin	1	6		
	[697 ‡]	Robert Mothral	1	5		
	[698 ‡]	James Bozeman	1	1		
	[699 ‡]	David Bidwell	1	2		
	[700 ‡]	John Fraser	1	3		
	[701*‡]	John Ewing	1	7		
	[702 ‡]	Jonathan Bradshaw	1	3		
	[703*‡]	John Elliott	1	5		
	[704 ‡]	James A Simpson	1	2		
	[705 ‡]	Walter Higden	1	2		
	[706*‡]	William Lucas	1	5		
	[707*‡]	James Phillips	2	3		
	[708*‡]	Burnside Phillips	1	2		
	[709 ‡]	William Lock	1	3		
	[710 ‡]	Jeremiah Etheridge	1	8		
	[711*‡]	Bazzel Daniel	1	7		
	[712*‡]	James Boyd	1	5		
	[713*‡]	James Hood	2	6		
	[714*‡]	Richard Hanes	2	5		
	[715*‡]	William Lock	1	3		
	[716 ‡]	James Barker	1	5		
	[717 ‡]	William McDonald	1	1		
	[718*‡]	William Long	1	3		
	[719 ‡]	William Phinemon	2	6		
	[720*‡]	Daniel Boltinghouse	1	11		
	[721*‡]	James Devenport	1	2		
	[722*‡]	Julius Driggers	1	6		
	[723*‡]	Nelly Reed		6		
	[724 ‡]	Polly Hencely		1		
	[725 ‡]	Reubin Rushford	1	9		
	[726*‡]	Sephen Stanley	2	6		
	[727*‡]	James Potter	3	6		
	[728*‡]	Edmond Covington	1	9		
	[729 ‡]	James H Brooks	2	2		
	[730 ‡]	William Browder	1	8		
	[731*‡]	James Bryant	1	6		
	[732 ‡]	William Rigney	2	3		
	[733*‡]	Thomas Grey	3	4		1

CENSUS OF 1820 351

WHITE COUNTY (*Continued*)

Township	No.	Heads of families	White males 21 & upwards	All other white	Free people of color	Servants or slaves
	[734 ‡]	Benjamin Glayson	2	4		
	[735 ‡]	William Daniel	1	2		
	[736*‡]	John Tayler	1	9		
	[737 ‡]	Michael Dickerson	2	3		
	[738*‡]	Moses Thompson	1	10		1
	[739 ‡]	Richard Davis Junr.	1	4		
	[740*‡]	Walter Jacobs	1	10		
	[741*‡]	Richard Davis	1	4		
	[742*‡]	James Davis	1	2		
	[743*‡]	James Dunlap	1	9		
	[744*‡]	James Meredith	1	9		
	[745*‡]	John Kanada	1	7		
	[746 ‡]	Zepeniah Noble	1	2		
	[747*‡]	Amos Howell	1	8		
	[748 ‡]	Fleetwood Hanks	2	3		
	[749 ‡]	William Riley	1			
	[750*‡]	Elizabeth Thrash		6		
	[751*‡]	James Hamilton	1	8		
	[752 ‡]	Isaac Scott	2	5		
	[753*‡]	William Whitnell	1	3		
	[754*‡]	James Jaggers	1	7		
	[755 ‡]	Nathan Jaggers	1	1		
	[756*‡]	David Daniel	1	9		
	[757 ‡]	John Daniel	1	2		
	[758 ‡]	Levi Self	1	7		
	[759 ‡]	Hezekiah Self	1	4		
	[760 ‡]	Daniel Heasty	3	2		
	[761*‡]	John More	1	5		
	[762 ‡]	David Greathouse	1	7		
	[763*‡]	John Short	1	6		
	[764*‡]	Samuel Smith	1	4		
	[765*‡]	Josiah Daniel	1	8		
	[766*‡]	George Graham	2	3		
	[767*‡]	Henry Vansickles	1	3		
	[768*‡]	George Sturn	1	4		
	[769 ‡]	Martha Gilson	3	3		
	[770*‡]	William Gilson	1	1		
	[771 ‡]	John Vote	1	1		

WHITE COUNTY (Continued)

Township	No.	Heads of families	White males 21 & upwards	All other white	Free people of color	Servants or slaves
	[772 ‡]	David Bidwell	1	2		
	[773*‡]	Jonathan Stewart	1	6		
	[774*‡]	William Gross	1	5		
	[775*‡]	George Hoover	1	12		
	[776*‡]	David Hanks	2	9		
	[777*‡]	William Council	1	2		
	[778*‡]	James Con	1	9		
	[779 ‡]	Elias Turner	1	6		
	[780*‡]	Hamlet Underwood	1	1		
	[781 ‡]	John Uins	1	7		
	[782*‡]	Young Stokes	2	4		
	[783*‡]	James McNeal	1	3		
	[784*‡]	Willis Cherry	1	5		1
	[785*‡]	Francis Nash	1	3		
	[786*‡]	William Nash	1	5		
	[787 ‡]	James Nash	1	1		
	[788 ‡]	Samuel Bozeman	1	5		
	[789*‡]	Wily Hilliard	1	6		
	[790 ‡]	John Stailey	1	4		
	[791 ‡]	Jacob Staily	1	3		
	[792*‡]	Archibald Brown	1	4		
	[793 ‡]	Isam Hust	1	1		
	[794 ‡]	John McClalan	1	3		
	[795 ‡]	Thomas Craton	1	3		
	[796 ‡]	Ison Lemocks	1	1		
	[797*‡]	John G Robinson	1	4		
	[798*‡]	Thomas Harper	1	6		
			1005	3701	15	52

The foregoing is a list of the Inhabitants of White County Taken by me.

JESSE C LOCKWOOD
Commissioner

CENSUS OF 1820

WHITE COUNTY (Continued)

White County Commissioner Court

July Term 1820

On motion it is ordered that the order of Court appointing Richard Graham to take in the Censis, made at the December Term of this Court be recinded and it is ordered that Jesse C Lockwood be and he is hereby appointed a commissioner to take the Censis of this County agreeably to an act of assembly in such case made and provided etc.

A Copy
Attest
JAS RATCLIFF Clk

State of Illinois }
White County }

I, Jesse C. Lockwood of White County, do solemnly swear, that I will well & truly make a correct enumeration of all persons resident within the County of White to the best of my ability, and return the same to the Secretary of State, on or before the first Monday in December, in the year eighteen hundred & twenty

JESSE C. LOCKWOOD

Subscribed & sworn to this 1t. day of August A D 1820 before me.

JOHN CROW J P.

Corrected totals:
  Free white males of 21 years and upwards   1005
  All other white inhabitants   3706
                                                 ────
                                                 4711
  Negroes   67
    Free persons of color   15
    Servants or slaves   52
                                     ──
                                     67

                                        Total   4778

WHITE COUNTY (Continued)

Daniel Hay took the 1818 census for White County, certifying the returns on June 3. Jesse C. Lockwood took both the state and federal census for 1820, certifying both on November 22. The names on the 1820 lists correspond except that John Lesley's name appears twice in the federal census.

Discrepancies are as follows:
- 5 Pierson, Akillis
  - 1818. Pearson, Achelus
  - F1820. Pierson, Akillis
- 14 Story, George, Sr.
  - 1818. Story, George
  - F1820. Story, George
- 16 McLallan, John
  - 1818. McLelland, John
  - F1820. McLallan, John
- 19 Nation, Andrew
  - F1820. Nations, Andrew
- 20 Nation, John
  - F1820. Nations, John
- 36 Spillman, Samuel
  - 1818. Spilman, Saml.
  - F1820. Spillman, Samuel
- 40 Martin, James
  - 1818. Martin, James B.
  - F1820. Martin, James
- 44 Blag, Isaac
  - 1818. Blagg, Isaac
  - F1820. Blag, Isaac
- 58 Welsh, Joseph
  - F1820. Welch, Joseph
- 62 Grey, James
  - 1818. Gray, James
  - F1820. Grey, James
- 68 Weed, Hugh W.
  - F1820. Weed, Hugh M.
- 71 Paillie, John B.
  - F1820. Paillie, John
- 88 Veatch, Isaac
  - 1818. Veach, Isaac
  - F1820. Veatch, Isaac
- 89 Parks, Matthew
  - 1818. Park, Mathew
  - F1820. Park, Mathew
- 91 Veatch, Elias
  - 1818. Veach, Elias
  - F1820. Veatch, Elias
- 92 Forgison, John
  - 1818. Ferguson, John
  - F1820. Forgison, John
- 100 Mayes, James
  - 1818. Mays, James
  - F1820. Mays, James
- 101 Veatch, James
  - 1818. Veach, James
  - F1820. Veatch, James
- 102 Veatch, John
  - 1818. Veach, John
  - F1820. Veatch, John
- 108 Wilson, Matthew
  - 1818. Wilson, Mathew
  - F1820. Wilson, Matthew
- 111 Cameron, Thomas
  - 1818. Camron, Thomas
  - F1820. Cameron, Thomas
- 113 McCan, Bartholomew
  - F1820. McCann, Bartholomew
- 118 Riggin, Joshua
  - 1818. Riggan, Joshua
  - F1820. Riggan, Joshua
- 123 Ooley, Henry
  - 1818. Wooley, Henry
  - F1820. Ooley, Henry
- 125 Sumpter, Heny
  - F1820. Sumpter, Henry
- 127 Dosher, Adam
  - 1818. Dosier, Adam
  - F1820. Doshier, Adam
- 128 Stevens, Canaba
  - 1818. Stevens, Carnaby
  - F1820. Stevens, Carnaba
- 132 Hanes, John
  - 1818. Haynes, John
  - F1820. Hanes, John
- 133 Dosher, Elizabeth
  - F1820. Dosier, Elizabeth
- 134 Barber, John
  - 1818. Barbra, John
  - F1820. Barber, John
- 136 Cary, Susanna
  - F1820. Crary, Susanna
- 137 Dosher, Adam
  - F1820. Dosier, Adam
- 146 Burrell, David
  - F1820. Burrel, David
- 149 Hargrave, Jeremiah
  - 1818. Hargrave, Jerremiah
  - F1820. Hargrave, Jeremiah
- 152 Hamilton, Mordica S.
  - 1818. Hambleton, Mordica
  - F1820. Hamilton, Mordica
- 162 Sawyer, Absolem
  - F1820. Sawyer, Absolom
- 163 Williams, Casada B.
  - F1820. Williams, Cassada B.

CENSUS OF 1820

WHITE COUNTY (Continued)

167 Hawley, Pierce
    1818. Hawley, Pearce
    F1820. Hawley, Pierce
171 Ferrel, William
    F1820. Ferril, William
178 Kennel, Lemuel
    F1820. Kernel, Lemuel
184 Parmer, Frederick
    1818. Farmer, Frederick
    F1820. Palmer, Frederick
186 Parmer, William
    1818. Farmer, William
    F1820. Palmer, William
187 Garrison, Absolem
    1818. Garrison, Absolum
    F1820. Garrison, Absolem
192 Barns, William
    1818. Barnes, William
    F1820. Barns, William
194 Holiby, John
    F1820. Holliby, John
199 Caine, William
    1818. Cain, William
    F1820. Caine, William
204 Badger, Edmond W.
    1818. Badger, Edward
    F1820. Badger, Edmond W.
214 Wicker, Thomas
    1818. Wickers, Thomas
    F1820. Wicker, Thomas
216 Hunt, William
    1818. Hurt, William
    F1820. Hunt, William
219 Cricel, George
    1818. Crisle, George
    F1820. Cricel, George
223 Heard, Charles
    1818. Herd, Charls
    F1820. Heard, Charles
225 Shearley, Moses
    F1820. Shearly, Moses
226 Malden, Ennis
    1818. Maulding, Ennes
    F1820. Malden, Ennis
230 Shearly, Nimrod
    1818. Shirley, Nimrod
    F1820. Shearley, Nimrod
231 Gore, John
    1818. Gore, John C.
    F1820. Gore, John
232 Hungate, William
    1818. Hungate, William
    F1820. Hungot, William
235 Vance, Jordan
    1818. Vance, Jorden
    F1820. Vance, Jordan

236 Hodges, Hiram
    1818. Hodge, Hiram and William
    F1820. Hodges, Hiram
238 Minnus, John
    1818. Manus, John
    F1820. Minnus, John
246 Hurd, Charles
    1818. Herd, Charls
    F1820. Hurd, Charles
247 Hardister, John
    1818. Hardesty, John
    F1820. Hardister, John
250 Townsend, John
    1818. Townsand, John
    F1820. Townsend, John
251 Hurd, Stephen
    F1820. Heard, Stephen
253 Perrey, Redman
    F1820. Perry, Redman
257 More, Jeremiah
    1818. More, Jerremiah
    F1820. More, Jeremiah
260 Veatch, William
    1818. Veach, Wm.
    F1820. Veatch, William
261 Malden, Ambrose
    1818. Maulding, Ambrose
    F1820. Malden, Ambrose
263 Malden, James
    1818. Maulding, James
    F1820. Malden, James
273 Griffeth, John
    1818. Griffith, John
    F1820. Griffeth, John
277 Daly, John
    F1820. Dailey, John W.
279 Trammel, Gerrard
    1818. Trammel, Jarrot
    F1820. Trammel, Jerrard
280 Cumpton, John B.
    1818. Compton, John B.
    F1820. Cumpton, John B.
283 Kimzey, Elijah
    1818. Kimsey, Elijah
    F1820. Kimzey, Elijah
288 Wheeler, William, Sr.
    1818. Wheeler, William
    F1820. Wheeler, William
294 Hyatt, Jesse
    1818. Hiatt, Jesse
    F1820. Hyatt, Jesse
295 Phipps, James
    1818. Fips, James
    F1820. Phipps, James

WHITE COUNTY (Continued)

301 Gatlin, Edward
    1818. Gatland, Edward
    F1820. Gatlin, Edward
306 Hog, Samuel
    1818. Hogg, Saml
    F1820. Hog, Samuel
312 Brady, Jacob
    F1820. Braden, Jacob
324 Jewett, Isaac
    F1820. Juitt, Isaac
325 Hardister, William
    1818. Hardisty, William
    F1820. Hardister, William
333 Nichols, George
    1818. Nicols, George
    F1820. Nichols, George
334 Grinds, Adonjah
    F1820. Grinds, Adonijah
338 McKenzie, George
    1818. McKinsey, George
    F1820. McKenzie, George
343 Watson, Robert
    1818. Watson, Robert, Jr.
    F1820. Watson, Robert
350 Maberry, Jesse
    1818. Mayberry, Jesse
    F1820. Maberry, Jesse
352 Maberry, Solomon
    1818. Mayberry, Solloman
    F1820. Maberry, Solomon
354 Maberry, David
    1818. Mayberry, David
    F1820. Maberry, David
355 Maberry, Frederick
    1818. Mayberry, Frederick
    F1820. Maberry, Frederick
367 Boler Jack, Joel
    F1820. Bolerjack, Joel
374 Forrister, Jacob
    1818. Forrester, Jacob
    F1820. Forrister, Jacob
377 McMurty, John
    1818. McMurtry, John
    F1820. McMurtry, John
378 McMurty, Henry
    1818. McMurtry, Henry
    F1820. McMurtry, Henry
382 Vineyard, John
    1818. Vinyard, John
    F1820. Vineyard, John
385 Jordan, William
    1818. Jorden, William
    F1820. Jordan, William
390 McGehee, William, Sr.
    1818. McGehee, William
    F1820. McGeehee, William

391 Satterfield, Isaac
    1818. Saturfield, Isaac
    F1820. Satterfield, Isaac
392 McGeehee, William, Jr.
    1818. McGehee, William
    F1820. McGeehee, William, Jr.
397 Satterfield, George
    1818. Saturfield, George
    F1820. Satterfield, George
398 Satterfield, George, Jr.
    1818. Saturfield, George
    F1820. Satterfield, George, Jr.
399 McGeehee, Elisha
    F1820. McGeehee, Elish
400 Trousdell, Alexander
    1818. Trousdale, Alexd.
    F1820. Trousdell, Alexander
401 Trousdell, James
    1818. Trousdale, James
    F1820. Trousdell, James
407 Johns, Evens
    1818. Johns, Even
    F1820. Johns, Evens
410 Pierce, Jesse
    1818. Pearce, Jesse
    F1820. Pierce, Jesse
412 Pierce, Moses, Sr.
    1818. Pearce, Moses
    F1820. Pierce, Moses, Sr.
416 More, Abner
    F1820. More, Allen
421 Taylor, Joseph
    F1820. Tayler, Joseph
424 Dagley, Thomas
    1818. Dagley, Thomas
    F1820. Daglee, Thomas
428 Dagley, Samuel
    1818. Dagley, Samuel
    F1820. Daglee, Samuel
430 Alvin, Joshua
    1818. Albin, Joshua
    F1820. Alvin, Joshua
434 Tayler, Merrit
    1818. Tayler, Merret
    F1820. Tayler, Merrit
436 Witherow, William
    1818. Withro, William
    F1820. Witherow, William
437 Harget, William
    1818. Hargate, William
    F1820. Harget, William
438 Dewey, Joshua
    1818. Dewey, Joshua
    F1820. Drewey, Joshua

WHITE COUNTY (Continued)

452 Langford, John
    1818. Lankford, John
    F1820. Langford, John W.
453 Owens, Philip
    F1820. Owen, Phillip
454 Nevit, William
    F1820. Nevitt, William
455 Edlin, Clemont
    F1820. Edlin, Clement
457 Trousdell, John C.
    F1820. Trousdell, John
460 Naught, George
    1818. Knott, George
    F1820. Naught, George
464 Naught, Isaac
    1818. Knott, Isaac
    F1820. Naught, Isaac
466 Oneal, Hezekiah
    1818. ONeill, Hezekiah
    F1820. Oneal, Hezzekiah
468 Pierce, Hosey
    1818. Pearce, Hosea
    F1820. Pierce, Hosea
475 Brown, Wallis
    F1820. Rowin, Wallis
476 Madcalf, Manuel
    1818. Metcalf, Emanuel
    F1820. Madcalf, Manuel
478 Patten, Joseph
    1818. Patton, Joseph
    F1820. Patten, Joseph
481 Young, Christopher
    1818. Young, ———
    F1820. Young, Christopher
484 Gillison, John
    1818. Gillison, John
    F1820. Gilson, John
493 Hart, Thomas
    F1820. Heart, Thomas
497 Widows, Peter
    1818. Widdows, Peter
    F1820. Widows, Peter
500 Ridgway, David W.
    F1820. Ridway, David W.
501 Lee, Green
    F1820. Lee, Gree
504 Myers, Henry
    1818. Mires, Henry
    F1820. Myers, Henry
509 Standifer, Archibald
    1818. Standefore, Archd.
    F1820. Standiferd, Archibald
510 Myers, John
    1818. Mires, John
    F1820. Myers, John
511 Swords, Griffin
    1818. Sowerd, Griffin
    F1820. Swords, Griffin
512 Carlisle, Robin
    1818. Carlile, Robert
    F1820. Carlisle, Robin
516 Auxer, Abraham
    1818. Auxier, Abraham
    F1820. Auxer, Abraham
522 Calvin, Neptune
    F1820. Calvin, Nepture
526 Kickendall, Noah
    1818. Kuykendall, Noah
    F1820. Kirkindall, Noah
528 McCown, George, Jr.
    1818. McCown, George
    F1820. McCown, George
529 McCown, George
    1818. McCown, George
    F1820. McCown, George, Sr.
531 Barnet, John C.
    F1820. Barnet, John G.
532 Hubbard, Mulekiah
    1818. Hubbard, Malleki
    F1820. Hubbard, Malakiah
537 Buckels, Robert
    F1820. Buckles, Robert
538 Williams, Aaron
    1818. Williams, Aron
    F1820. Williams, Aaron
539 Williams, Roly
    1818. Williams, Roley
    F1820. Williams, Roly
545 Allen, William B.
    1818. Allen, William
    F1820. Allen, William
546 Williams, Aaron
    1818. Williams, Aron
    F1820. Williams, Aaron
548 Pomroy, Joseph
    1818. Pumroy, Joseph
    F1820. Pomroy, Joseph
550 Vine, William
    1818. Vines, William
    F1820. Vines, William
551 Mobly, Charles
    1818. Mobley, Charles
    F1820. Mobly, Charles
553 Hanna, John, Sr.
    1818. Hanna, John
    F1820. Hanna, John
554 Hamilton, Alexander
    1818. Hammelton, Alexd.
    F1820. Hamilton, Alexander

WHITE COUNTY (Continued)

559 Maze, Thomas
    1818. Mays, Thomas
    F1820. Maze, Thomas
560 Davison, Harvey P.
    F1820. Davidson, Harvey P.
564 Anderson, John E.
    1818. Anderson, John
    F1820. Anderson, John
566 May, Balem
    1818. May, Balaam
    F1820. May, Baalem
567 Bowye, Ann
    1818. Bowie, Anna
    F1820. Bowye, Ann
568 Bryant, Benjamin
    1818. Bryon, Benjn.
    F1820. Briant, Benjamin
569 Robinson, William
    1818. Robertson, William
    F1820. Robinson, William
571 Brown, Willim
    1818. Brown, William
    F1820. Brown, William
573 Merril, William
    1818. Merrill, William
    F1820. Merril, William
574 Logan, George
    F1820. Logan, George R.
582 Cottenner, Frederick
    F1820. Cottener, Frederick
589 McCollister, Thomas
    1818. Mccallister, Thos
    F1820. McCollister, Thomas
591 Slocum, John C.
    1818. Slocumb, John C.
    F1820. Slocum, John C.
593 Slocum, Samuel
    1818. Slocumb, Saml.
    F1820. Slocum, Samuel
599 Thornbury, Thomas
    1818. Thornsberry, Thomas
    F1820. Thornbury, Thomas
600 Dosey, Halbert
    1818. Dorsey, Halyard
    F1820. Dorsey, Haliard
601 Kiger, John
    F1820. Kiger, John, Sr.
604 Vodris, Peter
    F1820. Voris, Peter
605 Vodris, James
    1818. Voris, James
    F1820. Voris, James
606 Read, John
    1818. Read, John
    F1820. Reed, John

607 Chapel, Cumstock
    1818. Chappel, Comstock
    F1820. Chapel, Cumpstock
608 Hurt, Absolem
    1818. Hurt, Absolum
    F1820. Hurt, Absolem
614 McCollister, Edward
    1818. Mccallister, Edward
    F1820. McCollister, Edward
615 McCollister, Simon
    1818. Mccallister, Simon
    F1820. McCollister, Simon
616 McCollister, James
    1818. Mccallister, James
    F1820. McCollister, James
621 Craig, John C.
    1818. Craig, John
    F1820. Craig, John C.
622 Wilson, John J.
    1818. Wilson, John
    F1820. Wilson, John J.
623 Wilson, Ervin
    1818. Wilson, Arvin
    F1820. Wilson, Ervin
626 Stewart, Elam
    1818. Stewert, Elam
    F1820. Stewart, Elam
627 Southart, Thomas
    1818. Southerd, Thomas
    F1820. Southart, Thomas
629 Goodwin, Joseph
    1818. Gooden, Joseph
    F1820. Goodwin, Joseph
633 Burrel, Joseph
    1818. Burrell, Joseph
    F1820. Burrel, Joseph
634 Matthews, John
    1818. Mathews, John
    F1820. Matthews, John
640 Collins, Michael C.
    1818. Collins, Michael
    F1820. Collins, Michael C.
644 Cottrell, Prier
    F1820. Cottrell, Pierce
650 Finley, James
    1818. Finly, James
    F1820. Finley, James
653 Pool, Arter
    1818. Pool, Arthur
    F1820. Pool, Arter
658 McIntyre, John
    1818. McIntire, John
    F1820. McIntyre, John
660 Griffith, Abraham
    1818. Griffith, Abraham
    F1820. Griffeth, Abraham

WHITE COUNTY (*Continued*)

662 Patten, Phillip
    1818. Patton, Philip
    F1820. Patten, Phillip
665 Brown, Daniel
    1818. Brown, Daniel, Jr.
    F1820. Brown, Daniel
674 Drigger, Isaac
    1818. Driggers, Isaac
    F1820. Triggers, Isaac
679 McHauz, Reubin
    F1820. McHawse, Reubin
680 Driggers, Absolem
    1818. Driggins, Absolam
    F1820. Driggers, Absolem
681 Stanley, William
    1818. Stanley, William
    F1820. Stanly, William
682 Elliott, Benjamin
    F1820. Elliot, Benjamin
683 Phillips, Alexander
    1818. Philips, Alexd.
    F1820. Philips, Alexander
684 Herring, Jesse
    1818. Hearing, Jesse
    F1820. Herring, Jesse
687 Underwood, Phillip
    1818. Underwood, Philip
    F1820. Underwood, Phillip
690 Williams, Auther
    F1820. Williams, Arthur
693 Stewart, Eli
    1818. Stewert, Eli
    F1820. Stewart, Eli
696 Hodkin, James
    1818. Hodkins, James
    F1820. Hodkin, James
699 Bidwell, David
    F1820. Bidwell, Daniel
705 Higden, Walter
    F1820. Higdon, Walter
707 Phillips, James
    1818. Philips, James
    F1820. Philips, James
708 Phillips, Burnside
    1818. Philips, Burnside
    F1820. Philips, Burnside
711 Daniel, Bazzel
    1818. Daniel, Bazil
    F1820. Daniel, Bazzel
714 Hanes, Richard
    1818. Haynes, Richd.
    F1820. Hanes, Richard
722 Driggers, Julius
    1818. Driggers, Julas
    F1820. Driggers, Julius
723 Reed, Nelly
    1818. Read, Nelly
    F1820. Read, Nelly
725 Rushford, Reubin
    F1820. Rutherford, Reubin
726 Stanley, Sephen
    1818. Stanley, Stephen
    F1820. Stanly, Stephen
728 Covington, Edmond
    1818. Covington, Edmon
    F1820. Carrington, Edmond
731 Bryant, James
    1818. Bryant, James
    F1820. Briant, James
733 Grey, Thomas
    1818. Gray, Thomas
    F1820. Grey, Thomas
736 Tayler, John
    1818. Taylor, John
    F1820. Tayler, John
737 Dickerson, Michael
    F1820. Dickison, Michael
745 Kanada, John
    1818. Kenneday, John
    F1820. Kanada, John
746 Noble, Zepeniah
    F1820. Nobles, Zepheniah
750 Thrash, Elizabeth
    1818. Thrash, Betsey
    F1820. Thrash, Elizabeth
751 Hamilton, James
    1818. Hambleton, James
    F1820. Hamilton, James
753 Whitnell, William
    1818. Whitnell, William
    F1820. Whitnal, William
759 Self, Hezekiah
    F1820. Self, Hezzekiah
765 Daniel, Josiah
    1818. Daniels, Josiah
    F1820. Daniel, Josiah
767 Vansickles, Henry
    1818. Vansicle, Henry
    F1820. Vansickles, Henry
770 Gilson, William
    1818. Gilston, William
    F1820. Gilson, William
773 Stewart, Jonathan
    1818. Stewert, Jonathan
    F1820. Stuart, Jonathan
774 Gross, William
    1818. Cross, William
    F1820. Cross, William
777 Council, William
    1818. Counsil, William
    F1820. Council, William

WHITE COUNTY (Concluded)

778 Con, James
   1818. Conn, James
   F1820. Con, James
784 Cherry, Willis
   1818. Cherry, Willis
   F1820. Cheny, Willis
789 Hilliard, Wily
   1818. Hilyard, Wiley
   F1820. Hilliard, Wily

790 Stailey, John
   F1820. Staily, John
793 Hust, Isam
   F1820. Husk, Isam
794 McClalan, John
   F1820. McClallin, John
797 Robinson, John G.
   1818. Robeson, John
   F1820. Robinson, John G.

INDEX

INDEX

Aanderson, Elizabeth, 84.
Aarnet, see Arnet.
Aaron, John, 108.
Aarstrong [Armstrong], Sasanah [Susanah, Susannah], 149, 181.
Abanatha, see Abenathey.
Abar, John, 75.
Abbernatha, Joseph, 268.
Abbernathar [Abernatha], Miles, 266, 285.
Abbet [Abbot], James, 123, 126.
Abbet [Abbot], John, 123, 126.
Abbet, see Abbett.
Abbett [Abbet], George, 219, 232.
Abbey, Richard, 1.
Abbot, Samuel, 240.
Abbot, see Abbet and Abbott.
Abbott [Abbot], Christopher, 316, 322.
Abbott [Abbot], John, 316, 322.
Abdik, see Updyke.
Abenathey [Abanatha, Abernathy], James M. [James], 300, 309.
Abenathy [Abernatha], Robert, 267, 286.
Abenerthy, Battee, 273.
Abenerthy [Abernatha], Robert [Robert, Jr.], 273, 288.
Abernatha, see Abbernathar, Abenathy, and Abenerthy.
Abernathy, see Abenathey.
Abner [Abney], Absolem [Abner, Absolom], 87, 97.
Abner, James R., 342.
Abner [Abney], William, 87, 97.
Abney, see Abner.
Abrahams, Lewis, 199.
Acard, see Acord.
Ackless, Richard, 206.
Acord [Acard], Jonus [Jonas], 106, 118.
Adair, William, 270.
Adams, Baly [Baily], 62, 71.
Adams, Eli, 86.
Adams, Hannah, 265.
Adams, Henry, 197.
Adams, James, 59, 88, 261.
Adams, John, 65, 167, 239, 312.
Adams [Addams], John R., 38, 50.
Adams, Joseph, 194.
Adams, Nancy [Nancey], 63, 71.
Adams, Richard, 89.
Adams, Thomas, 125, 296.
Adams, Thriston [Tressy], 269, 287.
Adams, Willaby [William], 141, 177.
Adams, William, 39.

Addams, see Adams.
Addison, Thomas, 91.
Adkin, see Adkins.
Adkins, Chansa [Charles], 26, 31.
Adkins, Cornelius, 244.
Adkins [Atkins], John [John, Sr.], 145, 179.
Adkins [Atkins], John [John, Jr.], 146, 180.
Adkins [Adkin, Atkins], William, 146, 180.
Adkins [Atkins], William [William, Jr.], 148, 181.
Adkinson [Adkison], Elijah, 276, 289.
Adkison [Atkinson], John, 88, 97.
Adkison [Atkinson], Joseph, 88, 97.
Adkison, see Adkinson and Atkinson.
Adlesperger, Peter, 205.
Aekin, see Akin.
Aester [Herte], C. P., 227, 236.
Agin, John, 211.
Aidelott [Aydolett], Zadock [Zadoc], 75, 92.
Aiken, Thomas, 8.
Aikles, William, 193.
Aikman, David, 196.
Aikman, see Akeman.
Akeman [Aikman], David, 142, 178.
Aken, Fanny, 65.
Aken, James, 64.
Akens, Christain, 197.
Akers, Thomas, 78.
Akers, William, 78.
Akin [Aekin], William, 113, 119.
Albert [Ulbert], Jacob, 122, 126.
Albert, M. [Michial], 108, 119.
Albert, Simon, 110.
Albert [Ulbert], William, 122, 126.
Albin, see Aluin and Alvin.
Alburt, Justice, 156, 185; see also Allcut and Desiles.
Alcorn, see Allcorn.
Alexander, Alexander, 246.
Alexander, Daniel, 334.
Alexander, David, 267.
Alexander, David D. [John D.], 15, 23.
Alexander, Hugh, 267.
Alexander, John, 35, 206, 317.
Alexander, John B., 39.
Alexander, Joshua C., 16.
Alexander, Samuel, 221.
Alexander, William, 202, 270.
Alexander [Alexandria], William M., 2, 5.
Alexander, see Alexandria.
Alexandria [Alexander], Nelson, 147, 180.

Alexandria, see Alexander.
Alison, Joseph, 54.
Alison, see Allison.
Allard, August [Agust], 242, 254.
Allard, William, 133.
Allcorn, Elijah, 248.
Allcorn [Alcorn], Josiah, 250, 255.
Allcut, Miran, 185; see also Alburt and Desiles.
Allen, Archabald [Archibald], 266, 285.
Allen, Benjamin, 169.
Allen, Car, 2.
Allen, Chesley [Chesly], 258, 282.
Allen, Danel [Daniel], 157, 185.
Allen, E. [Edward], 222, 234.
Allen, Elizabeth, 313.
Allen, George, 173.
Allen, Ichabod, 267.
Allen, Ira, 200.
Allen, Isaac, 122.
Allen, James, 64, 66, 198, 200.
Allen, James [James M.], 168, 190.
Allen, Jesse, 133.
Allen, John, 2, 168, 169, 250.
Allen, Nesbit [Nezebe], 3, 5.
Allen, Polly, 317.
Allen, Rauben [Reuben], 65, 73.
Allen, Rhody [Rody], 124, 127.
Allen, Rowlen P. [Rowland P.], 159, 186.
Allen, Samuel, 168, 270.
Allen, Susannah, 241.
Allen, Thomas, 168, 169.
Allen, William, 195, 250.
Allen, William, Sr., 258.
Allen, William, Jr. [William], 258, 282.
Allen, William B. [William], 346, 357.
Allen, Zachariah, 168.
Allen, see Allin.
Allender, Joshua, 37.
Allery, Baptiste, 195.
Allery, Battece [Baptiest], 279, 291.
Allexander, Rewben, 196.
Alley, John C., 156.
Allfin [Alphin], Shelten [Sheton], 257, 282.
Allin [Allen], George C., 156, 185.
Allison [Alison], Daniel, 39, 51.
Allison [Alison], Edward, 39, 51.
Allison, Ezra H., 36.
Allison [Alison], Frederick, 47, 54.
Allison [Alison], Isaac, 48, 54.
Allison, John, 48.
Allison [Alison], Jonathan [Johnathan], 39, 51.
Allison, Phebe, 48, 54.
Allison [Alison], Richard, 46, 53.
Allison [Alison], Samuel, 46, 53.
Allison, Thomas, 15.

Alphin, Reuben, 82.
Alphin, see Allfin.
Altom, James, 10.
Alton, Reubin, 83.
Alton [Olfan], Shelton, 166, 190.
Aluin [Albin], James, 83, 95.
Alvey, James, 89.
Alvin, Isaac, 342.
Alvin [Albin], Joshua, 342, 356.
Amalin, Alexi, 200.
Ambrose, William, 144.
Ames, Zepheniah, 270.
Amlah, see Amley.
Amley [Amlah], Lewis [Louis, Jr.], 278, 291.
Amley [Amlah], Lewis, Sr. [Louis, Sr.], 278, 291.
Ammermon [Amormon], Stephen, 65, 72.
Amormon, see Ammermon.
Amos, Abraham, 211.
Amos, Mary, 201, 211.
Anderson, Alexander, 270.
Anderson, Amos, 247.
Anderson, Benjamin, 15.
Anderson, Betsey, 36.
Anderson, Caleb, 36.
Anderson, Carter, 265.
Anderson, David, 155, 251.
Anderson, Dickey, 37.
Anderson, Ezekiel [Ezekel], 36, 50.
Anderson, George, 36, 86.
Anderson, Ignatius [Ignatious], 7, 22.
Anderson, Isaac, 316.
Anderson, Jacob, 167.
Anderson, James, 251, 266, 316.
Anderson, James B. [James], 29, 32.
Anderson, John, 163, 193, 338.
Anderson, John, Sr., 251.
Anderson, John, Jr., 248.
Anderson, John E. [John], 346, 358.
Anderson, John G., 346.
Anderson, John P. [John M.], 262, 284.
Anderson, Joshua, 36.
Anderson, Reuben, 261.
Anderson, Robert, 57, 339.
Anderson, Robert W., 144.
Anderson, Susanah, 316.
Anderson, Thomas, 39.
Anderson, William, 163.
Andress, see Andrews.
Andrew, John, 60.
Andrews, Amos, 199.
Andrews, Arba, 122.
Andrews [Andrus], Archabald [Archibal, Archibald], 312, 320.
Andrews, James, 59, 157.
Andrews [Andress], Nathanial S. [Nathan],

INDEX 365

122, 126.
Andrus, *see* Andrews.
Angelo, Benjamin, 264.
Angelo, John, 264.
Anglan, Elisha, 58.
Anglin, Adrian, 58.
Ankeney, *see* Ankeny.
Ankeny, Jacob, 110.
Ankeny [Ankeney], John, 113, 120.
Ano, John, 60.
Ano, Mary, 57.
Anson, Abraham [Abraham W.], 293, 305.
Anthis, George, 59.
Anthis, John, 58.
Anthis, Larkin, 60.
Antle, Michael, 166.
Antwine, 281.
Anyan, Mary, 295.
Aplen [Apling], Jessy [Jesse], 66, 73.
Aples, Samuel, 198.
Aplin, *see* Appling.
Apling, *see* Aplen *and* Appling.
Appling [Aplin, Apling], Pleasant, 317, 322.
Arcana, Joseph, 197.
Archer, Cavel [Covill], 140, 177.
Archer, Charles K., 27.
Archer, Hezekiah, 19.
Archer, Israel, 19.
Archer, James, 342.
Archer, John, 342.
Archer, Moses, 166.
Archer, William, 166.
Archer, William B., 27.
Archer, Zachariah, 27.
Armstrong, Aaron [Aron], 149, 181.
Armstrong, Abner, 56.
Armstrong, Andrew, 155.
Armstrong, Elsberry, 329.
Armstrong, Ephraim D., 59.
Armstrong, George, 148.
Armstrong, James, 65.
Armstrong, Jesse [Jessee], 165, 189.
Armstrong, John, 59, 91, 216, 336.
Armstrong, Josiah [Joshua], 153, 183.
Armstrong, Nathaniel, 63.
Armstrong, Richard, 28.
Armstrong, Robert, 67, 155, 165.
Armstrong, Thomas, 155.
Armstrong, William, 155.
Armstrong, *see* Aarstrong *and* Atterberry.
Arnet [Aarnet], John, 69, 74.
Arnet [Arnett], John, 141, 177.
Arnet [Arnett], Nathan, 69, 74.
Arnet [Arnett], Thomas [Thomas, Sr.], 167, 190.
Arnett, Jacob, 200.
Arnett, Thomas, Jr., 199.

Arnett, *see* Arnet.
Arnold, Andrew, 39.
Arnold, David, 297.
Arnold, Jacob, 60.
Arnold, James, 198.
Arnold, John, 60.
Arnold, John K., 61.
Arnold, Thomas, 104.
Arnold, William, 60.
Arpant, Francis, 57.
Arpant, Francis, Jr., 57.
Arpant, Joseph, 57.
Arterbury, Richard, 344.
Arthur, Benjamin, 37.
Arthur, Samuel, 318.
Arthurlana, *see* Arthurloney.
Arthurloney [Arthurlana], John, 256, 282.
Arundel, *see* Arundle.
Arundle [Arundel], William, 205, 212.
Asbel, *see* Asbell.
Asbell [Asbel], John, 42, 52.
Ashbrooke, Levi, 38.
Ashbrooke, Thomas, 38.
Ashbrooke, William C., 38.
Asher, Robison, 13.
Asher, Thomas, 13.
Asherst [Aster], Michael, 168, 190.
Ashmore, Amos, 28.
Ashmore, James, 28.
Ashmore, Samuel, 28.
Askins, Philoman, 196.
Asten, *see* Aston.
Aster, *see* Asherst.
Astin, *see* Aston.
Aston [Asten, Astin], William, 144, 179.
Atcheson, George, 205.
Atcheson, Matthew, 281.
Atcheson, William, 267.
Atcheson, *see* Atchison.
Atchison [Atcheson, Atchisson], Barton, 123, 126.
Atchison [Attchasen], Joseph T. [Joseph], 86, 96.
Atchison [Atchisson], William, 123, 126.
Atchison, *see* Hatchison.
Atchisson, *see* Atchison.
Athernton, John, 4, 6.
Atherton [Etherton], Aron, 4, 6.
Atherton [Etherton], John, 4, 6.
Atherton, Martin, 2.
Atherton [Etherton], Moses, 4, 6.
Atherton [Etherton], Samuel, 4, 6.
Atison [Haduson], Richard, 151, 183.
Atkins, James, 237, 239.
Atkins, Robert, 200.
Atkins, Spencer, 240.
Atkins, *see* Adkins *and* Atkinson.

Atkinson [Atkins], Henry, 315, 321.
Atkinson, Mahlon, 211.
Atkinson [Adkison], R. C. [Robert, Robert C.], 217, 231.
Atkinson, see Adkison.
Attchasen, see Atchison.
Atterberry [Armstrong], S. [Simon], 223, 234.
Atwater, see Atwaters.
Atwaters [Atwater], Joshua, 141, 177.
Aurel, see Averill.
Ausburn [Osburn], William, 106, 118.
Ausburn, see Coburn and Osbourn.
Austin, Ralf [Ralph], 20, 24.
Auston, see Oston.
Autire, Antoine, 239.
Autire, Michel, 240.
Auxer [Auxier], Abraham, 345, 357.
Auxer, Benjamin, 337.
Auxier, see Auxer.
Avaline, Francis, 41.
Avant, see Avents.
Avents [Avant], Harberd [Harbert], 122, 126.
Averill [Aurel], Philo, 219, 231.
Axley, Elisha, 201.
Axley, James, 210.
Axley, Robert, 296.
Axley, see Axly.
Axly [Axley], Elijah, 207, 212.
Aydelott [Aydelett], Levi, 75, 92.
Aydolett, see Aidelott and Aydelott.
Ayers, William, 317.
Ayers, see Ayres.
Ayres [Ayers], Russel, 317, 322.

Babcock, Joseph, 58.
Babcock, Joshua, 7.
Babee, see Beebe.
Bacchus [Bachus], John, 238, 253.
Baccus, John, 248.
Bace [Bates], James, 142, 178.
Bachus, Enock, 37.
Bachus, see Bacchus.
Bacon, Ira W. [Ira], 141, 177.
Bacon, Joel, 139.
Bacon, Oran, 195.
Badger, Edmond W. [Edward], 336, 355.
Badgley, Aaron, 262.
Badgley, Abraham, 263.
Badgley [Badley], Anthony, 262, 284.
Badgley, Hiram, 262.
Badgley, Ichabod, 263.
Badgley, Isaac, 263.
Badgley, Jobe [Job], 262, 284.
Badley, see Badgley.
Bagbey, see Bagby.

Bagby [Bagbey], John, 87, 97.
Baggett, Thomas, 36.
Baggs [Beggs], Alexander [Alexandria], 1, 5.
Baggs, see Beggs.
Bagley, David, 202.
Bags, George, 249.
Bags, John, 249.
Bailes [Bales], Elijah, 316, 322.
Bailey, David, 58.
Bailey, John, 293.
Bailey [Balies], Samuel, 220, 232.
Bailey, see Baily.
Baily, Isaac J., 202.
Baily, Robert, 202.
Baily [Bailey], Samuel, 203, 211.
Bain, Daniel, Sr., 326.
Bain, Moses, 91.
Bain, see Bane.
Baird, Charles, 200.
Baird, James, 245.
Baird, John, 248.
Baird, Thomas, 59.
Baird, see Beard.
Baismauve, Jacob, 196.
Baitman, Asail, 123.
Baits, Isaac, 339.
Baker, Abednigo, 19.
Baker, Absolem [Absolam, Absolum], 164, 189.
Baker, Alsworth, 196.
Baker, Benjamin, 71.
Baker, Charles, 19.
Baker, Coonrad [Coonrod], 69, 74.
Baker, Edmond [Edmund], 65, 73.
Baker, Elias, 20.
Baker, Elizabeth, 314.
Baker, Geter [Jeter], 80, 94.
Baker, Green, 332.
Baker, Horrace E. [Horace E.], 34, 49.
Baker, Jacob, 167, 347.
Baker, James, 20.
Baker, Jeptha, 28.
Baker, John, 28, 347.
Baker, John C., 67.
Baker, Joseph, 84.
Baker, Martin, 170.
Baker, Nathan [Nathen], 129, 135.
Baker, Reuben T., 58.
Baker, Richmond, 19.
Baker, Robert, 7.
Baker, Samuel, 46.
Baker, Solomon, 245.
Baker, Thomas, 152.
Baker, William, 69, 71, 100, 110, 170.
Baker, William R., 59.
Baker, see Barker.
Balden, see Baldwin.

INDEX

Baldin, Isaac, 79.
Baldin, William, 77.
Baldwin, Francis, 204.
Baldwin [Balden], Joseph, 218, 231.
Baldy, David, 45.
Bales, Emely, 152.
Bales, *see* Bailes.
Balies, *see* Bailey.
Ball, Aaron [Aron], 39, 51.
Ball, Adanijah, 247.
Ball, Adinegah [Adonigah], 106, 118.
Ball, Strauder [Strother], 164, 189.
Ball, *see* Bell.
Ballard, Blan, 240.
Ballard, Jeremiah, 60.
Ballard, Joseph, 57.
Ballard, Stephen, 266.
Ballard, Washington C. [Washington], 245, 254.
Baltzele [Baltzell], John, 300, 309.
Baltzell, *see* Baltzele.
Balze, Jesse, 337.
Bamber, John, 91.
Bandy, Elihu [Ellihu], 317, 322.
Bane [Bain], James, 131, 135.
Bane, John, 132.
Bane, Robert, 195.
Bane, *see* Bany.
Banes, Robert, 193.
Banham, *see* Bonham.
Banks, Alexander, 58.
Banks, Elijah, 58.
Banks, James, 59.
Banks, Thomas, 60.
Bankson, *see* Bankston.
Bankston [Bankson], Andrew, 315, 321.
Bankston, Richard, 67.
Bany [Bane], Robert A., 138, 176.
Bapest, Daniel, 210.
Barbarah [Barnaba], John, 156, 185.
Barbary, Joseph, 278.
Barb Barb, Lewis, 196.
Barbeau, Andrew, 242.
Barbeau [Barbo], Antoine, 242, 254.
Barbeau [Barbo], Batiste, 242, 254.
Barbeau, Henry, 242.
Barbee, Joke, 144.
Barbee, *see* Barbie.
Barber [Barbour], John, 149, 181.
Barber [Barbra], John, 334, 354.
Barber, Joseph, 8, 296.
Barbie, Joshua, 44.
Barbie [Barbee], William, 41, 52.
Barbo, Silas, 253.
Barbo, *see* Barbeau.
Barbour, Alexander, 248.
Barbour, Barbra, *see* Barber.

Barcroft, Aaron, 194.
Barger [Berger], Jacob, 80, 94.
Baringer, *see* Barrener.
Bark, William, 195.
Barker, Caleb, 260.
Barker, Daniel, 203.
Barker [Baker], Isaac N. [Isaac M.], 88, 97.
Barker, Jacob, 339.
Barker, James, 350.
Barker, John, 293.
Barker, Joseph, 197.
Barker, Joshua, 8.
Barker, Lewis [Lues], 218, 231.
Barker, Rachel, 20.
Barker, Sammuel [Lemuel], 249, 255.
Barker, Samuel, 341.
Barker, Susanna, 204, 212.
Barker, Thomas, 299.
Barker, William, 65.
Barker, Zebediah, 212.
Barklet, *see* Bartlett.
Barlow, James, 18.
Barlow, Jesse, 34.
Barlow, John W. [John], 35, 49.
Barlow, Lemuel, 59.
Barlow, Thomas, 89.
Barmore, William, 210.
Barnaba, John, 198.
Barnaba, *see* Barbarah.
Barnes, Ebenezar [Ebenezer], 163, 188.
Barnes, *see* Barns.
Barnesback [Barnsback], Gorge [George], 149, 181.
Barnet [Burnet], Alexander, 258, 282.
Barnet, George D., 143.
Barnet, John, 3, 250.
Barnet [Barnett], John [John C.], 147, 180.
Barnet, John C. [John G.], 345, 357.
Barnet [Barret], Luke, 264, 284.
Barnet, William, 250.
Barnett, Bazel, 85.
Barnett, David, 84.
Barnett, Henry, 197.
Barnett, James C. [James], 85, 96.
Barnett, John, 85.
Barnett, Joseph, 91.
Barnett, Thomas, 194.
Barnett, *see* Barnet.
Barney, George, 59.
Barney, William, 61.
Barnhill, Alexander, 77.
Barnhill, Mrs. Anna, 326.
Barnhill, David, 67.
Barns, Calvin, 320.
Barns, James, 7.
Barns [Barnes], Joshua, 12, 23.
Barns [Barnes], William, 336, 355.

Barnsback, see Barnesback.
Barnum, Pliny, 218.
Barr, James, 37.
Barrener [Baringer, Barringer], Henry, Sr. [Henry], 294, 305.
Barret, John, 281.
Barret, see Barnet.
Barrettel, Francis, 253.
Barrettel, Joseph, 243.
Barrick, William, 206.
Barrik, Peter, 44.
Barriner, Henry, Jr., 296.
Barriner [Barringer], Peter, 297, 307.
Barringer, see Barrener and Barriner.
Barritt, William, 210.
Barrough, Heman, 57.
Barrow, —— [John], 114, 120.
Barrow, David, 168.
Barrow, John, 168, 193, 244.
Barrow, Nancy, 139.
Barten, see Barton.
Bartlet, James, 29, 204.
Bartlet [Bartlett], Joseph, 142, 178.
Bartlet, Phillip, 336.
Bartlet, William, 29.
Bartlett, J., 224.
Bartlett, Michael, 84.
Bartlett [Barklet], W. [William, Willice], 224, 234.
Bartlett, William, 305.
Bartlett, William B., 193.
Bartlett, see Bartlet.
Bartleys, Robert, 38.
Barton, Elihu, 195.
Barton, John, 272.
Barton, Joseph, 239.
Barton, Joseph L., 143.
Barton, William, 159, 187, 273.
Barton [Barten], William, 295, 306.
Barton, see Bartrau.
Bartrau [Barton], Simon, 277, 290.
Basey [Basye], Isaa [Isaac], 267, 286.
Bashar [Brashar], Ithra, 41, 51.
Basset, see Bassett.
Bassett [Basset], Ery [Irie], 218, 231.
Bassitt, Josh. [Josia], 218, 231.
Baswell, see Boswell.
Basye, see Basey.
Bateman, Abraham, 10.
Bates, Samuel, 278.
Bates, Seth H., 42.
Bates, Thomas, 193, 320.
Bates, William, 77.
Bates, see Bace.
Bathe [Bayth], George, 43, 52.
Bathe, James, 43.
Bathrick, Daniel, 12.

Batson, William, 325.
Batteau [Batto, Bitto], John, 314, 321.
Battel, John, 172.
Battel, Lewis, 172.
Battelton, see Batterton.
Batterton [Battelton], Amos [Moses], 149, 181.
Batto, see Batteau.
Baty, John, Sr., 249.
Baty, John, Jr. [John], 249, 255.
Baugh, George, 327.
Baugh, John, 12.
Baugher [Boier], Jacob, 85, 96.
Baugher, see Boher.
Bawlin [Bowlin, Bowling], Benjamin, 9, 22.
Bayeau [Boyeau], Tousaint, 47, 54.
Bayth, see Bathe.
Baze, see Boyes.
Beach, Peter, 313.
Beadle [Beedle], Samuel, 262, 284.
Beag [Beck], Henry, 148, 181.
Beaird, Joseph A., 201.
Beaird, see Beard.
Beal, James, 11.
Beal [Bell], Luther, 80, 95.
Beall, Joshua, 58.
Beall, see Bell.
Bealls, Jesse, 59.
Beaman [Beeman, Beman], James, 173, 192.
Beamon [Beeman], Ormon [Orman], 139, 176.
Bean, Daniel, 261.
Bear [Beer], Joseph [Josep], 262, 284.
Bear, Peter, 262.
Beard, Elizabeth, 47.
Beard, James Y., 38.
Beard, Joseph, 39.
Beard [Baird, Beaird], William, 150, 182.
Beard, William A., 267.
Beard, see Beyard.
Beare [Beer], Henry, 262, 284.
Beare [Beer], William, 262, 284.
Beas [Best], James, 153, 184.
Beasley, Boswell, 57.
Beason [Cleson], Elijah E. [Elijah], 156, 185.
Beat, Alexander, 247.
Beat, Nicholas, 247.
Beatis [Bols], William, 157, 185.
Beatt [Beauatt], Louis, 240, 254.
Beatt, see Beuatt.
Beaty, Robert, 15.
Beauatt, see Beatt and Beuatt.
Beauchamp, Manlove, 56.
Beauchamp, William, 57.
Beaumont, James S., 210.
Beaver, Joel, 273.

INDEX

Beaver, Lawrence, 132.
Bebee, *see* Beebe.
Beck, John, 14, 346.
Beck, Paul, 14.
Beck, Stephen, 347.
Beck, *see* Beag.
Beckmore, *see* Vickmore.
Beckus, Benjamin, 347.
Beckwith, Benjamine [Benjamin], 42, 52.
Beckwith, Silas, 42.
Bedell, Moses, 61.
Bedwell, Samuel, 43.
Beebe [Babee, Bebee], Clarke [Charles], 168, 190.
Beech, Enoch, 327.
Beedle, *see* Beadle.
Beeman, *see* Beaman, Beamon, *and* Caiman.
Been, William, 241.
Beer, *see* Bear *and* Beare.
Beers, Moses, 210.
Beesely [Buseby], Howel, 249, 255.
Befra, John Baptist, 194.
Beggs, Alexander [Alexandria], 295, 306.
Beggs [Baggs], Archabel [Archabald, Arichibel], 295, 307.
Beggs [Baggs], Isaac, 295, 306.
Beggs [Baggs], John, 295, 306.
Beggs [Baggs], Robert, 296, 307.
Beggs, *see* Baggs.
Begold, Joshua, 320.
Beldeback, *see* Bilderback.
Belemon [Bellemey], Jesse [Jessee], 153, 183.
Belemont, Isaac, 194.
Belford, B. [Bengamin, Benjamin], 222, 233.
Belford [Bellford], William, 222, 233.
Bell [Belle], Francis, 168, 190.
Bell [Beall], James, 75, 92.
Bell [Belle], Jesse [Jessee], 141, 177.
Bell, John, 60, 160.
Bell, John S., 197.
Bell, Joseph, 29.
Bell [Belle], Nathaniel, 270, 287.
Bell [Ball], Resin [Risen], 29, 32.
Bell, Robert, 58.
Bell, *see* Beal.
Bellaugh, Reubin, 341.
Belle, *see* Bell.
Bellemey, *see* Belemon.
Bellford, *see* Belford.
Belsha, *see* Belska.
Belska [Belsha], George, 196.
Belt, Loyd [Lloyd], 265, 285.
Beman, *see* Beaman.
Benedict, Aaron, 46.
Benedict, James, 46.
Benefield, John, 37.

Benefield, Robert, 37.
Benett, John R., 193.
Bennet [Bennit], Ann [Anna], 261, 283.
Bennet, James B., 53.
Bennet, *see* Bennett *and* Bennit.
Bennett, Edward, 57.
Bennett, Elizabeth, 46, 53.
Bennett, Emma, 57.
Bennett, George, 46.
Bennett, H., 225.
Bennett [Bennet], H. [Aard], 225, 235.
Bennett, Henry, 57.
Bennett, J., 224.
Bennett, Nancy, 57.
Bennett [Bennet], Richard, 217, 231.
Bennett, William, 58.
Bennett, *see* Buennet.
Bennit [Bennet], Marget [Margret], 299, 309.
Bennit, *see* Bennet.
Benson, Henry, 113.
Benson, William, 200.
Benston, Oliver, 193.
Bentson, William, 197.
Berberick, Frederick, 7.
Berdin [Burden], Reubin, 171, 191.
Berger, *see* Barger.
Bergess [Burgess], Thomas, 137, 175.
Berkey [Berky], Daniel, 263, 284.
Berks, Richard, 325.
Berky, *see* Berkey.
Berly, Thomas, 200.
Bernash, *see* Burnaugh.
Berns [Burnes], Crawford, 65, 72.
Berns [Burnes, Burns], Elijah, 66, 73.
Berns [Burnes, Burns], Stephen [Steaphen], 66, 73.
Berns [Burnes, Burns], William, 66, 73.
Beron, *see* Bobo.
Berrey [Berry], John, 39, 51.
Berry, Arthur, 12, 238.
Berry, Elijah C., 12.
Berry, Enoch, 335.
Berry, Frederick, 312.
Berry, George, 334.
Berry, James, 3, 145.
Berry, Joel, 335.
Berry, John, 91.
Berry [Bery], John, 85, 96.
Berry, John F., 247.
Berry, John M. [John], 143, 179.
Berry, Jonathan, 17.
Berry, Nancy, 315.
Berry, Samuel, 196.
Berry, William, 91, 238.
Berry, William H., 315.
Berry, *see* Berrey *and* Bery.

Bery [Berry], Jeremiah [Fortnates], 163, 188.
Bery, see Berry.
Besley, Coles, 59.
Bess, David H., 199.
Best, see Beas.
Bethel, see Bethell.
Bethell [Bethel, Bethle], Chester, 86, 97.
Bethle, see Bethell.
Betts, Josiah, 238.
Betwood, Edmond F., 198.
Beuatt, Antoine, 243.
Beuatt [Beatt], Benjamin, 243, 254.
Beuatt [Beauatt], Joseph, 243, 254.
Beuatt [Beauatt], Michel, 243, 254.
Beuatt [Beatt], Zenia, 243, 254.
Bevanue, Madame [Modlen], 238, 253.
Bevanue, Antoine, 243.
Bevanue, Henry, 239.
Bevens, Charles, 196.
Beyard [Beard], J., 226, 236.
Bice, Samuel, 281.
Biddle, Richard, 91.
Biddle, see Bittle.
Bidwell, Daniel, 349.
Bidwell, David, 352.
Bidwell, David [Daniel], 350, 359.
Bigerstaff, Samuel, 335.
Bigerstaff, see Biggerstaff.
Biggerstaff, John, 1.
Biggerstaff [Bigerstaff], William, 4, 6.
Biggs, Noah, 34.
Biggs, William, Sr. [William], 265, 285.
Biggs, William, Jr., 257.
Biggs, see Bigs.
Bigs [Biggs], James, 41, 52.
Bilderback, Charles, 246.
Bilderback [Beldeback], D. [Daniel], 110, 119.
Bilderback, Ephraizm, 250.
Bilderback, James, 246.
Bilderback, John, 250.
Bilderback, William, 246.
Bileyu [Bilyeu], Joseph, 9, 22.
Billingsley [Billingsly], Bazel [Bazzel], 294, 306.
Billingsly, see Billingsley.
Bilyeu, see Bileyu.
Binion, William, 59.
Binkerton, see Pinkerton.
Biram [Byran, Byrum], Alexandria S. [Alexander], 141, 177.
Bird, James, 325.
Bird, John J., 193.
Birdon, see Burdin.
Birkbeck, Morris, 57.
Birkbeck, Richard, 57.

Bishop, Benjamin, 10, 125.
Bishop, David, 138.
Bishop, Edward, 138.
Bishop, John, 337.
Bishop, Rodah [Rhody], 146, 180.
Bishop, William, 206.
Biss, James, 196.
Bissell, Jerajah, 195.
Bissniss, Joseph, 199.
Bittle [Biddle], John, 104, 118.
Bitto, see Batteau.
Bivens, Wheeler, 132, 135.
Bizel [Bizzell], Isaac, 295, 306.
Bizzel, see Bizel.
Blacburn [Blackburn], John, 149, 182.
Black, Andrew, 199.
Black, C. P., 320.
Black, David, 40.
Black, David R., 197.
Black, James, 15, 57, 159, 246.
Black, John, 25, 28, 91.
Black, Maryann [Marian, Mary Ann], 159, 186.
Black, Rebecca, 28.
Black, Thomas, 28, 160.
Black, William, 28, 83.
Blackburn, Thomas, 58.
Blackburn, William, 57.
Blackburn, see Blacburn.
Blackford, Mary, 345.
Blackford, Nathaniel, 345.
Blackford, Reuben, 60.
Blackford, Z. [Zefenia], 221, 233.
Blackman [Blackmon], Remember, 26, 31.
Blackman, William, 314.
Blackman, see Blakeman.
Blackmon, see Blackman.
Blackmore, Washburn, 37.
Blackshire, Luke, 195.
Blackwel [Blackwell], David, 279, 292.
Blackwell, David, 239.
Blackwell, Robert, 12, 238.
Blackwell, see Blackwel.
Blag [Blagg], Isaac, 332, 354.
Blagg, see Blagg.
Blain [Blair], William, 163, 188.
Blair, Alx., 214.
Blair, Colbert [Colbin], 14, 23.
Blair, Enos, 14.
Blair, George, 156.
Blair, Gorge [George], 262, 284.
Blair, James, 262.
Blair, John, 14.
Blair, Thomas, 245.
Blair, see Blain.
Blake, John, 27.
Blakeman, Curtis, 156.

INDEX 371

Blakeman [Blackman], Elijah P. [Elijah], 156, 185.
Blalock [Blalocke], Henry, 89, 98.
Blalocke, see Blalock.
Blanchard, Seth, 17.
Blanchard, William P., 58.
Blaney, Robert, 193.
Blaney, see Blany.
Blanford, Henry, 139.
Blankenship [Blankeship], William, 65, 73.
Blankenship, see Blankingship.
Blankeship, see Blankenship.
Blankingship [Blankenship], John, 65, 72.
Blany [Blaney], John, 169, 190.
Blany, Robert, 200.
Blay, Antoine, 241, 242.
Blay, Charles, 242.
Blay, Joseph, 241.
Blaze, Jacob, 29.
Blessenden, John, 56.
Blesset, Mrs. Anna, 324.
Blesset, George T., 327.
Bleu, Solomon, 335.
Bliss, Joel, 60.
Bliss, Stephen, 60.
Blizzard, James, 7.
Blodeau, see Blundau.
Blodgett, Amesa, 210.
Bloom, John, 256.
Blundau [Blodeau], John B., 277, 290.
Boalter [Bolton], John, 173, 192.
Bobo [Beron], Charles, 277, 291.
Boez, Edmund, 8.
Bogard, Abraham [Abram], 35, 49.
Bogard, Benjamin, 58.
Bogard, John, 161.
Bogard, Joseph P., 56.
Bogardus, John L. [J. S.], 226, 236.
Bogart, Joseph, 59.
Boges, see Boggess and Bogus.
Boggard, Samuel, 199.
Boggess [Boges, Bogus], Joel, 294, 305.
Boggs, Francis, 37.
Boggs, Jesse, 204.
Bogle, William, 59.
Bogus [Boges], Henry, 220, 233.
Bogus, see Boggess.
Bohan, see Bohn.
Bohanan [Buckana], Joseph, 279, 291.
Boher [Baugher], George, 41, 52.
Bohham, see Bonham.
Bohn [Bohan], Elizabeth, 28, 31.
Boice, John, 199.
Boier, see Baugher.
Boland, David, 26.
Bolen, see Bowlen.

Boler Jack [Bolerjack], Joel, 341, 356.
Boler Jack, John, 341.
Boles, James, 8.
Boles [Bolls], John, 67, 74.
Boll, Stephen, 199.
Bolls, see Boles.
Bols, see Beatis.
Boltinghouse, Daniel, 60, 350.
Bolton, see Boalter and Boulton.
Boman, John, 3.
Boman [Bomon], Randolph, 268, 286.
Boman, see Bowman.
Bomon, see Boman.
Bond, George, 87.
Bond, Maston, 338.
Bond, Moses, 337.
Bond, Shadrach, 238.
Bondter, John, 91.
Bone [Boon], Squire [Square], 299, 309.
Bone [Boon], Mary, 302, 310.
Boneau, Pierre, 244.
Boner [Bonner], Alexandria [Alexander], 142, 177.
Boneue [Bono], Joseph, 275, 289.
Bonham [Bohham], Daniel, 257, 282.
Bonham, Mallakiah [Malachiah], 262, 284.
Bonham, Samuel, 262.
Bonham [Banham], William, 262, 284.
Bonneau, Nicholas, 57.
Bonner, Henery [Henry], 141, 177.
Bonner, see Boner.
Bono [Boon], Peter, 47, 54.
Bono, see Boneue.
Bonsley, John, 57.
Boon, William, 110.
Boon, see Bone and Bono.
Boother, John, 211.
Borah, George, 325.
Borah, John, 328.
Boran, Tarlton, 60.
Borders, Andrew, 245.
Boren [Borin], Bazel, 296, 307.
Boren [Borin], Hozea [Hosea, Hoza], 295, 307.
Boren [Borin], John, 296, 307.
Boren, see Borin.
Borin, John, Jr., 305.
Borin [Boren], Willis, 130, 135.
Borin, see Boren.
Boring, Dorsey [Dossy], 271, 287.
Borna, Jacob, 196.
Borna, see Borney.
Borney [Borna], John [Jacob], 144, 179.
Boroff, John, 194.
Borough, see Borow.
Borow [Borough], Joseph, 150, 182.
Bosarth, Joseph, 336.

Bosso [Bozenu], Nichlas [Nicholas], 275, 289.
Bostwick, Clement, 258.
Boswell [Baswell], Henry, 318, 323.
Botsford [Bottsford], Moss K., 261, 283.
Bottsford, *see* Botsford.
Boucher, John, 259.
Boughman, John, 91.
Boulton [Bolton], George [Charles], 155, 184.
Bourt, Martin, 156.
Boutwell, Alexander K., 76.
Boutwell, Leony C. [Leony, Loney], 77, 93.
Boutwell, Stephen, 76.
Bove, *see* Bovee.
Bovee [Bove], John, 326, 330.
Boveneau [Bovinu], John, 275, 289.
Bovinu, *see* Boveneau, Bovneu, *and* Bovoneau.
Bovneu [Bovinu], Nichles [Nicholas], 276, 290.
Bovoneau [Bovinu], John, 277, 290.
Bovy, Alexy, 239.
Bower, Jacob, 162.
Bowerman, Jacob, 244.
Bowerman, Jessee, 245.
Bowerman, Jonathan, 106.
Bowie, *see* Bowye.
Bowlen [Bolen], James, 171, 192.
Bowles, John, 110.
Bowlin, *see* Bawlin.
Bowling, James, 127.
Bowling, *see* Bawlin.
Bowls, Mary, 281.
Bowman, Abraham, 199, 299.
Bowman, Andrew, 9, 22.
Bowman [Boman], Benjn. [Bengeman, Bengman], 220, 232.
Bowman, Henry, 56.
Bowman, Mary, 57.
Bowye [Bowie], Ann [Anna], 346, 358.
Bowyer, Jacob, 157.
Bowyer, *see* Boyer.
Box, Stephen, 271.
Boyd, Andrew, 337.
Boyd, George, 193.
Boyd, Henry, 337.
Boyd, James, 350.
Boyd, Joel, 60.
Boyd, John, 40.
Boyd, Jonathan, 197.
Boyd, Joseph, 320.
Boyd, Thomas, 60.
Boyd, William, 61.
Boyeau, *see* Bayeau.
Boyer [Bowyer], George P. [John B.], 69, 74.
Boyer, Heny, 77.

Boyes [Baze], David, 86, 96.
Bozarth [Bozier], Israel, 220, 232.
Bozeman, Jacob, 348.
Bozeman, James, 350.
Bozeman, Samuel, 336, 352.
Bozenu, *see* Bosso.
Bozier, *see* Bozarth.
Bracken, Henry, 88.
Bracket, Willis, 260.
Brackman, William, 89.
Bradberry, *see* Bradbury.
Bradburn, James, 197.
Bradbury, *see* Bradbury.
Bradbury [Bradberry], Elisha, 40, 51.
Bradbury [Bradburry], William, 40, 51.
Braden, *see* Brady.
Bradford, Abner, 123.
Bradford, David, 14.
Bradford, George, 123.
Bradford, John, 312.
Bradford, Samuel, 123.
Bradley, Charles [Chals], 1, 5.
Bradley, Jacob, 146.
Bradley, James, 193, 250.
Bradley, Joshua, 253.
Bradley, *see* Bradly.
Bradly [Bradley], Rubin [Reuben], 206, 212.
Bradner [Braner], John, 215, 230.
Bradsby, James, 288.
Bradsby, Mary, 272, 288.
Bradsby, William H., 318.
Bradshaw, Absolum [Absalum], 202, 211.
Bradshaw, Elijah, 117.
Bradshaw, James, 207.
Bradshaw, John, 159, 294.
Bradshaw, Jonas, 147.
Bradshaw, Jonathan, 350.
Bradshaw, Nancy [Ann, Anne], 147, 180.
Bradshaw, Thomas, 327, 330.
Brady [Braden], Jacob, 339, 356.
Brady, John, 78.
Brady, Peter, 198.
Brady, Thomas, 197.
Brag [Bragg], William, 170, 191.
Bragg, *see* Brag.
Brake, John, 313.
Braken, William, 1, 6.
Bramblet, Bramblett, *see* Bramlett.
Bramlet, Elkanah, 327.
Bramlett [Bramblet], Benjamine [Benj., Benjamin], 85, 96.
Bramlett [Bramblet], Henry, 86, 96.
Bramlett, Nathan, 86.
Bramlett [Bramblett], Reuben [Reubin], 85, 96.
Braner, *see* Bradner.

INDEX 373

Brasele, *see* Brazel *and* Brazil.
Braselton [Brasilton], Benjamin, 320.
Brashar, *see* Bashar.
Brasilton, *see* Braselton.
Brassell, *see* Brazel.
Bratney, Robert, 249.
Braton, Mary, 9.
Bratten [Bratton], George W., 35, 50.
Bratton, Andrew, 328.
Bratton, *see* Bratten.
Brawdy, Richard, 47.
Brawdy, William, 47.
Brazel, David, 170.
Brazel, Richard, 13.
Brazel [Brasele, Brassell], Robert, 154, 184.
Brazel, *see* Brazule.
Brazelton [Brazleton], Benjamin, 7, 22.
Brazil [Brasele], George, 132, 136.
Brazleton, *see* Brazelton.
Brazule [Brazel], William, 272, 288.
Breach, *see* Breath.
Breath [Breach], James, 159, 186.
Breden [Breton], James, 138, 176.
Brembery, *see* Brimbery.
Brenchley, John, 57.
Brents, Joshua, 200.
Breton, *see* Breden *and* Britan.
Brewer, Henry, 258.
Brewer, Hubbard, 258.
Brewer, Jacob, 313.
Brewer, Peggy, 281.
Brewer, Richard, 240.
Brewer, Stephen [Henry], 258, 282.
Brewer, William M., 263.
Brewer, *see* Bruer.
Brewin, William, 148.
Brian, *see* Bryon.
Briant, Daniel, 343.
Briant, James, 343.
Briant, *see* Bryant.
Brickey [Bricky], Jarrot, 258, 282.
Bricky, Preston, 241.
Bricky, *see* Brickey.
Bridgeman, Joseph, 281.
Bridgeman [Bridgman], Nathan, 85, 96.
Bridger, *see* Bridges.
Bridgers [Bridges], George, 143, 178.
Bridges, Allen, 164.
Bridges, Gorge [George], 268, 286.
Bridges, John, 129.
Bridges, William, 270.
Bridges [Bridger], William, 276, 290.
Bridges, *see* Bridgers.
Bridgewater [Bridgwater], Zacariah [Zachariah], 15, 23.
Bridgman, *see* Bridgeman.
Bridgwater, *see* Bridgewater.

Brigam, Ebenezer, 281.
Brigance [Brigum], Clinton, 86, 96.
Briggman, William, 85.
Briggs, Robert, 15.
Bright [Brite], David [Daniel], 28, 31.
Bright, Hinson, 43.
Bright, Jacob, 58.
Bright, Tobias, 268.
Brigman, John, 37.
Brigum, *see* Brigance.
Brill, Solomon, 341.
Brimberry [Brimbery], Isaac, 40, 49, 51.
Brimberry, Jacob, 49.
Brimberry, *see* Brimbery.
Brimbery [Brembery, Brimberry], Samuel, 45, 53.
Brimbery, *see* Brimberry.
Brines, Henry, 15.
Brines, James, 15.
Brisco, *see* Briscow.
Briscow [Brisco, Brosco], John, 163, 189.
Bristo, *see* Bristow.
Bristow [Bristo], Thomas, 167, 190.
Britain [Britton], Ivins E. [Evens E.], 162, 188.
Britan [Breton], William, 161, 187.
Brite, *see* Bright.
Britton, Charleton, 26.
Britton, David L., 193.
Britton, *see* Britain.
Broad, John [John B.], 164, 189.
Broad, Moses, 164.
Broadwell, Backster, 194.
Brock, John, 200.
Brock, Mary, 272, 288.
Brock, Oliver, 288.
Brock, Solomon, 193.
Brockett, Benjamin, 332.
Brockett, Thomas, 332.
Brockway, Elias, 60.
Brockway, Jonathan Niles, 199.
Brook, *see* Bruce.
Brooks, James H., 350.
Brooks, Mary, 58.
Brooks, Thomas, 58.
Brooks [Brucks], Z. [Zaphne], 110, 119.
Broom, John, 273.
Brosco, *see* Briscow.
Browder, Jonathan, 316.
Browder, William, 350.
Browen, *see* Brownin.
Brown, Widow, 214.
Brown, Aaron B. [Aron B.], 132, 136.
Brown, Abbert, 168.
Brown, Abraham, 298.
Brown, Alexander, 45.
Brown, Alosyus [Aloscous, Alosysus], 26, 31.

Brown, Aquilla, 250.
Brown, Archibald, 352.
Brown, Armstead H. [Armstead], 294, 305.
Brown, Ben, 114.
Brown, Charles, 153.
Brown, Clade [Chad], 137, 176.
Brown, Colyer [Colier, Collier], 315, 322.
Brown, Daniel, 153, 349.
Brown, Daniel [Daniel, Jr.], 349, 359.
Brown, David, 5, 293, 305.
Brown, Erastus, 138.
Brown, Francis, 11, 237, 242.
Brown, George, 315.
Brown, George, Sr., 296.
Brown, George, Jr. [George 3d], 293, 305.
Brown, George H., 303.
Brown, Green B. [Greenberry], 2, 5.
Brown, Henry, 163, 197, 264.
Brown, J. [Joseph], 225, 235.
Brown, Jacob, 155, 302.
Brown, James, 293.
Brown, James P., 196.
Brown, Jehugh [John], 157, 185.
Brown, Jerremiah [Jeremiah], 5, 293, 305.
Brown, Jesse, 91.
Brown, John, 1, 59, 79, 157, 298, 315, 325, 349.
Brown, Jonithan [Jonathan], 138, 176.
Brown, Joseph, 4, 195.
Brown, Joshua, 166.
Brown, Martin [Mertain], 219, 232.
Brown, R., Sr. [Richard, Sr.], 112, 119.
Brown, Richard, 1.
Brown, Richard [Richard, Jr.], 112, 119.
Brown, Samuel, 56, 57, 147, 214, 315.
Brown, Thomas, 28, 56, 218.
Brown [Rowin], Wallis, 344, 357.
Brown, Warren, 237.
Brown, William, 7, 59, 112, 335.
Brown, William G., 268.
Brown, Willim [William], 346, 358.
Brown, see Browne.
Browne [Brown], Coleman [Coalman], 85, 96.
Browne, John, 81.
Browne [Brown], John, 86, 96.
Browne [Brown], Mavil [Marvel], 86, 96.
Browne, Michael, 85.
Browne, Novel, 84.
Browne [Brown], Thomas, 85, 96.
Browne, Thomas C., 81.
Browne [Brown], William, 86, 96.
Brownfield, John, 207.
Brownfield, Richard, 207.
Brownfield, Theron, 205.
Brownfield, William, 37.
Brownin [Browen], Benjamin, 257, 282.

Browning, Elisha, 131.
Browning, John, 62, 71.
Bruce [Brook], James, 168, 190.
Bruce, John, 302, 332.
Bruce, Robert, 341.
Brucks, see Brooks.
Bruer, John, 196.
Bruer [Brewer], William M. [William], 108, 118.
Bruington, John, 220.
Brumley, Daniel, 328.
Brunt, John, 258.
Brush, Alkenerey, 194.
Brush, William, 196.
Brusko [Bruzeer], Henry, 275, 289.
Bruyatt, Joseph, 281.
Bruzeer, see Brusko.
Bryan, Abner, 294.
Bryan, Daniel, 208.
Bryan [Bryant], Elijah, 294, 306.
Bryan, William, 205.
Bryans, see Bryant.
Bryant [Briant, Bryon], Benjamin, 346, 358.
Bryant [Briant], James, 350, 359.
Bryant [Bryans], James, 36, 50.
Bryant, Prince, 208, 209, 210.
Bryant, see Bryan.
Brynes, Patience, 59.
Bryon [Brian], Abner, 110, 119.
Bryon, see Bryant.
Buchannon, see Buckhanon.
Buck, James, 314.
Buck, Joseph, 145.
Buck, Warner [Warner, Sr.], 83, 95.
Buck, William, 145.
Buckana, see Bohanan.
Buckels [Buckles], Robert, 345, 357.
Buckhanan, John, 59.
Buckhanan, Joseph R., 58.
Buckhanan, Thomas, 57.
Buckhanan, Victor, 59.
Buckhanon [Buchannon], Joseph [John], 166, 190.
Buckles, John, 58.
Buckles, see Buckels.
Buckley, Peter, 199.
Buckner, Widow, 215.
Buckner, Henry, 45.
Buckner, James, 215.
Buckstan, see Buckston.
Buckston [Buckstan], John, 83, 95.
Buel [Buell], Daniel, 240, 254.
Buell, see Buel.
Buennet [Bennett], William, 148, 181.
Buffington, Abraham, 91.
Buffington, Philip C., 91.
Buffington, Richard, 85.

INDEX

Bugg, Henry, 332.
Bullard, John, 275.
Bully [Buya], Joseph, 278, 291.
Bunday [Bundy], Dorcas [Dorcus], 122, 126.
Bundy, see Bunday.
Bunker, Abraham [Abram], 271, 287.
Bunting, John A., 58.
Buoyar, John, 173.
Burbank, M., 223.
Burbanks, Daniel, 338.
Burcess, Gilbert, 347.
Burdauk [Burdo], Jack [John], 275, 289.
Burden, Joab, 161.
Burden [Burdon], John, 294, 306.
Burden, Julie, 200.
Burden, see Berdin and Burdin.
Burdin [Birdon, Burden], Reuben, 88, 97.
Burdo, see Burdauk.
Burdon, see Burden.
Burge, Buennet [Bennet], 163, 188.
Burge [Byrum], Buennet, Jr., 163, 188.
Burges [Burgess], William, 9, 22.
Burgess, see Bergess and Burges.
Burgum, Joseph, 196.
Burk, David, 205.
Burk, James, 197.
Burn, Lewis, 200.
Burnaugh [Bernash], Michael, 278, 291.
Burnes, John, 91.
Burnes, see Berns.
Burnet, see Barnet.
Burnett, S., 227.
Burnett, William [Will], 83, 95.
Burns, C. C., 226.
Burns, Charles, 56.
Burns, George, 326.
Burns, Stephen, 87.
Burns, Thomas, 104.
Burns, see Berns and Byrns.
Burnside, James, Sr. [James], 9, 22.
Burnside, James, Jr., 9.
Burnside, John, 9.
Burr, Chauncey S., 237.
Burr, Labin, 26.
Burr, Theodore, 243.
Burrel [Burrell], Joseph, 348, 358.
Burrel, see Burrell.
Burrell [Burrel], David, 335, 354.
Burrell, see Burrel.
Burrows, James, 312.
Burruss, Nancy, 43.
Burt, Morton, 193.
Burton, Gibeon [Gideon], 312, 320.
Burton, John, 57, 337.
Burton, Samuel L., 100.
Burton, William, 56.
Busby, see Buzbe.

Buseby, see Beesely.
Busely [Busly], Richard, 248, 255.
Bush, see Rush.
Bushhart, George, 91.
Bushnel, Lyman, 210.
Bushnel, Solomon, 210.
Busly, see Busely.
Butcher, Catherine, 104, 118.
Butcher, George, 118.
Butcher, Jacob, 112.
Butcher, see Butsher.
Butler, Charles, 314.
Butler, Elijah, 83.
Butler, George, 57.
Butler, Isaac, 56.
Butler, James, 47, 325.
Butler, Joshua, 57.
Butler, Stephen, 2.
Butsher [Butcher], Samuel, 300, 309.
Butterfield, Jonas, 35.
Buttilet, Joseph, 242.
Buya, see Bully.
Buzan, Jesse, 281.
Buzbe [Busby], Levi, 129, 135.
Byars, see Byers.
Byers [Byars], John, 112, 119.
Byran, see Biram.
Byrd, John, 197, 258, 271.
Byrns [Burns], John, 257, 282.
Byrons, Samuel, 127.
Byrum, see Biram and Burge.

Cackson, see Cockram.
Cade, Simon, 80.
Cadwell, Abijah, 196.
Cadwell, Elisha [Abijah], 145, 179.
Cadwell, George, 145.
Cafen, see Coffin.
Caggle, Henry, 68.
Cahe, William, 166.
Caiman [Beeman], Samuel, 139, 176.
Cain, John, 173.
Cain, Michael, 81.
Cain, see Caine and Cane.
Caine [Cain], William, 336, 355.
Caines, Talton M., 83.
Cairnes, see Carnes.
Cairns, Coldwell [Caldwell], 203, 211.
Caithle, William, 91.
Calbert [Colbert], James, 82, 95.
Calbreath [Colbreath], John, 264, 285.
Calbreath, see Colbreath.
Caldwell, Curtice [Curtis], 123, 126.
Caldwell, David, 26.
Caldwell, James, 35.
Caldwell, John, 81.
Caldwell, Richard [Robert], 63, 72.

Caldwell, Samuel, 84.
Caldwell, William [Will], 78, 94.
Caldwell, see Coldwell.
Calhoun, Hugh, 61.
Calhound, George, 34.
Callahan, Cassandra, 348.
Callahan, Robert, 313.
Calogue, Elisha, 167.
Calogue, Semore, 166.
Calvert, David, 336.
Calvert [Clavert], J. [John, John, Sr.], 222, 233.
Calvert [Clavert], J. [John, John, Jr.], 222, 234.
Calvert, John D., 336.
Calvey, see Cawley.
Calvin, Luther, 173.
Calvin, Neptune [Nepture], 345, 357.
Calvy, Richard, 195.
Cambbell, see Campbell.
Cambell [Campbell], Darneal, 68, 74.
Cambell [Campbell], Robert, 68, 74.
Cambell [Campbell], William, 68, 74.
Cambple, see Campbell.
Camel, John, 348.
Cameron [Camron], Thomas, 334, 354.
Cammon [Campbell], John, 162, 188.
Cammore [More], William [William C.], 161, 187.
Camp, Hosea J., 18.
Camp, Telemanchus, 194.
Campbel, see Campbell.
Campbell [Cambbell], Alex. [Alexander], 329, 330.
Campbell, Alexander, 251.
Campbell, Archibald, 78.
Campbell, Benjamin, 171.
Campbell [Cambple], Charles, 80, 94.
Campbell, Dugal, 59.
Campbell, James, 59.
Campbell, John, 102, 163, 250.
Campbell [Campbel], John, 78, 94.
Campbell, John, Sr., 114.
Campbell, John, Jr., 114.
Campbell, John M., 102.
Campbell, Neil, 56.
Campbell, S. [Stephen], 223, 234.
Campbell, Samuel N., 61.
Campbell [Campble], Samuel R., 80, 94.
Campbell, T. [Thomas], 223, 234.
Campbell, William, 38, 115, 246.
Campbell, see Cambell and Cammon.
Campble, see Campbell.
Camron [Carmen], Elijah, 259, 282.
Camron, see Cameron.
Canada, Edmond, 196.
Canada, Jacob, 130.

Canada, Jesse, 130.
Canada, see Keneday.
Canady, Archibal [Archibald], 8, 22.
Canady, William, 198.
Cane [Cain], James, 80, 94.
Cane [Cain], Joseph, 79, 94.
Canel, Lawrence, 194.
Cann, James, 345.
Cannada, M., 114.
Cannon, Benjamin, 334.
Cannon, Cornelius, 60.
Cannon [Cowan], David, 170, 191.
Cannon, Thomas, 281.
Cantrall [Cantrell], Richard, 63, 71.
Cantrel, see Clanterman.
Cantrell, see Cantrall.
Cantrill, see Tenton.
Cantwell, James, 27.
Cantwell, Martin, 325.
Cape, Jabese, 194.
Capture [Carpenter], William, 161, 187.
Caral [Carrel], Edward, 157, 185.
Card, James, 14.
Card [Carr], James, 167, 190.
Carden, Robert, 100.
Carel, Jiles, 168.
Caret, Thomas C., 152.
Carick, Thomas, 193.
Carigan, see Carrigan.
Carker [Carraker], Daniel, 296, 307.
Carker [Karraker], Jacob, 297, 307.
Carland, see Carlen and Carlin.
Carlen [Carland], Thomas, 158, 186.
Carlile, James, 210.
Carlile, see Carlisle.
Carlin [Carland], James, 138, 176.
Carlisle [Carlile], Robin [Robert], 345, 357.
Carlock, Abraham, 165.
Carlock, George, 200.
Carlock, Isaac, 165.
Carlock, Moses, 336.
Carloo, see Cobic.
Carmel [Cormack], Ribers [Rivers], 171, 191.
Carmen, see Camron.
Carnes [Cairnes], Abraham [Abram], 37, 50.
Carnes, Jacob, 91.
Carnes [Kerns], William, 148, 181.
Carns, Peggy, 274.
Carns, Robert, 261.
Caron, see Carron.
Carpenter, Chester, 337.
Carpenter, Christopher, 273.
Carpenter, Cornelius, 60.
Carpenter, Ephraim, 197.
Carpenter, James, 80.
Carpenter, John, 239.
Carpenter, Nathan, 146.

INDEX

Carpenter, Robert, 60.
Carpenter [Cavender], S., 224, 234.
Carpenter, see Capture.
Carr, Abner, 260.
Carr, Coonrad [Conrod], 260, 283.
Carr, Henry [Henry, Sr.], 258, 282.
Carr, Henry [Henry, Jr.], 260, 283.
Carr, Jacob, 264.
Carr, James, 314.
Carr, Leonard, 206.
Carr, Samuel, 315.
Carr, see Card.
Carraker, see Carker.
Carrel, Josias, 195.
Carrel, see Caral and Carrol.
Carrell [Carvel], Jacob, 219, 232.
Carret [Scarrett], Isaac, 159, 186.
Carrick, Moses, 273.
Carrigan, James, 312.
Carrigan [Carigan], John, 312, 320.
Carrigan, William, 318.
Carrington, see Covington.
Carrol [Carrel], Harlin [Harlande, Starling], 76, 93.
Carron [Caron], John B., 277, 290.
Carry, James, 197.
Carson, Andrew, 327.
Carson, John, 325.
Carson [Crarson], Urier [Euriah], 87, 97.
Carter, Aliece [Ledsey], 316, 322.
Carter, Davis, 170.
Carter, Edward, 62.
Carter, Elijah, 294.
Carter, John, 79, 195, 316, 338, 343.
Carter [Parker], John H., 67, 74.
Carter, Josiah, 332.
Carter, Leonard, 246.
Carter, Molton, 295, 306.
Carter, Moreton [Morten], 129, 135.
Carter, Nancy, 306.
Carter, Oliver, 200.
Carter, Rex [Ricks], 129, 135.
Carter, Richard [Richard P.], 312, 320.
Carter, Shadrach B. A. [S. B. A.], 45, 53.
Carter, Susanah, 82.
Carvel, John, 194, 199.
Carvel, see Carrell.
Cary, Joshua, 203.
Cary [Crary], Susanna, 334, 354.
Casa, see Casey.
Casad [Cazad], Anthony W., 273, 288.
Case, Alven, 168.
Casebry, John, 194.
Casewill, John, 91.
Casey, Aaron, 14.
Casey, Abraham P., 123.
Casey, Abraham T., 127.

Casey, Green P., 124.
Casey, Iaac [Isaac], 124, 126.
Casey, John C., 124.
Casey, Levi, 13.
Casey [Casy, Kasey], Levi, 132, 136.
Casey [Cassy], Nicholas, 79, 94.
Casey [Kasey], Randolph, 131, 136.
Casey [Casa], Robert, 300, 309.
Casey, Thomas M., 123.
Casey, William, 123.
Casey, Zadoc [Zadok], 124, 127.
Cason, Seth, 327.
Casper, Peter, 300.
Cass, Lewis, 200.
Cassey, Antoine, 253.
Casslin [Casterlan, Casterline], Jonithan [Jonathan], 148, 181.
Cassner, James, 159.
Cassy, see Casey.
Casteel, Abraham, 281.
Casteel, Ely [Eli], 222, 233.
Casteel, Jacob, 143.
Casteel, John, 194.
Casterlan, Casterline, see Casslin.
Castlebury, Meredith, 316.
Caswell, Josiah, 82.
Caswell, William, 223.
Casy, see Casey.
Cates, Robert D., 329.
Catherington, Jonathan, 200.
Cathern, see Cothern.
Catline [Cottand], Seth, 269, 286.
Cato [Catto], Antoine, 238, 253.
Cato, Charles, 336.
Caton, see Cayton.
Catron, George W., 30.
Catt, Sebaston, 328.
Catter, James, 193.
Catter, see Coatter.
Catterton, Diler, 37.
Catto, see Cato.
Caudle, see Coddle.
Cavanah, Charles, 197.
Cavenah, Charles, 242.
Cavenah [Cavenaugh], Patrick, 243, 254.
Cavenaugh, see Cavenah.
Cavender, see Carpenter.
Cawan, see Cowan.
Cawerly, James F., 198.
Cawley [Calvey], William [William W.], 140, 176.
Cayton [Caton], John, 81, 95.
Cazad, see Casad.
Cells, Abraham, 169.
Cellums, see Kelloms.
Cervil, John, 298.
Chafey, Onatis, 37.

Chaffen, see Chaffin.
Chaffin [Chaffen], Elias, 83, 95.
Chaffin, Elias, Jr., 86.
Chaffin, James, 123.
Chaffin, Joseph, 12, 281.
Chaffin, see Chafin.
Chafin [Chaffin], Ellis, 319, 323.
Chales, see Charles.
Chalfin, Amos, 211.
Chalfin, Charlotte, 203, 211.
Chalfin, William, 203.
Chalfin, see Chalpen and Chalpin.
Chalpen [Chalfin], Seth, 202, 211.
Chalpin [Chalfin], Ellis [Elis], 202, 211.
Chambelain [Chamberlan], Louis, 239, 253.
Chamberla, see Chambo and Chamberlain.
Chamberlain [Chamberla], Antoine, 238, 253.
Chamberlain [Chamberla], Batiste, 240, 254.
Chamberlain [Chamberla], Mary, 238, 253.
Chamberlan, see Chambelain.
Chambers, Sally [Sarah], 273, 288.
Chambers, William, 35.
Chambo [Chamberla], Joseph Ar. [Joseph], 239, 253.
Chamlis, Sary, 68.
Champion, John, 319.
Chance, David R. [David], 259, 283.
Chance, Joseph, 268.
Chance, William, 205.
Chancey, Israel [Izrel], 217, 231.
Chancey [Chancy], Roswell [Raswell], 214, 229.
Chancy, Andrew, 217.
Chancy, see Chancey.
Chandlar, George, 148.
Chandler, Amos, 318.
Chandler, Anderson, 316.
Chandler, Ely [Eli], 217, 231.
Chandler [Chandlier], Isaac, 147, 180.
Chandler [Chanler], Isaac, 140, 177.
Chandler [Chanler], Richard W., 261, 283.
Chandler, Thomas, 140, 217.
Chandler, William, 148.
Chandler, see Chanler.
Chandlier, see Chandler.
Chanler [Chandler], Daniel, 217, 230.
Chanler, see Chandler.
Chapel [Chappel], Cumstock [Comstock, Cumpstock], 347, 358.
Chapell [Chapelle], Elizabeth, 237, 253.
Chapelle, see Chapell.
Chapin, see Chaping.
Chaping [Chapin], Lorenzo, 312, 320.
Chaping [Chapin], Samuel, 312, 320.
Chaple, Solomon, 91.
Chapley, see Chappin.
Chapman, A. [Avery, Mr.], 110, 119.

Chapman, Asa, 297.
Chapman, James W. [James], 161, 187.
Chapman, Jobe, 325.
Chapman, John, 194.
Chapman, Richard, 194.
Chapman, Samuel, 343.
Chapman, Samuel J., 132.
Chappel, see Chapel.
Chappin [Chapley], Hiram, 152, 183.
Charles [Chales], Elijah, Sr., 264, 285.
Charles, Elijah, Jr., 270.
Charles, Levin, 3.
Charleville, Andrew, 243.
Charleville, Batiste, 244.
Chase, Ashur, 196.
Chase, Sardis R., 58.
Chavis, see Cheeves.
Cheach, see Cheek.
Cheak [Cheek], Joel, 43, 52.
Cheak [Cheek], Nellis [Willis], 174, 192.
Cheek [Cheach], Isham [Isem], 81, 95.
Cheek, Nathan, 42.
Cheek, Shadrick, 62.
Cheek, see Cheak.
Cheeves [Chavis], William, 272, 288.
Chein, Jacco, 242.
Chenet, Antoine Z., 58.
Chenney, Robert, 193.
Chenny, Antoine, 243.
Chenny, James, 240.
Chenoweth [Chenowith], John, 27, 31.
Chenowith, see Chenoweth.
Chense, Daniel, Jr., 194.
Cheny, see Cherry.
Chermont, Pierre, 194.
Cherry, Benjamin, 171.
Cherry [Cheny], Willis, 352, 360.
Chesney, Alexander, 315.
Chesney, Benjamin, 315.
Chesney, Robert, 268.
Childers, William, 346.
Childres, William, 36.
Chiles [Kile], Adams [Adam], 156, 185.
Chilson, Jesse, 91.
Chilson, Nathaniel, 77.
Chilton, William, 200.
Chipps, A. [Amos], 226, 236.
Chism, John, 349.
Chitty, Benjamin, 68.
Choat, Squire, 130.
Chouven, Lopenne, 198.
Chrice [Crise], David, 298, 308.
Chrice [Crise], John, 296, 307.
Christian, Robert, 81.
Christle, Henry, 338.
Christmas, John, 277.
Christopher, John, 91.

INDEX 379

Christy, Enos, 239.
Christy, William, 197, 238.
Chuing, see Chuning.
Chuning [Chuing], Richard, 221, 233.
Church, Daniel [Daniel, Sr.], 172, 192.
Church, E., 227.
Churchill, Daniel S., 59.
Churchill, Joel, 59.
Churlin [Cleveland], John, 156, 185.
Cilbern, William D., 31.
Cimmel [Kimmel], Daniel [David], 293, 305.
Cimmel [Kimmel, Kimmell], John, 298, 308.
Cissel, Edward, 210.
Citter, Coonrod, 305.
Clain, Robert, 162.
Clampet, Nathan, 65.
Clanterman [Cantrel], Levi, 162, 188.
Clanton, Edward, 140.
Clap [Clapp], Adam, Sr. [Adam], 297, 308.
Clap [Clapp], Adam, Jr., 302, 311.
Clapp, William, 305.
Clapp, see Clap.
Clarey, Sarah, 18, 23.
Clarey, Spencer, 18, 23.
Clarey, Vatchel, 88.
Clark, Absolem [Absalum], 169, 191.
Clark, Alexander, 112.
Clark, Alexander [Elexander], 326, 330.
Clark, Alexander H. [Alexander], 79, 94.
Clark, Andrew, 327.
Clark, Baldwin, 57.
Clark, Benjamin, 59.
Clark, Benonia [Benona], 204, 212.
Clark, Edward, 203, 260.
Clark [Clarke], Ensley [Anesly, Ansley], 77, 93.
Clark, Felix, 203.
Clark, Hezekiah, 60.
Clark, Jacob, 203.
Clark, James, 245, 326, 345.
Clark, James, Sr., 327.
Clark, John, 58, 320, 327, 345.
Clark, Joseph, 328.
Clark [Clarke], Joseph, 75, 92.
Clark, Joshua, 267.
Clark, Nathaniel, 3.
Clark, O. S. [Owen S.], 224, 235.
Clark, Randolph, 58.
Clark, Robert, 253.
Clark, Samuel, 76.
Clark, Sarah, 245.
Clark, Solomon, 327.
Clark, Susan, 203.
Clark, William, 57, 60, 193, 327, 328.
Clark [Clerk], William, 18, 23.
Clark, see Clarke.
Clarke [Clark], Isaac, 151, 182.

Clarke [Clark], John, 145, 179.
Clarke, Lucy, 151, 182.
Clarke [Clark], Philip, 171, 191.
Clarke, William, 182.
Clarke, William M., 142.
Clarke, see Clark.
Clarkson, Constantine, 170.
Clary [Clery], Greggs [Veach], 215, 230.
Clary, John, 23.
Clary, John [John, Sr.], 165, 189.
Clary, John [John, Jr.], 165, 189.
Clary, Rhereh, 165.
Clary, William, 165.
Clavert, see Calvert.
Clay, Ezekiel [Ezekel], 229.
Clay, Isam [Isom], 214, 229.
Claypole, Abraham, 148.
Claypoole, George, 59.
Clayton, Joseph, 58.
Clayton, Suard [Sword], 108, 118.
Clayton, William, 91.
Clement, John, 244.
Clemmens, James, 58.
Clemmens, John, 58.
Clendenan, Harvey, 246.
Clendenan, John, 247.
Clendenan, see Clendenon.
Clendenon [Clendenan], James, 247, 254.
Clerk, see Clark.
Clery, see Clary.
Cleson, see Beason.
Cleveland, John, 193.
Cleveland, see Churlin.
Clevendure, George, 38.
Clevenger, Job, 227, 229.
Cliff, James, 347.
Cline, George, 110.
Cline, John, 110.
Cline, John [Andrew], 162, 188.
Cline [Elins], John, 162, 188.
Cline, William, 15.
Clinelow, Asa, 162.
Close, George, 324.
Cloud, George, 3.
Clover, Jacob, 206.
Cloyes, Nathan, 239.
Clubb, Rezin, 60.
Clubb, Samuel H., 58.
Cluts, Henry, 297.
Cluts [Clutts], Jacob, 300, 310.
Cluts, Philip, 300.
Clutts, see Cluts.
Coal, see Cole.
Coalbourn, see Coburn.
Coalman [Coleman], Robert, 139, 176.
Coatter [Catter, Coulter], Robert, 154, 184.
Cobble, see Corble.

Cobic [Carloo], Philip, 145, 179.
Coburn, Jonathan, 84.
Coburn [Ausburn], Obediah [Obadiah], 275, 289.
Coburn [Coalbourn], Paul, 81, 95.
Cochenny, Mary, 241.
Cochran, Alex., 108.
Cochran [Coghren], Andrew, 131, 136.
Cochran, Andrew P., 91.
Cochran, Betsy, 131.
Cochran, James, 114.
Cochran, John, 91, 250.
Cochran, Marget [Peggy], 294, 306.
Cochran, Mary, 131.
Cochran, Moses, 132.
Cochran, Nathaniel [Nathaniel H.], 39, 51.
Cochran [Cothran], Robert, 112, 119.
Cochran, Samuel, 106.
Cochran [Cocthrin, Cotron], Wateres [Waters], 112, 119.
Cochran, William, 114, 247.
Cochrane, see Corhern.
Cockram [Cackson], Mason, 172, 192.
Cockrem, see Cockrum.
Cockrum [Cockrem], James, 313, 320.
Cocks, see Cox.
Cocthrin, see Cochran.
Coddle [Caudle], Ransom, 259, 282.
Coddle, William, 253.
Code, Edward, 11.
Coffe, see Coffee.
Coffee [Coffe], Newton, 14, 23.
Coffin [Cafen], B. [Barnabus], 218, 231.
Coffin [Coffman], Harris, 149, 182.
Coffman, Daniel, 237.
Coffman, Jacob, 337.
Coffman, see Coffin.
Coghren, see Cochran.
Coil [Coyle], John, 20, 24.
Coil, Nicholas, 193.
Colbert, Harrison, 253.
Colbert, see Calbert.
Colborne, see Coleman.
Colbreath, John [John H.], 269, 287.
Colbreath [Calbreath], William S., 263, 284.
Colbreath, see Calbreath.
Coldwell [Caldwell], George, 141, 177.
Coldwell [Caldwell], James, 80, 94.
Coldwell [Caldwell], James, 169, 191.
Coldwell, Samuel, 84.
Cole, Edward, 312.
Cole [Coal], Edy [Eady], 36, 50.
Cole, George, 8.
Cole, John, 219.
Cole, Richard, 312.
Cole, Robert, 8.
Cole, Samuel, 56.

Coleans, Abijah, 195.
Coleborn, Thomas, 210.
Coleen [Colien], Pierre, 243, 254.
Coleen, see Colene.
Coleman, Abigal, 195.
Coleman, Benjamine, 84.
Coleman, Daniel T., 293.
Coleman [Colborne], Ebenezer, 202, 211.
Coleman, Elisha H. [Elisha F.], 130, 135.
Coleman, Seth, 201.
Coleman, see Coalman.
Colene [Coleen], Francis, 147, 180.
Coliar [Colier], John, 215, 229.
Colien, see Coleen.
Colier [Colliers], Michael, 293, 305.
Colier, see Coliar.
Collard, Richard, 332.
Collens, see Collins.
Collett, see Cottet.
Collians, see Collins.
Collier, Edward, 57.
Collier, James, 57, 60.
Collier, Stephen, 281.
Colliers, see Colier.
Collins [Collens], Abraham [Ambrose], 167, 190.
Collins, Anson, 148.
Collins, John, 56, 333.
Collins [Collians], John, 169, 191.
Collins, Michael C. [Michael], 348, 358.
Collins, William, 3.
Colt, Anson, 199.
Colwell, John, 346.
Colwell, Stephen, 349.
Comeins [Cummins], John [William], 165, 189.
Comer, Allen, 19.
Comins [Cummins, Cummons], Josiah [Josias], 172, 192.
Commerce, Rickets, 281.
Compass [Compnio], Margaret, 279, 291.
Compnio, see Compass.
Compton, Elijah, 60.
Compton, John, 61.
Compton, John L., 57.
Compton, Levi, 56.
Compton, see Cumpton.
Comwell, Titus, 197.
Con [Conn], James, 352, 360.
Conant, N., 114.
Conaway, Hugh, 149.
Conaway, see Coneway, Connaway, and Conway.
Coneway [Conaway], James, 29, 32.
Coneway [Conoway], Jesse [Jessee], 149, 181.
Conger, John, 62.

INDEX

Conger, see Congor.
Congor [Conger], Isaac, 161, 187.
Coniers, see Conyers.
Conley [Conly], Alexandria [Alexander], 151, 183.
Conley, Edmon, 150.
Conley, Hesley [Hesey, Hesse], 151, 183.
Conley, Isaac, 151.
Conly, Willis, 198.
Conly, see Conley.
Conn, Curtis [Curtus], 247, 254.
Conn, Robert, 251.
Conn, see Con.
Connaway [Conaway], John, 46, 53.
Connel, John M., 91.
Conner, David, 329.
Conner, Henry, 240.
Conner, James, 198, 237, 240.
Conner, see Connor.
Connery, see Ocanrey.
Connor [Conner], Benjamin F., 106, 118.
Conoway, see Coneway.
Conrod [Coonrod], Abraham [Abram], 44, 52.
Conrod, James, 44.
Converse, Seth, 205.
Conway, Clement C., 238.
Conway, Joseph, 196.
Conway [Conaway], Joseph, 217, 231.
Conyers [Coniers], John, 3, 5.
Cook, Charles, 341.
Cook, Elias R., 210.
Cook [Cooke], Elish [Elicia, Elisha], 87, 97.
Cook, Fedrick [Fredrick], 302, 310.
Cook, Henery [Henry], 142, 178.
Cook, Hugh, 302.
Cook, James, 3.
Cook, John, 79, 151, 223, 340.
Cook, Margaret, 91.
Cook, Robert, 123.
Cook, Turner, 87.
Cook, William, 223.
Cook, Zacheriah, 341.
Cooke, see Cook.
Cooksey [Kooksey], John [John M.], 274, 288.
Coombs, Matthew, 56.
Coone [Coons], David [David F.], 276, 290.
Coone [Koon], John, 274, 288.
Coonrad, Coon Red, see Coonrod.
Coonrod [Coonrad], George, 144, 179.
Coonrod, John, 324.
Coonrod [Coon Red], Stephen, 327, 330.
Coonrod, see Conrod.
Coons, Edward, 195.
Coons, see Coone.
Coop, David, 159.

Cooper, Cadwaleder [Cadwalider], 29, 32.
Cooper, Hardy, 130.
Cooper, Harmon, 320.
Cooper, Henry, 161.
Cooper, Jacob, 170.
Cooper, James, 57, 60.
Cooper, Jesse W., 204.
Cooper, John, 169, 170, 201, 318.
Cooper, John L., 131.
Cooper, Joseph, 91.
Cooper, Meredith [Merideth], 270, 287.
Cooper, Robert, 83.
Cooper, Stephen, 263.
Cooper, William, 148.
Cope, John, 296.
Cope, Yost [Youst], 296, 307.
Copeland, Obid, 76.
Copeland, see Copland.
Coper, John, 200.
Copfil, James, 200.
Copland, James, 132.
Copland [Copeland], John, 132, 136.
Copland [Copeland], William, 131, 135.
Coppenborger, Jacob, 200.
Coppenbrger [Copperbarger], George, 272, 288.
Copperbarger, see Coppenbrger.
Coppinberger, see Cottonbarger.
Corban, Isaac, 67.
Corble [Cobble], Adam, 300, 309.
Corder, David H., 66.
Corder, James, 67.
Corgen, see Corgin.
Corgin [Corgen], Patrick, 302, 310.
Corhern [Cochrane], Hugh S., 140, 177.
Corie, William, 58.
Cormac [McCormick], Ruth, 207, 213.
Cormack, John, 194.
Cormack, see Carmel and Kermack.
Cormock, David, 195.
Cornel, see Cornell.
Cornelius, Joseph, 274.
Cornell [Cornel], Daniel, 27, 31.
Cornell [Cornel], Heli, 28, 31.
Corrandle, see Crandle.
Cort, see Court.
Corter, Polly, 59.
Cortrecht, John, 59.
Cortright, Daniel, 30.
Costley [Costly], William, 158, 186.
Costly, see Costley.
Cothern [Cathern], Hiram, 69, 74.
Cothran, see Cochran.
Cotner, David, 293.
Cotron, see Cochran.
Cottand, see Catline.
Cottener, see Cottenner.

Cottenner [Cottener], Frederick, 347, 358.
Cottet [Collett], Robert, 174, 192.
Cottle, David, 193.
Cottle, William, 193.
Cotton, Elias, 91.
Cotton, Elihu, 91.
Cotton, J. [John], 220, 232.
Cotton, John, 263.
Cottonbarger [Coppinberger], John, 161, 187.
Cottrell, Prier [Pierce], 348, 358.
Couch, James, 249.
Couch, Levi, 61.
Coulter, *see* Coatter.
Council, Reddick, 248.
Council, Samuel T., 349.
Council [Counsil], William, 352, 359.
Council, *see* Counsel.
Counsel [Council], Hardin [Hardy], 162, 188.
Counsil, *see* Council.
Court, William, 196.
Court [Cort], William, 145, 179.
Courtney, John H., 345.
Courtney, William, 200.
Cousart, *see* Cowsart *and* Cowsert.
Coventry, John C., 199.
Coventry, Sally, 147.
Covington [Carrington], Edmond [Edmon], 350, 359.
Cowan [Cawan], Dd. [D., David], 226, 236.
Cowan, Joel, 28.
Cowan [Cowen], William, 222, 233.
Cowan, *see* Cannon, Cowhen, *and* Cowin.
Cowen, William, 198.
Cowen, *see* Cowan *and* Cowin.
Cowhen [Cowan], Thomas, 261, 283.
Cowhick, Cowhill, *see* Cowwich.
Cowin, John, 91.
Cowin [Cowan, Cowen], Matthew, 137, 175.
Cowles, Alfred, 281.
Cowles, Edward, 238.
Cowling, Henry, 56.
Cowsart [Cousart], James, 214, 229.
Cowsart [Cousart], Thomas, 214, 229.
Cowsert [Cousart], Robt. [Robart], 214, 229.
Cowwich [Cowhick, Cowhill], Thomas, 167, 190.
Cox, Abicha, 193.
Cox, Abner, 132.
Cox, Absolom [Absalom], 249, 255.
Cox, Alexander, 82.
Cox, Ansel, 166.
Cox [Cocks], Anthony, 29, 31.
Cox, Benjamin, 314.
Cox, Bolen, 195.
Cox, Bowling [Bolen], 160, 187.
Cox, Charles, 314.

Cox, Daniel, 196.
Cox, Elizabeth [Jessee], 160, 187.
Cox, Henry, 87.
Cox, Isaac, 15.
Cox [Cocks], James, 27, 31.
Cox [Cocks], James, 29, 32.
Cox, Jane, 112.
Cox, Jarrot, 196.
Cox, John, 64, 195.
Cox, Mathew T. [Matthew], 265, 285.
Cox, Micajah, 147.
Cox, Nathaniel, 82.
Cox, Samuel, 3.
Cox, Thomas, 137, 256, 329.
Cox, Thomas [Thomas, Sr.], 296, 307.
Cox, Thomas, Jr. [Thomas S.], 302, 310.
Cox, William, 86, 274.
Coy [McCoy], David, 165, 189.
Coykendoll [Kaykendall], Peter, 28, 31.
Coyle, *see* Coil.
Cozad, Joseph, 75.
Crabb, Francis T., 261.
Crabell [Grable], David [David A.], 85, 96.
Craddock, John, 59.
Crafford [Crofford], William, 86, 96.
Crafford [Crawford], James, 221, 233.
Craford [Crawford], James, 270, 287.
Craft, Jacob, 301.
Craft, Thomas, 301.
Craften, *see* Crafton.
Crafton [Craften], Robert, 298, 308.
Crafton [Craften], Robert W. [Robert], 300, 309.
Crag, *see* Craig.
Craglo, Cragloe, *see* Craglole.
Craglole [Craglo, Cragloe], William, 300, 309.
Craig, Bazel, 294.
Craig [Crag], Hugh, 294, 306.
Craig, John C. [John], 348, 358.
Craig, Samuel, 334.
Craig, Sarah, 294.
Craig, *see* Craigg.
Craigg [Craig], Robert, 143, 178.
Crain [Crane], James, 167, 190.
Crain [Crane], Middleton [Philo M.], 158, 186.
Crain [Crane], Thomas, 157, 186.
Crain, *see* Crane.
Craly, Thomas, 167.
Cramwell, John, 197.
Cran, John, 157.
Crandal, James, 173.
Crandle [Corrandle], Gurdon [Jordan B.], 16, 23.
Crane [Crain], Squire, 108, 118.
Crane, Benjamin, 246.
Crane, James, 117.

Crane [Crain], Jhasper [Jesper], 68, 74.
Crane, Joel, 246.
Crane, John, 246.
Crane, Lemuel, 67.
Crane, Mathew, 67.
Crane, Silas, 270.
Crane, Smith [Samuel], 262, 284.
Crane [Crain], Spencer, 68, 74.
Crane [Crain], Thomas, 113, 119.
Crane, see Crain.
Cranshaw, E., 91.
Cranshaw, John, 91.
Crarson, see Carson.
Crary, see Cary.
Crasley, Samuel, 197.
Craten [Crayton], William, 317, 322.
Craton, Joseph, 349.
Craton, Thomas, 352.
Cravel, Allen, 117.
Cravens, Jesse, 344.
Cravins, Jesse, 91.
Craw, John, 333.
Craw, see Crow.
Crawder, Charles, 195.
Crawford, Abel, 195.
Crawford, George, 227.
Crawford, James [James L.], 221, 233.
Crawford, John, 60, 62, 198.
Crawford, John [J.], 227, 236.
Crawford, Josiah, 9.
Crawford, Mason, 63.
Crawford, Samuel, 193, 244.
Crawford, Thomas, 249.
Crawford, William, 193.
Crawford, see Craford and Crofford.
Crayton, see Craten.
Creal [Kreel], John, 318, 323.
Creamer, see Cremer.
Creath, George, 100.
Cremer [Creamer], John P. [Philip], 279, 292.
Crenshaw, Abraham, 91.
Crenshaw, Daniel, 124.
Cress, Jacob, 16.
Cresswell, see Criswell.
Crews, Andrew, 325.
Crews, John, 45.
Cricel [Crisle], George, 337, 355.
Cright [Crite], George, 303, 311.
Crill, see Gill.
Crimes, Jacob, 195.
Crimes, see Simes.
Crip, Jacob, 193.
Cripps, see Crips.
Crips, John, 305.
Crips [Cripps], John, 301, 310.
Crise, see Chrice.

Crisle, see Cricel.
Crisp, William M. [William], 16, 23.
Cristlar [Cristler], Silas, 247, 255.
Cristler, see Cristlar.
Criswell [Cresswell], David [Walter J.], 173, 192.
Crite, see Cright.
Crochett, James [J.], 226, 236.
Crochett [Crochitt, Crocket], John, 226, 236.
Crochitt, see Crochett.
Crocker, Arthur, 313.
Crocker, Elisha, 45, 49.
Crocker, Elizabeth, 313.
Crocker, Jacob, 313.
Crocker, James, 273.
Crocker, John, 267, 272.
Crocker, Josiah, 266.
Crocker [Croker], Stephen, 296, 307.
Crocker, William, 314.
Crocket, see Crochett.
Crofferd, Robert, 153.
Crofford [Crawford], Alexandria [Alexander], 162, 188.
Crofford, see Crafford.
Croft [Crofts], A., 223, 234.
Crofts, see Croft.
Croggins, see Scroggins.
Croker, see Crocker.
Cronk, see Crunk.
Croom [Crum], Daniel, 137, 175.
Crosby, Hezekiah, 139.
Crose, James, 339.
Crose, John, 339.
Crose, Michael, 339.
Crose, Phillip, 339.
Crose, Solomon, 341.
Crosier, see Crozier.
Crosieure, Simeon, 194.
Croson, see Crosson.
Cross, Arthur, 117, 244.
Cross, John, 60.
Cross, John [J.], 225, 235.
Cross, Jos., 114, 225.
Cross, Jos. [J.], 225, 235.
Cross, Samuel, 60.
Cross, see Crouse and Gross.
Crossen, see Crosson.
Crosson [Croson, Crossen], Michael, 205, 212.
Crosswite, Harvey, 130.
Crouch, Adam, 345.
Crouch, Edward, 67.
Crouse [Cross], J., 224, 235.
Crow, Jesse [Mary], 114, 120.
Crow, John, 353.
Crow, Joshua, 29.
Crow, Lewis, 1.
Crow, Rheuben [Rubin], 29, 32.

Crow [Craw], Robert [Robet], 114, 120.
Crow, William, 114.
Crow, see Croy.
Crowder, William B., 173.
Crowel, James, 150.
Crowell, William A., 56.
Crowl, John, 298.
Crown, Davis, 199.
Croy, Joshua, 164.
Croy [Crow], William, 164, 189.
Crozier, John C., 241.
Crozier [Crosier], Samuel, 250, 255.
Cruce, Peter, 305.
Cruce, see Cruse.
Crum, see Croom.
Crunk [Cronk], Andrew, 62, 71.
Crunk, James, 130.
Cruse [Cruce], Adam, 294, 306.
Cruse [Cruce], Henry, 299, 308.
Cruse, Henry, Jr., 303.
Cruson, William, 85.
Cryder, Henry, 80.
Cuberson [Culbertson], Alexander [Alexande], 268, 286.
Cuday [Cude, Cuddy], Lee, 296, 307.
Cuddeting, Joseph, 167.
Cuddy, Cude, see Cuday.
Culberson, Joseph, 348.
Culbertson, see Cuberson.
Culbreath, William, 343.
Culliam, John, Jr., 194.
Cullison, see Kullison.
Cullom, Edward N., 34.
Cullom, Francis, 44.
Cullom, William, 49.
Culp, Henry, 299.
Cummings, see Cummons.
Cummins, see Comeins, Comins, and Cummons.
Cummons [Cummins], Benjamine [Benjamin], 85, 96.
Cummons [Cummings], Thomas, 85, 96.
Cummons [Cummins], Thornton, 77, 93.
Cummons [Cummins], William [Will, Sr.], 77, 93.
Cummons [Cummins], William [William, Jr.], 85, 96.
Cummons, see Comins.
Cumpton [Compton], John B., 338, 355.
Cuningham [Cunningham], Patten [Peter], 38, 50.
Cunningham, John, 58.
Cunningham, William, 59.
Cunningham, see Cuningham.
Currie, John, 57.
Curry, Joseph, 247.
Curry, Martha, 250.

Curry, William A., 91.
Curtice, see Curtis.
Curtis, Henry, 8.
Curtis, John [John G.], 172, 192.
Curtis [Curtice], John, 219, 232.
Curtis, L. [Lewis], 223, 234.
Curtis, see Curtiss.
Curtiss [Curtis], Joseph, 26, 31.
Cusick, Henry, 61.
Cymons, see Simons.

Dabbs, James, 144.
Dacator [Decocashe], Gebriel [Gabriel], 277, 290.
Dace, Denis [Dennis], 204, 212.
Dace, Harmon, 210.
Dace, Mary, 204, 212.
Dace, Michael, 212.
Dacoto [Dacuto], Battece [J. Baptiest], 278, 291.
Dacuto, see Dacoto.
Daggot, Smith, 237.
Daglee, see Dagley.
Dagley [Daglee], Samuel, 342, 356.
Dagley [Daglee], Thomas, 342, 356.
Dail, William, 77.
Dailey [Daly], John, 300, 309.
Dailey, see Daly.
Daily, R., 113.
Daimwood, Boston, 78.
Daimwood [Damewood], John G. [John], 79, 94.
Dains, Levi, 204.
Dair, see Dare.
Dake, Arnold B., 59.
Dale, Jervis, 60.
Dale, John, 338.
Dalen, Elihu, 170.
Daley, Michael, 196.
Dalson [Dolson], James, 49.
Dalton, Ishom [Isham], 150, 182.
Daly [Dailey], John [John W.], 338, 355.
Daly, see Dailey.
Dames, see Dooms.
Damewood, see Daimwood.
Dammel [Domran], George, 164, 189.
Dammern, see Damron.
Damore, Madame, 241.
Damren, see Damron.
Damron, Charles, 66.
Damron [Dammern], John [John, Sr.], 66, 73.
Damron [Damren], John [John, Jr.], 66, 73.
Damron, William, 133.
Danel [Daniel, Daund], Walker, 158, 186.
Danes, Benjamin, 211.
Danes, Cloe, 249.

INDEX

Daney, see Denny.
Danford, Philip, 204.
Danforth, Cyrus, 57.
Danforth, Joseph, 326.
Daniel, Barton, 11.
Daniel, Bazzel [Bazil], 350, 359.
Daniel, David, 351.
Daniel, Delila, 11.
Daniel, Jeremiah, 11.
Daniel, John, 198, 218, 351.
Daniel [Daniels], Josiah, 351, 359.
Daniel, Martin, 11.
Daniel, Nicholas, 179; see also Daniel Neles.
Daniel, Robert, 11.
Daniel [Dannel], Thomas, 158, 186.
Daniel, William, 11, 83, 351.
Daniel [Daniels], William, 3, 5.
Daniel, see Danel and Daroneal.
Daniels, Aaron, 197.
Daniels, see Daniel.
Danley, Samuel, 161.
Dannel, see Daniel.
Dannie, Antoine, 238, 239.
Dannie, Battiste, 238.
Dannie, Charles, 240.
Dannie, Michel, 238.
Dannie, Michel B. [Michel], 238, 253.
Danogin, see Dunigan.
Dar [Dare], Hubbard, 79, 94.
Dar, see Dare.
Darbe, see Darby.
Darby, John F., 197.
Darby [Darbe], Joseph, 276, 290.
Dare [Dair, Dar], Matthew [Mathew], 146, 180.
Dare, see Dar.
Darnal, Darnall, see Darneal.
Darneal [Darnal, Darnell], Isaac, 316, 322.
Darneal [Darnall, Darnell], William, 316, 322.
Darneal, see Daroneal.
Darnell, see Darneal.
Daroneal [Darneal], Barten [Barton], 163, 188.
Daroneal [Daniel], John, 163, 188.
Darr, William, 198.
Dart, see Darte.
Darte [Dart], William [Will], 78, 93.
Darter, Henry, 259.
Darus, John Bte., 57.
Daugherty [Doerty], Elizabeth, 305.
Daugherty, see Dorety and Dougherty.
Daund, see Danel.
Davenport, James, 91.
Davenport [Devanpert], Marmaduk S. [M. D., M. S.], 89, 98.
Davenport [Devanport, Devenport], Otho, 89,
90, 91, 98.
Davice [Davis], Thomas, 137, 175.
Davice, see Devise.
Davidson, Ephraim, 196.
Davidson [Davison], George, 18, 23.
Davidson, James, 158.
Davidson, James W., 268.
Davidson, John [John, Sr.], 145, 179.
Davidson, John [John, Jr.], 161, 188.
Davidson, Matthew, 157.
Davidson, Samuel, 281.
Davidson, Thomas [Thomas G.], 137, 175.
Davidson, William, 157, 199, 333.
Davidson, William M., 199.
Davidson, see Davison.
Davies, see Davis.
Davinport, Peter I., 59.
Davis, Aaron, 108.
Davis, Benjamin, 256.
Davis, C. [Clement], 112, 119.
Davis, Charles, 138.
Davis, David, 160.
Davis, Denis, 199.
Davis, Denny [Dennis], 141, 177.
Davis, E. [Eliphaz, Eliphus], 112, 119.
Davis, Edward, 303.
Davis, Elijah, 260.
Davis, Enock, 27.
Davis, Enock [Enoch], 27, 31.
Davis, Frances, 245.
Davis, George, 14, 66, 298.
Davis, Gorge, 271.
Davis, H., Sr. [Hezekiah, Hezekiah, Sr.], 112, 119.
Davis, Henry, 200, 331.
Davis, Hezekiah, Jr., 117.
Davis, Jacob, 117, 332.
Davis, James, 108, 199, 351.
Davis, James C., 269.
Davis [Davies], James E., 123, 126.
Davis, Jarrl, 84.
Davis, Jesse, 117.
Davis, Jesse [Joshua], 160, 187.
Davis, Joel, 200.
Davis, John, 69, 160, 200.
Davis, John [John, Jr., John E.], 160, 187.
Davis, John [John E.], 193.
Davis, John S., 249.
Davis, Jonathan, 20.
Davis, Joshua, 253.
Davis, Matthias, 108.
Davis, Morris, 160.
Davis, Nat [Nathaniel], 302, 310.
Davis, Nathaniel, 245, 276.
Davis, Oliver, 195.
Davis, Othencall, 198.
Davis, Patrick, 78.

Davis, Peggy, 28.
Davis, Peter, 197.
Davis, Ralph, 114.
Davis, Richard, 351.
Davis, Richard, Jr., 351.
Davis, Robert, 170, 317, 341.
Davis, Rowland, 198.
Davis, Samuel, 117, 140, 194, 199.
Davis, Thomas, 160, 199, 347.
Davis, William, 102, 106, 164, 195, 341.
Davis, William B., 326.
Davis, see Davice.
Davison [Davidson], Harvey P., 346, 358.
Davison [Davidson], Msiah [Masias], 295, 306.
Davison, Samuel, 328.
Davison [Davidson], William, 294, 306.
Davison, see Davidson.
Dawsen, see Dawson.
Dawsey, John, 91.
Dawson, James, 60, 122.
Dawson, Thomas, 58.
Dawson [Dawsen], Thomas, 76, 93.
Day, Benjamin, 162.
Day, Calvin, 264.
Day, Edward, 152.
Day, George, 243.
Day, Jesse B., 344.
Day, Levi, 262.
Day, William, 199.
Dayal, Isaac, 199.
Dayle, Thomas, 199.
Dayless, John W., 197.
Deades [Deeds], Jacob, 139, 176.
Deads [Dees, Deeze], Lewis [Levi, Levy], 152, 183.
Deal [Dyal], Martain [Martin], 274, 288.
Deal, see Dial.
Dean, Jacob, 161.
Dean, John, 305.
Dean [Deen], Joshua, 161, 187.
Dean, see Deen and Denn.
Deane, William, 199.
Dearman [Dorman], William, 219, 232.
Deas, see Dees.
Deason [Deson], John, 106, 118.
Deaton, James, 269.
Deaton, John, 268.
Deats, Samuel, 338.
Deboc, Batest, 148.
De Bom, see Debond.
Debond [De Bom], George, 149, 181.
Debord, Solomon, 341.
Debord, William, 341.
Decamp, Charles, 198.
Decamp, Jacob, 198.
De Camp, Samuel G. J., 196.

Decen [Deeson], Samuel, 66, 73.
Dechamp, see Decompt.
De Chein, see Duldumin.
Deck, Jacob, 144.
Deck, John, 144.
Decker, Isaac, 34.
Decker, Moses, 61.
Declue [De Clue], Michel, 242, 254.
Decocashe, see Dacator.
Decompt [Dechamp], Joseph, 277, 290.
Dedricks, see Rice.
Deeds, John, 108.
Deeds, see Deades.
Deen, Jacob, 46.
Deen [Dean], Thomas, 302, 311.
Deen, see Dean.
Dees, Caleb, 195.
Dees, David, 218.
Dees [Deas], John, 317, 323.
Dees, William, 317.
Dees, see Deads.
Deeson, see Decen.
Deeze, see Deads.
Degannie, Madame, 242.
Delaney [Delany], Mary, 130, 135.
Delaney [Delany], Patience, 295, 306.
Delaney [Delany], William, 295, 306.
Delany, Fielden [Fielding], 161, 187.
Delany, see Delaney.
Delap, Daniel, 35.
Delap, William, 44.
Delaplane [Deleplain], John, 141, 177.
Delaplane [Deleplain], Joshua, 140, 177.
Delaplane [Deleplain], Samuel, 138, 176.
Delaplane, see Diliplane.
De Laygest [Legyster], John [John B.], 277, 290.
Deleplain, see Delaplane and Diliplane.
Delo, see Dillow.
Delodge, see Delong.
De Long, Cornelius, 59.
Delong [Delodge], Joseph, 277, 290.
Delson, see Ditson.
Demaret [Demarris], Joseph, 78, 93.
Demarris, see Demaret.
Demars, Louis [Lewis], 248, 255.
Dement, Alizabeth [Elizabeth], 67, 74.
Dement, Francis, 277.
Demick, see Dimy.
Demon, Robert, 198.
Denahoo, Jacob, 334.
Denison, Robert, 58.
Denison, William, 58.
Denn [Dean], Robert A., 82, 95.
Denney, James, 15.
Denney, William W., 197.
Dennis, John, 348.

INDEX 387

Dennis, John H., 261.
Dennis, see Denny.
Denny [Dennis], Prissilly [Pricilia, Priscilly], 137, 175.
Denny [Daney], Watel [Walter], 143, 178.
Denton, Jessee, 195.
Denton, John, 10.
Denton, Jonithan [Jonathan], 151, 183.
Denton, Samuel, 150.
Depew, John, 57.
Deprest, see Dupriest.
Depue, Mary, 253.
Deputy, William, 60.
Deratt, Louis, 68, 71.
Dereckson, John, 197, 198.
Derham [Durham], William, 88, 97.
Deron, John, 113.
Deruse, Akan, 243.
Deruse, Joseph, 253.
Deruse, Pierre, 243.
Deruse, Thomas, 238.
Derush, see Rush.
Desheat [Deshiels], Teague [Tague], 279, 292.
Desherley, see Desherly and Desily.
Desherly [Desherley, Dezurley], Charles, 144, 179.
Deshiels, see Desheat.
Desiles, Justice, 185; see also Alburt and Allcut.
Desily [Desherley, Dezurley], Antwine [Antoine, Antonio], 172, 192.
Deson, see Deason.
Deuvcelbliss, William, 281.
Devanpert, Devanport, see Davenport.
Devenport, James, 350.
Devenport [Devinport], Joseph, 273, 288.
Devenport, see Davenport and Devenporte.
Devenporte [Devenport], George, 166, 190.
Devinport, see Devenport.
Devise [Davice], Robt. [Robart], 220, 232.
Devore, Phillip, 328.
Dew, John, 273.
Dewey [Drewey], Joshua, 343, 356.
Dewral [Durall], Mary [Ephraigm], 301, 310.
Deyer [Dyer], Chs. [C., Charels], 226, 236.
Dezurley, see Desherly and Desily.
Dial [Deal], James, 41, 51.
Dial, Larkin, 245.
Diamond, see Dimond.
Dickason, George, 213.
Dickerson, Caleb, 56.
Dickerson, Lewis, 56.
Dickerson, Mary, 208, 213.
Dickerson [Dickison], Michael, 351, 359.
Dickison, Richard, 172.

Dickison, see Dickerson.
Dickson, Gorge [George], 270, 287.
Dickson, James, 194.
Dickson, Joseph, 170.
Dickson, Mary, 138.
Dickson, Samuel, 269.
Dickson, see Dixon.
Dicky, John, 246.
Dicron, Robert E., 198.
Dielle, Joseph, 57.
Dieumy [Dio], Francis [Pierre], 144, 179.
Dilard, see Dillard.
Dilch, see Ditch.
Diley, Richard, 172.
Diliplane [Delaplane, Deleplain], Benjamin, 147, 180.
Diliplane [Delaplane, Deleplain], John, 147, 180.
Dillard, Austin, 76.
Dillard, Ishmael [Ishmail], 207, 212.
Dillard, James, 76.
Dillard [Dilard], Jos. [Josaph, Joseph], 220, 232.
Dillen, Michael, 240.
Dillen, Waller, 193.
Dillinger, H. [Henry], 112, 119.
Dillinger, Val. [Valantine, Valentine], 110, 119.
Dillingham, Michael [Mich.], 87, 97.
Dillingham, William, 87.
Dillow [Delo], Jacob, 302, 311.
Dillow [Delo], John, 297, 307.
Dillow [Delo], Michael [Michel], 297, 307.
Dillow [Delo], Peter, Sr. [Peter, 2nd], 300, 310.
Dillow [Delo], Peter, Jr. [Peter], 302, 311.
Diment, David, 74.
Dimeral, see Dimmery.
Dimmery [Dimeral], David, 84, 96.
Dimmie, Samuel, 210.
Dimond, John, 8.
Dimond [Diamond], Robert, 17, 23.
Dimy [Demick], Judithan [Judthan], 217, 231.
Dio, Pierre, 196.
Dio, see Dieumy.
Diou [Dira], Francis, 145, 179.
Dira, see Diou.
Ditch [Dilch], David, 202, 211.
Ditch, Jonathan [Jonathan M.], 248, 255.
Diterline, see Ditterline.
Ditson, David, 166.
Ditson [Delson], Jesse, 166, 190.
Ditterline [Diterline], J. [John], 223, 234.
Ditterline [Diterline], S. [Samuel], 223, 234.
Divers, John, 201.
Divine, Nathaniel J. [Nathaniel], 247, 254.

388 ILLINOIS HISTORICAL COLLECTIONS

Dix, John, 91.
Dixon, Abraham, 201.
Dixon, Amos, 210.
Dixon, Francis, 58.
Dixon, Henry, 201.
Dixon, Joseph, 58.
Dixon, Nathan, 201.
Dixon, Samuel, 201.
Dixon [Dickson], Samuel, 17, 23.
Dixon, Samuel D., 100.
Dixon, Solomon, 201.
Doane, Henry, 198.
Docker, W. A. [William A.], 76, 93.
Dockery, Matthew, 349.
Dod [Dodd], William, 298, 308.
Dodd, Michael, 11.
Dodd, see Dod.
Dodds, Joseph, 159.
Doddy, Alanson, 329.
Doddy, Daniel, 329.
Dodge, Bazzle [Bazel], 78, 94.
Dodge, Henry S., 237.
Dodge, Peter, 193.
Dodge, Stanly, 258.
Dodge, see Dogit.
Dods, Joseph, 124.
Doerty, see Daugherty.
Dogit [Dodge], Richard, 166, 190.
Doliens, Charles, 196.
Dollahan, John, 36.
Dolson, Stephen, 205.
Dolson, see Dalson.
Domran, see Dammel.
Donald, George, 19.
Donelson, William, 195.
Doneo, Laurence, 196.
Donley, Jacob, 305.
Dooms [Dames], Wd. [W.], 225, 235.
Dorety [Daugherty], Dennis, 66, 73.
Dorman, see Dearman.
Dorres, see Dorris.
Dorris, James S., 12.
Dorris [Dorriss], James S., 100, 117.
Dorris [Dorres], Thomas M. [Thomas], 62, 71.
Dorriss, J. S., 99.
Dorriss, see Dorris.
Dorrity, John, 324.
Dorsey, see Dosey.
Dorvan, Joseph, 242.
Dosey [Dorsey], Halbert [Haliard, Halyard], 347, 358.
Dosher [Doshier, Dosier], Adam, 334, 354.
Dosher [Dosier], Adam, 334, 354.
Dosher [Dosier], Elizabeth, 334, 354.
Doshier, Dosier, see Dosher.
Dotchin, John, 193.

Dotey, see Doty.
Dotson, Thomas, 82.
Doty, Daniel, 113.
Doty [Dotey], William, 113, 120.
Dougherty, George, 305.
Dougherty [Daugherty], George, 221, 233.
Dougin, James, 210.
Douglas, Alexander, 341.
Douglas, Samuel, 249.
Douglass, R., 224.
Dougless, see Duglass.
Douthit, David, 348.
Dow, David, 319.
Dowdy, James, 155.
Dowler, Thomas, 276.
Downing, James, 151.
Downing, William, 151.
Doyal, see Doyl.
Doyl [Doyal, Doyle], Thomas, 131, 135.
Doyle, see Doyl.
Dragoo, John, 340.
Drake, James, 82.
Drake, Samuel, 35, 297.
Drakes, John, 281.
Draper, Chakley [Chalkley], 45, 53.
Dreine, Benjamine, 198.
Drennon, see Drunnian.
Dresskill, see Driskill.
Drew, Charles, 210.
Drew, James H., 336.
Drew, John, 329.
Drewey, see Dewey.
Drewry [Drurey], L. [Louis, Lues], 223, 234.
Driar [Dryer], John, 163, 188.
Drigger [Driggers, Triggers], Isaac, 349, 359.
Driggers [Driggins], Absolem [Absolam], 349, 359.
Driggers, Julius [Julas], 350, 359.
Driggers, see Drigger.
Driggins, see Driggers.
Drikel, see Driskill.
Driskel, see Driskill.
Driskell [Drikel], Isabella, 268, 286.
Driskell, see Driskill.
Driskill [Driskel], David B. [Beechem], 266, 285.
Driskill [Dresskill, Driskell], Elias, 45, 53.
Droddy, Aaron [Aron], 242, 254.
Drody, John, 202.
Drum [Drumm], John, 169, 190.
Drumm, see Drum.
Drummon, see Drunnion.
Drunnian [Drennon], William, 159, 187.
Drunnion [Drummon], Joseph, 160, 187.
Drurey, see Drewry.
Drury, Madame, 242.
Drury, Raphael, 204.

INDEX

Dry, Daniel, 104.
Dryer, see Driar.
Dryton, Thomas [Thomas B.], 217, 230.
Dubois, Henry, 58.
Dubois, Jane, 47.
Dubois, Pierre, 56.
Duce, Augustus, 198.
Du Chemin, see Duldumin.
Du Cleau, Antoine, 244.
Duel, Absolum H. [Absolem H.], 66, 73.
Duey, Abel, 78.
Duff, Abraham, 166.
Duff, Philip [Phillip], 9, 22.
Duffey, Francis, 333.
Dugger, Jeret [Jarrot, Jarrott], 154, 184.
Dugger, John, 193.
Dugger, Willey [Wesley, Westley], 154, 184.
Duglass [Dougless], Joseph, 272, 288.
Duit [Duitt], John, 293, 305.
Duitt, see Duit.
Dukes, Araminta, 58.
Dukes, William, 336.
Duldumin [De Chein, Du Chemin], Daniel, 112, 119.
Duleu, Elijah, 197.
Dummet, William, 59.
Dun, see Dunn.
Dunagan, Dunagin, Dunagun, see Dunigan.
Duncain [Duncan], Robert, 269, 287.
Duncan, James, 279.
Duncan, James M., 117.
Duncan, Jo. [Joseph], 112, 119.
Duncan, John, 8.
Duncan [Dunkin], John, 68, 74.
Duncan, John S., 114.
Duncan, Martin [Martin A.], 68, 74.
Duncan, Matthew, 99, 112, 115, 117.
Duncan, Nancy, 10.
Duncan, Robert, 10.
Duncan, Samuel, 7.
Duncan, Sarah, 10.
Duncan, William, 10.
Duncan, see Duncain, Duncane, and Dunkin.
Duncane [Duncan, Dunkin], Henry, 87, 97.
Dunegan, Ann, 199.
Dunesmore [Dunsmore], Daniel [David], 163, 189.
Dunham, Ephraim, 59.
Dunigan [Dunagin, Dunagun], Andrew, 157, 185.
Dunigan [Danogin, Dunagan], Ann [Anne], 137, 175.
Dunkin [Duncan], Joseph, 144, 179.
Dunkin [Duncan], Rice, 151, 183.
Dunkin, see Duncan and Duncane.
Dunlap, James, 351.
Dunlap, **John**, 38.

Dunlap, Joseph, 27.
Dunlap, Thomas, 43.
Dunlap [Dunlapt], William, 65, 73.
Dunlap, William, Sr. [William], 43, 52.
Dunlap, William, Jr., 43.
Dunlapt, see Dunlap.
Dunn, Jacob, 198.
Dunn, James, 84, 169.
Dunn, John, 56, 202.
Dunn [Dun], Sampson, 84, 96.
Dunn, Samuel, 204.
Dunn, Shaderick [Shadric, Shedrick], 88, 97.
Dunn, William, 7.
Dunsmore, Sefus [Joseph], 163, 189.
Dunsmore, see Dunesmore.
Dunsworth, Thomas, 129.
Dupey, see Dupuy.
Dupriest [Deprest], Jeffery [Jeffrey], 84, 96.
Dupriest, William, 124.
Dupuy [Dupey], James, 269, 286.
Dupuy [Dupey], Joseph, 269, 286.
Dupuy [Dupey], William, 269, 286.
Durall, see Dewral.
Durham, Lewis, 1.
Durham, Silas, 2.
Durham, see Derham and Durram.
Durley, Asa, 56.
Durley, Rhutia, 18.
Durley, see Harley.
Durram [Durham], William, 295, 306.
Dustin, Timothy, 247.
Dutton, Asel, 80.
Dutton, David, 172.
Duvall, Daniel, 168.
Duvall, John, 76.
Duvall, William, 76.
Dyal, see Deal.
Dye, Alexander, 206.
Dye, Harrison, 206.
Dye, Randle, 62, 71.
Dyer, Ab. [A., Abiga], 226, 236.
Dyer, Andrew F., 58.
Dyer, William, 226.
Dyer, see Deyer.

Eachols, see Echols.
Eaden [Eden, Edon], James, 314, 321.
Eades, Solomon, 317.
Eads [Edes], Thomas, 275, 289.
Eads, see Edes.
Eagleton, James, 27.
Eals, Labin, 206.
Earles, James, 197.
Earnst, Christian, 59.
Easen, Pomeroy, 320.
East, Henry, 154.
East, James, 154.

390   ILLINOIS HISTORICAL COLLECTIONS

East, Thomas, 108.
Eastas [Eastess], Byrd [Bird], 264, 284.
Eastep, see Estep.
Easterbrook, John, 195.
Eastess, see Eastas.
Easton, Richard, 45.
Eastwood, Abner, 347.
Eastwood, David, 346.
Eastwood, Jacob, 203.
Eastwood, John, 346.
Eatherton [Etherton], Samuel, 104, 118.
Eaton, Benjamin, 39.
Eaton, Benjamine [Benjamin, Benjamin, Jr.], 44, 52.
Eaton, Jesse, 28.
Eaton, John, 39, 302.
Eaton, Joseph, 40.
Eaton, Richard, 39.
Eaton, Stephen, 39.
Eaves, see Eves.
Eberman, Auther [Arthur], 207, 213.
Eberman, John, 200.
Eberman, see Everman.
Eblin, Samuel, 17, 122.
Echols [Eachols], Jasiel [Jesse], 296, 307.
Echols, John, 305.
Echols [Eachols], William, 303, 304, 305, 311.
Eckard, see Eckerd.
Eckburn, see Keagmen.
Eckerd [Eckard], John, 275, 289.
Eddor, Samuel, 198.
Edds, Thomas, 47.
Eddy, Henry, 91.
Eddy, Horatice, 199.
Eden, see Eaden.
Edes [Eads], Mathias [Matthew], 161, 187.
Edes, see Eads.
Edgar, John, 237.
Edgar, Sillis, 238.
Edgar, William, 245.
Edington, John, 10.
Edlin, Clemont [Clement], 343, 357.
Edline, Pierre, 59.
Edmondson, James, 58.
Edon, see Eaden.
Edward [Edwards], Washington, 104, 118.
Edwards, Charles, 342.
Edwards, James P., 2.
Edwards, John, 20, 345.
Edwards, John [J.], 225, 235.
Edwards, K. [Kinian], 112, 119.
Edwards, Ninian, 196.
Edwards, Philip, 40.
Edwards, Susanah [Susanna], 317, 322.
Edwards, see Edward.
Edwars, Calvin, 81.

Eedes, Moses, 146.
Egerster, Ephraim, 173.
Elam, Edward, 18.
Elder, John, 16, 345.
Eldred, see Eldrid.
Eldrid [Eldred], Jehosifat [Jehoshephat], 151, 182.
Eldrid, Warde [Ward], 151, 182.
Eldrid [Eldred], William, 151, 182.
Eldridge, see Eldrige.
Eldrige [Eldridge], Samuel, 271, 287.
Elems, see Elms.
Elidge, William, 196.
Elins, see Cline.
Eliott, see Elliott.
Elkin [Elkins], John, 130, 135.
Elkin [Elkins], Joshua, 131, 136.
Elkin, Richard, 129.
Elkin, Whitney, 131.
Elkin [Elkins], William, 129, 135.
Elkins, see Elkin.
Ellams [Ellems, Elms], James, 294, 306.
Ellams [Elms], Marget [Margret], 294, 306.
Elledge, Daniel, 326.
Elledge, Isaac, 326.
Elledge, John, 326.
Elledge, William, 326.
Ellems, see Ellams.
Elles [Ellis], John, 18, 23.
Ellet [Elliot], Thomas, 325, 330.
Ellice, see Ellis.
Elliot, Thomas, 328.
Elliot, see Ellet and Elliott.
Elliott [Eliott], Andrew, 166, 190.
Elliott [Elliot], Benjamin, 349, 359.
Elliott, Erasmus, 319.
Elliott, Jacob, 210.
Elliott, John, 350.
Elliott, William, 245.
Ellis, Benjamin, 345.
Ellis, Elizabeth, 41.
Ellis, Jacob, 166.
Ellis, James, 60.
Ellis [Ellice], James, 220, 232.
Ellis [Ells], James, 293, 305.
Ellis, John, 63.
Ellis, John [J.], 227, 236.
Ellis, Jonathan, 305.
Ellis, Levi, 166.
Ellis, William, 75, 344.
Ellis, see Elles.
Ellison, Andrew, 200.
Ellison, Isaac, 57.
Ellott, James, 42.
Ellott, William, 42.
Ells, see Ellis.
Elmore, Christopher, 301.

INDEX

Elmore [Elmoy], Jesse [Jessee], 113, 119.
Elmore, William, 91.
Elmoy, see Elmore.
Elms [Elems], David, 130, 135.
Elms, see Ellams.
Embree, James, 61.
Embree, John, 59.
Emeret, see Emerich.
Emerich [Emeret, Emmertt], Henery [Henry], 145, 179.
Emiett [Emmett, Emret], Andrew, 146, 180.
Emmerson, Allen, 60.
Emmerson, Ryal, 57.
Emmerson, William, 331.
Emmertt, see Emerich.
Emmett, see Emiett.
Emmons, Charles, 36.
Emret, Sally, 196.
Emret, see Emiett.
Emthan, Jonithan, 166.
Enard [Inard], Abner, 164, 189.
Enes, see Enness and Ennis.
Enesley [Insley], Joseph, 163, 188.
England, Stephen, 162.
England, Thomas, 57.
English, Isabella, 251.
Enloe, Asahel [Ashel], 17, 23.
Ennes, see Enos.
Enness [Enes, Ennis], Jesse [Jessee], 173, 192.
Ennis [Enes], William, 142, 177.
Ennis, see Enness.
Enochs, Sarah, 271.
Enocks, John, 195.
Enos [Ennes], Parseal P. [Pascal P., Pascoll P.], 152, 183.
Ensminger, Emanuel, 83.
Eoff, Gerret, 12.
Eply, Andrew, 333.
Ervin, Abraham, 64.
Ervin [Irvin], Charles, 88, 97.
Ervin [Erwin], Richard, 64, 72.
Ervin, see Irwin.
Ervine [Irvin], Thomas, 262, 284.
Erwin, Robert, 60.
Erwin, see Ervin.
Esbill, Henry, 198.
Esry, Essarey, see Essrey.
Essey, John, 152.
Essrey [Essarey], Jesse, 28, 31.
Essrey [Essarey, Esry], John, 27, 31.
Esstes [Estes], Elisha, 329, 330.
Este, see Estes.
Estep, Elijah, 19.
Estep, Enoch, 20.
Estep [Eastep], James, 274, 289.
Estes [Este, Estis], Chism, 89, 98.

Estes, see Esstes and Estis.
Estis [Estes], Absolum [Absalom, Absolem], 64, 72.
Estis [Estes], George, 206, 212.
Estis [Estes], Joseph, 64, 72.
Estis, see Estes.
Eter, see Etter.
Etheridge, Jeremiah, 350.
Etherton, see Atherton and Eatherton.
Ethridge [Ethrige], Jonas [Jonathan], 221, 233.
Ethrige, see Ethridge.
Etter [Eter], Peter, 151, 183.
Eubank, see Eubanks and Ewbanks.
Eubanks [Eubank], James, 64, 72.
Eubanks, Molton [Molten], 216, 230.
Eubanks, William, 341.
Evans, Bazil [Bazal], 38, 50.
Evans [Evin, Evins], Benjamine [Benjamin], 45, 53.
Evans, Elijah [Elijha], 295, 306.
Evans [Evens], George, 294, 306.
Evans, John, 36.
Evans [John, Jr.], 317, 322.
Evans [Evens], John, 45, 53.
Evans, John A. [John, Jr.], 313, 321.
Evans, Joseph, 278.
Evans [Evenas], Oen [Owen], 294, 306.
Evans, Shelton, 240.
Evans, Thomas, 38.
Eveland, Frederick, 198.
Eveland, Isaac, 194.
Eveland, Evelin, see Evlin.
Evenas, see Evans.
Evens, Jeremiah, 10.
Evens, John, 11.
Evens, see Evans and Ivins.
Everitt, William, 202.
Everitt, see Evret.
Everly, William, 57.
Everman [Eberman], Joseph, 152, 183.
Everman [Evermon], William, 39, 51.
Evermon, see Everman.
Eves [Eaves], Benjamin, 149, 181.
Evin, see Evans.
Evins, Aron, 328.
Evins, James, 205.
Evins, Joseph, 210.
Evins, Lewis, 199.
Evins, Samuel, 210.
Evins, see Evans.
Evlin [Eveland, Evelin], John, 172, 192.
Evlin [Evelin], Moses, 172, 192.
Evret [Everitt], David, 270, 287.
Ewbank, see Ewbanks.
Ewbanks [Eubank], William, 65, 72.
Ewbanks [Ewbank], William, 67, 74.

Ewell, Joshua, 56.
Ewing, Elexander [Alexander], 27, 31.
Ewing, Elijah, 62.
Ewing, James, 327.
Ewing, John, 69, 71, 350.
Eyman, Abraham, 256.
Eyman, Christopher [Henry], 261, 283.
Ezell, Archibal, 11.
Ezell, Thomas, 347.
Ezell, Thomas R., 334.

Fade [Fall], David, 75, 92.
Fagan, William, 161.
Faggot, George, 299.
Faherty, Edmund, 240.
Faherty, Patrick, 241.
Faherty, see Flauharty.
Fail, George, 58.
Fail, Henry, 58.
Fail, John, 37.
Fail, Joseph, 37.
Fain, see Fane.
Faires, see Ferris.
Falkner, J., 226.
Falkner, James [J.], 227, 236.
Falkner, see Fartner.
Fall, see Fade.
Fane [Fain], Jesse, 131, 135.
Faning, see Fannon.
Fannon [Faning], Henry, 154, 184.
Fannon, Peter, 125.
Fannon, see Fanon.
Fanon [Fannon], George, 153, 183.
Fanon [Fannon], Joseph, 153, 183.
Fansherp, Isaac, 127.
Faris, Alexan, 198.
Faris, George W., 325.
Faris, see Farris.
Farley, Adam, 347.
Farley, Edward, 347.
Farley, Francis, 348.
Farley, John, 276.
Farley, William, 328.
Farmer, see Parmer.
Farmings, George, 196.
Farnham, Joshua, 45.
Farnham, see Farnum.
Farnum [Farnham], James, 26, 31.
Farr, Archibald, 345.
Farraer [Farriree, Ferrierd], Francis [Franey], 277, 290.
Farrar, see Farrer.
Farrer [Farrar], Robert, 266, 285.
Farriree, see Farraer.
Farris [Pharis], James, Sr. [James], 193.
Farris, John, 62, 195.
Farris [Ferris], T. T., 225, 235.

Farris [Faris], William, 62, 71.
Farris, see Pharis and Pharris.
Fartner [Falkner], John [J.], 225, 235.
Fatman, Nathan, 318.
Fay, Jonathan B., 195.
Feasle [Feezle], Jacob [Jacob W.], 86, 96.
Feehans [Fuan], Martin, 157, 185.
Feezle, see Feasle.
Fellows, Joseph, 281.
Fellows, Willis, 197.
Felps [Phelps], Fredrich [Frederick], 124, 127.
Felps, John, 124.
Felps, Zadoc, 124, 127.
Felps, see Phelps.
Fenatia, see Finatia.
Ferdin [Furden], Joseph, 79, 94.
Fergeson [Ferguson], Andrew, 270, 287.
Fergurson, Nelson, 123.
Ferguson, C. [K.], 225, 235.
Ferguson, Daniel, 240.
Ferguson [Furguson], Isaac, 156, 185.
Ferguson, John, 200.
Ferguson, Thomas [T.], 227, 236.
Ferguson, see Fergeson, Firguson, Forgison, and Furgason.
Ferrander, Mary, 253.
Ferrel [Ferrill], Thomas, 300, 309.
Ferrel [Ferril], William, 335, 355.
Ferrierd, see Farraer.
Ferril, Ferrill, see Ferrel.
Ferris, Edward, 341.
Ferris [Pharris], George, 38, 50.
Ferris, James, 196.
Ferris [Faires], R. [Robert], 223, 234.
Ferris, Robert, 197.
Ferris, see Farris.
Fesler [Festler], Joseph, 34, 49.
Festler see Fesler.
Fettinger, Henry, 59.
Fettinger, Samuel, 61.
Feygabush, Tobias, 80.
Fiatt, see Friet.
Field, George, 60.
Field [Fields], Henry, 208, 213.
Field [Fields], Robert, 218, 231.
Field, see Fields.
Fields [Field], D. [Daniel], 226, 236.
Fields, James, 75.
Fields, Joshua, 333.
Fields, Obadeah [Obediah], 247, 254.
Fields, Stephen, 82.
Fields, Thomas, 331.
Fields, William, 333.
Fields, see Field.
Fife [Fiffe], Thomas, 37, 50.
Fifer, Adam, 112.

INDEX

Fiffe, see Fife.
Figgins, Daniel, 42.
Fike [Fyke], Able [Abel], 265, 285.
Files, Henry, 19.
Files, John, 344.
Files, John, Jr., 344.
Files, William, 344.
Finatia [Fenatia], Jacob, 207, 213.
Finch [French], James, 156, 185.
Finch, Joel, 138.
Finch, Lephod [Leford], 156, 185.
Finch, William, 75.
Findley, Howard, 159.
Findley [Finley], John, 157, 185.
Findley [Finley], John, 159, 186.
Findley [Finley], Moses, 174, 192.
Findley [Finley], Thomas, 169, 190.
Findley, William, 159.
Fineren, see Finnian.
Finley, Andrew, 15.
Finley, James, 193.
Finley [Finly], James, 348, 358.
Finley, John, 199, 210.
Finley, William S., 91.
Finley, see Findley.
Finly, see Finley.
Finney, James, 133.
Finney, John, 294.
Finnian [Fineren], John, 113, 120.
Fips, see Phipps.
Firguson [Furguson], Alston, 170, 191.
Firguson [Ferguson, Furguson], John, 170, 191.
Firguson [Ferguson], Joseph, 170, 191.
Firguson [Ferguson, Furguson], Thomas, 172, 192.
Firguson [Furgeson], William, 170, 191.
Fish, Elisha, 262.
Fish, Thomas, 58.
Fisher, Comfort, 281.
Fisher, Francis, 210.
Fisher, Grammer [Grammar], 301, 310.
Fisher, Jacob, 239.
Fisher, James, 164.
Fisher, Jane, 301.
Fisher, Joseph, 164.
Fisher, Joshua [Joseph], 164, 189.
Fisher, Merradith W., 78.
Fisher, Thomas, 300.
Fisher, William, 250.
Fisk, A. F. [A. J., Abram G.], 223, 234.
Fisk, R. [Robart], 223, 234.
Fitch, Chester, 46.
Fitch, Elisha, 46.
Fitch, John G., 328.
Fitchgerral, James, 325.
Flach [Flock], Christian, 303, 311.

Flack, see Flacke.
Flacke [Flack], John, 106, 118.
Flaery, Louis, 281.
Flagg, Nathaniel, 197.
Flanary, see Flanery.
Flanery, Abraham, 68.
Flanery [Flanary], Elijah, 68, 74.
Flanery, see Flannery.
Flanigan [Flanigin], Thomas, 154, 184.
Flanigin, see Flanigan.
Flannery [Flanery], E. [Eliga, Elijha], 223, 234.
Flatt, Edward, 329.
Flauharty [Faherty], Pattrick [Patrick], 258, 282.
Fleetewood [Fleetwood], Hatton [Haton], 88, 97.
Fleetewood [Fleetwood], Wiley, 88, 97.
Fleetwood, see Fleetewood.
Fleming, William, 91.
Fleming, see Flemming.
Flemming, James, 338.
Flemming [Fleming], Samuel, 27, 31.
Fletcher, Houson, 84.
Fletcher, Joab [Job], 159, 187.
Flinn, John, 42.
Flinn, Obid [Obadiah], 79, 94.
Flinn, William, 79.
Flint, John, 337.
Flint, William, 79.
Flipper, see Flippo.
Flippo [Flipper], William, 41, 51.
Flock, see Flach.
Flood, William, 43.
Flower, George, 56.
Flower, Richard, 56.
Flutcher, Thomas, 325.
Foley, James, 333.
Foley [Folid, Folly], Richard, 83, 95.
Foley, William, 336.
Folid, see Foley.
Folks [Foulks], Christopher, 266, 285.
Folly, see Foley.
Ford, Elias, 112.
Ford, Elizabeth, 208.
Ford, Robert C., 33, 34, 48, 49.
Ford [Froo], Samuel, 67, 74.
Fordice, Jairus, 59.
Forehand [Forhand], Jarvis, 16, 23.
Forgison [Ferguson], John, 333, 354.
Forhand, see Forehand.
Forister [Forrester], John, 75, 92.
Forister [Forster], William, 79, 94.
Fornestake [Fornostock], John [Jacob], 167, 190.
Fornostock, see Fornestake.
Forquer, George, 210.

Forquer, William, 207.
Forrester, John, Jr., 91.
Forrester, see Forister and Forrister.
Forrister, Ila, 2.
Forrister [Forrester], Jacob, 341, 356.
Forrister, John, 341.
Forrister, William, 341.
Forster, Fedrick [Federic], 67, 74.
Forster, Henry, 67.
Forster, see Forister.
Forsythe, Thomas, 335.
Fortner, John, 144.
Fortune, Louis, 243.
Foss, George, 7.
Foss, John, 316.
Foster, Asa [Asey], 214, 229.
Foster, Daniel, 198.
Foster, Hardy, 9.
Foster, James, 250.
Foster, Lanslot [Lancelot], 124, 127.
Foster, Oliver, 138.
Foster, Robert, 251.
Foster, Robert M., 198.
Foster, Thomas, 27, 148.
Foster, William, 204.
Fouke, Philip, 237.
Foulks, see Folks.
Fountain, Edward, 139.
Fowler, Daniel, 145.
Fowler, Elisha, 206.
Fowler, James, 206, 248.
Fowler, Jason, 1.
Fowler, Mason, 200.
Fowler [Fowuler], Samuel, 2, 5.
Fowler, William, 248, 260.
Fowuler, see Fowler.
Fox, Amos, 3.
Fox, James N. [J. N.], 225, 235.
Fox, John, 45.
Fox, P., 225.
Fox, William, 113.
Foxwell, Edward, 270.
Fraker, John, 260.
Francis, John, 210.
Francis, Solomon, 171.
Frankfort, John, 241.
Franklin, Ebenezer, 194.
Franklin, George, 247.
Franklin, John, 174.
Fraser, John, 350.
Frasure, Lydia, 186.
Fray, Daniel, 200.
Frazer [Freazer], Ezekiel, 80, 94.
Frazer [Freazer], John, 75, 92.
Frazer, Robert, 61.
Frazey, Levi, 37.
Frazier, John, 158, 186.

Frear, Richard, 58.
Freazer, see Frazer.
Free, Absolom P. [Absalom P., Absolam P.], 269, 286.
Free [Tree], Andrew, 259, 283.
Freeman, Elisha, 14.
Freeman, Richard, 57.
Freeman, Richman, 281.
Freeman, William, 14.
French, Joseph, 113, 195.
French, Levy [Levi], 102, 117.
French, Martha, 316.
French, Peter, 64.
French, Stephen, 161.
French, T. [Samuel], 113, 119.
French, Zeba, 59.
French, see Finch.
Frier, Richard, 343.
Friet [Fiatt, Fryatt], Robert, 301, 310.
Frizel [Frizell, Frizzle], William, 64, 72.
Frizell, Frizzle, see Frizel.
Froo, see Ford.
Frost, Widow, 225.
Frost, Epraim P., 210.
Frost, William, 121.
Fruit [Fruitt], Edward [Edmond, Edmund], 142, 178.
Fruitt, see Fruit.
Fry [Try], Joseph, 210.
Fry, Nathan, 57.
Fry [Frye], Philip, 169, 190.
Fry, William, 194.
Fryatt, see Friet.
Frye, see Fry.
Fryer, Thomas, 197.
Ftubblefield, see Stubelfield.
Fuan, see Feehans.
Fulfer, Isaac, 127.
Fulfer, Jessee, 127.
Fulford, Josiah, 333.
Fulherson [Fulkison], R. [Richard], 222, 233.
Fulkison, see Fulherson.
Fuller, Abner, 26.
Fuller, Abraham, 84.
Fuller, Cathorine [Catharine], 81, 95.
Fuller, Claton, 336.
Fuller, Jacob, 122.
Fuller, Marvin, 113.
Fulton, Aaron, 197.
Fulton, David, 241.
Fulton, Harriet, 253.
Fulton, John, 44.
Fulton, Rosannah, 241.
Fulton, Thomas, 249.
Fultze, Jacob, 202.

INDEX 395

Funderburgh, *see* Funderburk *and* Funderburth.
Funderburk [Funderburgh], Daniel, 155, 184.
Funderburth [Funderburgh], Henry, 170, 191.
Funk, Daniel, 44.
Funk, Gabriel [Gabril], 44, 52.
Funk, John [John, Sr.], 44, 52.
Funkhouser, Christopher, 344.
Funkhouser, Isaac, 344.
Funkhouser, John, 332.
Funkhouser, Young, 332.
Funkhouser, *see* Funkhowser.
Funkhowser [Funkhouser], Robert R. [Robert, Robert M.], 77, 93.
Fuqua [Fuquay], William D., 106, 118.
Fuquay, *see* Fuqua.
Furden, *see* Ferdin.
Furgason [Ferguson], James, 88, 97.
Furgeson, *see* Firguson.
Furguson, *see* Ferguson *and* Firguson.
Furlong, John, 197.
Furphy, *see* Murphey.
Furr, *see* Tir.
Fursea, John, 244.
Fursea, Solomon, 245.
Fury, Peter, 3.
Fyke, *see* Fike.

Gadwin [Godwin], Wilkison [Wilkinson, Wilkson], 297, 307.
Gaer, Ransom, 20.
Gaily [Galey], Isaac, 63, 72.
Gaines [Gains], Stephen, 46, 53.
Gains, *see* Gaines.
Galaher, *see* Gallaher.
Galaton, Solomon, 197.
Galey, *see* Gaily.
Gallaher [Galaher], Peter, 110, 119.
Gallamon, Asa, 222, 229.
Gallant, Mary, 58.
Gallispi, *see* Gillaspy.
Galloway, Adam, 58.
Gambla, *see* Gamlah *and* Gamlau.
Gamlah [Gambla], Peter [Pear], 278, 291.
Gamlau [Gambla, Gumlah], Mashec [Michael], 278, 291.
Ganda, *see* Goodeau.
Gandrow [Jandro], Lewis [Louis], 276, 290.
Gard, Seth, 61.
Garden, *see* Goodon.
Gardner, Charles, 59.
Gardner, Joseph, 60.
Gardner, Thomas, 61.
Gardner, *see* Girner.
Garetson, James, 212.
Garner [Garnor, Gernor], Charles [Charels], 100, 117.

Garner [Garnor], Francis, 112, 119.
Garner, Jarrett, 85.
Garner, John, 87, 297.
Garner, Moses B., 332.
Garner, Walter, 336.
Garner [Garnor], William [William F.], 102, 117.
Garnor, *see* Garner.
Garrard, *see* Garritt.
Garrason, Amos, 78.
Garret [Garrett], Hezekiah [Hisakiah], 66, 73.
Garret [Garrett], Mosses [Moses], 67, 73.
Garret, Richard, 67.
Garret, Robert, 146.
Garretson, *see* Garritson.
Garrett, *see* Garret *and* Garritt.
Garrish, Edward, 201.
Garrison, Absolem [Absolum], 336, 355.
Garrison, David, 329.
Garrison, James, 336, 346.
Garrison, Margaret, 19.
Garrison, Samuel, 329.
Garrison, Thomas, 334.
Garrison, Zimry [Zemra], 88, 97.
Garritson [Garretson], Mary, 206, 212.
Garritt [Garrard, Garrett], Jacob [Jacob, Jr.], 44, 52.
Garritt [Garrett, Gerrard], William, Sr., 44, 52.
Garritt [Garrett, Gerrard], William, Jr. [William], 44, 52.
Garvin, Hannah, 337.
Garvis, Moses, 210.
Garvy [Jarver, Jarvis], Enos [Aneas], 275, 289.
Garvy [Jarver, Jarvis], Lewis [Louis, Lous], 275, 289.
Garwood [Gorwood], James, 46, 53.
Gasaway, *see* Gassaway *and* Gazeway.
Gascal, *see* Gaskell *and* Gaskill.
Gash, James, 324.
Gash, John B., 327.
Gaskell [Gascal, Gaskill], Jonathan, 269, 287.
Gaskil [Gaskill], David, 150, 182.
Gaskil [Gaskill], S. T. Venas [Sylvanus, Sylvenus], 150, 182.
Gaskill [Gascal], Paul, 266, 285.
Gaskill, *see* Gaskell *and* Gaskil.
Gaskins [Ghastings], John, 87, 97.
Gaskins [Ghastings], Thadah [Thadius], 88, 97.
Gasler [Gazley], Thomas T., 272, 288.
Gassaway [Gasaway], John, 86, 96.
Gassaway [Gasaway], Thomas, 86, 97.
Gasten, Gastin, *see* Gaston.
Gaston, Eli [Elihu], 83, 95.

Gaston, James, 246, 327.
Gaston, John, 83.
Gaston, Margaretta, 248.
Gaston [Gasten, Gastin], Mathew, 1, 5.
Gaston, Robert, 325.
Gaston, Robert R., 327.
Gaston, Samuel, 122.
Gaston, Stepen [Stephen], 244, 254.
Gaston, William, 248.
Gaston [Gastin], William, 106, 118.
Gates, Hiram, 197.
Gates, Peter, 77.
Gates [Grafts], Samuel, 172, 192.
Gates, Vaulentine [Valentine], 261, 283.
Gatewood, Phillip, 328.
Gatland, see Gatlin.
Gatlin [Gatland], Edward, 339, 356.
Gatlin, Sally, 339.
Gaurd, see Guard.
Gavott [Gavt], B. F. [Benjamin F.], 221, 233.
Gavt, see Gavott.
Gay, John H., 263.
Gazeway [Gasaway], William, 67, 74.
Gazley, see Gasler.
Gear, Charles, 138.
Gear [Gracie], John, 144, 179.
Gearling, William, 293.
Gearvis [Jarvice, Jarvis], John, 152, 183.
Gelespy, see Gillispie.
George, Jahue [Jehue], 160, 187.
Geory, John, 198.
Gephart, John, 81.
Gernor, see Garner.
Gerrard, see Garritt.
Geving [Green], R. [Richard], 224, 235.
Ghasting, Wilson, 91.
Ghastings, see Gaskins.
Ghaston, Robert, 91.
Gholtson, Nathaniel, 340.
Gibbins, James, 196.
Gibbs, Austin [Hauston V., Orton], 158, 186.
Gibbs, Benjamin, 58.
Gibbs, Elijah, 42.
Gibbs, Richard, 137.
Gibson [Gillem], H. W. [William H.], 218, 231.
Gibson, James, 337.
Gibson [Gipson], James, 47, 54.
Gibson, William, 195, 216.
Gier, see Gire.
Gifford, Abraham, 211.
Gifford [Gilferd], Joshua, 39, 50.
Giger, Henry, 171.
Giger, John, 155.
Gilar [Guiler, Guyler], William, 259, 282.
Gilbert [Gillbert], David, 173, 192.

Gilbreath, Hugh, 274.
Gilbreath [Gilbreth], James, 315, 322.
Gilbreth, see Gilbreath.
Gilbrith, see Gilworth.
Gilerland [Gillerland], Thomas, 149, 181.
Gilferd, see Gifford.
Gilgasper, David, 158.
Gilham, Clamons [Clement], 146, 180.
Gilham, Erades, 196.
Gilham, Ezekiel, 197.
Gilham, J. C., 197.
Gilham, James H., 146.
Gilham, Jane, 194.
Gilham, Rydus C., 193.
Gilham, see Gillam and Gillham.
Gilihan [Gilliham], Robert, 108, 118.
Gill [Crill], Caleb [Caloss], 161, 188.
Gill, David, 82.
Gill, James, 106.
Gill, John, 35.
Gill, Thomas, 35, 57.
Gill, William, 100.
Gillam, Charles, Sr., 13.
Gillam, Charles, Jr., 13.
Gillam, Henry, 47.
Gillam [Gilham, Gillham], Thomas, 263, 284.
Gillard, Thomas, 66.
Gillaspie, John, 91.
Gillaspie, William, 260.
Gillaspie, see Gillispie.
Gillaspy [Gallispi], Robert, 19, 24.
Gillbert, see Gilbert.
Gillehan, see Gilliland.
Gillem, see Gibson.
Gillerland, Martin, 195.
Gillerland, Thomas, 197.
Gillerland, see Gilerland.
Gilles [Gillis], James, 100, 117.
Gillet [Jillet], Limon [Lemon], 150, 182.
Gillet, see Gillett.
Gillett [Gillet], David, 218, 231.
Gillham [Gilham], Charles, 157, 185.
Gillham [Gilham], David [David M.], 137, 175.
Gillham [Gilham], Isaac, 141, 177.
Gillham [Gilham], Isaac, 146, 180.
Gillham [Gilham], Isham [Isom], 139, 176.
Gillham [Gilham], James, 142, 178.
Gillham [Gilham], James, 145, 179.
Gillham [Gilham], John, 137, 175.
Gillham [Gilham], John [John D.], 157, 185.
Gillham [Gilham], John, Sr. [John], 197.
Gillham [Gilham], Samuel, 137, 175.
Gillham [Gilham], Thomas, 146, 180.
Gillham, William, 157.
Gillham [Gilham], William, 141, 177.
Gillham [Gilham], William, 146, 180.

INDEX 397

Gillham [Gilham], William, 157, 185.
Gillham, see Gillam.
Gilliham, see Gilihan.
Gilliland [Gillehan], Thomas, 316, 322.
Gillis, see Gilles.
Gillison [Gilson], John, 344, 357.
Gillispie [Gelespy, Gillaspie], J. P. [John P.], 225, 235.
Gillospel, Mathew, 85.
Gilmore, Ephraim, 195.
Gilmore, James, 59.
Gilmore, John, 20, 21, 315.
Gilson, Martha, 351.
Gilson [Gilston], William, 351, 359.
Gilson, see Gillison.
Gilston, see Gilson.
Gilworth [Gilbrith], John C. [John], 75, 92.
Ginger, Henry, 12.
Ginger, see Gingor.
Gingles [Ingles, Jingles], Elizabeth, 143, 178.
Gingles, Samuel, 198.
Gingor [Ginger], John, 216, 230.
Gipson, Robert, 161.
Gipson [Gripeson], Robert, 161, 187.
Gipson, see Gibson.
Gire [Guyer], Aaron, 45, 53.
Gire [Guyer], Exum [Axim], 45, 53.
Gire [Gier, Guyer], Jesse, 45, 53.
Girner [Gardner], Andrew, 162, 188.
Githen, John, 115.
Gittle, Samuel, 91.
Gladney, Samuel, 249.
Glagow, see Glasgow.
Glasgow, James C. [James], 260, 283.
Glasgow, William, 334.
Glasgow [Glagow], William, 261, 283.
Glass, Dudley [Dudly], 219, 231.
Glass, James, 256.
Glass, John, 219, 261.
Glass, see Gloss.
Glasscock, Joseph, 58.
Glayson, Benjamin, 351.
Glen, George, 241.
Glenn, Isac [Isaac], 108, 118.
Glenn, John, 37, 112.
Glenn, Jonathan, 15.
Glenn, Rowland [Robert], 108, 118.
Glenn, Thomas, 108.
Glenn, see Glexen.
Gless, see Gloss.
Glexen [Glenn], John, 166, 190.
Glice, John, 274.
Gloss [Glass], D. B. [David], 226, 236.
Gloss [Glass, Gless], F. [Frances, Francis], 222, 234.
Gloss [Glass], J. [Joseph], 222, 234.
Gloss [Glass], Jon. [John], 222, 234.

Glover, Charles C., 245.
Glover, J. [Joseph], 224, 235.
Glover, John, 259.
Glover, John [J.], 225, 235.
Glover, Reuben [R., Ruben], 225, 235.
Glover, William, 224, 225.
Go, Joseph, 194.
Goble, George, 38.
Goda, see Goodane.
Godair, John Batiste [John B.], 242, 254.
Godair, Zemry, 253.
Godan, see Goodeau.
Goddard [Godric], Joseph, 263, 284.
Goddard [Gorda], Margaret, 278, 291.
Goddard [Godric], Ruben [Reuben], 263, 284.
Godfrey, Hanson, 316.
Godric, see Goddard.
Godthard, see Gothard.
Godwin, see Gadwin.
Goen [Goins], Edward, 36, 50.
Goen [Goins], Isaac, 36, 50.
Goen [Goin], Isaac, 46, 53.
Goen, Jacob, 38.
Goen, Jasen, 36.
Goen [Goin], Lewis, 37, 50.
Goff, Bernard, 49.
Goff, David, 49.
Goff, Elmond, 34, 49.
Goforth, William G. [William P.], 261, 283.
Goin, see Goen.
Going, John, 121.
Going [Goings], Pleasant, 122, 126.
Going, William, 122.
Going, see Gooen.
Goings, see Going and Gooen.
Goins, see Goen.
Golahar, see Golaher.
Golaher [Golahar, Goliher], John, 47, 54.
Golaher [Goliher], John, Jr. [John], 47, 54.
Golder, Jacob, 197.
Golder, John R., 197.
Goldsmith, William, 202.
Goliher, see Golaher.
Goltson, Benjamin, 343.
Goltson, Francis, 343.
Goltson, John, 343.
Good, Daniel, 171.
Good, James [Jonas], 143, 179.
Good, John, 142.
Good, Thomas, 149.
Good, William, 142.
Goodall, Widow, 221.
Goodane [Goda, Gouda], Peter [Pear], 279, 292.
Goodbread, see Goodbred.
Goodbred [Goodbread], Joseph, 106, 118.
Goodeau [Ganda, Godan], Lewis [Louis],

276, 290.
Gooden, see Goodwin.
Goodin, Levi, 200.
Goodin, Lewis, 41.
Goodin, see Gooding.
Gooding [Goodner], Cornelius, 256, 280, 281.
Gooding, Fransess [Francis], 257, 282.
Gooding, Isaac, 256.
Gooding [Goodin], Robert, 256, 281.
Goodman, Archabald, 68.
Goodman, James, 68.
Goodner, Benjamin, 257.
Goodner, Coonrod [Conrad], 256, 282.
Goodner, see Gooding.
Goodon [Garden, Gordon], Henry [Henry T.], 170, 191.
Goodrich, Nathan, 123.
Goodridge, Sewel, 39.
Goodsel, Jacob, 193.
Goodwin, Elijah, 348.
Goodwin [Gooden], Joseph, 348, 358.
Gooen [Going, Goings], William, 146, 180.
Gorda, see Goddard.
Gorden, Elisha, 337.
Gorden, James, 317.
Gorden, William, 281.
Gordin, William, 246.
Gordon, Redman, 210.
Gordon, William, 196.
Gordon, see Goodon.
Gore, Daniel, 295.
Gore, John [John C.], 337, 355.
Gore, John [John W.], 131, 135.
Gore, Joshua [Joshua, Sr.], 129, 135.
Gore, Joshuay [Joshua], 295, 306.
Gore, Rubin, 205.
Gore, Thomas, 295.
Gorwood, see Garwood.
Gosner, Peter, 210.
Goss, David, 46.
Goss, Leonard, 20.
Goss, Solomon, 202.
Goss, William, 77.
Gothard [Godthard], William, 131, 136.
Gott, John, 332.
Gouda, see Goodane.
Gouge, William, 131.
Gould, Aaron, 57.
Gould, Thomas, 58.
Gowdy, Robert, 334.
Grable, David, 86.
Grable, see Crabell.
Grace [Gracia], Joseph, 144, 179.
Gracia, Joseph, 193.
Gracia, see Grace.
Gracie, see Gear.
Gracy, William, 20.

Grafts, see Gates and Grots.
Grage [Graig], Jacob, 171, 191.
Grage [Gragg, Gregg], Titus, 171, 191.
Gragg [Graig], John, 172, 192.
Gragg, see Grage.
Graham, Aaron, 56.
Graham, George, 351.
Graham, Jane [Jinny], 303, 311.
Graham, John, 334.
Graham [Grham], Levy [Levi], 1, 5.
Graham, Richard, 333, 353.
Graham, Robert, 349.
Graham, see Grayham and Sanfrey and Graham.
Graig, see Grage and Gragg.
Gramarr, Pierre, 57.
Grammar, see Grammer.
Grammer [Grammar], John, 293, 305.
Grammer [Grammar], William, 299, 309.
Granger, Abaham, 89.
Granger, John, 86.
Gransfield, Samuel, 56.
Grant, Alexander, 56.
Grant, John, 333.
Grant, Roland [Rowland], 257, 282.
Granwell [Greenwell], William, 44, 52.
Grate [Grote], William, 206, 212.
Grate, see Grote.
Graves [Gravis], Frederic [Fredrick], 131, 136.
Graves, John, 197.
Graves, John S. [John], 131, 136.
Graves, Mary, 2, 6.
Graves, Nelson, 349.
Graves, Richard, 349.
Graves, Thomas, 83.
Graves, William, 260.
Gravis, see Graves.
Gray, Barnet, 250.
Gray, Daniel T., 324.
Gray, James, 56, 158, 250.
Gray, John, 56.
Gray, Joseph, 198.
Gray, Rober [Robert S.], 324, 330.
Gray, Rowland, 133.
Gray, Samuel, 141.
Gray, William, 194, 293.
Gray, see Grey.
Grayham [Graham], George, 145, 179.
Grayson, John, 61.
Greathouse, Daniel, 60.
Greathouse, David, 351.
Greathouse, Enoch, 59.
Greathouse, Hiram, 340.
Greaton, David, 206.
Green, Bowling [Bolin], 315, 321.
Green, Burdet [Burdit], 204, 211.

INDEX

Green, George, 8, 200.
Green, James, 8, 56.
Green, Jesse [Jessey], 216, 230.
Green, Jesse [Jessey], 217, 230.
Green, John, 173.
Green, Joseph, 261.
Green, Lewis, 336.
Green, Mary, 338.
Green, Reuben [Ruben], 216, 230.
Green, Richard, 249.
Green, Robert, 195.
Green, Thomas, 300.
Green, Wiley, 199.
Green, Wiley [Willy], 158, 186.
Green, William, 65, 117, 158, 325, 344.
Green, see Geving.
Green House [Greenhouse], ———— [Renfrew], 295, 307.
Greenleaf, Mayo, 210.
Greennah [Greenye], Joseph [Josep], 275, 289.
Greenup, William C., 237.
Greenwell, see Granwell.
Greenwood, Fleming, 122.
Greenwood, Garrison [Garrelson], 122, 126.
Greenwood, James, 81, 198.
Greenwood, John W., 79.
Greenye, see Greennah.
Gregg, Daniel, 201.
Gregg [Greggs], Harmon, 39, 51.
Gregg [Greggs], John, 40, 51.
Gregg, see Grage.
Greggs, John, 40.
Greggs, see Gregg.
Gregory, Christian, 305.
Gregory, Jacob, 305.
Gregson, John, 258.
Gressham, see Grishum.
Grey [Gray], James, 332, 354.
Grey [Gray], Thomas, 350, 359.
Grey, William, 43, 349.
Grham, see Graham.
Gribbin, see Gribbins.
Gribbins [Gribbin, Griblens], James, 144, 179.
Griblens, see Gribbins.
Grider, see Gryder.
Gridley, Hezakiah, 138.
Grifeiths, see Griffy.
Griffeith, Joshua, 197.
Griffen [Griffin], Isaac, 259, 283.
Griffen, Jacob, 199.
Griffeth [Griffith], Daniel, 274, 289.
Griffeth [Griffith], John, 338, 355.
Griffeth, John B., 60.
Griffeth, Thomas, 74.
Griffeth, see Griffith.
Griffin, Francis [William W.], 155, 185.

Griffin, Jesse [Jessy], 312, 320.
Griffin, Joseph, 241.
Griffin, Nancey, 146.
Griffin, Peggy, 197.
Griffin, William, 146, 206.
Griffin, see Griffen.
Griffith, Abm. [A.], 223, 234.
Griffith [Griffeth], Abraham, 349, 358.
Griffith, John, 247.
Griffith, William, 223.
Griffith, see Griffeth.
Griffy [Grifeiths], Patsy, 67, 74.
Griffy, William, 16.
Grigery, Charles, 198.
Grigery, John, 301.
Griggery, James, 84.
Griggory, John, 8.
Griggs, Jesse, 113.
Grimes, Henry, 344.
Grimes [Grines], Philip, 158, 186.
Grinds, Adonjah [Adonijah], 340, 356.
Grines, see Grimes.
Gripeson, see Gipson.
Grisham, see Grissim.
Grishum [Gressham], John, 132, 136.
Grissim [Grisham], Austin, 19, 24.
Grist [Griste], John, 275, 289.
Griste, see Grist.
Griswood, Cyrus, 198.
Grizel, see Grizell.
Grizell [Grizel], Isaac, 217, 231.
Grizzel, Gilbert, 339.
Groats, see Grots.
Grogan, Spencer, 132.
Grose, Rebecca, 340.
Gross [Cross], William, 352, 359.
Grote [Grate], Nicholas, 204, 211.
Grote, see Grate.
Grots [Grafts, Groats], Sarah [Sally], 148, 180.
Ground, James, 156.
Grovener, Grovenor, see Grovner.
Groves, Daniel, 58.
Groves, Jacob, 28.
Groves, John, 56, 84.
Grovner [Grovener, Grovenor], Parker, 110, 119.
Grub, see Grubb.
Grubb [Grub], William, 112, 119.
Gryder [Grider], Cornelius, 75, 92.
Guard [Gaurd], Timothy, 86, 96.
Guiler, see Gilar.
Guinn, John, 114.
Gullet [Gullick], Ebeniah [Beniah], 143, 178.
Gullet [Gullick], Ira, 143, 178.
Gullet [Gullick], John, 143, 178.

Gullick, see Gullet.
Gumlah, see Gamlau.
Gunterman, Caleb, 142.
Gunterman [Guntryman], Jacob, 142, 178.
Gunterman, John [John, Sr.], 172, 192.
Gunterman, John [John, Jr.], 172, 192.
Gunterman, Peter, 172.
Guntryman, see Gunterman.
Gunvill [Gunville], Joseph, 275, 289.
Gunville, see Gunvill.
Gurley, Anson, 130.
Gurley, Benjamin, 130.
Guthery [Guthrie], Beverley [Beverly], 149, 181.
Guthery [Guthrie], Dempsey [Demcy], 149, 181.
Guthery [Guthrie], William, 149, 181.
Guthrie, Nancy, 241.
Guthrie [Gutry], Nancy, 258, 282.
Guthrie, see Guthery.
Gutry, see Guthrie.
Guy, Francis, 198.
Guyer, see Gire.
Guyler, see Gilar.
Gwin, William, 244.

Hacker, Absolem, 1.
Hacker, George, 1.
Hacker, John S. [John], 293, 305.
Hackerty, Alizabeth, 302.
Hackett, Martha, 35.
Hackins, see Hawkins.
Hacock [Hecock], Matthew, 158, 186.
Haddock, Joseph P., 57.
Haddox, see Maddux.
Hade, William, 196.
Hadely [Hadley], John, 149, 181.
Haden, James, 198.
Hadley, see Hadely.
Hadon, see Haydon.
Hadsheall, Samuel, 198.
Haduson, see Atison.
Hafsey [Hufsey], Samuel, 217, 231.
Hagar, John, Sr., 199.
Hagar, Stephen, 40.
Hagelar, Chiles W., 143.
Hagelar, Isaac, 143.
Hageler [Hagler], Benjamin J. [Benjamin], 155, 184.
Hageler [Hagler], Cleavland [Cleveland], 141, 177.
Hageler [Hagler], William R. [William], 155, 184.
Hagerman, Benjamin, 314.
Hagle [Hagler], John, 104, 118.
Hagle [Hagler], Phillip, 104, 118.
Hagler, Jacob, 104, 155.

Hagler [Hagter], Peter, 104, 118.
Hagler, see Hageler and Hagle.
Hagter, see Hagler.
Hail, Thomas, 281.
Hail, see Hale and Hill.
Hailey, Elizabeth, 11.
Hailey, James, 12.
Hailey [Haly], John, 11, 23.
Hailman, Christian, 80.
Haines, see Hains.
Hains [Haines, Hanes], James, 162, 188.
Hains, Philip, 146.
Hairston [Hurston], James, 297, 308.
Hairston [Harsten], John, 297, 308.
Haker [Hawker], John, 149, 181.
Halcomb, see Holcomb.
Halderburn [Holderbaum], John, 113, 120.
Halderman, see Holderman.
Hale, Benjamin, 196.
Hale [Hail], James, 217, 230.
Hale, see Hayle.
Halfacre, see Huffard.
Halfoway, Isaac, 195.
Hall, Achibald, 91.
Hall, Alferd, 327.
Hall, Andrew, 327.
Hall, Benjamin, 299.
Hall, David, 328.
Hall, Easther [Eastor], 150, 182.
Hall, Elisha, 342.
Hall, Harry, 197.
Hall, Henry, 9, 327.
Hall, Isaac, 86, 243.
Hall, James, 156, 199, 339.
Hall, James, Sr., 100.
Hall, James, Jr., 100.
Hall, James, 3d, 100.
Hall, John, 13, 57, 87, 91, 151, 327.
Hall, Joseph, 13.
Hall, Mary, 56.
Hall, Mathew, 87.
Hall, Ralph, 78.
Hall, Ransom, 332.
Hall, Resin, 332.
Hall, Richard, 76, 327.
Hall, Samuel, 272.
Hall, Thomas, 169, 271.
Hall, William, 13, 87, 91, 339.
Hall, William [William, Sr.], 151, 182.
Hall, William [William, Jr.], 151, 182.
Hall, see Hawl.
Halladay [Holliday, Holloday], David, 100, 117.
Halley, Abijah, 57.
Hallick, see Hallock.
Hallock [Hallick], Z. [Zeblen], 217, 231.
Halman, Phillip J., 336.

INDEX

Halton, James, 194.
Haly, *see* Hailey.
Ham, Moses, 123.
Hambleten [Hamilton], Samuel, 159, 186.
Hambleton [Hamilton], Adam, 160, 187.
Hambleton, Daniel H., 203.
Hambleton [Hamilton], James, 169, 191.
Hambleton, Nethaniel [Nat., Nethniel], 203, 211.
Hambleton [Hamilton], Thomas, 167, 190.
Hambleton, Thomas M., 203.
Hambleton, *see* Hamilton.
Hambrick [Hemrick], Joseph, 301, 310.
Hamelton, *see* Hamilton.
Hamer, James, 198.
Hamerson, *see* Harmanson.
Hamilton [Hammelton], Alexander, 346, 357.
Hamilton [Hamelton], George, 215, 229.
Hamilton, Hedman, 199.
Hamilton, J. [John], 222, 233.
Hamilton, James, 197.
Hamilton [Hambleton], James, 351, 359.
Hamilton, John, 226.
Hamilton [Hambleton], John, 78, 93.
Hamilton [Hambleton], Mordica S. [Mordica], 335, 354.
Hamilton [Hamelton], Robt. [Robart, Robert], 221, 233.
Hamilton, Samuel, 197.
Hamilton, William, 240.
Hamilton, William P., 59.
Hamilton, *see* Hambleten, Hambleton, *and* Hammont.
Hammelton, *see* Hamilton.
Hammon, *see* Hammond.
Hammond, Asa, 58.
Hammond [Hammons], John, 276, 289.
Hammond [Hammon], Michael, 208, 213.
Hammond, Peter, 108.
Hammons, *see* Hammond.
Hammont [Hamilton], Samuel, 150, 182.
Hampton, James, 86.
Hampton [Hamton], Smith, 87, 97.
Hamton, *see* Hampton.
Hance, Jacob, 199.
Hance, John, 195, 199.
Hancock, John, 42.
Hancock, R., 226.
Hancock, *see* Handcock.
Hand, George, 340.
Hand, Jeremiah, 263.
Hand, *see* Hann.
Handcock [Hancock], Bennet, 129, 135.
Handcock [Hancock], John [John O.], 272, 287.
Handlon [Hanley], Mathias [Nathias], 142, 178.

Handy, James, 197.
Handy, John, 29, 315.
Handy, Samuel, 29.
Handy, Stephen, 29.
Handy, Thomas, 29.
Hanes, Aaron, 194.
Hanes, Barnabus, 194.
Hanes [Haynes], John, 334, 354.
Hanes [Haynes], Richard, 350, 359.
Hanes, *see* Hains.
Haney [Hany], David, 79, 94.
Haney, William, 61.
Hanill, James, 198.
Hanin [Hanon], James, 7, 22.
Hanin [Hanon], Jesse, 7, 22.
Hanin [Hanon], Samuel, 11, 22.
Hankes [Hanks], Joshua, 156, 185.
Hanks, David, 352.
Hanks, Fleetwood, 351.
Hanks, Joseph, 59.
Hanks, Joshua, 138.
Hanks, *see* Hankes.
Hanley, *see* Handlon.
Hanly, Frances, 253.
Hann [Hand, Henn], John, 114, 120.
Hanna [Hannah], George, 221, 233.
Hanna, James, 346.
Hanna, John, Sr. [John], 346, 357.
Hannah, Brice, 84.
Hannah, J. [John], 222, 234.
Hannah, James, 222.
Hannah, William, 221.
Hannah, *see* Hanna.
Hanner, John, 145.
Hanon, *see* Hanin.
Hanson, Jacob, 195.
Hany, Alden, 124.
Hany, Francis, 124.
Hany, *see* Haney.
Harben, George, 199.
Harber [Harbin], Levi [Levy], 163, 189.
Harbin, *see* Harber.
Harden, Alfred, 198.
Harden, James, 198.
Harden, John, 197.
Harden, *see* Hardin.
Hardesty, Hezekiah, 57.
Hardesty, *see* Hardister.
Hardey, *see* Hardy.
Hardican, Joseph, 139.
Hardin [Herrington], Archer G. [Archery G.], 152, 183.
Hardin [Harden], Jehu, 40, 51.
Hardin, Jeptha, 91.
Hardin, Robert, 82.
Hardin, Sarah, 210.
Hardin [Harden], Thomas, 40, 51.

ILLINOIS HISTORICAL COLLECTIONS

Hardister [Hardesty], John, 337, 355.
Hardister [Hardisty], William, 339, 356.
Hardisty, see Hardister.
Hardy [Hardey], Jacob, 268, 286.
Harford [Herefore], Jessee [Jesse], 85, 96.
Harford [Herefore], Melachi [M.], 85, 96.
Hargate, see Harget.
Harget [Hargate], William, 343, 356.
Hargrave, Bennet, 341.
Hargrave, George, 345.
Hargrave, Jeremiah [Jerremiah], 335, 354.
Hargrave [Hartgrave], John [John, Sr.], 299, 309.
Hargrave, John, Jr., 300.
Hargrave, Robert, 297.
Hargrave, Samuel, 333.
Hargrave, Seth, 331.
Hargrave, Willis, 332.
Harison [Harrison], Henory [Henry], 29, 32.
Harlan [Harlin], Bonham, 7, 22.
Harland, Eligah, 329.
Harland, Elijah, 344.
Harland [Harlin], George, 148, 181.
Harlen, Charles W., 195.
Harlen [Harlin], Silas [Silus], 35, 49.
Harley [Durley], Joshua [Jehu], 160, 187.
Harlin, see Harlan, Harland, and Harlen.
Harlow, Overton, 124.
Harlow, Sylvanus [Silvanus], 250, 255.
Harlston, Paul, 241.
Harman [Harmon], William, 150, 182.
Harmanson [Hamerson], Nathaniel [Nat.], 64, 72.
Harmon, Catharine, 253.
Harmon, Francis, 10, 124.
Harmon, George, 165.
Harmon, Jacob, 250.
Harmon, John W., 193.
Harmon, Joseph, 247.
Harmon, see Harman.
Harn, William, 57.
Harness, Isaac, 61.
Harness [Harnis], Job [Jobe], 34, 49.
Harness, Joseph, 8.
Harness, Sarah, 58.
Harnet, Hiram, 253.
Harney, see Horney.
Harnis, see Harness.
Harper, Daniel, 161.
Harper, Elijah, 36.
Harper, Ephraem, 139.
Harper, Henry, 36.
Harper, I. [Isaac], 222, 233.
Harper, John, 123.
Harper [Harpr], Lincoln [Lincolen], 219, 232.
Harper, Thomas, 352.

Harpr, see Harper.
Harrass [Harris], Adley [Adloc], 143, 178.
Harrass [Harris], Benjamin, 154, 184.
Harrass [Harris], Edwin [Ervin], 143, 178.
Harrass [Harris], John, 143, 178.
Harrass [Harris], Jonithan L. [Jonathan L.], 143, 178.
Harrass [Harris], Robert W., 143, 178.
Harrel, Charles [Charles W.], 140, 177.
Harrel, see Herrald.
Harrgton [Harrington], Drury [Drewry], 112, 119.
Harriman [Harryman], Charles, 318, 323.
Harriman, John, 46.
Harriman [Harryman], Joshua, 318, 323.
Harrington, Charles W., 326.
Harrington, W. O. [Wiley O.], 113, 120.
Harrington, see Harrgton and Herrington.
Harris, Archabald, 124.
Harris, Edward, 133.
Harris, Eli, 39.
Harris, Eli G., 193.
Harris, Eligah, 324.
Harris, Elijah, 58, 88.
Harris, Ephrefram [Ephraim], 261, 283.
Harris, George, 269.
Harris, Isaac, 326.
Harris, Israel [Isral], 35, 49.
Harris, John R., 12.
Harris, Nathan, 324.
Harris, Richard, 89, 342.
Harris, Robert, 342.
Harris, Sampson, 63.
Harris, Samuel, 39.
Harris, William, 281.
Harris, see Harrass.
Harrison, Benjamine [Benjamin], 80, 94.
Harrison, George, 82, 274.
Harrison, John, 61.
Harrison, Lemuel, 65.
Harrison, Thomas, 256.
Harrison, see Harison and Harrisson.
Harriss, Henry, 146.
Harrisson [Harrison], Andrew U., 65, 72.
Harrisson [Harrison], Cudworth, 68, 74.
Harryman, see Harriman.
Hars, William, 152.
Harsford, William, 84.
Harsler, see Horsler.
Harsten, see Hairston.
Hart, Alexandria [Alexander], 138, 176.
Hart, Caleb, 250.
Hart, Edward D., 346.
Hart, Eli, 274.
Hart, James, 266, 275.
Hart, John, 271.
Hart [Heart], Thomas, 344, 357.

INDEX

Hart, William, 18, 266.
Hartgrave, see Hargrave.
Hartgroves, Charles, 326.
Hartline, George, 296.
Hartline, Samuel, 297.
Harvel [Horvell], Squire, 140, 177.
Harvel, see Harvell.
Harvell [Harvel], Merrit [Meret], 1, 5.
Harvell, Simion, 2.
Harvey, Benjamin, 346.
Harvic [Harvick], Adam, 130, 135.
Harvic [Harvick], Jacob, 133, 136.
Harvick, see Harvic.
Haskin, Samuel, 196.
Haskin, see Haskins and Hauskins.
Haskins [Haskin], Asahel [Ashers], 47, 53.
Haskins, James C., 78.
Haskins, Lemuel, 61.
Haskins, Robert, 206.
Haskins [Haskin], Robert, 46, 53.
Haskins, see Hoskins.
Hassle [Hastel], Zacheas [Zachaus, Zacheus], 27, 31.
Hassley, James, 141.
Hastel, see Hassle.
Hastin, George, 92.
Hasting, William, 19.
Hatch, Isaac J., 204.
Hatch, Ralph, 338.
Hatch, William, 58.
Hatch and McCawley, 324.
Hatchel, see Hatsel.
Hatchison [Atchison], John, 167, 190.
Hatchison [Atchison], Samuel, 167, 190.
Hatfield, Aaron, 29.
Hatfield, Adam S., 43.
Hatfield, Buckner, 78.
Hatfield, Harmon [Herman], 274, 288.
Hatfield, John, 57.
Hathaway, Widow, 217.
Hathaway, Eleezer [Eleazer], 272, 288.
Hathorn, David, 239.
Hathorn, James, 239.
Hathorn, Samuel, 250.
Hatsel [Hatchel], Mary, 84, 95.
Hatton, see Hutton.
Haukes [Hawks], Joseph, 297, 308.
Hauskins, Isaac, 147.
Hauskins [Haskin], Lemmons [Samuel], 147, 180.
Hauze, Benjamin, 346.
Hauze, William, 334.
Hawdsheall, Jacob, 198.
Hawes [Haws], Widow, 215, 229.
Hawes [Haws], John, 215, 229.
Hawes, see Haws.
Hawk, Isaac, 28.

Hawk [Hawks], John, 146, 180.
Hawk, Joseph, 28.
Hawk [Hawks], Philip, 146, 180.
Hawk, Robert, 201.
Hawker, see Haker.
Hawkey, Emma, 315.
Hawkins, Isaah [Josiah], 270, 287.
Hawkins, James, 132.
Hawkins, John, 131.
Hawkins [Hackins], Lemuel, 316, 322.
Hawkins, Marshal [Marshal D.], 270, 287.
Hawkins, William, 145.
Hawks, see Haukes and Hawk.
Hawl [Hall], John, 63, 71.
Hawley, Isaac, 200.
Hawley, Pierce [Pearce], 335, 355.
Hawley, William L., 259.
Hawley, see Holey.
Haws, Coleman [Colman], 214, 229.
Haws [Hawes], Jaramiah [J.], 83, 95.
Haws, see Hawes.
Hawthorn, Robert, 334.
Haxy [Hoxey], John, 153, 184.
Hay, Daniel, 333, 354.
Hay, John, 278.
Hayden, Joab [Jacob], 263, 284.
Haydon [Hadon], William, 250, 255.
Hayes, Calvin, 92.
Hayes, John, 79.
Hayes [Hays], John, 221, 233.
Hayes, Joseph, 79.
Hayes, Moses, 79.
Hayes, Samuel, 92.
Hayes, Solomon, 198.
Hayes, see Hays.
Hayl, see Hayle.
Hayle [Hale], Enoch, 267, 286.
Hayle, Isaac, 259.
Hayle [Hale, Hayl], Robart [Robert], 267, 286.
Haymon [Haymour], S., 226, 236.
Haymour, see Haymon.
Haynes, see Hanes.
Hayns, Daniel, 173.
Hays [Haze], Henry, 196.
Hays, John, 278.
Hays, John C., 16.
Hays [Hayes], Robt. [Robart, Robert], 221, 233.
Hays, William, 199, 215.
Hays, William H., 239.
Hays, Zachariah, 270.
Hays, see Hayes.
Hayter [Hiter], Abraham, 142, 178.
Hayward, Caleb, 130.
Hayworth, George, 160.
Haze, see Hays.

Hazel, *see* Hazele.
Hazele [Hazel], Daniel, 221, 233.
Hazele [Hazel], King, 221, 233.
Hazell [Hazzel], Samuel, 221, 233.
Hazlewood [Hazzelwood], Cliff [Clif], 297, 307.
Hazlewood, James, 297.
Hazzel, *see* Hazell.
Hazzelwood, *see* Hazlewood.
Heacock, *see* Hecock.
Head, Henery [Henry], 140, 177.
Headen [Hendricks], Andrew, 169, 190.
Headick [Hendricks], Michael, 169, 191.
Headrick, Charles, 198.
Heady, Ira, 167.
Heady, Sally, 195.
Heady, Sarah, 344.
Heady, Thomas, 344.
Heard [Herd], Charles [Charls], 337, 355.
Heard, *see* Hurd.
Hearing, *see* Herring.
Hearn, Dennis, 41.
Hearn, Edmon [Edman, Edmond], 43, 52.
Hearn, Mary, 41.
Hearn [Hern], William, 43, 52.
Hearndon, John L., 59.
Heart, *see* Hart.
Heasty, Daniel, 351.
Heater [Heeter], John, 132, 136.
Heath, William, 261.
Heazleton, Gervase, 61.
Heck, Jacob, 343.
Hecock [Heacock, Heycock], Esec [Esir, Esok], 45, 53.
Hecock [Heacock], Russel E. [Russell E.], 298, 308.
Hecock, *see* Hacock.
Heddy, Aaron, 82.
Heddy, Absolem, 3.
Heddy, Samuel, 82.
Heeter, *see* Heater.
Hefferd, Joseph, 326.
Helm, Huy, 114.
Helm, John, 267.
Helmstutter, Christ, 92.
Helterbran, David, 194.
Helverstine, Jacob, 36.
Hempstead, Stephen, 199.
Hemrick, *see* Hambrick.
Hence, John, 215.
Hencely, Polly, 350.
Hencely, Samuel, 349.
Henceson, James, 339.
Henderlight [Hinderlite], William, 270, 287.
Hendershot [Hendershott], David, 143, 178.
Hendershott, *see* Hendershot.
Henderson, Adam, 269.

Henderson, Benjamin, 100, 117.
Henderson, David, 45.
Henderson, Edward, 88.
Henderson, Hugh [Hew], 28, 31.
Henderson, James, 88, 168, 202.
Henderson, John, 117.
Henderson, Robert, 88, 100.
Henderson, Sherrod, 88.
Henderson, William, 18.
Henderson, Wilson, Sr. [Wilson], 88, 97.
Henderson, Wilson, Jr., 88.
Hendly, Samuel, 68.
Hendricks, Nathaniel, 60.
Hendricks, *see* Headen, Headick, *and* Hendrix.
Hendrix [Hendricks], John, 262, 284.
Hendrixon [Hendrixson], John, 131, 135.
Hendrixson, *see* Hendrixon.
Hendry, Abraham, 133, 135.
Hening, *see* Hennery.
Henley, *see* Henly.
Henly, John [J.], 225, 236.
Henly [Henley], John [J.], 225, 235.
Henn, *see* Hann.
Hennery [Hening], Ezekel [Ezekiel], 100, 117.
Hennis, Martin, 171, 191.
Henry, Evin [Evan], 297, 308.
Henry, James, 194.
Henry, Samuel, 42, 257.
Henry, Samuel Y. [Samuel], 245, 254.
Henry, Thomas, 257.
Hensley, Charles, 59.
Hensley, James, 60.
Hensley, Joseph, 122.
Hensley, Leftridge, 122.
Hensley, Robert, 122.
Henson, Allen, 108.
Henson, Benjamin, 108.
Henson, Giles, 108.
Henson, Green [G. W. G.], 106, 118.
Henson, Marvelle [Marvill], 108, 118.
Henson, *see* Hinson.
Herald, Cader, 341.
Herald [Herrald, Herreld], James, 113, 120.
Herald, Joel, 334.
Herbert, Thomas F., 318.
Herd, *see* Heard *and* Hurd.
Herefore, *see* Harford.
Herin, *see* Herring.
Herington [Herrington], John, 150, 182.
Herington [Herrington], Whitmell [Whitmill], 152, 183.
Hern, *see* Hearn.
Herod, John, 95.
Herral, Elias, 132.

INDEX

Herrald [Harrel, Herril], Theopolis [Theophilus], 313, 321.
Herrald, see Herald and Herrold.
Herreld, see Herald.
Herren [Herron], John, 143, 178.
Herren, see Herring and Herron.
Herril, see Herrald.
Herrin, see Herring and Herron.
Herring [Herren], David, 69, 74.
Herring [Herren], Isaac, 69, 74.
Herring, James, 69.
Herring [Hearing], Jesse, 349, 359.
Herring, John, 58.
Herring [Herren], Johnathan [Jonathan], 69, 74.
Herring [Herin, Herrin], Moses, 268, 286.
Herring [Herren], Riding B. [Redding B.], 206, 212.
Herrington, Daniel, 47.
Herrington [Harrington], Zenas [Zenos], 121, 126.
Herrington, see Hardin and Herington.
Herrod, Nancy, 83, 95.
Herrold [Herrald], Thomas, 87, 97.
Herron [Herrin], Major [Majer], 317, 322.
Herron [Herrin], Benjamin, 271, 287.
Herron [Herren, Herrin], Lewis [Louis], 274, 289.
Herron [Herrin], Simon, 317, 322.
Herron, William, 196.
Herron, see Herren.
Herte, see Aester.
Hervey, Beauchamp, 57.
Hesmith, see Highsmith.
Hess, John, 303.
Hethcock, see Hethcot.
Hethcot [Hethcock], Rachal [Rachel], 220, 232.
Hewey, see Hughey.
Hewit, see Hewitt.
Hewitt, George, 145.
Hewitt [Hewit], John, 158, 186.
Hewitt, Timothy, 195.
Hewley, Hiram R., 7.
Heycock, see Hecock.
Hiars, see Hyers.
Hiatt, see Hyatt.
Hibarger [Hybarger], Jacob, 293, 305.
Hickason, see Hickerson.
Hickcox, George W. [George], 248, 255.
Hickenbottom, Pullem, 325.
Hickerson [Hickason], William L. [William], 11, 23.
Hickey [Hickle], John, 146, 180.
Hickle, John, 196.
Hickle, see Hickey.
Hickman, Gorge [George], 259, 282.

Hickman [Hicman], Isaac, 259, 283.
Hicks, Aaron, 121.
Hicks, Henry, 196.
Hicks, Isaac, 124.
Hicks, James, 124.
Hicks, Job, 193.
Hicks, Marvel S., 57.
Hicks, William, 124.
Hicks [Hix], William, 45, 53.
Hicks, see Hix.
Hickum, William, 69.
Hicman, see Hickman.
Hide, Isaac, 81, 217.
Hiet, George [John], 3, 6.
Higden [Higdon], Walter, 350, 359.
Higdon, see Higden.
Higgains [Higgins], Martin [Marten], 163, 188.
Higgins, Elizabeth, 139.
Higgins, Fillemen [Fill, Philemon], 158, 186.
Higgins, George, 61.
Higgins, George W., 61.
Higgins, Hiram, 195.
Higgins, Isaac, 58.
Higgins, John, 61, 272.
Higgins, Ransom, 61.
Higgins, Robert, 59.
Higgins, Thomas, 13.
Higgins, Timothy, 258.
Higgins, William, 61.
Higgins, see Higgains and Higins.
Higginson, James, 349.
Highsmith, John, 35.
Highsmith [Hismith], Richard M. [Richard], 35, 50.
Highsmith, Thomas, 35.
Highsmith [Hesmith], William, 35, 50.
Highsmith, William [William, Jr.], 36, 50.
Higins, William, 162.
Higins [Higgins], William, 162, 188.
Hilebart [Hillebart], James C., 29, 32.
Hileman, George, Sr., 305.
Hileman, George, Jr., 297.
Hileman, Jacob, 296.
Hill, Doctor [Docter], 40, 51.
Hill, Allen, 218.
Hill, Burrel [Burrell], 267, 286.
Hill, Charles, 40, 83.
Hill, David, 260.
Hill, Fergus, 40.
Hill, George, 67.
Hill, Henry, 14.
Hill [Hail], Hezek [Hezakiah, Hizekia], 221, 233.
Hill, Isaac, 9, 337.
Hill, James, 10, 15, 173, 217.
Hill, Jeremiah, 200.

Hill, John, 9, 14, 40, 69, 163, 169, 251, 300.
Hill, Jonathan, 315.
Hill, M. B. [Widow B.], 220, 232.
Hill, Nathaniel, 268.
Hill, Peter, 263.
Hill, Pheneas [Phineas], 163, 188.
Hill, Robert, 16, 144, 193, 251.
Hill, Ruth, 260.
Hill, Samuel, 20, 174, 240, 257, 341.
Hill, Starling, 67.
Hill, Thomas, 14, 158.
Hill, William, 268, 269, 274.
Hillard, see Hilliard.
Hillebart, see Hilebart.
Hillhouse, William, 320.
Hilliard [Hillard], Nediam [Nedian], 327, 330.
Hilliard [Hilyard], Wily [Wiley], 352, 360.
Hilt, William, 267.
Hilten, see Hilton.
Hilton, Andrew, 204.
Hilton, Daniel, 204.
Hilton [Hilten], Seth, 318, 323.
Hilyard, see Hilliard.
Hinch, Pretree [Peter], 163, 188.
Hinch, William, 150, 193.
Hinckley, Timothy, 258.
Hincle, see Hinkle.
Hinde, Thomas S., 58.
Hinderlite, see Henderlight.
Hindman, John, 58.
Hindman, Robert [John], 246, 254.
Hinds, Joseph, 11.
Hines, John, 197.
Hines, Robert, 154.
Hines, William, 197.
Hinkle, Elijah, 170.
Hinkle [Hincle], Justus, 170, 191.
Hinkley, Nathaniel, 194.
Hinnon, Sarah, 191.
Hinson [Henson], Benjamin, 8, 22.
Hinson [Henson], John, 8, 22.
Hinson [Henson], Phillip [Philip], 77, 93.
Hinton, Even [Evans], 8, 22.
Hinton, Samuel, 256.
Hinton, Vachel, 256.
Hinton, William, 14, 153, 256.
Hinup, Daniel, 297.
Hismith, see Highsmith.
Hitchcock, Martin, 75.
Hitchcock [Hitchcox], Stephen, 313, 320.
Hitchcox, see Hitchcock.
Hiter, see Hayter.
Hiticks, William, 194.
Hix, Hilyard, 203.
Hix [Hicks], Vines [Barnes, Vynes], 157, 186.

Hix, see Hicks.
Hizer, William G. [William], 238, 253.
Hoag, see Hoage.
Hoage [Hoag], George [G.], 225, 235.
Hobb, Victor, 198.
Hobbs, James, 335.
Hobbs, John, 193.
Hobbs, William, 335.
Hobson, Christopher, 80.
Hobson, John, 260.
Hobson, Mary, 260.
Hockam, see Hocum.
Hocker, see Hooker.
Hockin, Amy, 320.
Hocksey [Hoxey], William, 142, 178.
Hocum [Hockam], S. [Silas], 222, 233.
Hodg, see Hodge.
Hodge, Alexander, 245.
Hodge [Hodg], Amos, 81, 95.
Hodge, David, 199.
Hodge, Erastes, 199.
Hodge, George, 221.
Hodge, James, 195.
Hodge, John, 92.
Hodge, Joseph, 199.
Hodge [Hodges], Seth, 151, 182.
Hodge, William, 195, 355.
Hodge, see Hodges and Hog.
Hodges [Hodge], Ebenezer, 138, 176.
Hodges [Hodge], Hiram, 337, 355.
Hodges, Seth, 281.
Hodges, William, 92.
Hodges, see Hodge.
Hodgin, Jeremiah, 47.
Hodkin [Hodkins], James, 350, 359.
Hodkins, see Hodkin.
Hofner, John, 296.
Hofner, Marten [Martin], 296, 307.
Hog [Hodge], Jonithan [Jonathan], 162, 188.
Hog [Hogg], Samuel, 339, 356.
Hogan, Daniel, 195.
Hogan, Isaac, 80.
Hogan, John, 204.
Hogan, Joseph, 201.
Hogan, Pattrick [Patrick], 271, 287.
Hogan, Sarah, 204.
Hogan, William, 206.
Hogg, Frs. [Frances], 215, 229.
Hogg, see Hog.
Hoggshead [Hoggshed, Hogshead], James, 261, 283.
Hoggshed, Hogshead, see Hoggshead.
Hogue, David, 29.
Hogue, Jeremiah, 43.
Hoisington, Joseph, 56.

INDEX

Holady [Holliday], Misalent [Milicent], 149, 181.
Holanback, see Hollenback.
Holaway, Thomas, 340.
Holbrook, Jacob, 19.
Holcomb [Halcomb], William, 261, 283.
Holcomb [Halcomb], Zachariah [Zacabiah], 281.
Holcomb, see Holkomb.
Holder, David D., 114.
Holderbaum, see Halderburn.
Holderman [Halderman], Christian, 207, 212.
Holedy, see Holiday.
Holeshouser, see Holshouser.
Holey [Hawley], Aaron, 171, 191.
Holiby [Holliby], John, 336, 355.
Holiby, Robert, 56.
Holiday [Holedy, Holladay], Robert, 45, 53.
Holkomb [Holcomb], Joel, 262, 284.
Holladay, see Holiday.
Holland, John, 348.
Holland [Hollen], Leven L. [Edmund], 299, 309.
Holland, Matthew, 143.
Holland, William, 88, 162.
Hollen, see Holland.
Hollenback [Holanback], Lawrance [Laurence, Lawrence], 28, 31.
Holley, see Holly.
Holliby, see Holiby.
Holliday, Elizabeth, 117.
Holliday, see Halladay and Holady.
Hollinshead, Mary, 4.
Holloday, Alexander, 15.
Holloday, see Halladay.
Holloman, Malchi [Maleki], 244, 254.
Holloway, John, 56.
Holly [Holley], William F., 3, 5.
Holman, Frederick, 12.
Holmes, Bryon, 92.
Holmes [Homes], John, 221, 233.
Holmes, see Homes.
Holshouser [Holeshouser], Michael, 297, 308.
Holt, Harmon, 9.
Holt, Robert, 122.
Holts, Samuel, 274.
Homes [Holmes], William, 298, 308.
Homes, see Holmes.
Honeycut, see Honeycutt.
Honeycutt [Honeycut], Arthel [Hartwell], 170, 191.
Hood, Aaron, 140.
Hood, Dempsey [Demcy, Demps], 123, 126.
Hood, James, 76, 350.
Hood, Sarah, 345.
Hood, William, 348.
Hook, William, 261.

Hooker, Ira A., 79.
Hooker, Ira E., 17.
Hooker, J., 115.
Hooker, Jabez, 62.
Hooker, John, 65.
Hooker [Hocker], N. [Neman], 222, 233.
Hooker, William, 65.
Hookham, Edward T., 56.
Hooler, N. H. H., 81.
Hooper, James, 11.
Hoopper, Clariden, 324.
Hoosar [Hoozer, Howzer], Jacob [Jacob, Sr.], 264, 284.
Hoosong [Husong], Daniel, 147, 180.
Hoosong [Husong], Jacob, 155, 185.
Hoosong, James, 143.
Hoosong [Husong], James, 155, 185.
Hoover, George, 352.
Hoozer, see Hoosar.
Hopewell, Henry, 347.
Hopkins, Andrew, 106.
Hopkins, Ezekiel, 200.
Hopkins, Jacob, 257.
Hopkins, James, 106.
Hopkins, John, 104, 301.
Hopkins, Rheubin, 149.
Hopkins, William H., 200.
Hopkinson, see Hopkison.
Hopkison [Hopkinson], Henry, 139, 176.
Hopper, Thomas, 123.
Hopson, Thomas, 336.
Hopton, John, 18.
Horine, Abram, 239.
Horn, Harmon, 325.
Horner, Nathan [Naathan], 272, 287.
Horner, Nichlas, 272.
Horney [Harney], Samuel, 265, 285.
Horrel, Benedict, 240.
Horsler [Harsler], Abraham, 63, 72.
Horsler, James, 195.
Horton, Daniel, 194.
Horvell, see Harvel.
Hosick, Alexander, 331.
Hosick, William, 331.
Hoskins, Isaac, 199.
Hoskins [Haskins], William, 158, 186.
Hotchkiss, Miles, 237.
House, Henry, 245.
House, Micajah, 245.
Houser, Christopher, 293.
Houston, William, 46.
How, James, 65.
Howard, Abraham, 159.
Howard, Aron [Aaron], 299, 309.
Howard, Blackston, 145.
Howard, David, 276.
Howard, Henry, 78.

Howard, John, 154, 216.
Howard, Joseph, 154.
Howard, Thomas, 4.
Howard, William, 10, 38, 205.
Howel, David, 274.
Howel, Thomas, 267.
Howel, Wallace, 198.
Howel, William L., 127.
Howel, see Howell.
Howell, Amos, 351.
Howell, Lewis, 84, 340.
Howell [Howel], William, 11, 22.
Howerton, James, 294.
Howsong [Hussong], Conrad [Conrod], 18, 23.
Howzer, see Hoosar.
Hoxcy, John, 199.
Hoxey, John, 193.
Hoxey, see Haxy and Hocksey.
Hubbard [Hubbart], Ansel, 172, 192.
Hubbard, Ephraim [Ephrim], 79, 94.
Hubbard, Jesse, 345.
Hubbard, John, 78.
Hubbard, Malachi, 56.
Hubbard, Mulekiah [Malakiah, Malleki], 345, 357.
Hubbard, Peter, 18.
Hubbard, Simon M., 67.
Hubbart, see Hubbard.
Hubberd, Hal, 125.
Huberd [Hurlburt], Matthew, 161, 188.
Hubert, Baley, 200.
Hubs, Jaramiah, 83.
Huddleston, Charles, 130.
Hudelston, see Hudleton.
Hudleton [Hudelston], Abm. [Abram], 219, 232.
Hudson, David, 158.
Hudson, see Hutson.
Huey, see Hughey.
Huff, John, 10.
Huff, Samuel, 122.
Huffard [Halfacre], Isaac, 162, 188.
Huffman, Daniel, 13.
Huffman, Michael, 13.
Huffman, Robert, 7.
Hufsey, see Hafsey.
Huggans, James, 246.
Huggans, Robert, 245.
Huggins, David, 318.
Huggins, Lewis, 318.
Huggins, Pattrick [Patrick], 259, 283.
Huggins, William, 318.
Hughes, David, 58.
Hughes, John, 58.
Hughes [Huse], Levi, 1, 5.
Hughes [Huse], Oen [Owen], 300, 309.
Hughes, Racheal [Rachael], 248, 255.

Hughes [Hughs], Robert, 269, 287.
Hughes, William, 58.
Hughes, see Hughs and Hugs.
Hughey [Hewey, Huey], John, 313, 321.
Hughey [Hewey, Huey], Thomas, 313, 321.
Hughs [Hughes, Huse], John, 299, 309.
Hughs [Hughes, Huse], Nathaniel, 297, 308.
Hughs, Samuel, 349.
Hughs [Hughes, Huse], William, 298, 308.
Hughs, see Hughes.
Hughson, see Huston.
Hugs [Hughes], Jonathan, 295, 307.
Huit [Huitt], Albert [Albertt], 207, 212.
Huitt, John, 174.
Huitt, see Huit.
Hulbert, Benjamin, 59.
Hull, Daniel, 202.
Hull, James, 210, 218.
Hull, Jonathan, 342.
Hull, Nortan [Norton], 239, 253.
Hull, Pelick, 61.
Hulm, see Woollum.
Humes, Joseph, 75.
Humphress, Pendleton, 210.
Humphreys, James, 197.
Humphris, Humphry, see Umphrais.
Hungate [Hungot], William, 337, 355.
Hungerford, Barney, 219.
Hungerford, James, 34.
Hungot, see Hungate.
Hunsak, see Hunsaker.
Hunsaker, Abraham, Sr. [Abraham], 300, 309.
Hunsaker, Abraham, Jr., 302.
Hunsaker, David, 293.
Hunsaker, George, Sr. [George], 293, 305.
Hunsaker, George, Jr., 296.
Hunsaker, Jacob, Sr., 302.
Hunsaker, Jacob, Jr., 303.
Hunsaker, John, Sr. [John], 296, 307.
Hunsaker, John, Jr. [John, 2d], 301, 310.
Hunsaker, Joseph, Sr. [Joseph], 296, 307.
Hunsaker, Joseph, Jr., 293.
Hunsaker, Samuel, Sr., 293.
Hunsaker [Hunsak], Samuel, Jr., 296, 307.
Hunt, David, 61.
Hunt, Henry, 58.
Hunt, James, 57.
Hunt, John, 7, 57, 325.
Hunt, Peyton, 79.
Hunt [Hurt], William, 336, 355.
Hunter, A., 224.
Hunter, Elizabeth, 193.
Hunter, Elizabeth [Elisabeth], 144, 179.
Hunter, George, 139.
Hunter, Henry, 69.
Hunter, John, 139.

INDEX

Hunter, John, Sr. [John], 19, 24.
Hunter, John, Jr., 19.
Hunter, Joseph, 19.
Hunter, Samuel, 19.
Hunter, William, 18.
Huntington, Ebenezer, 195.
Hurd [Herd], Charles [Charls], 337, 355.
Hurd, Martha, 247.
Hurd [Heard], Stephen, 337, 355.
Hurlburt, see Huberd.
Hurley, Priastly, 210.
Hurr, David, 218.
Hurst, James, 200.
Hurst, see Hust.
Hurston, see Hairston.
Hurt, Absolem [Absolum], 347, 358.
Hurt, see Hunt.
Husband, David, 240.
Husbands, Flour, 195.
Husbands, Thomas, 195.
Husbands, William, 195.
Huse, Charles M., 196.
Huse, Elizabeth, 81.
Huse, John S., Sr. [John S.], 326, 330.
Huse, Sanford, 194.
Huse, see Hughes *and* Hughs.
Husey, see Huzzer.
Husk, Philo, 335.
Husk, Larry [Lany], 161, 188.
Husk, William, 336.
Husk, see Hust.
Huskey [Husky], John, 298, 308.
Huskey [Husky], Jonathan, 299, 309.
Husky, see Huskey.
Husong, see Hoosong.
Hussey, Adney, 203.
Hussey, Asa, 203.
Hussong, see Howsong.
Hust [Hurst], Elijah, 161, 188.
Hust [Husk], Isam, 352, 360.
Huston, Henry, 60.
Huston [Hughson], Isaac, 312, 320.
Huston, James, 60, 140.
Huston, John, 19, 60.
Huston [Hutson], William, 217, 230.
Hutchcrafft, see Hutchcraft.
Hutchcraft [Hutchcrafft], John, 82, 95.
Hutchens [Hutchinson], Abraham, 162, 188.
Hutcheson, Catharine, 272.
Hutcheson, see Hutchison.
Hutchings, see Hutchins.
Hutchins [Hutchings], Fitz, 3, 6.
Hutchins, James, 57.
Hutchins [Hutchings], John R. [John], 317, 322.
Hutchinson, William, 114.
Hutchinson, see Hutchens.

Hutchison and Stewart [Hutcheson and Stewart], 207, 213.
Hutson, Chamlin [Chamberlin], 65, 72.
Hutson, Moses, 83.
Hutson [Hudson], William, 297, 307.
Hutson, see Huston.
Hutton, George, 157.
Hutton, Henry, 273.
Hutton [Hatton], Mary [Marthy], 35, 50.
Huzzer [Husey], Nathaniel [Nathan], 162, 188.
Hyatt [Hiatt], Jesse, 339, 355.
Hybarger, see Hibarger.
Hyers [Hiars], William, 114, 120.
Hyfall, see Hyfell.
Hyfell [Hyfall], B., 226, 236.
Hynes, William, 121.

Icenoggle, see Isenackle.
Icondro, Baptiste, 247.
Imgram [Ingram], George, 108, 118.
Inard, see Enard.
Ingersol, John, 59.
Ingland, John M., 193.
Ingles, see Gingles.
Inglis, Boon, 200.
Ingraham [Ingram], Jonas, 216, 230.
Ingraham, Philo, 61.
Ingram [Ingrum], George, 108, 118.
Ingram, see Imgram *and* Ingraham.
Ingrum, Peter, 199.
Ingrum, William, 122.
Ingrum, see Ingram.
Inkland, Nicholas, 194.
Inman, see Innman.
Inmand, Henry, 13.
Innman, A., 227.
Innman [Inman], Rufus, 7, 22.
Innman [Inman], Rufus, 11, 22.
Insley, see Enesley.
Ireland, Samuel, 197.
Iric, William, 320.
Irvin, Caleb, 133, 135.
Irvin, Samuel, 200.
Irvin, see Ervin, Ervine, *and* Irwin.
Irwin [Ervin, Irvin], Andrew, 299, 309.
Irwin [Ervin, Irvin], Hugh, 299, 309.
Irwin [Irvin], John, 251, 255.
Isaacs, James, 16.
Isbal [Isbell], Joseph, 165, 189.
Isbal [Isbell], Thomas, 165, 189.
Isbell, see Isbal.
Isenackle [Icenoggle], Jacob, 300, 309.
Isham, see Isom.
Isler, Henry, 207.
Isom, George W., 281.
Isom [Isham], Richard, 86, 96.

Ivins [Evens], John, 153, 184.
Ivory [Ivy], John, 66, 73.
Ivory [Ivy], Joseph [Josepth], 66, 73.
Ivy, see Ivory.

Jacaway, Jane, 198.
Jack, George, 261.
Jack, James, 9.
Jackman, Richard, 59.
Jackson, Alfred, 141.
Jackson, Andrew, 218.
Jackson, Benjamin [Bengamin], 63, 71.
Jackson, D., 224.
Jackson, Elizabeth, 336.
Jackson, George, 214.
Jackson, Hugh, 9.
Jackson, Isaac, 63.
Jackson, Ishom, 10.
Jackson, Jacob, 152.
Jackson, James, 59.
Jackson, Joel, 269.
Jackson, John, 43, 47, 124, 217, 264.
Jackson, John H., 43.
Jackson, John J., 47.
Jackson, Jonn. [Jonathan], 216, 230.
Jackson, Joseph, 84, 333.
Jackson, Low, 137.
Jackson, Martin, 335.
Jackson, Reubin [Reuben], 124, 127.
Jackson, Robert, 169.
Jackson, Samuel, 84.
Jackson, Shadrach [Shade], 141, 177.
Jacobs, Walter, 351.
Jad, Timothy, 92.
Jaggers, James, 351.
Jaggers, Nathan, 351.
James, Benjamin, 20.
James, George, 299.
James, James A., 205.
James, John C. [John], 203, 211.
James, Thomas, 204.
James, William, 42, 269.
James [Jones], Wylie [Whyley], 221, 233.
Jameson, Alexander, 203.
Jameson [Jamison], John, 205, 212.
Jamesson, see Jimmeson.
Jamison, see Jameson and Jimmeson.
Jammason [Jimason], Andrew, 85, 96.
Janderow, see Joneroy.
Jandra, Papu, 195.
Jandro, see Gandrow.
Janes, Belus, 194.
Janes, see Jones.
Jarrard, Jarret, see Jarrot.
Jarrot [Jarret], Isaac, 108, 118.
Jarrot, Nickles [Nicholas], 277, 290.
Jarrot [Jarrard], Thomas, 256, 282.

Jarver, see Garvy.
Jarvice, see Gearvis.
Jarvis, Fanlin [Franklin], 281.
Jarvis, John, 268.
Jarvis, Parker, 264.
Jarvis, see Garvy and Gearvis.
Jaundron [Jeondro], John [Baptiste], 237, 253.
Jaundron, Joseph, 243.
Jeffcoat, John, 57.
Jeffers, Joseph, 210.
Jeffers, Ralph, 45, 49.
Jefferson, Luke, 197.
Jeffries, Thomas, 44.
Jelly, Andrew, 253.
Jemison [Jimerson], Samuel, 29, 32.
Jenkens, see Jenkins.
Jenkins, Joab [Job], 271, 287.
Jenkins [Jinkens], Mathew [Matha], 219, 232.
Jenkins [Jenkens], Thomas, 112, 119.
Jenkins, see Jinkens.
Jennings, David, 59.
Jentry, Zimriah, 318.
Jeondro, see Jaundron.
Jervy, Joseph, 194.
Jesseps, George, 326.
Jesseps, James, 326.
Jewett [Juitt], Isaac, 339, 356.
Jewit, Gilmon, 210.
Jillet, see Gillet.
Jimason, see Jammason.
Jimerson, see Jemison.
Jimmeson [Jamesson, Jamison], Gorge [George], 267, 286.
Jimmison, William, 121.
Jingles, see Gingles.
Jinkens [Jenkins], John, 294, 306.
Jinkens, see Jenkins.
Joab [Jobe], Robert, 146, 180.
Jobe, see Joab.
Johetee [Johntee], Peter, 276, 290.
John, 281.
Johns, Evens [Even], 342, 356.
Johns, Zepheniah, 342.
Johnsen, see Johnston.
Johnson [Jonston], Widow, 215, 229.
Johnson, Abraham, 269.
Johnson [Johnston], Andrew, 80, 94.
Johnson, Benjamin, 19.
Johnson [Johnston], Benjamin, 149, 181.
Johnson [Jonston], Betsey [Betsy], 219, 232.
Johnson, Catharine, 78.
Johnson, Charles, 19.
Johnson, Collins M., 2.
Johnson, Curtis, 85.
Johnson [Johnston], Daniel, 139, 176.

INDEX 411

Johnson, Frances, 130.
Johnson, George, 84.
Johnson, Hardy, 132.
Johnson, Henry, 4, 259.
Johnson, Isaac, 339, 342.
Johnson, James, 122, 144.
Johnson [Johnston], James, 166, 190.
Johnson, James M., 1.
Johnson, Jesse, 325.
Johnson, Joel, 130.
Johnson, John, 158, 198, 327, 339.
Johnson, John W., 257.
Johnson, Joseph, 240.
Johnson, Lewis, 124.
Johnson [Johnston], Lewis, 220, 233.
Johnson, Malkem [Malcom, Malcomb], 265, 285.
Johnson, Matthew, 130.
Johnson, Pedrick, 281.
Johnson, Peter, 305.
Johnson [Johnston], Polly [Milley], 153, 184.
Johnson [Johnston], Robert B. [Robert], 114, 120.
Johnson [Johnston], Samuel, 150, 182.
Johnson, Thomas, 29, 341.
Johnson [Johnston], Thomas, 80, 94.
Johnson [Johnston], Thomas, 146, 180.
Johnson [Johnston], Thomas, 153, 184.
Johnson, William, 2, 3, 5, 6, 12, 212.
Johnson [Johnston], William, 114, 120.
Johnson [Johnston], William, 158, 186.
Johnson [Johnston], William, 160, 187.
Johnson, see Johnston.
Johnston, Andrew, 193.
Johnston, Charles, 210.
Johnston [Jonston], Charles [Charels], 219, 232.
Johnston [Johnson], David, 314, 321.
Johnston [Jonson], Henry, 37, 50.
Johnston [Johnsen], Hugh, 313, 320.
Johnston, James, 58, 60, 247.
Johnston [Johnson], James, 20, 24.
Johnston [Johnson], James, 26, 31.
Johnston [Johnson], James, 41, 49, 51.
Johnston, Jarvis, 197.
Johnston [Johnsen], John [John, Sr.], 313, 321.
Johnston [Johnson], John, 257, 282.
Johnston [Johnson], John, Sr. [John], 46, 53.
Johnston [Johnsen], John, Jr. [John S.], 313, 321.
Johnston [Johnson], John, Jr., 46, 53.
Johnston, John L., 61.
Johnston [Johnson], Joseph, 316, 322.
Johnston, McHenry, 20.

Johnston, Robert, 40.
Johnston, Samuel, 246.
Johnston, Tabitha, 207, 212.
Johnston, William, 40, 60.
Johnston [Johnsen], William, 313, 321.
Johnston [Johnsen], William [William Sr.], 313, 321.
Johnston [Johnsen], William [William, Jr.], 318, 323.
Johnston, see Johnson.
Johntee, see Johetee.
Joiner, Widow, 216, 217.
Joiner, Abm. [Abram], 215, 229.
Joiner, Cage, 216.
Joiner, Hickman, 215.
Joiner, John, 216.
Joiner, Levi [Levy], 216, 230.
Joiner, Lot, 216.
Joiner, R., 224.
Joiner, William, Sr. [William], 216, 230.
Joiner, William, Jr. [William], 216, 230.
Jolleff, see Jolliff.
Jolliff [Jolleff], Elijah, 124, 127.
Jondra, see Joneroy.
Joneroy [Janderow, Jondra], Batist [Baptiste], 148, 181.
Jones, Abraham, 59.
Jones, Ahira, 345.
Jones, Benjamin, 63, 314.
Jones, Bennet [Benett], 194.
Jones, Cadwallader, 60.
Jones [Janes], Charles, 256, 282.
Jones, Clayborn, 195.
Jones, Edmund W. B. [Edmund B. W.], 293, 305.
Jones, Elizabeth, 39.
Jones, Enoch, 198.
Jones, Enock [Enoch], 36, 50.
Jones, Ezekel [Ezekiel], 266, 285.
Jones, Gabriel, 249.
Jones, Henry, 264, 345.
Jones, Ignatious, 329.
Jones, Isaac, 10.
Jones, Jacob, 26.
Jones, James, 131.
Jones, James M., 199.
Jones, Jeremiah, 221.
Jones, Jesse, 320.
Jones, John, 69, 141.
Jones, John C., 3.
Jones, John H., 332.
Jones, Joseph, 57.
Jones, Joseph [Josiah], 155, 184.
Jones, Joseph P., 40.
Jones, Lasandrew [Cassandra], 67, 74.
Jones, Martin, 10, 22, 140.
Jones, Matthew, 345.

Jones, Michael, 78, 237.
Jones, Moses, 63.
Jones, Nathan [Naathan], 266, 285.
Jones, Nathaniel, 63.
Jones, Rebecca [Rebecka], 63, 72.
Jones, Richard T., 91.
Jones, Robert, 324.
Jones, Samuel B., 153.
Jones, Stephen, 110, 153, 196.
Jones, Thomas, 3, 40, 193, 195.
Jones, Wiley, 63.
Jones, William, 141, 142, 193, 216, 325.
Jones [Jons], William, 219, 231.
Jones, see James.
Jons, see Jones.
Jonson, see Johnston.
Jonston, Jesse, 15.
Jonston, see Johnson *and* Johnston.
Jordan, Caleb, 60.
Jordan, Elias, 60.
Jordan, James, 56.
Jordan [Jourdan], James, 65, 73.
Jordan, John, 20.
Jordan [Jorden], John, 121, 126.
Jordan, Joseph, 121.
Jordan, Joshua, 60.
Jordan, Reuben, 56.
Jordan, Thomas, 121.
Jordan, Thomas [Thomas, Jr.], 121, 126.
Jordan, William, 12, 60, 124.
Jordan, William [William, Sr.], 121, 126.
Jordan [Jorden], William, 341, 356.
Jordan, *see* Jorden *and* Jourdan.
Jorden [Jordan], Britton [Briton], 315, 322.
Jorden, *see* Jordan.
Jordon, James, 194.
Jorney [Journey], Elizabeth, 271, 287.
Jourdan [Jordan], Elias, 62, 71.
Jourdan, Francis, 67.
Jourdan, *see* Jordan.
Journey, John, 281, 287.
Journey, *see* Jorney *and* Juney.
Joy, George, 64.
Joy, Joseph, 247.
Joy, Levi, 56.
Judd, Elizeph [Eleazer], 156, 185.
Judy, Samuel, 147, 196.
Juitt, *see* Jewett.
Juney [Journey], William, 163, 188.
Juntum, Tuson, 196.
Jurney, Nancy, 13.
Just, Henry, 77, 82.
Just, Thomas, 82.

Kain, John, 318.
Kanada [Kenneday], John, 351, 359.
Kane, Alexander H., 80.

Kane, Elias K., 238.
Karnes, John, 86.
Karr, Henry, 241.
Karraker, *see* Carker.
Karson, James, 9.
Kasey, *see* Casey.
Kay, Agnes P., 152.
Kaykedall, *see* Kuykendal.
Kaykendall, *see* Coykendoll.
Keagmen [Eckburn], Zechariah [Zecheriah], 167, 190.
Kearney, Thomas, 58.
Keen, Daniel, 60.
Keen, Peter, 58.
Kees [Keys], Isaac [Isaac, Sr.], 160, 187.
Kees [Keys], Isaac [Isaac, Jr.], 160, 187.
Keeth [Koetah], Elizabeth, 98.
Keeth, Robert, 89, 98.
Keisterson [Kesterson], Robert, 218, 231.
Keistirson [Kesterson], Larken, 218, 231.
Keistirson [Kesterson], Peter, 218, 231.
Keith, Abner, 299.
Kelleay [Kelley, Kelly], William, 78, 94.
Kelley, Ebenezer, 60.
Kelley, Freeman, 204.
Kelley, Henry, 57.
Kelley, John, 204.
Kelley, Zebedee, 281.
Kelley, *see* Kelleay *and* Kelly.
Kellog, *see* Kelog.
Kellogg, Elisha, 199.
Kellogg, Lymon, 199.
Kelloms [Cellums], Margaret [Peggy C.], 165, 189.
Kelly, Abner O. [Abnor O.], 149, 181.
Kelly, D. H. [David W.], 113, 120.
Kelly, Elijah, 166.
Kelly, George, 194.
Kelly, Henry, 152, 166, 194.
Kelly, Hezekiah L., 196.
Kelly, Ira, 141.
Kelly [Kelley], John, 166, 190.
Kelly, Oliver [Oliver L.], 159, 186.
Kelly, Stephen, 110.
Kelly, William, 166.
Kelly, *see* Kelleay.
Kelog [Kellog], Elijah, 40, 51.
Keltner [Rittiner], Henry, 164, 189.
Keltner [Rettener], Solomon, 164, 189.
Kelton, Thomas, 87.
Kenada, *see* Keneday.
Kenady [Kennedy], Thomas, 45, 53.
Kenchalow, Daniel, 329.
Kendall, Stephen, 199.
Keneday [Canada, Kenada], Gorge F. [George F.], 274, 289.
Keneday [Canada], Neal [Neill], 272, 288.

INDEX

Kenedy, Hannah, 240.
Kenedy, Joseph, 43.
Kenedy, *see* Kennedy.
Keney, William, 84.
Kennady [Kennedy], James, 40, 51.
Kenneday, *see* Kanada.
Kennedy, Demsey, 318.
Kennedy [Kenedy], Jacob, 219, 232.
Kennedy, James, 57.
Kennedy [Kenedy], Thomas, 217, 231.
Kennedy, *see* Kenady *and* Kennady.
Kenneipp, Solomon, 59.
Kennel [Kernel], Lemuel, 335, 355.
Kenyon [Kinyon], Joseph, 314, 321.
Keown, *see* Kown.
Kerlogg, John, 12.
Kermack [Cormack], Lewis, 150, 182.
Kernel, *see* Kennel.
Kerns, *see* Carnes.
Kerr, James, 196.
Kershaw, Margaret, 56.
Kesler, Constantine, 294.
Kesler, John, 303.
Kesterson, William, 83.
Kesterson, *see* Keisterson *and* Keistirson.
Keys, Willard, 194.
Keys, *see* Kees.
Kichens, *see* Kitchins.
Kickendall [Kirkindall, Kuykendall], Noah, 345, 357.
Kidd, J. C. [J.], 223, 234
Kidd, Robert, 202.
Kidwell, James, 43.
Kiger, John [John, Sr.], 347, 358.
Kiger, John, Jr., 347.
Kikendall [Kuykendoll, Kuykindall], Lewis, 80, 94.
Kilbourn, Mary, 27, 31, 193.
Kile, *see* Chiles.
Killwell, James, 199.
Kimbell, Henry, 239.
Kimmel, Peter, 113.
Kimmel, Samuel, 89.
Kimmel, Kimmell, *see* Cimmel.
Kimsey, *see* Kimzey.
Kimzey, David, 338.
Kimzey [Kimsey], Elijah, 338, 355.
Kincade, Hugh, 61.
Kincaid [Kinkead], Andrew, 263, 284.
Kincaid [Kinkead], James, 263, 284.
Kindead, *see* Kinkaid.
Kinder, George, 141.
Kinder, Jacob, 145.
Kinder, Voluntine [Volentine], 145, 179.
King, C. [Charles], 223, 234.
King, George, 332.
King, James, 222.

King, John, 9.
King, Lawdy [Lowdy], 216, 230.
King, Peter, 148.
King, Salley, 157.
King, Mrs. Susannah, 327.
King, William, 63, 266.
Kings, Rufus, 195.
Kingsbury, Denison, 145.
Kingsbury, James, 145.
Kingston, Abraham, 199.
Kingston, David, 198.
Kingston, George, 161.
Kingston, John, 266.
Kingston, Paul, 265.
Kingston, Reard [Richard], 155, 184.
Kingston, William, 155.
Kinkade [Kinkaid], Samuel [Samuel J.], 157, 185.
Kinkade, *see* Kinkead.
Kinkaid [Kindead, Kinkand], William T., 263, 284.
Kinkaid, *see* Kinkade.
Kinkand, *see* Kinkaid.
Kinkead [Kinkade], George W., 37, 50.
Kinkead, *see* Kincaid.
Kinner, James, 92.
Kinney, Andy [Andey], 202, 211.
Kinney, Biram, 172.
Kinney, Daniel, 41.
Kinney, Isaac, 44.
Kinney, Jacob, 166.
Kinney, Joseph, 203.
Kinney, William, 265, 281.
Kinsall, John, 85.
Kinsay, Nietry, 197.
Kinters, *see* Winters.
Kinyon, *see* Kenyon.
Kirby, Cirus, 200.
Kirby, Syrus, 8.
Kirk, John, 64.
Kirkindall, *see* Kickendall.
Kirkindoll, Stephen, 154.
Kirkpartrack [Kirkpatrick], William, 165, 189.
Kirkpatrick, David, 16.
Kirkpatrick, Francis, 18.
Kirkpatrick, Hugh, 16.
Kirkpatrick, James, 17.
Kirkpatrick, James G. [James], 18, 23.
Kirkpatrick, John, 15, 18.
Kirkpatrick, Josiah, 15.
Kirkpatrick, Thomas, 14, 17.
Kirkpatrick, *see* Kirkpartrack, Kirkpattrick, *and* Patrick.
Kirkpattrick [Kirkpatrick], Francis, 206, 212.
Kitchell, Joseph, 34.

Kitchell, Nancy, 35.
Kitchell, Wickliff, 34.
Kitchens, see Kitchins.
Kitchins [Kichens, Kitchens], Charles, 169, 191.
Kithcart, David, 246.
Knapp, Samuel C., 333.
Kneel, see Neal.
Kneely, see Nelly.
Knight [Night], David, 265, 285.
Knight, George, 60.
Knight, James, 26, 195.
Knight, Richard, 142, 153.
Knight, Stephen, 57.
Knight, Thomas, 27.
Knighton [Nighting], Thomas, 274, 288.
Knott, see Naught.
Knotts, Thomas, 195.
Knotts, see Nots.
Knowlan, see Nowlen.
Koetah, see Keeth.
Kokenower, Abraham, 301.
Kooksey, see Cooksey.
Koon, see Coone.
Kown [Keown], James, 199.
Kreel, see Creal.
Kullison [Cullison], William, 218, 231.
Kunland, David, 197.
Kuykendal [Kaykedall, Kuykendall], Daniel, 46, 53.
Kuykendall, Joseph, 128, 129, 134, 135.
Kuykendall, see Kickendall and Kuykendal.
Kuykendoll, Kuykindall, see Kikendall.

Labarb, Baptiste, 196.
Labasere, see Labasha.
Labasha [Labasere, Labisya], Lewis [Louis], 278, 291.
Labisya, see Labasha.
Labour [Lawler], Partrach [Patrick], 145, 179.
Labrea, Antwine, 248.
Laby, Simeon, 194.
La Cavy, Batiste, 241.
Lacey, Ann, 257.
Lacey [Lacy], Barbary, 37, 50.
Lacey, Caleb, 257.
Lacey, John, 246, 256.
Lacey, Stephen, 256.
La Chance, Madame, 242.
Lackey, Adam, Sr. [Adam], 36, 50.
Lackey, Adam, Jr., 36.
Lackey, see Leaky.
Lacompt, Lacont, see Lacoumpt.
Lacoumpt [Lacourse], Antwine, 279, 291.
Lacoumpt [Lacompt, Lecomptre], Basel [Bazil, Brazil], 277, 290.

Lacoumpt [Lacounpt, Lecomptre], Battice [Baptiest, Batise], 277, 290.
Lacoumpt [Lacompt, Lecomptre], Juliann [Julian], 277, 290.
Lacoumpt [Lacompt, Lacont], Lewis [Louis], 278, 291.
Lacounpt, see Lacoumpt.
Lacounts [Lacours, Lecourse], Battice, Sr. [Baptist, Batise], 275, 289.
Lacours, see Lacounts.
Lacourse, see Lacoumpt.
Lacroy, Baptiste, 194.
Lacy, Elliot, 326.
Lacy, see Lacey.
Lad [Ladd], Timothy, 152, 183.
Ladd, Milton, 132.
Ladd, see Lad.
Laden [Layton], Thomas, 29, 32.
Ladison [Larrison], Ab. [A.], 225, 235.
Laffarty, see Lafferty.
Lafferty [Laffarty], Cornelius [Cornelus], 81, 95.
Laflam, see Laplumb.
La Fleau, see La Flue.
La Flue [La Fleau], Ursula, 243, 254.
Lafond, T. A., 60.
Lafranbroo, Lafromba, see Lafumba.
Lafumba [Lafranbroo, Lafromba], John [John B.], 276, 290.
Lagow, Richard, 44.
Lagow, Wilson, 35.
Lahone, John Baptiste, 195.
Lahone, Pierre, 195.
Lair, William B., 156.
Laird, see Larde.
Lairs, see Larn.
Laitham, Richard, 200.
Laitham, see Latham.
Lakins, see Lakons.
Lakons [Lakins], Joseph, 165, 189.
Lalar, Jacob, 197.
Lalong [Lolande], Battice [Baptieste], 277, 290.
Lamar, see Lemnor.
Lamarsh [Lemarche], Joseph [Josett], 277, 290.
Lamasters, see Lemasters.
Lamatte [Lemette], Johaim [Joachim], 278, 291.
Lamb, Abner, 30.
Lamb, Benjamin, 30.
Lamb, Cornelius, 30.
Lamb, John, 41, 341.
Lamb, Solomon, 258.
Lambert, Elisha, 197.
Lambert, Jesse, 276.
Lamer [Lamore], Henry, 301, 310.
Lamer [Lamour], Joseph, 300, 310.

INDEX

Lameur [Lamure], Louis [Francis], 238, 253.
Lamn, John, 69.
Lamore, see Lamer.
Lamorse, see Mar.
Lamott, Joseph, 58.
Lamour, see Lamer.
Lampens, see Lampins.
Lamphire, Elijah, 47.
Lampins [Lampens], W. [Wood], 222, 234.
Lampkins, Jeptha [Jopthah], 150, 182.
Lampley, see Lamply.
Lamply [Lampley], Thomas, 63, 72.
Lamure, see Lameur.
Lanahan, see Langham.
Land, Aaron, 266.
Land, Josep [Joseph], 268, 286.
Land, Moses, 268.
Land, Moses, Jr., 274.
Land, Phillip [Philip], 259, 283.
Land, Robert, 346.
Landers, Henry, 154.
Landers, Jacob, 154.
Landers, John, 297.
Landes, Simon, 14.
Lane, Daniel, 26.
Lane, James, 339.
Lane, John, 335.
Lane, Joseph, 59.
Lane, Lewis, 338.
Lane, Roland, 58.
Lane, see Lean.
Lanear, see Leneur.
Lang, Francis, 198.
Langdon, Samuel, 132.
Langford [Lankford], John [John W.], 343, 357.
Langham [Lanahan], John, 4, 6.
Langleey, ———, 114.
Langley [Langly], John, 298, 308.
L'Anglois, Francois, 56.
L'Anglois, John Bte., 56.
Langloy, Francis, 242.
Langloy, Stephen, 242.
Langly, William, 104.
Langly, see Langley.
Languedoc, Andro, 57.
Languedoc, Charlo, 57.
Languedoc, Louis, 57.
Langworthy, Agustus [Augustus], 139, 176.
Langworthy, Rodolphus [Reodolphus], 138, 176.
Langworthy, Stephen, 147.
Lanier, Thomas, 83.
Lankeston, Jaconeas, 200.
Lankford, see Langford.
Lansdown, James, 59.
Lanterman, Daniel A., 140.

Lanterman, James, 58.
Lanterman, John, 166.
Lanterman, Peter, 166.
Lanton [Larton], Jacob, 162, 188.
Laong, William, 148.
Lapage, Madam [Terrage], 278, 291.
Lapage, Joseph, 277.
Lapansa, see Lapoxey.
Laparsu, see Lapois.
Lapash, see Lapaugh.
Lapasse, see Lapois.
Lapaugh [Lapolh], Joseph, 275, 289.
Lapaugh [Pupah], Joseph, 278, 291.
Lapaugh [Lapash], Peter, 278, 291.
Laplumb [Laflam], Phillip [Philip], 275, 289.
Lapois [Laparsu, Lapasse], Francis, 278, 291.
Lapolh, see Lapaugh.
Lapoxey [Lapansa], Anthony [Antwine], 278, 291.
Larama [Laurum], Hugh [Hubert], 275, 289.
Larama [Laremore, Larimy], Lewis [Louis], 264, 285.
Larama [Laremire], Lewis, Sr. [Louis], 278, 291; see also St. Garnaw and St. Jeremy.
Larama [Loise], Paul, 275, 289.
Lard, J. [James], 223, 234.
Lard, John, 317.
Lard, Sammuel [Samuel, Jr.], 250, 255.
Lard, Samuel, Sr., 250.
Lard, see Larde.
Larde [Laird, Lard], James, 163, 188.
Larde [Laird, Lard], John, 154, 184.
Laremire, Laremore, Larimy, see Larama.
Larkin [Larkins], Edward, 144, 179.
Larkins, Edward, 199.
Larkins, see Larkin.
Larn [Lairs], Samuel, 164, 189.
Larrence [Lawrence], Jesey [Jessee], 150, 182.
Larrens, Calvin, 237.
Larrison, see Ladison.
Larsoan, Madame, 242.
Larton, see Lanton.
Lashang [Lewis], Abm. [A.], 225, 235.
Lashway, John B., 210.
Lasley [Lastley], John, 115, 120.
La Source, Pascal, 243.
Lassater, James, 335.
Laster [Luster], John, 39, 51.
Lasters, see Lemasters.
Lastley, Alexander, 250
Lastley, see Lasley.
Lastly, Hugh, 248.
Latau, see Lataue.

416   ILLINOIS HISTORICAL COLLECTIONS

Lataue [Latau], Joseph, 278, 291.
Latham [Laitham], James [John], 161, 187.
Latham [Lethem], William, 215, 230.
Lathem, Samuel, 132.
Latherham, James, 92.
Lathop [Lathrop], Charles, 44, 52.
Lathrop, Fayette, 210.
Lathrop, see Lathop.
La Toural, Joseph, 242.
La Toural, Yasaint [Yosaint], 242, 254.
Latter, Joseph, 197.
Lature, Henry, 47.
Laughlin, Alexandria [Alexander, Alexn.], 146, 180.
Laughlin, John, 18.
Laughlin, John L. [John Lewis, Lewis], 312, 320.
Laughlin, Michael, 200.
Laurum, see Larama.
Lavalette [Lavelit], Louis [Lewis, Lois], 46, 53.
Lavelit, see Lavalette.
Lavety, Russell, 197.
Lavine, James, 198.
Lavisee [Lavisse], David, 202, 211.
Lavisse, see Lavisee.
Lavoilete, August, 56.
Lavoilete, Françoise, 57.
Lavoilete, William, 56.
Lavoilette, Francis, 60.
Law, see Low.
Lawel [Lisle], Andrew, 154, 184.
Lawland, Morris, 198.
Lawland, see Lowrler.
Lawler, Patrick, 196.
Lawler, see Labour.
Lawless, Samuel, 198.
Lawless, see Lollis.
Lawrance [Lawrence], Samuel, 156, 185.
Lawrance, William, 195.
Lawrance, see Lawrence.
Lawrence [Lawrance, Leawrance], Ester [Easter, Esther], 297, 308.
Lawrence, John B., 210.
Lawrence, Richard, 210.
Lawrence, Solomon, 195.
Lawrence, see Larrence and Lawrance.
Lawrison, John, 151.
Laws, Moses, 58.
Lawson, David, 241.
Lawson, William, 60.
Layne, John, 244.
Layton, see Laden.
Lazier, Joseph, 57.
Leach [Leech], John, 266, 285.
Leach, see Leech.
Leak [Leek], Harmon, 106, 118.

Leak, Richard, 197.
Leaky [Lackey, Lecky], George, 217, 231.
Lealer, Thomas, 195.
Lean [Lane], James [J.], 223, 234.
Lear, Samuel, 198.
Learner, Mrs., 242.
Leathers, Charles, 210.
Leaviett, see Leavitt.
Leavitt [Leaviett], Abijah, 248, 255.
Leawrance, see Lawrence.
Lechance, see Lechanoe.
Lechanoe [Lechance], Joseph, Sr., 276, 290.
Lechanoe [Lesance], Joseph, Jr., 276, 290.
Leck [Lick], Herman, 269, 286.
Lecky, see Leaky.
Lecompt, Susannah, 241.
Lecomptre, see Lacoumpt.
Lecourse, see Lacounts.
Lecuras, Amos, 199.
Ledbetter, Asa, 12, 82.
Ledbetter, Henry, 12, 82.
Ledbetter, James, 85.
Ledbetter, Sarah, 92.
Lee, ———, 210.
Lee, Abijah, 121.
Lee, Beno [Benoni, Benony], 217, 231.
Lee, Charles, 343.
Lee, Green [Gree], 344, 357.
Lee, Harvey, 320.
Lee, Henry, 10, 13.
Lee, James, 13, 248.
Lee, James [James, Sr.], 218, 231.
Lee, John, 14, 20, 123, 271, 333.
Lee, Lemuel, 121.
Lee, Levi, 42.
Lee, Loyd, 11.
Lee, Nancey [Elizabeth], 154, 184.
Lee, Nancy, 335.
Lee, Rebecka, 230.
Lee, Richard, 216, 230.
Lee, Samuel, 20, 195.
Lee, Stephen, 43.
Lee, Thomas, 327.
Lee, William, 276.
Leech, Anthony, 59.
Leech [Leach], Isiah [Josia], 220, 232.
Leech, John, 60.
Leech, Jonathan, 58.
Leech [Leach], Nefel, 220, 232.
Leech, Thomas, 61.
Leech, William, 57.
Leech, see Leach.
Leek, Henry, 59.
Leek, see Leak.
Leeland [Leland], Silas, 243, 254.
Leeper, John, 17, 210.

INDEX

Leeper, *see* Leiper *and* Leper.
Lefavre, Francis, 198.
Legg, *see* Legge.
Legge [Legg], Edward, 45, 53.
Leggit [Leggitt], Abraham [Abraham A.], 159, 186.
Leggitt, Abraham A., 199.
Leggitt, *see* Leggit.
Legyster, *see* De Laygest.
Leightebarger, *see* Litebarger.
Leiper [Leeper], John, 218, 231.
Leland, William, 222.
Leland, *see* Leeland.
Lemain, Andrew, 194.
Leman [Lemen], Joseph, 271, 287.
Leman [Lemen], Robert, 265, 285.
Lemar, *see* Lemnor.
Lemarche, *see* Lamarsh.
Lemasters [Lamasters], Isaac, 35, 50.
Lemasters [Lasters], James, 43, 52.
Lemasters, Richard, 44.
Lemen, James, 204, 281.
Lemen, Josiah, 204.
Lemen, Moses, 204.
Lemen [Lemmon], William, 204, 211.
Lemen, *see* Leman *and* Lemon.
Lemette, *see* Lamatte.
Lemington, John, 194.
Lemmon, *see* Lemen.
Lemmons [Lemons], George, 301, 310.
Lemmons, *see* Lemons.
Lemnor [Lamar, Lemar], S. [J., Solomon], 225, 236.
Lemocks, Ison, 352.
Lemon, Robert, 281.
Lemon [Lemen], William, 203, 211.
Lemons [Lemmons], Samuel, 38, 50.
Lemons, *see* Lemmons.
Lenard [Leonard], Zepheniah [Zephaniah], 273, 288.
Lence [Lense], Boston [Boysten], 301, 310.
Lence [Lense], Davolt [Davault, Davoult], 301, 310.
Lence, George, Jr. [George], 297, 308.
Lence [Lense], John [John, Sr.], 298, 308.
Lence [Lense], John, Jr., 301, 310.
Lence, Michael, 305.
Lence, Peter, 296.
Leneur [Lanear], Samuel, 38, 50.
Lennon, Q. L. [James L.], 113, 120.
Lense, *see* Lence.
Leonard, Cutler, 27.
Leonard, Frances, Jr., 196.
Leonard, John, 193.
Leonard, John [J.], 226, 236.
Leonard, Lawrence, 196.
Leonard, Newil [Newel, Nuel], 29, 32.

Leonard, Polly, 195.
Leonard, Walter, 47.
Leonard, *see* Lenard.
Leper [Leeper], James, 202, 211.
Lepherd, Nicholas, 199.
Le Roy, Semore, 196.
Le Roy, Simon, 196.
Lerton [Lurton], Jacob, 170, 191.
Lesance, *see* Lechanoe.
Lesley, John, 348, 354.
Lethem, *see* Latham.
Letherlaird, George, 60.
Leven, James, 194.
Levens, Othiel, 241.
Levens, Thomas, 241.
Levens, *see* Levins.
Levery, Pierre, 239.
Levingston, Abram, 77.
Levingston, Joshua [Elisha], 3, 5.
Levins [Levens], Isaiah, 202, 211.
Lewis, And. [A.], 225, 235.
Lewis, David, 61.
Lewis [Louis], Elijah, 271, 287.
Lewis, George, 158.
Lewis [Lues], George [G.], 224, 235.
Lewis [Lues], H. [Henery], 224, 235.
Lewis, Isaac, 41.
Lewis, Isaiah, 58.
Lewis, J., 225.
Lewis, Jacob [J.], 225, 235.
Lewis, John, 20, 56, 156.
Lewis [Louis], John, 137, 175.
Lewis, Jonathan, 57.
Lewis, Joseph, 221.
Lewis, Nicholas, 196.
Lewis, Paul, 58.
Lewis, Peter, 38.
Lewis, Richard, 328.
Lewis, Samuel, 299.
Lewis, William, 27, 313, 328.
Lewis, Wolcot, 258.
Lewis, Zepheniah [Zephenah], 46, 53.
Lewis, *see* Lashang.
Leyrle, *see* Lierly.
Leytell [Lytle], Henry, 217, 231.
Lially, Henry, 305.
Lially, *see* Lierley.
Lick, *see* Leck.
Liddle, William, 59.
Lierley [Lially], Jacob, 302, 310.
Lierly [Leyrle], Henry, 298, 308.
Light, John, 305.
Lilburn, George, 195.
Liles [Lisle], Daniel, 170, 191.
Limbaugh, Limboch, *see* Linbeau.
Limerick, *see* Limrick.
Limmerick [Nimrick], Peter L., 273, 288.

Limrick [Limerick], John, 80, 94.
Linbeau [Limbaugh, Limboch], Michael [Michel], 298, 308.
Linch, Isaac, 273.
Linch, Patrick, 194.
Linch [Linck, Lynch], Solomon, 273, 288.
Linck, see Linch.
Lincoln, Elijah, 316.
Linder, Jacob, 174.
Lindley, David, 172.
Lindley, John, 17.
Lindley, Joseph, 193.
Lindley, Mark, 200.
Lindley, Samuel, 9.
Lindley [Lindly], Samuel, 35, 49.
Lindley, Simon, 163.
Lindley, see Lindly and Linnley.
Lindly [Lindley], William, 20, 24.
Lindly, see Lindley.
Lindsay, George W., 34.
Lindsey, James, 239.
Lindsey, William, 115.
Lindsey [Linsey], William, 112, 119.
Lindsley, see Linsey and Linsley.
Lingle, Antoney [Anthony], 298, 308.
Lingle, Daniel, 295.
Lingle, Jacob, Sr. [Jacob], 301, 310.
Lingle, Jacob, Jr., 299.
Lingle, John, 299.
Lingle, Paul, 301.
Lingle, Peter, 293.
Link, Christain, 158.
Linn, Aneas, 198.
Linn [Lynn], Thomas, 157, 185.
Linn, William, 114.
Linnley [Lindley], John, 154, 184.
Linsey [Lindsley], John, 166, 190.
Linsey, see Lindsey.
Linsley [Lindsley], Martin [Martin L.], 173, 192.
Linsly, Jacob, 198.
Linton, Lawson, 34.
Linton, William, 149.
Lions, Margaret, 174, 192.
Lipe, see Lupe and Lype.
Lipincott, Thomas, 139.
Lisenbay, see Lisenby.
Lisenby [Lisenbay], Widow, 216, 230.
Lisenby [Lisenbay], Betsy, 217, 230.
Lisenby [Lizenby], James, 131, 135.
Lisenby [Lizenby], Jeremiah, 132, 136.
Lisle, see Lawel and Liles.
Litebarger [Leightebarger], C. [Conrad], 113, 120.
Litener, Jacob, 92.
Litleton [Littleton], Ely [Eli], 300, 309.
Litleton [Littleton], John, 300, 310.

Litteral, Lot, 17.
Little, James, 41.
Little, James, Sr., 13.
Little, James, Jr., 13.
Little, Joseph [Jasper], 41, 52.
Little, Lewis, 43.
Little, Nancy, 63.
Little, Robert, 131.
Little, Samuel, 10, 85, 166, 245.
Little, Thomas, 173.
Little, William, 10.
Little, Wright, 85.
Littlefield, John, 100.
Littlefield, Samuel, 26.
Littleton, Jacob, 299.
Littleton, see Litleton.
Liveley [Lively], John, 269, 286.
Lively, Amos, 248.
Lively, James, 248.
Lively, John, 245.
Lively, Joseph, 248.
Lively, Reuben, 248.
Lively, Shadrach [Shadrach, Sr.], 244, 254.
Lively, Shadrach [Shadrach, Jr.], 249, 255.
Lively, see Liveley.
Livergood, John, 326.
Livinston, John P., 281.
Lizenby, see Lisenby.
Lloyd, see Loid.
Lock, Geradis [Gerades, Gerardis], 205, 212.
Lock, James, 244, 325.
Lock, John, 205.
Lock, Jonas, 338.
Lock, Moses, 205.
Lock, Richard, 325, 338.
Lock, Samuel, 205.
Lock, Samuel T., 324.
Lock, William, 350.
Lockaleer [Lockler], Major [Magey], 66, 73.
Lockard, William, 27.
Locke, David, 58.
Lockhart, see Lockheart.
Lockheart [Lockhart], Andrew, 159, 186.
Lockler, see Lockaleer.
Lockwood, Jesse C., 331, 352, 353, 354.
Loften, Samuel, 92.
Lofton, Easter [Esther], 196.
Lofton, John, 328.
Lofton, John [John G.], 157, 185.
Lofton, Thomas, 157.
Lofton, William, 161.
Logan, Adam, 76.
Logan, Alexander, 346.
Logan, Fleming, 92.
Logan, George, 343.

Logan, George [George R.], 346, 358.
Logan, Isaac, 334.
Logan, James, 76.
Logan, Thomas, 346.
Logsdon, John, 151.
Logsdon, Joseph, 92.
Logsdon [Logson], Joseph, 81, 95.
Logsdon [Logston], Margarett [Margaret, Peggy], 81, 95.
Logson, Logston, see Logsdon.
Loid [Lloyd], Robert H., 300, 309.
Loise, see Larama.
Lolande, see Lalong.
Loller, John, 81.
Lollis [Lawless], William, 141, 177.
Long, Christopher, 194.
Long, George, 343.
Long, Jacob, 28.
Long, John, 47.
Long, Samuel, 348.
Long, Thomas, 17.
Long, William, 350.
Lonis [Lounis, Lounius], John, 65, 73.
Looney, David, 244.
Lorin, Olive [Alive], 37, 50.
Lorton, Henry, 9.
Lorton, John, 9.
Lorton, Joseph, 171.
Lorton, Robert, Sr., 8.
Lorton, Robert, Jr., 8.
Lorton, Thomas, 8.
Lott, see Lotti.
Lotti [Lott], George, 160, 187.
Louis, Joseph Gran, 241.
Louis, see Lewis.
Lounis, Lounius, see Lonis.
Loup, Henry, 194.
Louzader, Isaac, 320.
Love, James M., 27.
Love, John, 193.
Loveland [Lovelands], Merreness [Merriness W.], 268, 286.
Lovelands, see Loveland.
Lovetetty [Lovlety], John, 216, 230.
Lovlety, see Lovetetty.
Low, Amos, 312.
Low [Law], Anthony, 81, 95.
Low, John, 318.
Low, Quillar [Aquilla], 167, 190.
Low, Thomas, 42.
Low, William, 43.
Low, see Lowe.
Lowden, Thomas C., 69.
Lowe [Low], David [David, Sr.], 272, 288.
Lowe, Gorge [George, Jr.], 265, 285.
Lowell, Daniel, 200.
Lowery [Lowry], Joseph, 82, 95.

Lowly, James, 154.
Lowrie, Joseph, 26.
Lowrie, see Lowry.
Lowrler [Lawland], Mason [Morris], 170, 191.
Lowry [Lowrie], Charles, 273, 288.
Lowry, see Lowery.
Lucas, John, 113, 349.
Lucas, Robert, 58.
Lucas, William, 350.
Lues, see Lewis.
Lugart, Nathan, 200.
Lumley, see Lunley.
Lunce, Jacob, 259.
Lunceford [Luncford], Jacob, 257, 282.
Luncford, see Lunceford.
Lunley [Lumley], Thomas, 169, 190.
Lupe [Lipe], George, 104, 118.
Lurton, see Lerton.
Lusadder [Luzaden], Jacob, 108, 118.
Lusby, Thomas, 205.
Lusk, see Luske.
Luske [Lusk], John T., 141, 177.
Luster, Archibal, 13.
Luster, David, 12.
Luster, Henry, 12.
Luster, Philip, 11.
Luster, see Laster.
Luzaden, see Lusadder.
Lybarger, Samuel, 238.
Lynch, see Linch.
Lynn, see Linn.
Lyon, Thomas, 318.
Lyons, James, 192.
Lyons, Richard, 272.
Lype, Henry, 104.
Lype [Lipe], John [John, Sr.], 104, 118.
Lype [Lipe], John [John, Jr.], 106, 118.
Lype [Lipe], Jonas, 106, 118.
Lype [Lipe], Leonard, 106, 118.
Lysles, George, 133.
Lytle, see Leytell.

Maberry [Mayberry], David, 340, 356.
Maberry [Mayberry], Frederick, 340, 356.
Maberry, Frederick, Sr., 340.
Maberry, Frederick, Jr., 340.
Maberry [Mayberry], Jesse, 340, 356.
Maberry [Mayberry], Solomon [Solloman], 340, 356.
McAdams, John, 16.
McAdams, Joseph, Sr., 16.
McAdams, Joseph, Jr., 16.
Mcadams, William, 154.
Mcaester [McCaster], Mary, 138, 176.
Mcafee [McAfee, McKee], Kerenhappuch [Carry Happy, Happa], 140, 177.

ILLINOIS HISTORICAL COLLECTIONS

Mcalean [McClenham], Robert, 162, 188.
Mcalee [McLilley], Samuel [Samuel, Sr.], 154, 184.
Mcalee [McLilley], Samuel [Samuel, Jr.], 154, 184.
Macalle [McLilley], John, 154, 184.
McAlley, David, 196.
McBane, John, 38.
McBride, Felix [Felex], 122, 126.
McBride, Hannah, 305.
McBride, James, 17.
McBride, John, 249.
McBride, Thomas, 249.
McBride, William, Sr., 249.
McBride, William, Jr., 250.
McBroom, Isaac, 335.
McCabe, James, 28.
McCabe, Robert, 28.
Mccallister, see McCollister.
McCallum, Edward, 210.
McCan, Arthur, 75.
McCan, Barny [Barney], 215, 229.
McCan [McCann], Bartholomew, 334, 354.
McCan, John, 265.
McCann, James, 270.
McCann, see McCan.
McCants, Elias, 196, 197.
McCants, John, 193, 198.
McCants, Thompson, 193.
McCart, Edward, 313.
McCarter, Mary, 197.
McCarty, J. [John], 224, 235.
M'Caslin, MCassahan, see McCastlin.
McCaster, see Mcaester.
McCastlin [M'Caslin, McCastlins], James, 83, 95.
McCastlin [MCassahan, McCastlins], Webster, 83, 95.
McCastlins, see McCastlin.
McCawley, John, 328.
McCawley, see Hatch and McCawley.
McCiver, see McKeever.
McClain, Charles, 88.
McClain, see McClane and McLane.
McClalan [McClallin], John, 352, 360.
McClallin, see McClalan.
McClane, James, 3, 6.
McClane [McClain], James, 1, 5.
M'Clane, Margaret, 66.
M'Clane, Robert, 64.
McClane, Thomas, 58.
M'Clane, see McLean.
McClarkin, see McClerkin.
McClary, John, 59.
McClean, William B., 333.
McClean, see Mclean and McLean.
McClees, William, 37.

McCleland [McClernand], Fatima [Fatina], 80, 94.
McClendon, see McLinden.
McClenham, see Mcalean.
McClerkin [McClarkin], James, 248, 255.
McClernand, see McCleland.
M'Clewer, MClewer, see McClure.
McClintic, see McClintick.
McClintick [McClintic], Joseph, 260, 283.
McClinton, John, 251.
McClinton, Samuel, 251.
McCluer, see McClure.
McClure [MClewer], Andrew, 38, 50.
McClure, James, 38.
McClure [M'Clewer], John, 27, 31.
McClure [McCluer], John, 204, 212.
McClure, Robert, 266.
McClure [MClewer], Samuel, 39, 51.
McColam, McColem, see McCollum.
McCollister [Mccallister], Edward, 347, 358.
McCollister [Mccallister], James, 347, 358.
McCollister, John, 82, 347.
McCollister, Robert, 82.
McCollister [Mccallister], Simon, 347, 358.
McCollister [Mccallister], Thomas, 347, 358.
McCollum [McColam, McColem], Jacob, 220, 232.
McConel [McConnell, M'Connell], Hugh, 79, 94.
McConel, Mary, 198.
McConel, Robert, 2.
McConnel, William, 200.
M'Connell, McConnell, see McConel.
McCool, Benjn. [Bengman, Benjamin], 220, 232.
McCool, Jessee [Jessey, Jessey, Sr.], 219, 232.
McCool, Joseph, 76.
M'Cool, McCoole, see McCooll.
McCooll [M'Cool, McCoole], Abraham T. [A. T. M., Abriham], 75, 92.
M'Coppin, see McCoupin.
McCorcle, see McCorkle.
McCord, Charles, 317.
McCord, David, 15, 36.
McCord, David J. [David], 317, 322.
McCord, James, 17.
McCord, Robert, 15, 36.
McCord, Samuel H., 36.
McCorkle [McCorcle], Andrew, 257, 282.
McCorkle, Joseph, 133.
McCorkle, Richard B., 57.
McCormac, Andrew, 251.
McCormac, Henry, 56.
McCormac [McCormick], John, 208, 213.
McCormick, George [G.], 224, 234.

INDEX 421

McCormick, John, 224.
McCormick, William, 224.
McCormick, see Cormac and McCormac.
McCorpin, Thomas H., 42.
McCoupin [M'Coppin], Preclla [Priscilla], 100, 117.
McCown, George [George, Sr.], 345, 357.
McCown, George, Jr. [George], 345, 357.
McCoy, Ezekiel [Ezekel], 216, 230.
McCoy, James, 171, 346.
McCoy, Walter, 341.
McCoy, William, 91.
McCoy [M'Coy], William, 76, 93.
McCoy, see Coy.
McCracken, Aquilla, 325.
McCracken [McCrackin, McReaken], James, 313, 321.
McCracken, John, 328.
McCracken, Samuel, 328.
McCrackin, Robert, 251.
McCrackin, see McCracken.
McCrana, Thomas, 194.
McCrarey [McCreary], John, 87, 97.
M'Crary [Mcreerey], Alexandrew [Elexander], 63, 71.
McCrary [Mcrary], Benjamin, 39, 51.
McCrary, Horatio, 199.
M'Crary [McCrary, Mcreerey], Robert, 62, 71.
McCrary, see Mcrey.
McCraven, McCravens, see Mcraven.
McCreary, see McCrarey.
McCroy [M'Koy], Alexander, 83, 95.
McCullom, see McCullum.
McCullough [McCully], John, 262, 284.
McCullum [McCullom], John [John T.], 159, 186.
McCully, see McCullough.
McDaniel, Abraham, 92.
McDaniel [McDonald], Adam, 269, 286.
McDaniel [McDonald], Gorge [George], 271, 287.
McDaniel, Henry, 10.
MC.Daniel, James, 68.
McDaniel, James, 207.
McDaniel [McDanold], Linvil [Lenvil, Linville], 207, 213.
McDaniel [McDonul], Robert, Sr., 249, 255.
McDaniel, Robert, Jr., 249.
McDaniel [McDonald, McDonold], Samuel, 273, 288.
M'Daniel, Walter, 66.
MacDaniel [McDaniel], Zacheriah [Zachariah], 296, 307.
McDaniel, see MacDaniel, McDonald, and McDonel.

Mcdanold, Walter, 88.
McDanold, see McDaniel.
McDavid, Anthony, 210.
McDavid, John, 202.
McDavid, William, 14.
McDiarman, George, 196.
McDill, John, 246.
McDill, Thomas, 253.
McDonald [McDaniel], Alexander [James], 39, 51.
McDonald [McDonold], James, 203, 211.
McDonald, William, 210, 350.
McDonald, see McDaniel.
McDonel [McDaniel], Daniel, 146, 180.
McDonold, see McDaniel and McDonald.
McDonough, James, 244.
McDonough, Stace, 248.
McDonul, see McDaniel.
MC.Dowel, Nelson, 68.
McDowel, see McDowell.
McDowell [McDowl], Robert, 41, 52.
McDowell [McDowel], Samuel, 35, 50.
McDowell, William, 41.
McDowl, see McDowell.
Mcdurum, Samuel, 172.
Mace, Henry, 267.
Macefield [Mansfield], Roswell, 75, 92.
McElhany, see Mucklehany.
M'Elvane [Muckelvane], Robert, 102, 117.
MC.Elyea [McElyea, Mceya], William, 67, 74.
Mcentire [McIntire], Benjamin, 173, 192.
McErtosh, see McIntosh.
Mceya, see MC.Elyea.
Mcfaddin, Catharine, 156.
McFail, John, 16.
Mcfamd [McFane], David, 172, 192.
McFane, see Mcfamd.
Mcfarland [McFarlen], James, 88, 97.
McFarland, see Mcfarlin.
McFarlen, see Mcfarland and McFarlin.
McFarlin [McFarlen], Achilles, 216, 230.
McFarlin, James, 245.
McFarlin, John, 240.
Mcfarlin [McFarland, McFarlin], Watty [Walter], 169, 191.
Mcfatridge, William, 128, 133.
McFearson [McPhearson], James, 149, 181.
McFeron, John, 253.
McFerron, Andrew, 249.
M'Ferron, John, 237.
McFerron, Robert, 249.
McGahey, see Magaha.
McGath [McGerth], James, 29, 32.
McGeehee, Elisha [Elish], 342, 356.
McGeehee, Stephen, 341.

McGeehee [McGehee], William, Jr. [William], 341, 356.
McGeehee, see McGehee.
McGehee, Henry, 75.
McGehee, James, 75.
McGehee [McGhee], William, 92.
McGehee [McGeehee], William, Sr. [William], 341, 356.
McGehee, see McGeehee.
McGerth, see McGath.
McGhee, see McGehee.
McGines, McGinnes, see Maginnis.
McGinness [Meginness], John, 129, 135.
McGinness, Richard, 129.
McGinness, Samuel, 129.
McGinness, William, 129.
McGinnis, Abraham, 18.
MC.Ginty, Alexandrew, 69.
McGlaughlin [M'Lauflen, McLaughlin], John, 75, 92.
McGlaughlin, Levi, 85.
McGoon, Alexander, 78.
McGowan, see McGowen.
McGowen [Megowen], Alexander, 131, 136.
McGowen, James, 198.
McGowen, John, 131, 135.
McGowen [McGowan, Megowen], Samuel, 132, 136.
McGregor, Henry, 60.
McGrew, Pattrick, 206.
McGuire, Thomas, 264.
McGuire, see Magirer.
McHauz [McHawse], Reubin, 349, 359.
McHawse, see McHauz.
McHenery, see McHenry.
McHenry, Daniel, 345.
McHenry [McHenery], John, 220, 232.
McHenry [McHenery], Joseph, 220, 232.
McHenry, William, 345.
McInder, Richard, 79.
Mcines, Charles, 147.
Mcines, Elias, 147.
Mcines, John, 147.
Mcines, William, 147.
McIntire, Alfred, 82.
McIntire, see Mcentire and McIntyre.
Macintorsh [Mcintosh, McIntosh], Thomas, 295, 307.
McIntosh [McErtosh], Aaron, 129, 135.
McIntosh, John, 60.
McIntosh, William, 1, 59.
Mcintosh, McIntosh, see Macintorsh, Mackentorsh, and Makintorsh.
McIntyre, Hugh, 320.
McIntyre [McIntire], John, 349, 358.
McIntyre, Polly, 332.
McIver, see McKeever.

McKane, Jesse, 208.
McKee, Benjamine, 198.
McKee, Henry, 258.
McKee, James, 220.
McKee, John, 150, 155.
McKee, Mary, 196.
McKee, Robert, 196.
McKee, Samuel, 210.
McKee, Stewart, 210.
McKee, William, 346.
McKee, see Mcafee.
McKeever [McCiver, McIver], Robert, 312, 320.
McKeever [McCiver], Samuel, 312, 320.
McKelvy, Alexander, 250.
McKelvy, Hugh, 253.
McKeney, M'Kenney, see McKinney.
McKenny, see McKinny.
Mackentorsh [McIntosh, Mcintosh], John, 299, 309.
McKenzie [McKinsey], George, 340, 356.
McKillen, Widow, 218.
M'Kinney, Archd., 114.
McKinney [M'Kenney], Charles, 108, 118.
McKinney [McKeney], Hampton, 196.
McKinney, James, 17, 35.
McKinney, John, 35.
McKinney [McKinny], John, 159, 186.
McKinney [M'Kinny], Joseph, 100, 117.
McKinney, Owen, 197.
McKinney, Thomas, 56.
McKinny, James, 199.
McKinny [McKenny], Jeremiah, 122, 126.
McKinny [McKenny], John, 122, 126.
McKinny [McKenny], Joseph, 122, 126.
M'Kinny, McKinny, see McKinney.
McKinsey, Alexander, 14.
McKinsey, see McKenzie.
McKinsy, see McKinzie.
McKinzie [McKinsy], Allen, 1, 5.
McKinzie, David, 2.
McKinzie [McKinsy], Stephen, 2, 5.
McKnight, Robert, 198.
M'Koy, see McCroy.
McLallan [McLelland], John, 331, 354.
McLallan, Samuel, 331.
McLallan, William, 331.
McLamore [McLimore], John H., 260, 283.
McLane [McClain], James, 261, 283.
McLane [McClain], Samuel, 274, 289.
M'Lauflen, see McGlaughlin.
McLaughlin, David, 57.
McLaughlin, Robert K., 12.
McLaughlin, Robert K. [R. K.], 267, 286.
McLaughlin, see McGlaughlin.
McLean [M'Clane], John, 92.
McLean [McClean], John, 216, 230.

INDEX 423

Mclean [McClean], Robert D. [R. D.], 80, 94.
McLeef, Benjamin, 60.
McLeef, John, 60.
Mclehanny, see Mucklehany.
McLelland, see McLallan.
McLilley, see Mcalee and Macalle.
McLimore, see McLamore.
McLin, David W., 333.
McLin, James S., 333.
McLinden [McClendon], F. [Frederick], 222, 234.
McMahan, Constantine, 58.
McMahan, Isaac, 149.
McMahan, Robert, 149.
McMahan, Robert [Robert, Jr.], 150, 182.
McMahen, Isaac, 148.
McManus, Bernard, 57.
McMeans [McMeen], Joseph, 207, 213.
McMeen, see McMeans.
McMellen, see McMillen.
McMillen [M'Millin], H., Jr. [Hugh], 115, 120.
McMillen, James, 59.
McMillen [McMellen, M'Millin], William, 100, 117.
McMillen, see McMillon.
McMillian [McMilliom, McMillion], Paul, 259, 283.
McMillin, Ann, 249.
McMillin, James, 253.
McMillin, John, 246, 249.
M'Millin, see McMillen and McMuthey.
McMilliom, McMillion, see McMillian.
McMillon [McMillen, M'Millin], Hugh [Hugh, Sr.], 100, 117.
McMullin, Samuel, 347.
McMurdo, James, 246.
McMurphy, Dd., 216.
McMurry, William, 267.
McMurtry, Abraham [Abram], 258, 282.
McMurty, see McMurty and McMuthey.
McMurty [McMurtry], Henry, 341, 356.
McMurty [McMurtry], John, 341, 356.
McMuthey [McMurtry, McMuttrey], George, 203, 211.
McMuttrey, see McMuthey.
McNabb, Alexander, 204.
McNabb, Archibald, 242.
McNabb, see Macneal.
McNail, Able [Abel, Abel A.], 269, 286.
McNail, William [William B.], 266, 285.
McNair, John, 60.
McNair, Robert, 59.
Mcnary, James, 168.
McNary, James, 123, 199.
McNeal, James, 352.

Macneal [McNabb], William, 163, 188.
McNeel, see McNeil.
McNeer, see McNeir.
McNeil [McNeel], Samuel, 325, 330.
McNeir, John, 17.
McNeir [McNeer], Moses, 29, 32.
McNemar, Jeremiah, 339.
McNight, see Night.
McNorten, see McNorton.
McNorton [McNorten], William, 131, 135.
McNulty, Hugh, 227.
McNulty, James, 248.
Mcnut, Charles, 171.
Macom, see Malcom.
Macomson, see Makemson.
McPhearson, see McFearson.
Mcquorter, Sarah, 328.
Mcrary, see McCrary.
Mcraven [McCraven, McCravens], Benjamin, 303, 311.
McReaken, see McCracken.
Mcreerey, see M'Crary.
Mcrey [McCrary], Calvin [Horatio], 152, 183.
McReynolds, Hugh, 18.
McRoberts, James, 201.
McRoberts, William, 108.
Macry, Elisha, 145.
McSpanon, James, 85.
McSpanon [M'Sparner], John, 85, 96.
M'Sparner, see McSpanon.
McWilliams, Alexander, 16.
Madcalf, John, 346.
Madcalf [Metcalf], Manuel [Emanuel], 344, 357.
Maddox, John P., 71.
Maddox [Maddux], Wingate, 312, 320.
Maddox, see Maddux.
Maddux [Maddox], Alexander, 318, 323.
Maddux [Maddox], Alexander [Alexander, Jr.], 314, 321.
Maddux [Haddox], Gilleous [Gilless, Gillis], 313, 320.
Maddux [Maddox], Leonard, 315, 321.
Maddux [Maddox], Lewis [Leven, Levin], 315, 321.
Maddux [Maddox], Zachariah, 315, 321.
Maddux, see Maddox.
Madglen, see Madlin.
Madison, James, 92.
Madlin [Madglen, Modglen], Lincy [Linsey], 214, 229.
Madlock [Medlock], Henry, 79, 94.
Magaha [McGahey], David, 44, 52.
Magill, James, 272.
Maginnes, Samuel, 295.

Maginnis [McGines, McGinnes], Patrick, 295, 306.
Maginnis [McGines, McGinnes], William, 295, 306.
Magirer [McGuire], Thomas [Thomas J.], 152, 183.
Magoon, Reuben, 57.
Mahan, A., 226.
Mahan, Alexander, 331.
Mahan, John, 246.
Mahu, see Mayhoe.
Mahuel, see Mahurin.
Mahurin [Mahuel], Samuel, 142, 177.
Main, Mecum, 43.
Mais [Morrs], Christopher [Cristopher], 44, 52.
Majors, James, 60.
Makemson [Macomson], James [Janes], 257, 282.
Makintorsh [McIntosh], Charles, 296, 307.
Malcom [Macom], Peter, 267, 286.
Malcom, see Malcum.
Malcum [Malcom], John, 40, 51.
Malden [Maulding], Ambrose, 338, 355.
Malden [Maulding], Ennis [Ennes], 337, 355.
Malden [Maulding], James, 338, 355.
Malden, Lee, 338.
Mallett [Mallott], Wheeler, 34, 49.
Mallingly, see Mattingly.
Mallinly, see Mattingley.
Mallors, William, 147.
Mallory, Eleson, 196.
Mallott, see Mallett.
Malone, see Mayland.
Maloney, David, 92.
Malthrop, see Molthrop.
Mamnon, see Manan.
Man, Frederick, 253.
Man [Mann], Robert, 249, 255.
Man [Mann], William, 249, 255.
Manan [Mamnon, Mannen], Thomas, 148, 181.
Manen [Manon], Welden [Weldon], 65, 72.
Mangram, see Mangrem.
Mangrem [Mangram, Mangum], Henry 131, 135.
Mangum, see Mangrem.
Maning [Mannan], John, 275, 289.
Maning, Mary, 194.
Maning, see Manning.
Mann, John, 58.
Mann, see Man.
Mannan, see Maning.
Mannen, see Manan.
Manning, J., 115.
Manning [Maning], J. [John], 224, 235.
Manning, James, 318.
Manning, William, 222.
Manon, see Manen.
Mansco [Mansker], Samuel, 246, 254.
Mansco [Mansker], William [Samuel], 246, 254.
Mansell, Robert, 40.
Mansfield, see Macefield.
Mansker, see Mansco.
Mantley, see Mattby.
Manuel, James, 153.
Manuel, Tropa, 243.
Manus, see Minnus.
Manvill, see Manville.
Manville [Manvill], Ira, 268, 286.
Manville, Josef [Joseph], 278, 291.
Mar [Lamorse, Mars], Louis [Lewis, Sr.], 144, 179.
Marcom, see Marcum.
Marcum [Marcom], Marvel, 35, 50.
Mares, Nathan, 44.
Mares [Marso], Peter [Pierre], 148, 181.
Margoto, Michel, 244.
Margrave, Jesse, 15.
Margrave, John, 15.
Margrave, see Margraves.
Margraves [Margrave], Thomas, 86, 96.
Marimaid, Jesse, 92.
Markes, David, 168.
Markley, see Merclay.
Marllo, Henry, 273.
Marlo [Marlow], Gabriel [Gabrele], 275, 289.
Marloe [Marlow], John, 269, 287.
Marlow, see Marlo and Marloe.
Marney, Benjamin, 207.
Marney, James, 262.
Marney, Jonathan, 57.
Marr, Alexander, 198.
Marray, John, 241.
Marrison, see Morrison.
Marrs, Thomas, 203.
Mars, see Mar.
Marsh, Shewbell, 210.
Marsh, Thomas, 248.
Marshal [Marshau], Battece [Baptiest], 278, 291.
Marshall, Daniel, 81.
Marshall, John, 80.
Marshall [Marshel], Robert, 112, 119.
Marshall, Samuel, 75.
Marshau, see Marshal.
Marshel, see Marshall.
Marso, see Mares.
Martain [Martin], James, 277, 290.
Marten, James, 198.
Marter [Martin], Peter [Pierre], 148, 181.

Martin, A., 92.
Martin, A. G., 12.
Martin, Adam, 198.
Martin, Clem, 56.
Martin, Daniel, 44.
Martin, Henry, 327.
Martin, Hugh, 59.
Martin, Isaac, 349.
Martin, James, 27, 60.
Martin, James [James B.], 332, 354.
Martin, James B., 325.
Martin, James H., 132.
Martin, Joel, 81.
Martin, John, 44, 58, 60, 332.
Martin [Marton], John, 86, 96.
Martin, Joseph [Joseph, Sr.], 325, 330.
Martin, Joseph [Joseph, Sr.], 327, 330.
Martin, Owen, 327.
Martin, Philip, 12, 315.
Martin, Robert, 92.
Martin, Samuel, 122.
Martin, William, 29, 58, 100.
Martin, see Martain and Marter.
Marton, David, 100.
Marton, see Martin.
Marvel [Marvell, Mavern], Barnabas, 34, 49.
Marvell, see Marvel.
Mary, 281.
Mason, Bennet [Bennit], 259, 282.
Mason, Hail, 158.
Mason, Isaac, 342.
Mason, Jane, 269.
Mason, Robert, 198.
Mason, Thomas, 58.
Mason, Thomas [Tomas], 276, 290.
Mason, see Mayson.
Massey [Massy], Shadrach [Shedrick], 108, 118.
Massey, William, 194.
Massey, see Massie.
Massie [Massey], Burwell, 14, 23.
Massie, John, 56.
Massock, David, 197.
Massy, see Massey.
Masterson, Benjamin, 210.
Matheney [Matheny], Daniel [Samuel], 272, 288.
Matheney [Matheny], Noah, 266, 285.
Matheny, Charles R. [Charls R.], 265, 285.
Matheny [Mattheney], Collins, 313, 321.
Matheny, see Matheney.
Mather, John, 56.
Mather, see Mathers.
Mathers [Mather, Matthers], Elijah [Elihu, Elihue], 148, 181.
Mathes, Edward, 199.

Mathews, Samuel, 41.
Mathews, William, 40.
Mathews, see Matthews.
Mathis [Matthews], Absolem [Absalom], 164, 189.
Mathis [Mathus], Andrew, 156, 185.
Mathis [Matthews], Daniel, 164, 189.
Mathis [Matthews], Matthew, 131, 135.
Mathis [Matthews], Samuel, 131, 135.
Mathis, see Matice and Mattis.
Mathus, see Mathis.
Matice [Mathis], George, 151, 182.
Matier, Henry, 47.
Matis, James, 162.
Matney, see Mattingley.
Matson, Luke, 47.
Mattby [Mantley], Frederick [Frereck], 76, 93.
Mattheis, 281.
Mattheney, see Matheny.
Matthers, see Mathers.
Matthews, Benjamin, 58.
Matthews [Mathews], John, 348, 358.
Matthews, see Mathis.
Mattingley [Mallinly, Matney], Edward, 77, 93.
Mattingley [Mattoney], Zacheriah [Zachariah], 77, 93.
Mattingly, Richard, 201.
Mattingly [Mallingly], William, 37, 50.
Mattis [Mathis], Flebin [Clibon], 171, 191.
Mattis [Metts], John, 172, 192.
Mattis [Metts], William, 172, 192.
Mattison, John, 214.
Mattoney, see Mattingley.
Mattox, Mrs., 226.
Maugham, John K., 320.
Mauldin [Maulding], John, 78, 93.
Maulding, see Malden and Mauldin.
Mauzy, John A., 257.
Mauzy, Silas, 257.
Mavern, see Marvel.
Maxant [Maxaw, Maxey], Francis, 264, 285.
Maxaw, see Maxant.
Maxell, Hugh H., 239.
Maxell, John, 239.
Maxey [Maxy], Bennet N. [Benet N.], 124, 126.
Maxey, Buennet [Bennett], 138, 176.
Maxey, Edward, 123.
Maxey, Elihu, 124.
Maxey [Maxy], Hennery B. [Henry B.], 123, 126.
Maxey [Maxy], William, 124, 126.
Maxey, see Maxant.
Maxwell, Hugh, 121.

Maxwell, Martin, 122.
Maxwell, Richard, 79.
Maxwell, Robert, 121.
Maxwell, William, 121.
Maxy, see Maxey.
May, Alfred, 346.
May, Balem [Baalem, Balaam], 346, 358.
May, Benjamin, 301.
May, Daniel, 328.
May, John, 302.
May, Joseph, 154, 195.
May, Rubin, 207.
May, Samuel, 210.
May, William L., 150.
Mayberry, see Maberry.
Mayes [Mays], James, 333, 354.
Mayfield, Elijah, 339.
Mayfield, Isaac, 340.
Mayhoe [Mahu], William, 272, 288.
Mayland [Malone], Jonithan, 173, 192.
Mayo, Johnathan, 26.
Mays, see Mayes and Maze.
Mayson [Mason], James, 153, 184.
Mayson [Mason], Paris, 153, 183.
Maze [Mays], Thomas, 346, 358.
Meacham, Adit, 139.
Meacham, Eathan, 196.
Mead [Mede], Alansen [Alanson], 276, 290.
Means, Robert, 158.
Mears, William, 261.
Mears, see Meers.
Meason [Meson], Mr. [John], 218, 231.
Mede, see Mead.
Medford, John, 172.
Medley, Joel, 317.
Medlock, see Madlock.
Medows, James, 200.
Meeker, Daniel, 196.
Meeks, Suddith [Judey, Judith], 77, 93.
Meeks, Thomas, 193.
Meers [Mears], Edwin, 15, 23.
Meginness, see McGinness.
Megowen, see McGowen.
Meguire, George W., 22.
Mekel, Mary, 153.
Melrose, Archibald, 60.
Melrose, William, 60.
Melton, John, 328.
Melton, Ruben, 327.
Melton [Milton], Thomas, 164, 189.
Melton, Tilman, 57.
Me Me [Meme], —— [Baptiste], 148, 181.
Menard, Francis, 243.
Menard, John, 240.
Menard, Peter, 248.
Menece, see Mineace and Minneace.
Menees, see Mineace.

Merclay [Markley], Frederck [Frederick], 43, 52.
Meredith, Daniel, 16.
Meredith, James, 351.
Meredith [Merideth], Samuel, 220, 232.
Meret, see Merrit.
Merett, see Merit.
Merideth, see Meredith.
Merit [Merett], Benjamin, 145, 179.
Merit [Merritt], Benjamin, 145, 179.
Merrell [Merril, Merrylls], Silvester [Sylvester], 264, 285.
Merril [Merrill], William, 346, 358.
Merril, see Merrell.
Merrill, see Merril.
Merritt [Meret], Ephraim, 324, 330.
Merritt, see Merit.
Merrylls, see Merrell.
Meson, see Meason.
Messenger, John, 263.
Messer, Richard, 130.
Metcalf, see Madcalf.
Metta, Mettee, see Metty.
Metts, see Mattis.
Metty [Metta, Mettee], James [Jacques], 143, 178.
Micenhamer, see Micenhimer and Misenhimer.
Micenhimer [Micenhamer], David, 297, 307.
Micenhimer [Micenhamer], John, 303, 311.
Micenhimer [Micenhamer], Moses, 296, 307.
Micenhimer [Micenhamer], Peter, 297, 307.
Michad, John, 12.
Michael, John, 83.
Michael, Mathew, 92.
Michael, see Mitchell.
Michaels, George, Jr., 60.
Michaels, John, 60.
Michaels, Moses, 61.
Michel [Michiel], Sion H., 62, 71.
Michel, see Mitchell.
Michiel, see Michel.
Mick [Micks], Charles, 89, 98.
Micks, see Mick.
Middlecoff [Middlecough], John, 260, 283.
Middlecough, see Middlecoff.
Middleton, Benoni [Benjamin], 41, 51.
Middleton, Henry, 92.
Middleton, Reuben [Rueben], 317, 322.
Middleton, Robert, 269.
Middleton, William, 314.
Midelton, John, 218.
Mikael, Barnabas, 16.
Milan, see Milton.
Milegan [Milligan], John, 65, 73.
Miles, Burd E., 10, 22.
Miles, Josias, 200.

Miles, Stephen, 210.
Milikin, see Millegin.
Mill, see Mills.
Millagan, Ferguson, 200.
Millegin [Milikin], Jacob, 299, 309.
Millekin, see Millikin.
Miller, Adam, 144, 194, 348.
Miller, Alfred, 167.
Miller, Alsey, 58.
Miller, Charles, 64.
Miller, Christian, 296.
Miller, David, 165, 302.
Miller, Francis, 335.
Miller, George, 40, 51.
Miller, George, Sr., 48.
Miller, Henry, 204, 348.
Miller, Heugh [Hew, Hugh], 29, 32.
Miller, Hugh, 173.
Miller, Hugh, Jr., 29.
Miller, Jacob, 165.
Miller, James, 30, 165, 169, 211, 333.
Miller, Jesse, 208.
Miller, John, 64, 194, 198, 199, 204, 251, 305.
Miller, Joseph, 260.
Miller, Lemuel, 335.
Miller, Marget [Margaretta], 146, 180.
Miller, Michael, 203.
Miller, Moses, 165.
Miller, Nancy, 51.
Miller, Patcy, 281.
Miller, Peter, 59, 331.
Miller, Peter [Peter, Sr.], 298, 308.
Miller, Rachel, 35, 50.
Miller, Richard, 211.
Miller, Robert, 35, 203, 331.
Miller, Rubin [Reuben], 203, 211.
Miller, Solomon, 165.
Miller, Susan [Sarah], 316, 322.
Miller, Uriah, 194.
Miller, William, 50, 64, 260, 328, 335.
Millian, see Million.
Milligan, John, 114.
Milligan, see Milegan.
Milligen, see Millikin.
Millikin [Millekin, Milligen], Alexander [Alexandria], 1, 5.
Million, Benjamin, 160.
Million [Millian], Benjamin, 274, 289.
Million, Bennet [Bennett], 274, 289.
Million [Millian], Daniel, 263, 284.
Mills [Mill], Edward, 36, 50.
Mills, Elisha, 214.
Mills, Henry J., 61.
Mills, John, 77.
Mills, John [John W.], 46, 53.
Mills, Thomas, 46.

Millsted [Milstead], Joseph, 269, 287.
Mils [Mise], David [Aaron], 160, 187.
Milstead, see Millsted.
Milton, Absalom, 61.
Milton, Andrew, 11.
Milton, Lazerous, 195.
Milton [Milan], Ranson [Ransom], 199.
Milton, see Melton.
Minah, Lunah, 92.
Mineace [Menece, Menees], Benjamin, 294, 305.
Miner, Daniel L., 86.
Miner [Minor], Thomas D., 124, 127.
Minneace [Menece], John, 299, 309.
Minnus [Manus], John, 337, 355.
Minor, see Miner.
Minsen, see Minson.
Minson [Minsen], Absalem [Abraham], 317, 323.
Minter, John, 149.
Mires [Myres], Isaac, 161, 187.
Mires, see Myers.
Mise, see Mils.
Misenhammer [Misen Hammer], Mathias, 328, 330.
Misenhimer [Micenhamer], Jacob, 296, 307.
Mishaw, Lewis, 301.
Mitchel [Mitchell], Edward, 264, 285.
Mitchel, Gorge, 259.
Mitchel, James, 260.
Mitchel, Peter, 264.
Mitchel [Mitchell], Samuel, 270, 287.
Mitchel, see Mitchell.
Mitchell, Jesse, 342.
Mitchell [Michael, Mitchel], Jessee [Jesse], 88, 97.
Mitchell, John, 58.
Mitchell [Mitchel], John, 206, 212.
Mitchell [Michel], Robert, 88, 97.
Mitchell, William, 40.
Mitchell, see Mitchel.
Mitchum, Aden E., 173.
Mizner, Henry C., 202.
Moberley, see Mobly.
Mobley, Benjamine, 87.
Mobley, Edward, 76.
Mobley, see Mobly.
Mobly [Mobley], Charles, 346, 357.
Mobly [Moberley, Mobley], Isaac, 69, 74.
Modgelon [Modglen], William, 219, 232.
Modglen, see Madlin, Modgelon, Modglin, and Mogelon.
Modglin, Henry, 201.
Modglin, John [John, Sr.], 201, 211.
Modglin [Modglen], John, 222, 234.
Modglin [Modglen], William, 215, 229.
Modlin, Lincey, 215, 229.

428   ILLINOIS HISTORICAL COLLECTIONS

Moffet [Moffitt], James, 157, 185.
Moffit, David, 18.
Moffitt, see Moffet.
Mogelon [Modglen], Strongman [Straingman], 215, 229.
Mogget, Samuel, 167.
Moize, Charlo, 57.
Molany, Daniel, 92.
Molthrop, John, 315.
Molthrop [Malthrop], John A., 315, 321.
Momance, John Bte., 57.
Monday, James, 141.
Money, see Mooney.
Monholand, John, 210.
Montgomery, Andrew, 43.
Montgomery, J. [James], 222, 233.
Montgomery, John, 19, 334.
Montgomery, John [J.], 225, 235.
Montgomery, Robert, 42.
Montgomery, William, 142, 171.
Montroy, Antwine, 247.
Montroy, Baptiste [John B.], 247, 254.
Montroy, Francis, 251.
Moody, Andrew, 20.
Moody, Benjamin, 274.
Moody, Robert, 344.
Moody, William, 92.
Mooney, Brian [Bryant], 272, 288.
Mooney [Money], Samuel, 202, 211.
Moor, Alliot, 194.
Moor, Hardin, 196.
Moor [Moore], William, 76, 93.
Moor, see Moore and More.
Moore, Abel, 140.
Moore, Abm. [A.], 226, 236.
Moore, Alexandria, 156.
Moore, Andrew, 18.
Moore [More], Charles, 161, 187.
Moore, Curtis, 281.
Moore, Daniel [Daniel G.], 171, 191.
Moore [Moor], David, 151, 182.
Moore, Enoch, 205.
Moore [Moor], F. [Frances], 227, 236.
Moore [Moor], George, 140, 177.
Moore [Moor], Isaac, 29, 32.
Moore, J. Milton, 205.
Moore, Jacob, 168.
Moore, James, 34, 173, 267.
Moore, James B., 201.
Moore [Moor], James E. [James], 30, 32.
Moore, Jane, 271.
Moore [More], Jesse [Jessy], 314, 321.
Moore, John, 169, 206, 210.
Moore [Moor], John, 34, 49.
Moore, Lydia, 15.
Moore, Philip, 13.

Moore, Risden, Sr. [Risdon, Risdon, Sr.], 265, 285.
Moore, Risdon, Jr., 269.
Moore, Robert, 246, 273.
Moore [More], Robert, 86, 96.
Moore, Thomas, 262.
Moore [More], Thomas, 148, 181.
Moore [More], Thomas L. [Thomas], 314, 321.
Moore, Warrick [Worrick], 279, 292; see also Moore Warrick.
Moore, William, 140, 199, 281.
Moore, William [William, Jr.], 270, 287.
Moore, William, Sr., 265.
Moore, William D., 264.
Moore, see Moor and More.
Moorehead [Morehead], Richard, 148, 181.
Mordock, John, 245.
More, Abner [Allen], 342, 356.
More [Moore], Anderson, 62, 71.
More [Moore], Isaac, 168, 190.
More, James, 337.
More, Jeremiah [Jerremiah], 338, 355.
More, John, 337, 351.
More [Moore], John, 62, 71.
More, Joseph, 343.
More, Peggy, 125.
More, Robert, 338.
More [Moor], Robert, 62, 71.
More [Moore], Thomas, 62, 71.
More, see Cammore and Moore.
Moredock, John, 205.
Morehead, Elickander, 200.
Morehead, see Moorehead.
Morehouse, Thaddeus, 38.
Moreland, Garner [Gardner], 75, 92.
Moreland, Hazel [Hazel, Sr.], 78, 94.
Moreland, Hazle [Hazel, Jr.], 75, 93.
Moreland, Vincent, 344.
Moreson, see Morrison.
Morgain, see Morgan.
Morgan, Abraham, 301.
Morgan, Antoney [Anthony], 300, 309.
Morgan, Arthur, 257.
Morgan, Henry, 332.
Morgan, James, 46.
Morgan, John, 92, 257.
Morgan, John H. [John], 316, 322.
Morgan, Jonathan, 198.
Morgan [Morgain], Joshuay [Joshua], 293, 305.
Morgan [Morgen], Lenard [Leonard], 293, 305.
Morgan, Levi, 345.
Morgan, Nathan, 148.
Morgan, Robert, 144.
Morgan, Sympson, 27.

INDEX 429

Morgan, William, 200, 256.
Morgan [Morgen], William [William, Sr.], 301, 310.
Morgan, William H., 194.
Morgen, see Morgan.
Morice, John, 171.
Morice, see Morris.
Morin, Elizabeth, 172.
Moris, see Morris.
Morison [Morrison], Nathaniel, 147, 180.
Morow, see Morrow.
Morrill, Abraham, 60.
Morris, Eli, 45.
Morris, George, 349.
Morris, Isaac, 57.
Morris, Jefferson, 41.
Morris, John [Batisted], 238, 253.
Morris [Morice], John, 217, 231.
Morris, Nancy, 36.
Morris, Oliver, 125, 126.
Morris, Robert H., 326.
Morris [Morriss], Samuel, 83, 95.
Morris [Moris], Sian, 36, 50.
Morris, Travis [Treves], 221, 233.
Morris, William, 138, 248.
Morris, Zachariah, 9.
Morris, see Morriss.
Morrison [Marrison, Moreson], Guy, 277, 290.
Morrison, John, 258.
Morrison, Joseph [Joseph, Jr.], 45, 53.
Morrison, Noble, 76.
Morrison, Phoebe, 253.
Morrison, Robert, 237.
Morrison, William, 238.
Morrison, see Morison.
Morriss [Morris], Elizabeth, 269, 286.
Morriss, see Morris.
Morrow, John, 108.
Morrow [Morow], Samuel M. [Samuel Mills], 214, 229.
Morrow, Thomas, 106.
Morrow, William, 168.
Morrs, see Mais.
Mors, see Morse.
Morse, John, 332.
Morse [Mors], John, 219, 232.
Morse, Robert, 140.
Morse, Samuel, 200.
Morton, Joseph, 315.
Morton, Oliver, 193.
Mosbey, see Mosby.
Mosby [Mosbey, Moseby], Benjamine [Benjamin], 81, 95.
Moseby, see Mosby.
Moss, David, 60.
Moss, Matthew, 174.

Mothral, Robert, 350.
Mott, Henry [Henery], 215, 229.
Mott, James P., 217.
Mott, Platt, 217.
Moulinaix, James, 210.
Mounce, Absolum, 328.
Mounce, Mary, 58.
Mounce, Smith, 59.
Mount, Elizabeth, 130.
Movell, see Movill.
Movill [Movell], John, 145, 179.
Mowry, John, 298.
Moyers, Isaac, 194.
Moze, Polite, 173.
Muckelvane, see M'Elvane.
Mucklehany [McElhany, Mclehanny], Joseph, 299, 309.
Mud, James, 240.
Mud, Thomas, 240.
Mull, Benedick, 301.
Mundy, Edward, 58.
Mundy, Samuel, 59.
Munford, James, 246.
Muns, Thomas, 151.
Murphey [Furphy], Francis [Francies], 294, 305.
Murphey [Murphy], Hiley [Hila, Hyly], 294, 306.
Murphey [Murphy], James, 1, 5.
Murphey, Jeremiah, 40.
Murphey, Lewis, 26.
Murphey, Moses, 40.
Murphey, William, 26.
Murphey, see Murphy.
Murphrey, Jeremiah, 253.
Murphrey, John, Sr., 245.
Murphry, James, 245.
Murphry, John, Jr., 245.
Murphy [Murphey], Alx. [Alexander], 221, 233.
Murphy [Murphey], James, 220, 232.
Murphy, John, 3.
Murphy [Murphey], John, 81, 95.
Murphy, Samuel L., 68.
Murphy, see Murphey.
Murray [Murry], John B., 297, 308.
Murry, Arthur, 258.
Murry, Bland, 69.
Murry, James, 92.
Murry, Rachel, 261.
Murry, see Murray.
Musick, Robert, 200.
Myers, Elizabeth, 344.
Myers [Mires], Henry, 344, 357.
Myers [Mires], John, 345, 357.
Myers [Mires], Joseph, 7, 22.

Myers [Myre], Lewis W. [Louis W., Luois W.], 261, 283.
Myers, Samuel, 115.
Myers [Mires], Stephen, 7, 22.
Myers, William, 7.
Myers, see Myres.
Myre, see Myers.
Myres [Myers], Rebeca [Rebecca], 44, 52.
Myres, see Mires.

Naff, Henry, 207.
Naff, Jacob, 210.
Nail, see Neal.
Nall, Nathan, 342.
Nangle, Daniel, 197.
Nangle, John, 65.
Nantz, James, 9.
Nash, Alexander, 264.
Nash, Francis, 352.
Nash, James, 352.
Nash, Moses, 167.
Nash, Stephen, 199.
Nash, Tim., 115.
Nash, William, 173, 352.
Nation [Nations], Andrew, 331, 354.
Nation, Christopher, 334.
Nation [Nations], John, 331, 354.
Nations, see Nation.
Naught [Knott], George, 343, 357.
Naught [Knott], Isaac, 343, 357.
Nawsham, see Newsham.
Neal [Nail], Edward, 278, 291.
Neal, Jessee, 200.
Neal, Joseph, 73.
Neal [Kneel], Lytle [Little], 87, 97.
Neal, Nancy, 65, 73.
Neal, Thomas, 312.
Neal, William, 65, 164.
Nealous [Nichols], Walker, 152, 183.
Nealy, John, 49.
Nealy, see Neely.
Neavel, see Nevils.
Nee [Neel], James, 100, 117.
Neece, James, 68.
Neece [Nees], James, 64, 72.
Needeham [Needham], John, 83, 95.
Needham, see Needeham.
Needle, James, 200.
Neel, see Nee and Neill.
Neeley, Matthew, 57.
Neeley, see Neely and Nelly.
Neely [Neeley], Charles, 27, 31.
Neely, Jacob, 13.
Neely, James [J., John], 224, 235.
Neely [Nealy], Mathew [Matthew], 34, 49.
Neely, Sarah, 34, 49.
Neely, William, 224.
Neely, see Nelly.

Neep [Neip], Samuel [S. and Co.], 115, 120.
Nees, see Neece.
Neesbet, see Neesbt.
Neesbt [Neesbet], Elexander, 328, 330.
Neil, John O., 196.
Neill [Neel], Joseph, 219, 231.
Neip, see Neep.
Neles, Daniel, 144, 179; see also Nicholas Daniel.
Nelly [Neeley], Henry, 170, 191.
Nelly [Kneely], J., 224, 235.
Nelly [Neely], Joseph, 170, 191.
Nelson, Daniel, 108.
Nelson, Delphus [Delphy S.], 162, 188.
Nelson, James, 3, 169.
Nelson, John, 3, 68, 320.
Nelson, Reubin, 342.
Nelson, Thomas, 205, 210.
Nelson, William, 19, 170, 240.
Nelton, Leonard, 206.
Nemo [Nimmo], Wesley G., 297, 308.
Neslor, John, 56.
Nevens, John, 197.
Nevet [Nevit], Joseph, 276, 290.
Nevils [Neavel], Enoch, 325, 330.
Nevins, John, 193.
Nevit [Nevitt], William, 343, 357.
Nevit, see Nevet.
Nevitt, see Nevit.
New, John, 195.
Newal, Thomas, 196.
Newby, John, 78.
Newcom, see Newcomb.
Newcomb [Newcom], John, 274, 289.
Newel [Nuel], Eli, 27, 31.
Newell, John, 80, 84.
Newell, Samuel, 60.
Newhouse, Samuel, 200.
Newland, Eli, 40.
Newland [Newlin], James, 44, 52.
Newland, John, 40.
Newland [Newlin], John [John, Jr.], 39, 51.
Newland, Nathaniel, 40.
Newland, Thomas, 39.
Newland, William, 40.
Newles [Nuel], James, 154, 184.
Newlin, see Newland.
Newman, George, 336.
Newman, John, 141, 142.
Newman, Joseph, 195.
Newman, Simon, 334.
Newman, Simpson, 86.
Newman, William, 141.
Newman, Zadok [Zadock, Zedock], 141, 177.

INDEX

Newport, Richard, 41.
Newsham [Nawsham], Edward, 258, 282.
Newten, see Nuten.
Newton, Charles, 320.
Newton, see Nuten.
Nichlas, Easther, 273.
Nichlas [Nicols], Jules [James], 273, 288.
Nichlas [Nicols], Sarah, 273, 288.
Nicholas, Madame, 241.
Nicholas, Alexander, 243.
Nicholas [Nichols], John [Nohn], 314, 321.
Nicholas, Madame Pachon [Madame Pacho], 242, 254.
Nicholas, Robert, 10.
Nicholas [Nichols], Thomas, 9, 22.
Nicholas [Nichols], William, 10, 22.
Nichold, see Nichols.
Nichols, George, 42.
Nichols [Nicols], George, 340, 356.
Nichols [Nichold], J. C., 226, 236.
Nichols [Nicols], William, 269, 286.
Nichols, see Nealous, Nicholas, and Nicklas.
Nick [Nix], Tempel [Temple], 174, 192.
Nicklas [Nichols, Nicols], Theophilus M., 268, 286.
Nicols, see Nichlas, Nichols, and Nicklas.
Night [McNight], Thomas M. [Thomas], 64, 72.
Night, see Knight.
Nighting, see Knighton.
Niles, Henry, 198.
Nimmo, see Nemo.
Nimon, Jacob, 196.
Nimrick, see Limmerick.
Nisbet, Samuel, 246.
Nisbitt, A. M. C. H., 19.
Nisbitt, Jane, 19.
Nix, Ambrose, 147.
Nix, David [Davis], 147, 180.
Nix, Ephraim, 197.
Nix, John, 147.
Nix, see Nick.
Nixon, David, 199.
Nixson, William, 195.
Noah, see North.
Noble, H., Sr. [Henry, Sr.], 112, 119.
Noble, H., Jr. [Henry, Jr.], 112, 119.
Noble, Henry, 298.
Noble, William D., 259.
Noble [Nobles], Zepeniah [Zepheniah], 351, 359.
Nobles, Elijah, 249.
Nobles, Zephaniah, 318.
Nobles, see Noble.
Noel, Ephragn [Ephraigm, Ephrem], 302, 310.
Noland, Nolin, see Nowlin.
Nooe, Alexander, 243, 247.

Nooe, Henry, 241.
Norante, see Norington.
Norington [Norante], Daniel, 84, 96.
Norman, Isaac G., 200.
Norman, John, 195, 197.
Norman, William, 199.
Norris, John, 68.
Norris, Thomas, 146.
Norris, William, 36, 68.
North, Darius, 343.
North [Noah], Hessel [Asa], 152, 183.
North, Sidney, 333.
Northcraft [Northcroft], James [James F.], 267, 285.
Northcroft, see Northcraft.
Norton, Asa, 46.
Norton, Jacob, 127.
Norton, John J. [John T.], 16, 23.
Norton, Reuben [Reubin, Rubin], 39, 51.
Norton, Samuel, 38.
Norton, Sophia, 82.
Norton, Stephen, 38.
Norton, Stephen, Sr., 46.
Norton, Zacariah, 203.
Nots [Knotts], Thomas, 160, 187.
Novall, Terrace, 237.
Novall, see Novet.
Novet [Novall], Root [Roseat], 278, 291.
Nowland, Bennett, 198.
Nowland, Louis, 281.
Nowland, see Nowlin.
Nowlen [Knowlan], Nathaniel, 312, 320.
Nowlin [Noland, Nowland, Nowling], Bennet [Bennett], 170, 191.
Nowlin, James, 257.
Nowlin, John, 8.
Nowlin, Lewis, 206.
Nowlin [Nolin], Samuel, 204, 211.
Nowling, see Nowlin.
Nuckles, James, 193.
Nuel, see Newel and Newles.
Null, Bolsor [Bolsam, Bolser], 259, 283.
Null, see Nulle.
Nulle [Null], Henry [Henry, Jr.], 258, 282.
Nuten [Newten, Newton], Joseph, 66, 73.

Oaoten, see Woton.
Oarinduff [Orindorff], Chapter [Christopher], 162, 188.
Oates [Oats], Mary, 318, 323.
Oats, see Oates.
Oby, William, 237.
Ocanrey [Connery], Morris [Maurice], 78, 93.
Ockletree, James, 58.
Odam, see Odum.
Odell, see Odle.
Odem, see Odum.

Oder, J., 114.
Odle, B. F., 223.
Odle [Odell], Caleb [Calot], 143, 178.
Odle, Fanny [Fanney], 63, 71.
Odle, John, 87.
Odle, Roubin [Rouban], 69, 74.
Odom [Odrien], Moses, 76, 93.
Odrien, see Odom.
Odum [Odam, Odem], Demcy [Dempsey], 67, 73.
Odum [Odam], Kinchen [Kinching], 65, 71, 72.
Ogle, Benjamin, 158, 267.
Ogle, Jacob, Sr., 271.
Ogle, Jacob, Jr., 266.
Ogle, Joseph, 270.
Ogle, Joseph, Sr., 271.
Ogle, Joseph, Jr., 265.
Ogle, Samuel, 262.
Ogle, William, 141.
Oglesby, Joshua, 267.
Oharra, see Oharrah.
Oharrah [Oharra], Henry, 240, 254.
Oins, see Owens.
Oldham, George, 62.
Oldridge, James, 301.
Olever, see Oliver.
Olfan, see Alton.
Oliver, Batiste, 241.
Oliver, James, 211.
Oliver [Olever], John, 129, 135.
Oller, Arthur, 2.
Oller, George, Sr. [George], 1, 5.
Oller, George, Jr., 2.
Oller, John, 2.
Oller, John, Sr., 2, 6.
Oller, Leonard, 2.
Olney, Nathan, 75.
Olver, James, 56.
Oman, George, 59.
Omelvany, see Omelveny.
Omelveny [Omelvany], Samuel [S., Samul], 214, 228, 229.
Oneal [ONeill], Hezekiah [Hezzekiah], 343, 357.
Oneal, Peter, 343.
O'Neill, Hugh, 13.
O'Neill, John, 13.
ONeill, see Oneal.
Onjer, Ferdinand, 253.
Onstot, David, 162.
Ooley [Wooley], Henry, 334, 354.
Ooley, John, 334.
Ooten, see Wootan and Woton.
Orange, Daniel, 57.
Orcut, Berthena, 156.
Orendorf, see Orenduff.
Orenduff [Orendorf], William, 315, 322.

Organ, Bennett, 38.
Orindorff, see Oarinduff.
Orr, Alexander, 9.
Orr, James, 38.
Orr, Joseph, 239.
Orr, Thomas, 239.
Orsbern, Joseph, 64.
Orsbern, Stephen, 64.
Orsborn, see Osborn.
Ortin [Orton], James, 313, 321.
Ortin [Orton], John M. T. [John], 313, 321.
Orton, see Ortin.
Osamus [Osmus, Osymus], Peter, 264, 284.
Osborn [Orsborn, Osbourn], Francis [Frances], 205, 212.
Osbourn [Ausburn], Thomas, 276, 290.
Osbourn, see Osborn.
Osbourne, Joseph, 57.
Osburn, Henry, 132.
Osburn, see Ausburn.
Osgood, Hannah, 59.
Osmus, John, 8.
Osmus, Philip [Phillip], 9, 22.
Osmus, see Osamus.
Osten, see Oston.
Oston [Auston, Osten], Elijah [Eliga], 26, 31.
Ostrander, John, 115.
Osymus, see Osamus.
Oterbury, Israel, 138.
Otey, James S., 33, 34.
Ottwell, see Otwell.
Otwell [Ottwell], William, 147, 180.
Outhouse, Hardy, 314.
Outhouse, John, 313.
Outhouse, Meredy [Meredith], 314, 321.
Outhouse, Peter, 313.
Overbay, see Overby.
Overby [Overbay], Lemuel, 217, 231.
Overstreet, James, 57.
Owen, Ezra, 239.
Owen, Franklin, 241.
Owen, John, 327.
Owen [Owens], Joseph, 86, 96.
Owen, Lemuel, 239.
Owen, Nathan, 325.
Owen, Robert, 92.
Owen, Walter, 325.
Owen, see Owens.
Owens, Charles, 249.
Owens, John [James], 219, 232.
Owens [Oins], Joseph, 29, 32.
Owens, Michael, 117.
Owens [Owen], Phillip, 343, 357.
Owens [Owen], Robert, 82, 95.
Owens, Samuel, 150.
Owens, Sary, 62, 71.

INDEX 433

Owens, Simeon, 196.
Owens, Simmean, 78.
Owens, Thomas, 56, 62.
Owens [Owen], Willis, 80, 94.
Owens, see Owen and Owins.
Owings, see Owins.
Owins [Owens, Owings], John, 150, 182.
Owins [Owings], Simeon [Simion, Simms], 152, 183.
Owsey, William, 193.

Pace [Page], Joel, 64, 72.
Pace [Page], Joel, 123, 126.
Pace, Spencer, 127.
Pacely [Parsley], Robert, 17, 23.
Pacely [Pusley], William, 16, 23.
Paddock, see Padock.
Padfeld, see Padfield.
Padfield, Joseph, 266, 281.
Padfield, Thomas, 281.
Padfield, William, Sr. [William], 272, 288.
Padfield, William, Sr. [William], 273, 288.
Padfield [Padfeld], William Jr., 273, 288.
Padock [Paddock], Gaaius [Gaines], 152, 183.
Padon, John, 268.
Padon, William, 281.
Padrick, see Pedrick.
Page, David, 240.
Page, Jesse, 39.
Page, William, 123.
Page, see Pace.
Paillie, John B. [John], 333, 354.
Pain, Olaney, 195.
Paine, Daniel, 58.
Paine, Enoch, 238.
Paine, see Pane.
Paint, see Painter.
Painter, John, 56.
Painter [Paint], John, 199.
Painter, Jonas, 35.
Painter, Joseph, 193.
Palmer [Palmon], Widow, 218, 231.
Palmer, Joseph, 298.
Palmer, Solomon, 117.
Palmer, see Parmer.
Palmon, see Palmer.
Palmor, John, 231.
Pamer [Pammer], Ambrose, 206, 212.
Pammer, see Pamer.
Pane [Paine, Payne], Cristopher [Christopher], 156, 185.
Pane, see Payne.
Pankee [Pankey, Panky], Hampton [Hamton], 88, 97.
Pankey, Lewis [Lues], 218, 231.
Pankey [Panky], William, 218, 231.
Pankey, see Pankee.

Panky, see Pankee and Pankey.
Pantier, David, 83.
Pantus, James, 76.
Paren, James M., 92.
Paridee, see Perredu.
Parish, Joseph, 57, 193.
Park, see Parke and Parks.
Parke [Park, Parks], James, 142, 177.
Parkenson, see Parkison.
Parker, 281.
Parker, Benjamine [Benjamin], 43, 52.
Parker, Daniel, 28.
Parker, Elijah, 337.
Parker, Francis, 293.
Parker, George, 42, 87.
Parker, Isaac, 43, 166, 171.
Parker, J., 225.
Parker, James, 60, 210.
Parker, James, Sr., 42.
Parker, James, Jr., 42.
Parker, James W. [James], 28, 31.
Parker, John, 28, 89, 281.
Parker, Jonathan, 42, 332.
Parker, Mary, 45.
Parker, Moses, 140.
Parker, Samuel, 42.
Parker, Stephen, 339.
Parker, William, 2, 42, 195, 294.
Parker, see Carter.
Parkerson, Parkinson, see Parkison.
Parkison, Alx., 214.
Parkison [Parkinson], Daniel, 170, 191.
Parkison [Parkenson], Washington, 154, 184.
Parkison [Parkerson], William, 144, 179.
Parks, Arthur, 245.
Parks, David, 3.
Parks, Francis, 195.
Parks, Hugh [Hue], 88, 97.
Parks, Matthew, 200.
Parks [Park], Matthew [Mathew], 333, 354.
Parks, Nicholas, 68.
Parks, Samuel, 67, 246.
Parks, see Parke.
Parmeley [Parmerly, Parmley], Giles [Gils, Jiles], 300, 309.
Parmer [Farmer, Palmer], Frederick, 336, 355.
Parmer [Palmer], James, 152, 183.
Parmer, Polly, 69.
Parmer [Farmer, Palmer], William, 336, 355.
Parmerly, Parmley, see Parmeley.
Parrett, see Parrott.
Parris, Lewis [Luess], 82, 95.
Parrish, Gilford, 16.
Parrish [Pash], Lewis [Louis], 277, 290.

Parrott, J., 224.
Parrott [Parrett], J., 225, 235.
Parsley, see Pacely.
Parsons, Henry [Henrey], 66, 73.
Parviance, see Pervines.
Pascal, Abram, 237.
Pascal, see Paschal.
Paschal [Pascal], Nicholas, 243, 254.
Pash, see Parrish.
Pasia, Joseph, 238.
Pate, Anthony, 271, 281.
Pate, Joseph, 265.
Pate, Mathew [Matthew], 272, 283.
Pate, Parrott [Parrett, Parrot], 87, 97.
Pate, William, 87, 265.
Paten, see Peyton.
Patengale, see Patongill.
Paterson [Patterson], Josiah, 295, 306.
Paterson [Patterson], Levy [Levi], 295, 306.
Patillo, John S., 342.
Paton [Patton], Andrew [Andrew V.], 173, 192.
Patongill [Patengale, Petingill], Daniel, 144, 179.
Patree [Roundtree, Rountree], Jesse [Jessee], 155, 185.
Patrick, Charles, 25, 30, 31.
Patrick [Kirkpatrick], John K. [John], 65, 72.
Patten, John, 335.
Patten [Patton], Joseph, 344, 357.
Patten [Patton], Phillip [Philip], 349, 359.
Patten [Patton], Thomas, 41, 51.
Patterson, Arthur, 256.
Patterson, Charles, 207.
Patterson, Greenbury [Green B.], 260, 283.
Patterson, Hardin, 171.
Patterson, James, 245.
Patterson, Joseph, 87.
Patterson, Joshua, 157.
Patterson, Josiah, 265.
Patterson, Luke, 205.
Patterson, Perregrin, 12.
Patterson, Solomon, 207.
Patterson, see Paterson.
Patton, Josiah, 16.
Patton, Robert, 85.
Patton, see Paton and Patten.
Paul, Peter, 247.
Paul, Stephen, 198.
Paupa, see Paupau and Paupaugh.
Paupau [Paupa, Pupah], Paul, 278, 291.
Paupaugh [Paupa, Pupah], Joseph, 278, 291.
Paver [Pavo], Stephen [Akan], 239, 253.
Pavo, see Paver.

Paxton, Amos, 240.
Payne, Adams, 204.
Payne, Laben [L.], 226, 236.
Payne, Nathaniel, 198.
Payne, Olney, 60.
Payne [Pane], William, 246, 254.
Payne, see Pane.
Payton, William, 13.
Pea, James, 274.
Pea, John, 270.
Peach, William, 241.
Peacock, Benjamin, 58.
Peacock, Etheldred, 130.
Peacock, see Pecock.
Peake [Pike], John, 168, 190.
Pealet, Joseph, 277.
Pealet [Pelette, Petitte], Lewis [Louis], 277, 290.
Pearce, Daniel, 152.
Pearce, Francis, 151.
Pearce, James, 153.
Pearce [Pierce], James, 154, 184.
Pearce [Pierce], James S. [James], 142, 177.
Pearce [Pierce], Robert A. [Robert], 165, 189.
Pearce [Pierce], Solomon, 165, 189.
Pearce, see Pierce.
Pearcifield [Purcefield], Jeramiah [Jeremiah], 165, 189.
Pearcy [Piercy], John, 168, 190.
Pearson, see Pierson.
Peas [Pease], Abraham, 163, 188.
Pease, Anbrose [Obrose], 45, 53.
Pease, see Peas.
Peck, Heney [Henry], 156, 185.
Peckard, Alpheus [Alppeus], 47, 54.
Pecock [Peacock], James U., 302, 310.
Peddigrew [Pettygrew, Pettygrove], James M., 77, 93.
Pedrick [Padrick], Caleb, 244, 254.
Peebles, see Peeples.
Peeples [Peebles], Robert, 75, 92.
Pehny [Penney, Penny], Hiram, 220, 232.
Peirce, David, 316, 322; see also Caleb Pierce.
Peirce [Pierce], Elijah, 316, 322.
Peirce, see Pierce.
Pelate [Petitte], Michael, 278, 291.
Peleau, John Baptist, 47.
Pelette, see Pealet.
Pelham, Markus [Marcus], 207, 212.
Pelkey, Baptiste, 194.
Pelky, Madame, 57.
Pelletier, Pierre, 57.
Pembrook, Enos, 139.
Penfold, Abraham, 57.

INDEX

Penfold, Jacob, 56.
Penington [Pennington], Absolom [Absalom], 269, 286.
Penington, Riggs, 64.
Peninton, Benjamin, 214, 229.
Penn, Joseph, Sr. [Josep, Sr., Joseph], 272, 288.
Penn, Joseph, Jr., 272.
Penn, Philip, 153.
Penn, William, 266.
Penney, Solomon, 200.
Penney, see Pehny and Penny.
Pennington, see Penington.
Penny [Penney], John, 164, 189.
Penny [Penney], John, 165, 189.
Penny [Penney], Robert, 164, 189.
Penny [Penney], Robert, 165, 189.
Penny, William, 148, 164.
Penny [Penney], William, 165, 189.
Penny, William B., 148.
Penny, see Pehny and Perry.
Penrod, Allin [Allen], 299, 309.
Penrod, Andy [Andrew], 300, 310.
Penrod, David, 300.
Penrod, Emanuel, 298.
Penrod, John, 298.
Penrod, Lewis [Louis], 295, 307.
Penrod, Samuel, Sr., 300.
Penrod, Samuel, Jr., 299.
Penrod, Sollomon [Soloman, Solomon], 298, 308.
Pensano, Francis, 277.
Pensino, see Pensono.
Pensono [Pensino, Pincinneau], Lewis [Louis], 275, 289.
Pensono [Pesano, Pincinnsau], Lewis [Louis, Louision], 277, 290.
Pensono, Tadale [Hideal], 279, 291.
Pentecost, Ruth, 264.
Penvine, Francis, 281.
Peoples, Thornton [Thorton], 266, 285.
Pera, Madame, 239, 253.
Peradee, see Perredu.
Percyfield, Henry, 200.
Perdew, see Perdue.
Perdue [Perdew], Ezekiel [Ezekel], 29, 32.
Pereau [Pereu], Lewis [Louis], 277, 290.
Pereu, see Pereau.
Peril, Stephen, 163.
Perkens, see Pirkins.
Perkings [Perkins, Pirkins], Reece [Isaac, Rees], 65, 72.
Perkins, Absalom, 314.
Perkins, Edward, 165.
Perkins, Isaac, 171.
Perkins, Jesse [Jessee], 266, 285.
Perkins, Joshua, 267.
Perkins, Lewis, 34.
Perkins, Samuel, 34.
Perkins, Solomon, 270.
Perkins, Stephen, 76.
Perkins, see Perkings, Pirkins, and Purkins.
Permeture, Thomas, 156.
Pero, Peter, 253.
Peroginn, John, 42.
Peroginn, Peter, 42.
Perredu [Paridee, Peradee], Battice [Baptiest, Batese], 276, 290.
Perrey [Perry], Redman, 337, 355.
Perry [Penny], Franklin [Frenklen], 220, 232.
Perry, John, 250.
Perry [Pery], Samuel, 28, 31.
Perry, William B., 62.
Perry, see Perrey.
Persell, see Purcell.
Persol [Purcell], Edwin [Edward], 26, 31.
Person, Joseph, 44.
Pervines [Pervunce], Alexandria [Alexander], 164, 189.
Pervines, John, 164.
Pervines [Parviance, Purvines], William, 150, 182.
Pervo, see Provou.
Pervunce, see Pervines.
Pery, see Perry.
Pesano, see Pensono.
Peteet, see Pettette.
Peter, see Peters.
Peters [Petters], William C. T. [William C.], 80, 94.
Peters [Peter], Zachariah [Zacheriah], 160, 187.
Peterson, John, 132.
Peterson, Thomas, 1.
Petet, see Petit.
Petingill, see Patongill.
Petit [Petet], David, 247, 255.
Petit, Henry, 193, 247.
Petit, Jonathan, 250.
Petite, David M., 194.
Petitte, see Pealet and Pelate.
Petters, see Peters.
Pettet [Pettit], James, 262, 284.
Pettet, Solomon, 194.
Pettett, John R., 194.
Pettette [Peteet], Isaac, 216, 230.
Pettigrew, Charles, 77.
Pettilla [Pitilla], James, 222, 233.
Pettis, Benjamin, 38.
Pettit, see Pettet.
Petty, Moses, 59.
Pettygrew, Pettygrove, see Peddigrew.
Pew, Bethel, 83.
Peyton [Paten], Thomas B., 2, 5.

Pharis [Farris], George [George W.], 153, 184.
Pharis [Farris], Smith, 153, 184.
Pharis, see Farris and Pharris.
Pharr, Ephraim, 56.
Pharris [Farris, Pharis], James [James, Jr.], 150, 182.
Pharris, see Ferris.
Phelps, Amos, 35.
Phelps, David, 39.
Phelps, Elias, 200.
Phelps, Frederick, 10.
Phelps, Jacob, 342.
Phelps, John, 112.
Phelps [Felps], John, 10, 22.
Phelps, Mary, 112.
Phelps, William, 132.
Phelps [Felps], Zadock [Zedoch], 10, 22.
Phelps, see Felps.
Philips, John, 92.
Philips [Phillips], John, 317, 323.
Philips, Peasley, 193.
Philips, Sally, 92.
Philips, Thomas, 242.
Philips, William, 200.
Philips, see Phillips.
Phillips [Philips], Alexander, 349, 359.
Phillips [Philips], Benjamin, 264, 284.
Phillips [Philips], Burnside, 350, 359.
Phillips [Philips], Daniel, 262, 284.
Phillips [Philips], David, 266, 285.
Phillips [Philips], Jacob, 64, 72.
Phillips [Philips], James, 2, 5.
Phillips [Philips], James, 267, 286.
Phillips [Philips], James, 350, 359.
Phillips, Jeremiah, 258.
Phillips, John, 68, 210.
Phillips, Joseph, 264.
Phillips, Peter, 64.
Phillips [Philips], Samuel M. [Samuel], 1, 5.
Phillips [Philips], William, 262, 284.
Phillips, see Philips.
Phillpott, Benjamin, 330.
Phinemon, William, 350.
Phipps, Benjamin, 339.
Phipps [Fips], James, 339, 355.
Phipps, John, 60.
Phipps, Loch, 332.
Phipps, William, 59.
Piatt [Pyott], Abraham, 69, 74.
Piatt [Pyatt], Henry, 14, 23.
Piatt, see Pyatt.
Pichy [Richey], Alexandria [Alexander], 159, 187.
Pickering, Isaac, 324.
Pickford, John, 67.
Pickford, William, 69.
Pickly, John, 172.
Pierce, Abner, 338.
Pierce [Peirce], Caleb, 322; see also David Peirce.
Pierce [Peirce], Daniel, 267, 286.
Pierce, David, 342.
Pierce [Pearce], Hosey [Hosea], 343, 357.
Pierce, Jarvis, 333.
Pierce [Pearce], Jesse, 342, 356.
Pierce [Pearce], Moses, Sr. [Moses], 342, 356.
Pierce, Moses, Jr., 342.
Pierce, Philip, 195.
Pierce, Stephen, 194.
Pierce, see Pearce and Peirce.
Pierceau [Pierson], Jonah [Josiah], 271, 287.
Piercy, see Pearcy.
Pierson [Pearson], Akillis [Achelus], 331, 354.
Pierson, see Pierceau.
Piggot [Piggott], Levi, 205, 212.
Piggott, see Piggot.
Pigott, John, 196.
Pike, see Peake.
Pile [Pyle], John, 102, 117.
Pile [Pyle], William, 102, 117.
Piles, James, 121.
Piles, Joshua, 121.
Piles, Leonard, 121.
Piles [Pyle], Nicholas, 100, 117.
Piles [Pyle], Nicholas, 317, 322.
Piles [Pyle], Samuel, 273, 288.
Pilkinton, Thomas, 155.
Pillars, John, 244.
Pillars [Spellers], John, 166, 190.
Pincinneau, Pincinnsau, see Pensono.
Pinkard, Nathaniel, 137.
Pinkard, William G., 137.
Pinkerton [Binkerton], James, 169, 191.
Pinkstaff, Andrew, 36.
Pinkstaff, John, 36.
Piper, Edward H., 33, 34.
Piper, John, 153.
Piper, Jonithan, 160.
Piper, Netter [Nutter], 153, 184.
Piper, Robert, 195.
Piper, Thomas, 157.
Pipp, Patrick, 197.
Pirkins [Perkens, Perkins], Ephran [Ephraim], 266, 285.
Pirkins, see Perkings.
Pitilla, see Pettilla.
Pitt, Mrs., 223.
Pixley, Joe, 58.
Plant, Robert, 164.

INDEX

Plant, Williamson [William], 19, 24.
Plasant [Pleasant], Frank, 279, 292.
Plaster, Joseph, 63.
Pleasant, see Plasant.
Pleasants, Thomas, 197, 198.
Pleasants, Thomas R., 199.
Plough, Philip, 56.
Plugh, Nimrod, 48.
Pogue, Robert, 144.
Pollard, Elijah, 60.
Polls, William, 86.
Pomely, Samuel, 221.
Pompter, John, 151.
Pomroy [Pumroy], Joseph, 346, 357.
Ponner, Alexy, 242.
Ponner, Joseph, 241.
Ponner, see Punner.
Pool, Arter [Arthur], 348, 358.
Pool, James, 61.
Pool, John, 47.
Pool, Joseph R. G., 80.
Pool, Stephen, 166.
Pool, Thomas, 349.
Pool, William, 61, 348.
Poorman, Jacob, 28.
Poorman, Jacob, Jr., 27.
Pope, Nathaniel, 237.
Pore, James, 3.
Porter, Benjamin A. [Benjamin], 247, 254.
Porter, Daniel, 250.
Porter, David, 34, 162.
Porter, Guin, 167.
Porter, James, 193.
Porter, John, 36, 161, 271.
Porter, Joseph, 167.
Porter, Polly, 226.
Porter, Rebecah [Rebecca, Rebecka], 271, 287.
Porter, Reder, 167.
Porter, Robert, 35.
Porter, Robin, 336.
Porter, see Pourter.
Portmess, see Potmess.
Posey, Hetty [Hester], 315, 321.
Posey, Leaiden [Leeaiden], 312, 320.
Posey, see Pozia.
Postelwyt, Elizabeth, 272, 287.
Postleweight, John, 287.
Potmess [Portmess, Potmicer], Peter, 301, 310.
Potmicer, see Potmess.
Potter, Andrew, 199.
Potter, Hannah, 258.
Potter, James, 195, 350.
Potter, R. [Reuben], 223, 234.
Potter, Rial [Royal], 165, 189.

Potts, Anthony, 276.
Potts, Isaak L. [Isaac], 76, 93.
Pourter, Andrew, 211.
Pourter [Porter], Thomas, 206, 212.
Powel [Powell], James, 168, 190.
Powel, John, 172.
Powel [Powell], John, 159, 187.
Powel, Samuel, 202.
Powell, Daniel, 340.
Powell, Green, 76.
Powell, Nicholas, 77.
Powell, Nicholas [Nicholas, Sr.], 76, 93.
Powell, see Powel.
Powers, Elijah, 8.
Powers, George, 113.
Powers, John, 8, 57.
Powers, Samuel, 17.
Powers, Thomas, 19.
Powlas, see Powles.
Powles [Powlas], Peter, 297, 307.
Pozia [Posey], Jubilee, 149, 181.
Prat, Nathaniel, 193.
Prater, Edward, 137.
Prater, Holle, 13.
Prengel, see Pringall.
Prentice, John O., 279.
Preston, Ann, 281.
Preston, Ezekiel, 202.
Preston, Joseph, 61.
Prevo, Samuel, 29.
Prewit, see Pruitt.
Price, Calven [Calvin], 303, 311.
Price, David, 47.
Price, Henry, 47.
Price, Israel, 36.
Price, Jerimiah [Richard], 46, 53.
Price, John, 42, 305.
Price, Leonard, 318.
Price, Michael, 36.
Price, Peter, 47.
Price, William, 3.
Prichard, Elizabeth [Mrs.], 263, 284.
Prichard, see Pritchit.
Pricket [Prickett], Gorge [George], 271, 287.
Pricket, John, 20.
Prickett, see Pricket.
Priestly, James, 198.
Prim, John, 162.
Prim, Thomas, 200.
Primm, John, 256.
Primm, Joseph, 256.
Primm, Thomas, 261.
Pringall [Prengel], William, 220, 232.
Pringle, James, 4.
Pritchard, Deborah, 57.
Pritchard, see Pritchit.

Pritchet, John, 327.
Pritchit [Prichard, Pritchard], Elisha [Abisha], 148, 181.
Procter, David, 337.
Procter, John, 338.
Procter, Joseph, 339.
Procter, Littlepage, 338.
Proctor, John, 60.
Prout, Sherman, 57.
Provins, Ebenser, 150.
Provo, Bartholemew [Bartholmew], 278, 291.
Provou [Pervo], Mark, 1, 5.
Prow, Reuben, 193.
Prowitt, see Pruett.
Pruett [Prowitt, Pruit], Jacob, 89, 98.
Pruett, see Pruitt.
Pruit, see Pruett.
Pruitt, Abraham [Abram], 138, 176.
Pruitt, Dorotha [Dolley], 139, 176.
Pruitt [Prewit], Fields, 8, 22.
Pruitt, Isaac, 158.
Pruitt, James, 157, 168.
Pruitt, Soloman [Solomon], 139, 176.
Pruitt [Pruett], Soloman [Solomon], 165, 189.
Pruitt, Solomon, 195.
Pruitt, William, 138.
Pryor, Jos. E., [J.], 226, 236.
Pugh, George, 60.
Pugsley, Charles, 56.
Pulham [Pullam, Pullem], Robert, 137, 175.
Pulham, see Pulliam.
Pullam, Pullem, see Pulham.
Pullham [Pulliam, Pulliem], Alcey [Alsa, Alsey], 169, 191.
Pulliam [Pulham], David [Davis], 259, 283.
Pulliam [Pulham], James, 263, 284.
Pulliam, John, 263.
Pulliam, Thomas, 58, 259.
Pulliam, Pulliem, see Pullham.
Pumphrey, Nancy, 37.
Pumroy, see Pomroy.
Punner [Ponner], Izado [Izedo], 241, 254.
Pupah, see Lapaugh, Paupau, and Paupaugh.
Purcefield, see Pearcifield.
Purcell, Brice, 34.
Purcell [Persell], Jonathan [Johnathan], 34, 49.
Purcell, see Persol.
Purkins [Perkins], Elisha M., 124, 127.
Purkins, Ephraim, 92.
Purse, Charles, 146.
Pursley, William, 10.
Purvines, see Pervines.
Pusley, see Pacely.
Putman, Elijah, 166.

Putnam, Ebenezer, 60.
Putnam, Samuel, 60.
Pyatt [Piatt], E. [Ebenezer], 112, 119.
Pyatt [Piatt], Samuel, 114, 120.
Pyatt, see Piatt.
Pyle, Abner, 102.
Pyle, Thomas, 117.
Pyle, see Pile and Piles.
Pyott, see Piatt.

Quarles, James, 106.
Quick, Aaron, 263.
Quick, Isaac, 274.
Quick, Jacob, 38.
Quick, Thomas, 281.
Quigley, Aaron, 266.
Quigley, John, 173.
Quigley, William, 144.
Quinney, 12.

Rader, Philip, 201.
Ragan [Rager], Henry B., 173, 192.
Ragan, Marke, 143.
Ragar [Ruyar], Lewis [Louis], 278, 291.
Rager, see Ragan.
Raggen, William, 37.
Ragin [Riggin], John, 155, 184.
Ragin, Marke, 155.
Ragland [Raglen, Ragline], George, 77, 93.
Ragland [Raglen, Ragline], Haley [Haly], 77, 93.
Raglen, Ragline, see Ragland.
Raily [Richey], John, 165, 189.
Rainor [Raner], Samuel, 210.
Rale [Ruelle], Joseph, 277, 290.
Ralls, Edward, 241.
Ralls [Rawles, Rolls], Rawleigh [Raleigh, Rolly], 258, 282.
Ralsion [Robison], Jacob, 219, 232.
Ralston, Hugh, 201.
Ralston, see Rolston.
Ramey, George, 201.
Ramis, William, 197.
Ramsay [Ramsey], John, 316, 322.
Ramsay [Ramsey], John H., 316, 322.
Ramsey, Elexander, 328.
Ramsey, Elizabeth, 334.
Ramsey, Isham, 149.
Ramsey, James, 325.
Ramsey [Ransey], James, 143, 178.
Ramsey, Samuel, 58, 281.
Ramsey, William, 60.
Ramsey [Ranscy], William [James], 143, 178.
Ramsey, see Ramsay.
Randle, Josias, Jr., 199.
Randle, Pyram [Parham], 200.

INDEX 439

Randle, Robert W., 12.
Randle, Thomas, 200.
Randle, see Randol.
Randleman, Henry, 256.
Randleman, Jacob, 257.
Randol [Randle], Elizabeth, 152, 183.
Randol [Randle], Isham, 159, 186.
Randol, Josiah [Josias], 159, 186.
Randol, Payton [Peyton], 152, 183.
Randolph, Elijah, 349.
Raner, see Rainor.
Ranes, Patrick [Partrick], 245, 254.
Raney, Isaac, 245.
Raney, John, 246.
Rangerton, Thomas, 193.
Rankin, James, 58.
Rankin, William, 58.
Rannals [Reynoalds, Runnels], John, 278, 291.
Ransam, Amherst, 281.
Ranscy, Ransey, see Ramsey.
Ransom, Merritt, 193.
Ransom, Thomas, 198.
Rants, Robert, 197.
Rape, Jacob, 170.
Rape, Peter, 170.
Raper, Richard, 260.
Rapert [Raport], Daniel, 204, 211.
Raport, see Rapert.
Rasco, Jessy [Jesse], 102, 117.
Rasons, Joseph, 197.
Ratcliff, Charles, 259.
Ratcliff, James, 333, 353.
Ratcliff, Michael [Michel], 259, 282.
Ratcliff, William, 276.
Ratcliff, see Ratliff.
Ratclift [Ratliff], Richard, 66, 73.
Rathbone [Rathbourn], Edman [Camon], 37, 50.
Rathbone, S., 223.
Rathbourn, see Rathbone.
Ratliff [Ratcliff], James, 164, 189.
Ratliff [Ratcliff], Joab [James], 164, 189.
Ratliff [Ratcliff], John, 164, 189.
Ratliff [Ratcliff], Tompson [Thomas], 164, 189.
Ratliff [Ratcliff], William, 164, 189.
Ratliff, see Ratclift.
Rattan, John, 139.
Rattan, Richard, 168.
Rattan, Thomas, 169.
Raviel, Antwine [Anthony], 247, 254.
Rawles, see Ralls.
Rawlin, Drury, 167.
Rawlings, James, 60.
Rawlings, Nancy, 57.
Rawlings, see Rowlings.

Rawlins [Rollins], Hosea, 313, 321.
Rawson, see Rowson.
Ray, Biram [Abiram], 316, 322.
Ray, John, 27.
Ray, Martin, 27.
Ray, Thomas, 196, 271.
Ray, see Rhea.
Rayboy, John Baptise, 194.
Rayhill, George, 281.
Rayhill, Jacob, 266.
Raynolds, see Reynolds.
Read, Charles, 208.
Read, James, 347.
Read [Reed], James, 148, 181.
Read [Reed], John, 154, 184.
Read [Reed], John, 347, 358.
Read [Reed], Samuel, 150, 182.
Read, William, 345.
Read [Reed], William, 173, 192.
Read, see Reed.
Reader [Reeder], Amos, 153, 183.
Readman, see Redman.
Rearden, William, 333.
Reatherford, John, 328.
Reau, see Reum.
Reavell, see Reaville.
Reaves [Rieves], Isaac, 151, 183.
Reaves [Reeves], John, 132, 136.
Reaville [Reavell], David, 42, 52.
Reavis [Revise], Alexandria [Alexander], 165, 189.
Reavis [Rieves], Isaac, 167, 190.
Reavis, see Revis and Reviss.
Recaw, Antwine, 248.
Rechey, see Richie.
Redding, James, 159.
Reddon, James, 195.
Redell [Riddle], John, 299, 308.
Redell [Riddle], Thomas, 302, 310.
Redfern, see Redford.
Redfield, Amos, 199.
Redfield, R. [Rural], 113, 120.
Redford [Redfern], John, 215, 230.
Redkin [Redkins], William [William S.], 226, 236.
Redkins, see Redkin.
Redman, Abraham, 198.
Redman [Readman, Redmond], Samuel, 271, 287.
Redmond, see Redman.
Redpath [Redpeth], James, 268, 286.
Redpeth, see Redpath.
Reece, John D., 69.
Reed, Andre [Andrew], 220, 232.
Reed, Charles, 320.
Reed, Eli, 56.
Reed, Isaac, 8.

440   ILLINOIS HISTORICAL COLLECTIONS

Reed [Reeder], Isaac, 257, 282.
Reed, Jacob, 197.
Reed, James, 9.
Reed, John, 3, 314.
Reed, Joseph, 78.
Reed [Read], Joseph, 123, 126.
Reed [Read], Nelly, 350, 359.
Reed, Samuel, 130.
Reed, Thomas, 84, 220.
Reed, see Read and Rieds.
Reeder, Isaac, 216.
Reeder, Levy, 194.
Reeder, Philip, 197.
Reeder, see Reader and Reed.
Reel, George, 241.
Reese, see Reess.
Reess [Reese], Hampton [Edward H.], 102, 118.
Reeves, see Reaves.
Reichercker, John, 197.
Reiley [Riley], Isaac, 79, 94.
Reiley [Reily, Riley], Joseph, 79, 94.
Reily, see Reiley.
Reives [Rives], John C., 92.
Reives, see Rieves.
Relay [Reley], Morace [Morice], 216, 230.
Reley, see Relay.
Rellens, see Rollins.
Renfro, Mark, 132.
Renfro, see Renfrow.
Renfrow, Isaac, 9.
Renfrow [Renfro], Jesse [Jessee], 155, 185.
Renfrow, Joseph, 155.
Renfrow [Rentfrow], Joseph, 150, 182.
Renfrow, Joshua, 14.
Renfrow [Renfro, Rentfrew], Margaret [Margerett], 150, 182.
Rengold [Ringgold], John, 261, 283.
Renneo [Rieno], Antoine [Antwine], 275, 289.
Rensaw, James, 343.
Renshaw, Abraham [Absalom], 150, 182.
Renshaw, Elijah, 150.
Rentelman, see Rentleman.
Rentfrew, see Renfrow.
Rentfrow, James, 193.
Rentfrow, see Renfrow.
Rentleman [Rentelman], Jacob, 298, 308.
Ressell [Russel, Russell], Dowell [James M. D., James W.], 88, 98.
Retherford, see Rutherford.
Rettener, see Keltner.
Rettenghouse [Rettenhouse, Rettonhouse], Peter, 264, 285.
Rettenhouse, see Rettenghouse and Rittenhouse.
Rettonhouse, see Rettenghouse.

Reum [Reau], Batiste [Baptiste], 238, 253.
Revis [Reavis], Charles, 7, 22.
Revis [Reavis], Harris, 13, 23.
Revis [Reavis], Isham [Ishom], 10, 22.
Revis, Ishom, 17.
Revis, see Reviss.
Revise, see Reavis.
Reviss [Reavis, Revis], Henery [Henry], 142, 178.
Reynoalds, see Rannals.
Reynold, see Reynolds.
Reynolds, Benjamin, 59.
Reynolds, Daniel, 83.
Reynolds, David, 294.
Reynolds, Huston [Husten], 159, 186.
Reynolds, James, 147.
Reynolds, Jesse, 45.
Reynolds, Joseph, 144, 169.
Reynolds, Joseph L., 198.
Reynolds, Levi, 159.
Reynolds [Raynolds], Mary, 110, 119.
Reynolds, Milleton [Milikin], 294, 306.
Reynolds, Robert [Robert, Sr.], 147, 180.
Reynolds [Reynold], Robert [Robert, Jr.], 147, 180.
Reynolds, Samuel, 198.
Reynolds, Thomas, 147, 175, 244.
Reynolds [Runnels], William, 84, 96.
Reynolds, William L. [William], 237, 253.
Rhea, Andrew B. [Andrew], 35, 49.
Rhea, James, 40.
Rhea [Ray], Thomas, 153, 184.
Rhoads, George, 195.
Rhodes, Claybourn, 197.
Rhodes, Clayburn, 195.
Rhodes, William, 332.
Rial, Whitmill, 11.
Rian [Ryan], John, 138, 176.
Rian, see Ryan.
Rice, Abel, 331.
Rice, B. [Benjamin], 92.
Rice [Dedricks], Daniel D. [Daniel], 151, 183.
Rice, Green P., 17.
Rice, Thomas [Thomas K.], 146, 180.
Rice, William, 65.
Rice, William D. [William], 154, 184.
Richard, 315, 322.
Richardson, Abraham, 348.
Richardson, George, 145.
Richardson, James, 198, 247.
Richardson, Jane, 47, 54.
Richardson, John, 29, 194.
Richardson [Richason], John, 64, 72.
Richardson, John B., 54.
Richardson, Joseph, 49.
Richason, see Richardson.

INDEX

Riche, William, 251.
Richerfuse, see Rickafuse.
Richey, Adam, 339.
Richey, see Pichy, Raily, Richie, and Richy.
Richie [Rechey, Richey], J. [James], 223, 234.
Richison, Abel [Able], 215, 230.
Richley, see Ripley.
Richy [Richey], John, 172, 192.
Rickafoos, see Rickafuse.
Rickafuse [Richerfuse, Rickafoos], Christopher, 316, 322.
Ricker, Rufus, 122.
Riddle, David, 315.
Riddle, Richard, 89.
Riddle, see Redell.
Rider [Ryder], John, 263, 284.
Ridgeway, Caleb, 328.
Ridgley, William, 59.
Ridgway [Ridway], David W., 344, 357.
Ridgway, John, 333.
Ridway, see Ridgway.
Rieds [Reed], John, 77, 93.
Rieno, see Renneo.
Rieves, Gustavus, 92.
Rieves [Reives], James, 86, 96.
Rieves, see Reaves and Reavis.
Rigg, Charles, 58.
Rigg [Riggs], Clement [Clemment], 263, 284.
Rigg [Riggs], Hosea, 263, 284.
Rigg, Samuel, 60.
Riggan, see Riggin.
Riggin [Riggan], Joshua, 334, 354.
Riggin, see Ragin.
Riggins, Morth, 195.
Riggins, see Rigin.
Riggs, Scott [Scot], 39, 51.
Riggs, William, 207.
Riggs, see Rigg.
Right [Wright, Write], James, 298, 308.
Right, Thomas, 331.
Right, William, 207.
Right, see Wright and Write.
Rightenour, see Rightnour.
Rightnour [Rightenour], George, 215, 230.
Rigin [Riggins], Henery [Henry], 152, 183.
Rigney, William, 350.
Riley, Anderson, 154.
Riley, Barney [Barnebas], 17, 23.
Riley, Jacob, 332.
Riley, Jeremiah, 13.
Riley, William, 351.
Riley, see Reiley.
Rines [Ryan, Ryans], William, 137, 175.
Ringgold, see Rengold.
Ripley, Arnold, 197.

Ripley [Richley], Benjamin, 112, 119.
Ripley, William, 115.
Ripper, John, 200.
Rite, see Wright.
Riter [Ritter], Daniel, 298, 308.
Ritheghouse [Rittenhouse], William, Sr. [William], 274, 289.
Rittenghouse [Rittenhouse], Elijah [Elijah, Sr.], 274, 289.
Rittenhouse, Elijah [Eligah], 267, 286.
Rittenhouse, Mary, 274.
Rittenhouse [Rettenhouse], William [William, Sr.], 261, 283.
Rittenhouse, see Ritheghouse, Rittenghouse, and Rittinghouse.
Ritter, see Riter.
Rittiner, see Keltner.
Rittinghouse [Rittenhouse], Elijah [Elijah, Sr.], 261, 283.
Rives, see Reives.
Roach, David, 149, 199.
Roach, Enenor, 89.
Roach, John, 151, 205.
Roach, John [John D.], 256, 282.
Roach, Mathew [Matthew], 256, 282.
Roach, Thomas, 276.
Roads, Abm. [Absalem], 219, 232.
Roads, Clayburn, 199.
Roan, James, 198.
Roan, Thomas, 198.
Roas, see Rose.
Robans [Robins], William, 273, 288.
Robarts, see Roberts.
Robbins, Joseph, 317.
Robbins, William, 42.
Robbins, see Robins.
Robenet, Roberds, see Roberts.
Roberson, Tiry, 326.
Roberson, see Robertson.
Robertes [Roberts], Lius [Elias], 157, 185.
Roberts, Andrew, 171.
Roberts, Archable, 324.
Roberts, Edmond, 334.
Roberts, Edmund, 237.
Roberts, Isaiah, 210.
Roberts, James, 121.
Roberts, John, 66, 110, 166.
Roberts [Robarts], John [J.], 226, 236.
Roberts [Roberds], John B., 302, 311.
Roberts, John T., 281.
Roberts, Joseph, 20.
Roberts, Levi, 172.
Roberts, Margaret, 47.
Roberts, Moses, 47.
Roberts [Robenet], R. [Richard, Richart], 223, 234.
Roberts, Thomas, 194, 250.

Roberts, Thomas R. [Thomas], 63, 71.
Roberts, William, 110, 171.
Roberts, William A. [William], 69, 74.
Roberts, William F., 202.
Roberts, see Robertes.
Robertson [Robinson], Aaron, 268, 286.
Robertson, David, 147.
Robertson, Hardy, 200.
Robertson [Robinson], Isreal [Israel], 270, 287.
Robertson, James, 145, 245.
Robertson [Roberson], James, 295, 306.
Robertson [Robinson], James, 269, 287.
Robertson [Robinson] James [John], 140, 177.
Robertson [Robinson], James S. [James], 259, 282.
Robertson, Joab [Job], 151, 183.
Robertson, John, 159, 257.
Robertson [Roberson], John, 310.
Robertson [Robinson], John, 65, 72.
Robertson [Robinson], John, 140, 177.
Robertson [Robinson], John B., 260, 283.
Robertson, John P., 262.
Robertson, Joseph, 245.
Robertson [Robinson], Joseph, 159, 186.
Robertson [Roberson], Marada [Merriday], 64, 72.
Robertson, Richard [Richard, Sr.], 245, 254.
Robertson, Richard, Jr., 251.
Robertson, Sarah, 301, 310.
Robertson, Thomas, 348.
Robertson, Vincent, 302.
Robertson, William, 147, 152, 245.
Robertson, see Robinson and Robison.
Robeson, see Robinson.
Robinet, Joseph, 75.
Robinett, Thomas, 35.
Robins [Robbins], Hiram, 156, 185.
Robins, John, 206.
Robins, Marmeduke, 13.
Robins, Nathaniel, 13.
Robins, William, 157.
Robins, see Robans.
Robinson [Robison], A. [Allen], 226, 236.
Robinson, Edw., 221.
Robinson [Robertson], Hugh, 88, 97.
Robinson [Robison], Hugh, 214, 229.
Robinson, J., 114.
Robinson, James, 220.
Robinson, John, 38, 57, 75, 100.
Robinson [Robeson], John G. [John], 352, 360.
Robinson, Joshua, 123.
Robinson, Labon, 79.
Robinson [Robertson], Lucy, 123, 126.
Robinson, Marke, 89.

Robinson, Mary, 81.
Robinson [Robison, Rollinson], R. [Richard D.], 224, 235.
Robinson, Richard, 30.
Robinson, Sarah [Sally], 78, 94.
Robinson, Thomas M., 75.
Robinson, William, 82.
Robinson [Robertson], William, 346, 358.
Robinson, see Robertson and Robison.
Robison [Robertson], Alexander, 17, 23.
Robison, David, 206.
Robison [Robinson], Gideon, 18, 23.
Robison, Hugh, 19.
Robison [Robertson], Thomas, 14, 23.
Robison [Robinson], William, 19, 23.
Robison, see Ralsion and Robinson.
Roch [Rock], Peter, 279, 291.
Rock, Anthony [Antwine Couin], 277, 290
Rock, see Roch.
Rockwell, Jay T., 253.
Rodden, David, 169.
Rodden, Robert, 195.
Roderick, Daniel, 243.
Roderick, Gague, 237.
Roderick, George, 342.
Roderick, Peter, 237, 243.
Rodes, Thomas, 26.
Rodger, see Rodgers.
Rodgers [Rodger, Rogers], Benjamin, 62, 71.
Rodgers, Isham, 56.
Rodgers [Rogers], James, 63, 72.
Rodgers, Joseph, 56.
Rodgers [Rogers], William [Williams], 63, 72.
Rodgers, see Rogers.
Roe, Isaac F., 199.
Rogers, Elisha B., 320.
Rogers [Rodgers], Mathew [Matthew], 162, 188.
Rogers [Rodgers], Robert, 106, 118.
Rogers, Sollomon, 302.
Rogers [Rodgers], William, 157, 185.
Rogers, see Rodgers.
Rohrer, John, 80.
Rolan, James, 13.
Rolan, see Roland.
Roland [Rolan], John, 68, 74.
Roland [Rolan], Ragsdale, 68, 74.
Rollens, Mical [Michill, Mikel], 65, 72.
Rollings, Nathan, 59.
Rollings, see Rollins and Rowlin.
Rollins, James, 59, 60.
Rollins [Rollings], James, 123, 126.
Rollins, Michael, 38.
Rollins [Rellens], Nathan, 42, 52.
Rollins, Province, 42.
Rollins, see Rawlins.
Rollinson, see Robinson.

Rolls, Daniel, 197, 198.
Rolls, *see* Ralls.
Rolston [Ralston], Isaac, 221, 233.
Romey, Nancey, 193.
Rondeau, *see* Rondo.
Ronderman, Adam, 197.
Rondo [Rondeau], William, 227, 236.
Ronnalds, *see* Runnolds.
Rood [Rude], Hankerson [Hankersen], 89, 98.
Root, Benjamin [Benjamine], 137, 175.
Root, Hyram, 102.
Roper, David, 313.
Roper, George, 214.
Roper, John, 115.
Rose [Roas], Elbert, 215, 230.
Rose [Roas], Henry [Henery], 218, 231.
Rose [Rows], James, 279, 291.
Rose, Jonathan, 332.
Rose, Martin, 139.
Rose [Roas], Pleasant, 216, 230.
Rose [Roas], Sharon [Sherman], 216, 230.
Rose [Roas], Thomas, 215, 230.
Rose, *see* Rows.
Rosen, *see* Rowson.
Ross, Widow, 217.
Ross, Asa, 335.
Ross, Bateman, 44.
Ross, Ephraim, 45, 49.
Ross, Ethan E., 193.
Ross, Harrington, 194.
Ross, Henry J., 194.
Ross, John, 130, 256.
Ross, Joshua [John], 219, 231.
Ross, Leonard, 194.
Ross, Osin M., 142.
Ross, Thomas, 253.
Ross, William, 194.
Rossin, Thomas, 342.
Rosson, Ephraim, 20.
Roundtree, William, 313.
Roundtree, *see* Patree.
Rountree, Hiram, 11.
Rountree, *see* Patree.
Rouse, L. [Lewis], 223, 234.
Rouse, *see* Rowse.
Row, Michael, 334.
Rowden, Nathaniel, 157.
Rowden, William, 157.
Rowe, Hezekiah, 316.
Rowe, John, 314.
Rowe, Stephen, 316.
Rowe, William, 270.
Rowin, *see* Brown.
Rowland, James H., 2.
Rowley, Ezra, 29.
Rowlin [Rollings], James, 168, 190.

Rowlings, Ecker, 197.
Rowlings [Rawlings], Moses M., 79, 94.
Rows [Rose], John, 140, 177.
Rows, *see* Rose.
Rowse [Rouse], I. [Isaac], 223, 234.
Rowson [Rawson, Rosen], Abner, 81, 95.
Roy, Andrew, 242.
Roy, Francis, 173.
Roy, John Batiste, 242.
Roy, Scene [Charles], 141, 177.
Royal [Ryal], Thomas, 4, 6.
Royboalt [Runbolt], Rachael [Rachel], 144, 179.
Royer, Henry, 239.
Ruark, James, 59.
Ruark, John C., 59.
Ruark, Rezin, 60.
Ruben, James, 162.
Rubey [Ruby], Charles, 271, 287.
Ruble, Jesse, 199.
Ruby, David, 39.
Ruby, *see* Rubey.
Rude, Elijah, 92.
Rude, *see* Rood.
Ruelle, *see* Rale.
Rule, Aaron, 16, 154.
Rule, Henry, 273.
Rumal, John, 3.
Runbolt, *see* Royboalt.
Runnels, *see* Rannals, Reynolds, *and* Runnolds.
Runnolds [Ronnalds, Runnels], Barnibald [Barnabas], 26, 31.
Rupe, John, 297.
Rush [Bush], Abraham, 169, 191.
Rush, John, 221.
Rush [Derush], John D. [John], 262, 284.
Rushes [Russel], Niclis [Nicholas], 150, 182.
Rushford [Rutherford], Reubin, 350, 359.
Rusle, *see* Russle.
Russel, Abraham, 132.
Russel, Edmond, 1.
Russel, Elizabeth, 1.
Russel, George, 315.
Russel, John, 2, 117.
Russel, John [John O.], 132, 136.
Russel [Russell], John, 139, 176.
Russel [Russell], Nancy [Anna], 261, 283.
Russel, Nathan, 2.
Russel, William, 131.
Russel, *see* Ressell, Rushes, Russell, *and* Russle.
Russell, David B., 88.
Russell, George, 329.
Russell [Russel], John, 14, 21, 22.
Russell, Nicholas, 199.
Russell, William, 17, 327.

Russell, *see* Ressell *and* Russel.
Russle [Russel], Phillip [Philip], 68, 74.
Russle [Rusle], Soloman, 67, 73.
Rust, Isaac, 244.
Rutan, John D., 113.
Ruth, Frederick, 348.
Rutherford, James B., 17.
Rutherford, John, 170.
Rutherford [Retherford], John, 2, 5.
Rutherford, Richard, 196.
Rutherford, William, 265.
Rutherford, *see* Rushford *and* Ruthorford.
Ruthorford [Rutherford], John, 173, 192.
Rutledge, James, 331.
Rutledge, Thomas, 333.
Rutledge, William, 331.
Ruvia, Antoine, 242.
Ruyar, *see* Ragar.
Ryal, *see* Royal.
Ryan, James, 43, 57.
Ryan, James J., 314.
Ryan, William, 43.
Ryan [Rian], William, 257, 282.
Ryan, *see* Rian *and* Rines.
Ryans, Henry, 196.
Ryans, *see* Rines.
Rybolt, Richard, 179.
Ryder, *see* Rider.

Sabin, Liman [Lyman], 83, 95.
Sacket, Almeran, 3.
Sacket, Reuben, 242.
Sackett, Simon, 193.
Sackrider, John, 44.
Sagan [Segan], Batiste, 238, 253.
Sagan [Segan], Batiste, 243, 254.
Sagan [Segan], Louis, 243, 254.
Sage, William, 137.
St. Andre, *see* St. Anthony.
St. Anthony [St. Andre], Nichlas [Nicholas], 276, 289.
St. Clair, *see* Sinclair.
St. Garnaw, Louis, 291; *see also* Larama *and* St. Jeremy.
St. Jeremy, Louis, 291; *see also* Larama *and* St. Garnaw.
St. John, Andrew, 155.
St. John, Lewis [Louis], 278, 291.
St. Piere, Joseph, 238.
St. Piere, Mary, 238.
Salems, Daniel, 195.
Saler [Saylor], John, 273, 288.
Sales, Elizabeth, 263.
Sales [Sayles], James, 161, 187.
Salisbury [Sallisbury, Salsbury], Jeffrey [Jefry], 44, 52.
Sallisbury, Salsbury, *see* Salisbury.

Salter, Joseph, 198.
Sames [Sams], David, 303, 311.
Sames [Sams], Rice [Riece], 299, 308.
Sames [Sams], Thomas, 296, 307.
Sammons, James, 265.
Sammons, Robert, 302.
Sample, William, 262.
Samples, David, 155, 199.
Samples, John, 9.
Samples, William, 9.
Sampson, William, 165.
Sams, William H., 59.
Sams, *see* Sames.
Samuels, Reuben, 281.
Sanders, Anthony, 26.
Sanders, Hanah, 199.
Sanders [Sandress], Hanner [Hanna, Hannah] 142, 178.
Sanders, James, 328.
Sanders, John, 64.
Sanders, Peter, 80.
Sandford, Isaac, 26.
Sandress, *see* Sanders.
Sands, John, 92.
Sanduskia, *see* Sandusky.
Sandusky [Sanduskia, Sendusky], John, 64, 72.
Sandusky [Sanduskia], Killion [Kellion], 64, 72.
Sanford, Enoch, 17.
Sanfrey, A., and Graham [Sanfrey and Graham], 326, 330.
Sarns, Lott, 58.
Satley [Sattirly], Robert, 171, 191.
Satterfield [Saturfield], George, 342, 356.
Satterfield [Saturfield], George, Jr. [George], 342, 356.
Satterfield [Saturfield], Isaac, 341, 356.
Satterlee, Archibald, 335.
Satterlee, Robert, 335.
Satterly, Archibald, 200.
Sattirly, *see* Satley.
Saturfield, *see* Satterfield.
Saturly, William, 60.
Saunders, Widow, 224.
Saunders, George, 178.
Savag [Savage], William, 158, 186.
Savage, Eli, 276.
Savage, James, 276.
Savage, James [William], 276, 290.
Savage, Lydia, 316.
Savage, *see* Savag.
Saven, *see* Savern.
Savern [Saven], Francis, 277, 290.
Sawyer, Absolem [Absolom], 335, 354.
Sawyer, James, 199.
Sayles, *see* Sales.

Saylor, see Saler.
Scandland, see Scantlin.
Scantlin [Scandland], Gideon, 149, 181.
Scarrett, Nathan, 199.
Scarrett, see Carret.
Schenbarger, see Shinbarger and Shinberger.
Schoolcraft, Isaac, 344.
Schuffelberger [Shufelbargr], Abm. [Absolem], 219, 232.
Schwartz, see Swartz.
Scimmus, John, 200.
Scoby, James, 40.
Scoby, John, 210.
Scott, Alexander, 264.
Scott, Benjamin, 210.
Scott, Dallis [Dalis], 164, 189.
Scott, Daniel, 340.
Scott, David, 208.
Scott, Dickson [Dixen], 218, 231.
Scott, Eli, 163.
Scott, Gabriel, 58.
Scott, George, 210.
Scott, Isaac, 320, 351.
Scott, Isaac B. [I. B.], 226, 236.
Scott, J. [Joshua], 222, 234.
Scott, J. D. [James D.], 217, 231.
Scott, Jehu, 205.
Scott, John, 58, 163, 168, 211.
Scott, John [John, Sr.], 259, 283.
Scott, John [John, Jr.], 267, 286.
Scott, Joseph, 76, 265.
Scott, Levi, 173.
Scott, Nimrod, 76.
Scott, Robert [R.], 226, 236.
Scott, Samuel, 159, 265.
Scott, Samuel [Samuel, Sr.], 260, 283.
Scott, Sarah, 265.
Scott, William, 142, 170, 199, 315.
Scott, William [William, Sr.], 265, 285.
Scovel, see Scovil.
Scovil [Scovel], Benjamin, 204, 211.
Scovil, Ira, 202.
Scovil, Norman, 202.
Scraggins, see Scrgins.
Scranton, James, 198.
Scrgins [Scraggins], Prier, 153, 183.
Scribner, William, 17.
Scridamore, see Scridmore.
Scridmore [Scridamore], George, 12, 23.
Scroggin [Scroggins], Barten, 76, 93.
Scroggin [Scroggins], Carter, 76, 93.
Scroggin [Scroggins], Humphrey, 76, 93.
Scroggin [Scroggins], John, 83, 95.
Scroggins [Croggins], Chatten [Chattin], 82, 95.
Scroggins, see Scroggin.
Scroud [Stroud], Asa, 171, 191.

Scroud, Simeon, 171.
Scroxtable, David, 166.
Scudder, Isaac, 249.
Scudder, Ralph, 249.
Scutton, Oliver, 156.
Sealy [Seely], Walter J., 141, 177.
Sealy, William, 152, 163.
Seaton, Peter C., 92.
Seeds, Hugh, 59.
Seeds, James, 57.
Seeds, Moses, 57.
Seely, see Sealy.
Seemore [Semore], Young, 123, 126.
Seers, Thomas, 8.
Seever, see Severo.
Segan, see Sagan.
Segar, Jacob, 145.
Self, Hezekiah [Hezzekiah], 351, 359.
Self, Levi, 351.
Sellars, see Sellers.
Sellers [Sellars], William, 214, 229.
Selley, Joseph, 60.
Sells, Jacob, 195.
Semore, see Seemore.
Sendusky, see Sandusky.
Servington, John, 56.
Severo [Seever], John, 263, 284.
Severs, James, 155.
Seward, Israel, 16.
Seward, Samuel, 7.
Seward, Thomas, 145.
Sexton, Jacob, 79.
Sexton, Joab, 42.
Sexton, Joshua, 81.
Sexton, Samuel, 336.
Seybold, see Sibool.
Shadle, John, 61.
Shadwick, Iram, 195.
Shahan [Sheehen], John, Sr. [John], 205, 212.
Shahan, John, Jr. [John], 205, 212.
Shalovel, Mitchael [Mitchall], 247, 254.
Shanan, Mary, 198.
Shane, Daniel, 194.
Shane, George, 141.
Shannan, see Shannon.
Shannon, Charles, 63.
Shannon [Shannan], John, 113, 119.
Sharewood [Sherwood], Edward, 76, 93.
Sharewood [Sharwood, Sherewood], Moses, 76, 93.
Sharoon, William, 140.
Sharp, David, 273.
Sharp, Henry, 315.
Sharp, Jonathan, 314.
Sharp, Levi, 27.
Sharp, Robert, 123.

Sharp, Samuel, 314.
Sharp, Syrus [Cyrus], 30, 32.
Sharp, see Sharpe.
Sharpe [Sharp], Christopher H., 78, 93.
Sharto, see Shautaue.
Shartrau, see Sheretau.
Sharwood, see Sharewood.
Shatrau [Shatre], Battice [Baptieste], 277, 290.
Shatre, see Shatrau.
Shatzer, Benjamin, 63.
Shautaue [Sharto], Thomas, 279, 291.
Shaver, John, 1.
Shaver, Michael, 39.
Shaver, Simeon [Simion], 3, 5.
Shaw, Greenberry [Greenbery], 41, 51.
Shaw, J. [James], 222, 234.
Shaw, James, 40, 49, 325.
Shaw, Jessee [Jesse], 88, 97.
Shaw, John, 172.
Shaw, Joseph, 28, 41.
Shaw, Luthern, 195.
Shaw, Nathaniel, 172.
Shaw, Smith, 35, 200.
Shean, William, 8.
Shear, William, 210.
Shearer, David, 130.
Shearley [Shearly], Moses, 337, 355.
Shearley, see Shearly.
Shearly [Shearley, Shirley], Nimrod, 337, 355.
Shearly, see Shearley.
Shearman, see Sherman.
Sheehen, see Shahan.
Sheepherd, see Sheppard.
Sheffield, Daniel, 60.
Sheilds, John, 12.
Shelbey, see Shelby.
Shelby, Abram, 131.
Shelby [Shelvey], C. [Charels, Charles], 223, 234.
Shelby, David, 335, 336.
Shelby, Isaac, 332.
Shelby [Shelveny, Shelvery], Jacob, 215, 230.
Shelby, Jonathan, 60.
Shelby [Shelbey, Shelvey], Rees [Reece], 215, 229.
Shelby, William, 130.
Shelly, Jahue [John], 167, 190.
Shelton, James, 161, 194, 199.
Shelton, Johnsem, 155.
Shelton, Joseph, 345.
Shelton, Mathias [Matthias, Nathius], 154, 184.
Shelton, Thomas, 163.
Shelton, William, 171, 294.
Shelveny, Shelvery, see Shelby.

Shelvey, see Shelby and Shilby.
Shephard, see Shepherd.
Shepherd [Shephard], Alizebeth [Elizabeth], 302, 310.
Shepherd, Elihu H., 281.
Shepherd [Shephard], Jacob, 299, 309.
Shepherd, James, 257.
Shepherd, Peter, 164.
Shepherd, Rowlin [Robert], 164, 189.
Shepherd, Samuel, 167, 199.
Shepherd, see Sheppard.
Sheppard [Sheepherd], James R. [James], 203, 211.
Sheppard [Shepherd], Jonathan, 206, 212.
Shepperd, Thomas, 56.
Sherarer, John, 92.
Sheretau [Shartrau], Towe [Toashez], 278, 291.
Sherewood, see Sharewood.
Sherill, see Sherrill.
Sherman [Shearman], Joab [Job J.], 147, 180.
Sherman [Shearman], Lewis [Lurana], 147, 180.
Sherril [Sherrill], Ambros [Ambrose], 301, 310.
Sherrill [Sherill], Aventon [Avington], 210.
Sherrill, see Sherril.
Sherwood, Salmon, 312.
Sherwood, see Sharewood.
Shetler, Jacob, 29.
Shickle, Jacob, 84.
Shidler, Peter, 38.
Shields, Booker, 60.
Shields, John, 34.
Shilby [Shelvey], Even, 215, 230.
Shills, George, 167.
Shin [Simms], Charles, 145, 179.
Shinalt, John, 347.
Shinbarger [Schenbarger], Lawrence, 281.
Shinbarger, see Shinberger.
Shinberger [Schenbarger, Shinbarger], John [Baptiest, Batise], 275, 289.
Shingelton, see Singleton.
Shinn, Caleb, 70.
Shinn, John [John, Jr.], 155, 185.
Shipley, James, 334.
Shipley, John, 347.
Shipley, Robert, 347.
Shipman, George, 18.
Shirkee, see Shuckey.
Shirley, see Shearly.
Shives, John, 56, 344.
Shockney [Shokney], Dd. [David], 222, 234.
Shokney, see Shockney.
Shook, Aaron, 262.
Shook, Daniel, 206.

INDEX

Shook, David [Benjamin, Daniel], 40, 51.
Shook, Jonas, 263.
Shook, Samuel [Samuel, Sr.], 264, 284.
Shook, Samuel [Samuel, Jr.], 259, 283.
Shook, Solomon, 201.
Shores, Hiram, 325.
Shores, Reuben [Ruben], 325, 330.
Shormac, *see* Shumake.
Short, Bennet, 320.
Short, Denard, 244.
Short, Eli, 247.
Short, Green W., 140.
Short, Hubbard, 7.
Short, Jacob, 260.
Short, John, 17, 351.
Short, Moses, 266.
Short, Patsey, 314.
Short, Wilim [William], 162, 188.
Short, *see* Shorte.
Shorte [Short], Stepen [Stephen], 142, 177.
Shotwell, Henry, 197.
Shoulders, Samuel, 43.
Shoults [Shultz], Charles [Jacob], 66, 73.
Shoults, David, 66.
Shoults [Shultz], John [John M.], 66, 73.
Shoults [Shultz], John R. [John], 66, 73.
Shoults [Shultz], Soosan [Susan, Susannah], 66, 73.
Shrader, Jacob, 57.
Shuckey [Shirkee], Peter, 276, 290.
Shufelbarger, *see* Shuffelberger.
Shufelbargr, *see* Schuffelberger.
Shuffelberger [Shufelbarger], Jacob, 219, 232.
Shultz, *see* Shoults.
Shumake [Shormac], Berrimon [John B.], 85, 96.
Shutwell, George, 193.
Sibool [Seybold, Sybold], Robert, 150, 182.
Sibool [Seybold, Sybold], Samuel, 150, 182.
Sidman [Steadman, Stedman], Benjamin, 173, 192.
Sidney, Samuel, 197.
Siena, Briant [Bryant], 43, 52.
Siena, John, 41.
Sifford, Peter, 301.
Sights, Charles, 348.
Sikes, John, 253.
Silkwood, Brazilla, 314.
Silkwood, Brazilla [Basil], 314, 321.
Silkwood, Hyram, 320.
Silkwood, James, 267.
Silkwood, Obediah [Obadiah], 268, 286.
Silkwood, Solomon, 197, 314.
Silsbe, Enos, 121.
Silvely, Jesse, 165.
Sim [Sin], William, 226, 236.
Simco, Samuel, 59.

Simerman [Zimmerman], Mathias, Sr., 299, 308.
Simerman [Simmerman], Mathias, Jr. [Mathias], 303, 311.
Simes, George, 156.
Simes [Crimes], Jacob, 163, 188.
Simes [Simmons], Josiah [Josias], 160, 187.
Simkens, Simkins, *see* Simpkins.
Simkye [Sippy], John, 276, 290.
Simmerman, *see* Simerman.
Simmon [Simmons], Levi, 268, 286.
Simmons, David, 20.
Simmons, George, 193.
Simmons, James, 171.
Simmons [Simons], Jasper, 214, 229.
Simmons, John, 273.
Simmons, John [J.], 223, 234.
Simmons, S. [Samuel], 222, 233.
Simmons, Stephen, 61.
Simmons, *see* Simes, Simmon, *and* Sims.
Simms, James, 159.
Simms, *see* Shin *and* Sims.
Simonds, William, 57.
Simons [Cymons], Daniel, 313, 320.
Simons, John, 173.
Simons, *see* Simmons.
Simonton, David, 241.
Simonton, William, 237.
Simpkin, *see* Simpkins.
Simpkins [Simkens], George [G.], 225, 235.
Simpkins [Simpkin], Jerrimiah [Jeremiah], 270, 287.
Simpkins [Simkins], John G., 67, 74.
Simpkins, William, 56.
Simpson, Widow, 224.
Simpson, Daniel, 92.
Simpson, Gideon, 271.
Simpson [Simson], Isaac, 86, 96.
Simpson, James, 262.
Simpson, James A., 350.
Simpson, Lewis J. [Lewis], 133, 136.
Simpson, Samuel S., 131.
Simpson, William, 133, 271.
Simpson, William [William, Sr.], 133, 136.
Simpson, *see* Simson.
Sims [Simmons, Simms], Austin [Augustin, Augustus], 153, 184.
Sims, John, 166.
Sims, *see* Symes *and* Symmes.
Simson [Simpson], Polly [Mary], 220, 232.
Simson, Tolliver [Toliver], 324, 330.
Simson [Simpson], William, Sr., 324, 330.
Simson, *see* Simpson.
Sin, *see* Sim.
Sinard [Sinnard], Abraham, 165, 189.
Sinclair [St. Clair], Robert, 137, 175.
Sinclair, *see* Sinclare.

448 ILLINOIS HISTORICAL COLLECTIONS

Sinclare [Sinclair], James W. [James M.], 76, 93.
Singilton, see Singleton.
Singleton, James, 271.
Singleton, John, 146.
Singleton [Shingelton, Singilton], Spires [Spyres, Squire], 217, 230.
Singleton, William, 343.
Sink, Daniel, 205.
Sinnard, see Sinard.
Sinnet, John, 171.
Sippe, Sippi, see Sippy.
Sippy [Sippe, Sippi], Abraham, 146, 180.
Sippy, see Simkye.
Siratt [Sirratt], John, 66, 73.
Siratt [Sirratt, Suratt], Joseph, 66, 73.
Sirkle, George, 328.
Sirratt, see Siratt.
Siter, Coonrad, 300.
Sitton [Sutton], James, 130, 135.
Sivey, Jacob, 220.
Skeen, Aaron, 13.
Skellinger, Silas, 243.
Skidmore, John W. L., 198.
Skidmore, Philip, 56.
Skiner [Skinner], William, 152, 183.
Skinner, Andrew, 215.
Skinner, Benjamin, 58.
Skinner, Ephraim, 117.
Skinner, Henry [Henery], 215, 229.
Skinner, see Skiner.
Slack, Andrew, 78.
Slade, Charles, 320.
Slade, Charles [Charles, Sr.], 316, 322.
Slankard, George [George, Sr.], 221, 233.
Slankard [Slankford], George [Georg, Jr.], 221, 233.
Slankard, Henry, 133.
Slankard, Herman [Hickman], 220, 232.
Slankard, Joshua, 221.
Slankford, see Slankard.
Slater, James, 248.
Slater, Samuel, 193.
Slater, see Slator and Slatten.
Slaton [Slayton], George, 273, 288.
Slator [Slater], Elijah, 163, 188.
Slatten [Slater], Joseph, 153, 183.
Slavens, see Slavings.
Slavings [Slavens], Stewart [Steward], 313, 320.
Slawson, Jesse, 47.
Slayton, see Slaton.
Sloan, James, 87.
Sloan, Thomas, 57.
Slocham [Slokum], Thomas, 158, 186.
Slocum, Charles, 347.
Slocum [Slocumb], John C., 347, 358.

Slocum [Slocumb], Samuel, 347, 358.
Slocumb, John [John S.], 324, 330.
Slocumb, Samuel, 324.
Slocumb, see Slocum.
Slokeham, Jacob, 195.
Slokeum, Samuel, 197.
Slokum, see Slocham.
Sloo, Thomas [Thomas, Sr.], 78, 93.
Sloo, Thomas, Jr., 338.
Small, William, 57, 261.
Smart, Bennet, 199.
Smart, see Smarte.
Smarte [Smart], Peter, 155, 185.
Smarte [Smart], Wiley, 158, 186.
Smerls, see Smirl.
Smiley [Smily], George, 297, 307.
Smiley [Smily], Hugh, 260, 283.
Smily, see Smiley.
Smirl [Smerls], James C. [James], 121, 126.
Smith, Aaron, 8, 199.
Smith, Abraham, 151.
Smith, Adam, 202.
Smith, Adam, Sr., 11.
Smith, Adam, Jr., 11.
Smith, Allen, 264.
Smith, Anderson, 151.
Smith, Asa, 60, 167.
Smith, Asahel, 320.
Smith, Aseab, 246.
Smith, Benjamin, 60, 69, 138, 194, 344.
Smith, Benjamin R., 346.
Smith, Betsey, 259.
Smith, Carter, 347.
Smith [Smyth], Charles [Charels], 218, 231.
Smith, Christain, 198.
Smith, David, 8, 165, 200.
Smith, Delilah [Delila], 274, 288.
Smith, Ebenezer, 172.
Smith, Elias, 210.
Smith, Elijah, 264.
Smith, Elisha, 275.
Smith, Enoch, 195.
Smith, Francis, 58, 332.
Smith, George, 41.
Smith, Guy W., 56, 59.
Smith, Hambleton, 202.
Smith, Hanah, 199.
Smith, Hanna [Hannah], 148, 181.
Smith, Hardy, 3.
Smith, Headley [Hadly], 160, 187.
Smith, Henry, 11.
Smith, Isaac, 67, 167.
Smith, Ivin [Evan, Even], 160, 187.
Smith [Storry], J. H., 225, 235.
Smith, Jacob, 268, 281.
Smith, James, 17, 62, 104, 173, 257, 259.
Smith, James [James H.], 272, 288.

INDEX

Smith, Jeramah [Jeremiah], 162, 188.
Smith, Joel, 16.
Smith, John, 11, 17, 59, 68, 83, 85, 112, 160, 161, 172, 187, 206, 258, 316, 333, 335.
Smith, John C., 132.
Smith, John M., 172.
Smith, Joseph, 143, 162.
Smith, Joseph [Josep], 266, 285.
Smith, Leroy, 3.
Smith, Lester [Leister], 258, 282.
Smith, Lewis, 84.
Smith, Martin, 92.
Smith, Mary, 282.
Smith, Michael, 242.
Smith, Milton [Milliton], 129, 135.
Smith, Nancy, 211.
Smith, Nicholas, 1, 6.
Smith, Olif, 152.
Smith, Peter, 9, 197.
Smith, Philip, 161.
Smith, Phillip [Philip], 272, 288.
Smith, Randolph, 339.
Smith, Ransalier N., 59.
Smith, Richard, 142.
Smith, Richard W., 338.
Smith, Robert, 241, 259, 282, 336.
Smith, Ruth, 347.
Smith, Rutha, 187.
Smith [Smyth], S. [Samuel], 226, 236.
Smith, Samuel, 8, 100, 114, 260, 338, 351.
Smith, Simeon, 333.
Smith, Sion, 248.
Smith, Susannah, 137.
Smith, Theopholus W. [Theopholas], 143, 178.
Smith, Thomas, 56, 86, 104, 137, 142, 146, 337.
Smith, William, 1, 60, 81, 195, 247, 318.
Smith, William H., 342.
Smith, Zadock [Zedock], 20, 24.
Smith, see Smyth.
Smock, Widow, 218.
Smoot, Armsted [Armstord], 77, 93.
Smoot, John, 77.
Smothers, Thomas, 63.
Smyth [Smith], Andrew, 298, 308.
Smyth [Smith], Barney, 295, 306.
Smyth [Smith], John, 303, 311.
Smyth [Smith], John F. [John], 2, 4, 5.
Smyth [Smith], Maryann [Maryan], 2, 5.
Smyth [Smith], Michael, 296, 307.
Smyth [Smith], Thomas, 301, 310.
Smyth, see Smith.
Snell, Lewis, 92.
Snider, Augustus, 348.
Snider, Fielding, 332.

Snider, J. [John], 223, 234.
Snider, Jacob, 141, 302.
Snider [Snyder], Jacob, 276, 290.
Snider, John, 59, 332.
Snider, Solomon, 68.
Snider, see Snyder.
Snipes, Jesse, 46.
Snipes, John T. [John], 46, 53.
Snipes, Mark, 46.
Snodgrass, Archibald, 244.
Snodgrass [Snotgrass], James [James, Sr.], 170, 191.
Snodgrass [Snotgrass], James [James, Jr.], 170, 191.
Snodgrass [Snotgrass], Joseph, 142, 178.
Snodgrass, Robert, 121.
Snodgrass, Thomas, 294.
Snotgrass, see Snodgrass.
Snow, James, 219.
Snyder [Snider], Abraham [Abram], 27, 31.
Snyder, H. F., 115.
Snyder, see Snider.
Soalivan, see Sullivan.
Socia, see Souldan.
Sollemell, H., 115.
Sorrels, Richard, 114.
Sorrels, Sam, 114.
Sosha, see Souldan.
Souldan [Socia, Sosha], Michael, 276, 290.
Southart [Southerd], Thomas, 348, 358.
Southerd, see Southart.
Southwick, Jesse [Jessee], 163, 188.
Soward, S. [Charels], 214, 229.
Sowerd, see Swords.
Spalding [Spaulding, Spawling], Elijah [Elezer], 45, 53.
Span, John, 119.
Span, Mary [Mary Ann], 110, 119.
Spance [Spencer], John, 92.
Sparks, Able, 16.
Sparks, David, 271.
Sparks, Sally, 261.
Spaulding, Spawling, see Spalding.
Speaks, William, 138.
Spears, Robert, 84.
Spellers, see Pillars.
Spence, Daniel, 293.
Spencer, Major, 59.
Spencer, Benjamin, 138.
Spencer, Elisha, 57.
Spencer, Francis, 138, 194.
Spencer [Sponsor], James, 42, 52.
Spencer [Sponsor], Jesse, 38, 50.
Spencer, Joel, 3.
Spencer, John H., 143.
Spencer, Ruben S., 327.

Spencer, Stephen W., 194.
Spencer, William, 58, 60.
Spencer, see Spance.
Spens, George, 198.
Spensor, see Spencer.
Spevy, see Spivy.
Spicers, Solomon, 200.
Spigue, William, 194.
Spiller, Elijah [Eligah], 68, 74.
Spiller, William, 68.
Spillman [Spilman], Samuel, 332, 354.
Spilman, see Spillman.
Spiqrey, see Spivy.
Spivy [Spevy, Spiqrey], Exum [Axim], 45, 53.
Spratt, William, 18.
Sprigg, Joseph, 239.
Spriggins, Thomas, 210.
Spring, Sidney, 58.
Springer, John, 137.
Springer, Nathaniel, 195.
Sprinkle, Michael, 77.
Sprinkle, Peter, 263.
Sprouce [Sprous], Samuel, 297, 308.
Srous, see Sprouce.
Squires, Amos, 146.
Squires, Michael, 199.
Squires, see Squirs.
Squirs [Squires], Michael, 148, 181.
Stafford, Bird, 89.
Stafford, John, 28.
Stafford, Oliver, 335.
Staggs, see Stags.
Stags [Staggs], Samuel [Samuel C.], 68, 74.
Stailey [Staily], John, 352, 360.
Staily, Jacob, 352.
Staily, see Stailey.
Stallians [Stallings], John, 144, 179.
Stallians [Stallings, Stallion], Samuel, 144, 179.
Stallians [Stallion], William, 145, 179.
Stallians, see Stallions.
Stallings, Stallion, see Stallians.
Stallions [Stallians], Marget [Margaret], 160, 187.
Stamm, George, Sr. [George], 238, 253.
Stamm, George, Jr. [George], 237, 253.
Stanard [Standard], William, 129, 135.
Standard, John, 130.
Standard, Thomas, 129.
Standard, see Stanard and Standerd.
Standefore, see Standifer.
Standerd [Standard], Thomas, 295, 306.
Standerd [Standard], Willis, 295, 306.
Standerford, see Standiver.
Standifer [Standefore, Standiferd], Archibald, 345, 357.

Standiferd, see Standifer.
Standiver [Standerford], Anderson, 300, 309.
Standley [Stanley], Thomas, 88, 97.
Stanfield, see Stanphell.
Stanlay, see Stanly.
Stanley, James, 329.
Stanley, Mark, 349.
Stanley [Stanly], Sephen [Stephen], 350, 359.
Stanley [Stanly], William, 349, 359.
Stanley, see Standley and Stanly.
Stanly [Stanlay, Stanley], John, 262, 284.
Stanly, see Stanley.
Stanphell [Stanfield], Temprence [Temperance], 272, 288.
Stark, David W., 46.
Stark, see Starke.
Starke [Stark], Jesse, 142, 178.
Starke [Stark], Jonithan [Jonathan], 152, 183.
Starkey, Jesse, 196.
Starkey, John, 335.
Starkey, see Starky.
Starky, Jesse [Jessee], 139, 176.
Starky [Starkey], John, 139, 176.
Starnater [Starnatur], John, 318, 323.
Starnatur, see Starnater.
Starr, Absolom [Absolem], 45, 53.
Starr, Barnet, 45.
Starr, Daniel, 205.
Starr, Elisha, 202.
Starr, John, 45.
Staten, see Staton.
Staton [Staten, Statton], Ezechael [Ezekel, Ezekiel], 302, 310.
Staton, Jos., 115.
Staton, Peter, 329.
Statton, see Staton.
Steadman, see Sidman.
Steal [Steele], Andrew [Andrew C.], 294, 306.
Steal [Steel], John, 154, 184.
Stean [Steen], James, 144, 179.
Stedman, see Sidman.
Steel, Hugh, 117.
Steel, John, 17, 266.
Steel, John [James], 214, 229.
Steel, Peter, 332.
Steel, Samuel, 267.
Steel, William, 240, 315.
Steel, see Steal.
Steele, Archibald, 244.
Steele, George, 244.
Steele, James, 244.
Steele, John, 244.
Steele, John, Sr., 244.
Steele, John, Jr., 244.

INDEX

Steele, *see* Steal.
Steen, *see* Stean.
Stephens, Isaac, 169.
Stephens, James, 210.
Stephens, John, 199.
Stephens, Leonard, 249.
Stephens, Rheubin, 2.
Stephens, *see* Stevens.
Stephenson, Benjamin, 149.
Stephenson, James, 2.
Stephenson [Stepheson], James, 325, 330.
Stephenson, Ruff, 197, 199.
Stephenson, Thomas B., 196.
Stephenson [Stepheson], William, 8, 22.
Stephenson, Zachariah, 258.
Stepheson, *see* Stephenson.
Stepleford, Noah, 57.
Sterns, Abraham, 11.
Sterrel [Stull], James, 247, 254.
Sterret [Sterrett, Sterrit], Thomas, 207, 212.
Sterret [Sterrett], William, 207, 212.
Sterrett, Sterrit, *see* Sterret.
Stevens, B., 227.
Stevens, Canaba [Carnaba, Carnaby], 334, 354.
Stevens [Stephens], Charles, 315, 321.
Stevens, Elizabeth, 347.
Stevens, Fanny, 338.
Stevens, John, 218, 348.
Stevens, Noah, 334.
Stevens, William, 334.
Stevenson, William, 210.
Steward, Hew, 326.
Steward, James, 193.
Steward, John, 92, 210.
Steward, Joshua, 281.
Steward, William, 15.
Steward, *see* Stewart *and* Stuard.
Stewart, Alexander, 344.
Stewart, David, 34.
Stewart [Stewert], Elam, 348, 358.
Stewart [Stewert], Eli, 349, 359.
Stewart, Ephraim, 200.
Stewart, James, 38.
Stewart [Steward], James, 161, 188.
Stewart, John, 56, 60.
Stewart, Jonathan, 349.
Stewart [Stewert, Stuart], Jonathan, 352, 359.
Stewart, Josiah, 333.
Stewart [Steward], Peter, 314, 321.
Stewart, Robert, 18.
Stewart [Steward], Samuel, 315, 322.
Stewart, Scoby, 55, 58.
Stewart, *see* Hutchison and Stewart.
Stewert, *see* Stewart.
Stice, Charles, 14.

Stice, Nancy, 151.
Stice, Robert, 171.
Stiff, Jessee [Jesse], 87, 97.
Stilley, Stephen, 92.
Stilley, *see* Stilly.
Stillman, *see* Tollman.
Stillwell, Richard, 275.
Stilly, Catherine [Caty], 64, 72.
Stilly [Stilley], Davis, 67, 73.
Stilly, Jourdan, 67.
Stilly, Stephen [Steaphen], 66, 73.
Stilson, Lara, 92.
Stilwell, John, 59.
Stilwell, Samuel, 60.
Stiner [Styner], Bennet [Bennit], 268, 286.
Stinson, James, 83.
Stockton [Stocton], David [Davis], 144, 179.
Stockton, James, 138.
Stockton [Stogdon], Robart [Robert], 259, 283.
Stockton, Rura, 196.
Stockwell, Elizabeth, 46.
Stocton, Stogdon, *see* Stockton.
Stoker, James, 253.
Stoker, Joseph, 18.
Stokes, Edmund, 77.
Stokes, John, 168, 295.
Stokes, Young, 352.
Stokes, Young F. [Young], 295, 306.
Stokey, *see* Stookey.
Stone, Captain, 56.
Stone, David, 198.
Stone, Gardner, 208.
Stone, John, 169, 340.
Stone, Solomon, 324.
Stone, William, 57.
Stong, Jacob, 203.
Stong, *see* Story.
Stookey [Stokey], Daniel, 256, 282.
Stookey, Simon, 256.
Storey, George, 219.
Storey, John, 215.
Storey, *see* Story.
Stork, Jonathan, 193.
Storm [Stow], Arthur, 222, 233.
Storm, Jacob, 222.
Storry, *see* Smith.
Story, Andrew, 331.
Story, George, Sr. [George], 331, 354.
Story, George, Jr., 331.
Story, John, 331.
Story [Stove], John, 153, 183.
Story [Storey], N. [Nethan], 215, 229.
Story, Robert, 331.
Story [Stong], Solomon, 205, 212.
Stotton, Olaver, 171.
Stout, Christley [Christopher], 137, 175.

452   ILLINOIS HISTORICAL COLLECTIONS

Stout, Daniel, 261.
Stout, David [John], 157, 185.
Stout, George, 163.
Stout, Henry, 266.
Stout, John, 137.
Stout, Jonathan, 77.
Stout, William, 262.
Stove, see Story.
Stovell, Elizabeth, 199.
Stow, see Storm.
Strader, Benjamin, 92.
Strahan, see Stratian.
Straigh, Straight, see Strait.
Strait [Straigh, Straight], Isrual [Israel], 259, 282.
Strang, see Strong.
Stratian [Strahan], James, 251, 255.
Straton, Benjamine, 79.
Stratten, Hezekiah, 34.
Stratton, Charles, 249.
Stratton, Joseph, 199.
Street, Anthoncy, 328.
Street, James, 16.
Street, Joseph M., 81.
Strickland, Joseph, 200.
Strickland, see Stricklin, Striman, and Stritlen.
Stricklin [Stricktin], Harmon, 87, 97.
Stricklin [Strickland], Jonathan, 87, 97.
Stricklin [Strickland], William, 87, 97.
Stricktin, see Stricklin.
Striman [Strickland], Readman [Redman], 171, 191.
Stritlen [Strickland], Witte [Wiatt], 171, 191.
Stroad [Stroud], Levi, 269, 287.
Stroad [Stroud], Peter, 263, 284.
Strong [Strang], Daniel, 313, 320.
Stroud, John, 200.
Stroud, see Scroud and Stroad.
Struton, see Strutton.
Strutton [Struton], John, 26, 31.
Stuard [Steward], James, 66, 73.
Stuart, William, 253.
Stuart, see Stewart.
Stubb, see Stubbs.
Stubbins, Christopher [Christopher B.], 167, 190.
Stubblefield, John, 18.
Stubblefield, Wyatt, 18, 23.
Stubblefield, see Stubblfield and Stubelfield.
Stubblfield [Stubblefield], William, 18, 23.
Stubblield, see Wyatt Stubblefield.
Stubbs [Stubs], John [J.], 224, 234.
Stubbs [Stubb, Stubs], M. [Moses], 224, 235.
Stubbs, R., 224.

Stubelfield [Ftubblefield, Stubblefield], Thomas, 268, 286.
Stublefield, Lemuel, 253.
Stubs, see Stubbs.
Stucer, Thomas, 196.
Stucker, Davis [Davies], 221, 233.
Stucker, W. [Willice, Willis], 222, 233.
Stufelbeam, see Stuffelbeam.
Stuffelbeam [Stufelbeam], John E., 38, 50.
Stuffelbeam [Stuflebeam], Michael, 39, 51.
Stuflebeam, see Stuffelbeam.
Stull, Nicholas, 124.
Stull, see Sterrel.
Stults, Samuel, 59.
Stuntz, John, 264.
Stupp, James, 193.
Sturdevan, Roswel [Roswell], 269, 286.
Sturn, George, 351.
Sturn, Henry, 348.
Sturn, Phillip, 348.
Stutson, Isaac, 79.
Stutson, John S., 139.
Styner, see Stiner.
Sudevoit, see Sudriott.
Sudriott [Sudevoit], Charles, 46, 53.
Sugg, see Suggs.
Suggs [Sugg], Aquilla, 19, 24.
Suillevin, see Sullivan.
Sulivan [Sulliven], James, 157, 185.
Sulivan [Sullivan], John, 156, 185.
Sullivan [Soalivan, Suillevin], Edward, 63, 71.
Sullivan, James, 281.
Sullivan, Sulliven, see Sulivan.
Sumers, see Summers.
Summers, Edward [Edward D.], 260, 283.
Summers, John, 210.
Summers, Jonston [Johnson], 298, 308.
Summers [Sumers], Thomas, 301, 310.
Sumner, Benjamin, 59.
Sumner, Richard, 298.
Sumner, William, 298.
Sumpter, Benjamin, 326.
Sumpter, Heny [Henry], 334, 354.
Sumpter, John, 344.
Suratt, see Siratt.
Sur Petite, Antonio, 196.
Suton [Sutton], Aaron, 139, 176.
Sutten, see Sutton.
Suttle [Suttler], Jessee [Jesse], 296, 307.
Suttler, see Suttle.
Sutton [Sutten], Edmond, 2, 5.
Sutton, William, 86.
Sutton, see Sitton and Suton.
Swader, John, 196.
Swafford, John W., 63.
Swafford, Samuel, 62.

INDEX 453

Swagart, Jonas, 274, 289.
Swaggard, Elizabeth, 289.
Swaggard, see Swaggart.
Swaggart [Swaggard, Swaggert], Gorge [George, Goorge], 275, 289.
Swaggert, see Swaggart.
Swan, see Swann.
Swane, Charles, 106.
Swann [Swan], Francis [Frances], 273, 288.
Swanson, Dempsey, 137, 156.
Swanson, Polly, 137.
Swanwick, Thomas, 246.
Swartz [Schwartz], C. [Catherine], 112, 119.
Swaton, John, 92.
Swearingen, Daniel S., 314.
Sweet, Jeptha, 100.
Sweet, Joseph, 339.
Sweet, Pelick, 339.
Sweet, Robert, 339.
Sweet, Theophilus, 339.
Sweeten, William, 339.
Swenerton, see Swinington.
Swicher, see Swidden.
Swidden [Swicher], John, 156, 185.
Swinerton, see Swinington.
Swinington [Swenerton, Swinerton], James G., 138, 176.
Swords [Sowerd], Griffin, 345, 357.
Sybold, see Sibool.
Sydner, Washington, 198.
Symes [Sims, Symmes], Hall, 44, 52.
Symmes [Sims, Syms], William, 315, 321.
Symmes, see Symes.
Syms, see Symmes.

Tacket, see Tichet.
Taft, Robert, 261.
Taggart, Daniel, 248.
Taggart, John, 247.
Tague, Joshua, 68.
Tailor, Aaron, 64.
Tailor [Taylor], Armstead [Amsterd], 138, 176.
Tailor [Taylor], Edward, 142, 178.
Tailor [Taylor], Edward [Edmond], 159, 187.
Tailor [Taylor], Elijah [Eljah], 64, 72.
Tailor [Taylor], Henry, 149, 181.
Tailor [Taylor], Isaac, 169, 190.
Tailor, James, 161, 168.
Tailor [Taylor], John, 160, 187.
Tailor, see Taylor.
Tait, Nathaniel, 59.
Talbert [Tolbott], William, 88, 97.
Talbot [Talbott], Thomas [Thomas W.], 260, 283.
Talbot, see Tolbert.

Talbott, Elijah, 207.
Talbott, Joshua, 206.
Talbott, see Talbot and Tolbott.
Talby, Pleasant, 92.
Talent, see Tallant.
Tallant [Talent], John, 270, 287.
Talor [Taylor], John S. [John], 154, 184.
Talton, Townsend, 339.
Talton, see Tarlton.
Tanahill [Tannehill, TannyHill], James, 258, 282.
Tangua, Francis, 242.
Tann, Austin, 36.
Tannehill, see Tanahill.
Tanner, John, 89.
TannyHill, see Tanahill.
Tara, see Terveya.
Tarcourt, see Turcothe.
Tarence [Torance, Torrence], Matthew, 159, 186.
Tarlton, Charles, 92.
Tarlton [Talton], George [T., Townsen], 85, 96.
Tarlton, Robert M., 80.
Tase [Teas], George, 152, 183.
Tash, James, 2.
Tash, Mary, 2.
Tayler [Taylor], John, 351, 359.
Tayler, Merrit [Merret], 343, 356.
Tayler, see Taylor.
Taylor, Abraham [Abram], 34, 49.
Taylor, Benjamin, 61.
Taylor, Billington, 204.
Taylor, Cornelius [Cornelious], 37, 50.
Taylor, D. S. [David S.], 226, 236.
Taylor, Edmund, 11.
Taylor, George, 8, 194.
Taylor [Tailor], Gideon [Gidion], 63, 71.
Taylor, Giles, 89.
Taylor, Henry, 257.
Taylor, Isaac, 37.
Taylor, Jackson, 244.
Taylor, James, 27, 115, 130, 207, 243, 272, 324.
Taylor, James W. D., 59.
Taylor, John, 9, 197, 253, 326, 329.
Taylor, Joseph, 281.
Taylor [Tayler], Joseph, 342, 356.
Taylor [Tayler], Joseph [Isaiah], 87, 97; see also Sarah Taylor.
Taylor, Josiah, 46.
Taylor, Rachel, 194.
Taylor, Samuel, 243.
Taylor, Sarah, 87, 97; see also Joseph Taylor.
Taylor, Thomas, 102.
Taylor, Thomas, Sr., 207.
Taylor, Thomas, Jr., 207.

Taylor, Walter, 9.
Taylor [Taytor], Walter, 104, 118.
Taylor, William, 89, 102, 194, 313.
Taylor, *see* Tailor, Talor, Tayler, *and* Traylor.
Taytor, *see* Taylor.
Teadford, Walter, 83.
Teas, *see* Tase.
Teasley, William, 56.
Tebeau [Teoboc], John B., 194.
Tebo, *see* Teebo.
Tedford, *see* Tetford.
Teebo [Tebo], Madame Charlo, 242, 254.
Teebo [Tebo], Francis, 242, 254.
Teebo [Tebo], Henry, 241, 254.
Teeter [Teter], John, 257, 282.
Teeter, *see* Teter.
Telton, *see* Tilton.
Temple, James, 320.
Temple, Ritchard [Richard], 260, 283.
Tenant, Gorge, 274.
Tenegar, Henry, 164.
Tennelly, Hugh, 197.
Tenton [Cantrill], Wiett [Wyatt], 162, 188.
Teoboc, *see* Tebeau.
Terman [Turman], Jacob, 315, 321.
Terner, *see* Turner.
Ternour [Tonish], Terrace, 238, 253.
Terongy, Terrace, 243.
Terrango [Terrongy], Ferrander [Besons], 238, 253.
Terrell, Stephen, 195.
Terrongy, *see* Terrango.
Terry, Stephen T. [Stephen], 270, 287.
Terveya [Tara], Thomas, 278, 291.
Tesson, Albert, 196.
Teter [Teeter, Teters], Philip, 149, 181.
Teter, Solomon, 263.
Teter, *see* Teeter.
Teterick [Tetrick, Tetricks], Peter, 269, 287.
Teters, *see* Teter.
Tetford [Tedford], Walter, 294, 306.
Tetrick, Tetricks, *see* Teterick.
Tettrick, Abraham, 13.
Teulia, Joseph, 243.
Thacher, *see* Thacker.
Thacker [Thacher], David, 314, 321.
Thacker, Thomas, 58.
Thacker, William, 12.
Thackston, *see* Thaxton.
Thaxton [Thockson], Larkin, 140, 177.
Thaxton [Thackston], William, 168, 190.
Thockson, *see* Thaxton.
Thomas, Anthony M., 263.
Thomas, David, 219.
Thomas, Edmond, 281.
Thomas, Edward, 275.
Thomas, Elizabeth, 79.

Thomas, James D., 268.
Thomas, Jesse B., 153.
Thomas, John, 13, 167, 169, 270.
Thomas, John D., 267.
Thomas, Joseph, 160.
Thomas, Norris A., 160.
Thomas, Robert, 268.
Thomas, Samuel, 169.
Thomas, Thurston [Thruston], 240, 254.
Thomas, *see* Thompson.
Thomason, *see* Thompson *and* Tommason.
Thompsen, *see* Thompson.
Thompson, Abner, 117.
Thompson, Adam, 343.
Thompson, Alexandria [Alexander], 153, 184.
Thompson, Archibald [Archibald, Sr.], 250, 255.
Thompson, Archibald [Archibald, Jr.], 248, 255.
Thompson, B. [Benegar], 224, 235.
Thompson, Charles, 39.
Thompson, David, 59.
Thompson, Drewry, 339.
Thompson, Elizabeth, 11.
Thompson, Enoch, 62.
Thompson, Evan [Eden, Even], 110, 119.
Thompson, H. O., 211.
Thompson, Isaac, 114.
Thompson, Isaaih, Ky., 115.
Thompson, Israel, 301.
Thompson, James, 92, 196, 237, 252, 253, 317, 318.
Thompson, James, Sr., 250.
Thompson [Thomason], James, Jr. [John], 251, 255.
Thompson, James P. [James B.,], 75, 93.
Thompson, John, 40, 45, 81, 110, 210.
Thompson [Thompsen], John, 318, 323.
Thompson [Tompson], John, 62, 71.
Thompson, John, Sr., 193.
Thompson, John, Jr., 194.
Thompson [Thompsen], John, Jr., 318, 323.
Thompson, Jonas, 305.
Thompson, Joseph, 62.
Thompson, Moses, 251, 351.
Thompson, Neal, 75.
Thompson [Thomas], Nevel [Nevil], 65, 72.
Thompson [Thomason, Thomsen], Richard, 318, 323.
Thompson, Robert, Sr., 251.
Thompson, Robert, Jr., 250.
Thompson, Samuel, 197, 251.
Thompson, Thomas, 77, 92, 337.
Thompson, Thomas [T.], 224, 235.
Thompson, William, 92, 210, 250, 344.
Thompson [Thompsen], William, 317, 322.

INDEX

Thompson [Thompsen], William, Jr., 318, 323.
Thompson, see Thomson and Tompson.
Thomsen, see Thompson.
Thomson [Thompson], Samuel H., 273, 288.
Thomson [Thompson], William, 275, 289.
Thomson, see Tommason.
Thorn, Jacob, 79.
Thornbury [Thornsbury], Francis, 100, 117.
Thornbury [Thornsberry], Thomas, 347, 358.
Thornsberry, Thornsbury, see Thornbury.
Thornton, David, 298.
Thornton, John, 117, 199, 293.
Thornton, William [William, Sr.], 296, 307.
Thornton, William, Jr. [William, 2d], 293, 305.
Thorp, Henry B., 193.
Thralkel, William, 106, 118.
Thrash, Elizabeth [Betsey], 351, 359.
Thrasher, Issebell, 328.
Thread, John, 56.
Threlfall, William, 258.
Throgmorton, Joshuay [Joshua], 295, 306.
Thuston, John, 271.
Tichet [Tacket], Luke [Lues], 218, 231.
Tidinas, Thomas, 140.
Tiffin, Claiton [Clayton], 137, 175.
Tifft, David, 193.
Tifft, Royal, 149.
Tifney, George A., 239.
Tildon, Stephen, 246.
Tilford, William, 13.
Tille [Tilly], John, 272, 288.
Tille [Tilly], William, 272, 288.
Tilly, see Tille and Tolly.
Tilor, Henry, 327.
Tilor [Tyler], John, 124, 126.
Tilson, John, 16.
Tilten, see Tilton.
Tilton [Telton], Enoch, 318, 323.
Tilton, John, 57, 318.
Tilton [Tilten], Richard, 318, 323.
Tilton, Thomas, 318.
Times, Walter, 344.
Tindal, Thomas, 141.
Tindal, see Tindol.
Tindle, Reuben [Reuben W.], 246, 254.
Tindle, Robert, 246.
Tindle, see Tindol.
Tindol [Tindal, Tindle], Charles, 150, 182.
Tiner, Joshua, 69.
Tiner, Willis [Willes], 69, 74.
Tiner, see Turner.
Tingly, see Tinsley.
Tinsley, Isaac, 300.
Tinsley [Tingly], James, 302, 310.
Tinsley, Robert, 336.

Tippet, Luke, 58.
Tippey, see Tippy.
Tippy [Tippey], Abraham, 68, 74.
Tippy [Tippey], John, 68, 74.
Tir [Furr], Elenor [Eliver], 86, 97.
Titball, James, 173.
Tite, Voluntine, 77.
Titsworth, B. [Bengeman], 224, 235.
Titus, Nathan [Naathan, Nan], 267, 286.
Toberry, Thomas, 341.
Todd, John, 143.
Todd, Susanna [Widow], 210.
Toddle [Twadley], James, 170, 191.
Tolbert, Ellison [Elison], 248, 255.
Tolbert [Talbot], Fedrick [Fredrick], 302, 310.
Tolbert, William, 248.
Tolbott [Talbott], Thomas, 201, 211.
Tolbott, see Talbert.
Tolin, Isaac, 203.
Tolin, John, 203.
Tolley [Tolly], Benjamin, 89, 98.
Tolley [Tully], John, 121, 126.
Tollman [Tolman], Daniel, 144, 179.
Tollman [Stillman], Stephen, 161, 188.
Tolly [Tilly], Andrew, 276, 290.
Tolly, Cornelius, 149.
Tolly, Isham [Isom], 271, 287.
Tolly, James, 270.
Tolly, see Tolley.
Tolman, see Tollman.
Tombs, William, 343.
Tome, John, 61.
Tommason [Thomason, Thomson], William, 78, 94.
Tompson, George, 147.
Tompson [Thompson], James, 143, 178.
Tompson [Thompson], John, 153, 183.
Tompson [Thompson], Morgan, 152, 183.
Tompson [Thompson], William, 142, 178.
Tompson, see Thompson.
Tonish, see Ternour.
Tope, Fedrick, Sr. [Fedrick, Fredrick, Sr.], 298, 308.
Tope, Fedrick, Jr. [Fredrick, Jr.], 300, 310.
Tope, Jacob, 300.
Tope, John, 300.
Torance, Torrence, see Tarence.
Tosier [Tozier], Samuel, 270, 287.
Toulouce, Camila, 238.
Toulouce, Joseph, 243.
Town, Epharim [Ephraim], 275, 289.
Towns, Randall [Randel], 215, 230.
Townsand, Townsen, see Townsend.
Townsend [Townsen], Edmond [Edmun], 313, 321.
Townsend, Jesse, 15.

Townsend [Townsand], John, 337, 355.
Townsend, Martha, 316.
Townsend [Townzen], Whitfield, 272, 288.
Townzen, see Townsend.
Tozier, see Tosier.
Tracy, see Trasey.
Tramell, Elizabeth, 67.
Tramell [Trammell], Phillip [David], 66, 73.
Tramell, Thomas, 66.
Trammel, Gerrard [Jarrot, Jerrard], 338, 355.
Trammel, see Tramell.
Trasey [Tracy], William, 85, 96.
Trask, Joseph, 211.
Trask, Marvin, 211.
Travers, see Travis.
Travis [Travers], Daniel, 38, 50.
Travis, Francis, 17.
Travis, William, 60.
Traylor [Taylor], Archabald [Archibal, Archibald], 314, 321.
Treace [Treece, Trees], Jacob, 298, 308.
Treace, John, 303.
Tree, see Free.
Treece, Trees, see Treace.
Triggers, see Drigger.
Trimble, Thomas, 34.
Trip, Andy, 294, 306.
Trip [Tripp], Hiram, 298, 308.
Trip [Tripp], John, 294, 306.
Trip [Tripp], William, 300, 309.
Tripe, see Tripp.
Triplet, Elizabeth [Elizebeth], 206, 212.
Triplet [Triplett], Nimrod [Minrod], 206, 212.
Triplett, see Triplet.
Tripp [Tripe], Jenny [Jinny], 306.
Tripp, see Trip.
Trobley [Trombley], Tocan [Isom], 279, 291.
Trockwell, David, 200.
Tromble, see Trumbeau.
Trombley, see Trobley.
Trotier, August, Jr., 281.
Trotier, Augustice [August, Sr., Augestine], 275, 289.
Trotier, Francis, 275.
Trotier, Joseph, 277.
Trousdale, see Trousdell.
Trousdell [Trousdale], Alexander, 342, 356.
Trousdell, James, 342.
Trousdell [Trousdale], James, 342, 356.
Trousdell, John C. [John], 343, 357.
Trout, Jacob, 60, 201.
Troutman, James, 18.
Troutman, John, 15.
Trowbridge, Calvin, 38.
Troy, Charles, 194.

Trucky, Joseph, 242.
Trull, James, 67.
Trumbeau [Tromble], Ames [Amal], 277, 290.
Truskit, William, 11.
Trusoe [Trusoo, Tuzer], Nichlas [Nicholas], 275, 289.
Trusoo, see Trusoe.
Trusty, Wiley, 341.
Try, see Fry.
Tull, C., 226.
Tully, Dorcus, 127.
Tully, see Tolley.
Tumbleson [Tumbleston], Ezekel [Zekiah], 100, 117.
Tumbleston, see Tumbleson.
Tunell [Tunnel, Tunnell], Calvin, 158, 186.
Tunnel, see Tunell and Tunnell.
Tunnell [Tunnel], James [James, Sr.], 174, 192.
Tunnell, see Tunell.
Tunstel, Thomas T., 77.
Tunstell, Edmund, 12.
Tupper, Henry, 194.
Turcothe [Tarcourt, Turcotte], Francis, 277, 290.
Turcotte, see Turcothe.
Turman, see Terman.
Turmon, Giles, 302.
Turnar, see Turner.
Turner, Alexander, 58.
Turner, Andrew, 151.
Turner, Archibald, 166.
Turner, Elias, 352.
Turner, Elijah, 346.
Turner [Terner], Ezekiel [Ezekel], 39, 51.
Turner, George, 326.
Turner, Israel, 171.
Turner [Tiner], J., 224, 234.
Turner, James, 203, 211, 324.
Turner [Turney], James, 243, 254.
Turner, John, 151.
Turner [Turnar], John, 216, 230.
Turner, Lazeraus [Lazerous], 66, 73.
Turner, Mathew, 217.
Turner, Robert, 57.
Turner [Terner], Ruth, 39, 51.
Turner, S. [Samuel], 222, 234.
Turner, Samuel, 77, 203, 211.
Turner, Thomas, 59.
Turner, William, 248.
Turney, Anthoney B., 327.
Turney, Isaiah, 324.
Turney, John, 329.
Turney, Michael, 324.
Turney, see Turner.
Turpen, see Turpin.

INDEX

Turpin [Turpen], Nathan [Nathen], 2, 5.
Turus, Samuel, 279.
Tuzer, see Trusoe.
Twadey, James, 198.
Twadley, James, 200.
Twadley, see Toddle.
Twasure, Thomas, 194.
Twedy, see Tweedy.
Tweedy [Twedy, Twiddy], John, 300, 309.
Twiddy, see Tweedy.
Twist, Ebian [Eddey], 156, 185.
Twist, Moses, 156.
Twist, Solomon, 198.
Twitchell, Moses, 217.
Twitty, Russel, 198.
Tyler, see Tilor.
Tyner, James, 59.
Tyner, Lucy, 56.
Tyner, Thomas, 59.

Uins, John, 352.
Ulbert, see Albert.
Ulm, Edward, 60.
Umphrais [Humphris, Humphry], Charles, 65, 72.
Umprey, William, 122.
Umstead, Stephen, 167.
Underwood, Hamlet, 352.
Underwood, John, 342.
Underwood, Phillip [Philip], 349, 359.
Underwood, Samuel, 82.
Upchurch, Samuel [John], 86, 96.
Updike, Gilbert, 291.
Updyke [Abdik], Olive, 277, 291.
Upton, David, 335.
Upton, John, 336.
Ury, see Woory.
Usher, Caton, 315.
Ussel [Uzzel, Uzzell], Jurden [Jordan, Jorden], 154, 184.
Utchler, John, 124.
Utter, Henry, 61.
Uzzel, Uzzell, see Ussel.

Valain, Francis, 198.
Valentine, Jacob, 196.
Valliant, Antoin, 198.
Vallie, Francois, 60.
Valuntine [Volentine], Ichebod [Ichabod], 205, 212.
Van [Von], Jacob, 246, 254.
Van, Matthew, 253.
Vanansdol [Vanasdal, Vanosdole], Richard, 273, 288.
Vanarsdol [Vanasdol, Vanosdol], Simon, 275, 289.
Vanasdal, see Vanansdol.

Vanasdol, see Vanarsdol.
Vanatta, Aaron, 42.
Vanbuskurk, Larence, 197.
Vance, Andrew, 337.
Vance [Vancel], Gideon, 160, 187.
Vance, John, 121, 337.
Vance, John C., 20.
Vance, Jordan [Jorden], 337, 355.
Vance, Nicholas, Jr., 92.
Vance, P., 223.
Vance, Samuel, 338.
Vance [Vancel, Vann], Samuel, 160, 187.
Vance, Thomas, 239.
Vancel, see Vance and Vancil.
Vancell, Adam, 195.
Vancil [Vancel, Vancill], Edmon [Edmond, Edmund], 298, 308.
Vancil, Edmon, Jr., 301.
Vancil [Vancel, Vancill], Isaac, 299, 309.
Vancil [Vancill], John, Sr., 299, 309.
Vancil [Vancill], John Jr., 301, 310.
Vancil [Vancel, Vancill], Jonas [Jonas P.], 301, 310.
Vancil, Penrod, 195.
Vancill, see Vancil.
Vancraft, James, 173.
Vandagriff [Vandergrifft], Thomas, 163, 188.
Vandegriff, see Vandergriff.
Vandergriff [Vandegriff], William, 313, 320.
Vandergrifft, see Vandagriff.
Vanderhoof, Cornelius, 59.
Vanderveer, Arthur T., 56.
Vanhooser [Van Hooser], Abraham [Abraham, Jr.], 155, 184.
Vanhooser [Van Hooser], Voluntine [Valentine], 155, 184.
Van Hooser, see Vanhoser and Vanhooser.
Vanhooser, see Vanhoser.
Vanhoser [Van Hooser, Vanhooser], Abraham [Abraham, Sr.], 151, 182.
Van Houter, William, 26.
Vanlandingham, O. C., 80, 94.
Vanmeter, Joseph, 78.
Vanmetre, Amasa, 36.
Van Metre, Thomas, 196.
Van Metre, see Vermetre.
Vann, see Vance.
Vanosdol, see Vanarsdol.
Vanosdole, see Vanansdol.
Van Pelt, Darick, 194.
Vansee [Vansel], Adam, 104, 118.
Vansel, Jonas, 106.
Vansel, see Vansee.
Vansickles [Vansicle], Henry, 351, 359.
Vansicle, see Vansickles.
Vanstuter, Adam, 200.
Vanstuter, Peter, 200.

Vanwikle, *see* Vanwinkle.
Vanwinkel [Vanwinkle], Job, 268, 286.
Vanwinkle [Vanwikle], Daniel, 43, 52.
Vanwinkle, David, 43.
Vanwinkle, Greenbury [Greenlee], 43, 52.
Vanwinkle, Helmer, 67.
Vanwinkle, *see* Vanwinkel.
Vanzant, Cornelius, 336.
Vanzant, John, 335.
Varick, Nancy, 195.
Varnen, *see* Varner.
Varner [Varnen], Abraham, 265, 285.
Varner, George, 16.
Varner, Jacob, 156.
Varner, Vanwincle, 274.
Varnum [Vernum], Fredreck [Frederick], 203, 211.
Varnum, *see* Vernum.
Vastal, *see* Vestal.
Vaudry, *see* Voodree.
Vaughan [Von], George, 219, 232.
Vaughan [Von], John, 218, 231.
Vaughan, Luke, 220.
Vaughan, *see* Vaughn.
Vaughn [Vaughan], Daniel, 207, 212.
Vaughn, John, 261.
Vaughn, Joseph [Josiah], 138, 176.
Vaughn, Sarah [Sally], 147, 180.
Vaughn, Thomas, 260.
Vaughn, William, 158.
Vaught, John E., 349.
Vaught, Thomas F., 92.
Veach, John, 42, 132.
Veach, *see* Veatch.
Veatch [Veach], Elias, 333, 354.
Veatch [Veach], Isaac, 333, 354.
Veatch [Veach], James, 333, 354.
Veatch [Veach], John, 333, 354.
Veatch [Veach], William, 338, 355.
Verdan, Levi, 14.
Verdan, William, 14.
Vermetre [Van Metre], William, 165, 189.
Vermillion, Benjamin, 122.
Vernum [Varnum], Moses, 203, 211.
Vernum, *see* Varnum.
Vestal [Vastal], William, 259, 283.
Vials, *see* Viles.
Vicary [Vickery, Vickory], John, 141, 177.
Vickerey, John, 81.
Vickery, *see* Vicary.
Vickmore [Beckmore], Patsey [Martha], 144, 179.
Vickory, *see* Vicary.
Viles [Vials, Voiles], Samuel, 158, 186.
Vilnave, Joseph, 59.
Vina, Abraham, 200.
Vinard [Vinyard], George, 214, 229.

Vinard, *see* Vineyard.
Vincant [Vincent], Michael [Mitchell], 277, 291.
Vincen, *see* Vinson.
Vincent, *see* Vincant *and* Vinson.
Vine [Vines], William, 346, 357.
Vines, *see* Vine.
Vineyard, Adam, 271.
Vineyard, Catharine, 270.
Vineyard [Vinyard], David, 296, 307.
Vineyard [Vinyard], George, 296, 307.
Vineyard, Isaak, 246.
Vineyard, John, 249.
Vineyard [Vinyard], John, 341, 356.
Vineyard, Phillip [Philip], 274, 289.
Vineyard, Rosanna, 12.
Vineyard [Vinard], William, 155, 184.
Vinny, Rebecca, 171.
Vinsan [Vinson], Jaramiah [Jeremiah], 77, 93.
Vinson [Vincen], Edmund [Edmond], 87, 97.
Vinson [Vincent], Isham [Isom], 158, 186.
Vinson, James, 56.
Vinson [Vincent], William, 166, 190.
Vinson, *see* Vinsan.
Vinyard, Daniel, 216.
Vinyard, John, 296.
Vinyard, William, 198.
Vinyard, *see* Vinard *and* Vineyard.
Virgin, Brice, 268.
Virgin, Hiram [Hyram], 317, 322.
Virgin, William, 267.
Vodra, *see* Voodry.
Vodris [Voris], James, 347, 358.
Vodris [Voris], Peter, 347, 358.
Voiles, Jonathan, 15.
Voiles, *see* Viles.
Volentine, *see* Valuntine.
Volintine, Hardy, 19.
Volintine, William, 20.
Vollwinder, Henry, 117.
Volner, Samuel, 133, 135.
Von, *see* Van *and* Vaughan.
Voodra, Peter, 281.
Voodra, *see* Voodree *and* Voodry.
Voodree [Voodra], Francis, 279, 292.
Voodree [Vaudry, Voodra], Lewis [Louis], 279, 292.
Voodry [Vodra], Francis, 277, 291.
Voodry [Vodra], James [Yeyum], 278, 291.
Voris, *see* Vodris.
Vote, John, 351.

Wadderman, *see* Warderman.
Waddle, David, 13.
Waddle, James, 198.
Waddle, Jesse [Jessee], 146, 180.

Waddle, John, 65, 146.
Waddle, Obediah [Obadiah], 142, 178.
Waderman, see Warderman.
Wadkens, see Wadkins and Watkins.
Wadkins, Absolum, 13.
Wadkins, Joseph, 200.
Wadkins [Wadkens, Watkins], Spencer [Speser], 66, 73.
Wadkins, see Watkins.
Wadle [Woodall], William, 146, 180.
Wadley, Jacob, 194.
Wadley, Thomas, 102.
Wadsworth, see Wardsworth.
Wafer, James, 15.
Wafer, Thomas, 15.
Wafferd, see Waughford.
Waggener, see Wagoner.
Waggoner, John, 148, 199, 275.
Waggoner, Peter [Petter], 140, 176.
Waggoner [Wagner], William [Will], 85, 96.
Waggoner, see Wagner.
Waggonner, John, 60.
Wagner [Waggoner], Jacob, 158, 186.
Wagner, see Waggoner and Wagoner.
Wagoner [Waggener, Wagner], Jacob, 293, 305.
Wait, Silas Lee, 20.
Wait, Thomas B., 194.
Wakefield, Diana [Dianna], 11, 23.
Wakefield, George, 200.
Wakefield, Henry, 332.
Wakefield, John A., 11.
Waker [Walker], Jessey [Jesse, Jessee, Sr.], 270, 287.
Walbert, Mary, 348.
Walden, Susanna, 342.
Walden, see Waldin.
Waldin [Walden], Benjamin [Benj.], 84, 96.
Waldrop, see Waldrope.
Waldrope [Waldrop], John, 41, 51.
Waldrope [Waldrop], John [John, Jr.], 35, 50.
Waldrope [Waldrop], William, 41, 51.
Waldrup [Walldrupe], Samuel, 302, 310.
Waler, see Waller.
Walker, Benjamin, 106, 196.
Walker, Bryant, 60.
Walker, Charles P. [Charles], 258, 282.
Walker, David, 260.
Walker, Francis, 237.
Walker, George R., 79.
Walker, Harles [Archer], 152, 183.
Walker, Henry, 259, 271.
Walker, Jacob W., 193.
Walker, James, 145, 320.
Walker, James [James, Sr.], 273, 288.

Walker, James [James, Jr.], 266, 285.
Walker, Jesse, Jr. [Jessee, Jr.], 281.
Walker, John, 193, 269, 324.
Walker, John J., 17.
Walker, Joseph, 295.
Walker, Reuben, 145.
Walker, Robert S., 144.
Walker, Samuel A. [Samuel], 153, 183.
Walker, William, 266, 281, 314, 343.
Walker [Welker], William, 1, 5.
Walker, Zacheriah [Zachariah], 295, 306.
Walker, see Waker.
Wall, William, 315.
Wall, see Walls.
Wallace, Jacob, 82.
Wallace, James, 200.
Wallace, Thomas, 214.
Wallace, William, 12, 200.
Wallace, see Wallis.
Walldrupe, see Waldrup.
Wallen, James, 127.
Waller, Eli, 345.
Waller, John W., 63.
Waller, Joseph, 301, 337.
Waller [Waler], Richard, 63, 71.
Waller, Thomas, 87, 199.
Walling, John, 121.
Wallingford, Joseph, 92.
Wallis, George, 202.
Wallis [Wallace], John, 139, 176.
Wallis, Morgan, 344.
Walls [Wall], Thomas, 150, 182.
Walser, George, 56.
Walter [Waters], William, 165, 189.
Walters, Abraham, 43.
Walters, Isaac, 44.
Walters, Isaiah, 193.
Walters, Jacob, 44.
Walton, Joseph, 262.
Walton and White, 326.
Waltrip, Luke, 168.
Waltrip, William, 168.
Walts, George, 335.
Wammock, Benjamine, 82.
Wammock [Wormack], Green, 82, 95.
Wammock, Rebakah, 82, 95.
Wanzer, Ephraim, 58.
Ward, Able [Abel], 265, 285.
Ward, Daniel, 64.
Ward, Eli, 267.
Ward, James, 14, 108.
Ward, John, 14, 265.
Ward, Joshua, 193.
Ward, Mark, 259.
Ward, Mary, 14.
Ward, Solomon, 211.
Ward, William, 194.

Warde, Hiram, 172.
Warden, Clarke, 57.
Warden, Elisha, 57.
Warderman [Wadderman, Waderman], Henry, 205, 212.
Wardsworth [Wadsworth], John, 312, 320.
Wardsworth, Rachel, 173.
Wardsworth [Wadsworth], Thomas, 312, 320.
Ware, Malichi, 122.
Ware, see Were.
Warfield, John, 338.
Warick, see Warnick.
Wark, James, 281.
Warlock, see Warnick.
Warner, Alexander Z., 56.
Warnick [Warick, Warlock], J. L. [Julies], 224, 235.
Warnick, John, 12.
Warnick, Nathan [Abram, Nethan], 216, 230.
Warren, Edward, 316.
Warren, James, 326.
Warren, John, 10.
Warren, William, 326.
Warren, see Warrin.
Warrick [Warwick], John, 171, 191.
Warrick, Moore, 292; see also Warrick Moore and Worrick.
Warrin [Warren], Harden [Hardy], 155, 184.
Warrin, Peter, 158.
Warrington, Oswald, 59.
Warthon [Wathen], Joseph, 84, 96.
Warwick, see Warrick.
Wary, Vachel G., 92.
Wasen, James, 190.
Washburn, Ruth, 317.
Wason [Wauson], Bekey [Rebecca], 168, 190.
Waters, Hiram, 92.
Waters, Isaac, 138.
Waters, S. [Shedrick], 226, 236.
Waters, Thomas, 221.
Waters, see Walter and Watters.
Wathen, see Warthon.
Watkins [Wadkins], Beverly, 316, 322.
Watkins [Wadkens], Daniel, 215, 230.
Watkins, Hennery, 124.
Watkins, Hennery [Henry], 123, 126.
Watkins, Lewis, 123, 126.
Watkins, Samuel, 89.
Watkins [Wadkins], Thomas, 316, 322.
Watkins, William, 324.
Watkins, see Wadkins.
Watley [Whatley], Henry, 9, 22.
Wats [Watt, Watts], James, 151, 183.
Wats, see Watts.
Watson, Gilbert, 143.

Watson, Hugh, 18.
Watson, James, 193, 340.
Watson, Jesse, 328.
Watson, John, 37, 258.
Watson, Robert [Robert, Jr.], 340, 356.
Watson [Watston], Robert, 81, 95.
Watson, William, 140, 340.
Watston, see Watson.
Watt, see Wats.
Watters [Waters], Thomas, 222, 233.
Watts, Benjimin, 265.
Watts, Ezekiel, 41.
Watts [Wats], Haden, 312, 320.
Watts, James, 41, 49, 267.
Watts, Lot, 41.
Watts, Robert, 41.
Watts, Thomas, 41, 195.
Watts, see Wats.
Waughford [Wafferd], William, 4, 6.
Wauson, see Wason.
Wayne, Nathaniel, 43.
Wead [Weed], Ebenezar [Edward G.], 158, 186.
Weakly, see Weekly.
Weatherman, John, 195.
Weathero [Witherow], Ann [Nancy], 80, 94.
Weathers, Enoch, 196.
Weaver, John, 130.
Web [Webb], William, 158, 186.
Web, see Webb.
Webb [Web], Ely [Eli], 64, 72.
Webb, Henry, 338.
Webb, Henry L., 2.
Webb [Web, Well], Lazeraus [Lazarous, Lazerous], 64, 72.
Webb, Thomas, 59.
Webb, see Web.
Webster, Elijah, 210.
Webster, Francis, 314.
Webster, Judiah, 199.
Webster, Samuel, 281.
Webster, T., 223.
Weed, Edmond, 263.
Weed, Hugh W. [Hugh M.], 333, 354.
Weed, see Wead.
Weekly [Weakly], William [William D.], 65, 72.
Weeless [Wheelis], Elizabeth, 317, 322.
Weeless [Wheelis], Sarah, 317, 322.
Weeless [Wheeless, Wheelis], William, 317, 322.
Weir, Joseph, 245.
Weir, Samuel, 247.
Weirs, William, 60.
Welch, Andrew, 272.
Welch, Enoch, 199.
Welch, John, 28.

INDEX

Welch, Rufus, 196.
Welch, Thomas, 210.
Welch [Welsh], Thomas, 122, 126.
Welch, William, 196, 294.
Welch, see Welsh.
Weldney [Wilder], Randolph, 268, 286.
Welker, see Walker.
Welkerson, see Wilkerson.
Well, see Webb.
Wells, Alexandria [Alexander], 168, 190.
Wells, Carmi, 324.
Wells, Elijah, 102.
Wells, Ester, 35.
Wells, Joel, 343.
Wells, Joel, Sr., 84.
Wells, Joel, Jr., 84.
Wells, Joell, 77.
Wells, John, 37, 122, 197.
Wells [Wels], Joseph, 34, 49.
Wells, Levi, 266.
Wells, Lewis [Lewis, Sr.], 102, 117.
Wells, Lewis [Lewis, Jr.], 102, 117.
Wells, Lucy, 82.
Wells, Mercy [Mary], 270, 287.
Wells, Thomas, 102.
Wells, Unnah, 326.
Wels, see Wells.
Welsh [Welch], John, 313, 321.
Welsh [Welch], Joseph, 332, 354.
Welsh, see Welch.
Welsher, Abraham, 60.
Welty, John, 104.
Welty, Joseph, 104.
Wenkfield, James, 200.
Wentworth [Wintworth, Witworth], Elijah, 114, 120.
Were [Ware], John, 265, 285.
Werst, James, 112.
West, Asa, 295.
West, Benjamin, 302.
West, David L., 270.
West, Edward, 60.
West, Emanual [Emanuel J.], 139, 176.
West, Emanuel J., 195, 196.
West, Hezekiah, 130, 135.
West, Isaac, 152, 198.
West, James, 102.
West, John, 295.
West, Tilghiman H., 269.
West, Washenton [Washington], 260, 283.
West, William, 61.
Westbrook [Westbrooke], James, 132, 136.
Westbrooke, see Westbrook.
Westerfield, Peter, 82.
Westfall, Isaac, 37.
Westfall, James, 37.
Westfield, Silas, 172.

Westfield, Walter, 265.
Westnor, George, 41.
Westrope, William, 37.
Wetmore, Hartshorn, 197.
Whaley, James, 212.
Whaley, Nancy, 206, 212.
Whaley, William B. [Baker], 205, 212.
Whalin, see Whaling.
Whaling [Whalin], James, 240, 254.
Whatley, see Watley.
Wheeler, Edward, 26.
Wheeler, George, 56.
Wheeler, Henry, 338.
Wheeler, William, Sr. [William], 338, 355.
Wheeler, William, Jr., 339.
Wheeler, Willis, 340.
Wheeless, Wheelis, see Weeless.
Wheelock, E. L. R., 19.
Wheelock, Simon, 196.
Whipple, Daniel, 194.
Whiswell [Wiswall], John R., 138, 176.
Whitacre, see Whitiker.
Whitaker, Alexander [Alexandria], 299, 309.
Whitaker, James, 303.
Whitaker, John, 297.
Whitaker, Richard, 301.
Whitchurch, William, 274.
Whitcomb, Samuel, 17.
White, Alexander, 317.
White, Ambrose, 14.
White, Anne, 8, 22.
White, Benjamine [Benjamin], 79, 94.
White, Benoni, 42.
White, Buennet [Banard], 169, 191.
White, Chauncey, 59.
White, Daniel, 313.
White, David, 22, 316.
White, David S., 154.
White, Eldrid [Edward], 160, 187.
White, Elisha, 332.
White, Hartshorn, 320.
White, Isaac, 18.
White, James, 47, 102, 131, 138, 163.
White, John, 15, 19, 49, 60, 155.
White, John, Jr., 59.
White, Joseph, 157, 312.
White, Leonard, 335.
White, Mary Ann, 264.
White, Richard, 19.
White, Robert, 154.
White, Robert G. [Robert], 18, 23.
White, Samuel, 15, 92, 199.
White, Samuel L., 78.
White, Tapley, 1.
White, Thomas, 29, 343.
White, Thomas, Sr. [Thomas], 19, 24.
White, Thomas, Jr., 18, 117.

White, William, 56.
White, William [Robert], 162, 188.
White, see Walton and White.
Whitehead, James, 193.
Whitehead, William, 147.
Whitenburg [Whittenburg], Joseph, 317, 323.
Whitenburg [Whittenburg], Samuel [Daniel], 317, 323.
Whiteside, Davis, 207.
Whiteside [Whitesides], Jacob, 263, 284.
Whiteside [Whitesides], James L. [James], 157, 185.
Whiteside [Whitesides], Joel [Uel], 142, 178.
Whiteside, John, 268.
Whiteside, John D., 201.
Whiteside, John J., 263.
Whiteside [Whitesides], John L., 257, 282.
Whiteside [Whitesides], Nancy, 144, 179.
Whiteside [Whitesides], Robert, 143, 178.
Whiteside, Samuel, 159.
Whiteside, Stephen, 260.
Whiteside [Whitesides], William B., 147, 180.
Whiteside [Whitesides], William L., 265, 285.
Whiteside, see Whitsid.
Whitesides [Whitsid, Whitsids], James A., 219, 232.
Whitesides, William H., 196.
Whitesides, see Whiteside and Whitsid.
Whitford, William, 328.
Whiticker [Whitiker], Mark, 215, 230.
Whitiker [Whitacre], Robert, 168, 190.
Whitiker, see Whiticker.
Whitlesy [Whitley], William, 26, 31.
Whitley, Elisha, 10.
Whitley, John, Sr. [John], 10, 22.
Whitley, John, Jr., 10.
Whitley, Mills, 10.
Whitley, Randle, 10.
Whitley, Samuel, 199.
Whitley, see Whitlesy.
Whitlock, Ambrose, 47.
Whitlock, Henery [Henry], 142, 177.
Whitlock, James, 59, 141, 195.
Whitly, Samuel, 63.
Whitmore, George, 193.
Whitmore, Solomon, 199.
Whitnal, see Whitnell.
Whitnell [Whitnal], William, 351, 359.
Whitney, James W., 138.
Whitney, Simeon, 168.
Whiton [Whitton], Easton, 14, 23.
Whitsid [Whiteside, Whitesides], Joel, 149, 181.
Whitsid, see Whitesides.

Whitside, John, 219.
Whitsids, see Whitesides.
Whittenburg, see Whitenburg.
Whitton, James, 37.
Whitton, Pleasant, 42.
Whitton, Robert, 42.
Whitton, see Whiton.
Wiat, William, 139.
Wiatt [Wyatt], John, 140, 176.
Wiatt, William, 140.
Wiatt, see Wyatt.
Wicker [Wickers], Thomas, 336, 355.
Wickers, see Wicker.
Widdows, see Widows.
Widen, Raphael, 238.
Widows [Widdows], Peter, 344, 357.
Wier, Joseph, 193.
Wigans [Wiggins], Samuel, 276, 289.
Wigger, William, 240.
Wiggins, see Wigans and Wigins.
Wight, see Wyatt.
Wigins [Wiggins], William C., 153, 183.
Wigle, Jacob, 302.
Wigle, John, 299.
Wilard, see Willard.
Wilbanks [Willbanks], Daniel, 268, 286.
Wilbanks [Willbanks], Joseph [Josph], 266 285.
Wilber [Wilbre], Joseph, 47, 53.
Wilber, see Willber.
Wilbre, see Wilber.
Wilcocks, see Willcocks.
Wilcoks, see Willcox.
Wilcox [Wilcx], Barbary, 3, 5.
Wilcox, Eli, 194.
Wilcox, Enoch, 329, 330.
Wilcox, Gad, 210.
Wilcox, Hazzard, 346.
Wilcox, see Willcox.
Wilcx, see Wilcox.
Wilder, James, 140.
Wilder, see Weldney.
Wilderman, Dorsey [Dossey], 264, 284.
Wilderman, Gorge [George], 264, 284.
Wilderman, Jacob, 264.
Wilderman, James, 264.
Wiley, John, 193, 197, 245.
Wiley, William, 245.
Wiley, see Willey.
Wilhitt [Willhite], Mathew [Matthew], 92.
Wilkens, Brient, 88.
Wilkerson, Jacceard, 253.
Wilkerson [Welkerson], John, 122, 126.
Wilkeson [Wilkison], Edmond P., 261, 283.
Wilkey [Wilky], Hester, 123, 126.
Wilkey [Wilky], Maxey [Mackeil, Maxwell], 123, 126.

INDEX

Wilkins, Andrew, 80.
Wilkins, David, 197.
Wilkins, John, 170.
Wilkins, Susan, 197.
Wilkins, Willaby, 89.
Wilkins, William, 38, 348.
Wilkinson, John [James], 218, 231.
Wilkison, see Wilkeson and Willkisson.
Wilks, Paul, 272.
Wilky, see Wilkey.
Will, Conrad, 100, 117.
Will, Henry, 239.
Willard [Wilard], Daniel, 45, 53.
Willard, Harry, 92.
Willard, Joseph, 29.
Willard [Williard], Nancy, 302, 310.
Willard, Simon, 106.
Willbanks, see Wilbanks.
Willber [Wilber], Alexander, 36, 50.
Willbern [Willbur], Robert, 164, 189.
Willbur, see Willbern.
Willcock, Simeon, 156.
Willcocks [Wilcocks], Jonithan [John], 161, 187.
Willcox [Wilcox], Isaac D., 132, 136.
Willcox [Wilcoks], Oshel [Ossian], 162, 188.
Willes, see Willis.
Willey [Wiley], Amus [Ames, Amos], 88, 97.
Willhite, see Wilhitt.
Willhoit, Enoch, 44.
William, see Williams.
Williams, Aaron [Aron], 345, 357.
Williams, Aaron [Aron], 346, 357.
Williams [Wms.], Aaron [Aron], 317, 322.
Williams, Abraham, 167.
Williams, Andrew, 200.
Williams, Auther [Arthur], 349, 359.
Williams, Casada B. [Cassada B.], 335, 354.
Williams, Charles, 89, 336.
Williams, Daniel, 59.
Williams, Elias, 200.
Williams, Elizabeth, 9, 196.
Williams, Henry, 19.
Williams, Henson, 60.
Williams, Isaac, 294.
Williams, J. [Joshua], 222, 234.
Williams, James, 214.
Williams, Jesse, 92.
Williams, Joel, 219, 220.
Williams, John, 10, 63, 86, 87, 215.
Williams, Jonathan, 349.
Williams, Joseph, 15, 58, 145.
Williams, Joseph T., 102.
Williams, Levi, 348.
Williams, Mary, 275.
Williams, Moses [Mosis], 27, 31.
Williams, Mumford, 114.

Williams, Rial, 62.
Williams [William], Richard, 194.
Williams, Roly [Roley], 345, 357.
Williams, Samuel, 26, 140.
Williams, Terry, 102.
Williams, Thomas, 1, 345.
Williams [Wilson], W. H. [William, William H.], 225, 235.
Williams, William, 195.
Williams, Zopher, 203.
Williams, see Wilson.
Williamson, J. [John], 223, 234.
Williamson, John, 148.
Williard, see Willard.
Willim, Henry, 79.
Willis, David P., 80.
Willis, Hardy [Archibald], 80, 94.
Willis, J. E. [James E.], 226, 236.
Willis [Willes], Jacob, 298, 308.
Willis, James, 2, 76.
Willis [Willes], James, 300, 309.
Willis, James [James, Jr.], 80, 94.
Willis, James W., 15.
Willis, John, 81, 198.
Willis, Malach C. [Malacah], 81, 95.
Willis, Merril, 338.
Willis, Samuel, 253.
Willis, William, 343.
Willkisson [Wilkison], Thomas, 65, 72.
Willson [Wilson], Aaron, 167, 190.
Willson, James, 140.
Willson, Jesse, 160.
Willson, see Wilson.
Wilmans, Frederick, 344.
Wilsher, William, 77.
Wilson, Alexr., 239.
Wilson, Benjamin, 41.
Wilson, Benjn. [Bengeman], 217, 231.
Wilson, Champion, 131.
Wilson, Edward, 257.
Wilson, Ervin [Arvin], 348, 358.
Wilson, George, 58, 249.
Wilson, Harrison, 75.
Wilson, Henry, 210.
Wilson, James, 16, 34, 239, 250, 335.
Wilson [Willson], James, 81, 95.
Wilson, Jeremiah, 59.
Wilson, John, 219, 339.
Wilson, John, Sr. [John], 76, 93.
Wilson [Wilton], John, Jr. [John], 76, 93.
Wilson, John B., 334.
Wilson, John J. [John], 348, 358.
Wilson, John M., 260.
Wilson, Jos., 221.
Wilson [Williams], Jos. [James], 220, 232.
Wilson, Joseph E., 3.
Wilson, Lemuel M., 81.

464   ILLINOIS HISTORICAL COLLECTIONS

Wilson, Matthew [Mathew], 334, 354.
Wilson, Moses, 249.
Wilson, Nicholas, 4.
Wilson, Otho, 257.
Wilson, Prudy, 240.
Wilson, Reuben [Reubin], 132, 136.
Wilson, Robert, 241, 331, 336.
Wilson, Russell F., 92.
Wilson, Thomas, 27, 248.
Wilson, William, 3, 34, 58, 220, 257.
Wilson, William P., 59.
Wilson, see Williams and Willscn.
Wilten [Wilton], Harry, 320.
Wilton, Harry, 312, 319, 320.
Wilton, Henry, 92.
Wilton, see Wilson and Wilten.
Wiltsey, John, 344.
Wily, Equiller, 69.
Wimon [Wineman], George, 145, 179.
Winchel, Stephen, 68.
Winchester, Alden, 27.
Winchester, Palemon H., 196.
Windsor, see Winser.
Wineman, see Wimon.
Winfield, David, 240.
Wing, William, 81.
Winn, Daniel, 204.
Winser [Windsor], Jephe [Jeptha], 150, 182.
Winson, Samuel, 271.
Winsor, John, 195.
Winstanly, Thomas, 258.
Winter, Jane, 247.
Winters, James, 195.
Winters [Kinters], John, 317, 322.
Winters, John D., 104.
Winters, Nathaniel [Nathan], 168, 190.
Winters, Zadochiah, 61.
Wintworth, see Wentworth.
Wiot, see Wyatt.
Wise, Daniel, 173.
Wise, Federic, 170.
Wise, Henry, 195.
Wise, Jacob, 193.
Wise, Jeptha, 130.
Wise, Joseph, 142, 195, 196.
Wisecoff [Wycock], John, 163, 188.
Wiswall, see Whiswell.
Wiswell, Jesse, 211.
Witherow [Withro], William, 343, 356.
Witherow, see Weathero.
Withro, see Witherow.
Witt, John, 220.
Witworth, see Wentworth.
Wiyet, see Wyet.
Wms., see Williams.
Wolcott, Tiba H., 45, 49.
Woldrech [Wolrick], Mary, 110, 119.

Woldrich [Wolrick], Adam, 108, 118.
Woldrige [Wolerick], Peter, 114, 120.
Wolerick, see Woldrige.
Wolf, Andrew, 132.
Wolf [Woolf], George, 302, 310.
Wolf [Woolf], Jacob, 299, 309.
Wolrick, see Woldrech and Woldrich.
Womel, Simon, 216.
Wood, Alexander, 61.
Wood, Alferd [Alfred], 124, 127.
Wood, Beder, 343.
Wood, Benjamin, 137.
Wood [Woods], Ephraim, 174, 192.
Wood, G. W., 12.
Wood, George, 57.
Wood, George [G.], 225, 235.
Wood [Woods], Isaac, 141, 177.
Wood [Woods], James, 167, 190.
Wood, Jeremiah, 59.
Wood, John, 20, 35, 57, 61.
Wood [Woods], John, 160, 187.
Wood, John [J.], 225, 235.
Wood, John C., 152.
Wood, John H., 268.
Wood, Jonathan, 43.
Wood, Joseph, 61.
Wood, Joseph [Joseph, Sr.], 41, 52.
Wood, Lee, 108.
Wood [Woods], Martin [Morton], 159, 187.
Wood, Millo, 14.
Wood, Richard, 153, 198.
Wood [Woods], Sampson, 174, 192.
Wood [Woods], Samuel, 143, 178.
Wood, Spencer, 59.
Wood, Thomas G., 78.
Wood, William, 56, 124.
Wood [Woods], William, 159, 187.
Wood [Woods], Young, 174, 175, 192.
Wood, see Woods.
Woodall [Woodoll], Elijah [Elijha P.], 299, 308.
Woodall, see Wadle.
Woodard, Joseph L., 197.
Woodbourn [Woodburn], Isaac, 138, 176.
Woodburn, see Woodbourn.
Woodham, George, 57.
Woodland, John, 57.
Woodland, William, 57.
Woodoll, see Woodall.
Woodrom, see Woodrum.
Woodrome, David, 207.
Woodrome, James, 207.
Woodrome, Joel, 207.
Woodrome [Woodrum], John, Jr., 315, 322.
Woodrome, William, 207.
Woodrum [Woodrom], John [James], 314, 321.

INDEX

Woodrum, see Woodrome.
Woods, Benjamin, 265.
Woods [Wood], David [Daniel], 104, 118.
Woods, John, 264.
Woods, Louis, 281.
Woods [Wood], Mason, 82, 95.
Woods, Richard, 199.
Woods, William C., 193.
Woods, see Wood.
Woodworth, Charles, 279.
Woodworth, Henry, 237.
Woodworth [Woodwourth], John S., 44, 52.
Woodwourth, see Woodworth.
Woolams [Woolens], Absolem [Absalon], 140, 176.
Woolens, see Woolams.
Wooley, see Ooley.
Woolf, see Wolf.
Woollen, John, 193.
Woollum [Hulm], Peter, 314, 321.
Woolsey, Jacob, 240.
Woory [Ury], John, 294, 305.
Wootan [Ooten, Wooten], James, 104, 118.
Wooten, Susanna, 302.
Wooten, see Wootan and Woton.
Worhengton [Worthington], Pheby [Phebe], 303, 311.
Worldley, see Worley.
Worley [Worldley], Isaac, 131, 136.
Worley, John, 202.
Worley, Joseph, 202.
Worley, Richard, 20.
Worley, William, 202.
Wormack, William, 95.
Wormack, see Wammock.
Worrel [Worrell], Lewis, 129, 135.
Worrell, see Worrel.
Worrick, 292; see also Moore and Warrick.
Wortham [Worthen], Nancey [Nancy], 112, 119.
Worthbacor, Abbias, 143.
Worthen, Robert, 66.
Worthen, see Wortham.
Worthington, Benjamin, 297.
Worthington, James, Jr. [James, James, Sr.], 296, 307.
Worthington, William, 297.
Worthington, see Worhengton.
Woton [Oaoten, Wooten], D. [Daniel], 113, 120.
Woton [Ooten], Henry, 113, 120.
Wray, Willson, 63.
Wren, Binus J., 57.
Wren, John, 69.
Wren, Nicholas, 121.
Wright, Abner, 148.
Wright [Right], Abner, 148, 181.

Wright, Andrew, 326.
Wright, Benjamin, 139, 176.
Wright, Crispen [Crispin], 250, 255.
Wright, David, 56, 141, 326.
Wright, George, 176.
Wright, Isom, 195.
Wright, Ison, 176.
Wright, James, 16.
Wright [Right], James, 141, 177.
Wright [Right], James [James, Jr.], 150, 182.
Wright, Jeremiah, 139, 176.
Wright, Jonathan, 326.
Wright, Joseph, 14, 58, 130.
Wright [Right], Lugar, 220, 232.
Wright, Peter, 265.
Wright, Reding, 221.
Wright, Reuben, 130.
Wright, Richard, 265.
Wright, Rosana [Rosanna], 11, 22.
Wright, William, 60, 267.
Wright [Rite], Zachariah, 67, 73.
Wright, see Right and Write.
Write [Wright], Josiah [Josias], 149, 182.
Write [Right, Wright], William, 139, 176.
Write, see Right.
Wyatt [Wight], Eli [Ailsy], 276, 289.
Wyatt [Wiatt], Micajah, 257, 282.
Wyatt [Wiot], Samuel, 133, 136.
Wyatt, see Wiatt.
Wycock, John, 195.
Wycock, see Wisecoff.
Wycoff, Henry, 37.
Wyet [Wiyet], Thomas, 241, 254.
Wyot, William, 210.
Wyzer, John B., 201.

Yald, Henry, 197.
Yaple, David, 198.
Yaple, John, 200.
Yaples, Jacob, 193.
Yarbor, see Yarbough.
Yarbough [Yarbor, Yarbrough], Absalom [Absalem], 318, 323.
Yarbrough, see Yarbough.
Yates, Jesse [Jessee], 151, 182.
Yates, Robert, 341.
Yoakum, James, 200.
Yoakum, see Yocam and Yorker.
Yocam [Yoakum], William, 164, 189.
Yoekum [Yokem], John, 16, 23.
Yokem, see Yoekum.
Yokum, see Yorker.
Yonar, John B., 281.
Yong [Young], John, 326, 330.
Yong, see Young.
Yongblood, see Youngblood.

York, Ezekiel, 46.
York, see Yorke.
Yorke [York], William, 140, 176.
Yorker [Yoakum, Yokum], Peter, 160, 187.
Yost, Henry, 63.
Yost, see Youst.
Young, Abner, 139.
Young, Arthur G. [A. G.], 83, 95.
Young, Benjamine, 198.
Young, Christopher, 344, 357.
Young, Drewery, 326.
Young, Henry, 59.
Young, James, 122.
Young, John, 139, 146, 247, 250.
Young, John S., 85.
Young, Richard M., 293.
Young, Samuel, 122.
Young [Yong], Samuel, 64, 72.
Young, Sparling, 59.
Young, Tapley, 17.
Young, Thomas, 44.
Young, William, 17, 44, 84, 224.
Young, William M., 15.
Young, see Yong.
Youngblood [Yongblood], Aaron, 62, 71.
Youngblood, Isaiah, 71.
Young Blood [Youngblood], J. [James], 225, 236.
Youngman, Adam, 240.
Youst [Yost], John, 305.

Zimmerman, see Simerman.

www.ingramcontent.com/pod-product-compliance
Lightning Source LLC
Chambersburg PA
CBHW050132240426
43673CB00043B/1645